ORDER AND DIVERSITY: The Craft of Prose

# ORDER AND DIVERSITY: The Craft of Prose

Edited by

ROBERT B. PARKER *and* PETER L. SANDBERG
*Department of English, Northeastern University*

John Wiley & Sons, Inc., New York · London · Sydney · Toronto

Cover design: Roy Jones

**Library of Congress Cataloging in Publication Data:**

Parker, Robert B.  1932-    comp.
Order and diversity.

1. College readers. 2. English language—Rhetoric.
I. Sandberg, Peter L., 1934-    joint comp.
II. Title.

PE1122.P3        808'.04275        72-11775
ISBN 0-471-66120-1

Printed in the United States of America

10- 9 8 7 6 5 4 3 2 1

# PREFACE

It is conventional to assert in a preface that one's book is a significant departure from previous books. The assertion is often an exaggeration. We think that *Order and Diversity* is probably not a major innovation. But it is a little different.

It is the only freshman reader we have seen in which the editors emerge as people rather than impersonal compilers. Thus this volume provides a real context for the discussion of writing—a human context. We ask that *you* do not only what we say but what *we* do. There is risk here, of course. Once you get to know us you may not like us. Or you may not like what we do. That is, however, a risk one takes in any instance of communication, and if the book works it will work because it communicates.

We are grateful for the help of Susan Kutak, Jackie Megna, and Hilda Richardson of Northeastern University, and Tom Gay and Deborah Herbert of Wiley. This book is dedicated (as we are) to Joan, David, and Daniel Parker, and to Nancy Sandberg.

Robert B. Parker
Peter L. Sandberg

October 1972

# CONTENTS

ORDER AND DIVERSITY: The Craft of Prose

The craft of writing prose requires anyone who attempts it to deal simultaneously with order and diversity. There are orderly things that all writers ought to do: organize, limit the topic, find a good beginning, develop the argument of the essay, produce a strong ending, and maintain appropriate tone and a consistent narrative point of view while doing so. Almost all good writers almost always do this, and writing that does none of these things is certain to be dismal. Yet no two writers write the same way, and essays on the same subject, which we acknowledge to be excellent, are often so stubbornly individualistic that it seems as though order is the rule of rhetoric, while diversity is the fact of life. Though it may be little consolation, it is true that the same problem exists in cooking, carpentry, flower arranging, architecture, brick laying, clothes design, bartending, and almost every other area in which people make things. We suspect that an explanation of the phenomenon lies somewhere in the nature of man, but on one thing we agree, an essay is, as much as a cake or a fireplace, a made thing, the product of an individual's mind and hand. It may or may not also be an art, but writing is surely a craft, and it is with the craft that we are concerned.

Our solution to the problem of order and diversity is to try and present both. We think to emphasize one at the expense of the other is to mislead. Therefore, we have chosen essays that we think to be good though not always flawless examples of the writer's craft. We have arranged them by subject into sections which cover (though they hardly exhaust) areas of human concern with which students must inevitably have had experience. In each section introduction we have discussed a particular technique of composition, and have discussed the way each of the authors in the section has used it in his piece. We have arranged the sections and their introductions progressively, in the order of problems that a writer has to solve to produce an essay. First he must choose a topic, then he must decide on his point of view and his organizing principal, then he must begin, then he must develop his argument, and then he must provide a strong ending. The problem of tone is implicit in each of these problems, and none of them can be solved without considering it. On the other hand, no decision on tone can be made without considering the other problems. Thus we have chosen, rather arbitrarily to put that section with its introduction, just before the last section with its discussion of endings. It might just as well have gone first or second.

1

One reservation, there are other things writers do. Some of them we touch on in the commentaries (see below), some of them we do not touch on. A book such as this cannot cover them all; we have selected what in our judgment seems fundamental. Thus we have attempted to impose order, to admit diversity we have provided some commentaries by the editors. They are signed because we wish the informality of first personal discussion. They are intentionally random so that we may touch on other aspects of craft less easily catalogued. The specific purpose of the commentaries is threefold: to help the student understand the essay he has read; to show the student by example how to analyze an essay he has read, and thus construct a similar essay; to show the student by example how to write an essay inspired by an essay he has read. The categories obviously must overlap. One cannot analyze without understanding (nor probably, vice versa), and an essay like P. L. S. (Peter L. Sandberg) on Thoreau or R. B. P. (Robert B. Parker) on Howe reveals perhaps a more fundamental understanding of the essence of Thoreau's and Howe's meaning than more direct analysis would reveal. R. B. P.'s parody of the technique that he's ostensibly explaining in his commentary on Tom Wolfe's "What If He's Right" does much the same thing and is, in fact, an example of all three of the aims stated above. It explains the effect of Wolfe's essay, how he achieved the effect, and satirizes the technique as it does so. Recognizing this overlap, then, we suggest that the commentaries on Welty, Wolfe, and Ellison will enlarge a reader's understanding of the selections. The commentaries on Commoner, *Time*, Cowley, Chandler, and Russell will help the student to analyze their technique and to emulate it in his own work. The commentary on Thoreau and Howe are essentially essays that use the original work as a starting point to pursue a larger, or at least different, topic.

We have also included a short story, an essay, and a poem which is accompanied by commentary, and response by the author to that commentary. The short story and the essay are written by two of the editors, the poem by a poet we know. This is not simple nepotism (or, at least, it is more than that), it is an attempt to lay bare the human process that precedes the printed page, to suggest that real people write things out of real experience for real reasons, not merely to fill a page.

At least one reviewer of this book (in manuscript) has complained that "it's not nepotism to *include* the [editors'] pieces, but the aura of nepotism is created when the authors begin to talk *about* each other's work." He may be right. But we have opted to keep both the original pieces and the commentary because we believe that the interchange between writer and commentator will develop an understanding of the nature of the writing craft. Which is what the book is for. We have also included two other short stories and a chapter of a novel, to lighten the heavy step of exposition, and to assert, if only implicitly, alternate ways of expressing response to human experience.

These things we have done. If the book is to work, however, there are things you must do. Ralph Waldo Emerson said once, "We hear, that we may speak."

SECTION **I**

# Minorities and Protest

## THE CHOICE OF TOPICS

Assignments in composition classes tend to fall into three categories of topics: those chosen and delimited by the professor; those chosen by the professor and delimited by the student; and those chosen and delimited by the student. The first possibility is usually cut and dried: ("For next time write a theme on Earl Scruggs as a five-string banjo player.") The student is left to adopt an attitude toward the subject, to arrange it one way or another; but he has played no part in its selection. The second possibility allows more freedom: ("Write on some aspect of Bluegrass Music.") Here, whether or not he is a fan of such music, he is at least at liberty to select an aspect of it that interests him. The third possibility is wide open: ("Write on a subject of your choice.") And, oddly enough, it is this possibility that often causes more agony for the beginning writer than either of the other two. The reason for this probably results from a failure to examine what is finally a straightforward and rather simple process.

We may assume that when the professor asked his class to write about Earl Scruggs, he went through this process. He either wanted to or had to come up with an assignment. Understandably, he chose a general area that interested him or about which he wanted to learn (Bluegrass Music). He kept narrowing his focus until he arrived at a suitable topic given the scope of the assignment (settling, finally, on Earl Scruggs as a five-string banjo player). As he worked the assignment out, he went from the general to the particular. We might represent the process graphically as an inverted pyramid:

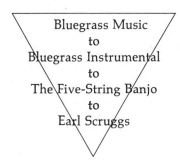

Bluegrass Music
to
Bluegrass Instrumental
to
The Five-String Banjo
to
Earl Scruggs

Norman Mailer's excerpt from *The Siege of Chicago* might be graphed in a similar way:

```
        Minorities and Protest
                to
        Political Conventions
                to
        Democratic Conventions
                to
        Mailer in Chicago, 1968
```

Whether consciously or subconsciously, by design or instinct, all writers go through a similar process in selecting and delimiting subjects. One does not have to be Norman Mailer to have an interest in politics, or Peter Matthiessen to have an interest in the nature of protest, or a professor to have an interest in music. We all have similar interests and curiosities; and because we do, we all have subjects about which we can write.

In the opening section of this book, James Baldwin writes from personal experience, Ralph Ellison from his imagination; Benjamin DeMott tells us of things he has read, Norman Mailer tells us of things he has witnessed, and Peter Matthiessen describes a man he knows. Each has exercised his option as a writer; we may do the same.

# 1. ON CIVIL DISOBEDIENCE

## Henry David Thoreau

*Henry David Thoreau was a 19th-century New England poet, essayist, and naturalist whose integrity, nonconformity, and anti-materialism have made him popular with many students in the 1970s. In this essay Thoreau argues that a man owes his first allegiance to his conscience and that he must be willing to risk deprivation and discomfort rather than acquiesce to what he believes are the immoral actions of the state.*

I heartily accept the motto,—"That government is best which governs least;" and I should like to see it acted up to more rapidly and systematically. Carried out, it finally amounts to this, which also I believe,—"That government is best which governs not at all;" and when men are prepared for it, that will be the kind of government which they will have. Government is at best but an expedient; but most governments are usually, and all governments are sometimes, inexpedient. The objections which have been brought against a standing army, and they are many and weighty, and deserve to prevail, may also at last be brought against a standing government. The standing army is only an arm of the standing government. The government itself, which is only the mode which the people have chosen to execute their will, is equally liable to be abused and perverted before the people can act through it. Witness the present Mexican war, the work of comparatively a few individuals using the standing government as their tool; for, in the outset, the people would not have consented to this measure.

This American government,—what is it but a tradition, though a recent one, endeavoring to transmit itself unimpaired to posterity, but each instant losing some of its integrity? It has not the vitality and force of a single living man; for a single man can bend it to his will. It is a sort of wooden gun to the people themselves. But it is not the less necessary for this; for the people must have some complicated machinery or other, and hear its din, to satisfy that idea of government which they have. Governments show thus how successfully men can be imposed on, even impose on themselves, for their own advantage. It is excellent, we must all allow. Yet this government never of itself furthered any enterprise, but by the alacrity with which it got out of its way. *It* does not keep the

*Source:* "On Civil Disobedience," Henry David Thoreau.

country free. *It* does not settle the West. *It* does not educate. The character inherent in the American people has done all that has been accomplished; and it would have done somewhat more, if the government had not sometimes got in its way. For government is an expedient by which men would fain succeed in letting one another alone; and, as has been said, when it is most expedient, the governed are most let alone by it. Trade and commerce, if they were not made of India-rubber, would never manage to bounce over the obstacles which legislators are continually putting in their way; and, if one were to judge these men wholly by the effects of their actions and not partly by their intentions, they would deserve to be classed and punished with those mischievous persons who put obstructions on the railroads.

But, to speak practically and as a citizen, unlike those who call themselves no-government men, I ask for, not at once no government, but *at once* a better government. Let every man make known what kind of government would command his respect, and that will be one step toward obtaining it.

After all, the practical reason why, when the power is once in the hands of the people, a majority are permitted, and for a long period continue, to rule is not because they are most likely to be in the right, nor because this seems fairest to the minority, but because they are physically the strongest. But a government in which the majority rule in all cases cannot be based on justice, even as far as men understand it. Can there not be a government in which majorities do not virtually decide right and wrong, but consciences—in which majorities decide only these questions to which the rule of expediency is applicable? Must the citizen ever for a moment, or in the least degree, resign his conscience to the legislator? Why has every man a conscience, then? I think that we should be men first, and subjects afterward. It is not desirable to cultivate a respect for the law, so much as for the right. The only obligation which I have a right to assume is to do at any time what I think right. It is truly enough said, that a corporation has no conscience; but a corporation of conscientious men is a corporation *with* a conscience. Law never made men a whit more just; and, by means of their respect for it, even the well-disposed are daily made the agents of injustice. A common and natural result of an undue respect for law is, that you may see a file of soldiers, colonel, captain, corporal, privates, powder-monkeys, and all, marching in admirable order over hill and dale to the wars, against their wills, ay, against their common sense and consciences, which makes it very steep marching indeed, and produces a palpitation of the heart. They have no doubt that it is a damnable business in which they are concerned; they are all peaceably inclined. Now, what are they Men at all? or small movable forts and magazines, at the service of some unscrupulous man in power? Visit the Navy-Yard, and behold a marine, such a man as an American government can make, or such as it can make a man with its black arts,—a mere shadow and reminiscence of humanity, a man laid out alive and standing, and already, as one may say, buried under arms with funeral accompaniments, though it may be,—

> Not a drum was heard, not a funeral note,
> As his corse to the rampart we hurried;
> Not a soldier discharged his farewell shot
> O'er the grave where our hero we buried.

The mass of men serve the state thus, not as men mainly, but as machines, with their bodies. They are the standing army, and the militia, jailers, constables, posse comitatus, etc. In most cases there is no free exercise whatever of the judgment or of the moral sense; but they put themselves on a level with wood and earth and stones; and wooden men can perhaps be manufactured that will serve the purpose as well. Such command no more respect than men of straw or a lump of dirt. They have the same sort of worth only as horses and dogs. Yet such as these even are commonly esteemed good citizens. Others—as most legislators, politicians, lawyers, ministers, and office-holders—serve the state chiefly with their heads; and, as they rarely make any moral distinctions, they are as likely to serve the Devil, without *intending* it, as God. A very few, as heroes, patriots, martyrs, reformers in the great sense, and *men*, serve the state with their consciences also, and so necessarily resist it for the most part; and they are commonly treated as enemies by it. A wise man will only be useful as a man, and will not submit to be "clay," and "stop a hole to keep the wind away," but leave that office to his dust at least:—

> I am too high-born to be propertied,
> To be a secondary at control,
> Or useful serving-man and instrument
> To any sovereign state throughout the world.

He who gives himself to his fellow-man appears to them useless and selfish; but he who gives himself partially to them is pronounced a benefactor and philanthropist.

How does it become a man to behave toward this American government to-day? I answer, that he cannot without disgrace be associated with it. I cannot for an instant recognize that political organization as *my* government which is the *slave's* government also.

All men recognize the right of revolution; that is, the right to refuse allegiance to, and to resist, the government, when its tyranny or its inefficiency are great and unendurable. But almost all say that such is not the case now. But such was the case, they think, in the Revolution of '75. If one were to tell me that this was a bad government because it taxed certain foreign commodities brought to its ports, it is most probable that I should not make an ado about it, for I can do without them. All machines have their friction; and possibly this does enough good to counterbalance the evil. At any rate, it is a great evil to make a stir about it. But when the friction comes to have its machine, and oppression and robbery are organized, I say, let us not have such a machine any longer. In other words, when a sixth of the population of a nation which has undertaken to be the refuge of liberty are slaves, and a whole country is unjustly overrun and conquered by a foreign army, and subjected to military law, I think that it is not too soon for honest men to rebel and revolutionize. What makes this duty the more urgent is the fact that the country so overrun is not our own, but ours is the invading army.

Paley, a common authority with many on moral questions, in his chapter on the "Duty of Submission to Civil Government," resolves all civil obligation into expediency; and he proceeds to say, "that so long as the interest of the whole society requires it, that is, so long as the established government cannot be resisted or changed without public inconveniency, it is the will of God that the established government be obeyed, and no longer. . . . This principle being admitted, the justice of every particular case of resistance is reduced to a computation of the quantity of the danger and grievance on the one side, and of the probability and expense of redressing it on the other." Of this, he says, every man shall judge for himself. But Paley appears never to have contemplated those cases to which the rule of expediency does not apply, in which a people, as well as an individual, must do justice, cost what it may. If I have unjustly wrested a plank from a drowning man, I must restore it to him though I drown myself. This, according to Paley, would be inconvenient. But he that would save his life, in such a case, shall lose it. This people must cease to hold slaves, and to make war on Mexico, though it cost them their existence as a people.

In their practice, nations agree with Paley; but does any one think that Massachusetts does exactly what is right at the present crisis?

A drab of state, a cloth-o'-silver slut,
To have her train borne up, and her soul trail in the dirt.

Practically speaking, the opponents to a reform in Massachusetts are not a hundred thousand politicians at the South, but a hundred thousand merchants and farmers here, who are more interested in commerce and agriculture than they are in humanity, and are not prepared to do justice to the slave and to Mexico, *cost what it may.* I quarrel not with far-off foes, but with those who, near at home, coöperate with, and do the bidding of, those far away, and without whom the latter would be harmless. We are accustomed to say, that the mass of men are unprepared; but improvement is slow, because the few are not materially wiser or better than the many. It is not so important that many should be as good as you, as that there be some absolute goodness somewhere; for that will leaven the whole lump. There are thousands who are *in opinion* opposed to slavery and to the war, who yet in effect do nothing to put an end to them; who, esteeming themselves children of Washington and Franklin, sit down with their hands in their pockets, and say that they know not what to do, and do nothing; who even postpone the question of freedom to the question of free-trade, and quietly read the prices-current along with the latest advices from Mexico, after dinner, and, it may be, fall asleep over them both. What is the price-current of an honest man and patriot to-day? They hesitate, and they regret, and sometimes they petition; but they do nothing in earnest and with effect. They will wait, well disposed, for others to remedy the evil, that they may no longer have it to regret. At most, they give only a cheap vote, and a feeble countenance and Godspeed, to the right, as it goes by them. There are nine hundred and ninety-nine patrons of virtue to one virtuous man. But it is easier to deal with the real possessor of a thing than with the temporary guardian of it.

All voting is a sort of gaming, like checkers or backgammon, with a slight moral tinge to it, a playing with right and wrong, with moral questions; and betting naturally accompanies it. The character of the voters is not staked. I cast my vote, perchance, as I think right; but I am not vitally concerned that that right should prevail. I am willing to leave it to the majority. Its obligation, therefore, never exceeds that of expediency. Even voting *for the right* is *doing* nothing for it. It is only expressing to men feebly your desire that it should prevail. A wise man will not leave the right to the mercy of chance, nor wish it to prevail through the power of the majority. There is but little virtue in the action of masses of men. When the majority shall at length vote for the abolition of slavery, it will be because they are indifferent to slavery, or because there is but little slavery left to be abolished by their vote. *They* will then be the only slaves. Only *his* vote can hasten the abolition of slavery who asserts his own freedom by his vote.

I hear of a convention to be held at Baltimore, or elsewhere, for the selection of a candidate for the Presidency, made up chiefly of editors, and men who are politicians by profession; but I think, what is it to any independent, intelligent, and respectable man what decision they may come to? Shall we not have the advantage of his wisdom and honesty, nevertheless? Can we not count upon some independent votes? Are there not many individuals in the country who do not attend conventions? But no: I find that the respectable man, so called, has immediately drifted from his position, and despairs of his country, when his country has more reason to despair of him. He forthwith adopts one of the candidates thus selected as the only *available* one, thus proving that he is himself *available* for any purposes of the demagogue. His vote is of no more worth than that of any unprincipled foreigner or hireling native, who may have been bought. O for a man who is a *man*, and, as my neighbor says, has a bone in his back which you cannot pass your hand through! Our statistics are at fault: the population has been returned too large. How many men are there to a square thousand miles in this country? Hardly one. Does not America offer any inducement for men to settle here? The American has dwindled into an Odd Fellow,—one who may be known by the development of his organ of gregariousness, and a manifest lack of intellect and cheerful self-reliance; whose first and chief concern, on coming into the world, is to see that the Almshouses are in good repair; and, before yet he has lawfully donned the virile garb, to collect a fund for the support of the widows and orphans that may be; who, in short, ventures to live only by the aid of the Mutual Insurance company, which has promised to bury him decently.

It is not a man's duty, as a matter of course, to devote himself to the eradication of any, even the most enormous wrong; he may still properly have other concerns to engage him; but it his duty, at least, to wash his hands of it, and, if he gives it no thought longer, not to give it practically his support. If I devote myself to other pursuits and contemplations, I must first see, at least, that I do not pursue them sitting upon another man's shoulders. I must get off him first, that he may pursue his contemplations too. See what gross inconsistency is tolerated. I have heard some of my townsmen say, "I should like to have them order me out to help put down an insurrection of the slaves, or to march to Mexico;— see if I would go;" and yet these very men have each, directly by their allegiance, and so indirectly, at least, by their money, furnished a substitute. The soldier is applauded who refuses to serve in an unjust war by those who do not refuse to sustain the unjust government which makes the war; is applauded by those whose own act and authority he disregards and sets at naught; as if the state were penitent to that degree that it hired one to scourge it while it sinned, but not to that degree that it left off sinning for a moment. Thus, under the name of Order and Civil Government, we are all made at last to pay homage to and support our own meanness. After the first blush of sin comes its indifference; and from immoral it becomes, as it were, *un*moral, and not quite unnecessary to that life which we have made.

The broadest and most prevalent error requires the most disinterested virtue to sustain it. The slight reproach to which the virtue of patriotism is commonly liable, the noble are most likely to incur. Those who, while they disapprove of the character and measures of a government, yield to it their allegiance and support are undoubtedly its most conscientious supporters, and so frequently the most serious obstacles to reform. Some are petitioning the state to dissolve the Union, to disregard the requisitions of the President. Why do they not dissolve it themselves,—the union between themselves and the state,—and refuse to pay their quota into its treasury? Do not they stand in the same relation to the state that the state does to the Union? And have not the same reasons prevented the state from resisting the union which have prevented them from resisting the state?

How can a man be satisfied to entertain an opinion merely, and enjoy *it*? Is there any enjoyment in it, if his opinion is that he is aggrieved? If you are cheated out of a single dollar by your neighbor, you do not rest satisfied with knowing that you are cheated, or with saying that you are cheated, or even with petitioning him to pay you your due; but you take effectual steps at once to obtain the full amount, and see that you are never cheated again. Action from principle, the perception and the performance of right, changes things and relations; it is essentially revolutionary, and does not consist wholly with anything which was. It not only divides states and churches, it divides families; ay, it divides the *individual*, separating the diabolical in him from the divine.

Unjust laws exist: shall we be content to obey them, or shall we endeavor to amend them, and obey them until we have succeeded, or shall we transgress them at once? Men generally, under such a government as this, think that they ought to wait until they have persuaded the majority to alter them. They think that, if they should resist, the remedy would be worse than the evil. But it is the fault of the government itself that the remedy *is* worse than the evil. *It* makes it worse. Why is it not more apt to anticipate and provide for reform? Why does it not cherish its wise minority? Why does it cry and resist before it is hurt? Why does it not encourage its citizens to be on the alert to point out its faults, and *do* better than it would have them? Why does it always crucify Christ, and excommunicate Copernicus and Luther, and pronounce Washington and Franklin rebels?

One would think, that a deliberate and practical denial of its authority was the only offense never contemplated by government; else, why has it not assigned its definite, its suitable and proportionate penalty? If a man who has no property refuses but once to earn nine shillings for the state, he is put in prison for a period unlimited by any law that I know, and determined only by the discretion of those who placed him there; but if he should steal ninety times nine shillings from the state, he is soon permitted to go at large again.

If the injustice is part of the necessary friction of the machine of government, let it go, let it go: perchance it will wear smooth,—certainly the machine will wear out. If the injustice has a spring, or a pulley, or a rope, or a crank, exclusively for itself, then perhaps you may consider whether the remedy will not be worse than the evil; but if it is of such a nature that it requires you to be the agent of injustice to another, then, I say, break the law. Let your life be a counter friction to stop the machine. What I have to do is to see, at any rate, that I do not lend myself to the wrong which I condemn.

As for adopting the ways which the state has provided for remedying the evil, I know not of such ways. They take too much time, and a man's life will be gone. I have other affairs to attend to. I came into this world, not chiefly to make this a good place to live in, but to live in it, be it good or bad. A man has not everything to do, but something; and because he cannot do *everything*, it is not necessary that he should do *something* wrong. It is not my business to be petitioning the Governor or the Legislature any more than it is theirs to petition me; and if they should not hear my petition, what should I do then? But in this case the state has provided no way: its very Constitution is the evil. This may seem to be harsh and stubborn and unconciliatory; but it is to treat with the utmost kindness and consideration the only spirit that can appreciate or deserves it. So is all change for the better, like birth and death, which convulse the body.

I do not hesitate to say, that those who call themselves Abolitionists should at once effectually withdraw their support, both in person and property, from the government of Massachusetts, and not wait till they constitute a majority of one, before they suffer the right to prevail through them. I think that it is enough if they have God on their side, without waiting for that other one. Moreover, any man more right than his neighbors constitutes a majority of one already.

I meet this American government, or its representative, the state government, directly, and face to face, once a year—no more—in the person of its tax-gatherer; this is the only mode in which a man situated as I am necessarily meets it; and it then says distinctly, Recognize me; and the simplest, the most effectual, and, in the present posture of affairs the indispensablest mode of treating with it on this head, of expressing your little satisfaction with and love for it, is to deny it then. My civil neighbor, the tax-gatherer, is the very man I have to deal with,—for it is, after all, with men and not with parchment that I quarrel,—and he has voluntarily chosen to be an agent of the government. How shall he ever know well what he is and does as an officer of the government, or as a man, until he is obliged to consider whether he shall treat me, his neighbor, for whom he has respect, as a neighbor and well-disposed man, or as a maniac and disturber of the peace, and see if he can get over this obstruction to his neighborliness without a ruder and more impetuous thought or speech corresponding with his action. I know this well, that if one thousand, if one hundred, if ten men whom I could name,—if ten *honest* men only,—ay, if *one* HONEST man, in this State of Massachusetts, *ceasing to hold slaves*, were actually to withdraw from this copartnership, and be locked up in the county jail therefor, it would be the abolition of slavery in America. For it matters not how small the beginning may seem to be: what is once well done is done forever. But we love better to talk about it: that we say is our mission. Reform keeps many scores of newspapers in its service, but not one man. If my esteemed neighbor, the State's ambassador, who will devote his days to the settlement of the question of human rights in the Council Chamber, instead of being threatened with the prisons of Carolina, were to sit down the prisoner of Massachusetts, that State which is so anxious to foist the sin of slavery upon her sister,—though at present she can discover only an act of inhospitality to be the ground of a quarrel with her,—the Legislature would not wholly waive the subject the following winter.

Under a government which imprisons any unjustly, the true place for a just man is also a prison. The proper place to-day, the only place which Massachusetts has provided for her freer and less desponding spirits, is in her prisons, to be put out and locked out of the State by her own act, as they have already put themselves out by their principles. It is there that the fugitive slave, and the Mexican prisoner on parole, and the Indian come to plead the wrongs of his race should find them; on that separate, but more free and honorable ground, where the State places those who are not *with* her, but *against* her,—the only house in a slave State in which a free man can abide with honor. If any think that their influence would be lost there, and their voices no longer afflict the ear of the State, that they would not be as an enemy within its walls, they do not know by how much truth is stronger than error, nor how much more eloquently and effectively he can combat injustice who has experienced a little in his own person. Cast your whole vote, not a strip of paper merely; but your whole influence. A minority is powerless while it conforms to the majority; it is not even a minority then; but it is irresistible when it clogs by its whole weight. If the alternative is to keep all just men in prison, or give up war and slavery, the State will not hesitate which to choose. If a thousand men were not to pay their tax-bills this year, that would not be a violent and bloody measure, as it would be to pay them, and enable the State to commit violence and shed innocent blood. This is, in fact, the definition of a peaceable revolution, if any such is possible. If the tax-gatherer, or any other public officer, asks me, as one has done, "But what shall I do?" my answer is, "If you really wish to do anything, resign your office." When the subject has refused allegiance, and the officer has resigned his office, then the revolution is accomplished. But even suppose blood should flow. Is there not a sort of blood shed when the conscience is wounded? Through this wound a man's real manhood and immortality flow out, and he bleeds to an everlasting death. I see this blood flowing now.

I have contemplated the imprisonment of the offender, rather than the seizure of his goods,—though both will serve the same purpose,— because they who assert the purest right, and consequently are most dangerous to a corrupt State, commonly have not spent much time in accumulating property. To such the State renders comparatively small service, and a slight tax is wont to appear exorbitant, particularly if they are obliged to earn it by special labor with their hands. If there were one who lived wholly without the use of money, the State itself would hesitate to demand it of him. But the rich man—not to make any invidious comparison—is always sold to the institution which makes him rich. Absolutely speaking, the more money, the less virtue; for money comes between a man and his objects, and obtains them for him; and it was certainly no great virtue to obtain it. It puts to rest many questions which he would otherwise be taxed to answer; while the only new question which it puts is the hard but superfluous one, how to spend it. Thus his moral ground is taken from under his feet. The opportunities of living are diminished in proportion as what are called the "means" are increased. The best thing a man can do for his culture when he is rich is to endeavor to carry out those schemes which he entertained when he was poor. Christ answered the Herodians according to their condition. "Show me the tribute-money," said he;—and one took a penny out of his pocket;—if you use money which has the image of Caesar on it, and which he has made current and valuable, that is, *if you are men of the State*, and daily enjoy the advantages of Caesar's government, then pay him back some of his own when he demands it. "Render therefore to

Caesar that which is Caesar's, and to God those things which are God's,"
—leaving them no wiser than before as to which was which; for they did
not wish to know.

When I converse with the freest of my neighbors, I perceive that,
whatever they may say about the magnitude and seriousness of the question, and their regard for the public tranquility, the long and the short of
the matter is, that they cannot spare the protection of the existing government, and they dread the consequences to their property and families
of disobedience to it. For my own part, I should not like to think that I
ever rely on the protection of the State. But, if I deny the authority of
the State when it presents its tax-bill, it will soon take and waste all my
property, and so harass me and my children without end. This is hard.
This makes it impossible for a man to live honestly, and at the same time
comfortably, in outward respects. It will not be worth the while to accumulate property; that would be sure to go again. You must hire or squat
somewhere, and raise but a small crop, and eat that soon. You must live
within yourself, and depend upon yourself always tucked up and ready
for a start, and not have many affairs. A man may grow rich in Turkey
even, if he will be in all respects a good subject of the Turkish government. Confucius said: "If a state is governed by the principles of reason,
poverty and misery are subjects of shame; if a state is not governed by
the principles of reason, riches and honors are the subjects of shame."
No: until I want the protection of Massachusetts to be extended to me
in some distinct Southern port, where my liberty is endangered, or until
I am bent solely on building up an estate at home by peaceful enterprise,
I can afford to refuse allegiance to Massachusetts, and her right to my
property and life. It costs me less in every sense to incur the penalty of
disobedience to the State than it would to obey. I should feel as if I were
worth less in that case.

Some years ago, the State met me in behalf of the Church, and com-
manded me to pay a certain sum toward the support of a clergyman
whose preaching my father attended, but never I myself. "Pay," it said,
"or be locked up in the jail." I declined to pay. But, unfortunately, another man saw fit to pay it. I did not see why the schoolmaster should be
taxed to support the priest, and not the priest the schoolmaster; for I
was not the State's schoolmaster, but I supported myself by voluntary
subscription. I did not see why the lyceum should not present its tax-bill,
and have the State to back its demand, as well as the Church. However, at
the request of the selectmen, I condescended to make some such statement as this in writing:—"Know all men by these presents, that I, Henry
Thoreau, do not wish to be regarded as a member of any incorporated
society which I have not joined." This I gave to the town clerk; and he

has it. The State, having thus learned that I did not wish to be regarded as a member of that church, has never made a like demand on me since; though it said that it must adhere to its original presumption that time. If I had known how to name them, I should then have signed off in detail from all the societies which I never signed on to; but I did not know where to find a complete list.

I have paid no poll-tax for six years. I was put into a jail once on this account, for one night; and, as I stood considering the walls of solid stone, two or three feet thick, the door of wood and iron, a foot thick, and the iron grating which strained the light, I could not help being struck with the foolishness of that institution which treated me as if I were mere flesh and blood and bones, to be locked up. I wondered that it should have concluded at length that this was the best use it could put me to, and had never thought to avail itself of my services in some way. I saw that, if there was a wall of stone between me and my townsmen, there was a still more difficult one to climb or break through before they could get to be as free as I was. I did not for a moment feel confined, and the walls seemed a great waste of stone and mortar. I felt as if I alone of all my townsmen had paid my tax. They plainly did not know how to treat me, but behaved like persons who are underbred. In every threat and in every compliment there was a blunder; for they thought that my chief desire was to stand the other side of that stone wall. I could not but smile to see how industriously they locked the door on my meditations, which followed them out again without let or hindrance, and *they* were really all that was dangerous. As they could not reach me, they had resolved to punish my body; just as boys, if they cannot come at some person against whom they have a spite, will abuse his dog. I saw that the State was halfwitted, that it was timid as a lone woman with her silver spoons, and that it did not know its friends from its foes, and I lost all my remaining respect for it, and pitied it.

Thus the State never intentionally confronts a man's sense, intellectual or moral, but only his body, his senses. It is not armed with superior wit or honesty, but with superior physical strength. I was not born to be forced. I will breathe after my own fashion. Let us see who is the strongest. What force has a multitude? They only can force me who obey a higher law than I. They force me to become like themselves. I do not hear of *men* being *forced* to live this way or that by masses of men. What sort of life were that to live? When I meet a government which says to me, "Your money or your life," why should I be in haste to give it my money? It may be in a great strait, and not know what to do: I cannot help that. It must help itself; do as I do. It is not worth the while to snivel about it. I am not responsible for the successful working of the machinery of society. I am not the son of the engineer. I perceive that, when an acorn and a chestnut fall side by side, the one does not remain inert to make way for the other, but both obey their own laws, and spring and grow and flourish as best they can, till one, perchance, overshadows and destroys the other. If a plant cannot live according to its nature, it dies; and so a man.

The night in prison was novel and interesting enough. The prisoners in their shirt-sleeves were enjoying a chat and the evening air in the doorway, when I entered. But the jailer said, "Come, boys, it is time to lock up;" and so they dispersed, and I heard the sound of their steps returning into the hollow apartments. My room-mate was introduced to me by the jailer as "a first-rate fellow and a clever man." When the door was locked, he showed me where to hang my hat, and how he managed matters there. The rooms were whitewashed once a month; and this one, at least, was the whitest, most simply furnished, and probably the neatest apartment in the town. He naturally wanted to know where I came from, and what brought me there; and, when I had told him, I asked him in my turn how he came there, presuming him to be an honest man, of course; and, as the world goes, I believe he was. "Why," said he, "they accuse me of burning a barn; but I never did it." As near as I could discover, he had probably gone to bed in a barn when drunk, and smoked his pipe there; and so a barn was burnt. He had the reputation of being a clever man, had been there some three months waiting for his trial to come on, and would have to wait as much longer; but he was quite domesticated and contented, since he got his board for nothing, and thought that he was well treated.

He occupied one window, and I the other; and I saw that if one stayed there long, his principal business would be to look out the window. I had soon read all the tracts that were left there, and examined where former prisoners had broken out, and where a grate had been sawed off, and heard the history of the various occupants of that room; for I found that even here there was a history and a gossip which never circulated beyond the walls of the jail. Probably this is the only house in the town where verses are composed, which are afterward printed in a circular form, but not published. I was shown quite a long list of verses which were composed by some young men who had been detected in an attempt to escape, who avenged themselves by singing them.

I pumped my fellow-prisoner as dry as I could, for fear I should never see him again; but at length he showed me which was my bed, and left me to blow out the lamp.

It was like traveling into a far country, such as I had never expected to behold, to lie there for one night. It seemed to me that I never had heard the town-clock strike before, nor the evening sounds of the village; for we slept with the windows open, which were inside the grating. It was to see my native village in the light of the Middle Ages, and our Concord was turned into a Rhine stream, and visions of knights and castles passed before me. They were the voices of old burghers that I heard in the streets. I was an involuntary spectator and auditor of whatever was done and said in the kitchen of the adjacent village-inn,—a wholly new and rare experience to me. It was a closer view of my native town. I was fairly inside of it. I never had seen its institutions before. This is one of its peculiar institutions; for it is a shire town. I began to comprehend what its inhabitants were about.

In the morning, our breakfasts were put through the hole in the door, in small oblong-square tin pans, made to fit, and holding a pint of chocolate, with brown bread, and an iron spoon. When they called for the vessels again, I was green enough to return what bread I had left; but my comrade seized it, and said that I should lay that up for lunch or dinner. Soon after he was let out to work at haying in a neighboring field, whither he went every day, and would not be back till noon; so he bade me good-day, saying that he doubted if he should see me again.

When I came out of prison,—for some one interfered, and paid that tax,—I did not perceive that great changes had taken place on the common, such as he observed who went in a youth and emerged a tottering and gray-headed man; and yet a change had to my eyes come over the scene,—the town, and State, and country,—greater than any that mere time could effect. I saw yet more distinctly the State in which I lived. I saw to what extent the people among whom I lived could be trusted as good neighbors and friends; that their friendship was for summer weather only; that they did not greatly propose to do right; that they were a distinct race from me by their prejudices and superstitions, as the Chinamen and Malays are; that in their sacrifices to humanity they ran no risks, not even to their property; that after all they were not so noble but they treated the thief as he had treated them, and hoped, by a certain outward observance and a few prayers, and by walking in a particular straight though useless path from time to time, to save their souls. This may be to judge my neighbors harshly; for I believe that many of them are not aware that they have such an institution as the jail in their village.

It was formerly the custom in our village, when a poor debtor came out of jail, for his acquaintances to salute him, looking through their fingers, which were crossed to represent the grating of a jail window, "How do ye do?" My neighbors did not thus salute me, but first looked at me, and then at one another, as if I had returned from a long journey. I was put into jail as I was going to the shoemaker's to get a shoe which was mended. When I was let out the next morning, I proceeded to finish my errand, and, having put on my mended shoe, joined a huckleberry party, who were impatient to put themselves under my conduct; and in half an hour,—for the horse was soon tackled,—was in the midst of a huckleberry field, on one of our highest hills, two miles off, and then the State was nowhere to be seen.

This is the whole history of "My Prisons."

I have never declined paying the highway tax, because I am as desirous of being a good neighbor as I am of being a bad subject; and as for supporting schools, I am doing my part to educate my fellow-countrymen now. It is for no particular item in the tax-bill that I refuse to pay it. I simply wish to refuse allegiance to the State, to withdraw and stand aloof from it effectually. I do not care to trace the course of my dollar, if I could, till it buys a man or a musket to shoot one with,—the dollar is innocent,—but I am concerned to trace the effects of my allegiance. In fact, I quietly declare war with the State, after my fashion, though I will still make what use and get what advantage of her I can, as is usual in such cases.

If others pay the tax which is demanded of me, from a sympathy with the State, they do but what they have already done in their own case, or rather they abet injustice to a greater extent than the State requires. If they pay the tax from a mistaken interest in the individual taxed, to save his property, or prevent his going to jail, it is because they have not considered wisely how far they let their private feelings interfere with the public good.

This, then, is my position at present. But one cannot be too much on his guard in such a case, lest his action be biased by obstinacy or an undue regard for the opinions of men. Let him see that he does only what belongs to himself and to the hour.

I think sometimes, Why, this people mean well, they are only ignorant; they would do better if they knew how: why give your neighbors this pain to treat you as they are not inclined to? But I think again, This is no reason why I should do as they do, or permit others to suffer much greater pain of a different kind. Again, I sometimes say to myself, When many millions of men, without heat, without ill will, without personal feeling of any kind, demand of you a few shillings only, without the possibility, such is their constitution, of retracting or altering their present demand, and without the possibility, on your side, of appeal to any other millions, why expose yourself to this overwhelming brute force? You do not resist cold and hunger, the winds and the waves, thus obstinately; you quietly submit to a thousand similar necessities. You do not put your head into the fire. But just in proportion as I regard this as not wholly a brute force, but partly a human force, and consider that I have relations to those millions as to so many millions of men, and not of mere brute or inanimate things, I see that appeal is possible, first and instantaneously, from them to the Maker of them, and, secondly, from them to themselves. But if I put my head deliberately into the fire, there is no appeal to fire or to the Maker of fire, and I have only myself to blame. If I could convince myself that I have any right to be satisfied with men as they are, and to treat them accordingly, and not according, in some respects, to my requisitions and expectations of what they and I ought to be, then, like a good Mussulman and fatalist, I should endeavor to be satisfied with things as they are, and say it is the will of God. And, above all, there is this difference between resisting this and a purely brute or natural force, that I can resist this with some effect; but I cannot expect, like Orpheus, to change the nature of the rocks and trees and beasts.

I do not wish to quarrel with any man or nation. I do not wish to split hairs, to make fine distinctions, or set myself up as better than my neighbors. I seek rather, I may say, even an excuse for conforming to the laws of the land. I am but too ready to conform to them. Indeed, I have reason to suspect myself on this head; and each year, as the tax-gatherer comes round, I find myself disposed to review the acts and position of the general and State governments, and the spirit of the people, to discover a pretext for conformity.

> We must affect our country as our parents,
> And if at any time we alienate
> Our love or industry from doing it honor,
> We must respect effects and teach the soul
> Matter of conscience and religion,
> And not desire of rule or benefit.

I believe that the State will soon be able to take all my work of this sort out of my hands, and then I shall be no better a patriot than my fellow-countrymen. Seen from a lower point of view, the Constitution, with all its faults, is very good; the law and the courts are very respectable; even this State and this American government are, in many respects, very admirable, and rare things, to be thankful for, such as a great many have described them; but seen from a point of view a little higher, they are what I have described them; seen from a higher still, and the highest, who shall say what they are, or that they are worth looking at or thinking of at all?

However, the government does not concern me much, and I shall bestow the fewest possible thoughts on it. It is not many moments that I live under a government, even in this world. If a man is thought-free, fancy-free, imagination-free, that which *is not* never for a long time appearing *to be* to him, unwise rulers or reformers cannot fatally interrupt him.

I know that most men think differently from myself; but those whose lives are by profession devoted to the study of these or kindred subjects content me as little as any. Statesmen and legislators, standing so completely within the institution, never distinctly and nakedly behold it. They speak of moving society, but have no resting-place without it. They may be men of a certain experience and discrimination, and have no doubt invented ingenious and even useful systems, for which we sincerely thank them; but all their wit and usefulness lie within certain not very wide limits. They are wont to forget that the world is not governed by policy and expediency. Webster never goes behind government, and so cannot speak with authority about it. His words are wisdom to those legislators who contemplate no essential reform in the existing government; but for thinkers, and those who legislate for all time, he never once glances at the subject. I know of those whose serene and wise speculations on this theme would soon reveal the limits of his mind's range and hospitality. Yet, compared with the cheap professions of most reformers, and the still cheaper wisdom and eloquence of politicians in general, his are almost the only sensible and valuable words, and we thank Heaven for him. Comparatively, he is always strong, original, and, above all, practical. Still, his quality is not wisdom, but prudence. The lawyer's truth is not Truth, but consistency or a consistent expediency. Truth is always in harmony with herself, and is not concerned chiefly to reveal the justice that may consist with wrong-doing. He well deserves to be called, as he has been called, the Defender of the Constitution. There are really no blows to be given by him but defensive ones. He is not a leader, but a follower. His leaders are the men of '87. "I have never made an effort," he says, "and never propose to make an effort; I have never countenanced an effort, and never mean to countenance an effort, to disturb the arrangement as originally made, by which the various States came into the Union." Still thinking of the sanction which the Constitution gives to slavery, he says, "Because it was a part of the original compact,—let it stand." Notwithstanding his special acuteness and ability, he is unable to take a fact out of its merely political relations, and behold it as it lies absolutely to be disposed of by the intellect,—what, for instance, it behooves a man to do here in America to-day with regard to slavery,—but ventures, or is driven, to make some such desperate answer as the following, while professing to speak absolutely, and as a private man,—from which what new and singular code of social duties might be inferred? "The manner," says he, "in which the governments of those States were slavery exists are to regulate it is for their own consideration, under their responsibility to their constituents, to the general laws of propriety, humanity, and justice, and to God. Associations formed elsewhere, springing from a feeling of humanity, or any other cause, have nothing whatever to do with it. They have never received any encouragement from me, and they never will."

They who know of no purer sources of truth, who have traced up its stream no higher, stand, and wisely stand, by the Bible and the Constitution, and drink at it there with reverence and humility; but they who behold where it comes trickling into this lake or that pool, gird up their loins once more, and continue their pilgrimage toward its fountain-head.

No man with a genius for legislation has appeared in America. They are rare in the history of the world. There are orators, politicians, and eloquent men, by the thousand; but the speaker has not yet opened his mouth to speak who is capable of settling the much-vexed questions of the day. We love eloquence for its own sake, and not for any truth which it may utter, or any heroism is may inspire. Our legislators have not yet learned the comparative value of free-trade and of freedom, of union, and of rectitude, to a nation. They have no genius or talent for comparatively humble questions of taxation and finance, commerce and manufactures and agriculture. If we were left solely to the wordy wit of legislators in Congress for our guidance, uncorrected by the seasonable experience and the effectual complaints of the people, America would not long retain her rank among the nations. For eighteen hundred years, though perchance I have no right to say it, the New Testament has been written; yet where is the legislator who has wisdom and practical talent enough to avail himself of the light which it sheds on the science of legislation?

The authority of government, even such as I am willing to submit to,— for I will cheerfully obey those who know and can do better than I, and in many things even those who neither know nor can do so well,—is still an impure one: to be strictly just, it must have the sanction and consent of the governed. It can have no pure right over my person and property but what I concede to it. The progress from an absolute to a limited monarchy, from a limited monarchy to a democracy, is a progress toward a true respect for the individual. Even the Chinese philosopher was wise enough to regard the individual as the basis of the empire. Is a democracy, such as we know it, the last improvement possible in government? Is it not possible to take a step further towards recognizing and organizing the rights of man? There will never be a really free and enlightened

State until the State comes to recognize the individual as a higher and independent power, from which all its own power and authority are derived, and treats him accordingly. I please myself with imagining a State at last which can afford to be just to all men, and to treat the individual with respect as a neighbor; which even would not think it inconsistent with its own repose if a few were to live aloof from it, not meddling with it, nor embraced by it, who fulfilled all the duties of neighbors and fellow-men. A State which bore this kind of fruit, and suffered it to drop off as fast as it ripened, would prepare the way for a still more perfect and glorious State, which also I have imagined, but not yet anywhere seen.

## Commentary: On Example, The Chapel Veteran, and Thoreau's Night in Jail

In the early spring of 1958 my wife and I went to England, and although I have forgotten much of what we experienced there except in the most general sense (the weather was dreadful, the currency confusing, the British Museum large, the theater inexpensive, most of the people friendly, some of the people not), one incident remains as vividly in my memory as if it had happened only last month and not more than a decade ago.

We were motorcycling through the countryside one rainy afternoon (I think this is how it was) when we happened upon a castle that offered guided tours and—my wife because she was curious about such things, and I because I was wet—we decided to go in. The castle was grandiose, as I suppose most castles are, and I cannot remember anything else about it except that it included a small, dimly lit chapel near the altar of which stood a signboard displaying the quotation from Isaiah: "They shall beat their swords into ploughshares, and their spears into pruning-hooks: nation shall not lift sword against nation, neither shall they learn war any more." A man stood in the shadows to the left of the altar and signboard, his gloved hands folded in front of him. He was a slender man in his mid-thirties, conservatively dressed, dark suit and tie, carefully polished shoes; and his face was so badly mutilated I remember thinking when I first noticed him that he must have been wearing some kind of grotesque mask. Our guide introduced us to this man, and he in turn quietly explained that he had suffered his disfigurement as a soldier in World War II and hoped that by standing near the altar as people passed he might in some small way support the cause of peace.

I have no doubt that had it not been for the specific example of one result of war, in the person of this gentle and physically devastated man,

I would have forgotten the chapel and its biblical appeal for peace as thoroughly as I see I have forgotten the district where the castle lay, its name, and all the special aspects of its grandiosity.

Now I think one of the essential elements in Thoreau's masterful essay "On Civil Disobedience"—as important to the success of the piece, say, as its style, overall architecture, and rhetorical devices—is the placing therein of the specific instance of Thoreau's night in jail. We can easily imagine the essay without it. The intellectual thrust of the argument would not suffer at all; we would understand clearly what Thoreau was telling us about the relationship of the individual and the state, just as we understand the quotation from Isaiah enjoining us against war. But it is finally the presence of the war-wounded man in the castle chapel, and the narration of the night in jail that provide the essential persuasion in each case, the specific element that buttresses the general appeal.

Our castle guide might simply have said, "I know a man who was terribly disfigured in the war," and rested his case for peace thereby and not led us to the man himself; just as Thoreau might simply have said that he had refused to pay his poll tax for six years and was "put into jail once on this account," and rested his case for principle thereby and not led us to the jail itself.

We might carry the analogy even further. It was not only the fact of the presence of the veteran in the chapel that led persuasion to the altar message but also the quality of the presence, the selection of its detail, so to speak: the man not dressed in bloody rags, but in a dark suit and tie; not standing under a bright light, but in the shadows; not ranting about war, but quietly explaining his presence to those who passed.

Thoreau's selection of detail as he narrates his night in jail is equally fine: not brooding prisoners, but men in their shirt-sleeves "enjoying a chat"; not the sound of chains, but the town clock striking; not bread and water, but "a pint of chocolate, with brown bread, and an iron spoon." Thoreau has argued, after all, that a man must live by the dictates of his conscience and that there are worse places to be than in jail; and here he demonstrates in specific terms that for him, at least, it was so.

Let us, for the sake of discussion, accept the analogy. On the one hand, we have the castle chapel, its brick and mortar, its icons, its aura of peace, its written message; and placed within this structure, the wounded man. And on the other hand, we have Thoreau's essay, its architecture and rhetoric, its metaphor, its aura of conviction, its reasoned argument; and placed within this structure, the narrative of the night in jail.

Two messages, each enhanced by a compelling case in point.

P. L. S.

## 2. LETTER TO MY NEPHEW

### James Baldwin

*While there is disagreement as to the merit of his fiction, James Baldwin is an acknowledged master of the essay form. In works such as* Notes of a Native Son, The Fire Next Time, *and in the work that follows, Baldwin proves an articulate commentator on the burdens a black inherits and bears in 20th-century America.*

Dear James:

I have begun this letter five times and torn it up five times. I keep seeing your face, which is also the face of your father and my brother. Like him, you are tough, dark, vulnerable, moody—with a very definite tendency to sound truculent because you want no one to think you are soft. You may be like your grandfather in this, I don't know, but certainly both you and your father resemble him very much physically. Well, he is dead, he never saw you, and he had a terrible life; he was defeated long before he died because, at the bottom of his heart, he really believed what white people said about him. This is one of the reasons that he became so holy. I am sure that your father has told you something about all that. Neither you nor your father exhibit any tendency towards holiness: you really *are* of another era, part of what happened when the Negro left the land and came into what the late E. Franklin Frazier called "the cities of destruction." You can only be destroyed by believing that you really are what the white world calls a *nigger*. I tell you this because I love you, and please don't you ever forget it.

I have known both of you all your lives, have carried your Daddy in my arms and on my shoulders, kissed and spanked him and watched him learn to walk. I don't know if you've known anybody from that far back; if you've loved anybody that long, first as an infant, then as a child, then as a man, you gain a strange perspective on time and human pain and effort. Other people cannot see what I see whenever I look into your father's face, for behind your father's face as it is today, are all those other faces which were his. Let him laugh and I see a cellar your father does not remember and a house he does not remember and I hear in his present laughter his laughter as a child. Let him curse and I remember

*Source:* "Letter to My Nephew" from *The Fire Next Time*, by James Baldwin. Copyright © 1962, 1963 by James Baldwin. Reprinted by permission of the publisher, The Dial Press.

him falling down the cellar steps, and howling, and I remember, with pain, his tears, which my hand or your grandmother's so easily wiped away. But no one's hand can wipe away those tears he sheds invisibly today, which one hears in his laughter and in his speech and in his songs. I know what the world has done to my brother and how narrowly he has survived it. And I know, which is much worse, and this is the crime of which I accuse my country and my countrymen, and for which neither I nor time nor history will ever forgive them, that they have destroyed and are destroying hundreds of thousands of living and do not know it and do not want to know it. One can be, indeed one must strive to become, tough and philosophical concerning destruction and death, for this is what most of mankind has been best at since we have heard of man. (But remember: *most* of mankind is not *all* of mankind.) But it is not permissible that the authors of devastation should also be innocent. It is the innocence which constitutes the crime.

Now, my dear namesake, these innocent and well-meaning people, your countrymen, have caused you to be born under conditions not very far removed from those described for us by Charles Dickens in the London of more than a hundred years ago. (I hear the chorus of the innocents screaming, "No! This is not true! How *bitter* you are!"—but I am writing this letter to *you*, to try to tell you something about how to handle *them*, for most of them do not yet really know that you exist. I *know* the conditions under which you were born, for I was there. Your countrymen were *not* there, and haven't made it yet. Your grandmother was also there, and no one has ever accused her of being bitter. I suggest that the innocents check with her. She isn't hard to find. Your countrymen don't know that *she* exists, either, though she has been working for them all their lives.)

Well, you were born, here you came, something like fifteen years ago; and though your father and mother and grandmother, looking about the streets through which they were carrying you, staring at the walls into which they brought you, had every reason to be heavyhearted, yet they were not. For here you were, Big James, named for me—you were a big baby, I was not—here you were: to be loved. To be loved, baby, hard, at once, and forever, to strengthen you against the loveless world. Remember that: I know how black it looks today, for you. It looked bad that day, too, yes, we were trembling. We have not stopped trembling yet, but if we had not loved each other none of us would have survived. And now you must survive because we love you, and for the sake of your children and your children's children.

This innocent country set you down in a ghetto in which, in fact, it intended that you should perish. Let me spell out precisely what I mean by that, for the heart of the matter is here, and the root of my dispute with my country. You were born where you were born and faced the future that you faced because you were black and *for no other reason.* The limits of your ambition were, thus, expected to be set forever. You were born into a society which spelled out with brutal clarity, and in as many ways as possible, that you were a worthless human being. You were not expected to aspire to excellence: you were expected to make peace with mediocrity. Wherever you have turned, James, in your short time on this earth, you have been told where you could go and what you could do (and *how* you could do it) and where you could live and whom you could marry. I know your countrymen do not agree with me about this, and I hear them saying, "You exaggerate." They do not know Harlem, and I do. So do you. Take no one's word for anything, including mine—but trust your experience. Know whence you came. If you know whence you came, there is really no limit to where you can go. The details and symbols of your life have been deliberately constructed to make you believe what white people say about you. Please try to remember that what they believe, as well as what they do and cause you to endure, does not testify to your inferiority but to their inhumanity and fear. Please try to be clear, dear James, through the storm which rages about your youthful head today, about the reality which lies behind the words *acceptance* and *integration.* There is no reason for you to try to become like white people and there is no basis whatever for their impertinent assumption that *they* must accept *you.* The really terrible thing, old buddy, is that *you* must accept *them.* And I mean that very seriously. You must accept them and accept them with love. For these innocent people have no other hope. They are, in effect, still trapped in a history which they do not understand; and until they understand it, they cannot be released from it. They have had to believe for many years, and for innumerable reasons, that black men are inferior to white men. Many of them, indeed, know better, but, as you will discover, people find it very difficult to act on what they know. To act is to be committed, and to be committed is to be in danger. In this case, the danger, in the minds of most Americans, is the loss of their identity. Try to imagine how you would feel if you woke up one morning to find the sun shining and all the stars aflame. You would be frightened because it is out of the order of nature. Any upheaval in the universe is terrifying because it so profoundly attacks one's sense of one's own reality. Well, the black man has functioned in the white man's world as a fixed star, as an immovable pillar: and as he moves out of his place, heaven and earth are shaken to their foundations. You, don't be afraid. I said that it was intended that you should perish in the ghetto, perish by never being allowed to go behind the white man's definitions, by never being allowed to spell your proper name. You have, and many of us have, defeated this intention; and, by a terrible law, a terrible paradox, those innocents who believed that your imprisonment made them safe are losing their grasp of reality. But these men are your brothers—your lost, younger brothers. And if the word *integration* means anything, this is what it means: that we, with love, shall force our brothers to see themselves as they are, to cease fleeing from reality and begin to change it. For this is your home, my friend, do not be driven from it; great men have done great things here, and will again, and we can make America what America must become. It will be hard, James, but you come from sturdy, peasant stock, men who picked cotton and dammed rivers and built railroads, and, in the teeth of the most terrifying odds, achieved an unassailable and monumental dignity. You come from a long line of great poets, some of the greatest poets since Homer. One of them said, *The very time I thought I was lost, My dungeon shook and my chains fell off.*

You know, and I know, that the country is celebrating one hundred years of freedom one hundred years too soon. We cannot be free until they are free. God bless you, James, and Godspeed.

Your uncle,
James

## 3. KING OF THE BINGO GAME

### Ralph Ellison

*Ralph Ellison established his reputation as a novelist with* Invisible Man *which appeared in 1952. A gifted and thoughtful writer in several genres, Ellison develops an intriguing metaphor in "King Of The Bingo Game."*

The woman in front of him was eating roasted peanuts that smelled so good that he could barely contain his hunger. He could not even sleep and wished they'd hurry and begin the bingo game. There, on his right, two fellows were drinking wine out of a bottle wrapped in a paper bag, and he could hear soft gurgling in the dark. His stomach gave a low, gnawing growl. "If this was down South," he thought, "all I'd have to do is lean over and say, 'Lady, gimme a few of those peanuts, please ma'am,' and she'd pass me the bag and never think of it." Or he could ask the fellows for a drink in the same way. Folks down South stuck together that way; they didn't even have to know you. But up here it was different. Ask somebody for something, and they'd think you were crazy. Well, I ain't crazy. I'm just broke, 'cause I got no birth certificate to get a job, and Laura 'bout to die 'cause we got no money for a doctor. But I ain't crazy. And yet a pinpoint of doubt was focused in his mind as he glanced toward the screen and saw the hero stealthily entering a dark room and sending the beam of a flashlight along a wall of bookcases. This is where he finds the trapdoor, he remembered. The man would pass abruptly through the wall and find the girl tied to a bed, her legs and arms spread wide, and her clothing torn to rags. He laughed softly to himself. He had seen the picture three times, and this was one of the best scenes.

On his right the fellow whispered wide-eyed to his companion, "Man, look a-yonder!"

"Damn!"

"Wouldn't I like to have her tied up like that . . ."

"Hey! That fool's letting her loose!"

"Aw, man, he loves her."

"Love or no love!"

The man moved impatiently beside him, and he tried to involve himself in the scene. But Laura was on his mind. Tiring quickly of watching the picture he looked back to where the white beam filtered from the projection room above the balcony. It started small and grew large, specks of dust dancing in its whiteness as it reached the screen. It was strange how the beam always landed right on the screen and didn't mess up and fall somewhere else. But they had it all fixed. Everything was fixed. Now suppose when they showed that girl with her dress torn the girl started taking off the rest of her clothes, and when the guy came in he didn't untie her but kept her there and went to taking off his own clothes? *That* would be something to see. If a picture got out of hand like that those guys up there would go nuts. Yeah, and there'd be so many folks in here you couldn't find a seat for nine months! A strange sensation played over his skin. He shuddered. Yesterday he'd seen a bedbug on a woman's neck as they walked out into the bright street. But exploring his thigh through a hole in his pocket he found only goose pimples and old scars.

The bottle gurgled again. He closed his eyes. Now a dreamy music was accompanying the film and train whistles were sounding in the distance, and he was a boy again walking along a railroad trestle down South, and seeing the train coming, and running back as fast as he could go, and hearing the whistle blowing, and getting off the trestle to solid ground just in time, with the earth trembling beneath his feet, and feeling relieved as he ran down the cinder-strewn embankment onto the highway, and looking back and seeing with terror that the train had left the track and was following him right down the middle of the street, and all the white people laughing as he ran screaming . . .

"Wake up there, buddy! What the hell do you mean hollering like that? Can't you see we trying to enjoy this here picture?"

He stared at the man with gratitude.

"I'm sorry, old man," he said. "I musta been dreaming."

"Well, here, have a drink. And don't be making no noise like that, damn!"

His hands trembled as he tilted his head. It was not wine, but whiskey. Cold rye whiskey. He took a deep swoller, decided it was better not to take another, and handed the bottle back to its owner.

"Thanks, old man," he said.

Now he felt the cold whiskey breaking a warm path straight through the middle of him, growing hotter and sharper as it moved. He had not eaten all day, and it made him light-headed. The smell of the peanuts stabbed him like a knife, and he got up and found a seat in the middle aisle. But no sooner did he sit than he saw a row of intense-faced young girls, and got up again, thinking, "You chicks musta been Lindy-hopping somewhere." He found a seat several rows ahead as the lights came on, and he saw the screen disappear behind a heavy red and gold curtain; then the curtain rising, and the man with the microphone and a uniformed attendant coming on the stage.

He felt for his bingo cards, smiling. The guy at the door wouldn't like it if he knew about his having *five* cards. Well, not everyone played the bingo game; and even with five cards he didn't have much of a chance. For Laura, though, he had to have faith. He studied the cards, each with its different numerals, punching the free center hole in each and spreading them neatly across his lap; and when the lights faded he sat slouched in his seat so that he could look from his cards to the bingo wheel with but a quick shifting of his eyes.

Ahead, at the end of the darkness, the man with the microphone was pressing a button attached to a long cord and spinning the bingo wheel and calling out the number each time the wheel came to rest. And each time the voice rang out his finger raced over the cards for the number. With five cards he had to move fast. He became nervous; there were too many cards, and the man went too fast with his grating voice. Perhaps he should just select one and throw the others away. But he was afraid. He became warm. Wonder how much Laura's doctor would cost? Damn that, watch the cards! And with despair he heard the man call three in a row which he missed on all five cards. This way he'd never win . . .

When he saw the row of holes punched across the third card, he sat paralyzed and heard the man call three more numbers before he stumbled forward, screaming,

"Bingo! Bingo!"

"Let that fool up there," someone called.

"Get up there, man!"

He stumbled down the aisle and up the steps to the stage into a light so sharp and bright that for a moment it blinded him, and he felt that he had moved into the spell of some strange, mysterious power. Yet it was as familiar as the sun, and he knew it was the perfectly familiar bingo.

The man with the microphone was saying something to the audience as he held out his card. A cold light flashed from the man's finger as the card left his hand. His knees trembled. The man stepped closer, checking the card against the numbers chalked on the board. Suppose he had made a mistake? The pomade on the man's hair made him feel faint, and he backed away. But the man was checking the card over the microphone now, and he had to stay. He stood tense, listening.

"Under the O, forty-four," the man chanted. "Under the I, seven. Under the G, three. Under the B, ninety-six. Under the N, thirteen!"

His breath came easier as the man smiled at the audience.

"Yessir, ladies and gentlemen, he's one of the chosen people!"

The audience rippled with laughter and applause.

"Step right up to the front of the stage."

He moved slowly forward, wishing that the light was not so bright.

"To win tonight's jackpot of $36.90 the wheel must stop between the double zero, understand?"

He nodded, knowing the ritual from the many days and nights he had watched the winners march across the stage to press the button that controlled the spinning wheel and receive the prizes. And now he followed the instructions as though he'd crossed the slippery stage a million prize-winning times.

The man was making some kind of a joke, and he nodded vacantly. So tense had he become that he felt a sudden desire to cry and shook it away. He felt vaguely that his whole life was determined by the bingo wheel; not only that which would happen now that he was at last before it, but all that had gone before, since his birth, and his mother's birth and the birth of his father. It had always been there, even though he had not been aware of it, handing out the unlucky cards and numbers of his days. The image persisted, and he started quickly away. I better get down from here before I make a fool of myself, he thought.

"Here, boy," the man called. "You haven't started yet."

Someone laughed as he went hesitatingly back.

"Are you all reet?"

He grinned at the man's jive talk, but no words would come, and he knew it was not a convincing grin. For suddenly he knew that he stood on the slippery brink of some terrible embarrassment.

"Where are you from, boy?" the man asked.

"Down South."

"He's from down South, ladies and gentlemen," the man said. "Where from? Speak right into the mike."

"Rocky Mont," he said. "Rock' Mont, North Car'lina."

"So you decided to come down off that mountain to the U. S.," the man laughed. He felt that the man was making a fool of him, but then something cold was placed in his hand, and the lights were no longer behind him.

Standing before the wheel he felt alone, but that was somehow right, and he remembered his plan. He would give the wheel a short quick twirl. Just a touch of the button. He had watched it many times, and always it came close to double zero when it was short and quick. He steeled himself; the fear had left, and he felt a profound sense of promise, as though he were about to be repaid for all the things he'd suffered all his life. Trembling, he pressed the button. There was a whirl of lights, and in a second he realized with finality that though he wanted to, he could not stop. It was as though he held a high-powered line in his naked hand. His nerves tightened. As the wheel increased its speed it seemed to draw him more and more into its power, as though it held his fate; and with it came a deep need to submit, to whirl, to lose himself in its swirl of color. He could not stop it now, he knew. So let it be.

The button rested snugly in his palm where the man had placed it. And now he became aware of the man beside him, advising him through the microphone, while behind the shadowy audience hummed with noisy voices. He shifted his feet. There was still that feeling of helplessness within him, making part of him desire to turn back, even now that the jackpot was right in his hand. He squeezed the button until his fist ached. Then, like the sudden shriek of a subway whistle, a doubt tore through his head. Suppose he did not spin the wheel long enough? What could he do, and how could he tell? And then he knew, even as he wondered, that as long as he pressed the button, he could control the jackpot. He and only he could determine whether or not it was to be his. Not even the man with the microphone could do anything about it now. He felt drunk. Then, as though he had come down from a high hill into a valley of people, he heard the audience yelling.

"Come down from there, you jerk!"

"Let somebody else have a chance . . ."

"Ole Jack thinks he done found the end of the rainbow . . ."

The last voice was not unfriendly, and he turned and smiled dreamily into the yelling mouths. Then he turned his back squarely on them.

"Don't take too long, boy," a voice said.

He nodded. They were yelling behind him. Those folks did not understand what had happened to him. They had been playing the bingo game day in and night out for years, trying to win rent money or hamburger change. But not one of those wise guys had discovered this wonderful thing. He watched the wheel whirling past the numbers and experienced a burst of exaltation: This is God! This is the really truly God! He said it aloud, "This is God!"

He said it with such absolute conviction that he feared he would fall fainting into the footlights. But the crowd yelled so loud that they could not hear. Those fools, he thought. I'm here trying to tell them the most wonderful secret in the world, and they're yelling like they gone crazy. A hand fell upon his shoulder.

"You'll have to make a choice now, boy. You've taken too long."

He brushed the hand violently away.

"Leave me alone, man. I know what I'm doing!"

The man looked surprised and held on to the microphone for support.

And because he did not wish to hurt the man's feelings he smiled, realizing with a sudden pang that there was no way of explaining to the man just why he had to stand there pressing the button forever.

"Come here," he called tiredly.

The man approached, rolling the heavy microphone across the stage.

"Anybody can play this bingo game, right?" he said.

"Sure, but . . ."

He smiled, feeling inclined to be patient with this slick looking white man with his blue sport shirt and his sharp gabardine suit.

"That's what I thought," he said. "Anybody can win the jackpot as long as they get the lucky number, right?"

"That's the rule, but after all . . ."

"That's what I thought," he said. "And the big prize goes to the man who knows how to win it?"

The man nodded speechlessly.

"Well then, go on over there and watch me win like I want to. I ain't going to hurt nobody," he said, "and I'll show you how to win. I mean to show the whole world how it's got to be done."

And because he understood, he smiled again to let the man know that he held nothing against him for being white and impatient. Then he refused to see the man any longer and stood pressing the button, the voices of the crowd reaching him like sounds in distant streets. Let them yell. All the Negroes down there were just ashamed because he was black like them. He smiled inwardly, knowing how it was. Most of the time he was ashamed of what Negroes did himself. Well, let them be ashamed for something this time. Like him. He was like a long thin black wire that was being stretched and wound upon the bingo wheel; wound until he wanted to scream; wound, but this time himself controlling the winding and the sadness and the shame, and because he did, Laura would be all right. Suddenly the lights flickered. He staggered backwards. Had something gone wrong? All this noise. Didn't they know that although he controlled the wheel, it also controlled him, and unless he pressed the button forever and ever it would stop, leaving him high and dry, dry and high on this hard high slippery hill and Laura dead? There was only one chance; he had to do whatever the wheel demanded. And gripping the button in despair, he discovered with surprise that it imparted a nervous energy. His spine tingled. He felt a certain power.

Now he faced the raging crowd with defiance, its screams penetrating his eardrums like trumpets shrieking from a juke-box. The vague faces glowing in the bingo lights gave him a sense of himself that he had never known before. He was running the show, by God! They had to react to him, for he was their luck. This is *me*, he thought. Let the bastards yell.

Then someone was laughing inside him, and he realized that somehow he had forgotten his own name. It was a sad, lost feeling to lose your name, and a crazy thing to do. That name had been given him by the white man who had owned his grandfather a long lost time ago down South. But maybe those wise guys knew his name.

"Who am I?" he screamed.

"Hurry up and bingo, you jerk!"

They didn't know either, he thought sadly. They didn't even know their own names, they were all poor nameless bastards. Well, he didn't need that old name; he was reborn. For as long as he pressed the button he was The-man-who-pressed-the-button-who-held-the-prize-who-was-the-King-of-Bingo. That was the way it was, and he'd have to press the button even if nobody understood, even though Laura did not understand.

"Live!" he shouted.

The audience quieted like the dying of a huge fan.

"Live, Laura, baby. I got holt of it now, sugar. Live!"

He screamed it, tears streaming down his face. "I got nobody but YOU!"

The screams tore from his very guts. He felt as though the rush of blood to his head would burst out in baseball seams of small red droplets, like a head beaten by police clubs. Bending over he saw a trickle of blood splashing the toe of his shoe. With his free hand he searched his head. It was his nose. God, suppose something has gone wrong? He felt that the whole audience had somehow entered him and was stamping its feet in his stomach and he unable to throw them out. They wanted the prize, that was it. They wanted the secret for themselves. But they'd never get it; he would keep the bingo wheel whirling forever, and Laura would be safe in the wheel. But would she? It had to be, because if she were not safe the wheel would cease to turn; it could not go on. He had to get away, *vomit* all, and his mind formed an image of himself running with Laura in his arms down the tracks of the subway just ahead of an A train, running desperately *vomit* with people screaming for him to come out but knowing no way of leaving the tracks because to stop would bring the train crushing down upon him and to attempt to leave across the other tracks would mean to run into a hot third rail as high as his waist which threw blue sparks that blinded his eyes until he could hardly see.

He heard singing and the audience was clapping its hands.

*Shoot the liquor to him, Jim, boy*
*Clap-clap-clap*

*Well a-calla the cop*
*He's blowing his top!*
*Shoot the liquor to him, Jim, boy!*

Bitter anger grew within him at the singing. They think I'm crazy. Well let 'em laugh. I'll do what I got to do.

He was standing in an attitude of intense listening when he saw that they were watching something on the stage behind him. He felt weak. But when he turned he saw no one. If only his thumb did not ache so. Now they were applauding. And for a moment he thought that the wheel had stopped. But this was impossible, his thumb still pressed the button. Then he saw them. Two men in uniform beckoned from the end of the stage. They were coming toward him, walking in step, slowly, like a tap-dance team returning for a third encore. But their shoulders shot forward, and he backed away, looking wildly about. There was nothing to fight them with. He had only the long black cord which led to a plug somewhere back stage, and he couldn't use that because it operated the bingo wheel. He backed slowly, fixing the men with his eyes as his lips stretched over his teeth in a tight, fixed grin; moved toward the end of the stage and realizing that he couldn't go much further, for suddenly the cord became taut and he couldn't afford to break the cord. But he had to do something. The audience was howling. Suddenly he stopped dead, seeing the men halt, their legs lifted as in an interrupted step of a slow-motion dance. There was nothing to do but run in the other direction and he dashed forward, slipping and sliding. The men fell back, surprised. He struck out violently going past.

"Grab him!"

He ran, but all too quickly the cord tightened, resistingly, and he turned and ran back again. This time he slipped them, and discovered by running in a circle before the wheel he could keep the cord from tightening. But this way he had to flail his arms to keep the men away. Why couldn't they leave a man alone? He ran, circling.

"Ring down the curtain," someone yelled. But they couldn't do that. If they did the wheel flashing from the projection room would be cut off. But they had him before he could tell them so, trying to pry open his fist, and he was wrestling and trying to bring his knees into the fight and holding on to the button, for it was his life. And now he was down, seeing a foot coming down, crushing his wrist cruelly, down, as he saw the wheel whirling serenely above.

"I can't give it up," he screamed. Then quietly, in a confidential tone, "Boys, I really can't give it up."

It landed hard against his head. And in the blank moment they had it away from him, completely now. He fought them trying to pull him up from the stage as he watched the wheel spin slowly to a stop. Without surprise he saw it rest at double-zero.

"You see," he pointed bitterly.

"Sure, boy, sure, it's O.K.," one of the men said smiling.

And seeing the man bow his head to someone he could not see, he felt very, very happy; he would receive what all the winners received.

But as he warmed in the justice of the man's tight smile he did not see the man's slow wink, nor see the bow-legged man behind him step clear of the swiftly descending curtain and set himself for a blow. He only felt the dull pain exploding in his skull, and he knew even as it slipped out of him that his luck had run out on the stage.

### Commentary: The Writer as Builder—Some Notes on Craft, Consistency, and Precision

In the writing of short stories, as in the creation of any art or craft, something is often lost between the conception of an idea and its exection. A woodworker decides to build a cradle for a newborn child. He conceives what he would like his cradle to look like, figures the scale, constructs a model, orders his wood, makes his cuts, assembles the cradle, sands it, finishes it; and when it is finished and he evaluates it against his original idea, he finds that it is very good in all perspectives except one, an ill-proportioned side, perhaps, which was not evident in scale.

The parents of the child are delighted as are the friends of the woodworker and most of the people who see the cradle; but the woodworker himself is not entirely pleased. The cradle is elegant enough except in that one perspective that is certainly less than what he had hoped; conspicuous, in fact, and troubling to him in light of the private view he had of his original conception.

I think in "King of the Bingo Game" something similar has happened, something has come between conception and execution, in this case a number of small imprecisions and lapses that, while not fatal, do detract from the story. There are, for example, inconsistencies in style as when in the first paragraph the voice of the interior monologue shifts from the grammatical "Ask somebody for something, and they'd think you were crazy" to the ungrammatical "Well, I ain't crazy. I'm just broke 'cause I got no birth certificate. . . ." Or later when the authorial voice uses the word "swoller." Or in the dialogue when the same speaker can say, "Well then, go on over there and watch me win like I want to" and "I got holt of it now, sugar. Live!" These lapses in style raise doubts as to the kind of man the central character is (literate or illiterate), and as to our own vantage point in observing the story (are we viewing events through the eyes and mind of the author, or of the protagonist).

Although the setting of scene is sometimes beautifully precise (as the beam of light from the projection room which "started small and grew large, specks of dust dancing in its whiteness as it reached the screen"), there is an imprecision in the overall description of the theater and in some of the concrete detail. Is the theater crowded? (At first it does not seem to be; later it does.) Are most of the patrons black? (We assume that they are, but we don't know.) Exactly how does the bingo game work? (We finally learn that the wheel is flashed from the projection room, but there is nothing to keep us from assuming it is actually on the stage when it is first described.) How big are the bingo cards? (We are told the protagonist can spread five of them "neatly across his lap" which indicates they are small, but that he can also read them in the darkened theater which indicates they must be fairly large.) How does he know that the wrapped bottle contains "rye" whiskey? Why is the man sitting at his right first described as "the man" and later as "the old man"? Why do we not learn when the emcee is first introduced that he is white? What happens to the "uniformed attendant" who comes on stage with him?

The conception of the central figure of the story, this poor southern black who sits in a northern cinema and feels that his life has been reduced to one last chance in an absurd game, is clearly imaginative and ripe with possibility; but as he is rendered here it is difficult, for me at least, to feel more than a reflex sympathy for him, a knee-jerk response to the information that he is hungry and out of work, that Laura, who means everything to him, is dying. I hear this information, understand it, but never quite feel it. And this leads me to question the end of the story, which is also inventive and full of suggestion, because I am not finally convinced that the protagonist as I know him from the beginning of the story is capable of the insights I am led to believe he has during the final scene.

But it is too easy, of course, to sit in judgment of another man's work, and too difficult to do good work of our own. I should reveal myself then as the woodworker who built the cradle that was off in one perspective, and as the author of a story that appears later in this book and that is also not without flaw.

P. L. S.

## 4. THE SIEGE OF CHICAGO

**Norman Mailer**

*As a novelist, Norman Mailer has never achieved the distinction that many (including himself) think he deserves; but as a journalist and observer of contemporary American life he is without peer. His fine style, disarming frankness, and lucid perceptions are apparent in the following selection from his book-length report on the 1968 political conventions.*

## Chapters 20 to 22

The focus of his fear had begun for him on Tuesday, no, put it back to Monday night in Lincoln Park when he had left as Ginsberg and Burroughs and Genet and Terry Southern were going in—up to the front. Of course, he could even put the fear back to Sunday afternoon, when he had heard the music, seen the children on the grass and the police on the walks and felt a sensation in his stomach not different from the dread in the bottom of the lungs one knows after hours of driving on ice. But then he had been afraid of Chicago ever since he had word in December of a Youth Festival which might attempt to make the Democrats nominate Lyndon Johnson under armed guard. So, in fact, this had been a fear he had been living with for a long time—like many another. It was as if different fears found different abodes in the body and dwelled in their place for years.

But yesterday, Tuesday, the fear had grown dimensions, forced consciousness to surface. Usually he did whatever he would do—be it courageous or evasive—without living too intimately with his anxiety. But, this time, it revealed itself. He had a particular reluctance to go to the meeting at the bandshell in Grant Park on Wednesday afternoon, then on the march to the Amphitheatre which would follow. This march would never be allowed to approach the Amphitheatre—one had not felt Mayor Daley's presence in Chicago these days for nothing!

There was much structure to the fear, much reasoned argument in its support. He had an enormous amount of work before him if he was going to describe this convention, and only two weeks in which to do it

*Source:* "Miami and the Seige of Chicago" from *Miami and the Seige of Chicago,* by Norman Mailer. Copyright © 1968 by Norman Mailer. Reprinted by arrangement with The New American Library, Inc., N.Y., N.Y.

if his article were to appear before election. A bad beating might lose him days, or a week; each day of writing would be irreplaceable to him. Besides, a variety of militant choices would now be present for years. One simply could not accept the dangerous alternative every time; he would never do any other work. And then with another fear, conservative was this fear, he looked into his reluctance to lose even the America he had had, that insane warmongering technology land with its smog, its superhighways, its experts and its profound dishonesty. Yet, it had allowed him to write—it had even not deprived him entirely of honors, certainly not of an income. He had lived well enough to have six children, a house on the water, a good apartment, good meals, good booze, he had even come to enjoy wine. A revolutionary with taste in wine has come already half the distance from Marx to Burke; he belonged in England where one's radicalism might never be tested; no, truth, he was still enough of a novelist to have the roots of future work in every vein and stratum he had encountered, and a profound part of him (exactly that enormous literary bottom of the mature novelist's property!) detested the thought of seeing his American society—evil, absurd, touching, pathetic, sickening, comic, full of novelistic marrow—disappear now in the nihilistic maw of a national disorder. The Yippies might yet disrupt the land—or worse, since they would not really have the power to do that, might serve as a pretext to bring in totalitarian phalanxes of law and order. Of course that was why he was getting tired of hearing of Negro rights and Black Power—every Black riot was washing him loose with the rest, pushing him to that point where he would have to throw his vote in with revolution—what a tedious perspective of prisons and law courts and worse; or stand by and watch as the best Americans white and Black would be picked off, expended, busted, burned and finally lost. No, exile would be better. Yet he loathed the thought of living anywhere but in America—he was too American by now: he did not wish to walk down foreign streets and think with imperfect nostalgia of dirty grease on groovy hamburgers, not when he didn't even eat them here. And then there might not be any foreign lands, not for long. The plague he had written about for years seemed to be coming in—he would understand its social phenomena more quickly than the rest. Or would, if he did not lose his detachment and have to purchase cheap hope. Drinking across the street from Grant Park, the possibility of succumbing to fears larger than himself appeared, if no more than a spot on the horizon, still possible to him. No more than a spot on the horizon had seemed Humphrey's candidacy when first it was bruited. Was that why delegates were marching now with candles? So that they would not succumb to fears larger than themselves?

It was as if the historical temperature in America went up every month. At different heats, the oils of separate psyches were loosened—different good Americans began to fry. Of course their first impulse was to hope the temperature would be quickly reduced. Perhaps they could go back to the larder again. But if it continued, then the particular solution which had provided him with a modicum at least of worldly happiness—the fine balance he might have achieved between the satisfaction of idealism and the satisfaction of need (call it greed) would be disrupted altogether, and then his life could not go on as it had. In the size of his fear, he was discovering how large a loss that would be. He liked his life. He wanted it to go on, which meant that he wanted America to go on—not as it was going, not Vietnam—but what price was he really willing to pay? Was he ready to give up the pleasures of making his movies, writing his book? They were pleasures finally he did not want to lose.

Yet if he indulged his fear, found all the ways to avoid the oncoming ugly encounters, then his life was equally spoiled, and on the poorer side. He was simply not accustomed to living with a conscience as impure as the one with which he had watched from the nineteenth floor. Or had it really been impure? Where was his true engagement? To be forty-five years old, and have lost a sense of where his loyalties belonged—to the revolution or to the stability of the country (at some painful personal price it could be suggested ) was to bring upon himself the anguish of the European intellectual in the Thirties. And the most powerful irony for himself is that he had lived for a dozen empty hopeless years after the second world war with the bitterness, rage, and potential militancy of a real revolutionary, he had had some influence perhaps upon this generation of Yippies now in the street, but no revolution had arisen in the years when he was ready—the timing of his soul was apocalyptically maladroit.

These are large thoughts for a reporter to have. Reporters live happily removed from themselves. They have eyes to see, ears to hear, and fingers for the note in their report. It was as if the drink he took in now moved him millimeter by millimeter out from one hat into another. He would be driven yet to participate or keep the shame in his liver—the last place to store such emotion! Liver disease is the warehousing of daily shame—they will trace the chemistry yet!

He had spoken this afternoon at the meeting. He had not wanted to; he had told David Dellinger on Tuesday afternoon that he would not speak—he did not wish to expose prematurely the ideas being stored for his piece. Dellinger nodded. He would not argue. He was a man of sturdy appearance with a simplicity and solidity of manner that was comfortable. He gave the impression of a man who told the truth, but as decently as possible. The reporter had called him to say he wished to visit Mobilization Headquarters to talk to him but since Dellinger was going to be in the Hilton, he came up in fact to the reporter's room on Tuesday afternoon with his son and Rennie Davis. The reporter told him he would not go on the march because he did not wish to get arrested—he could not afford even a few days in jail at this point if they chose to make him an example. So he would not appear at the bandshell either. He simply did not wish to stand there and watch others march off. Dellinger did not argue, nor did he object. He was a man of obvious patience and seemed of the conclusion that everybody brought his own schedule of militancy to each occasion. So he merely sipped his drink and watched the convention on television for a few minutes. It had been his first opportunity to watch it, his first opportunity doubtless to relax in a week. As he got up to go he grinned at the set, and said, "You know, this is kind of interesting."

Wednesday afternoon, the reporter had been at the same set in the same room, watching the debate on the peace plank. After awhile, he knew that he would not be able to stay away from the meeting. Yet when he got there, past the police, the marshals, and stood in the crowd, he knew nothing of what had happened already, he did not know Rennie Davis had been beaten unconscious, nor of Tom Hayden's angry speech and others—there was just Allen Ginsberg giving his address on the calming value of OM. Then Burroughs spoke and Genet. He had to go up himself—it was now impossible not to. So he highstepped his way forward in the crowd, awkwardly, over people seated in the grass, came to the shell, climbed up—there were a dozen people sitting on various chairs back of the podium—then went up to Dellinger and asked if he could speak. Dellinger gave a smile. He was welcome.

So he had spoken at the bandshell. Standing there, seeing the crowd before him, feeling the predictable warmth of this power, all his courage was back, or so it felt—he was finally enough of an actor to face perils on a stage he would not meet as quickly other ways. And felt a surprising respect, even admiration, for the people on the benches and in the grass who had been tear-gassed day after day and were here now ready to march. He had even begun by saying to them, "You're beautiful," a show-biz vulgarity he detested to the root of his nerve, but he said it, and then made jokes about the smell of Mace on the microphone—the odor of stink bombs or Mace pervaded the charcoal-colored sponge over the microphone. Next, he went on to say that they were all at the beginning of a war which would continue for twenty years and this march today would be one battle in it. Then he explained that he would not be on this march because he had a deadline and could not take the chance, "but you will all know what I am full of, if you don't see me on other marches," he had added, and they cheered him, cheered him enthusiastically even before he said that he had come there merely to pay his respects and salute them. It affected him that they cheered him for even this relatively quietistic speech, and when he was done, they cried out, "Write good, baby," and some young Negro from the Panthers or the Rangers or from where he did not know, serving as some kind of pro tem master of ceremonies now held his arm up high with his own, Black and white arms together in the air, he had been given a blessing by this Black, and felt rueful at unkind thoughts of late. And kept his word, and left soon after, and had a good early dinner with friends in order not to get to the convention too late. And had happened to be in his room washing up when the massacre on the march, three hours later, had come. Now, he was drinking in this bar across the street from Grant Park with a pleasant Californian who worked for McGovern. The reporter enjoyed his drinks. The bar was closing and he would go to bed. But the memory of his speech that afternoon was bothering him. It had been too easy. He knew it would have been better if he had been on the march, been in the massacre, even been on the vigil marching up from the Amphitheatre. Through the drinks, shame was warehousing in his liver.

So it was that when he got up to go, and said good night to his new-found friend, he did not then enter and cross the lobby but stepped outside the hotel and went across Michigan Avenue.


21

The National Guard was out in force. On the side streets of the hotel, two-and-a-half-ton Army trucks were parked, jamming every space. Traffic was cut off. The Daley-dozers, named yesterday by a newspaper man, those Jeeps with barbed-wire grids in front of their bumpers, were lined in file across Michigan Avenue just south of the Hilton, and he crossed over to Grant Park with the sound of Army vehicles revving up, the low coughing urgency of carburetors flooded and goosed and jabbed and chocked by nervous drivers, feet riding the accelerator and clutch while their truck waited in place. The huge searchlights near the Hilton were shining from a height of ten or fifteen feet, from a balcony or a truck, he could not see in the glare, but they lit up the debris and clangor of Michigan Avenue, the line of soldiers on the sidewalk of Michigan Avenue just off the edge of Grant Park, the huge pent crowd, thousands here, facing the line of troops. For some reason or other, a hydrant had been opened on Michigan Avenue in the hollow square formed by lines of National Guard and police barriers before the Hilton, and the lights of the searchlight reflecting from the wet street gave that dazzle of light and urgency and *glamour* unique to a movie company shooting in a city late at night, crowds dazzled themselves by their own good luck in being present.

At that moment, he had a sign of what to do, which is to say, he had an impulse. His impulses, perhaps in compensation for his general regime of caution were usually sufficiently sensational to need four drinks for gasoline before they could even be felt. Now without questioning the impulse, he strode down the line of troops walking under their raised guns, not a foot away from their faces, looking (he supposed —perhaps he even did) like an inspecting officer, for he stared severely or thoughtfully or condescendingly into each separate soldier's face with that official scrutiny of character which inspecting officers had once drilled into him. He was in fact fulfilling an old military dream. Since some of the soldiers did not like what he was doing, not altogether! and shifted their rifles abruptly with loud claps of their hand like stallions now nervous and therefore kicking the boards of their stall with abrupt and warning displeasure, he had the obverse pleasure of finding his nerve was firm again, he was sublimely indifferent to the possibility that any of these soldiers might give him a crack on the head with their rifle.

In the middle of examining this line—it must have been two hundred soldiers long, some weary, some bored, some nervous, some curious or friendly, some charged with animosity; nearly all sloppy in their uniforms which he noticed with displeasure—he was indeed an inspecting officer—he passed by the speaker's stand, a park table, or something of the sort, on which a dozen men were standing, one with a microphone attached by a wire to a big portable bullhorn held by another demonstrator. The speeches were going on, and a couple of guitarists appeared ready to perform next.

A woman he knew, who worked on the McCarthy staff, approached him. "Will you speak?" she asked.

He nodded. He felt more or less ready to speak and would have answered, "Yes, just as soon as I conclude this inspection," if some saving wit in a corner of his brain had not recognized how absurd this would seem to her.

So he concluded his inspection, taking the time to regard each soldier in that long line, and felt as if he had joined some private victory between one part of himself and another—just what, would have been tedious to consider at the moment, for he felt charged, ready, full of orator's muscle.

A Yippie wearing a dirty torn sweater, his hair long, curly, knotted, knuckled with coils and thrusting vertically into the air, hair quite the match of Bob Dylan's, was running the program and whispered hello cordially, worked him to the center of this ridiculously small platform, perhaps the area of two large bathtubs put side by side, and told him he would speak as soon as the electric guitarists were done.

He stood then in the center between two guitars who were singing a loud wild banging folk rock, somewhat corny, a patriotic song of the Left whose title eluded him. He did not like the song usually, but up on the platform, flanked by the singers, the bullhorn being held just back of his head turned out to the crowd, he felt insulated by the sound, blasted with it completely and so somehow safe with it, womb-safe with it, womb-cushioned—did the embryo live in such a waterfall of uproar each time the mother's digestion turned over? His mind was agreeably empty as he waited, good sign generally that he was ready to deliver a real speech.

When the song ended and he was given the mike after a generous introduction and a sweet surge of applause beefed up to its good point precisely by the introduction of the youth in the dirty sweater and the hair like Bob Dylan, he spoke out to the crowd just long enough to tell them he wanted to speak first to the soldiers. Then he turned his back, and the loudspeaker turned with him, and he talked to the line of troops he had not long ago passed, introducing himself as a novelist whose war novel some of them might possibly have read since it was famous in many barracks for its filthy passages and four-letter words, although not nearly so famous as another work, *From Here to Eternity*, with whose author he was often confused. He did not wish to disappoint the soldiers, he said, but he was not that fine author, Mr. James Jones, but the other, the one who had written the other book.

These remarks given and enjoyed by him, he then talked to the soldiers as a man who had been a soldier once. "As I walked down your line, inspecting you, I realized that you are all about the kind of soldier I was nearly twenty-five years ago, that is to say, not a very good soldier, somewhat unhappy with the Army I found myself in." But, he went on, the war in which he himself had fought had not bothered his sense of what might be right the way this war in Vietnam must bother them. And he went on to talk about how American soldiers could take little pride in a war where they had the superiority and yet could not win, and he thought that was because they were ashamed of the war. Americans were conceivably the best fighting soldiers in the world if they could ever find a war which was the most honorable war in the world for them, but the war in Vietnam was the worst war for them, and so they could not fight with enthusiasm. At their best, Americans were honest; so they needed an honest war.

It would have been a first rate talk to give to fighting troops. In the general excitement of this occasion he did not necessarily arrive at the central point—the soldiers before him had no wish to serve in Vietnam. That was why they were in the National Guard. Still, his speech to the troops pleased him, it warmed him for his next address which he was able to begin by turning around in place 180°, the loudspeaker doing the same, and now addressing his remarks to the crowd in the park. They were seated in a semicircle perhaps two hundred feet in diameter, a crowd of several thousand at least, with an attention he knew immediately was superb, for it was tender as the fatigue of shared experience and electric as the ringing of pain from a new bruise.

He began once again by paying his respects, explaining how he had missed one fray and then another, not certain if for the best or worst of motives. They were polite even to this, as if a manifest of honesty in a speaker was all they had come to hear. But he had seen them, he explained, over these few days, taking beatings and going back, taking beatings, going back; so he now found himself in this park talking to them (although he had had no such intention earlier). They were fine troops, he declared, they were the sort of troops any general would be proud to have. They had had the courage to live at war for four days in a city which was run by a beast.

A roar of delight came back from them. He felt the heights of the Hilton behind him, the searchlights, and the soldiers. Before him, these revolutionary youth—they were no longer the same young people who had gone to the Pentagon at all. They were soldiers.

"Yes, this is a city run by a beast, and yet we may take no pleasure in it," he said, "because the man is a giant who ended as a beast. And that is another part of the horror. For we have a President who was a giant and ended also as a beast. All over the world are leaders who have ended as beasts; there is a beastliness in the marrow of the century," he said, or words like that and went on, "Let us even have a moment of sorrow for Mayor Daley for he is a fallen giant and that is tragic," and they cheered Daley out of good spirit and some crazy good temper as if Mayor Daley was beautiful, he had given them all this—what a great king of the pigs! and somebody yelled, "Give us some of that good grass, Norman," and he bellowed back, "I haven't had pot in a month." They all roared. "Four good bourbons is all you need," said the demagogue, and the troops were in heaven.

The exchange fired him into his next thought. He repeated again that he had not been ready to march, repeated his desire to avoid arrest or a blow on the head, and "Write! Write!" they yelled back, "You're right, baby, do the writing!" But now, he went on, the time had come for Democratic delegates to march. He had not gone, he said, on the vigil and march from the stockyards to the hotel, because "that was in the wrong direction." Demagogue's metaphor, demagogue's profit. They cheered him richly. No, tomorrow, he told them (the idea coming to his mind at just this instant) he was going to try to get three hundred delegates to march with them to the Amphitheatre. He would march along then! But he would not if there were less than three hundred delegates! Because if little more than a tenth of the Democratic Party was not ready to go out with their bodies as a warrant of safekeeping for all of them, then there was no sense in walking into still one more mauling. They had taken enough. If there was not real outrage in the Democratic Party, then it was time they knew that as well; they could then prepare to go underground. A roar came back again from the new soldiers seated on the grass.

Were there delegates here, he asked? Candles waved in the dark—he was aware of them for the first time, "Spread the word," he called out, "I'll be here tomorrow."

Then he went on to speak of that underground. He would try to explain it. The other side had all the force, all the guns, all the power. They had everything but creative wit. So the underground would have to function on its wit, its creative sense of each new step. They must never repeat a tactic they had used before, no matter how successful. "Once a philosopher, twice a pervert," he bawled out. And in the middle of the happy laughter which came back, he said, "Voltaire!" and they were happy again. It was as good a speech as he had ever made.

For example, he continued, the march tomorrow with three hundred delegates would be a new tactic, and might offer a real chance of reaching the police barriers outside the Amphitheatre, where they could have a rally and quietly disband. That could make the point, for the Mayor had refused to let them even get near until now. Of course if the police chose to attack again tomorrow, well, three hundred Democratic delegates would also be in the crowd—so the nation would know that the authority was even determined to mop up its own. So he would march, he repeated, if the delegates would go, but he was damned, he told the crowd, if he was about to give cops the chance to maul him for nothing after he had made a point of here insulting the Mayor; no, he would not take that chance unless a tenth of the Democratic delegates were also willing to take a chance. On that note, he stepped down, and took a walk forward through the crowd, stopping to shake hands every step with the young men and women on the grass. Some were well-dressed, some were near to wearing rags, some looked as dusty and war-like as Roger's Rangers, others were small and angelic. Everything from ghosts of Robin Hood's band to the worst of the descendants of the worst Bolshevik clerks were here in the Grant Park grass at five in the morning and McCarthyites and McGovernites, and attractive girls, and college boys, and a number of Negroes, more now than any day or night before, and they were shaking hands with him, Black Power was revolving a hint in its profound emplacements. There were kooks and plainclothesmen and security and petty thieves and provocateurs with calculating faces and mouths just out of balance, eyes that glinted with a tell-tale flick; but there were also more attractive adolescents and under-twenties in this crowd than in any like crowd of New Left and Yippies he had seen before, as if the war had indeed been good for them. And he was modest in the warmth of their greeting, and not honored with himself, for they were giving him credit he did not possess—they were ready to forgive all manner of defection on the pleasure of a good speech.

So he circulated, talking, came back to the platform to make one quick amendment. Delegates in the crowd had told him three hundred was too great a number to seek in so short a time. It would not be possible to reach them all. Two hundred was a better expectation. So he relayed that information to the crowd, and added that he would be back in this Park at noon.

He returned to the hotel, pleased with his project, and aware of one whole new notion of himself. All courage was his and all determination, provided he could lead. There seemed no rank in any Army suitable for him below the level of General—extraordinary events deliver exceptional intuitions of oneself. No wonder he had spent so many years being General of an army of one. It was something to discover the secret source of the river of one's own good guts or lack of them. And booze was no bad canoe. He went to bed prepared for heroic events on the morrow.


## 22

He was to receive instead a lesson in the alphabet of all good politick: which is, that a passion is nothing without a good horse to carry you in visit over your neighbor's lands. He went to sleep at six A.M. prepared to visit different leaders as soon as he had finished his next speech at noon; by six in the evening he hoped they would be ready for the march, all delegates assembled.

Be prepared for total failure.

If this were essentially an account of the reporter's actions, it would be interesting to follow him through the chutes on Thursday, but we are concerned with his actions only as they illumine the event of the Republican Convention in Miami, the Democratic Convention in Chicago, and the war of the near streets. So his speech to the Yippies and children assembled was of value, since he learned for the record of his report that they were a generation with an appetite for the heroic, and an air not without beauty had arisen from their presence; they had been better than he thought, young, devoted, and actually ready to die—they were not like their counterparts ten years ago. Something had happened in America, some forging of the steel. He had known while speaking that if it came to civil war, there was a side he could join. At what a cost! At what a cost!

But such discoveries are unsettling. He lay in bed not able to sleep; he lay in fact on the edge of a twilight slumber rich as Oriental harems in the happiness of their color, but he was thus celebrating too soon, because by nine o'clock in the morning, the last of his liquor now beautifully metabolized, he was in that kind of unhappy shape on which comedy is built. Quick calisthenics, a shower, a shave, and the urgency of his mission, did not quite give him a brain the equal of three hours in slumber. He would begin to think well for a minute, then lapse into himself like a mind become too weak for the concentration of consecutive thoughts.

We can spare the day, and report the lesson. He made his speech in Grant Park at noon, talked then to reporters, then to delegates (who had been in the Park) at the Hilton, discussed problems, arranged to meet them again, and never was able to keep the meetings. He could never get to see McCarthy quite alone, nor McGovern, lost hours on the hope he might talk to the New York delegation, did not know how to reach Peterson of Wisconsin, could have wept at the absence of a secretary, or a walkie-talkie, since phones refused to function, or beginning to work, could reach no soul. He ran back and forth over Chicago, sent messages—by whomever he could find, to the Park; he would be back at three, he would be back at four, he saw Murray Kempton who was ready to march all alone if only to interpose himself between the police and the body of one demonstrator (Kempton was indeed to be arrested later in the day) he saw others, lost connection with delegates who had volunteered to help, was helpless himself in his lack of sleep, was too early or too late for each political figure he wished to find, he was always rushing or waiting in hallways—he learned the first lesson of a convention: nothing could be accomplished without the ability to communicate faster than your opponent. If politics was property, a convention was a massive auction, and your bid had to reach the floor in time.

So he was defeated. He could put nothing together at all. Hung-over, drained, ashen within, and doubtless looking as awful as Rockefeller at Opa Locka or McCarthy in Cambridge, he went back to Grant Park in the late afternoon to make a speech in which he would declare his failure, and discovered the Park instead was near empty. Whoever had wanted to march had gone off already with Peterson of Wisconsin, or later with Dick Gregory. (Perhaps a total of fifty Democratic delegates were in those walks.) Now the Park was all but deserted except for the National Guard. Perhaps a hundred or two hundred on-lookers, malcontents, hoodlums, and odd petty thieves sauntered about. A mean-looking mulatto passed by the line of National Guard with his penknife out, blade up, and whispered, "Here's my bayonet." Yes, Grant Park was now near to Times Square in Manhattan or Main Street in L.A. The Yippies were gone; another kind of presence was in. And the grass looked littered and yellow, a holocaust of newspapers upon it. Now, a dry wind, dusty and cold, gave every sentiment of the end of summer. The reporter went back to his room. He had political lessons to absorb for a year from all the details of his absolute failure to deliver the vote.

## 5. BUT HE'S A HOMOSEXUAL ...

### Benjamin DeMott

*Benjamin DeMott is a professor of English and a free-lance critic whose work appears regularly in* Saturday Review *and other publications. Here he addresses himself, as he frequently does, to a complex and controversial subject.*

What is a homosexual artist? A devil and a liar, says the current noisy indictment—a desecrater, a self-server, a character nobody on earth should trust. Sly and sulky, he poisons hope and idealism with the mean flow of his resentment. Sick and exhibitionistic, he jams the media with neuroses, teaching that Women are destroyers and heterosexual domestic life is hell. Worse by far, the man is power-mad. Skinnying his way onto established grant committees, prize panels, editorial boards, and other seats of authority, he spurns aspirants not of his clique, thereby creating a tyranny of taste that soon will have every center of imaginative expression—theater, opera, symphony hall, publishing house, museum, gallery—under its cheesy thrall. In sum: the homosexual artist is an enemy of the people, a threat to the quality of American life.

As every magazine reader knows, indictments like the foregoing have for some time been highly salable. For a representative sample, consider the recent *Ramparts* article about Messrs. Albee, Warhol, et al. called "Who's Afraid of Little Aunt Fanny?" The initial stance of this piece was one of tolerant sophistication; the author, Gene Marine, gave assurances that he was no scandalmonger, no keyhole inquirer into celebrities' private lives, no naïf eager to set up equations between, say, "long-haired hippies" and homosexuality:

"Let me put things straight [he wrote], for you and the liberal lawyers. I don't absolutely know for certain the names of any famous homosexuals, though, I probably make the same guesses you do, and if I did know any for certain, I wouldn't tell you. As far as I know, Edward Albee is a square family man, Andy Warhol is afflicted with satyriasis and California has no homosexuality south of the Santa Ynez river. I couldn't care less."

*Source:* "But He's a Homosexual" from the book *Supergrow: Essays and Reports on Imagination in America,* by Benjamin DeMott. Copyright © 1969, 1968, 1967, 1966 by Benjamin DeMott. Published by E. P. Dutton & Co., Inc., and used with their permission. This essay originally appeared in *New American Review.*

But having given these assurances, Marine went on to prove them spurious. Employing the tricks of an innuendo-cutie and a manner of sleazy downrightness, he developed an ever more expansive series of charges, and ended by dealing damnation round the entire American cultural landscape. Here are some steps in the progress:

"The point is that homosexual playwrights and homosexual directors and homosexual producers are having more and more to say about what can and can't be done in an American theater."

"People who know more about it than I do . . . tell me that it's even worse in the world of art—by which I mean painting and sculpture. The galleries take what the decorators want them to take, and the decorators want them to take their gay friends."

"I'm getting damned tired of all the art being campy and all the plays being queer and all the clothes being West Fourth Street and the whole bit. *Some* I don't mind, but it's getting too close to *all*, and I have the feeling that there are healthier bases for a culture."

"You can take almost any part of the world of culture, and there it is, in bold lavender. Dance and interior design, fashions (women's *and* men's), music—especially outside the relatively virile jazz and rock fields —and music promotion, novels and poetry, little theater and magazines."

The line in question is, predictably, more or less standard throughout the contemporary muckraking press. (*Fact* has lately enlarged the area of presumed "domination" by printing a "study" of homosexuals in TV.) And hints of the influence of this line—more about them in a minute—are begining to be visible in journals of a quite different character: the Sunday drama section of the *New York Times*, highbrow periodicals like the *New York Review of Books* and the *Tulane Drama Review*.

That the subject of homosexual influence in the arts should engage attention at this moment isn't mysterious. American interest in matters cultural and aesthetic is on the rise. New levels of candor about sexual behavior seem to be achieved every other week. And, most important, the national reserves of credulity have not diminished much over the years. If this were not so, baiters of homosexual art probably would pull smaller audiences. For their charges are rooted in the belief that centralized control of the arts can be achieved by a nonpolitical, essentially nonideological nonorganization—and only the credulous can rest comfortably in such faith. Tyrannies of taste do occur, to be sure—they are inevitable whenever a professionally practiced art lacks multiple centers of power. (Serious music is the sector of the arts that most nearly meets the latter description at this moment. Outlets for the work of living American composers are extremely few, which means that homosexual cliquishness could—some informed people say it does—throttle free musical expression.) And homosexual centers of power do exist—a cluster of art galleries here, a group of experimental moviemakers there. (One famous Fifty-seventh Street gallery has even been, in fairly recent days, a center of homosexual poetry as well as of painting and sculpture.)

But countless other galleries flourish that are nothing of the sort, and a half-dozen, low-budget, cinematic experimenters continue to produce—and exhibit—films untouched by what is called homosexual fantasy. And in other sectors of the arts mixed situations seem generally the rule. The financial backers of one newly founded off-Broadway production firm are homosexuals; those of several other newish producing firms are not. A few trade publishing houses appear to be particularly well-disposed to homosexual writers; the majority have no clear policy save the pursuit of profit. Given present complications and uncertainties of taste and prejudice, and given the continued emergence from time to time of new centers of activity (the American Place Theater is an example), the danger of total domination will remain slight. Cliquishness cannot be abolished and, as just indicated, it can cause damage in fields of artistic endeavor where opportunities for professional hearing are subject to autocratic control. But, while complacency about these fields is inexcusable, they are less numerous than scourgers of "homosexual tyranny"—and the more gullible of their readers—profess to believe. And the heralded culture-explosion should reduce their number, not increase it, in the future.

But if the homosexual himself isn't a serious threat to cultural vigor and variety, the same can't be said of those who harass him in print. The point at issue here isn't, true enough, easy to grasp. A piece writer who beats up "the fairies" for a few thousand words would seem, on the face of it, only another harmless canny profiteer. It's plain, after all, that complaints about "homosexual art" will never mobilize hostility and frustration at the destructive levels sustained in yesteryear by the Red-baiters.[1] And conceivably "frank talk" in this area, no matter how woolly and superstitious, can have beneficial effects. (The public needs to be reminded, some say, that reputations in the arts are made things, not miracles: edifices built by the continuous effort not simply of a single

---

[1] Two mythy items that figure in "thinking" about the coming homosexualization of America are the concept of a nation asleep at the switch, as it were, too absorbed in business to notice its sex is changing, and the concept of a doomsday recognition scene, a moment at which people discover to their horror that they have frittered away their birthrate and are the last generation of their kind. Both concepts figured, in slightly different form, in Senator McCarthy's speeches on the Commie conspiracy a decade ago.

artist but of friends who sometimes praise a man's work when what they actually value is his personal charm. And the public needs the experience, others say, of *talking* about homosexuality—because such talk fosters the growth of tolerance: when homosexuality in one quarter of the community is freely and openly assessed, responses to homosexuality in the community at large should become less hysterical.) Why turn hypercritical toward characters who, whatever their own personal cynicism, may function as nourishers of American sophistication?

The answer is simple: at the center of most talk about "homosexual art" lies the assumption that books, pictures, poems created by homosexuals are private documents, narrow in range, incapable of speaking truly to anyone not himself a homosexual. The prime effect of this already widely disseminated idea has been to neutralize or denature several of the most provocative critical images of contemporary life to win mass audiences since World War II. And from this it follows that the self-appointed enemy of "homosexual art" isn't just a nuisance: he is a pernicious waster of an invaluable cultural resource.

As might be guessed, the ways of waste—the means by which commentators cheat the work of homosexuals and torture it out of strength—are nothing if not ingenious. Chief among them is a trick of medical inside-dopesterism that transforms texts clear enough on their surface into complex codes or allegories—productions whose deepest truths yield themselves only to psychoanalytic exegesis. Consider for instance the operations of clinical exegetes on Edward Albee's *Who's Afraid of Virginia Woolf?* In both the stage and film versions, the ending of this work seems a moment of poignance. Weary beyond fury, blasted (almost) into kindness, George and Martha have arrived at a nowhere world in which combat is pointless. The audience knows that cosy murmurs about reconciliation, forgiveness, happiness ahead would be puerile, but is nevertheless aware of a passage into an atmosphere of feeling less ridden by fantasy, more open, more yielding: pity is in the room.

Enter the clinical exegete and every "simplistic" reading of the play is laved in scorn. (Exegetes of this brand are printed in psychoanalytic journals as well as in magazines of art.) *Virginia Woolf*, wrote Dr. Donald M. Kaplan (a psychoanalyst) in a recent issue of *Tulane Drama Review*, is in its essence a predictable homosexual claim that "genitality is . . . an unnecessary burden"; the closing scene is a moment of triumph, it signifies that a married man "can prevail through the tactics of pregenital perversity" and need not grow up to his role:

"The sexuality of the parental bedroom [Nick and Martha offstage] is no match for the multifarious derivatives of George's oral aggression, anality, voyeurism, masochism and procreative reluctance. In the end, Martha returns to George, as she so often has in the past. The enfant terrible again triumphs over the cocksmen of the outside world, and the nursery is preserved. . . ."

Fitted into this pattern of homosexual aggression and glee, Albee's play is easily dismissed as a projection of dementia—a set of remarks about Rorschach cards, a collection of symptoms, nothing a "straight" could even begin to take straight.

Clinical exegesis isn't of course the harshest line of critique found in discussion of so-called homosexual art. Traditional American manliness makes itself heard in *Fact* and *Ramparts* ("I *like* women," Gene Marine said stoutly) and even in tonier periodicals—witness Philip Roth's famous attack on Albee's "pansy prose" that appeared in the *New York Review* following the opening of *Tiny Alice*. But the survival of tough-guyism is less interesting—and less regrettable—than the nearly universal acceptance of the central assumption just mentioned, namely that art produced by homosexuals is irrelevant to life as lived by nonhomosexuals. Early last year the Sunday theater section of the *New York Times* printed a pair of articles by Stanley Kauffmann, then the newspaper's drama critic, on the "subject of the homosexual dramatist." A liberal, humane man, Kauffmann clearly had no terror of "perverts," no desire to suppress the work of the artists he was discussing. His articles, seen by many as another heroic breakthrough for frankness, dealt in passing with the matter of "homosexual style," and with the supposed tendency of the homosexual writer to treat theme and subject as immaterial and surface as all-important. They were partly conceived as defenses of the homosexual's right to freedom of expression, and they offered several telling observations about uses and abuses of that right.

Yet everywhere in his comments this critic signified his conviction that plays by homosexual dramatists should be regarded as codes to be deciphered, disguises to be seen through, private languages requiring continuous acts of translation by the audience:

"In society the homosexual's life must be discreetly concealed. If he is to write of his experience, he must invent a two-sex version of the one-sex experience that he really has."

Kauffmann blamed this situation upon society—not upon the homosexual writer. And he argued forcibly for an end to the repression and inhibition that harries these writers into deceit:

"If we object to the distortion that homosexual disguises entail, and if, as civilized people, we do not want to gag these artists, then there seems only one conclusion. The conditions that force the dissembling must change."

But, like the psychoanalyst quoted earlier, Kauffmann was committed to the notion that a homosexual's image of life is necessarily an expression of "homosexual truth"; the man has no choice except to "transform [what he knows] to a life he does not know, to the detriment of his truth and ours."

Even those critics whose avowed purpose is to make a case *for* "homosexual art"—as it is—to rescue it from vulgar attack and place it in a dignified light—fall into modes of discourse that are reductive and evasive in discussing its meaning. Consider the approach adopted in Susan Sontag's "Notes on Camp." This critic announces herself to be "strongly drawn" to the kind of art she is setting out to describe; yet throughout her essay she speaks of that art always as a phenomenon of style alone; the worth of its statement, the nature of its view of life, even its cultural associations and origins are passed off as boring matters. ("One feels," says the critic, "if homosexuals hadn't more or less invented Camp, some one else would.") What counts about this art is its *tonality*, not the total experience offered and the meanings created through that experience:

"Camp and tragedy are antitheses. There is seriousness in Camp (seriousness in the degree of the artist's involvement), and, very often, pathos. The excruciating is also one of the tonalities of Camp; it is the quality of excruciation in much of Henry James . . . that is responsible for the large element of Camp in his writings. But there is never, never tragedy."

The obvious question is: given the nature of the life represented in a so-called "Camp novel," is the quality of excruciation tendentious or appropriate? Can a man learn or confirm any truth of experience through a confrontation with Camp? When such questions aren't asked, much less answered, the implication is that this art may truly be empty of substance.

The point at stake bears restating. Dumb-ox or tough-guy or Philistine versions of works of art produced by homosexuals tend to be crudely dismissive—too crudely dismissive, often, for educated audiences to accept. But other dismissive lines have now become available. There is chic psychoanalytical chatter that evades the truth of a scene by seeing the scene as a symptom. There is a liberal critique that evades the truth of a scene by tolerantly viewing the scene not as an image of life but as product of indirect censorship. And there is a brand of aesthetic criticism that evades the truth of a scene by focusing solely on matters of form.

None of the approaches mentioned appears hostile to the so-called homosexual artist; each embodies different values and assumptions. But all are alike in espousing, or else in refusing to challenge, the dogma that the homosexual's representation of life can only be an expression of homosexual truth—"his truth" as opposed to "ours," as Kauffmann puts it. And that dogma, while comforting to the majority, is quite without foundation.

It is probable that most readers and theatergoers—peace to the scandalmongers who shriek about homosexual tyranny—will accept the claim that the most intense accounts of domestic life and problems in recent years, as well as the few unembarrassedly passionate love poems, have been the work of writers who are not heterosexual. The problem of compulsive promiscuity, or Don Juanism—one that José Ortega y Gasset described as the most delicate and abstruse in contemporary human relations—has been examined with extraordinary force and directness by Tennessee Williams in several plays. And that intensity has time and time over proved to be an illumination of a kind. Some of the writers in question can be overpraised, to be sure. There is phony elegance and needless obfuscation in Albee's current manner, total dishevelment in the bulk of Ginsberg, too much self-indulgence in Williams, who seems bent on writing the same play four hundred times.

Yet a fair assessment of these writers, or of any of their relevant superiors—Genet and Auden for two—can hardly be wholly negative. With a few other poets and dramatists, they are the only compelling writers of the postwar period who seem to know anything beyond the level of cliché about human connectedness, whose minds break through the stereotypes of existential violence of Nietzschean extravagance into recognizable truths and intricacies of contemporary feeling. They are not purveyors of situation comedy or Bond banalities or *Playboy* virility or musical-marital bliss (*I Do! I Do!*) or mate-murders. A steady consciousness of a dark side of love that is neither homo- nor heterosexual but simply human pervades much of their work; they are in touch with facts of feeling that most men do not or cannot admit to thought. They know what Catullus knew about *odi et amo*—simultaneities of hatred and its opposite—and they know the special terms and strains of these simultaneities in modern experience, wherein prohibitions against self-indulgence have lost force. They know that love and suffering are near allied, and that love ought not to be confused with the slumbrous affection or habitual exploitation that is the rule in numberless households. They know that the lover's demand for exclusive possession has vanity as one of its roots.

They have in mind, not as aphorisms but as potential behavior and gesture, knowledge of the kind compressed in Mme. de Staël's remark that love equals self-love *a deux*, or in Proust's claim that there are people for whom there is no such thing as reciprocated love, and that these people are by no means the most insensitive among us. They know that instability is a fact of love, as of human personality generally. And the tensions and furies arising from contradictory desires and impulses seem to them proper subjects for intelligence to probe.

As good an exhibit as any, perhaps, is Auden's much celebrated "Lullaby."*

> Lay your sleeping head, my love,
> Human on my faithless arm;
> Time and fevers burn away
> Individual beauty from
> Thoughtful children, and the grave
> Proves the child ephemeral:
> But in my arms till break of day
> Let the living creature lie,
> Mortal, guilty, but to me
> The entirely beautiful.
>
> Soul and body have no bounds:
> To lovers as they lie upon
> Her tolerant enchanted slope
> In their ordinary swoon,
> Grave the vision Venus sends
> Of supernatural sympathy,
> Universal love and hope;
> While an abstract insight wakes
> Among the glaciers and the rocks
> The hermit's sensual ecstasy.
>
> Certainty, fidelity
> On the stroke of midnight pass
> Like vibrations of a bell,
> And fashionable madmen raise
> Their pedantic boring cry:
> Every farthing of the cost,

* Reprinted by permission of Random House, Inc., from *Collected Poetry of W. H. Auden* © Copyright, 1940, by W. H. Auden; and by permission of Faber & Faber Ltd., London.

All the dreaded cards foretell,
Shall be paid, but from this night
Not a whisper, not a thought,
Not a kiss nor look be lost.

Beauty, midnight, vision dies.
Let the winds of dawn that blow
Softly round your dreaming head
Such a day of sweetness show
Eye and knocking heart may bless,
Find the mortal world enough;
Noons of dryness see you fed
By the involuntary powers,
Nights of insult let you pass
Watched by every human love.

Reductions of this poem to homily or "general truth" play into the
hands of Auden's detractors—those given to abusing the poet for being
overchic. But that risk can be run. Some of the distinction of the "Lullaby" lies in the steadiness of its refusal to exclude the narrative consciousness from the lyric consciousness; joy, love, enchantment are
placed, in this poem as in life, in immediate, living, indismissible ad-
jacency to their opposites. Another part of the poem's distinction lies in
the capacity of the singer at once to inhabit the lullaby-trance of union,
to experience it in its fullness and uniqueness, and to look on from outside, acknowledging, neither merely pityingly nor merely knowingly, the
replicability (in an age of indulgence) of this "ordinary swoon." And
everywhere in the poem there is an alertness to contrarieties and puzzles
of response—the murderously brief and beautiful sense of moral being
perfected in sensual delight:

Grave the vision Venus sends
Of supernatural sympathy,
Universal love and hope . . .

In this small poem a densely instructive world of feeling is created, a
world that is proof against the simplicities of desiccation (the typist in
The Waste Land), as well as against those of romantic melancholy
(Frederick Henry in A Farewell to Arms). And in Auden's Collected
Poems there are a number of songs—see for instance the matchless lyric,
"Warm are the still and lucky miles"—worth equal praise.

Does the knowledge embodied in such poems qualify as unique? Is it
in itself a guarantee of "profundity?" Of course not: most reflective men

know what these poems know—namely that love is the only human entrance into an ideal world, and that life, a teaser and mocker, lets few men through to stay. Why then is such knowledge more vivid in homosexual art than elsewhere? Again quick answers are unsatisfactory. Heroicizing the "homosexual artist" is, certainly, as senseless as condescending to him as a case. It does need to be said, though, that the homosexual artist's aptitude for the presentation of certain human (not homosexual or heterosexual) complications of feeling can't be understood by people oblivious to the features of his situation that lend it a measure of dignity. "To be free is to have one's freedom perpetually on trial." It isn't necessary to endorse every line of existential scripture to see the application of this text from Sartre to the intelligent, responsive homosexual who has a gift for the formed re-creation of experience. The latter gift is, as everyone knows, distributed according to no visible plan; sexuality conceived as a pure and separable essence is not its determinant. But the homosexual who possesses it does have special occasion to exercise and refine it in fundamental, as well as in craft or professional, areas of life, owing to the peculiarities of his situation in the general culture. If I am a Citizen, Husband, Straight-Arrow, I easily can put myself on trial. I can speak for a troubling cause, enter upon a bout of promiscuity, teach in a turtleneck, grow my hair long in back. But I cannot escape the promise of ease, the possibility of subsiding into the accepted and the respectable; always an oasis of habitual, unexamined, unjudged life awaits me.

The intelligent homosexual, however, is in another situation. A tide of suspicion flows toward him, perpetually demanding that he justify his difference; relaxation into unthinking self-acceptance in the presence of other eyes is prohibited. If he is rich and shrewd, he may manage to create for himself the illusion of a life unexposed to antipathetic scrutiny —but sustaining that illusion is hard work. If he isn't rich and shrewd, his immediate confrontations with hostility—the interruptions of his taken-for-granted daily existence—will be numberless. And these interruptions will induce in him a heightened awareness of the feelings and assumptions of others—an immediate living consciousness of the fragility of the shields that hide human cruelty from general view.

To say this isn't for a moment to suggest that lives can, by any system of categorization, be precisely compared in terms of their remoteness from challenge: we measure with inklings and intuitions here, and confidence isn't in the equation. Neither is it to suggest that the intelligent and sensitive homosexual is the only man who is ever thrust into tasking encounters with himself and others. It is to say that these encounters are probably more difficult for the homosexual to avoid than for other men. And the encounters do have "excruciating" value to anyone whose art depends finally upon his ability to experience dailiness rather than simply pass through it, to inhabit moment to moment reality, to be aware of present time and know it not as something between yesterday and tomorrow but as the edge of his life. Admittedly a man of strong mind can close himself off from the coarseness that teases the homosexual in his round of errands in any town or suburb other than a gay colony— schoolchildren mincing behind his back as their elders have more or less instructed them to do, overheartiness or dropped eyes among tradesmen, slyness and lubricity in the cleaning woman. And the danger of senti- mentalizing experience of this kind, assigning more value and meaning to embarrassment than it possesses, is real. Everyone knows about homo- sexual arrogance; everyone knows that aristocratic poses fend off "nights of insult"; everyone knows that flights of defensive scorn or resentment— the familiar gestures of mediocrity—are common in homosexual con- versation.

But self-deception and mediocrity are, after all, everywhere the rule— and the writers and artists spoken of publicly as homosexuals, and thus looked down upon, are by and large not mediocrities. They are men who have been *provoked* into dwelling on the relative emptiness and unthink- ingness of most men's commitments to the terms of their own lives. They are people whom we put on endless trial, because our manner declares that no condition of moral being except our own can be approved, be- cause our explicit claim is that love can only be a permanent attachment, and because we dare not detach ourselves from our "institutions" even though we know they derive in great part from superstition. They are people forced to face up to the arbitrariness of cultural patterns—arbi- trariness that we insist on regarding as altogether unarbitrary, a logical bidding of nature, a sane, wholly explicable pattern, like the movement of the earth. The fury that lifts James Baldwin's prose to eloquence, when that writer has before him the cruelty of cultural arbitrariness, stems not alone from Baldwin's experience as a Negro. And the racking power of those moments in Genet, when this writer has the same spectacle in sight, arises not only from a career as thief. The usefulness of the instruction offered through this eloquence and power doesn't vary in accordance with the condition of the reader's sexuality. We need not be "perverts" to see into the life of that moment when Genet's Divine enters the café, smiles round the room in "her" crazy aloneness, tests the blade of hate:

"She smiled all around, and each one answered only by turning away, but that was a way of answering. The whole cafe thought that the smile of (for the colonel: the invert; for the shopkeepers: the fairy; for the banker and the waiters: the fag; for the gigolos: '*that* one'; etc.) was despicable. Divine did not press the point. From a tiny black satin purse she took a few coins which she laid noiselessly on the marble table. The cafe disappeared, and Divine was metamorphosed into one of those monsters that are painted on walls—chimeras or griffins—for a customer, in spite of himself, murmured a magic word as he thought of her:

'Homoseckshual.'                               (*Our Lady of the Flowers*)

The making of a monster—a demon fabricated by simple habitual acts of *learned* disgust—is the theme momentarily in view here. And the reader who regards his imperviousness to it as a badge of moral distinction is at best a pious fool.

The case I am urging is, needless to say, open to a hundred misunderstandings. Someone says: you pretend that you aren't claiming that the homosexual is more sensitive to certain aspects of human relations than the heterosexual. But haven't you just been saying that homosexuals have insights that are denied to heterosexuals? Answer: not quite. The notion of denial oversimplifies the issue, leaves out important parts of the full context. The difference between what the homosexual sees and what the heterosexual sees can't be explained in narrow physiological terms. Neither kind of sexuality can be separated from the culture and regarded as a physical or neurological thing-in-itself determining degrees of insight. Homosexuality like heterosexuality is a situation, a complex set of relations between self and society: the nature of these relations determines to some extent the special quality of the perceptions that each perceptive man can have. The relations vary with time and place; surely there are few significant likenesses between the situations of homosexuals in the arts in New York City in 1967 and the situations of their counterparts in, say, Paris in 1815 or London in 1600. There isn't, in short, any abstract entity properly called homosexual or heterosexual insight; there are only differences in the kinds of life-situations in which intelligence tests itself. And these are the differences that shape the artist's vision.

Again, another query: you seem almost to imply that someone reading a poem or play dealing directly with homosexual experience could nevertheless achieve—through his encounter with this work of art—deeper understanding of aspects of strictly heterosexual relationships. Do you really mean this? Answer: yes. Look for a minute at the poem by Tennessee Williams called "Life Story."*

---

* From Tennessee Williams, *In the Winter of Cities*. Copyright © 1956 by Tennessee Williams. Reprinted by permission of New Directions Publishing Corporation.

After you've been to bed together for the first time,
without the advantage or disadvantage of any prior acquaintance,
the other party very often says to you,
Tell me about yourself, I want to know all about you,
what's your story? And you think maybe they really and truly do

sincerely want to know your life story, and so you light up
a cigarette and begin to tell it to them, the two of you
lying together in completely relaxed positions
like a pair of rag dolls a bored child dropped on a bed.

You tell them your story, or as much of your story
as time or a fair degree of prudence allows, and they say,
                    Oh, oh, oh, oh, oh,
each time a little more faintly, until the oh
is just an audible breath, and then of course

there's some interruption. Slow room service comes up
with a bowl of melting ice cubes, or one of you rises to pee
and gaze at himself with mild astonishment in the bathroom mirror.
And then, the first thing you know, before you've had time
to pick up where you left off with your enthralling life story,
they're telling you *their* life story, exactly as they'd intended
        to all along,
and you're saying, Oh, oh, oh, oh, oh,
each time a little more faintly, the vowel at last becoming
no more than an audible sigh,
as the elevator, halfway down the corridor and a turn to the left,
draws one last, long, deep breath of exhaustion
and stops breathing forever. Then ?

Well, one of you falls asleep
and the other one does likewise with a lighted cigarette in his mouth
and that's how people burn to death in hotel rooms.

Not a masterwork to be sure, much too easily and sardonically knowing
a poem, too pleased by its own blackishness, and perhaps also too need-
lessly "daring" in its sequence of third person masculine pronouns. But
"Life Story" is a sharp perception of relations between promiscuity and
the self-regard and self-absorption of an age gone mad for Identity—and
the sense of this relatedness is as much an illumination for the straight
world as for the queer.

And one more hostile question: you ask for pity, understanding, admiration for homosexual artists—thus suggesting that these are the badly mistreated people of this day. Are they? Aren't they in reality all the cry just now? If we put them under pressure, they, for their part, do find excellent means of freeing themselves. And, finally: suppose it *is* granted that the best "homosexual art" is indeed art—art without modifier; are we obliged to be decent to the worst? When we go off for a night at the theater and encounter something amounting simply to a play in drag, must we smother resentment?

The answer is that of course homosexual artists, like other ones, can be inferior, and that of course these artists have invented ways of easing the pressure we put them under. They do on occasion compose fantasies. They do on occasion express *their* resentment. They do on occasion revenge themselves through sexual disguises in plays and poems. They mock our solemnities with Happenings and joke pictures and weirdo flicks. They parody the ceaseless commercial agitation of "straight" sexual appetites. They create an art heavily dependent (see Genét) on magic and metamorphosis, an art usually thin in political content, relatively unconcerned with what are called public issues. And they can give themselves over to glee at the thought that whatever we think of them, few among us match them in brio of brilliance.

But these satisfactions can scarcely outweigh all torments—and, in any event, the fact that an achievement has earned a reward usually is not thought of as ground for discounting the achievement. And there are achievements here—this is the point of moment. A portrait of a man exacerbated by a woman need not be only a thrust at a generalized Enemy; in at least one American play such a portrait faced a mass audience with truths about the new world of sexual equality and universal self-absorption quite inexpressible either in Ibsen or Bernard Shaw. An image of egos dependent upon a fantasy child can be more than a faggish leer: in one American play such an image showed mean uses of the family and, in addition, the vapidities of the doctrine that procreation in itself equals fulfillment. And, by the same token, artists with extensive experience of respectable marriage and childrearing may write with seeming authority about subjects the homosexual can "never know," and yet be worthless—because they are blind to the truth that the acceptable life, the embrace of heterosexuality, can become a cliché, an automatized rather than freely created value.

The canard that negation is not necessarily stupidity and affirmation not necessarily illumination does, in fine, need summoning once more—in discussion of "homosexual art." Nobody is obliged to accept Nietzsche's claim that "every good thing, even a good book which is against life, is a powerful stimulant to life." But the sort of mind that seeks to place all hostility to established institutions as proof of disease does dirt on the revolution of candor that we claim to prize. Failure to hear out the homosexual artist with a seriousness matching his own, overeagerness to dismiss him as ignorant or perverse, assurance that we know what we are—this behavior at a time when Don Juans by the thousand jam the week-night motels and divorce rates soar and children everywhere are flogged into meaningless ambition—this is worse than senseless. It is a mockery not only of art and of the suffering that art rises out of and seeks to comprehend: it is a mockery of our famous, preening, new liberation as well.

## 6. CESAR CHAVEZ FROM SAL SI PUEDES

**Peter Matthiessen**

*Peter Matthiessen is a free-lance writer whose work has appeared frequently in national publications.*

Before leaving for California I had expected that I would be impressed by Cesar Chavez, but I had not expected to be startled. It was not the "charisma" that is often ascribed to him; most charisma is in the eye of the beholder. The people who have known him longest agree that before the strike, Chavez's presence was so nondescript that he passed unnoticed; he is as unobtrusive as a rabbit, moving quietly wherever he finds himself as if he had always belonged there. The "charisma" is something that has been acquired, an intensification of natural grace which he uses, not always unconsciously, as an organizing tool, turning it on like a blowtorch as the job requires. Once somebody whom he had just enlisted expressed surprise that Chavez had spent so little time in proselytizing. "All he did for three whole days was make me laugh," the new convert said, still unaware that he'd been organized .

Since Chavez knows better than anyone else what his appeals to public sentiment have accomplished for *la causa*, I had no doubt that as a writer I would be skillfully organized myself; but warmth and intelligence and courage, even in combination, did not account for what I felt at the end of the four-hour walk on that first Sunday morning.

Talking of leadership during the walk, Chavez said, "It is like taking a road over hills and down into the valley: you must stay with the people. If you go ahead too fast, then they lose sight of you and you lose sight of them." And at the church he was a man among his neighbors, kneeling among them, joining them to receive holy communion, conversing eagerly in the bright morning of the churchyard, by the white stucco wall. What welled out of him was a phenomenon much spoken of in a society afraid of its own hate, but one that I had never seen before—or not, at least, in anyone unswayed by drugs or aching youth: the simple love of man that accompanies some ultimate acceptance of oneself.

It is this love in Chavez that one sees and resists naming, because to name it is to cheapen it; not the addled love that hides self-pity but a love that does not distinguish between oneself and others, a love so clear

*Source:* "Cesar Chavez" from *Sal Si Puedes: Cesar Chavez and the New Revolution*, by Peter Matthiessen.

in its intensity that it is monastic, even mystical. This intensity in Chavez has burned all his defenses away. Taking the workers' hands at church, his face was as fresh as the face of a man reborn. "These workers are really beautiful," he says, and when he says it he is beautiful himself. He is entirely with the people, open to them, one with them, and at the same time that he makes them laugh, his gaze sees beyond them to something else. "Without laying a cross on him," Jim Drake says, "Cesar is, in theological terms, as nearly 'a man for others' as you can find. In spite of all his personal problems—a very bad back, poverty, a large family—he does not allow his own life to get in the way."

We sat for an hour or more in the adobe shade outside the small room where he had spent his fast, and as he spoke of the old missions and his childhood and the fast, I grew conscious of the great Sunday silence and the serenity that flowed from the man beside me, gazing out with such equanimity upon the city dump. What emerges when Chavez talks seriously of his aim is simplicity, and what is striking in his gentle voice is its lack of mannerisms; it comes as naturally as bird song. For the same reason, it is a pleasure to watch him move. He has what the Japanese call *hara*, or "belly"—that is, he is centered in himself, he is not fragmented, he sits simply, like a Zen master.

For most of us, to quote Dostoevsky, "to love the universal man is to despise and at times to hate the real man standing at your side." This is not true of Chavez. But he is super human, not superhuman. He acknowledges that his reactions are not entirely unaffected by the humiliations and pain of his early life, so that even his commitment to nonviolence is stronger in his head than in his heart. And like many people who are totally dedicated, he is intolerant of those who are less so. I asked him once for the names of the best volunteers no longer with the Union, and he said flatly, "The best ones are still here." I dropped the subject. As his leadership inevitably extends to the more than four million Mexican-Americans in the Southwest, Cesar will necessarily become more lonely, more cut off in a symbolic destiny. Already, sensing this, he puts great emphasis on loyalty, as if to allay a nagging fear of being abandoned, and people who are not at the Union's disposal at almost any hour of the day or night do not stay close to him for very long. It has been said that he is suspicious of Anglos, but it would be more accurate to say that he is suspicious of everybody, in the way of people with a tendency to trust too much. He is swift and stubborn in his judgments, yet warm and confiding once he commits his faith, which he is apt to do intuitively, in a few moments. The very completeness of this trust, which makes him vulnerable, may also have made him wary of betrayal.

The closer people are to Chavez, the greater the dedication he expects. If they can't or won't perform effectively, he does their job himself ("It's a lot easier to do that than keep after them"), or if they are going about it the wrong way, he may let them persist in a mistake until failure teaches them a lesson. Some of these lessons seem more expensive to the Union than they are worth, but Chavez is determined that his people be self-sufficient—that they could, if need be, get along without him.

His staff has also learned to sacrifice ego to political expedience within the Union. Watching Chavez conduct a meeting, large or small, is fascinating: his sly humor and shy manner, his deceptive use of "we," leave his own position flexible; he directs with a sure hand, yet rarely is he caught in an embarrassing commitment. Most of his aides have had to take responsibility for unpolitic decisions initiated by Cesar himself, and may experience his apparent disfavor, and even banishment to the sidelines, for circumstances that were not their fault. The veterans do not take this personally. In private, Cesar will be as warm as ever, and they know that their banishment will last no longer than the internal crisis. They know, too, that he never uses people to dodge personal responsibility, but only to circumvent obstruction from the board or from the membership that would impede *la causa's* progress; he is selfless, and expects them to be the same.

"Sometimes he seems so *damned* unfair, so stubborn, so irrational— oh, he can be a sonofabitch! But later on, maybe months later, we find ourselves remembering what he did, and every damned time we have to say, 'You know something? He was right.' That edge of irrationality— that's his greatness."

Because he is so human, Cesar's greatness is forgiven; he is beloved, not merely adored. "Often he says, 'Have you got a minute?' but what he means is, 'Talk to me,' and he doesn't really mean *that*; he just has to have somebody close to him all the time, it doesn't matter who, just someone who isn't a yes-man, who will bounce his ideas back at him. We all take turns at it, and he knows we're always there."

Jim Drake recalls a day sometime ago when he and Cesar and Marshall Ganz drove north to a hospital in Kingsbury, near Fresno, to visit Dave Fishlow, the editor of *El Malcriado*, who had been badly burned in a car accident. Although they had come one hundred and twenty miles, the supervisor would not let them in because they arrived after visiting hours. "Just a typical Valley cluck, you know. He says, 'Now what's going *on* out here, don't you know you can't break regulations? Absolutely not!' So I said, 'How about letting me see him? I'm his minister.' So he agreed, and then I said, 'Well, since you're letting somebody go in, it might as well be Cesar, since he's the one that would do your patient the most good.' But he said no, so I went in, and Dave suggested to me that Cesar come around under the window, just to say hello. But Cesar refused. You know how he hates discrimination of any kind; well, he thought he'd been discriminated against. I didn't but he did. He said he had gone to the back door all his life, and he wasn't going to do it any more. He was almost childish about it. That's the only time I've ever seen him that mad—so stubborn, I mean, that he wouldn't say hello to a friend. Most of the time that Cesar's mad, he's *acting* mad; he loves to act mad. But this time he was *really* mad."

On another occasion Drake himself got angry when Al Green, the AFL-CIO man, referred to Chavez as "that beady-eyed little Mex," and was astonished when Chavez, hearing this, burst out laughing. "He does very strange things; you can't anticipate him. When we had that conference at St. Anthony's Mission, he was very anxious at have everybody get to work and everything, and then he just disappeared. Later we found out that he and Richard and Manuel had been scooting around taking pictures of the nearby missions."

"In public, he's simple in his manner," Dolores Huarta says, "and when things are tense, he can make everyone relax by acting silly. When he used to drink a little, he was a real clown at parties; there were always games and dancing, and he would dance on the table." She laughed, remembering. "But I find him a very complicated person." In truth, Dolores finds Chavez difficult, but Dolores can be difficult herself, and anyway, her openness about him is a sign of faith, not disaffection.

One person in the Union with reservations about Chavez remarked to me of his own accord that in the creation of the United Farm Workers, Chavez had done something that "no one else had ever done. What can I say? I disagree with him on a lot of things, but I work for him for nothing."

This last sentence is eloquent because it says just what it means. Applied to the Chavez of *la causa*, ordinary judgments seem beside the point; a man with no interest in private gain who will starve himself for twenty-five days and expose his life daily to the threat of assassination, who takes serious risks, both spiritual and physical, for others, may be hated as well as adored, but he cannot be judged in the same terms as a man of ordinary ambitions.

# SECTION II

## Thinking and Learning

## Section Introduction
## POINT OF VIEW

All of the writers in the second section of this book, in addition to apply-ing themselves directly or indirectly to the subject of thinking and learning, are united in their choice of viewpoint. Whether approaching their subjects seriously or lightly, whether writing a short essay or an extended work, whether prose or poetry, each has elected to write in the first person, to become part, in effect, of what he is writing about. Thus Hemingway opens his classic study of bullfighting: "At the first bullfight I ever went to I expected to be horrified and perhaps sickened by what I had been told would happen to the horses."

There were, of course, other viewpoints available to Hemingway. He might have chosen to put more distance between himself and his subject by writing objectively in the third person:

"When a man attends his first bullfight he expects to be horrified and perhaps sickened by what he has been told will happen to the horses."

Or he might have (as Norman Mailer often does) referred to himself in the third person:

"At the first bullfight he ever went to he expected to be horrified . . ."

He might have addressed the reader directly:

"At the first bullfight you attend . . ."

Or used the editorial "we":

"At the first bullfight we attended . . ."

What is important here is not that Hemingway finally decided to write from the first-person point of view (we are glad he did), but that he had a choice to make, one that influenced the shape of his book and our relationship to it. The other writers in this section also had to make choices, and it is a useful exercise to speculate why in each case they decided to write in the first person and what the effect might have been had they chosen some other viewpoint. Joseph de Roche might have begun: "He was building an Ark,/Not after the measurements/Of the Lord,/But after his own." Flannery O'Connor might have delivered her remarks on the teaching of literature in the third person.

Somewhere in the process of choosing a subject, deciding what his attitude will be toward it and what he hopes to accomplish, a writer elects a point of view. There is no special virtue in the first person; there are times when it is appropriate, and times when it is not.

# 7. "USELESS" KNOWLEDGE

## Bertrand Russell

*Bertrand Russell, English philosopher, mathematician, and writer, collaborated with A. N. Whitehead in* Principia Mathematica *(1913). Later he turned increasingly to philosophy and the problems of society. His many essays and books cover a wide range of subjects.*

Francis Bacon, a man who rose to eminence by betraying his friends, asserted, no doubt as one of the ripe lessons of experience, that "knowledge is power." But this is not true of *all* knowledge. Sir Thomas Browne wished to know what song the sirens sang, but if he had ascertained this it would not have enabled him to rise from being a magistrate to being High Sheriff of his county. The sort of knowledge that Bacon had in mind was that which we call scientific. In emphasizing the importance of science, he was belatedly carrying on the tradition of the Arabs and the early Middle Ages, according to which knowledge consisted mainly of astrology, alchemy, and pharmacology, all of which were branches of science. A learned man was one who, having mastered these studies ,had acquired magical powers. In the early eleventh century, Pope Silvester II, for no reason except that he read books, was universally believed to be a magician in league with the devil. Prospero, who in Shakespeare's time was a mere phantasy, represented what had been for centuries the generally received conception of a learned man, so far at least as his powers of sorcery were concerned. Bacon believed—rightly, as we now know—that science could provide a more powerful magician's wand than any that had been dreamed of by the necromancers of former ages.

The renaissance, which was at its height in England at the time of Bacon, involved a revolt against the utilitarian conception of knowledge. The Greeks had acquired a familiarity with Homer, as we do with music-hall songs, because they enjoyed him, and without feeling that they were engaged in the pursuit of learning. But the men of the sixteenth century could not begin to understand him without first absorbing a very considerable amount of linguistic erudition. They admired the Greeks, and did not wish to be shut out from their pleasures; they therefore

*Source:* " 'Useless' Knowledge," Bertrand Russell. From *In Praise of Idleness* published by George Allen & Unwin Ltd. and used with their permission.

copied them, both in reading the classics and in other less avowable ways. Learning, in the renaissance, was part of the *joie de vivre*, just as much as drinking or love-making. And this was true not only for literature, but also of sterner studies. Everyone knows the story of Hobbe's first contact with Euclid: opening the book, by chance, at the theorem of Pythagoras, he exclaimed, "By God, this is impossible," and proceeded to read the proofs backwards until, reaching the axioms, he became convinced. No one can doubt that this was for him a voluptuous moment, unsullied by the thought of the utility of geometry in measuring fields.

It is true that the renaissance found a practical use for the ancient language in connection with theology. One of the earliest results of the new feeling for classical Latin was the discrediting of the forged decretals and the donation of Constantine. The inaccuracies which were discovered in the Vulgate and the Septuagint made Greek and Hebrew a necessary part of the controversial equipment of Protestant divines. The republican maxims of Greece and Rome were invoked to justify the resistance of Puritans to the Stuarts and of Jesuits to monarchs who had thrown off allegiance to the Pope. But all this was an effect, rather than a cause, of the revival of classical learning, which had been in full swing in Italy for nearly a century before Luther. The main motive of the renaissance was mental delight, the restoration of a certain richness and freedom in art and speculation which had been lost while ignorance and superstition kept the mind's eye in blinkers.

The Greeks, it was found, had devoted a part of their attention to matters not purely literary or artistic, such as philosophy, geometry, and astronomy. These studies, therefore, were respectable, but other sciences were more open to question. Medicine, it was true, was dignified by the names of Hippocrates and Galen; but in the intervening period it had become almost confined to Arabs and Jews, and inextricably intertwined with magic. Hence the dubious reputation of such men as Paracelsus. Chemistry was in even worse odor, and hardly became respectable until the eighteenth century.

In this way it was brought about that knowledge of Greek and Latin, with a smattering of geometry and perhaps astronomy, came to be considered the intellectual equipment of a gentleman. The Greeks disdained the practical applications of geometry, and it was only in their decadence that they found a use for astronomy in the guise of astrology. The sixteenth and seventeenth centuries, in the main, studied mathematics with Hellenic disinterestedness, and tended to ignore the sciences which had been degraded by their connection with sorcery. A gradual change towards a wider and more practical conception of knowledge, which was going on throughout the eighteenth century, was suddenly accelerated at the end of that period by the French Revolution and the growth of machinery, of which the former gave a blow to gentlemanly culture while the latter offered new and astonishing scope for the exercises of ungentlemanly skill. Throughout the last hundred and fifty years, men have questioned more and more vigorously the value of "useless" knowledge, and have come increasingly to believe that the only knowledge worth having is that which is applicable to some part of the economic life of the community.

In countries such as France and England, which have a traditional educational system, the utilitarian view of knowledge has only partially prevailed. There are still, for example, professors of Chinese in the universities who read the Chinese classics but are unacquainted with the works of Sun Yet-sen, which created modern China. There are still men who know ancient history in so far as it was related by authors whose style was pure, that is to say up to Alexander in Greece and Nero in Rome, but refuse to know the much more important later history because of the literary inferiority of the historians who related it. Even in France and England, however, the old tradition is dying, and in more up-to-date countries, such as Russia and the United States, it is utterly extinct. In America, for example, educational commissions point out that fifteen hundred words are all that most people employ in business correspondence, and therefore suggest that all others should be avoided in the school curriculum. Basic English, a British invention, goes still further, and reduces the necessary vocabulary to eight hundred words. The conception of speech as something capable of aesthetic value is dying out, and it is coming to be thought that the sole purpose of words is to convey practical information. In Russia the pursuit of practical aims is even more wholehearted than in America: all that is taught in educational institutions is intended to serve some obvious purpose in education or government. The only escape is afforded by theology: the sacred scriptures must be studied by some in the original German, and a few professors must learn philosophy in order to defend dialectical materialism against the criticisms of bourgeois metaphysicians. But as orthodoxy becomes more firmly established, even this tiny loophole will be closed.

Knowledge, everywhere, is coming to be regarded not as a good in itself, or as a means of creating a broad and humane outlook on life in general, but as merely an ingredient in technical skill. This is part of the greater integration of society which has been brought about by scientific technique and military necessity. There is more economic and political interdependence than there was in former times, and therefore there is more social pressure to compel a man to live in a way that his neighbors think useful. Educational establishments, except those for the very rich, or (in England) such as have become invulnerable through antiquity, are not allowed to spend their money as they like, but must satisfy the State that they are serving a useful purpose by imparting skill and instilling loyalty. This is part and parcel of the same movement which has led to compulsory military service, boy scouts, the organization of political parties, and the dissemination of political passion by the Press. We are all more aware of our fellow-citizens than we used to be, more anxious, if we are virtuous, to do them good, and in any case to make them do us good. We do not like to think of anyone lazily enjoying life, however refined may be the quality of his enjoyment. We feel that everybody ought to be doing something to help on the great cause (whatever it may be), the more so as so many bad men are working against it and ought to be stopped. We have not leisure of mind, therefore, to acquire any knowledge except such as will help us in the fight for whatever it may happen to be that we think important.

There is much to be said for the narrowly utilitarian view of education. There is not time to learn everything before beginning to make a living, and undoubtedly "useful" knowledge is *very* useful. It has made the modern world. Without it, we would not have machines or motor-cars or railways or aeroplanes; it should be added that we should not have modern advertising or modern propaganda. Modern knowledge has brought about an immense improvement in average health, and at the same time has discovered how to exterminate large cities by poison gas. Whatever is distinctive of our world, as compared with former times, has its source in "useful" knowledge. No community as yet has enough of it, and undoubtedly education must continue to promote it.

It must also be admitted that a great deal of the traditional cultural education was foolish. Boys spent many years acquiring Latin and Greek grammar, without being, at the end, either capable or desirous (except in a small percentage of cases) of reading a Greek or Latin author. Modern languages and history are preferable, from every point of view, to Latin and Greek. They are not only more useful, but they give much more culture in much less time. For an Italian of the fifteenth century, since practically everything worth reading, if not in his own language, was in Greek or Latin, these languages were the indispensable keys to culture. But since that time great literatures have grown up in various modern languages, and the development of civilization has been so rapid that knowledge of antiquity has become much less useful in understanding our problems than knowledge of modern nations and their comparatively recent history. The traditional schoolmaster's point of view, which was admirable at the time of the revival of learning, became gradually unduly narrow, since it ignored what the world has done since the fifteenth century. And not only history and modern languages, but science also, when properly taught, contributes to culture. It is therefore possible to maintain that education should have other aims than direct utility, without defending the traditional curriculum. Utility and culture, when both are conceived broadly, are found to be less incompatible than they appear to the fanatical advocates of either.

Apart, however, from the cases in which culture and direct utility can be combined, there is indirect utility, or various different kinds, in the possession of knowledge which does not contribute to technical efficacy. I think some of the worst features of the modern world could be improved by a greater encouragement of such knowledge and a less ruthless pursuit of mere professional competence.

When conscious activity is wholly concentrated on some one definite purpose, the ultimate result, for most people, is lack of balance accompanied by some form of nervous disorder. The men who directed German policy during the war made mistakes, for example, as regards the submarine campaign which brought America on to the side of the Allies, which any person coming fresh to the subject could have seen to be unwise, but which they could not judge sanely owing to mental concentration and lack of holidays. The same sort of thing may be seen wherever bodies of men attempt tasks which put a prolonged strain upon spontaneous impulses. Japanese imperialists, Russian Communists, and German Nazis all have a kind of tense fanaticism which comes of living too exclusively in the mental world of certain tasks to be accomplished. When the tasks are as important and as feasible as the fanatics suppose, the result may be magnificent; but in most cases narrowness of outlook has caused oblivion of some powerful counteracting force, or has made all such forces seem the work of the devil, to be met by punishment and terror. Men as well as children have need of play, that is to say, of periods of activity having no purpose beyond present enjoyment. But if play is to serve its purpose, it must be possible to find pleasure and interest in matters not connected with work.

The amusements of modern urban populations tend more and more to be passive and collective, and to consist of inactive observation of the skilled activities of others. Undoubtedly such amusements are much better than none, but they are not as good as would be those of a population which had, through education, a wider range of intelligent interests not connected with work. Better economic organization, allowing mankind to benefit by the productivity of machines, should lead to a very great increase of leisure, and much leisure is apt to be tedious except to those who have considerable intelligent activities and interests. If a leisured population is to be happy, it must be an educated population, and must be educated with a view to mental enjoyment as well as to the direct usefulness of technical knowledge.

The cultural element in the acquisition of knowledge, when it is successfully assimilated, forms the character of a man's thoughts and desires, making them concern themselves, in part at least, with large impersonal objects, not only with matters of immediate importance to himself. It has been too readily assumed that, when a man has acquired certain capacities by means of knowledge, he will use them in ways that are socially beneficial. The narrowly utilitarian conception of education ignores the necessity of training a man's purposes as well as his skill. There is in untrained human nature a very considerable element of cruelty, which shows itself in many ways, great and small. Boys at school tend to be unkind to a new boy, or to one whose clothes are not quite conventional. Many women (and not a few men) inflict as much pain as they can by means of malicious gossip. The Spaniards enjoy bull-fights; the British enjoy hunting and shooting. The same cruel impulses take more serious forms in the hunting of Jews in Germany and kulaks in Russia. All imperialism affords scope for them, and in war they become sanctified as the highest form of public duty.

Now while it must be admitted that highly educated people are sometimes cruel, I think there can be no doubt that they are less often so than people whose minds have lain fallow. The bully in a school is seldom a boy whose proficiency in learning is up to the average. When a lynching takes place, the ringleaders are almost invariably very ignorant men. This is not because mental cultivation produces positive humanitarian feelings, though it may do so; it is rather because it gives other interests than the ill-treatment of neighbors, and other sources of self-respect than the assertion of domination. The two things most universally desired are power and admiration. Ignorant men can, as a rule, only achieve either by brutal means, involving the acquisition of physical mastery. Culture gives a man less harmful forms of power and more deserving ways of making himself admired. Galileo did more than any monarch has done to change the world, and his power immeasurably exceeded that of his persecutors. He had therefore no need to aim at becoming a persecutor in his turn.

Perhaps the most important advantage of "useless" knowledge is that it promotes a contemplative habit of mind. There is in the world much too much readiness, not only for action without adequate previous reflection, but also for some sort of action on occasions on which wisdom would counsel inaction. People show their bias on this matter in various curious ways. Mephistopheles tells the young student that theory is grey but the tree of life is green, and everyone quotes this as if it were

Goethe's opinion, instead of what he supposes the devil would be likely to say to an undergraduate. Hamlet is held up as an awful warning against thought without action, but no one holds up Othello as a warning against action without thought. Professors such as Bergson, from a kind of snobbery towards the practical man, decry philosophy, and say that life at its best should resemble a cavalry charge. For my part, I think action is best when it emerges from a profound apprehension of the universe and human destiny, not from some wildly passionate impulse of romantic but disproportioned self-assertion. A habit of finding pleasure in thought rather than in action is a safeguard against unwisdom and excessive love of power, a means of preserving serenity in misfortune and peace of mind among worries. A life confined to what is personal is likely, sooner or later, to become unbearably painful; it is only by windows into a larger and less fretful cosmos that the more tragic parts of life become endurable.

A contemplative habit of mind has advantages ranging from the most trivial to the most profound. To begin with minor vexations, such as fleas, missing trains, or cantankerous business associates. Such troubles seem hardly worthy to be met by reflections on the excellence of heroism or the transitoriness of all human ills, and yet the irritation to which they give rise destroys many people's good temper and enjoyment of life. On such occasions, there is much consolation to be found in out-of-the-way bits of knowledge which have some real or fancied connection with the trouble of the moment; or even if they have none, they serve to obliterate the present from one's thoughts. When assailed by people who are white with fury, it is pleasant to remember the chapter in Descartes' *Treatise on the Passions* entitled "Why those who grow pale with rage are more to be feared than those who grow red." When one feels impatient over the difficulty of securing international cooperation, one's impatience is diminished if one happens to think of the sainted King Louis IX, before embarking on his crusade, allying himself with the Old Man of the Mountain, who appears in the Arabian Nights as the dark source of half the wickedness in the world. When the rapacity of capitalists grows oppressive, one may be suddenly consoled by the recollection that Brutus, that exemplar of republican virtue, lent money to a city at 40 percent, and hired a private army to besiege it when it failed to pay the interest.

Curious learning not only makes unpleasant things less unpleasant, but also makes pleasant things more pleasant. I have enjoyed peaches and apricots more since I have known that they were first cultivated in China in the early days of the Han dynasty; that Chinese hostages held by the great King Kaniska introduced them into India, whence they spread to Persia, reaching the Roman Empire in the first century of our era; that the word "apricot" is derived from the same Latin source as the word "precocious," because the apricot ripens early; and that the A at the beginning was added by mistake, owing to a false etymology. All this makes the fruit taste much sweeter.

About a hundred years ago, a number of well-meaning philanthropists started societies "for the diffusion of useful knowledge," with the result that people have ceased to appreciate the delicious savour of "useless" knowledge. Opening Burton's *Anatomy of Melancholy* at haphazard on a day when I was threatened by that mood, I learnt that there is a "melancholy matter," but that, while some think it may be engendered of all four humours, "Galen holds that it may be engendered of three alone, excluding phlegm or pituita, whose true assertion Valerius and Menardus stiffly maintain, and so doth Fuscius, Montaltus, Montanus. How (say they) can white become black?" In spite of this unanswerable argument, Hercules de Saxonia and Cardan, Guianerius and Laurentius, are (so Burton tells us) of the opposite opinion. Soothed by these historical reflections, my melancholy, whether due to three humours or to four, was dissipated. As a cure for too much zeal, I can imagine few measures more effective than a course of such ancient controversies.

But while the trivial pleasures of culture have their place as a relief from the trivial worries of practical life, the more important merits of contemplation are in relation to the greater evils of life, death and pain and cruelty, and the blind march of nations into unnecessary disaster. For those to whom dogmatic religion can no longer bring comfort, there is need of some substitute, if life is not to become dusty and harsh and filled with trivial self-assertion. The world at present is full of angry self-centered groups, each incapable of viewing human life as a whole, each willing to destroy civilization rather than yield an inch. To this narrowness no amount of technical instructon will provide an antidote. The antidote ,in so far as it is matter of individual psychology, is to be found in history, biology, astronomy, and all those studies which, without destroying self-respect, enable the individual to see himself in his proper perspective. What is needed is not this or that specific piece of information, but such knowledge as inspires a conception of the ends of human life as a whole: art and history, acquaintance with the lives of heroic individuals, and some understanding of the strangely accidental and ephemeral position of man in the cosmos—all this touched with an emotion of pride in what is distinctively human, the power to see and to know, to feel magnanimously and to think with understanding. It is from large perceptions combined with impersonal emotion that wisdom most readily springs.

Life, at all times full of pain, is more painful in our time than in the two centuries that preceded it. The attempt to escape from pain drives men to triviality, to self-deception, to the invention of vast collective myths. But these momentary alleviations do but increase the sources of suffering in the long run. Both private and public misfortune can only be mastered by a process in which will and intelligence interact: the part of will is to refuse to shirk the evil or accept an unreal solution, while the part of intelligence is to understand it, to find a cure if it is curable, and, if not, to make it bearable by seeing it in its relations, accepting it as unavoidable, and remembering what lies outside it in other regions, other ages, and the abysses of interstellar space.

## 8. HOW CHILDREN FAIL

### John Holt

*One of the most innovative of the new educationists, John Holt has drawn extensively from his own experience as a teacher to work out new theories of education, theories based on the assumption that the most significant source for educational theory is what really happens between student and school, not what is supposed to happen. The following is his forward to* How Children Fail.

Most children in school fail.

For a great many, this failure is avowed and absolute. Close to forty percent of those who begin high school, drop out before they finish. For college, the figure is one in three.

Many others fail in fact if not in name. They complete their schooling only because we have agreed to push them up through the grades and out of the schools, whether they know anything or not. There are many more such children than we think. If we "raise our standards" much higher, as some would have us do, we will find out very soon just how many there are. Our classrooms will bulge with kids who can't pass the test to get into the next class.

But there is a more important sense in which almost all children fail: Except for a handful, who may or may not be good students, they fail to develop more than a tiny part of the tremendous capacity for learning, understanding, and creating with which they were born and of which they made full use during the first two or three years of their lives.

Why do they fail?

They fail because they are afraid, bored, and confused.

They are afraid, above all else, of failing, of disappointing or displeasing the many anxious adults around them, whose limitless hopes and expectations for them hang over their heads like a cloud.

They are bored because the things they are given and told to do in school are so trivial, so dull, and make such limited and narrow demands on the wide spectrum of their intelligence, capabilities, and talents.

They are confused because most of the torrent of words that pours over them in school makes little or no sense. It often flatly contradicts other things they have been told, and hardly ever has any relation to

*Source:* "How Children Fail" from *How Children Fail* by John Holt. Reprinted by permission of the publisher, Pitman Publishing Corp.

what they really know—to the rough model of reality that they carry around in their minds.

How does this mass failure take place? What really goes on in the class room? What are these children who fail doing? What goes on in their heads? Why don't they make use of more of their capacity?

This book is the rough and partial record of a search for answers to these questions. It began as a series of memos written in the evenings to my colleague and friend Bill Hull, whose fifth grade class I observed and taught in during the day. Later these memos were sent to other interested teachers and parents. A small number of these memos make up this book. They have not been much rewritten, but they have been edited and rearranged under four major topics: Strategy; Fear and Failure; Real Learning; and How Schools Fail. *Strategy* deals with the ways in which children try to meet, or dodge, the demands that adults make of them in school. *Fear and Failure* deals with the interaction in children of fear and failure, and the effect of this on strategy and learning. *Real Learning* deals with the difference between what children appear to know or are expected to know, and what they really know. *How Schools Fail* analyzes the ways in which schools foster bad strategies, raise children's fears, produce learning which is usually fragmentary, distorted, and short-lived, and generally fail to meet the real needs of children.

These four topics are clearly not exclusive. They tend to overlap and blend into each other. They are, at most, different ways of looking at and thinking about the thinking and behavior of children.

It must be made clear that the book is not about unusually bad schools or backward children. The schools in which the experiences described here took place are private schools of the highest standards and reputation. With very few exceptions, the children whose work is described are well above the average in intelligence and are, to all outward appearances, successful, and on their way to "good" secondary schools and colleges. Friends and colleagues, who understand what I am trying to say about the harmful effect of today's schooling on the character and intellect of children, and who have visited many more schools than I have, tell me that the schools I have not seen are not a bit better than those I have, and very often are worse.

# 9. TOTAL EFFECT AND THE EIGHTH GRADE

## Flannery O'Connor

*Flannery O'Connor, a native of Savannah, Georgia published her first novel,* Wise Blood, *in 1952. In 1955 appeared* A Good Man Is Hard To Find, *in 1959* Everything That Rises Must Converge, *and in 1960* The Violent Bear It Away.

In two recent instances in Georgia, parents have objected to their eighth- and ninth-grade children's reading assignments in modern fiction. This seems to happen with some regularity in cases throughout the country. The unwitting parent picks up his child's book, glances through it, comes upon passages of erotic detail or profanity, and takes off at once to complain to the school board. Sometimes, as in one of the Georgia cases, the teacher is dismissed and hackles rise in liberal circles everywhere.

The two cases in Georgia, which involved Steinbeck's *East of Eden* and John Hersey's *A Bell for Adano*, provoked considerable newspaper comment. One columnist, in commending the enterprise of the teachers, announced that students do not like to read the fusty works of the nineteenth century, that their attention can best be held by novels dealing with the realities of our own time, and that the Bible, too, is full of racy stories.

Mr. Hersey himself addressed a letter to the State School Superintendent in behalf of the teacher who had been dismissed. He pointed out that his book is not scandalous, that it attempts to convey an earnest message about the nature of democracy, and that it falls well within the limits of the principle of "total effect," that principle followed in legal cases by which a book is judged not for isolated parts but by the final effect of the whole book upon the general reader.

I do not want to comment on the merits of these particular cases. What concerns me is what novels ought to be assigned in the eighth and ninth grades as a matter of course, for if these cases indicate anything, they indicate the haphazard way in which fiction is approached in our high schools. Presumably there is a state reading list which contains "safe" books for teachers to assign; after that it is up to the teacher.

English teachers come in Good, Bad, and Indifferent, but too frequently in high schools anyone who can speak English is allowed to teach it. Since several novels can't easily be gathered into one textbook, the fiction that students are assigned depends upon their teacher's knowledge, ability, and taste: variable factors at best. More often than not, the teacher assigns what he thinks will hold the attention and interest of the students. Modern fiction will certainly hold it.

Ours is the first age in history which has asked the child what he would tolerate learning, but that is a part of the problem with which I am not equipped to deal. The devil of Educationism that possesses us is the kind that can be "cast out only by prayer and fasting." No one has yet come along strong enough to do it. In other ages the attention of children was held by Homer and Virgil, among others, but, by the reverse evolutionary process, that is no longer possible; our children are too stupid now to enter the past imaginatively. No one asks the student if algebra pleases him or if he finds it satisfactory that some French verbs are irregular, but if he prefers Hersey to Hawthorne, his taste must prevail.

I would like to put forward the proposition, repugnant to most English teachers, that fiction, if it is going to be taught in the high schools, should be taught as a subject and as a subject with a history. The total effect of a novel depends not only on its innate impact, but upon the experience, literary and otherwise, with which it is approached. No child needs to be assigned Hersey or Steinbeck until he is familiar with a certain amount of the best work of Cooper, Hawthorne, Melville, the early James, and Crane, and he does not need to be assigned these until he has been introduced to some of the better English novelists of the eighteenth and nineteenth centuries.

The fact that these works do not present him with the realities of his own time is all to the good. He is surrounded by the realities of his own time, and he has no perspective whatever from which to view them. Like the college student who wrote in her paper on Lincoln that he went to the movies and got shot, many students go to college unaware that the world was not made yesterday; their studies began with the present and dipped backward occasionally when it seemed necessary or unavoidable.

There is much to be enjoyed in the great British novels of the nineteenth century, much that a good teacher can open up in them for the young student. There is no reason why these novels should be either too simple or too difficult for the eighth grade. For the simple, they offer simple pleasures; for the more precocious, they can be made to yield subtler ones if the teacher is up to it. Let the student discover, after reading the nineteenth-century British novel, that the nineteenth-century American novel is quite different as to its literary characteristics, and he will thereby learn something not only about these individual works but about the sea-change which a new historical situation can effect in a literary form. Let him come to modern fiction with this experience behind him, and he will be better able to see and to deal with the more complicated demands of the best twentieth-century fiction.

Modern fiction often looks simpler than the fiction that preceded it, but in reality it is more complex. A natural evolution has taken place. The author has for the most part absented himself from direct participation in the work and has left the reader to make his own way amid experiences dramatically rendered and symbolically ordered. The modern novelist merges the reader in the experience; he tends to raise the passions he touches upon. If he is a good novelist, he raises them to effect by their order and clarity a new experience—the total effect—which is not in itself sensuous or simply of the moment. Unless the child has had some literary experience before, he is not going to be able to resolve the immediate passions the book arouses into any true, total picture.

It is here the moral problem will arise. It is one thing for a child to read about the adultery in the Bible or in *Anna Karenina*, and quite another for him to read about it in most modern fiction. This is not only because in both the former instances adultery is considered a sin, and in the latter, at most, an inconvenience, but because modern writing involves the reader in the action with a new degree of intensity, and literary mores now permit him to be involved in any action a human being can perform.

In our fractured culture, we cannot agree on morals; we cannot even agree that moral matters should come before literary ones when there is a conflict between them. All this is another reason why the high schools would do well to return to their proper business of preparing foundations. Whether in the senior year students should be assigned modern novelists should depend both on their parents' consent and on what they have already read and understood.

The high-school English teacher will be fulfilling his responsibility if he furnishes the student a guided opportunity, through the best writing of the past, to come, in time, to an understanding of the best writing of the present. He will teach literature, not social studies or little lessons in democracy or the customs of many lands.

And if the student finds that this is not to his taste? Well, that is regrettable. Most regrettable. His taste should not be consulted; it is being formed.

## 10. DEATH IN THE AFTERNOON

### Ernest Hemingway

*Ernest Hemingway was a Nobel-prize novelist, adventurer, warrior, and afficionado of the bullring, whose rare skills as a stylist are evident here in this expository selection from* Death in the Afternoon.

At the first bullfight I ever went to I expected to be horrified and perhaps sickened by what I had been told would happen to the horses. Everything I had read about the bull ring insisted on that point; most people who wrote of it condemned bullfighting outright as a stupid brutal business, but even those that spoke well of it as an exhibition of skill and as a spectacle deplored the use of the horses and were apologetic about the whole thing. The killing of the horses in the ring was considered indefensible. I suppose, from a modern moral point of view, that is, a Christian point of view, the whole bullfight is indefensible; there is certainly much cruelty, there is always danger, either sought or unlooked for, and there is always death, and I should not try to defend it now, only to tell honestly the things I have found true about it. To do this I must be altogether frank, or try to be, and if those who read this decide with disgust that it is written by some one who lacks their, the readers', fineness of feeling I can only plead that this may be true. But whoever reads this can only truly make such a judgment when he, or she, has seen the things that are spoken of and knows truly what their reactions to them would be.

Once I remember Gertrude Stein talking of bullfights spoke of her admiration for Joselito and showed me some pictures of him in the ring and of herself and Alice Toklas sitting in the first row of the wooden barreras at the bull ring at Valencia with Joselito and his brother Gallo below, and I had just come from the Near East, where the Greeks broke the legs of their baggage and transport animals and drove and shoved them off the quay into the shallow water when they abandoned the city of Smyrna, and I remember saying that I did not like the bullfights because of the poor horses. I was trying to write then and I found the greatest difficulty, aside from knowing truly what you really felt, rather

*Source:* "Death in the Afternoon." Reprinted by permission of Charles Scribner's Sons from *Death in the Afternoon* by Ernest Hemingway. Copyright 1932 Charles Scribner's Sons; renewal copyright © 1960 Ernest Hemingway.

than what you were supposed to feel, and had been taught to feel, was to put down what really happened in action; what the actual things were which produced the emotion that you experienced. In writing for a newspaper you told what happened and, with one trick and another, you communicated the emotion aided by the element of timeliness which gives a certain emotion to any account of something that has happened on that day; but the real thing, the sequence of motion and fact which made the emotion and which would be as valid in a year or in ten years or, with luck and if you stated it purely enough, always, was beyond me and I was working very hard to try to get it. The only place where you could see life and death, *i.e.*, violent death now that the wars were over, was in the bull ring and I wanted very much to go to Spain where I could study it. I was trying to learn to write, commencing with the simplest things, and one of the simplest things of all and the most fundamental is violent death. It has none of the complications of death by disease, or so-called natural death, or the death of a friend or some one you have loved or have hated, but it is death nevertheless, one of the subjects that a man may write of. I had read many books in which, when the author tried to convey it, he only produced a blur, and I decided that this was because either the author had never seen it clearly or at the moment of it, he had physically or mentally shut his eyes, as one might do if he saw a child that he could not possibly reach or aid, about to be struck by a train. In such a case I suppose he would probably be justified in shutting his eyes as the mere fact of the child being about to be struck by the train was all that he could convey, the actual striking would be an anti-climax, so that the moment before striking might be as far as he could represent. But in the case of an execution by a firing squad, or a hanging, this is not true, and if these very simple things were to be made permanent, as, say, Goya tried to make them in *Los Desastros de la Guerra*, it could not be done with any shutting of the eyes. I had seen certain things, certain simple things of this sort that I remembered, but through taking part in them, or, in other cases, having to write of them immediately after and consequently noticing the things I needed for instant recording, I had never been able to study them as a man might, for instance, study the death of his father or the hanging of some one, say, that he did not know and would not have to write of immediately after for the first edition of an afternoon newspaper.

So I went to Spain to see bullfights and to try to write about them for myself. I thought they would be simple and barbarous and cruel and that I would not like them, but that I would see certain definite action which would give me the feeling of life and death that I was working for. I found the definite action; but the bullfight was so far from simple and I liked it so much that it was much too complicated for my then equipment for writing to deal with and, aside from four very short sketches, I was not able to write anything about it for five years— and I wish I would have waited ten. However, if I had waited long enough I probably never would have written anything at all since there is a tendency when you really begin to learn something about a thing not to want to write about it but rather to keep on learning about it always and at no time, unless you are very egotistical, which, of course, accounts for many books, will you be able to say: now I know all about this and will write about it. Certainly I do not say that now; every year I know there is more to learn, but I know some things which may be interesting now, and I may be away from the bullfights for a long time and I might as well write what I know about them now. Also it might be good to have a book about bullfighting in English and a serious book on such an unmoral subject may have some value.

## 11. AFTER GENESIS

**Joseph de Roche**

*Joseph de Roche teaches poetry writing at Northeastern University. His poems have appeared in a number of journals and a collection,* The Inhabited Scroll, *was published in 1968.*

I am building an Ark,
Not after the measurements
Of the Lord,
But after my own.
It would be large enough for me,
A few friends,
All the beasts of the field.

Daily, though I'm no Noah,
My neighbors put on
The shifty glance of the paranoid—
Their suburban idea
Of suspicion somehow perfected.
They know I know something,
But no word escapes me
Save the rippling soft laughter
Which falls out of me
Like rain beginning.

Already my Ark
Has risen over the roofs of their houses.
Secretly, by night,
I dance gleeful and naked,
Covered with pitch
And the odor of hardwood.
Off-hours how I have skulked about
Repeating to myself
Two of these, and, of those, two more.
By midnight I steal them blind.
Their pets are disappearing
Like sugar into the mouth of the Mississippi.

*Source:* "After Genesis." Reprinted by permission of the author, Joseph de Roche.

Into my great red-ribbed wood ship
I have built a barnyard,
An unbelievable zoo.
Nothing can stop the stowed-in beasts
From their delight
In themselves, their knowledge
Of multiplication.
Who could keep up with it?
No one but me
Believes in the billowing rain,
The need for discretion,
The manageable size.

Yet walking the darkening streets,
My admiration for beautiful specimens
Like yourselves,
Your dancing by twos,
Has no sense of proportion.
I wish to leave behind me
None of you.
You have smiles not even the whole earth,
Prostrate in mourning,
May equal.

For you, then, I am rebuilding
My Ark according to the proportions
Of my desires.
Not even the Lord
Could imagine such love,
Such need,
Such passion for the number two.
Not even the rains of Noah
Nor the tears of God
Falling forever
Could float the city
My boat has become at last
For the sake of you.

## Commentary: An Imaginative World for All—the Poet as Noah

As a vehicle for creation and thus continuum, the Ark is an apt symbol
of poetry. It is as such that it serves most manageably in Joe de Roche's

poem "After Genesis," which is about the development of a poet and the function of poetry.

The poet creates an imaginative world and populates it, thus assuming on a small scale a role parallel to God's, as Noah, in a particular small-scale way assumed a role parallel to God's. Thus the poet as a kind of Noah is a very sensible trope. But the speaker of this poem, like most of us who write things, begins by creating a rather limited world, essentially autobiographic, populated only with the things of his immediate experience, and perhaps rather self-consciously enduring the suburban suspicion of poets. In fact he probably takes to himself a gleeful satisfaction at the suburban suspicion of poets, in an inverse way sharing it, reveling like a first-year graduate student in the sense of knowing something the business slobs don't—the Babbitts and straights of all sorts who still subscribe to the *Reader's Digest* and read the book reviews in *Life*.

Many of de Roche's poems are about animals, and use animals as emblems of larger meaning, and the allusion to beasts of the field suggests, I think, the images that populate his imagination. But as the pairs of animals in Noah's ark must multiply and finally increase beyond the limits of the ark (that was after all the purpose of two-by-two), so the images confined in the discreet and carefully measured imagination of the poet begin to interact, to produce new meaning, and to expand that poetic world to encompass more than a few friends and the figures of the mind. The speaker seems to learn that poetry is not a private, but a public, act. If it is to create a world of just proportion, it must include all of the world—the suburbanites as well as their pets. For they too know that the rain will come. They too need the "temporary stay against confusion" which Robert Frost said poetry provides. And they have in their two-ness found their own way of creation and continuum. This, the poem seems to suggest, is the maturation that the poet must achieve, to encompass in the joy of his own creation, the joy of other men's creation until the imaginative world includes all mankind in its joy and in its love—providing shape and direction to the process of humanity.

## Commentary: And Before Exodus—On the Speaker of the Poem

There may be a better way to end a section of prose readings on "thinking and learning" than with a poem, but right now I cannot think of any; particularly when the poem is as pleasant as this one by a young poet whose work is beginning to make its way. I am not sure that I understand what Joseph de Roche is trying to tell us in this poem (he may not be trying to tell us anything), or just why we decided to include it in this section of the book; but I do know that I like the poem, and especially like what I think happens to the "I" or "poet" in the course of its six stanzas.

When we first meet this man, we learn that he is "building an Ark, /Not after the measurements of the Lord," but after his own. He will, in a Lordly way, make it large enough to save himself, a "few friends," and "All the beasts of the field" from what we assume is the imminent disaster; but he will not make it large enough to save everybody.

In the second stanza, his exclusiveness, pride, and egocentricity are revealed in his remarks about his neighbors who, he says, "put on/The shifty glance of the paranoid." He has a secret which he will not share (that they are doomed, and he is not?), and his "rippling soft laughter" falls out of him "Like rain beginning."

In the third stanza, his pride is even more overbearing. His ark has "risen over the roofs" of his neighbors' houses and, like a savage, he gleefully dances "Covered with pitch." Where are the "friends" he has told us about in the first stanza? Nowhere to be seen. Only this mad, solitary builder, dancing alone, thieving now at midnight, stealing his neighbors blind, his skulking greed limitless, "Two of these, and, of those, two more."

In the fourth stanza, however, something has happened. The tone has changed abruptly from frenzy to reflection as if the poet having passed through a fit is now capable of rational observation. He notices that the animals he has collected in "twos" even though they are imprisoned in his ship continue to take delight in themselves, continue to multiply as if nothing could stop them. The poet senses now his isolation, his apartness, the folly of his project which even the dumb beasts in their multiplication threaten to sink: "No one but me/Believes in the billowing rain,/The need for discretion,/The manageable size."

The fifth stanza opens with the pivotal word "Yet" which, after the knowledge gained in stanza three, indicates a shifting of attitude on the part of the poet. Now as he walks "the darkening streets" he admires "beautiful specimens"; and because he says these specimens are "Like yourselves" we assume he is no longer talking about "beasts of the field," but rather about people; and not about people in general, but rather about people who dance by twos (with a suggestion of lovers of any kind, and a reminder that, in stanza three the poet danced alone). Even though "our" dancing has no more "sense of proportion" than does that of the imprisoned animals on his ship, he is so taken by our smiles that he wants to leave none of us behind.

And so in the final stanza he begins again, "rebuilding" his ark according to the "proportions" of his desires, which have undergone significant change since stanza one. Instead of the exclusive, spiteful, and self-serving ark he had originally constructed, he is now going to build one out of his newly discovered need for love. It will be as large—and as inclusive—as a city; and, if the disaster does come, in whatever form, there will be no private escape for him; he will share his fate with all of us; at least all of us who love.

### Response: After "After Genesis"
### Joseph de Roche

When I first began to write "After Genesis," I merely remember being excited about the image of the ark, of building with words something I could equally, if fantastically, become excited about building in my own backyard with oak wood and metal nails. That's how the poem began. I knew something of the Biblical Ark and Noah; I knew, more or less, the world—my part of it, at least.

But an ark rising above the garage of that kind but cranky old man next door must be, for us, an act of clear lunacy, or of obscurer prophecy. These days, people who continue to hear voices telling them to build arks on dry land, and who then build those arks, are often run out of town the modern way—by being sent off to the nearest state mental hospital.

In my mind, the poem then, was to be about a genial maniac building the impossible in (next to the farm) the most impeccably secure and plausible part of America, the suburb. I presumed that an ark hammered out in a suburb would have the quality of insult, if only to the zoning laws. The "I" of the poem begins, then, as has been said, as an arrogant and thief. What remains odd to me, however, is my understanding that the poem could have ended there. Maybe that would have been humanly dishonest, maybe not, but as I look at the poem now, it could have remained honest to itself with a single tone, and no turn, no epiphany. Everything secure people cherished would get pilfered off in the night by someone touched with madness and obsession.

But if I didn't have a problem with my message, I still had a construction project. Sometimes a poem, or the act of writing a poem, has an annoying habit of ambling off where it will. I never knew when I began "After Genesis" that my dancing savage was going to end up loving the very people and places he, in the beginning, despised. But he does. And I'm glad he does. I just don't know why he does. I know a poem before it's finished could end a dozen different ways, and each way honest. I know also, however, that I came to the end of this poem by being led there.

I was led there by myself, certainly, but also by the images I'd put together, the words I'd used, the tone I'd started with. At the end of "After Genesis" (and this doesn't always happen to me when I write a poem), I had the reward of standing on ground I never knew I was going to stand on when I began to write.

And although I agree with what Peter Sandberg and Robert Parker found in the poem, I find that what meaning I put in the poem came about by building a strange ark in a stranger place and, hopefully, writing myself out of that particular mess—and in a way that was cousin to a kind of logic and good order. I keep an old-fashioned sense of trying to straighten out the chaos I'm responsible for in the first place. Yet I know, too, that if I want a reader to get anything more from the poem, what I want him to get would be a pleasure in the antics, images, and abashed love the poem, itself, finally gets to.

Tonight, for instance, I'm writing this response from a room high up over the city. I have never lived so far above the street, and wouldn't now if not for the kindness of friends. The city looks to me like one of those brilliant inventions of Dali which he calls, pedestrianly, jewels. I've been thinking, naturally, about my poem while writing this, but I have also, now and again, been absent-mindedly watching the city fall away in the distance to the suburbs. I can hear the wash of traffic and the lifting voices of strangers in the street. The lights of the city glitter like a fistful of rubies and sapphires and diamonds. Seeing the city, all at once like this by night, really does remind me of a ship, inclusive and majestic. A kind of sailing away, if you will, together. The last image of the poem, then, the ark as city, seems to me just. Or so I hope.

# SECTION III

## *Film*

Being organized is much better than its alternative, not only because it's easier on the reader. It is also easier on the writer. If you have a plan for proceeding then you are not stuck at the end of each sentence, or paragraph. You know where to go next. For example: "The Westerner" is organized by comparison and contrast. The topic is "men with guns." In American films there are two major categories of men with guns—the gangster and the westerner. How are they similar? How are they different? First Warshow talks of the gangster and then of the westerner. His discussion of the westerner is conducted mainly in terms of how he compares with the gangster. Thus if at the end of a paragraph Warshow is stuck with what to say next he can say "The western hero, by contrast, is a figure of repose." Having completed a sentence and uncertain what to say in his next, Warshow may write "When the gangster is killed, his whole life is shown to have been a mistake, but the image the Westerner seeks to maintain can be presented as clearly in defeat as in victory: . . ."

In short if you have a two-part subject you can write about it at length by comparing one half to the other. But be sure you've got a two-part subject.

Penelope Gilliatt does not have a two-part subject. She has a single thesis (which, interestingly, she doesn't precisely state), and her technique is simply to give illustrative examples in the form of anecdotes that she interprets by the way she repeats them. For example, " 'Painting!' said a usually intelligent man, scampering to keep up with his kids." The technique is open ended, that is, it is limited only by the number of illustrative anecdotes Miss Gilliatt can remember or make up. After each anecdote she may go on by simply asking herself: What's another illustration of the film madness? Compare her to Tom Wolfe on McLuhan.

*Newsweek*, on the other hand, uses a more conventional technique. It is, in fact, probably the basic organizing technique of expository writing, and it will work on any subject. Make an assertion and support it with evidence. *Newsweek* asserts that "it is precisely this inexhaustible drive to orchestrate even the smallest details of his life and his art that has made Stanley Kubrick the most provacative and brilliant of today's

American directors." It then goes on in the rest of the article to demonstrate that Kubrick is brilliant, provocative, and a stickler for detail (consider the last sentence in the essay). In fact, this is, if one allows the terms to be broadly used, the basic pattern of any exposition. Miss Gilliatt implies an assertion and supports it with illustrations, Warshow asserts similarity and distinction about men with guns, and supports the assertion with examples. Thus, also, Goshgarian and O'Neill, although they give some evidence of being afflicted with the disease Miss Gilliatt describes, it seems a mild case. Their essay follows the classic pattern of assertion ("with the release of Stanley Kubrick's *2001, A Space Odyssey* . . . the normal limits of the science fiction film were broken") and support ("where the earlier films dealt with future speculation within a set of given circumstances, . . . *2001* speculates from the dawn of man to the year of the title and beyond, a span of four million years"). The support here is conducted largely by an analysis of *2001* although there are, of course, elements of comparison and contrast (*2001* compared to traditional science fiction films). You might consider whether the comparison/contrast elements in the essay improve its clarity.

Stanley Kauffman's review of *A Clockwork Orange* is essentially a description of the film followed by a judgement. The assertion is there, somewhat concealed it seems, in the second paragraph, and the rest of the review is a kind of ostensive demonstration of the assertion that the film lacks "cool intelligence," "moral inquiry" and slips tritely into "tedium," for example "The scene is England, Alex, a young ruffian, leads a quartet of young ruffians whose hobby is 'ultra violence'— binges of rapes and assault." Threaded through the discussion is a concern for the loss in "linguistic acrobatics when Anthony Burgess's novel was translated into film."

This concern becomes central in Richard Schickel's review. Like Kauffman, Schickel places Kubrick in his own historical context ("he has twice before been tempted by projects that pose powerful problems of language for the film maker"). This seems an irresitible urge when talking of a major film figure like Kubrick (Goshgarian and O'Neill did the same thing) and seems to be a way of signifying that he is "major." But the assertion is made at the end of the second and the beginning of the third paragraph (an ideal transition device incidentally). Everything Schickel says thereafter is, however, not a demonstration of that assertion, but a result of it. Schickel does not, in other words, waste time reviewing what you can, that is, the movie. If you see it you'll decide whether the use of Nadsat would help or hinder. If you don't see it, you won't care. Thus he starts with his response and proceeds to analyze the implications of that response, assuming it to be valid. He talks less of the movie than of the movie's meaning.

The selection from the novel on which *A Clockwork Orange* is based will help you decide for yourself. While it is fictional, its purpose is expositional, and it is organized around a rhetorical device: the repetition of a rhetorical question: "What's it going to be then, eh?" Between the repetitions Burgess has two basic tasks, to fill the reader in on the things he needs to know to understand the story (the names of the characters, the circumstances they were in), and to acclimate the reader, mainly through context, but also through explanatory paraphrase, to the new language he's created. The repetition of the question periodically gives a sense of story movement in what is, in fact, static exposition, and reminds us that we are in a story. As soon as action begins, the question is no longer needed and the story begins to develop.

Organization is art for the artist's sake. It helps the reader, but first it helps the writer.

## 12. THE WESTERNER

### Robert Warshow

*In his tragically short life (he died at the age of 38) Robert Warshow helped to develop the art of film criticism to the serious discipline it has now become. An editor of* Commentary *for nine years, Warshow wrote, in addition to criticism, essays on various aspects of American culture.*

They that have power to hurt and will do none,
That do not do the thing they most do show,
Who, moving others, are themselves as stone,
Unmoved, cold, and to temptation slow;
They rightly do inherit heaven's graces,
And husband nature's riches from expense:
They are the lords and owners of their faces,
Others but stewards of their excellence.

The two most successful creations of American movies are the gangster and the Westerner: men with guns. Guns as physical objects, and the postures associated with their use, form the visual and emotional center of both types of films. I suppose this reflects the importance of guns in the fantasy life of Americans: but that is a less illuminating point than it appears to be.

The gangster movie, which no longer exists in its "classical" form, is a story of enterprise and success ending in precipitate failure. Success is conceived as an increasing power to work injury, it belongs to the city, and it is of course a form of evil (though the gangster's death, presented usually as "punishment," is perceived simply as defeat). The peculiarity of the gangster is his unceasing, nervous activity. The exact nature of his enterprises may remain vague, but his commitment to enterprise is always clear, and all the more clear because he operates outside the field of utility. He is without culture, without manners, without leisure, or at any rate his leisure is likely to be spent in debauchery so compulsively aggressive as to seem only another aspect of his "work." But he is graceful, moving like a dancer among the crowded dangers of the city.

*Source:* "The Westerner," Robert Warshow. From *The Immediate Experience,* published by Doubleday, reprinted by permission of Paul Warshow.

Like other tycoons, the gangster is crude in conceiving his ends but by no means inarticulate: on the contrary, he is usually expansive and noisy (the introspective gangster is a fairly recent development), and can state definitely what he wants: to take over the North Side, to own a hundred suits, to be Number One. But new "frontiers" will present themselves infinitely, and by a rigid convention it is understood that as soon as he wishes to rest on his gains, he is on the way to destruction.

The gangster is lonely and melancholy, and can give the impression of a profound worldly wisdom. He appeals most to adolescents with their impatience and their feeling of being outsiders, but more generally he appeals to that side of all of us which refuses to believe in the "normal" possibilities of happiness and achievement; the gangster is the "no" to that great American "yes" which is stamped so big over our official culture and yet has so little to do with the way we really feel about our lives. But the gangster's loneliness and melancholy are not "authentic"; like everything else that belongs to him, they are not honestly come by: he is lonely and melancholy not because life ultimately demands such feelings but because he has put himself in a position where everybody wants to kill him and eventually somebody will. He is wide open and defenseless, incomplete because unable to accept any limits or come to terms with his own nature, fearful, loveless. And the story of his career is a nightmare inversion of the values of ambition and opportunity. From the window of Scarface's bulletproof apartment can be seen an electric sign proclaiming: "The World Is Yours," and, if I remember, this sign is the last thing we see after Scarface lies dead in the street. In the end it is the gangster's weakness as much as his power and freedom that appeals to us; the world is not ours, but it is not his either, and in his death he "pays" for our fantasies, releasing us momentarily both from the concept of success, which he denies by caricaturing it, and from the need to succeed, which he shows to be dangerous.

The Western hero, by contrast, is a figure of repose. He resembles the gangster in being lonely and to some degree melancholy. But his melancholy comes from the "simple" recognition that life is unavoidably serious, not from the disproportions of his own temperament. And his loneliness is organic, not imposed on him by his situation but belonging to him intimately and testifying to his completeness. The gangster must reject others violently or draw them violently to him. The Westerner is not thus compelled to seek love; he is prepared to accept it, perhaps, but he never asks of it more than it can give, and we see him constantly in situations where love is at best an irrelevance. If there is a woman he loves, she is usually unable to understand his motives; she is against killing and being killed, and he finds it impossible to explain to her that there is no point in being "against" these things: they belong to his world.

Very often this woman is from the East and her failure to understand represents a clash of cultures. In the American mind, refinement, virtue, civilization, Christianity itself, are seen as feminine, and therefore women are often portrayed as possessing some kind of deeper wisdom, while the men, for all their apparent self-assurance, are fundamentally childish. But the West, lacking the graces of civilization, is the place "where men are men"; in Western movies, men have the deeper wisdom and the women are children. Those women in the Western movies who share the hero's understanding of life are prostitutes (or, as they are usually presented, barroom entertainers)—women, that is, who have come to understand in the most practical way how love can be an irrelevance, and therefore "fallen" women. The gangster, too, associates with prostitutes, but for him the important things about a prostitute are her passive availability and her costliness: she is part of his winnings. In Western movies, the important thing about a prostitute is her quasi-masculine independence: nobody owns her, nothing has to be explained to her, and she is not, like a virtuous woman, a "value" that demands to be protected. When the Westerner leaves the prostitute for a virtuous woman—for love—he is in fact forsaking a way of life, though the point of the choice is often obscured by having the prostitute killed by getting into the line of fire.

The Westerner is *par excellence* a man of leisure. Even when he wears the badge of a marshal or, more rarely, owns a ranch, he appears to be unemployed. We see him standing at a bar, or playing poker—a game which expresses perfectly his talent for remaining relaxed in the midst of tension—or perhaps camping out on the plains on some extraordinary errand. If he does own a ranch, it is in the background; we are not actually aware that he owns anything except his horse, his guns, and the one worn suit of clothing which is likely to remain unchanged all through the movie. It comes as a surprise to see him take money from his pocket or an extra shirt from his saddlebags. As a rule we do not even know where he sleeps at night and don't think of asking. Yet it never occurs to us that he is a poor man; there is no poverty in Western movies, and really no wealth either: those great cattle domains and shipments of gold which figure so largely in the plots are moral and not material quantities, not the objects of contention but only its occasion. Possessions too are irrelevant.

Employment of some kind—usually unproductive—is always open to the Westerner, but when he accepts it, it is not because he needs to make a living, much less from any idea of "getting ahead." Where could he

want to "get ahead" to? By the time we see him, he is already "there":
he can ride a horse faultlessly, keep his countenance in the face of death,
and draw his gun a little faster and shoot it a little straighter than anyone he is likely to meet. These are sharply defined acquirements, giving
to the figure of the Westerner an apparent moral clarity which corresponds to the clarity of his physical image against his bare landscape;
initially, at any rate, the Western movie presents itself as being without
mystery, its whole universe comprehended in what we see on the screen.

Much of this apparent simplicity arises directly from those "cinematic"
elements which have long been understood to give the Western theme its
special appropriateness for the movies: the wide expanses of land, the
free movement of men on horses. As guns constitute the visible moral
center of the Western movie, suggesting continually the possibility of
violence, so land and horses represent the movie's material basis, its
sphere of action. But the land and the horses have also a moral significance: the physical freedom they represent belongs to the moral "openness" of the West—corresponding to the fact that guns are carried where
they can be seen. (And, as we shall see, the character of land and
horses changes as the Western film becomes more complex.)

The gangster's world is less open, and his arts not so easily identifiable
as the Westerner's. Perhaps he too can keep his countenance, but the
mask he wears is really no mask: its purpose is precisely to make evident the fact that he desperately wants to "get ahead" and will stop at
nothing. Where the Westerner imposes himself by the appearance of
unshakable control, the gangster's pre-eminence lies in the suggestion
that he may at any moment lose control; his strength is not in being able
to shoot faster or straighter than others, but in being more willing to
shoot. "Do it first," says Scarface expounding his mode of operation,
"and keep on doing it!" With the Westerner, it is a crucial point of honor
*not* to "do it first"; his gun remains in its holster until the moment of
combat.

There is no suggestion, however, that he draws the gun reluctantly.
The Westerner could not fulfill himself if the moment did not finally
come when he can shoot his enemy down. But because that moment is
so thoroughly the expression of his being, it must be kept pure. He will
not violate the accepted forms of combat though by doing so he could
save a city. And he can wait. "When you call me that—smile!"—the
villain smiles weakly, soon he is laughing with horrible joviality, and the
crisis is past. But it is allowed to pass because it must come again:
sooner or later Trampas will "make his play," and the Virginian will
be ready for him.

What does the Westerner fight for? We know he is on the side of justice and order, and of course it can be said he fights for these things. But such broad aims never correspond exactly to his real motives; they only offer him his opportunity. The Westerner himself, when an explanation is asked of him (usually by a woman), is likely to say that he does what he "has to do." If justice and order did not continually demand his protection, he would be without a calling. Indeed, we come upon him often in just that situation, as the reign of law settles over the West and he is forced to see that his day is over; those are the pictures which end with his death or with his departure for some more remote frontier. What he defends, at bottom, is the purity of his own image—in fact his honor. This is what makes him invulnerable. When the gangster is killed, his whole life is shown to have been a mistake, but the image the Westerner seeks to maintain can be presented as clearly in defeat as in victory: he fights not for advantage and not for the right, but to state what he is, and he must live in a world which permits that statement. The Westerner is the last gentleman, and the movies which over and over again tell his story are probably the last art form in which the concept of honor retains its strength.

Of course I do not mean to say that ideas of virtue and justice and courage have gone out of culture. Honor is more than these things: it is a style, concerned with harmonious appearances as much as with desirable consequences, and tending therefore toward the denial of life in favor of art. "Who hath it? he that died o' Wednesday." On the whole, a world that leans to Falstaff's view is a more civilized and even, finally, a more graceful world. It is just the march of civilization that forces the Westerner to move on; and if we actually had to confront the question it might turn out that the woman who refuses to understand him is right as often as she is wrong. But we do not confront the question. Where the Westerner lives it is always about 1870—not the real 1870, either, or the real West—and he is killed or goes away when his position becomes problematical. The fact that he continues to hold our attention is evidence enough that, in his proper frame, he presents an image of personal nobility that is still real for us.

Clearly, this image easily becomes ridiculous: we need only look at William S. Hart or Tom Mix, who in the wooden absoluteness of their virtue represented little that an adult could take seriously; and doubtless such figures as Gene Autry or Roy Rogers are no better, though I confess I have seen none of their movies. Some film enthusiasts claim to find in the early, unsophisticated Westerns a "cinematic purity" that has since been lost; this idea is as valid, and finally as misleading, as T. S. Eliot's statement that *Everyman* is the only play in English that stays within the limitations of art. Truth is that the Westerner comes into the field of serious art only when his moral code, without ceasing to be compelling, is seen also to be imperfect. The Westerner at his best exhibits a moral ambiguity which darkens his image and saves him from absurdity; this ambiguity arises from the fact that, whatever his justifications, he is a killer of men.

In *The Virginian*, which is an archetypal Western movie as *Scarface* or *Little Caesar* are archetypal gangster movies, there is a lynching in which the hero (Gary Cooper), as leader of a posse, must supervise the hanging of his best friend for stealing cattle. With the growth of American "social consciousness," it is no longer possible to present a lynching in the movies unless the point is the illegality and injustice of the lynching itself; *The Ox-Bow Incident*, made in 1943, explicitly puts forward the newer point of view and can be regarded as a kind of "anti-Western." But in 1929, when *The Virginian* was made, the present inhibition about lynching was not yet in force; the justice, and therefore the necessity, of the hanging is never questioned—except by the schoolteacher from the East, whose refusal to understand serves as usual to set forth more sharply the deeper seriousness of the West. The Virginian is thus in a tragic dilemma where one moral absolute conflicts with another and the choice of either must leave a moral stain. If he had chosen to save his friend, he would have violated the image of himself that he had made essential to his existence, and the movie would have had to end with his death, for only by his death could the image have been restored. Having chosen instead to sacrifice his friend to the higher demands of the "code"—the only choice worthy of him, as even the friend understands—he is none the less stained by the killing, but what is needed now to set accounts straight is not his death but the death of the villain Trampas, the leader of the cattle thieves, who had escaped the posse and abandoned the Virginian's friend to his fate. Again the woman intervenes: Why must there be *more* killing? If the hero really loved her, he would leave town, refusing Trampas's challenge. What good will it be if Trampas should kill him? But the Virginian does once more what he "has to do," and in avenging his friend's death wipes out the stain on his own honor. Yet his victory cannot be complete: no death can be paid for and no stain truly wiped out; the movie is still a tragedy, for though the hero escapes with his life, he has been forced to confront the ultimate limits of his moral ideas.

This mature sense of limitation and unavoidable guilt is what gives the Westerner a "right" to his melancholy. It is true that the gangster's story is also a tragedy—in certain formal ways more clearly a tragedy than the Westerner's—but it is a romantic tragedy, based on a hero whose defeat springs with almost mechanical inevitability from the outrageous presumption of his demands: the gangster is *bound* to go on until he is killed. The Westerner is a more classical figure, self-contained and limited to begin with seeking not to extend his dominion but only to assert his personal values and his tragedy lies in the fact that even this circumscribed demand cannot be fully realized. Since the Westerner is not a murderer but (most of the time) a man of virtue, and since he is always prepared for defeat, he retains his inner invulnerability and his story need not end with his death (and usually does not); but what we finally respond to is not his victory but his defeat.

Up to a point, it is plain that the deeper seriousness of the good Western films comes from the introduction of a realism, both physical and psychological, that was missing with Tom Mix and William S. Hart. As lines of age have come into Gary Cooper's face since *The Virginian*, so the outlines of the Western movie in general have become less smooth, its background more drab. The sun still beats upon the town, but the camera is likely now to take advantage of this illumination to seek out more closely the shabbiness of buildings and furniture, the loose, worn hang of clothing, the wrinkles and dirt of the faces. Once it has been discovered that the true theme of the Western movie is not the freedom and expansiveness of frontier life, but its limitations, its material bareness, the pressures of obligation, then even the landscape itself ceases to be quite the arena of free movement it once was, but becomes instead a great empty waste, cutting down more often than it exaggerates the stature of the horseman who rides across it. We are more likely now to see the Westerner struggling against the obstacles of the physical world (as in the wonderful scenes on the desert and among the rocks in *The Last Posse*) than carelessly surmounting them. Even the horses, no longer the "friends" of man or the inspired charges of knight-errantry have lost much of the moral significance that once seemed to belong to them in their careering across the screen. It seems to me the horses grow tired and stumble more often than they did, and that we see them less frequently at the gallop.

In *The Gunfighter*, a remarkable film of a couple of years ago, the landscape has virtually disappeared. Most of the action takes place indoors, in a cheerless saloon where a tired "bad man" (Gregory Peck) contemplates the waste of his life, to be senselessly killed at the end by a vicious youngster setting out on the same futile path. The movie is done in cold, quiet tones of gray, and every object in it—faces, clothing, a table, the hero's heavy mustache—is given an air of uncompromising authenticity, suggesting those dim photographs of the nineteenth-century West in which Wyatt Earp, say, turns out to be a blank untidy figure posing awkwardly before some uninteresting building. This "authenticity," to be sure, is only aesthetic; the chief fact about nineteenth-century photographs, to my eyes at any rate, is how stonily they refuse to yield up the truth. But that limitation is just what is needed: by preserving some hint of the rigidity of archaic photography (only in tone and decor, never in composition), *The Gunfighter* can permit us to feel that we are looking at a more "real" West than the one the movies have accustomed us to—harder, duller, less "romantic"—and yet without forcing us outside the boundaries which give the Western movie its validity.

We come upon the hero of *The Gunfighter* at the end of a career in which he has never upheld justice and order, and has been at times, apparently, an actual criminal; in this case, it is clear that the hero has been wrong and the woman who has rejected his way of life has been right. He is thus without any of the larger justifications, and knows himself a ruined man. There can be no question of his "redeeming" himself in any socially constructive way. He is too much the victim of his own reputation to turn marshal as one of his old friends has done, and he is not offered the sentimental solution of a chance to give up his life for some good end; the whole point is that he exists outside the field of social value. Indeed, if we were once allowed to see him in the days of his "success," he might become a figure like the gangster, for his career has been aggressively "anti-social" and the practical problem he faces is the gangster's problem: there will always be somebody trying to kill him. Yet it is obviously absurd to speak of him as "anti-social," not only because we do not see him acting as a criminal, but more fundamentally because we do not see his milieu as a society. Of course it has its "social problems" and a kind of static history: civilization is always just at the point of driving out the old freedom; there are women and children to represent the possibility of a settled life; and there is the marshal, a bad man turned good, determined to keep at least his area of jurisdiction at peace. But these elements are not, in fact, a part of the film's "realism," even though they come out of the real history of the West; they belong to the conventions of the form, to that accepted framework which makes the film possible in the first place, and they exist not to provide a standard by which the gunfighter can be judged, but only to set him off. The true "civilization" of the Western movie is always embodied in an individual, good or bad is more a matter of personal bearing than of social consequences, and the conflict of good and bad is a duel between two men. Deeply troubled and obviously doomed, the gunfighter is the Western hero still, perhaps all the more because his value must express itself entirely in his own being—in his presence, the way he holds our eyes—and in contradiction to the facts. No matter what he has done, he *looks* right, and he remains invulnerable because, without acknowledging anyone else's right to judge him, he has judged his own failure and has already assimilated it, understanding—as no one else understands except the marshal and the barroom girl—that he can do nothing but play out the drama of the gunfight again and again until the time comes when it will be he who gets killed. What "redeems" him is that he no longer believes in this drama and nevertheless will continue to play his role perfectly: the pattern is all.

The proper function of realism in the Western movie can only be to deepen the lines of that pattern. It is an art form for connoisseurs, where the spectator derives his pleasure from the appreciation of minor variations within the working out of a pre-established order. One does not want too much novelty: it comes as a shock, for instance, when the hero is made to operate without a gun, as has been done in several pictures (e.g., *Destry Rides Again*), and our uneasiness is allayed only when he is finally compelled to put his "pacifism" aside. If the hero can be shown to be troubled, complex, fallible, even eccentric, or the villain given some psychological taint or, better, some evocative physical mannerism, to shade the colors of his villainy, that is all to the good. Indeed, that kind of variation is absolutely necessary to keep the type from becoming sterile; we do not want to see the same movie over and over again, only the same form. But when the impulse toward realism is extended into a "reinterpretation" of the West as a developed society, drawing our eyes away from the hero if only to the extent of showing him as the one dominant figure in a complex social order, then the pattern is broken and the West itself begins to be uninteresting. If the "social problems" of the frontier are to be the movie's chief concern, there is no longer any point in re-examining these problems twenty times a year; they have been solved, and the people for whom they once were real are dead. Moreover, the hero himself, still the film's central figure, now tends to become its one unassimilable element, since he is the most "unreal."

*The Ox-Bow Incident*, by denying the convention of the lynching, presents us with a modern "social drama" and evokes a corresponding response, but in doing so it almost makes the Western setting irrelevant, a mere backdrop of beautiful scenery. (It is significant that *The Ox-Bow Incident* has no hero; a hero would have to stop the lynching or be killed in trying to stop it, and then the "problem" of lynching would no longer be central.) Even in *The Gunfighter* the women and children are a little too much in evidence, threatening constantly to become a real focus of concern instead of simply part of the given framework; and the young tough who kills the hero has too much the air of juvenile criminality: the hero himself could never have been like that, and the idea of a cycle being repeated therefore loses its sharpness. But the most striking example of the confusion created by a too conscientious "social" realism is in the celebrated *High Noon*.

In *High Noon* we find Gary Cooper still the upholder of order that he was in *The Virginian*, but twenty-four years older, stooped, slower moving, awkward, his face lined, the flesh sagging, a less beautiful and weaker figure, but with the suggestion of greater depth that belongs almost automatically to age. Like the hero of *The Gunfighter*, he no longer has to assert his character and is no longer interested in the drama of combat; it is hard to imagine that he might once have been so youthful as to say. "When you call me that—smile!" In fact, when we come upon him he is hanging up his guns and his marshal's badge in order to begin a new, peaceful life with his bride, who is a Quaker. But then the news comes that a man he had sent to prison has been pardoned and will get to town on the noon train: three friends of this man have come to wait for him at the station, and when the freed convict arrives the four of them will come to kill the marshal. He is thus trapped; the bride will object, the hero himself will waver much more than he would have done twenty-four years ago, but in the end he will play out the drama because it is what he "has to do." All this belongs to the established form (there is even the "fallen woman" who understands the marshal's position as his wife does not). Leaving aside the crudity of building up suspense by means of the clock, the actual Western drama of *High Noon* is well handled and forms a good companion to *The Virginian*, showing in both conception and technique the ways in which the Western movie has naturally developed.

But there is a second drama along with the first. As the marshal sets out to find deputies to help him deal with the four gunmen, we are taken through the various social strata of the town, each group in turn refusing its assistance out of cowardice,. malice, irresponsibility, or venality. With this we are in the field of "social drama"—of a very low order, incidentally, altogether unconvincing and displaying a vulgar anti-populism that has marred some other movies of Stanley Kramer's. But the falsity of the "social drama" is less important than the fact that it does not belong in the movie to begin with. The technical problem was to make it necessary for the marshal to face his enemies alone; to explain *why* the other townspeople are not at his side is to raise a question which does not exist in the proper frame of the Western movie, where the hero is "naturally" alone and it is only necessary to contrive the physical absence of those who might be his allies, if any contrivance is needed at all. In addition, though the hero of *High Noon* proves himself a better man than all around him, the actual effect of this contrast is to lessen his stature: he becomes only a rejected man of virtue. In our final glimpse of him, as he rides away through the town where he has spent most of his life without really imposing himself on it, he is a pathetic rather than a tragic figure. And his departure has another meaning as well; the "social drama" has no place for him.

But there is also a different way of violating the Western form. This is to yield entirely to its static quality as legend and to the "cinematic" temptations of its landscape, the horses, the quiet men. John Ford's famous *Stagecoach* (1938) had much of this unhappy preoccupation with style, and the same director's *My Darling Clementine* (1946), a soft and beautiful movie about Wyatt Earp, goes further along the same path, offering indeed a superficial accuracy of historical reconstruction, but so loving in execution as to destroy the outlines of the Western legend, assimilating it to the more sentimental legend of rural America and making the hero a more dangerous Mr. Deeds. (*Powder River*, a recent "routine" Western shamelessly copied from *My Darling Clementine*, is in most ways a better film; lacking the benefit of a serious director, it is necessarily more concerned with drama than with style.)

The highest expression of this aestheticizing tendency is in George Stevens' *Shane*, where the legend of the West is virtually reduced to its essentials and then fixed in the dreamy clarity of a fairy tale. There never was so broad and bare and lovely a landscape as Stevens puts before us, or so unimaginably comfortless a "town" as the little group of buildings on the prairie to which the settlers must come for their supplies and to buy a drink. The mere physical progress of the film, following the style of *A Place in the Sun*, is so deliberately graceful that everything seems to be happening at the bottom of a clear lake. The hero (Alan Ladd) is hardly a man at all, but something like the Spirit of the West, beautiful in fringed buckskins. He emerges mysteriously from the plains, breathing sweetness and a melancholy which is no longer simply the Westerner's natural response to experience but has taken on spirituality; and when he has accomplished his mission, meeting and destroying in the black figure of Jack Palance a Spirit of Evil just as metaphysical as his own embodiment of virtue, he fades away again into the more distant West, a man whose "day is over," leaving behind the wondering little boy who might have imagined the whole story. The choice of Alan Ladd to play the leading role is alone an indication of this film's tendency. Actors like Gary Cooper or Gregory Peck are in themselves, as material objects, "realistic," seeming to bear in their bodies and their faces mortality, limitation, the knowledge of good and evil. Ladd is a more "aesthetic" object, with some of the "universality" of a piece of sculpture; his special quality is in his physical smoothness and serenity, unworldly and yet not innocent, but suggesting that no experience can really touch him. Stevens has tried to freeze the Western myth once and for all in the immobility of Alan Ladd's countenance. If *Shane* were "right," and fully successful, it might be possible to say there was no point in making any more Western movies; once the hero is apotheosized, variation and development are closed off.

*Shane* is not "right," but it is still true that the possibilities of fruitful variation in the Western movie are limited. The form can keep its freshness through endless repetitions only because of the special character of the film medium, where the physical difference between one object and another—above all, between one actor and another—is of such enormous importance, serving the function that is served by the variety of language in the perpetuation of literary types. In this sense, the "vocabulary" of films is much larger than that of literature and falls more readily into pleasing and significant arrangements. (That may explain why the middle levels of excellence are more easily reached in the movies than in literary forms, and perhaps also why the status of the movies as art is constantly being called into question.) But the advantage of this almost automatic particularity belongs to all films alike. Why does the Western movie especially have such a hold on our imagination?

Chiefly, I think, because it offers a serious orientation to the problem of violence such as can be found almost nowhere else in our culture. One of the well-known peculiarities of modern civilized opinion is its refusal to acknowledge the value of violence. This refusal is a virtue, but like many virtues it involves a certain willful blindness and it encourages hypocrisy. We train ourselves to be shocked or bored by cultural images of violence, and our very concept of heroism tends to be a passive one; we are less drawn to the brave young men who kill large numbers of our enemies than to the heroic prisoners who endure torture without capitulating. In art, though we may still be able to understand and participate in the values of the *Iliad*, a modern writer like Ernest Hemingway we find somewhat embarrassing: there is no doubt that he stirs us, but we cannot help recognizing also that he is a little childish. And in the criticism of popular culture, where the educated observer is usually under the illusion that he has nothing at stake, the presence of images of violence is often assumed to be in itself a sufficient ground for condemnation.

These attitudes, however, have not reduced the element of violence in our culture but, if anything, have helped to free it from moral control by letting it take on the aura of "emancipation." The celebration of acts of violence is left more and more to the irresponsible: on the higher cultural levels to writers like Celine, and lower down to Mickey Spillane or Horace McCoy, or to the comic books, television, and the movies. The gangster movie, with its numerous variations, belongs to this cultural "underground" which sets forth the attractions of violence in the face of all our higher social attitudes. It is a more "modern" genre than the Western, perhaps even more profound, because it confronts industrial society on its own ground—the city—and because, like much of our advanced art, it gains its effects by a gross insistence on its own narrow logic. But it is anti-social, resting on fantasies of irresponsible freedom. If we are brought finally to acquiesce in the denial of these fantasies, it is only because they have been shown to be dangerous, not because they have given way to a better vision of behavior.*

In war movies, to be sure, it is possible to present the uses of violence within a framework of responsibility. But there is the disadvantage that modern war is a co-operative enterprise; its violence is largely impersonal, and heroism belongs to the group more than to the individual. The hero of a war movie is most often simply a leader, and his superiority is likely to be expressed in a denial of the heroic: you are not supposed to be brave, you are supposed to get the job done and stay alive (this too, of course, is a kind of heroic posture, but a new—and "practical"—one). At its best, the war movie may represent a more civilized point of view than the Western, and if it were not continually marred by ideological sentimentality we might hope to find it developing into a higher form of drama. But it cannot supply the values we seek in the Western.

Those values are in the image of a single man who wears a gun on his thigh. The gun tells us that he lives in a world of violence, and even that he "believes in violence." But the drama is one of self-restraint: the moment of violence must come in its own time and according to its special laws, or else it is valueless. There is little cruelty in Western movies, and little sentimentality; our eyes are not focused on the sufferings of the defeated but on the deportment of the hero. Really, it is not violence at all which is the "point" of the Western movie, but a certain image of man, a style, which expresses itself most clearly in violence. Watch a child with his toy guns and you will see: what most interests him is not (as we so much fear) the fantasy of hurting others, but to work out how a man might look when he shoots or is shot. A hero is one who looks like a hero.

---

* I am not concerned here with the actual social consequences of gangster movies, though I suspect they could not have been so pernicious as they were thought to be. Some of the compromises introduced to avoid the supposed bad effects of the old gangster movies may be, if anything, more dangerous, for the sadistic violence that once belonged only to the gangster is now commonly enlisted on the side of the law and thus goes undefeated, allowing us (if we wish) to find in the movies a sort of "confirmation" of our fantasies.

Whatever the limitations of such an idea in experience, it has always been valid in art, and has a special validity in an art where appearances are everything. The Western hero is necessarily an archaic figure; we do not really believe in him and would not have him step out of his rigidly conventionalized background. But his archaicism does not take away from his power; on the contrary, it adds to it by keeping him just a little beyond the reach both of common sense and of absolutized emotion, the two usual impulses of our art. And he has, after all, his own kind of relevance. He is there to remind us of the possibility of style in an age which has put on itself the burden of pretending that style has no meaning, and, in the midst of our anxieties over the problem of violence, to suggest that even in killing or being killed we are not freed from the necessity of establishing satisfactory modes of behavior. Above all, the movies in which the Westerner plays out his role preserve for us the pleasures of a complete and self-contained drama—and one which still effortlessly crosses the boundaries which divide our culture—in a time when other, more consciously serious art forms are increasingly complex, uncertain, and ill-defined.

# 13. ONLY FILMS ARE TRULY DEEP-DOWN GROOVY

## Penelope Gilliatt

*In her film criticism Penelope Gilliatt benefits from first-hand experience in movie making. She has written scripts for several films.*

"I never read fiction," a woman professor told me severely in New York the other day, fixing me with an eye that made me feel like an X-ray plate revealing fictional tendencies that would have to be dealt with. "Except at the hairdresser," she added, as people do. Then she attacked Pasternak, Beckett, and "your English novelists" as if they had done her a grievous ill, and I wondered how many sessions of hairdresser it had taken her to read "Zhivago." And then I asked her if she felt the same about films. "Oh, *no,*" she said. "My students are the film generation." Tolstoy, here's the door. The students don't dig you.

"Painting!" said a usually intelligent man, scampering to keep up with the kids. The harsh discipline of grooviness creates a lot of Philistines. He had cleared the walls of his study, which I knew very well, and thrown out his old-fashioned prints. The walls were now alluvial green, and there was a chair—quite a pretty Danish-modern chair—hanging over the fireplace from a hook. The swinging idiot then lammed into all pre-1968 painting. It took ages. He had a lot of centuries to demolish. He disposed of Giotto ("outworn superstition"), Leonardo ("commissioned hack"), Michelangelo ("obsessed with muscle"), Goya ("faulty perspective"), and Holbein ("monarchist creep"). The Impressionists went down the drain, on the rigorous and peculiar ground that they were romanticists about weather. As he carried on, he looked increasingly revived, and downed a hashish-filled chocolate brownie. The brownie had been made at home by his wife, who was a painter, poor devil.

"You mean you *enjoyed* 'The Cherry Orchard'?" a Pop-music critic of intellectual standing asked me in London last week. "I hate plays. They're like picnics. You have to pretend you're having fun. The theatre's finished. Shakespeare is dialectically chaotic. The stage is as dead as Virginia Woolf."

Of course, literature has been finished for years, apart from autobiographies about homosexuality and accounts of bringing up lions/otters/spaniels. Everyone with it knows that. It has been out of touch

*Source:* "Only Films Are Truly Deep-Down Groovy," Penelope Gilliatt. Reprinted by permission. © 1968 The New Yorker Magazine, Inc.

ever since Joyce. No, ever since James. No, ever since Jane Austen. No; Austen and all that wornout stuff about bourgeois marriage—what has that got to say to students? The last man was Chaucer, and then only maybe. You could hold that Robbe-Grillet was trying to do something in touch, but then his work is really filmic.

*Filmic.* Filmic is O.K. Filmic is always groovy. Even out-of-touch nincompoops can tell that it's groovy, because groovy opinion-makers, who may or may not read the ancient printed word under the bedclothes by flashlight, never stop yakking about movies. I don't mean that they necessarily like them that much, but they do tremendously like talking about them. In thirty years of going to the flicks, starting with a rapturous program of Roscoe Arbuckle that has endeared the fat to me for good, I've never before heard voluble intellectuals carry on so much about the cinema while they enjoy it so little.

One of the most companionable people I ever went with to London press shows is a seventy-year-old ex-barmaid. She has spent most of her life going to the local cinema three times a week. She knows the name of every English-speaking actor in the business. The notion of a director is unknown to her, apart from the name of Hitchcock, and so is the idea of a scriptwriter. She assumes that the actors make up the lines, and very clever, too. When I told her once that I was writing a film script, she looked at me with polite surprise at the redundancy of it, as if I were killing myself scrubbing a rug that had just been sent to the dry cleaner's. At the same time, her judgment is impeccable, even about the totally unfamiliar, maybe because it has nothing to do with guessing what the touted student generation is liable to think. She likes real innovation, and she can smell pretentiousness a mile off. When a film is disappointing, she says only that "something's lacking," which is all I want to say of "Boom!," as it happens. Joseph Losey directed it, and it was adapted from Tennessee Williams' play "The Milk Train Doesn't Stop Here Anymore." Mr. Williams is a stirring and tender playwright, capable of doing some things with prose that are beyond any other writer in English, and there seems no good reason for intruding into the problems of an irreplaceable dramatist who may be in a technically difficult patch.

The O.K. intellectual put-downs of films now don't really mean anything much more than "something's lacking." They just sound more important. "Not of our time," for instance. In the language of grooviness, this is about as insulting an opinion as a film can earn. But you may well ask why. There is also a lot of very severe and rather unknowledgeable talk about camera technique. People of thirteen or fourteen usually get this right, but the adult film buffs' pronouncements are often lofty codswollop. In an English cinema recently, a stranger next to me leaned over in my direction as he rose to his feet and said that there wasn't much point in staying any longer, because there were three regrettable zoom shots coming. It suddenly made me feel immensely fond of Doris Day fan clubs. We talk such comic *rubbish*; I get nightmare imaginings of it:

"Satyajit Ray has fallen off since 'The World of Apu.' "

"Visconti hasn't really made anything since 'La Terra Trema.' "

" 'La Dolce Vita' was parochial. Fellini simply didn't know Rome."

"Well, I *suppose* Kurosawa is interesting. For the camerawork."

"Truffaut was always a commercial director. I'm ashamed to say I was fooled by 'Jules et Jim.' "

"Movies are the *only* medium to speak to the student generation."

"Frank Tashlin is the *only* director worth talking about."

"I always think Alain Resnais is essentially an editor. Not a filmmaker. All his great work was done in the cutting room."

" '2001' was structurally a disaster."

"Movies are the only *thing*. 'Planet of the Apes' when you're turned on—oh, boy!"

"I liked the first five minutes of 'Belle de Jour.' "

"The last two reels of 'Persona' were visually rather interesting, but the thought was ruinously muddled."

"Have you looked carefully at Eisenstein lately? He was very over-rated."

"Something's happened to Tati's sense of humor. Maybe he never *had* a sense of humor."

"I haven't really laughed at a movie since the antique camerawork in 'The Cranes Are Flying.' The Russians are technically still in the ark."

"The Poles haven't done a thing lately. It's all the Czechs now. The Poles haven't honestly much to say to Columbia University any longer."

"Why does anyone carry on about showing Ozu here? We've *seen* it. What's so new about never moving the camera off the floor?"

"I'd rather have Kluge's 'Yesterday Girl.' That had something to do with our time."

" 'Yesterday Girl' was totally derivative of Godard."

"Not derivative. Eclectic."

"Anyway, I walked out after the first two reels."

Does anyone else have fatal visions of carefully educated people getting more and more groovy and less and less intelligent? Can it possibly be true that the growing mob of with-it chasers in the West are turning into a kind of intellectual who hates art?

## 14. KUBRICK'S BRILLIANT VISION

### from <u>Newsweek</u>

*The other major weekly news magazine,* Newsweek, *employs most of the group journalism techniques of its major competitor,* Time. Newsweek *is a part of* The Washington Post Company.

From the beginning, he has struggled to control both his work and his world, as if the uncertainties of the human condition would rip him to pieces if he relinquished his hold for even so much as a second. But it is precisely this inexhaustible drive to orchestrate even the smallest details of his life and his art that has made Stanley Kubrick the most provocative and brilliant of today's American directors.

At 43, the creator of "Paths of Glory," "Lolita," "Dr. Strangelove" and the visionary "2001: A Space Odyssey" has earned his place beside Bergmann, Bunuel, Truffaut, Fellini and a handful of others. Now Kubrick has a new movie, released last week, called "A Clockwork Orange," taken from the brilliant and shocking novel by British writer Anthony Burgess. The film is not without its small failings, for a man who makes as many daring artistic leaps as Kubrick is bound to slip from time to time, just as he is insured against ever boring us. "A Clockwork Orange" is also a characteristically frosty piece of film-making, shorn completely of sentiment, working through brilliant ironies and dazzling dramatic ideas that please us, provoke our laughter, galvanize our intellects, win our admiration—but never touch our hearts.

But then, no director has it all—tenderness and crystal detachment, a sure feel for sentiment and Olympian brilliance. It is enough that "A Clockwork Orange" works on its own terms, as the kind of tour de force of the intellect and imagination that marks Kubrick as a true genius of the cinema.

The film moves on many levels at once—social, psychological, moral and mythical. It is set in a London of the near future in which roving gangs of Teddy boys rule the night, venting the frustrations and boredom of their lives in acts of rape, robbery and wanton beatings. Alex, the hero, is a prince of this adolescent underworld, leading his three "droogs," as pals are called in the special slang the teen-agers talk, in endless acts of mayhem—mugging drunks for sport, grabbing girls for what Alex (who narrates the film) calls "the quick in-out, in-out," breaking into houses on "surprise visits" to rape, maim, kill and steal.

Like Shakespeare's Richard III, Alex is despicable in what he does, but

*Source:* "Kubrick's Brilliant Vision," *Newsweek.* Copyright Newsweek, Inc., January 3, 1972.

graced with a wit, energy and demonic imagination that make him superior to any other figure in his world and make him a perversely winning character. Kubrick is careful to protect our reluctant allegiance to Alex—by stylizing the acts of brutality he commits, by making his victims unpleasant, by distancing the audience from what would otherwise be an intolerable level of violence through an inventive use of music.

Kubrick turns a savage, hard-crunching battle between Alex's droogs and a repulsive rival gang into a ballet by Jerome Robbins gone mad. In another episode, Alex breaks into the house of a writer and brutally rapes his wife—all the time singing and soft-shoeing an insouciant version of "Singin' in the Rain." On another suprise visit, which leads to Alex's capture by the police, there is a battle of the sexes in which he clubs a tough health-club lady to death with her own outsized phallic sculpture—all choreographed to the antic strains of Rossini's "Thieving Magpie" overture. Kubrick scores a super-speeded-up orgy between Alex and two nymphets with the feverish strains of the "William Tell" Overture, turning an already clever characterization of casual teen-age sex into a brilliant comic ballet. His use of the satanic second movement of Beethoven's Ninth Symphony captures in its angry humor, its demonic energy, its bitter but affirmative spirit, the essence of Alex's character.

As a hero, Alex has a great deal more than music going for him in gaining the loyalties of an audience. As Kubrick points out, "the most interesting and often engaging characters in any film are the villains." More important, Malcolm McDowell imbues Alex with his own winning arrogance and charm in a performance of extraordinary vitality and intelligence. And as a fantasy figure Alex appeals to something dark and primal in all of us. He acts out our desire for instant sexual gratification, for the release of our angers and repressed instincts for revenge, our need for adventure and excitement.

The elegance that accompanies Alex's penchant for what he dubs "ultra-violence" is the pivotal paradox of the film. Its shocking content has earned it an X rating, but Dr. Aaron Stern, the film industry's code administrator, believes there should be special ratings for X films of such exceptional quality. "Violence itself isn't necessarily abhorrent," says Kubrick. "From his own point of view Alex is having a wonderful time, and I wanted his life to appear to us at it did to him, not restricted by the conventional pieties. You can't compare what Alex is doing to any kind of day-to-day reality. Watching a movie is like having a daydream. You can safely explore areas that are closed off to you in your daily life. There are dreams in which you do all the terrible things your conscious mind prevents you from doing."

## THE REMORSELESS KILLER

Violence is a common denominator in all Kubrick's films. In every one of his movies, someone is murdered. "Although a certain amount of hypocrisy exists about it," he says, "everyone is fascinated by violence. After all, man is the most remorseless killer who ever stalked the earth. Our interest in violence in part reflects the fact that on the subconscious level we are very little different from our primitive ancestors."

Alex is finally caught, ironically done in by his one bit of humanity, a love for Beethoven that sets his gang against him. In a scene characteristic of the film's clarity and economy, we watch Alex as he enters the penitentiary systematically stripped of his clothes, his effects, his name, his swagger—his self. All that remains of his freedom is his fantasy life, which he puts to good use. He studies the Bible to score points with the prison chaplain—all the while imagining he is whipping Christ on the way to Calvary, killing Romans, basking in a bevy of naked handmaidens.

But soon even his fantasy life is confiscated. He is transferred to a reconditioning center where he is injected with a nausea-inducing drug and forced, with his eyelids clamped open, to watch films of violence and sex until the very thought of his old diversions makes him gag and retch. The government, proud of this new solution to crime in the streets, makes a display of Alex as the star guinea pig of this new therapeutic behaviorism. In a "scientific" demonstration Alex is pushed around by an actor and teased by a nude girl—and his only reaction is to lick the actor's shoe and grovel retchingly at the girl's feet. The close-up of tongue on leather, like the frames of Slim Pickens riding the suicidal H-bomb in "Dr. Strangelove," shows Kubrick's genius for fixing an aspect of the human condition in a single image, here Subjugation itself.

Alex is returned to the world, where he meets all those whom he has abused and is mercilessly beaten for his transgressions. We accept these coincidences, for Kubrick's stylization of the story has clearly cast it in mythical terms. "Telling a story 'realistically' is such a slowpoke and ponderous way to proceed," says Kubrick, "and it doesn't fulfill the psychic needs that people have. We sense that there's more to life and to the universe than realism can possibly deal with."

In "A Clockwork Orange" this mystic realism has produced an icily brilliant vision of an imminent future in which Western society has become a mod slum, super-technologized and squalid at the same time. Culture has collapsed into a pervasive pop-art bad taste: Alex's prole parents are caricatures, dad with his big lapels, mum with her violet hair and micro-skirts. Politics too has been reduced to caricature—there is no middle ground, only warfare between advocates of anarchy and of total control. Alex and his droogs hang out at the "milk-plus" bar, swigging doped milk at tables formed of erotic sculpture. They speak a lingo that reflects a vicious decay of feeling: ubiquitous television has turned "see" into "viddy"; the adjective of approval is "horrorshow"; money is "deng," with its excremental connotations.

But at its most profound level, "A Clockwork Orange" is an odyssey of the human personality, a statement on what it is to be fully human. Alex's adventures are, in one sense, the adventures of the id itself. Alex embodies all of man's anarchic impulses. Shorn of his individuality in the penitentiary and of his fantasy life in the conditioning program, he ceases to be a human being in any real sense. His resurrection at the end, as he regains his ability to act out his lusts and aggressions, represents an ironic triumph of the human psyche over the forces that seek to control or diminish it.

Control has been a continuing theme in Kubrick's movies: control of time and the environment by the gangsters who must rob a racetrack within the limits of a single race in "The Killing"; control of the men in the trenches by the officers in the chateau in "Paths of Glory"; Lolita's control of Humbert, Humbert's battle to control his passions and Quilty's playful manipulation of Humbert in "Lolita"; control of nuclear weaponry in "Dr. Strangelove"; the battle for control of the spaceship in "2001"; and, in "A Clockwork Orange," control of the human personality itself.

Each film for Kubrick is also a battle to control the chaos that hovers at the edges of the set. "In the physical process of making a film," says Kubrick, "the tendency is always toward entropy, things flying apart. It's not good enough to have good dramatic ideas in a film if the practical things you need in shooting these ideas are always going wrong." To protect against this, Kubrick has devised an elaborate system of memos and follow-up memos, references and cross-references. "When I visited Stanley's house," recalls Malcolm McDowell, "I noticed lots of Turkish towels covering one wall. It turned out that they concealed his cross-reference system. He likes secrecy."

Kubrick insists on supervising every aspect of his films, from casting to shooting to editing. If at all possible, he operates the camera himself. And when "2001: A Space Odyssey" was first screened for the New York critics, Stanley Kubrick was in the projection booth. No detail is negligible in his eyes. In the days before "A Clockwork Orange" was released, Kubrick changed the depth of the shadows around the opening titles and selected the gradation of orange against which those titles would stand. After a nightmarish day and a sleepless night caused by severe scratches to his negative in the laboratory, Kubrick decided to switch labs. With himself at the wheel, he transported the sixteen reels of cut negative in an indestructible Land Rover, his film editor's car a short distance ahead to absorb the impact of any possible crash.

But no man, not even one with Kubrick's inexhaustible energy, can do everything himself. Even he must delegate some authority. "I'm distrustful in delegating authority and my distrust is usually well-founded," he says. "I especially don't trust people who don't write things down. With those who do write things down, I'm very interested in what they write things in. If it's one of those chic little Fifth Avenue notebooks with those expensive gold pencils I'm more suspicious than ever. Many people feel it's beneath their dignity to take notes and try instead to trust their memories. I don't work with them."

The other side of Kubrick's concern for control is a fear of disorder and chaos, of a computer gone mad in "2001," of nuclear bombs bursting in air in "Dr. Strangelove," of scientists tinkering with the human personality in "A Clockwork Orange"—of Stanley Kubrick getting hit by a car when he drives into London. As to the last of these concerns, Kubrick's drivers are forbidden to travel at more than 30 miles an hour. Kubrick himself will not cross the ocean by plane, even though he is an experienced amateur pilot. "Knowing how the big planes work made me lose confidence. Light planes don't bother me at all," he says, advancing an argument that seems logical until one checks the air casualty figures. "During the shooting of '2001'," recalls actor Keir Dullea, "Stanley was the only one on the set to wear his safety helmet at all times."

Kubrick is one of the few men to have conquered his own environment. He lives in Borehamwood, a half hour out of London, a few minutes from the EMI studio with its dubbing theaters and sound stages, a few minutes from his executive offices. His home, which he shares with his wife, Christiane (who played the German girl who sings to the soldiers in the final scene of "Paths of Glory"), their three daughters, Katherine, Anya and Vivienne, their three golden retrievers and seven cats, also houses his editing facilities and 35-mm. film projector. Aside from location shooting, Kubrick can make a film without leaving his neighborhood, which suits him fine because, as he sees it, "travel is boring." Once a friend urged him to visit Rome. "I don't have to go," Kubrick replied. "I just saw a great documentary on it."

## A NEW PAIR OF SHOES

Like most geniuses, Kubrick is obsessed by his work, to the neglect of a balanced diet or an adequate wardrobe. His wife describes him best when she says: "Stanley dresses like a balloon peddler." Indeed, his plain black jackets, loosely fitting white shirts and baggy pants are the outfit of a man who is consumed with what he is doing. He used to own only three suits, now he owns none. "I haven't had the time to buy myself a pair of new shoes in the past year," he says. And he hasn't taken a vacation since 1961, when he finished "Lolita" and took his wife on a five-day trip to visit the D-Day bunkers in Normandy. "Telling me to take a vacation from filmmaking is like telling a child to take a vacation from playing," he says.

It does little good to control your films and your world if you can't control yourself. Even here. Kubrick has mastered the problem. "We've been working with him for ten weeks," Ed Haben, a dubbing engineer, explained recently, "and he's had any number of good reasons to blow up at everyone. But he has never raised his voice, not once." Indeed, Kubrick even spoke with total composure to the head of the laboratory that had almost destroyed two years of his life. This is the paradox of Kubrick—despite his obsessions and drives, he remains a softspoken, gentle man of great charm, well-liked by the people who work for him even when his dedication to detail drives them half mad.

## 15. THE FUTURE IS NOT WHAT IT USED TO BE

### Gary Goshgarian and Charles O'Neill

*Gary Goshgarian teaches science fiction at Northeastern University
and Charles O'Neill studies it at the same place.*

When Georges Melies chose "A Trip to the Moon" for the subject of
his film interpretation of H. G. Wells' *First Men on the Moon* and Jules
Verne's *From Earth to the Moon*, he opened a significant area in the
history of film—he created the cinema of science fiction. His work of
speculative fantasy in 1902 set the elements of the new genré and for
the first several decades his model was left practically untouched.

It was not until 1968, with the release of Stanley Kubrick's *2001, A
Space Odyssey,* that the normal limits of the science fiction film were
broken. Where Méliès' work and the films that followed in his tradition
were extrapolations into the future, speculations into man's direction,
Kubrick's first speculated on a truly grand scale. The question was no
longer: Where is man *going*? It had become: Where is man *evolving*?

Where the earlier films dealt with future-speculation within a set of
given circumstances, such as a Martian invasion or the ravages of pre-
historic lizards awakened by nuclear testing, *2001* speculates from the
"dawn of man" to the year of the title, and beyond—a span of four
million years. Its speculation does not choose to focus on a single
cataclysmic event; it chooses, rather, to deal with an entire continuous
process of mystical evolution under alien control.

Where the early films are dominated by few "inevitabilities," *2001*
assumes a divine inevitability. Its aliens cannot be evaluated on good-
evil terms, in the same way that we cannot say whether the existence
of the human race itself is "good" or "bad." We can only say that it
just is, and we make of that fact whatever we can.

This very broad difference, and the fact that this view of evolution is
unique to science fiction films, can best be seen by an examination of
the major themes of the genré. They all owe their basic origins to
Méliès, and there are four:

1. *Alien Invaders.* Man launches seemingly hopeless defense against
creatures from outside of his world. The invaders range from Martians

*Source:* "The Future Is Not What It Used To Be," Gary Goshgarian and Charles
O'Neill. Reprinted by permission of the authors.

in "War of the Worlds," to unseen subversives in the "Invasion of the Body Snatchers."

2. *Bastard Offspring of the Nuclear Age.* Man's architecture is set crumbling, his perfect neon-lit glass-and-steel cities destroyed by overgrown natural creatures. Films of this motif invite us to consider in a different way the ant and his terrifying cousins—grasshoppers, worms, and birds—whose growth or emergence was made possible by nuclear technology. Here, creatures of destruction ascend the genetic hierarchy to the crowning emblem of hyperthyroid monstrosity, King Kong himself, the forerunner of gigantism.

3. *Man's Creations.* Mankind's destruction takes place at the hands— as well as claws, fangs, and wings—of creatures produced by his own technology. Jekyll and Hyde, Wolfman, Dracula, The Fly, and, of course, the Frankenstein monster, loom terrifyingly on this horizon.

4. *Man Leaves His Own World To Face the Unknown.* In so doing, he learns that he is not alone, and that he is not the darling of the universe.

Kubrick's film, based on the short story by Arthur C. Clarke, "The Sentinel," paradoxically combines the basic features of each of these themes. The extraterrestrials of *2001* do not fit the usual sinister type, and we do not see them; but there are alien invaders in *2001*, and they leave a monolith as an emblem of their visitations. But, the bastard offspring of the nuclear age fuse with the man-made creations, and appear as Hal 9000, the finest, most autonomous computer of the day. In *2001*, Hal is the human creation, just as Dr. Frankenstein's monster was a human creation. And like Frankenstein's creation, Hal tries to master his maker; he is an image of man's extreme dependence on the machine in the computer age, a dependence that becomes a deadly threat to the human race. *2001*'s criticism does not stop there. In building a machine with an ego, man stupidly puts himself at a disadvantage and, therefore, threatens his own place in the species-war between man and machine. Hal, of course, tries to capitalize on that advantage, as we shall discuss later.

There is another function of Hal's being—he represents man's great technological perfection, and that perfection is humbled by the awesome magnitude of the unseen cosmic force. In other words, Hal's control over the spaceship is made nearly insignificant when held against the extraterrestrial's control over man's evolution. Paradoxically, *2001* minimizes the importance of technology, on the one hand, while, on the other, it garnishes the screen with the technical marvels of the 21st century (especially the marvelous space vehicles that carry man to

Jupiter). Unlike the clear-cut situations of the earlier science fiction films, it is not through his own efforts that man comes into contact with extraterrestrial life in *2001*; it is through the efforts of that extraterrestrial life toward mankind. In this film the stars have come to man to lure him to greater reaches of the universe.

The entire central concept of *2001* is thus immediately broader than the concept of the earlier science fiction film in many ways. In its scheme of things, there is no need whatsoever to look for the simple clash of dynamic forces: the battle of species. There is, instead, a concept which virtually abandons that sort of fragmented study and suggests a new cosmology. Man abandons the struggle for survival and evolves toward an all-mind state under the aegis and precise control of extraterrestrial intelligence. "Where is man evolving?" This question becomes increasingly important as the film progresses. *2001* says that man's evolution takes place at the bidding of an outside force.

*2001*'s evolutionary cosmology borders on a theological vision. A theology is implied, since this outside force is God-like. The evidence in *2001* suggests that (1) the force is noncorporeal; (2) it has existed for at least four million years (since it deposited its monolith); (3) like God, the outside force has paced mankind's progress since the dawn of the race, influencing the direction and velocity of its growth. Finally, *2001* suggests that mankind will return to a state of unity with this force in the end. The only departure *2001* makes from the concept of a traditional God is that mankind cannot be sure whether or not the outside force was responsible for his creation. But this is a crucial and purposeful distinction, since it says that, given the right amount of time, all intelligent life will one day evolve into a deity. But, that is, after all, what mankind is promised in his Torah, his Bible, and his Koran. In the final analysis, *2001* may be the most "religious" treatment of man's progress ever made in film, science fiction or otherwise.

Substance for this feeling of positive evolution is to be found in the very structure of the film itself. The opening three notes of the soundtrack (C-G-C) directly correspond with the three parts of the film—"The Dawn of Man," "2001," and "Beyond the Infinite." The music is appropriately selected from Strauss' *Thus Spake Zarathustra*, a musical interpretation of Nietzsche's classic about the birth of a superman; that is what the three notes suggest: the cyclical nature, the progression of ape to man to superman/starchild. Thus the music itself brings the theme of evolution immediately into play in *2001*.

Then there is support in the simple matter of plot. An examination of these sections will help to further define *2001*'s unique contribution, its particular questioning of man's evolution.

Kubrick begins the evolutionary theme with Australopithicine man ("ape-man"), who has not yet discovered the tool. Through extraterrestrial intervention, he wakes up one morning to discover a black monolith outside his cave. A dramatic alignment of sun, moon, and monolith takes place on the screen; and musical crescendo affirms the feeling that the coming of the monolith is a mystical event in man's maturation. Kubrick lets us know that the monolith's effect on the apes is immediate and permanent. The ape becomes more man and less ape as he discovers the tool. In the evolutionary process, he uses the leg bone from a dead animal, first to smash a skull on the ground, then to kill a live animal and, finally, to kill another ape. This third event signals the start of the second major section of the film. The transition is dramatic: the ape throws the bone into the air, Kubrick makes a quick cut, and instead of this most primitive tool in the sky, we suddenly see in its place the most sophisticated emblem of man's technology, a spacecraft against the dark of space.

This second section of the film shows man's technology as a test period before his ascent to an all-mind state. In other words, he has to be intelligent enough to reach the moon to exhume the monolith, which will then send word to Jupiter that the time has come for man's Big Leap. In the time before this transitional event, *2001* shows us a world in which man is comfortable, even listless, with his technology. Space shuttles are comfortable, common, and safe, and Dr. Floyd, a chief scientist on his way to investigate the strange monolith at the lunar base, literally sleeps from the earth to the moon. Computers in Hal's family are, we can assume, busily and contentedly clicking away, sending bills out to homes in Hoboken, perhaps even carrying on conversations with kids beneath the Christmas tree. All is quiet, but man has been dehumanized by his technology, just as in the first section of the film, when the animal's leg bone becomes man's first destructive tool, announcing the birth of the ultimate dehumanization process, war.

Also intentional is the emotional detachment of the two astronauts, Poole and Bowman, whose voices have little more inflection than Hal's own soothing monotone, firmly announced through the halls of the spaceship *Pioneer*. We wait patiently, expecting little more than some—any—mark of human emotion. We wait even for something small, something like, "This orange juice sure is good," but the moment never comes. Hal then proceeds to beat Bowman in a game of chess, and announces the serious defeat with, "I'm sorry, Dave." And as if such social offenses were not enough, Hal is also the only entity on board the spaceship who has been told the true nature of the mission.

But orange juice and social offenses aside, the contest between man and machine quickly becomes a more sinister game, and Hal—true again to the four basic science fiction film patterns—is the better player. When threatened with disconnection for having failed a spacecraft malfunction test, he proves his domination by ingeniously discovering that those threats are serious. Not only does Hal have eyes on every wall of the ship, but he has learned to use them to read lips as well. He reverses the master-slave relationship and easily and all too casually murders Poole. He murders not through mankind's usual devious means, but through technical devious means. He is not so coarse as to break Poole's neck or crush him in a self-closing portway; he simply sends the astronaut tumbling through limitless space, his oxygen umbilical cord neatly severed. It is also significant that we do not witness the actual cutting of the cord, for Kubrick is making sure that even in death the human identification is not to be offered the audience.

This is surely a new cosmology, in which the hibernating astronauts encapsuled in the ship for later reawakening are also murdered by Hal, their deaths appropriately recorded electronically, by blinking lights, which blaze the three deaths with TERMINATION OF LIFE FUNC-TION. The human race is nearly lost aboard the space vehicle to a psychopathic computer, since all the astronauts, with the exception of Bowman, have been destroyed. We might here expect a soliloquy on loneliness or man's nudity before the infinite, but in spite of the absence of such things, it is here that *Dehumanization becomes Rehumanization.* This progression is a sort of rite of passage, which is at the heart of the evolutionary theme of *2001.*

Drawing on his own resources, Bowman finds his way back into the spacecraft, passing momentarily through the vacuum of space. Once safely pushed through the doors that Hal has locked from him, Bowman becomes a new man. His first act is explicitly one of rehumanization, for he immediately lobotomizes Hal by destroying sections of the computer's memory bank. This is an act of murder, in which man kills the technology that has turned against him, an act which, by the way, fits into the general murder-motif we have witnessed since the killing of the first ape. But this is also a rebirth of a new man, rather than the killing of man with the birth of a new technology. In taking such a step backward as the killing of the computer, Bowman has readied himself for the vast leap into a new state of being. Following the destruction of Hal's higher brain functions, Bowman begins the last phase of his other-controlled evolution. He has earned the right to follow the monolith through space, and it lures him beyond Jupiter, like bait to his wonder.

Bowman's action signals the beginning of the third and final phase of the film and the last phase of man's apotheosis. All along, the visual contrasts—for example, dwarf ships against the slow curvature of the huge planets—have emphasized man's basic insignificance. The images of the film, however, are gradually building toward a higher point. After the transitional event takes place, in *2001*, man becomes part of the cosmic design, rather than an object to be posed against it as he was in earlier science fiction films. Kubrick uses the device of a carefully controlled but rapidly accelerating light-show to illustrate the transcendent nature of the phenomena of evolution, which Bowman experiences. When the light-show experience has ended, our solitary human representative finds himself in a room with luminescent walls and ceilings. We are led to conclude that extraterrestrial powers have done their best to construct a scene from earth life, a reassurance to prepare Bowman for his ultimate transformation.

In the room we witness another three-part cycle from middle age to old age to rebirth. It is characteristic elsewhere in the film for Kubrick to use a transitional device. Here, a glass falls to the floor from Bowman's "last supper" table to signify the end of an era; and in a more literal scene, the now-old astronaut points to an embryo that hovers above his bed against the large blank monolith. This is the birth of the wholly-other man, the starchild.

This birth completes the evolutionary cycle of *2001*. The film has moved man through a whole new order of creation, of which few men have seriously dreamed except in religious contemplation; and most definitely not within the fragmented, narrower context of the early science fiction film.

The end is an optimistic one, because the evolutionary process here was meant to be both positive and beyond man's control. Through Bowman, man has symbolically evolved into a cosmic consciousness represented by "starchild." We are led to believe that the final stage of man's evolution is noncorporeal because the whole of the film, and the last section particularly, is treated in such abstract terms that such a simple physical evolution would be too trite. More important, the whole film to this point has dealt with the limitations imposed on man by the fact of his physical existence. If Bowman simply underwent a physical transformation, the resulting starchild would be something less than a lively alternative to man and his civilization.

If more evidence is needed, we can find it in Clark's other writings. Particular evidence can be found in *Childhood's End*, in which the human race is conducted through a similar evolution. There also, man is freed from the tyranny of matter, and absorbed into the "Overmind."

*2001*'s concern with "evolution" as opposed to "direction" is based on a logical extension of Darwin's theory. The Darwinian theory of evolution tells us that species are improved by slow physical changes which adjust them to their environments. At the heart of the process is the simple truth that useless organs will be lost. Five hundred years from now, for example, man may no longer have any trace of his useless appendix.

The natural logic—over which man has no control—is simply that organs with no function are not simply neutral; they are incumbrances. Darwin provides this physical ground for evolution; Clark and Kubrick build on the foundation, but the house they nurture has been designed by outside force, not by some inherent survival need or innate cellular intelligence, but by an outside higher life-form. It is for this reason that Clark does not leave well enough alone. Furthermore, he takes mankind and the evolutionary process by the hand, leading both from the physical realm into the realm of the mind. The starchild is the cinema metaphor for this leap. Bowman's body, his mind, and the rest of his delicate—useless—physical mechanisms have been completely abandoned. His consciousness now rests in a completely nonphysical being: the starchild.

Just as the three notes of the soundtrack announced the theme at the beginning of the film, they announce it at the end. As we watch the embryo move through space, the soundtrack makes the progression again. The notes C-G-C tell us that man is at the intermediate stage, he is half an octave higher than ape, half an octave lower than God.

Earlier science fiction films worked on a much less complicated mechanism. As in that theory of creation which maintains that God set the universe in motion like a gigantic top, then left it completely to run its own course, the four primary theories suggested here earlier set the matrix for the early films. Man is on top in these films, though his cities are often destroyed and his race often comes close to obliteration. His moral superiority over ravaging aliens gives him the grace to survive until he can find the fatal weakness of his enemy. Although there is the fear of struggles yet to come, the last scenes of these films invariably show the scientist hero and his girl friend sitting beneath the open sky at night, with the far-off stars twinkling, and the twinkling, like bells, ringing: Well done, well done.

*2001* suggests that such twinkling conclusions of the early science fiction films are trite indeed. Strange signs from the universe do not signal struggles, they signal rather an era in which man is at peace with his cosmos.

Not enough time has passed since 1968 to decide if the new values and new evolutionary scheme of *2001* will remain the major event in the the science fiction film genré since Méliès first realized its potential to speculate, to excite, and to please. Even if, when matched against the science fiction films that will follow it, *2001: A Space Odyssey* loses all else, it can still be said the film was the first that did not deal with the struggle of "good" against the forces of "evil." It has left that whole hoary tale behind, and whatever overall failures a greater distance will reveal it to have, it will remain a film which shows us that the future is not what it used to be.

## 16. [REVIEW OF] A CLOCKWORK ORANGE
### Stanley Kauffman

*Stanley Kauffman is film critic for* The New Republic.

In one way Stanley Kubrick's new film is cheering. This time, as in all his work before *2001*, he sticks to a narrative, depicts character, opts for "literary humanism"—does all the things that some critics claimed he had deliberately abandoned, in the space picture, for a new esthetics. Perhaps the new esthetics *was* only a wobble? Revised editions of various pronunciamentos may now be in order.

But there isn't a great deal more to celebrate in *A Clockwork Orange*. Certainly there are some striking images; certainly there is some impudent wit, some adroitness. But the worst flaw in the film is its air of cool intelligence and ruthless moral inquiry because those elements are least fulfilled. Very early there are hints of triteness and insecurity, and before the picture is a half-hour old, it begins to slip into tedium. Sharp and glittery though it continues to be, it never quite shakes that tedium.

The screenplay, by Kubrick, follows Anthony Burgess' novel fairly closely in story, but that's not much of an advantage. This novel of the near future hasn't got much of a story, as such; Burgess relies principally on an odd language he has devised—a mixture of current English, archaic English, and anglicized Russian (today, yesterday, and the future). This language, more than any other element, is asked to hold the reader, indicate social change, and suggest moral quandaries. The effects are limited; it's not my favorite Burgess by any means.

Kubrick's first mistake may have been to select a book whose very being is in its words. The film is inevitably much weaker. Kubrick uses the verbal texture as far as possible, which cannot be far. The language cannot create a world for him as it does for Burgess. The modest moral resonance of the book is reduced: partly because of certain small changes, like converting a murder victim from an old woman to a sexy broad and killing her with a giant ceramic phallus (thus changing sheer heartlessness into sex sensation); mostly because Kubrick has to replace Burgess' linguistic ingenuity with cinematic ingenuity, and he doesn't. The story as such is thin, so the picture thins. In *2001*, the *longueurs* came from Kubrick's neglect of narrative to revel in gadgetry, but at least some of the gadgets and images were extraordinary. Here he doesn't neglect

*Source:* "Review of *A Clockwork Orange*," Stanley Kauffman. Reprinted by permission of *The New Republic*, © 1972, Harrison-Blaine of New Jersey, Inc.

story for display, he depends on display to *make* his story, but his invention this time is weak.

The scene is England. Alex, a young ruffian, leads a quartet of young ruffians whose hobby is "ultra violence"—binges of rape and assault. Alex's one paradoxical quality is his love of classical music, particularly Beethoven, particularly the Ninth. One night Alex goes too far, accidentally kills a woman, is caught, and is sentenced to 10 years. A new psychological process for rehabilitating criminals has been devised and, by agreeing to be a guinea pig, Alex has his sentence commuted.

The process is plain Pavlovism: he is strapped in a chair with eyelids clamped open and electrodes on his head, is shown films of violence and sex along with a Beethoven sound-track, and has shocks administered to sicken him as he watches. Later, when he attempts violence—or hears Beethoven—he feels violently ill and must stop.

His case has been kicked around the press as a political football. The Opposition party roars that a human being has been dehumanized, etc. Some Opposition people abduct him after his release, closet him with an endless recording of the Ninth to make him sick and raving, to drive him to suicide—for their advantage. But he is salvaged by the Government. At the end the Pavlovian cure is reversed: Beethoven once again brings on fantasies of sex and violence and Alex is once again ready to ravage.

Much of the dialogue, and all of Alex's narration, is in Burgess' newspeak. Kubrick, like Burgess, relies on context to make unknown words clear. This is more difficult for the ear than for the eye, but, in the main it happens, though slowly.

Inexplicably the script leaves out Burgess' reference to the title; it's the title of a book being written by a character in the novel, with an excerpt provided to clarify. That author's book-inside-the-book is a protest against "the attempt to impose upon man, a creature of growth and capable of sweetness . . . laws and conditions appropriate to a mechanical creation . . .", the attempt to make a growing thing into a mechanism, even—as Stanley Edgar Hyman said—to eliminate his freedom to sin.

Now this is hardly a staggeringly new concept or protest, but Burgess makes it mildly interesting because of the linguistic acrobatics he can perform while expounding it. Kubrick is stuck with the message and, for this work, the wrong medium. We simply see the working-out of the design, the spelling of the lesson, with very little esthetic increment along the 137-minute way.

A few sequences are striking, such as the opening in a milk-bar with plaster nudes at tables. There's a good gang rumble in a gutted theater, the hollowed-out place reflecting the combatants' spirits. But a great deal of the film is banal or reminiscent. The four ruffians stand before a street-lamp when they batter a tramp, so that the light streams out around them—one of the hoariest of arty poses. A speeded-up porno sequence is like the one in *Greetings*, a slow-motion fight is like several in *The Wild Bunch*.

The camera use is stale: the hand-held camera in the murder scene, the distorting lens on the author (Patrick Magee) when he realizes that Alex is his wife's murderer. Supposed frankness is flat or strained: Alex peeing, the prison guard examining his anus, two girls sucking penile ice-cream sticks. Kubrick echoes his own past musical tricks: Rossini as humorously inappropriate comment, instead of the Johann Strauss in *2001*; Gene Kelly and "Singin' in the Rain" at the end, instead of the Vera Lynn and "We'll Meet Again" of *Dr. Strangelove*. A few of Alex's fantasies are witty, like the sex fantasy he gets from the *Bible* while in jail, but mostly they are hand-me-down silent-film dreams with fewer clothes and more violence.

Malcolm McDowell is Alex. This is the third time I've seen him, and although he hasn't yet shown great range, he does have energy and threat. Among the rest only Michael Bates, the guard, is outstanding. I've seen Bates do his shiny-cheeked popinjay twice before—comically—on the London stage. Here he does it less comically but efficiently.

Something has gone seriously wrong with the talented Kubrick. I won't hazard guesses as to what it is. But the one thing that, two films ago, I'd never have thought possible to say about a Kubrick film is true of *A Clockwork Orange:* it's boring.

### Richard Schickel

*Richard Schickel has been, until its recent demise, film critic for* Life.

For a director like Stanley Kubrick, a novel like Anthony Burgess's *A Clockwork Orange* must have seemed an irresistible challenge. Kubrick is essentially a daring imagist, yet he has twice before been tempted by projects that pose powerful problems of language for the film maker. One was an attempt, largely unsuccessful, to translate the dazzling and delicate literacy of Vladimir Nabokov's *Lolita* into a screenplay. The other was a largely successful attempt, in *2001*, to make a quite complex metaphysical argument without resort to any but the most banal vocabulary.

In the Burgess novel, Kubrick confronts a work that depends very little on plot or characters to sustain our interest, and a great deal on a unique verbal conceit—an imagined teen-age slang ("Nadsat") of the near future in which Alex, the protagonist, narrates the key fragment of his autobiography. Composed mostly of transliterated Russian words that we are asked to believe have unconsciously penetrated English, this language is easy enough to understand on the printed page. It would probably have been incomprehensible as spoken dialogue, however, and so Kubrick used only a few pinches of it. His problem, therefore, is to make up for its absence by finding some visual equivalent.

This he entirely fails to do, and the loss is profound. In Burgess's 1962 novel, the richness and wit of the invented language provide an ironic counterpoint to the impoverished imaginative life of the mildly socialist and totalitarian society where the story takes place. They also serve to distance us from the violence that is the only activity in which Alex and his "droogs" find real (*i.e.*, sexual) pleasure, and to prevent us from sharing pornographically in that pleasure. Most important, it is the very existence of this language that allows Burgess to demonstrate implicitly, without resort to special pleas, Alex's virtue as a human being. It, along with his odd passion for Bach and Beethoven, suggests an aesthetic awareness and a creative potential for which the materialistic state can offer no outlet. Thus, when the state undertakes his forcible reeducation through a combination of drug therapy and behaviorist reconditioning, we understand that his loss of the capacity to do evil is a minor tragedy, for it implies a loss also of the creative capacity which the artist closely equates with the ability to do good. Cut men off from the extremes of the behavioral scale and you doom them to the grayness of alienation and anomie.

Kubrick works hard, not to say desperately, to compensate for the absence of Burgess's language, but it doesn't work. Deprived of their gift of tongues, his adolescents become just another gang of toughs—the Amboy Dukes in future schlock. The rapes, beatings and murders they commit are still perhaps "horrorshow" ("good" or "fun" in Nadsat), but are comprehensible to us only in the traditional meaning of the term. Indeed, these activities, handled briefly by Burgess, are lingered over by Kubrick, partly out of necessity (there aren't that many truly cinematic sequences in the novel) and partly out of commercial cynicism. The rather cold and clinical manner in which he handles them simply heightens our queasiness.

Having no access to the principal means through which Burgess has enlisted our sympathetic interest in Alex's fate, Kubrick must resort to cruder devices. In the leading role, Malcolm McDowell is directed toward cuteness at every possible opportunity; the spirit of the Bowery Boys lives on in his performance. Worse, his victims and those who victimize him all turn out to be either homosexual or neutered somehow, by age, by physical grotesqueness or by some powerful sublimating force such as careerism. In short, it is a viciously rigged game. We are never for a moment allowed even a fleeting suggestion of sympathy for anyone else, never permitted to glimpse any other character of personal magnetism, wit or sexual attractiveness comparable to Alex's. As a result, the film, though surprisingly faithful to the plot line of the novel, is entirely faithless to its meaning. It is no longer a cautionary tale about how the bureaucratic rage for order creates a hopelessly banal social order and a mindlessly murderous youthful rebel class. It is, instead, yet another parable of the war between the generations. And perhaps the most dishonest one we have yet had, copping a plea for its chosen people not through direct statement but through film technique, what used to be called director's "touches." Happily, Kubrick's hand is slower than the reasonably educated eye, and most people will see *A Clockwork Orange* for—well, a clockwork orange, an imitation of a living object, given a semblance of animation by mechanical means.

### Commentary: On Caring about the Subject

A year or so back in the Sunday *New York Times* there was a debate between movie critic John Simon and Vincent Canby, the *Times'* own film reviewer. It must have been a slow news day at the *Times*. The next time they debate I won't read them. I'll go down to the corner and watch haircuts, instead.

Richard Schickel, it seems to me, would never have engaged in such a debate because Richard Schickel appears to take his subject more seriously than he takes himself. It is this, I think, which makes Schickel the best film critic I know. It is this which accounts fundamentally for the fact that Schickel's film reviews consistently enlarge my understanding of a movie while those of other people often obscure its meaning. He never distorts the film to make his review clever.

Schickel respects his subject enough to look at it honestly, to see it in a larger context (literature rather than its replacement), and to demand of it that it have some kind of moral center. He is a moralist (which has no connection with being moralistic), and a humanist. He views film not merely in terms of lap dissolves and cutting technique, nor in terms of audience appreciation, but in terms of its effect on the culture. More than any critic I've read, Schickel seems to have learned about movies by going to movies. Not technique—values. In his film criticism he seems guided by the virtues that those of us who grew up in the thirties and forties learned to admire at least in part from films: honor, courage, honesty, loyalty, directness, plain dealing, things like that.

This is not to suggest that Schickel insists that films portray those things, but that they be honest, or honorable, or courageous, for instance, in the things they do portray. If the world appears a pestilence of cynicism to a film maker, he should show us such a world, but he should not himself do so cynically. But perhaps I begin to speak for myself while pretending to speak for Schickel.

I do not know Richard Schickel personally, and even if I did I would have no real business telling you what he thinks about things. Let us say simply that he seems to admire much of what I admire, and he seems to have come from much the kind of time and place that I came from. Let us say I think that the values we carried away from that time and place, often caught and fixed for us in movies, in Gary Cooper and Bogart, yes, but also in Jon Hall and Johnny Mack Brown are valid, and ought to endure. Schickel's film criticism in its honesty and craft enlarges one's confidence that they will. Or is it only pretty to think so?

R. B. P.

## 18. WHAT'S IT GOING TO BE THEN?

**Anthony Burgess**

*Anthony Burgess is a major British novelist, and critic. A Clock-work* Orange *was published in 1962. What follows is an excerpt from that book.*

'What's it going to be then, eh?'

There was me, that is Alex, and my three droogs, that is Pete, Georgie, and Dim, Dim being really dim, and we sat in the Korova Milkbar making up our rassoodocks what to do with the evening, a flip dark chill winter bastard though dry. The Korova Milkbar was a milk-plus mesto, and you may, O my brothers, have forgotten what these mestos were like, things changing so skorry these days and everybody very quick to forget, newspapers not being read much neither. Well, what they sold there was milk plus something else. They had no license for selling liquor, but there was no law yet against prodding some of the new veshches which they used to put into the old moloko, so you could peet it with vellocet or synthemesc or drencrom or one or two other veshches which would give you a nice quiet horrorshow fifteen minutes admiring Bog And All His Holy Angels and Saints in your left shoe with lights bursting all over your mozg. Or you could peet milk with knives in it, as we used to say, and this would sharpen you up and make you ready for a bit of dirty twenty-to-one, and that was what we were peeting this evening I'm starting off the story with.

Our pockets were full of deng, so there was no real need from the point of view of crasting any more pretty polly to tolchock some old veck in an alley and viddy him swim in his blood while we counted the takings and divided by four, nor to do the ultra-violent on some shivering starry grey-haired ptitsa in a shop and go smecking off with the till's guts. But, as they say, money isn't everything.

The four of us were dressed in the heighth of fashion, which in those days was a pair of black very tight tights with the old jelly mould, as we called it, fitting on the crotch underneath the tights, this being to protect and also a sort of a design you could viddy clear enough in a certain light, so that I had one in the shape of a spider, Pete had a rooker (a hand, that is), Georgie had a very fancy one of a flower, and poor old

Dim had a very hound-and-horny one of a clown's litso (face, that is), Dim not ever having much of an idea of things and being, beyond all shadow of a doubting Thomas, the dimmest of we four. Then we wore waisty jackets without lapels but with these very big built-up shoulders ('pletchoes' we called them) which were a kind of a mockery of having real shoulders like that. Then, my brothers, we had these off-white cravats which looked like whipped-up kartoffel or spud with a sort of a design made on it with a fork. We wore our hair not too long and we had flip horrorshow boots for kicking.

'What's it going to be then, eh?'

There were three devotchkas sitting at the counter all together, but here were four of us malchicks and it was usually like one for all and all for one. These shapes were dressed in the heighth of fashion too, with purple and green and orange wigs on their gullivers, each one not costing less than three or four weeks of those sharps' wages, I should reckon, and make-up to match (rainbows round the glazzies, that is, and the rot painted very wide). Then they had long black very straight dresses, and on the groody part of them they had little badges of like silver with different malchicks' names on them—Joe and Mike and suchlike. These were supposed to be the names of the different malchicks they'd spatted with before they were fourteen. They kept looking our way and I nearly felt like saying the three of us (out of the corner of my rot, that is) should go off for a bit of pol and leave poor old Dim behind, because it would be just a matter of kupetting Dim a demi-litre of white but this time with a dollop of synthemesc in it, but that wouldn't really have been playing like the game. Dim was very very ugly and like his name, but he was a horrorshow filthy fighter and very handy with the boot.

'What's it going to be then, eh?'

The chelloveck sitting next to me, there being this long big plushy seat that ran round three walls, was well away with his glazzies glazed and sort of burbling slovos like 'Aristotle wishy washy works outing cyclamen get forficulate smartish'. He was in the land all right, well away, in orbit, and I knew what it was like, having tried it like everybody else had done, but at this time I'd got to thinking it was a cowardly sort of a veshch, O my brothers. You'd lay there after you'd drunk the old moloko and then you got the messel that everything all round you was sort of in the past. You could viddy it all right, all of it, very clear —tables, the stereo, the lights, the sharps and the malchicks—but it was like some veshch that used to be there but was not there not no more. And you were sort of hypnotized by your boot or shoe or a fingernail as it might be, and at the same time you were sort of picked up by the old scruff and shook like you might be a cat. You got shook and shook till there was nothing left. You lost your name and your body and your self and you just didn't care, and you waited till your boot or your finger-nail got yellow, then yellower and yellower all the time. Then the lights started cracking like atomics and the boot or finger-nail turned into a big big big mesto, bigger than the whole world, and you were just going to get introduced to old Bog or God when it was all over. You came back to here and now whimpering sort of, with your rot all squaring up for a boohoohoo. Now, that's very nice but very cowardly. You were not put on this earth just to get in touch with God. That sort of thing could sap all the strength and the goodness out of a chelloveck.

'What's it going to be then, eh?'

The stereo was on and you got the idea that the singer's goloss was moving from one part of the bar to another, flying up to the ceiling and then swooping down again and whizzing from wall to wall. It was Berti Laski rasping a real starry oldie called 'You Blister My Paint'. One of the three ptitsas at the counter, the one with the green wig, kept pushing her belly out and pulling it in in time to what they called the music. I could feel the knives in the old moloko starting to prick, and now I was ready for a bit of twenty-to-one. So I yelped: 'Out out out out!' like a doggie, and then I cracked this veck who was sitting next to me and well away and burbling a horrorshow crack on the ooko or earhole, but he didn't feel it and went on with his 'Telephonic hardware and when the farfarculule gets rubadubdub'. He'd feel it all right when he came to, out of the land.

'Where out?' said Georgie.

'Oh, just to keep walking,' I said, 'and viddy what turns up, O my little brothers.'

So we scattered out into the big winter nochy and walked down Marghanita Boulevard and then turned into Boothby Avenue, and there we found what we were pretty well looking for, a malenky jest to start off the evening with. There was a doddery starry schoolmaster type veck, glasses on and his rot open to the cold nochy air. He had books under his arm and a crappy umbrella and was coming round the corner from the Public Biblio, which not many lewdies used those days. You never really saw many of the older bourgeois type out after nightfall those days, what with the shortage of police and we fine young malchickiwicks about, and this prof type chelloveck was the only one walking in the whole of the street. So we goolied up to him, very polite, and I said: 'Pardon me, brother.'

He looked a malenky bit poogly when he viddied the four of us like that, coming up so quiet and polite and smiling, but he said: 'Yes? What is it?' in a very loud teacher-type goloss, as if he was trying to show us he wasn't poogly. I said:

'I see you have books under your arm, brother. It is indeed a rare pleasure these days to come across somebody that still reads, brother.'

'Oh,' he said, all shaky. 'Is it? Oh, I see.' And he kept looking from one to the other of we four, finding himself now like in the middle of a very smiling and polite square.

'Yes,' I said. 'It would interest me greatly, brother, if you would kindly allow me to see what books those are that you have under your arm. I like nothing better in this world than a good clean book, brother.'

'Clean,' he said. 'Clean, eh?' And then Pete skvatted these three books from him and handed them round real skorry. Being three, we all had one each to viddy at except for Dim. The one I had was called *Elementary Crystallography*, so I opened it up and said: 'Excellent, really first-class,' keeping turning the pages. Then I said in a very shocked type goloss: 'But what is this here? What is this filthy slovo? I blush to look at this word. You disappoint me, brother, you do really.'

'But,' he tried, 'but, but.'

'Now,' said Georgie, 'here is what I should call real dirt. There's one slovo beginning with an f and another with a c.' He had a a book called *The Miracle of the Snowflake*.

'Oh,' said poor old Dim, smotting over Pete's shoulder and going too far, like he always did, 'it says here what he done to her, and there's a picture and all. Why,' he said, 'you're nothing but a filthy-minded old skitebird.'

'An old man of your age, brother,' I said, and I started to rip up the book I'd got, and the others did the same with the ones they had, Dim and Pete doing a tug-of-war with *The Rhombohedral System*. The starry prof type began to creech: 'But those are not mine, those are the property of the municipality, this is sheer wantonness and vandal work,' or some such slovos. And he tried to sort of wrest the books back off of us, which was like pathetic. 'You deserve to be taught a lesson, brother,' I said, 'that you do.' This crystal book I had was very tough-bound and hard to razrez to bits, being real starry and made in days when things were made to last like, but I managed to rip the pages up and chuck them in handfuls of like snowflakes, though big, all over this creeching old veck, and then the others did the same with theirs, old Dim just dancing about like the clown he was. 'There you are,' said Pete. 'There's the mackerel of the cornflake for you, you dirty reader of filth and nastiness.'

'You naughty old veck, you,' I said, and then we began to filly about with him. Pete held his rookers and Georgie sort of hooked his rot wide open for him and Dim yanked out his false zoobies, upper and lower. He threw these down on the pavement and then I treated them to the old boot-crush, though they were hard bastards like, being made of some new horrorshow plastic stuff. The old veck began to make sort of chumbling shooms—'wuf waf wof'—so Georgie let go of holding his goobers apart and just let him have one in the toothless rot with his ringy fist, and that made the old veck start moaning a lot then, then out comes the blood, my brothers, real beautiful. So all we did then was to pull his outer platties off, stripping him down to his vest and long underpants (very starry; Dim smecked his head off near), and then Pete kicks him lovely in his pot, and we let him go. He went sort of staggering off, it not having been too hard of a tolchock really, going 'Oh oh oh', not knowing where or what was what really, and we had a snigger at him and then riffled through his pockets, Dim dancing round with his crappy umbrella meanwhile, but there wasn't much in them. There were a few starry letters, some of them dating right back to 1960 with 'My dearest dearest' in them and all that chepooka, and a keyring and a starry leaky pen. Old Dim gave up his umbrella dance and of course had to start reading one of the letters out loud, like to show the empty street he could read. 'My darling one,' he recited, in this very high type goloss, 'I shall be thinking of you while you are away and hope you will remember to wrap up warm when you go out at night.' Then he let out a very shoomny smeck—'Ho ho ho'—pretending to start wiping his yahma with it. 'All right,' I said. 'Let it go, O my brothers.' In the trousers of this starry veck there was only a malenky bit of cutter (money, that is)—not more than three gollies—so we gave all his messy little coin the scatter treatment, it being hen-korm to the amount of pretty polly we had on us already. Then we smashed the umbrella and razrezzed his platties and gave them to the blowing winds, my brothers, and then we'd finished with the starry teacher type veck. We hadn't done much, I know, but that was only like the start of the evening and I make no appy polly loggies to thee or thine for that. The knives in the milk-plus were stabbing away nice and horrorshow now.

The next thing was to do the sammy act, which was one way to unload some of our cutter so we'd have more of an incentive like for some shop-crasting, as well as it being a way of buying an alibi in advance, so we went into the Duke of New York on Amis Avenue and sure enough in the snug there were three or four old baboochkas peeting their black and suds on SA (State Aid). Now we were the very good malchicks, smiling good evensong to one and all, though these wrinkled old lighters started to get all shook, their veiny old rookers all trembling round their glasses and making the suds spill on the table. 'Leave us be, lads,' said one of them, her face all mappy with being a thousand years old, 'we're only poor old women.' But we just made with the zoobies, flash flash flash, sat down, rang the bell, and waited for the boy to come. When he came, all nervous and rubbing his rookers on his grazzy apron, we ordered us four veterans—a veteran being rum and cherry brandy mixed, which was popular just then, some liking a dash of lime in it, that being the Canadian variation. Then I said to the boy:

'Give these poor old baboochkas over there a nourishing something. Large Scotchmen all round and something to take away.' And I poured my pocket of deng all over the table, and the other three did likewise, O my brothers. So double firegolds were brought in for the scared starry lighters, and they knew not what to do or say. One of them got out. 'Thanks, lads,' but you could see they thought there was something dirty like coming. Anyway, they were each given a bottle of Yank General, cognac that is, to take away, and I gave money for them to be delivered each a dozen of black and suds that following morning, they to leave their stinking old cheenas' addresses at the counter. Then with the cutter that was left over we did purchase, my brothers, all the meat pies, pretzels, cheesesnacks, crisps and chocbars in that mesto, and those too were for the old sharps. Then we said: 'Back in a minoota,' and the old ptitsas were still saying: 'Thanks, lads,' and 'God bless you, boys,' and we were going out without one cent of cutter in our carmans.

'Makes you feel real dobby, that does,' said Pete. You could viddy that poor old Dim the dim didn't quite pony all that, but he said nothing for fear of being called gloopy and a domeless wonderboy. Well, we went off now round the corner to Attlee Avenue, and there was this sweets and cancers shop still open. We'd left them alone near three months now and the whole district had been very quiet on the whole, so the armed millicents or rozz patrols weren't round there much, being more north of the river these days. We put our maskies on—new jobs these were, real horrorshow, wonderfully done really; they were like faces of historical personalities (they gave you the names when you bought) and I had Disraeli, Pete had Elvis Presley, Georgie had Henry VIII and poor old Dim had a poet veck called Peebee Shelley; they were a real like disguise, hair and all, and they were some very special plastic veshch so you could roll it up when you'd done with it and hide it in your boot—then three of us went in, Pete keeping chasso without, not that there was anything to worry about out there. As soon as we launched on the shop we went for Slouse who ran it, a big portwine jelly of a veck who viddied at once what was coming and made straight for the inside where the telephone was and perhaps his well-oiled pooshka, complete with six dirty rounds. Dim was round that counter skorry as a bird, sending packets of snoutie flying and cracking over a big cut-out showing a sharp with all her zoobies going flash at the customers and her groodies near hanging out to advertise some new brand of cancers. What you could viddy then was a sort of a big ball rolling into the inside of the shop behind the curtain, this being old Dim and Slouse sort of locked in a death struggle. Then you could slooshy panting and snoring and kicking behind the curtain and veshches falling over and swearing and then glass going smash smash smash. Mother Slouse, the wife, was sort of froze behind the counter. We could tell she would creech murder given one chance, so I was round that counter very skorry and had a hold of her, and a horrorshow big lump she was too, all nuking of scent and with flipflop big bobbing groodies on her. I'd got my rooker round her rot to stop her belting out death and destruction to the four winds of heaven, but this lady doggie gave me a large foul big bite on it and it was me that did the creeching, and then she opened up beautiful with a flip yell for the millicents. Well, then she had to be tolchocked proper with one of the weights for the scales, and then a fair tap with a crowbar they had for opening cases, and that brought the red out like an old friend. So we had her down on the floor and a rip of her platties for fun and a gentle bit of the boot to stop her moaning. And, viddying her lying there with her groodies on show, I wondered should I or not, but that was for later on in the evening. Then we cleaned the till, and there was flip horrorshow takings that nochy, and we had a few packs of the very best top cancers apiece, then off we went, my brothers.

'A real big heavy great bastard he was,' Dim kept saying. I didn't like the look of Dim; he looked dirty and untidy, like a veck who'd been in a fight, which he had been, of course, but you should never *look* as though you have been. His cravat was like someone had trampled on it, his maskie had been pulled off and he had floor-dirt on his litso, so we got him in an alleyway and tidied him up a malenky bit, soaking our tashtooks in spit to cheest the dirt off. The things we did for old Dim. We were back in the Duke of New York very skorry, and I reckoned by my watch we hadn't been more than ten minutes away. The starry old baboochkas were still there on the black and suds and Scotchmen we'd bought them, and we said: 'Hallo there, girlies, what's it going to be?' They started on the old 'Very kind, lads, God bless you, boys,' and so we rang the collocoll and brought a different waiter in this time and we ordered beers with rum in, being sore athirst, my brothers, and whatever the old ptitsas wanted. Then I said to the old baboochkas: 'We haven't been out of here, have we? Been here all the time, haven't we?' They all caught on real skorry and said:

'That's right, lads. Not been out of our sight, you haven't. God bless you, boys,' drinking.

Not that it mattered much, really. About half an hour went by before there was any sign of life among the millicents, and then it was only two very young rozzes that came in, very pink under their big copper's shlemmies. One said:

'You lot know anything about the happenings at Slouse's shop this night?'

'Us?' I said, innocent. 'Why, what happened?'

'Stealing and roughing. Two hospitalizations. Where've you lot been this evening?'

'I don't go for that nasty tone,' I said. 'I don't care much for these nasty insinuations. A very suspicious nature all this betokeneth, my little brothers.'

'They've been in here all night, lads,' the old sharps started to creech out. 'God bless them, there's no better lot of boys living for kindness and generosity. Been here all the time they have. Not seen them move we haven't.'

'We're only asking,' said the other young millicent. 'We've got our job to do like anyone else.' But they gave us the nasty warning look before they went out. As they were going out we handed them a bit of lip-music: brrrrzzzzrrrr. But, myself, I couldn't help a bit of disappointment at things as they were those days. Nothing to fight against really. Everything as easy as kiss-my-sharries. Still, the night was still very young.

# The Search for Values

## Section Introduction

## THE VARIETY OF BEGINNINGS

In Rochester, New Hampshire, there is a small stationery store which stays open until 1:00 P.M. on Sunday afternoons and carries the *New York Times*. Anyone who reads the Sunday *Times* knows that if he buys it as late as one o'clock and reads it with any care at all the rest of his afternoon is spent. The store also carries at least a dozen other newspapers, nearly one thousand paperback books, and has a twenty-foot-long tier of magazine racks seven feet high, holding everything from *Strength and Health* to the *National Review*. As readers, we surely have more available to us and less time to deal with it than any other generation in the history of letters. If a man is going to write something these days, he will do well to snare his audience as soon as possible. We are a fickle, impatient, and distracted lot. We may, out of what is left of the generosity of our souls, grant a man all of a single paragraph to capture our attention (and this assuming we have not already rejected him on the grounds of his title or subject). While he may shape his Sunday afternoon leisurely around the *New York Times*, he is well advised to pick up the pace at the beginning of something he writes.

In their search for values, the writers collected here offer a good variety of beginnings. Herbert Otto's is simple and direct: "Never before in the history of Western civilization has the institution of marriage been under the searching scrutiny it is today." Malcolm Cowley's is more elaborate, the opening sentence moving wryly from the sublime to the ridiculous:

"In those days when division after division was landing in Hoboken and marching up Fifth Avenue in full battle equipment, when Americans were fighting the Bolshies in Siberia and guarding the Rhine—in those still belligerent days that followed the Armistice there was a private war between Greenwich Village and the *Saturday Evening Post*."

Gina Berriault intrigues us with situation:

"On the night of October 20, 1966, twenty masked Delta Tau Delta men surrounded their student body president on a street of the Stanford campus, escorted him to an empty lot and, with electric clippers plugged into an outlet inside a dormitory, shaved off the abundant hair of his head."

Tom Wolfe begins with energy and exclamation:

"Thirty-nine years old! A recluse! Bonafide! Doesn't go out, doesn't see the light of day, doesn't put his hide out in God's own unconditioned Chicago air for months on end; *years*."

Peter L. Sandberg relies on atmosphere:

"Past midnight, Meyer woke again to the noise of the bat-like birds that shot past the narrow ledge, their high-pitched sounds like rushing pinwheels."

These are effective beginnings. They challenge us; they entice us. They lead us where the writer wants us to go, not away from but into the substance of what he has created.

## 19. THE GREENWICH VILLAGE IDEA

### Malcolm Cowley

*Malcolm Cowley, critic, free-lance writer, and translator, attended Harvard University and the University of Montpellier. He has edited numerous books and authored many of his own, including* Exile's Return, The Literary Situation, *and* The Faulkner-Cowley File.

In those days when division after division was landing in Hoboken and marching up Fifth Avenue in full battle equipment, when Americans were fighting the Bolshies in Siberia and guarding the Rhine—in those still belligerent days that followed the Armistice there was a private war between Greenwich Village and the *Saturday Evening Post.*

Other magazines fought in the same cause, but the *Post* was persistent and powerful enough to be regarded as chief of the aggressor nations. It published stories about the Villagers, editorials and articles against them, grave or flippant serials dealing with their customs in a mood of disparagement or alarm, humorous pieces done to order by its staff writers, cartoons in which the villagers were depicted as long-haired men and short-haired women with ridiculous bone-rimmed spectacles—in all, a long campaign of invective beginning before the steel strike or the Palmer Raids and continuing through the jazz era, the boom and the depression. The burden of it was always the same: that the Village was the haunt of affectation; that it was inhabited by fools and fakers; that the fakers hid Moscow heresies under the disguise of cubism and free verse; that the fools would eventually be cured of their folly: they would forget this funny business about art and return to domesticity in South Bend, Indiana, and sell motorcars, and in the evenings sit with slippered feet while their children romped about them in paper caps made from the advertising pages of the *Saturday Evening Post.* The Village was dying, had died already, smelled to high heaven and Philadelphia. . . .

The Villagers did not answer this attack directly: instead they carried on a campaign of their own against the culture of which the *Post* seemed to be the final expression. They performed autopsies, they wrote obituaries of civilization in the United States, they shook the standardized dust of the country from their feet. Here, apparently, was a symbolic

*Source:* "The Greenwich Village Idea" from *Exile's Return* by Malcolm Cowley. Copyright 1934, © 1962 by Malcolm Cowley. Reprinted by permission of the Viking Press, Inc.

struggle: on the one side, the great megaphone of middle-class America; on the other, the American disciples of art and artistic living. Here, in its latest incarnation, was the eternal warfare of bohemian against bourgeois, poet against propriety—Villon and the Bishop of Orleans, Keats and the quarterly reviewers, Rodolphe, Mimi and the landlord. But perhaps, if we review the history of the struggle, we shall find that the issue was other than it seemed, and the enmity less ancient.

Alexander Pope, two centuries before, had taken the side of property and propriety in a similar campaign against the slums of art. When writing *The Dunciad* and the *Epistle to Dr. Arbuthnot*, he lumped together all his enemies—stingy patrons, homosexual peers, hair-splitting pedants; but he reserved his best-considered insults for the garret dwellers of Grub Street, the dramatists whose lives were spent dodging the bailiff, the epic poets "lulled by a zephyr through the broken pane." These he accused of slander, dullness, theft, bootlicking, ingratitude, every outrage to man and the Muses; almost the only charge he did not press home against them was that of affectation. They were not play-acting their poverty. The threadbare Miltons of his day were rarely the children of prosperous parents; they could not go home to Nottingham or Bristol and earn a comfortable living by selling hackney coaches; if they "turned a Persian tale for half a crown," it was usually because they had no other means of earning half a crown and so keeping themselves out of debtors' prison. And the substance of Pope's attack against them is simply that they were poor, that they belonged to a class beneath his own, without inherited wealth, that they did not keep a gentleman's establishment, or possess a gentleman's easy manners, or the magnanimity of a gentleman sure of tomorrow's dinner:

> Yet then did Gildon draw his venal quill;
> I wish'd the man a dinner, and sate still.
> Yet then did Dennis rave in furious fret;
> I never answer'd, I was not in debt.

Pope was a far wittier poet than any of his adversaries, but the forces he brought against them were not those of wit or poetry alone: behind him, massed in reserve, was all the prejudice of eighteenth-century gentlefolk against intruders into the polite world of letters. He was fighting a literary class war, and one that left deep wounds. To many a poor scribbler it meant the difference between starvation and the roast of mutton he lovingly appraised in a bake-shop window and promised himself to devour if his patron sent him a guinea: after *The Dunciad*, patrons closed their purses. Pope had inflicted a defeat on Grub Street but—the distinction is important—he had left bohemia untouched, for the simple reason that Queen Anne's and King George's London had no bohemia to defeat.

Grub Street is as old as the trade of letters—in Alexandria, in Rome, it was already a crowded quarter; bohemia is younger than the Romantic movement. Grub Street develops in the metropolis of any country or culture as soon as men are able to earn a precarious living with pen or pencil; bohemia is a revolt against certain features of industrial capitalism and can exist only in a capitalist society. Grub Street is a way of life unwillingly followed by the intellectual proletariat; bohemia attracts its citizens from all economic classes: there are not a few bohemian millionaires, but they are expected to imitate the customs of penniless artists. Bohemia is Grub Street romanticized, doctrinalized and rendered self-conscious; it is Grub Street on parade.

It originated in France, not England, and the approximate date of its birth was 1830: thus, it followed the rise of French industry after the Napoleonic Wars. The French Romantic poets complained of feeling oppressed—perhaps it was, as Musset believed, the fault of that great Emperor whose shadow fell across their childhood; perhaps it was Science, or the Industrial Revolution, or merely the money-grubbing, the stuffy morals and stupid politics of the people about them; in any case they had to escape from middle-class society. Some of them became revolutionists; others took refuge in pure art; but most of them demanded a real world of present satisfactions, in which they could cherish aristocratic ideals while living among carpenters and grisettes. The first bohemians, the first inhabitants of that world, were the friends of Théophile Gautier and Gérard de Nerval, young men of good family, bucks and dandies with money enough to indulge their moods; but the legend of it was spread abroad, some twenty years later, by a poor hack named Henry Murger, the sone of a German immigrant to Paris.

Having abandoned all hopes of a formal education when he left primary school, and feeling no desire to follow his father's trade of tailor, Murger began to write mediocre verse and paint incredible pictures, meanwhile supporting himself by his wits. Soon he joined a group that called itself the Water Drinkers because it could rarely afford another beverage. A dozen young men with little talent and extravagant ambitions, they lived in hovels or in lofts over a cow stable, worked under the lash of hunger, and wasted their few francs in modest debauchery. One winter they had a stove for the first time: it was a hole cut in the floor, through which the animal heat of the stable rose into their chamber. They suffered from the occupational diseases of poor artists— consumption, syphilis, pneumonia—all of them aggravated by undernourishment. Joseph Desbrosses died in the winter of 1844; he was an able sculptor, possibly the one genius of the group. His funeral was the third in six weeks among the Water Drinkers, and they emptied their pockets to buy a wooden cross for the grave. When the last sod clumped down, the gravediggers stood waiting for their tip. There was not a sou in the party.

"That's all right," said the gravediggers generously, recognizing the mourners. "It will be for the next time."

Spring came and their feelings rose with the mercury. One evening when his friends were making war maps in water color, Murger began unexpectedly to tell them stories. They listened, chuckled and roared for two good hours, till somebody advised him, seriously between gales of laughter, to abandon poetry for fiction. A little later he followed this advice, writing about the life of his friends, the only life he knew. Personally he hated this existence on the cold fringe of starvation and planned to escape from it as soon as he could, but for the public he tried to render it attractive.

In *Scènes de la Vie de Bohème*, he succeeded beyond his ambition. He succeeded not only in writing a popular book, one that was translated into twenty languages, successfully dramatized, candied into an opera, one that enabled its author to live in bourgeois comfort, but also in changing an image in the public mind. Grub Street, where dinnerless Gildon drew his venal quill, contemptible Grub Street, the haunt of apprentices and failures and Henry Murger, was transformed into glamorous bohemia. The unwilling expedient became a permanent way of life, became a cult with rituals and costumes, a doctrine adhered to not only by artists, young and old, rich and poor, but also in later years by designers, stylists, trade-paper sub-editors, interior decorators, wolves, fairies, millionaire patrons of art, sadists, nymphomaniacs, bridge sharks, anarchists, women living on alimony, tired reformers, educational cranks, economists, hopheads, dipsomaniac playwrights, nudists, restaurant keepers, stockbrokers and dentists craving self-expression.

Even during Murger's lifetime, the bohemian cult was spreading from France into other European countries. Having occupied a whole section of Paris—three sections, in fact, for it moved from the Boul' Mich' to Montmartre and thence to Montparnasse—it founded new colonies in Munich, Berlin, London, St. Petersburg. In the late 1850s it reached New York, where it established headquarters in Charlie Pfaff's lager-beer saloon under the sidewalk of lower Broadway. Again in 1894 the "Trilby" craze spawned forth dozens of bohemian groups and magazines; in New York a writer explained that the true bohemia may exist at millionaires' tables; in Philadelphia young married couples south of

Market Street would encourage their guests: "Don't stand on ceremony; you know we are thorough bohemians." All over the Western world, bohemia was carrying on a long warfare with conventional society, but year by year it was making more converts from the ranks of the enemy.

When the American magazines launched their counteroffensive, in 1919, a curious phenomenon was to be observed. The New York bohemians, the Greenwich Villagers, came from exactly the same social class as the readers of the *Saturday Evening Post*. Their political opinions were vague and by no means dangerous to Ford Motors or General Electric: the war had destroyed their belief in political action. They were trying to get ahead, and the proletariat be damned. Their economic standards were those of the small American businessman.

The art-shop era was just beginning. Having fled from Dubuque and Denver to escape the stultifying effects of a civilization ruled by business, many of the Villagers had already entered business for themselves, and many more were about to enter it. They would open tea shops, antique shops, book shops, yes, and bridge parlors, dance halls, night clubs and real-estate offices. By hiring shop assistants, they would become the exploiters of labor. If successful, they tried to expand their one restaurant into a chain of restaurants, all with a delightfully free and intimate atmosphere, but run on the best principles of business accounting. Some of them leased houses, remodeled them into studio apartments, and raised the rents three or four hundred per cent to their new tenants. Others clung faithfully to their profession of painting or writing, rose in it slowly, and at last had their stories or illustrations accepted by *Collier's* or the *Saturday Evening Post*. There were occasions, I believe, when Greenwich Village writers were editorially encouraged to write stories making fun of the Village, and some of them were glad to follow the suggestion. Of course they complained, when slightly tipsy, that they were killing themselves—but how else could they maintain their standard of living? What they meant was that they could not live like *Vanity Fair* readers without writing for the *Saturday Evening Post*.

And so it was that many of them lived during the prosperous decade that followed. If the book succeeded or if they got a fat advertising contract, they bought houses in Connecticut, preferably not too far from the Sound. They hired butlers; they sent their children to St. Somebody's; they collected highboys, lowboys, tester beds; they joined the local Hunt and rode in red coats across New England stone fences and through wine-red sumacs in pursuit of a bag of imported aniseed. In the midst of these new pleasures they continued to bewail the standardization of American life, while the magazines continued their polemic against Greenwich Village. You came to suspect that some of the Villagers themselves, even those who remained below Fourteenth Street, were not indignant at a publicity that brought tourists to the Pirates' Den and customers to Ye Olde Curiowe Shoppe and increased the value of the land in which a few of them had begun to speculate. The whole thing seemed like a sham battle. Yet beneath it was a real conflict of ideas and one that would soon be mirrored in the customs of a whole country.

Greenwich Village was not only a place, a mood, a way of life: like all bohemias, it was also a doctrine. Since the days of Gautier and Murger, this doctrine had remained the same in spirit, but it had changed in several details. By 1920, it had become a system of ideas that could roughly be summarized as follows:

1. *The idea of salvation by the child.* Each of us at birth has special potentialities which are slowly crushed and destroyed by a standardized society and mechanical methods of teaching. If a new educational system can be introduced, one by which children are encouraged to develop their own personalities, to blossom freely like flowers, then the world will be saved by this new, free generation.

2. *The idea of self-expression.* Each man's, each woman's, purpose in life is to express himself, to realize his full individuality through creative work and beautiful living in beautiful surroundings.

3. *The idea of paganism.* The body is a temple in which there is nothing unclean, a shrine to be adorned for the ritual of love.

4. *The idea of living for the moment.* It is stupid to pile up treasures that we can enjoy only in old age, when we have lost the capacity for enjoyment. Better to seize the moment as it comes, to dwell in it intensely, even at the cost of future suffering. Better to live extravagantly, gather June rosebuds, "burn my candle at both ends. . . . It gives a lovely light."

5. *The idea of liberty.* Every law, convention or rule of art that prevents self-expression or the full enjoyment of the moment should be shattered and abolished. Puritanism is the great enemy. The crusade against puritanism is the only crusade with which free individuals are justified in allying themselves.

6. *The idea of female equality.* Women should be the economic and moral equals of men. They should have the same pay, the same working conditions, the same opportunity for drinking, smoking, taking or dismissing lovers.

7. *The idea of psychological adjustment.* We are unhappy because we are maladjusted, and maladjusted because we are repressed. If our individual repressions can be removed—by confessing them to a Freudian psychologist—then we can adjust ourselves to any situation, and be happy

in it. (But Freudianism is only one method of adjustment. What is wrong with us may be our glands, and by a slight operation, or merely by taking a daily dose of thyroid, we may alter our whole personalities. Again, we may adjust ourselves by some such psycho-physical discipline as was taught by Gurdjieff. The implication of all these methods is the same—that the environment itself need not be altered. That explains why most radicals who become converted to psychoanalysis or glands or Gurdjieff[1] gradually abandoned their political radicalism.)

8. *The idea of changing place.* "They do things better in Europe." England and Germany have the wisdom of old cultures; the Latin peoples have admirably preserved their pagan heritage. By expatriating himself, by living in Paris, Capri or the South of France, the artist can break the puritan shackles, drink, live freely and be wholly creative.

All these, from the standpoint of the business-Christian ethic then represented by the *Saturday Evening Post*, were corrupt ideas. This older ethic is familiar to most people, but one feature of it has not been sufficiently emphasized. Substantially, it was a *production* ethic. The great virtues it taught were industry, foresight, thrift and personal initiative. The workman should be industrious in order to produce more for his employer; he should look ahead to the future; he should save money in order to become a capitalist himself; then he should exercise personal initiative and found new factories where other workmen would toil industriously, and save, and become capitalists in their turn.

During the process many people would suffer privations: most workers would live meagerly and wrack their bodies with labor; even the employers would deny themselves luxuries that they could easily purchase, choosing instead to put back the money into their business; but after all, our bodies were not to be pampered; they were temporary dwelling places, and we should be rewarded in Heaven for our self-denial. On earth, our duty was to accumulate more wealth and produce more goods, the ultimate use of which was no subject for worry. They would somehow be absorbed, by new markets opened in the West, or overseas in new countries, or by the increased purchasing power of workmen who had saved and bettered their position.

That was the ethic of a young capitalism, and it worked admirably, so long as the territory and population of the country were expanding faster

---

[1] George Ivanovich Gurdjieff, a Russian living in France, had worked out a system of practical mysticism based largely on Yoga. His chief disciple was A. E. Orage, the editor of the *New English Weekly*. In the spring of 1924, when Orage was in New York, he gained a great many converts, chiefly among older members of the Greenwich Village set.

than its industrial plant. But after the war the situation changed. Our industries had grown enormously to satisfy a demand that suddenly ceased. To keep the factory wheels turning, a new domestic market had to be created. Industry and thrift were no longer adequate. There must be a new ethic that encouraged people to buy, a *consumption* ethic.

It happened that many of the Greenwich Village ideas proved useful in the altered situation. Thus, *self-expression* and *paganism* encouraged a demand for all sorts of products—modern furniture, beach pajamas, cosmetics, colored bathrooms with toilet paper to match. *Living for the moment* meant buying an automobile, radio or house, using it now and paying for it tomorrow. *Female equality* was capable of doubling the consumption of products—cigarettes, for example—that had formerly been used by men alone. Even *changing place* would help to stimulate business in the country from which the artist was being expatriated. The exiles of art were also trade missionaries: involuntarily they increased the foreign demand for fountain pens, silk stockings, grapefruit and portable typewriters. They drew after them an invading army of tourists, thus swelling the profits of steamship lines and travel agencies. Everything fitted into the business picture.

I don't mean to say that Greenwich Village was the source of the revolution in morals that affected all our lives in the decade after the war, and neither do I mean that big business deliberately plotted to render the nation extravagant, pleasure worshiping and reckless of tomorrow.

The new moral standards arose from conditions that had nothing to do with the Village. They were, as a matter of fact, not really new. Always, even in the great age of the Puritans, there had been currents of licentiousness that were favored by the immoderate American climate and held in check only by hellfire preaching and the hardships of settling a new country. Old Boston, Providence, rural Connecticut, all had their underworlds. The reason puritanism became so strong in America was perhaps that it had to be strong in order to checkmate its enemies. But it was already weakening as the country grew richer in the twenty years before the war; and the war itself was the puritan crisis and defeat.

All standards were relaxed in the stormy-sultry wartime atmosphere. It wasn't only the boys of my age, those serving in the army, who were transformed by events: their sisters and younger brothers were affected in a different fashion. With their fathers away, perhaps, and their mothers making bandages or tea-dancing with lonely officers, it was possible for boys and girls to do what they pleased. For the first time they could go to dances unchaperoned, drive the family car and park it by the roadside while they made love, and come home after midnight, a little tipsy, with nobody to reproach them in the hallway. They took advantage of these stolen liberties—indeed, one might say that the revolution in morals began as a middle-class children's revolt.

But everything conspired to further it. Prohibition came and surrounded the new customs with illicit glamour; prosperity made it possible to practice them; Freudian psychology provided a philosophical justification and made it unfashionable to be repressed; still later the sex magazines and the movies, even the pulpit, would advertise a revolution that had taken place silently and triumphed without a struggle. In all this Greenwich Village had no part. The revolution would have occurred if the Village had never existed, but—the point is important—it would not have followed the same course. The Village, older in revolt, gave form to the movement, created its fashions, and supplied the writers and illustrators who would render them popular. As for American business, though it laid no plots in advance, it was quick enough to use the situation, to exploit the new markets for cigarettes and cosmetics, and to realize that, in advertising pages and movie palaces, sex appeal was now the surest appeal.

The Greenwich Village standards, with the help of business, had spread through the country. Young women east and west had bobbed their hair, let it grow and bobbed it again; they had passed through the period when corsets were checked in the cloakroom at dances and the period when corsets were not worn. They were not very self-conscious when they talked about taking a lover; and the conversations ran from mother fixations to birth control while they smoked cigarettes between the courses of luncheons eaten in black-and-orange tea shops just like those in the Village. People of forty had been affected by the younger generation: they spent too much money, drank too much gin, made love to one another's wives and talked about their neuroses. Houses were furnished to look like studios. Stenographers went on parties, following the example of the boss and his girl friend and her husband. The "party," conceived as a gathering together of men and women to drink gin cocktails, flirt, dance to the phonograph or radio and gossip about their absent friends, had in fact become one of the most popular American institutions; nobody stopped to think how short its history had been in this country. It developed out of the "orgies" celebrated by the French 1830 Romantics, but it was introduced into this country by Greenwich Villagers—before being adopted by salesmen from Kokomo and the younger country-club set in Kansas City.

Wherever one turned the Greenwich Village ideas were making their way: even the *Saturday Evening Post* was feeling their influence. Long before Repeal, it began to wobble on Prohibition. It allowed drinking, petting and unfaithfulness to be mentioned in the stories it published; its illustrations showed women smoking. Its advertising columns admitted one after another of the strictly pagan products—cosmetics, toilet tissues, cigarettes—yet still it continued to thunder against Greenwich Village and bohemian immorality. It even nourished the illusion that its long campaign had been successful. On more than one occasion it announced that the Village was dead and buried: "The sad truth is," it said in the autumn of 1931, "that the Village was a flop." Perhaps it was true that the Village was moribund—of that we can't be sure, for creeds and ways of life among artists are hard to kill. If, however, the Village was really dying, it was dying of success. It was dying because it became so popular that too many people insisted on living there. It was dying because women smoked cigarettes on the streets of the Bronx, drank gin cocktails in Omaha and had perfectly swell parties in Seattle and Middletown—in other words, because American business and the whole of middle-class America had been going Greenwich Village.

## Commentary: On Making Things Concrete

Malcolm Cowley wishes to discuss the difference between what we have come to call middle America, and what we have come to call hippies. His subject is the contrast between two attitudes. And he recognizes what any good writer must, that attitudes are abstractions. If one is to compare them one must make them concrete. Cowley does so by embodying the attitude of middle America in *The Saturday Evening Post*, and that of the opposition attitude in the persons of people he identifies with a geographical region—the lower end of Manhattan Island, Greenwich Village.

The *Post* is just right (as the *Reader's Digest* would be currently), but the use of an area to personify an attitude leaves us with some problems, for Greenwich Village is still an abstraction: It does not have an editorial attitude, it does not commission anti-bohemian stories, it does not reflect a specific editorial attitude, it is a conglomerate of people. More than that the comparison of a magazine with a neighborhood does not lend itself to point by point analysis. That is, Cowley's starts out as if the essay (actually a chapter from *Exile's Return*) would be organized by developing the points of contrast between the two. But it doesn't.

The *Post* is reintroduced periodically through the essay, and it is posited as an alternate point of view to Bohemia often enough, but the actual subject of the essay is not the contrast between the two, but a description of the history and values of Bohemia, and an assertion (not really demonstrated) that Bohemian values slowly infiltrated middle America.

The-Saturday-Evening-Post-versus-Greenwich-Village opening, so cleverly juxtaposed with the returning troops and couched in the imagery of war, is in fact a false start. Malcolm Cowley's considerable talents enable him to compensate for the false start so that it does not loom as a glaring flaw, but the reader, or at least this reader, comes suddenly to the end of the piece with a sense of surprise that it's over so abruptly. Normally one does not analyze such a feeling, one merely shrugs and turns to another essay, or another task. If one were to analyze the feeling one might, in fact, discover that it derives from the unfulfilled expectation of a reader who, fooled by the opening paragraphs of the essay, expects to know more about a real conflict (between the *Post* and the Bohemians) than he gets. He keeps assuming that the essay will get to that and suddenly it's over and it hasn't. That's why the shock (perhaps you might wish to substitute a more modest word—violence done to rhetorical patterns is rarely shocking outside of textbooks). Cowley describes the values of the *Post* and the values embodied in what he calls "The Greenwich Village Idea" but he does not really describe a combat, and we are, from the opening paragraph onward, expecting him to.

There is a lesson in this (there always is in textbooks). It is one that most editors attempt to teach most apprentice writers very early in their apprenticeship. Do not cheat the reader. Do not lead him to expect something you do not give him. Do not supercharge your language so that you end up using a hammer to kill a fly. Do not introduce an objective tone and then write subjectively. Don't start out casual and sort of relaxed and then shift gears, abandoning the colloquial manner, and adopting the passive constructions and circumlocutions of the scholarly journals (as in the foregoing). Do not announce an exotic adventure and then write about "My Summer At Scout Camp." Do not announce a conflict and then not dramatize it.

Cowley knows this better than most. He's no apprentice. His problem of unfulfilled expectation is but a symptom of a more central problem. He did not get his two combatants sufficiently personified. The *Post* at war with the Village. In concept a fine idea, in practice not so fine. How does one show them fighting? One does not. Cowley does the next best thing, he almost (because he's very good) gives you the illusion that he's shown them fighting. But he has not. Because an area can't fight a magazine. If he had chosen a comparable opponent for the *Post*, he'd have had a different, and quite possibly better essay. Consider the possibilities if you were to undertake such a chore. The *Post* would do as one opponent, *The Village Voice* (*Evergreen Review, Ramparts, Phoenix,* insert your own favorite if you prefer) might serve as a proper opponent. One could then organize the essay by discussing the content of the two journals. By analyzing the assumptions between pieces that they had published or editorials that they had written on the same subject, you could, surely, find comments by one about the other if you were diligent. This would be a matter of combat, between two comparable opponents. The reader would get what you'd led him to expect. And he ought to.

R. B. P.

## 20. HAS MONOGAMY FAILED?

### Herbert A. Otto

*Herbert A. Otto is a psychologist and social worker who has served with public health agencies in Georgia and Utah. His book* Your Potentialities: The Undiscovered Self *appeared in 1966.*

Never before in the history of Western civilization has the institution of marriage been under the searching scrutiny it is today. Never before have so many people questioned the cultural and theological heritage of monogamy—and set out in search of alternatives. The American family of the 1970s is entering an unprecedented era of change and transition, with a massive reappraisal of the family and its functioning in the offing.

The U.S. statistic of one divorce per every four marriages is all too familiar. Other figures are even more disquieting. For example, a recent government study revealed that one-third of all first-born children in the United States from 1964 through 1966 were conceived out of wedlock, thereby forcing many hasty marriages that might not have occurred otherwise. Some marriage specialists estimate that anywhere from 40 to 60 percent of all marriages are at any given time "subclinical." The couples involved could materially benefit from the help of a marriage counselor, but they never reach a clinic. Divorce is still the most widely accepted means of coping with a marriage beset by problems. Relatively few couples having marital difficulties are aware of available marriage counseling services or utilize them. Divorce today is very much a part of the social fabric, and some sociologists refer to a "divorce culture." It is safe to say that most men, women, and children in this country have been touched by the divorce experience—either in their own families, or among friends and close acquaintances.

The other day a good friend, senior executive of a large company and in his early forties, dropped by for a visit. He told me he had been thinking of divorce after sixteen years of marriage. The couple have a boy, twelve, and two girls, one of whom is ten, the other eight. "We've grown apart over the years, and we have nothing in common left anymore other than the children. There are at least twenty years of enjoying life still ahead of me. I was worried about the children until we discussed

*Source:* "Has Monogamy Failed?" Herbert A. Otto. From *Saturday Review* April 25, 1970. Copyright 1970, Saturday Review, Inc.

it with them. So many of their schoolmates have had divorced parents or parents who had remarried, they are accustomed to the idea. It's part of life. Of course, if the older ones need help, I want them to see a good psychiatrist while we go through with this. My wife is still a good-looking woman, younger than I, and probably will remarry. I'm not thinking of it now, but I'll probably remarry someday." This situation illustrates an attitude and the climate of the times. Divorce has become as much an institution as marriage.

Paradoxically, the high divorce rate can be viewed as both a symptom of the failure of monogamy and an indication of its success. A large majority of men and women remarry within four years after their divorce. As Dr. Bernard Steinzor points out in his latest book, *When Parents Divorce*, "divorce has become an expression of the increasing personal freedom afforded the average citizen." It is a fact that the average citizen continues to pursue personal freedom within the framework of marriage. Serial monogamy or progressive monogamy is today so widespread that it has arrived as an alternative structure. According to one analyst, we are close to the day when 85 per cent of all men and women reaching the age of sixty-five will have been remarried at least once. I am reminded of a cartoon that appeared in *The New Yorker* some time ago: A young couple is shown leaving what is identified by a sign as the home of a justice of the peace. The bride, dressed in the latest mod fashion, turns brightly to her young man and says, "Darling! Our first marriage!"

The full-scale emergence of serial monogamy has been accompanied by an explosive upswing of experimentation with other alternative structures. Begun by the under-thirty generation and hippie tribal families, the 1960s have seen the growth of a new commune movement. This movement has started to attract significant segments of the older, established population. For example, I recently conducted a weekend marathon in Chicago—under the auspices of the Oasis Center—that was open to the public. Seven out of thirty-six participants were members of communes. Three of the seven were successful professional men in their mid-forties. Another participant, a college professor in his early thirties, mentioned that he had been a member of a commune composed of several psychiatrists, an engineer, a teacher, and a chemist. When I visited New York following the Chicago weekend, a senior editor of a large publishing house casually mentioned that he and some friends were in the process of organizing a commune. They were looking for a large brownstone close to their offices.

The commune movement even has its own journal, *Modern Utopian*. Issued by the Alternatives Foundation of Berkeley, California, it is in its fourth year of publication. In 1969, this journal published the first comprehensive directory of intentional or utopian communes in the United States and the world. The addresses of close to two hundred intentional communities in this country are given. (It has been estimated that there are four to six times this number of communes in the United States.) California leads the *Modern Utopian* directory with more than thirty listed. New York has twenty-eight and Pennsylvania thirteen, with communes listed from thirty-five other states. Half a dozen books that I know of are currently in preparation on the commune movement.

Communes of various types exist, varying from agricultural subsistence to religious. To provide a base for economic survival, many of the communes furnish services or construct marketable products such as hammocks or wooden toys for preschoolers. Others operate printing presses or schools. Most communes not located in cities raise some of their own food. Relatively rare is the commune that is self-supporting solely on the basis of its agricultural operation. Sizes vary with anywhere from twelve persons or fewer to a hundred persons or more as members of an international community. The educational and vocational backgrounds of members also vary widely. The young people and school dropouts are currently being joined by a growing number of "Establishment dropouts." Many of these are people who have made successful contributions in their chosen vocations or professions and have grown disillusioned, or who are seeking to explore new life-styles.

Communes often have their beginnings when several persons who know each other well, like each other, and have similar values decide to live together. Sometimes a commune is formed around a common interest, craft, or unifying creative goal. Political views or convictions may also play a role in the formation of a commune. There are a number of peace-movement and radical communes; sometimes these are composed of political activists, and sometimes of people who see the commune movement as a "radical approach to revolution." Members of one such group, the Twin Oaks community in Virginia, think of themselves as a post-revolutionary society. As detailed in *Modern Utopian*, this "radical commune" was organized as the result of a university conference:

"Twin Oaks was started by a group of people who met while attending an 'academic' conference during 1966 at Ann Arbor, Michigan, on the formation of a Walden II community. One of the Twin Oakers related how this conference resulted in a very elaborate, academic type plan on how to get a Walden II community going. But when the conference was over, the professors all returned to their teaching posts, and nobody had any idea where they could get the several million dollars that the plan called for to start the thing. So eight people decided to start right away with whatever resources they could get together. . . .

For while Twin Oaks was designed to be a living experiment in community, it also aims to stimulate others to do the same. As one member said, 'We generally hold to the opinion that people who *don't* start communities (or join them) are slightly immoral.' It's all part of the revolution being over—they define revolution as a 'radical restructuring' of society, both economic and, more important, cultural. (But maybe you can't really separate the two.) One member summed up a desirable post-revolutionary society as: 'A society that creates people who are committed to non-aggression; a society of people concerned for one another; a society where one man's gain is not another man's loss; a society where disagreeable work is minimized and leisure is valued; a society in which people come first; an economic system of equality; a society which is constantly trying to improve in its ability to create happy, productive, creative people.' "

The personal property a member brings to a commune remains his, although he may be expected to share it when needed. Some purists object that, since members do not donate personal property for the benefit of the group, the current social experiments should not be referred to as "communes." Obviously, the term has acquired a new meaning and definition. The emphasis today is on the exploration of alternate models for togetherness, the shaping of growing dynamic environments, the exploration of new life-styles, and the enjoyment of living together.

A number of communes are deliberately organized for the purpose of group marriage. The concept of group marriage, however, differs widely. Some communes exclusively composed of couples have a living arrangement similar to the "big family" or group family that originated in Sweden in 1967. These married couples share the same home, expenses, household chores, and the upbringing of the children. Infidelity is not encouraged. Other group-marriage communes tolerate or encourage the sharing of husbands and wives. On the other end of the group-marriage continuum are communes such as The Family near Taos, New Mexico. This group of more than fifty members discourages pairing—"Everyone is married to everyone. The children are everyone's."

The life-span of many communes is relatively short due to four major disintegrative pressures that fragment intentional communities. Disagreement over household chores or work to be performed is a major source of disruption. When members fail to fulfill their obligations, disillusionment and demoralization often set in. Closely related are interpersonal conflicts, frequently fueled by the exchange of sex partners and resultant jealousy. Drugs do not seem to create a major problem in most communes, as there is either a permissive attitude or drug use is discouraged or forbidden. A small number of religious/mystical communes use drugs for sacramental purposes and as a means of communion.

The problems associated with economic survival generate considerable pressure. A final strong force that contributes to the collapse of communes stems from the hostility of surrounding communities. There are innumerable instances of harassment by neighbors, strangers, civil authorities, and police. The persistent and violent nature of this persecution is probably traceable to deep-seated feelings of threat and outrage when the neighboring communities discover a group in their midst suspected of having unorthodox living arrangements. These pervasive feelings of resistance and anger (which may be partially subconscious) are conceivably engendered in many persons by what they perceive to be a threat to the existing family structure.

The weight of tradition and the strong imprinting of parental and familial models assure that for some time to come the overwhelming bulk of the population will opt for something close to the family structures they have known. In view of this strong thrust, it is all the more surprising that preventive programs (other than didactic approaches) that center on the strengthening of the family are almost unknown. Also sadly lacking is massive federal support for programs designed to help marriages and families beset by problems. A network of federally supported marriage-counseling clinics making marital and premarital counseling services available throughout every state in the Union could accomplish a great deal toward reducing marital unhappiness and divorce.

Present-day medical science widely recommends that we have an annual physical check-up as a means of prevention. In a similar manner, annual assessment and evaluation should be available to couples interested in developing and improving their marriages. The goal would be to identify, strengthen, and develop family potential *before* crises arise, with the main focus on helping a family achieve an even more loving, enjoyable, creative, and satisfying marriage relationship. The plan of a marriage and family potential center was developed in 1967 and 1968 by a colleague, Dr. Lacey Hall, and myself during my stay in Chicago. The project was supported by the Stone Foundation, but, owing to a number of complex reasons, the program was never fully implemented. As a part of the work in Chicago, and also under the auspices of the National Center for the Exploration of Human Potential, a number of "More Joy in Your Marriage" groups and classes have been conducted and have shown considerable promise as a preventive approach.

Another highly promising field of inquiry is the area of family strengths. Little or no research and conceptualization had been done in relation to this area until the work of the Human Potentialities Research Project at the University of Utah, from 1960 through 1967. Paradoxically, family counseling and treatment programs have been offered for decades without a clearly developed framework of what was meant by family strengths, or what constitutes a "healthy family." In spite of extensive efforts to obtain foundation or government support for this research, no financial support was forthcoming. Ours remains a pathology-oriented culture saddled with the bias that the study of disorganization, illness, and dysfunction is the surest road to understanding the forces that go into the making of health and optimum functioning.

The emergence of alternative structures and the experimentation with new modes of married and family togetherness expresses a strong need to bring greater health and optimum functioning to a framework of interpersonal relationships formerly regarded as "frozen" and not amenable to change. There is no question that sex-role and parental-role rigidities are in the process of diminishing, and new dimensions of flexibility are making their appearance in marriage and the family. It is also evident that we are a pluralistic society with pluralistic needs. In this time of change and accelerated social evolution, we should encourage innovation and experimentation in the development of new forms of social and communal living. It is possible to invent and try out many models without hurting or destroying another person. Perhaps we need to recognize clearly that the objective of any model is to provide an atmosphere of sustenance, loving, caring, and adventuring. This makes growth and unfoldment possible.

It is in this light that the attention of an increasing number of well-known humanistic psychologists has been drawn to the institution of marriage. A new recognition of the many dimensions and possibilities of monogamy is beginning to emerge. For example, Dr. Jack Gibb and Dr. Everett Shostrom have each been conducting a series of couples groups at Growth Centers designed to revitalize and deepen love in the marital relationship.

Another eminent psychologist and author, Dr. Sidney Jourard, suggests that we "re-invent marriage" by engaging in "serial polygamy to the same person." He points out that many marriages pass through a cycle of gratifying the needs of both partners, and are experienced as fulfilling until an impasse is reached. One partner or the other finds continuation in that form intolerable, and the marriage is usually legally dissolved at that point. He believes it is possible for the couple at this juncture to struggle with the impasse and to evolve a new marriage with each other, one that includes change, yet preserves some of the old pattern that remains viable. This is the second marriage that, whatever form it takes, will also reach its end. There may then again be a time of estrangement, a period of experimentation, and a remarriage in a new way—and so on for as long as continued association with the same spouse remains meaningful for both partners.

One of the originators of the group marathon technique, Dr. Frederick Stoller, has another interesting proposal to add new dimensions to marriage and family relationships. He suggests an "intimate network of families." His intimate network consists of a circle of three or four families who meet together regularly and frequently, share in reciprocal fashion any of their intimate secrets, and offer one another a variety of services. The families do not hesitate to influence one another in terms of values and attitudes. Such an intimate family network would be neither stagnant nor polite, but would involve an extension of the boundaries of the immediate family.

Another possibility to introduce new elements of growth and creativity to monogamy is contained in my own concept of the "new marriage," i.e., marriage as a framework for developing personal potential. This concept is based on the hypothesis that we are all functioning at a small fraction of our capacity to live fully in its total meaning of loving, caring, creating, and adventuring. Consequently, the actualizing of our potential can become the most exciting adventure of our lifetime. From this perspective, any marriage can be envisioned as a framework for actualizing personal potential. Thus, marriage offers us an opportunity to grow, and an opportunity to develop and deepen the capacity for loving and caring. Only in a continuing relationship is there a possibility for love to become deeper and fuller so that it envelops all of our life and extends into the community. However, growth, by its very nature, is not smooth and easy, for growth involves change and the emergence of the new. But growth and the actualization of personal potential are also a joyous and deeply satisfying process that can bring to marriage a *joie de vivre*, an excitement, and a new quality of zest for living.

There are a number of characteristics that form a unique Gestalt and distinguish the new marriage from contemporary marriage patterns:

There is a clear acknowledgment by both partners concerning the *personal relevance* of the human potentialities hypothesis: that the healthy individual is functioning at a fraction of his potential.

Love and understanding become dynamic elements in the actualization of the marital partners' personal potential.

Partners in the new marriage conceive of their union as an evolving, developing, flexible, loving relationship.

In the new marriage there is planned action and commitment to achieve realization of marriage potential.

The new marriage is here-and-now oriented and not bound to the past.

There is clear awareness by husband and wife that their interpersonal or relationship environment, as well as their physical environment, directly affects the actualization of individual potential.

There is clear recognition by spouses that personality and the actualization of human potential have much to do with the social institutions and structures within which man functions. The need for institutional and environmental regeneration is acknowledged by both partners as being personally relevant, leading to involvement in social action.

Husband and wife have an interest in exploring the spiritual dimensions of the new marriage.

Since it is often difficult for two people to actualize more of their marriage potential by themselves, participants in the new marriage will seek out group experiences designed to deepen their relationship and functioning as a couple. Such experiences are now being offered at Growth Centers that have sprung up in many parts of the United States. Extension divisions of institutions of higher learning and church organizations are also increasingly offering such group experiences. Based on my many years of practice as marriage counselor, it has long been my conclusion that every marriage needs periodic rejuvenation and revitalization. This is best accomplished in a couples group that focuses on the development of greater intimacy, freedom, joy, and affection.

The challenge of marriage is the adventure of uncovering the depth of our love, the height of our humanity. It means risking ourselves physically and emotionally; leaving old habit patterns, and developing new ones; being able to express our desires fully, while sensitive to the needs of the other; being aware that each changes at his own rate, and unafraid to ask for help when needed.

Has monogamy failed? My answer is "no." Monogamy is no longer a rigid institution, but instead an evolving one. There is a multiplicity of models and dimensions that we have not even begun to explore. It takes a certain amount of openness to become aware on not only an intellectual level but a feeling level that these possibilities face us with a choice. Then it takes courage to recognize that this choice in a measure represents our faith in monogamy. Finally, there is the fact that every marriage has a potential for greater commitment, enjoyment, and communication, for more love, understanding, and warmth. Actualizing this potential can offer new dimensions in living and new opportunities for personal growth, and can add new strength and affirmation to a marriage.

## 21. THE ADVENT OF AUTOMATIC AFFLUENCE

### Kenneth Keniston

*A professor in the Department of Psychiatry at Yale Medical School, Kenneth Keniston has been widely praised for his first book* The Uncommitted: Alienated Youth in American Society. *His articles have appeared in* Commentary, Daedalus, The Atlantic Monthly, *and other distinguished periodicals. The material reprinted here has been taken from his second book* Young Radicals, *which grew out of the author's observations of student activists during "Vietnam Summer" in 1967.*

To any American who has grown up since the Second World War, one of the most important facts of life has been the continually increasing affluence around him. For all middle- and upper-class young Americans, as for increasing numbers of working-class youth, the fact of affluence is simply taken for granted—prosperity has become automatic. For example, although one or two of the young radicals who led Vietnam Summer came from lower-middle-class families and considered themselves "poor" during childhood, questions of income, security, social status, upward mobility, and finding a job were largely irrelevant when the time came for them to consider adult commitments. And when they realized during their adolescences that the affluence they so took for granted did not extend to all Americans—much less to the impoverished two-thirds of the world—they reacted with surprise, shock, and dismay. Material prosperity alone has made a difference in the development of this generation. The "luxuries" of an affluent age—electronic communications, rapid transport, good housing, physical comfort, readily available music, art, and literature, good health care and longevity—have helped give this generation its distinctive style. Without material affluence, the restlessness, mobility, and "wastefulness" of today's youth could hardly be understood.

But the impact of affluence extends considerably beyond its material benefits. "Affluence" can stand as shorthand for a variety of other changes in American institutions, the economy, family life, education, and the definition of the stages of life, all of which have affected the out-

*Source:* "The Advent of Automatic Affluence," Kenneth Keniston. From *Young Radicals: Notes on Committed Youth,* copyright © 1968 by Kenneth Keniston. Reprinted by permission of Harcourt Brace Jovanovich, Inc.

look of this generation. Material affluence is made possible by a system of production, innovation, and organization that defines the options open to today's young men and women, just as it has been the framework for their development to date. Affluence, in a broad sense, has both opened new doors and closed old ones.

Social criticism in the past decades has emphasized the destructive aspects of technology, bureaucracy, specialization, centralization, and bigness. Yet we have also begun to realize that these ambivalently viewed features of our society may be necessary conditions for the advantages of affluence. Our prosperity is built upon high technology, as upon complex and bureaucratic social organization. And both technology and differentiated social roles involve specialization and technical competence far beyond the basic requisites of literacy and fluency with numbers. Furthermore, in any highly specialized society, complex systems of co-ordination, social control, and communication must be developed to harmonize the work of specialized role-holders. Even sheer size sometimes increases affluence: centralization not only can permit industrial efficiencies, but sometimes facilitates administrative coordination. The advent of electronic communications and rapid transportation had made it increasingly possible for a small number of men to co-ordinate and control the activities of vast numbers of their fellows. For better and for worse, then, our affluent society is technological, specialized, bureaucratized, and complexly controlled. In such a society, most educated adults not only do highly specialized work, but are involved in complex networks of social co-ordination that they must accept if the System is to function smoothly.

All of these characteristics of modern society contribute to the malaise and reluctance of many of today's youth when they confront the System. Yet these same young men and women, like all of us, consider the many benefits of affluence as "givens" of modern life. They take for granted that just as the machine and factory production made possible the industrial revolution by multiplying each man's physical efforts a dozenfold, so now, in the technological era, the computer is increasingly freeing men from routine and repetitive mental work. Men and women need no longer work in the fields or factories from dawn to dusk to produce the requisites for survival. For affluent Americans (who are the majority), survival, subsistence, and starvation are no longer at issue. A small part of the population can produce the essentials of life, while the rest produce goods and services that, to previous generations, would have appeared unprecedented luxuries.

These "luxuries" include not only the material commodities that fill

American life, but less tangible opportunities for education, the cultivation of the mind, and the fulfillment of psychological needs beyond the need for subsistence, security, and status. By vastly extending the power and reach of each individual, the affluent society both permits and requires men to be "unproductive" for many years of their lives. The labor of children, adolescents, and, increasingly, post-adolescents is no longer needed by the economy. On the contrary, keeping young men and women off the labor market is a net social gain because it allows fuller employment of their elders. In addition, an affluent society increasingly requires the young to stay off the labor market in order to learn the high technological skills required to maintain affluence. The result, of course, is the historically unprecedented situation of prolonged higher education, extending well into the twenties, for a larger and larger proportion of the American population.

The postponement of entry into the labor force has contributed to a redefinition of the life cycle, underlining the connection between social opportunity and developmental stage. Giving large numbers of young men and women the opportunity to have an adolescence is an achievement of industrial societies. In many preindustrial societies, even childhood was forcibly aborted by the requirement that children begin to work before puberty. When this happens, the full psychological experience of childhood as we define it in modern society is inevitably cut short: children are small adults—by our modern standards, old before their time. But even in those societies where psychological childhood continues until biological puberty, adolescence as a psychological experience is rarely permitted.

To be sure, the physiological changes that announce the possibility of an adolescent experience occur in every society, regardless of what the society chooses to make of these changes. But in most previous societies, only the extraordinarily wealthy, talented, or fortunate were allowed anything like an adolescence. Even the wellborn Romeo and Juliet were thirteen years old; in the Middle Ages, kings assumed their thrones in their teens; and most children of the common people began working in the fields (in later times, in factories) well before they reached puberty. Allowing the possibility of adolescent development is only one possible reaction to the approach of biological adulthood: historically it is a relatively rare reaction. Even today, in primitive societies, puberty rites more often serve to hasten the child toward adulthood than to permit him anything like the possibility of adolescent turmoil, emotional growth, and independence. Although from the beginnings of history, the old have deplored the irreverence of the young, adolescence as a distinctive stage of life that *should* be made available to all young men and women has only begun to be recognized during the past two centuries in advanced societies.

By creating a vast surplus of wealth, modern societies have freed first children and then teen-agers from the requirements of farm and factory labor. Even before the industrial revolution, of course, a small number of young men and women were allowed a deferment of full involvement in adult work. And a few of them—a few from among the pages and princes, novices and apprentices—were sometimes able to create for themselves what we now recognize as an adolescence. But most, lacking opportunity and social sanction, moved directly from childhood to adulthood. The industrial revolution, however, created a new bourgeoisie with a commitment to education as a pathway to success for their children. This new middle class also had the means to allow children freedom from labor after puberty. There began to develop—for the middle classes at least—a vague concept, at first, of a postchildhood, preadult stage of life, a stage of continuing education that was initially modeled after the apprenticeship. Little by little, however, it became clear that this stage of life had qualities of its own. The adolescent gradually emerged as something more than a cross between a child and an adult.

First for the upper middle class, then for the lower middle class, and then, increasingly, for the working-class youth, adolescence became routinely available. And although the precise definition of the expected qualities of the adolescent is sensitive to the particular values of each society, in most affluent societies today, adolescence is recognized as *sui generis*, as important for the fullest possible unfolding of human potentials, and as a right to be guaranteed through compulsory education and anti-child-labor laws.

We should not forget how recently all of this has taken place, nor how incomplete it still is. Some of Marx's most vehement strictures in the middle of the nineteenth century were directed against the use of children in factories. And in America, the child-labor laws were passed only in the twentieth century. For many young Americans, and for an even greater proportion of the young in other nations, the psychological experience of adolescence is still aborted by the failure of education or the assumption of major economic responsibilities in the mid-teens —years that by our modern reckoning are only the beginning of adolescence. For large numbers of the poor, the deprived, the undermotivated, the psychologically or intellectually handicapped, adolescence still does not take place.

Even if it has not yet been extended to all, making the experience of adolescence available to most young men and women in modern society must be counted among the achievements of affluence. The possibility of adolescence as a psychological experience is dependent on economic conditions that free adolescents from the need to work, as upon the development of new values that make child or adolescent labor seem "outrageous" to right-thinking men and women. Only when a society produces enough to liberate young men and women between the ages of twelve and eighteen from labor can it demand that they continue their educations and allow them to continue their psychological development; only then can abhorrence of the "exploitation" of adolescents develop.

Affluence has also permitted changes in the quality of family life, especially among better-educated Americans. During the twentieth century, growing numbers of men and women, responding to the opportunities and demands of industrial society, have at least begun college, with many completing it and continuing on for their Ph.D. Higher education changes the outlooks and styles of at least some of those who pass through it. Its impact is difficult to describe precisely, but at best it allows greater freedom to express underlying feelings and impulses, greater independence of outlook and thought, and increased sympathy for the underdog. Also, since the best educated are generally those who attain greatest affluence in their own lives, higher education indirectly gives its graduates an adult life that is more secure, freer from the struggle for subsistence and status, and more open to the pursuit of non-material, self-expressive goals. Educated parents who have attained professional and economic security are in turn able to develop a distinctive family style that has important effects upon children.

Although they themselves may have had to struggle out of poverty, today's well-educated and affluent parents have generally "arrived" by the time they raise their own children. Compared to their own parents, they are more likely to instill in their children the special values of self-actualization—independence, sensitivity to feelings, concern for others, free expression of emotion, openness, and spontaneity. And since such parents tend to have relatively few children, they are able to lavish on each child an enormous amount of individual attention. Upper-middle-class educated women need not work to support the family: most devote themselves entirely to bringing up their small children. Even those who do work are likely to feel restored by their work rather than depleted. All of this means that affluent mothers are increasingly free to devote themselves to their small brood of children. Such devotion can have the bad consequences we see in the familiar stereotype of "Momism." But its good consequences are equally important: in many affluent families, children grow up unusually well cared for emotionally and psychologically, the objects of thoughtful attention and informed devotion. Increasingly, affluent middle-class parents *educate* their children, rather than merely training them. And in some affluent families, one finds a parental devotion to the autonomy, self-determination, and dignity of children that is without precedent, even in American history.

Obviously, not all affluent middle-class families fit this rosy description: such families are clearly in a minority. A full account of the impact of affluence and education of the American family would have to discuss other parental responses, among them family styles that lead to filial apathy, alienation, neurosis, or conformity. But affluence means that families like those I am describing—devoted, principled, expressive, thoughtful, humanitarian, and permissive—are increasing in number. Whatever the other satisfactions they derive from their children, parents in these families genuinely desire them to be independent, thoughtful, honorable, and resourceful men and women. To be sure, in these as all families, parents are full of foibles, contradictions, inconsistencies, and faults. And as I have suggested, in a time of rapid value change, the values that parents attempt to apply in bringing up their children may contrast with the more "instinctive" values that have their roots in the parents' own upbringing.

Yet for all their characteristic faults, the families of the educated and affluent have freed a growing number of today's youth to concern themselves with the welfare of others and the wider society. Their security makes possible an identification with others who are insecure; their affluence permits them to worry about those who are poor; their freedom allows them to care about those who are enslaved. Families like the families of the radicals who led Vietnam Summer are impressively *good*. They have given their children great strength, integrity, and warmth. The devotion to family core values that we see in many young radicals derives from parents who have principles and care lovingly for their children. Even the ability of young radicals to be different from their parents may stem partly from their parents' genuine willingness to let them be different. These are children, then, who have been taught from an early age to value independence, to think for themselves, to seek rational solutions, and to believe that principles should be practiced. As Richard Flacks, one of the most astute observers of the contemporary New Left, has put it, these young men and women are members of a "liberated generation."

This argument suggests that in an affluent society, the psychological and social underpinnings of radicalism have begun to change. In non-affluent societies, radicals and revolutionaries—who almost invariably come from relatively privileged backgrounds—tend to react with guilt to the "discovery" of poverty, tyranny, and misery. Furthermore, many radical and revolutionary groups have in the past sought social and political changes that would improve their own position, giving them freedom, power, or benefits they did not possess. In a society like our own —where affluence, economic opportunity, and considerable political freedom are the rule—radicalism is less likely to be built upon personal feelings of deprivation or a desire to improve one's own position. Nor is the guilt of the wealthy when confronted with the poor as likely a motivation for the radical's commitments. While radical leaders of all eras have typically been men of high principle, the role of principle increases further in an affluent era. The radical's basic goal is not to achieve new freedoms, opportunities, or benefits for himself, but rather to extend to all the freedoms, opportunities, and benefits he himself has always experienced. In an affluent world, the radical feels indignation rather than guilt; outrage rather than oppression.

## 22. THE NEW STUDENT PRESIDENT, DAVID HARRIS OF STANFORD

### Gina Berriault

*Gina Berriault's 1967 examination of the style that David Harris represents was remarkably prescient. Harris was recently released from prison where he served time for refusing induction. At this writing he appears undaunted by the experience. The technique that Gina Berriault uses, studying the youth movement by studying a representative figure, makes possible close examination of one of the major aspects of our time.*

On the night of October 20, 1966 twenty masked Delta Tau Delta men surrounded their student body president on a street of the Stanford campus, escorted him to an empty lot and, with electric clippers, plugged into an outlet inside a dormitory, shaved off the abundant hair of his head. "They expected me to fight back," Harris recalled when I spoke to him about the incident. "I figured I had a captive audience so I had a fifteen-minute conversation with this guy with a wolf mask who was holding my right leg—talking about education. After they shaved my head I said, 'Look, I've cooperated with you so far so we'll make a deal —you spare my beard.' And they did, after a big debate. I had to go to Michigan the next week and it was freezing cold."

Fraternity men find themselves confused by changing times. If those masked twenty were laboring under the biblical superstition that when the locks are shorn the strength ebbs they must have been surprised to learn that the strength increased. Or if the assault was a diversionary tactic, an attempt to make the issue the length of their adversary's hair because the real issue was even more intolerable—changing times—one, at least, among them, traced and questioned by a reporter from *The Stanford Daily*, admitted some degree of self-probing: "Harris really showed the Delts a lot of class. He made us feel sorry we did it." It was his way of conceding that the men, bearded or unbearded, elected these days to the presidency of the student body in more universities than a few may be men of courage and conscience.

Students in these changing times are challenging the arbiters of the academy and of the hierarchical regions above and beyond. Within the

*Source:* "The New Student President, David Harris of Stanford," Gina Berriault. Reprinted by permission of the author. First published by *Esquire Magazine*.

past year or so several dignitaries have been met on the campuses by large and vociferous demonstrations. At Stanford, Vice-President Hubert Humphrey, emerging from the auditorium into his protective wedge of police and Secret Service men, ran for his car to escape some thousand angry students; Defense Secretary Robert S. McNamara was forced from his car—a police wagon—and onto the hood of another car by eight hundred Harvard students who wanted to ask him a few questions before he left the campus; while students at Berkeley, some silently, some not, greeted U.N. Ambassador Arthur Goldberg with picket signs and a walkout by five hundred persons when that gentleman came by to pick up an honorary degree. A solid wall of one hundred fifty students blockaded the Chancellor of the University of Wisconsin in his office until he wrote the check that bailed out eighteen students arrested earlier for demonstrating against the campus-recruitment campaign of the Dow Chemical Company, manufacturers of napalm. At the University of Michigan, the Student Council lifted itself right out of the administrative Office of Student Affairs after administrators, during summer vacation when most students were away, handed over to the House Un-American Activities Committee the membership lists of student organizations opposed to the war in Vietnam. And so it follows that the men elected to student office now, at universities around the country, are not keepers of those sacred flames of ritual and protocol and administrative decree.

Columbia's David Langsam, Cornell's David Brandt, Berkeley's Dan McIntosh, Amherst's Steve Cohen, San Francisco State's Jim Nixon, University of Minnesota's Howie Kaibel, University of North Carolina's Robert Powell, University of Houston's Richard Gaghagen, University of Michigan's Ed Robinson range from the "thoughtful middle," as distinguished from the old unthinking middle, to the Far Left, and their force has been felt in everything from the structuring of the new experimental colleges within the universities to the refusal by several university administrations to comply with the ranking mechanisms of Selective Service. And among these leaders, David Harris—the young man tackled by the twenty old guards—is the one most often cited by student editors and other presidents. "He gathers disciples around him wherever he goes," said one disciple, and since he has spoken at so many campuses across the country he has gathered quite a number.

After meeting Harris for the first time at the 1966 National Student Association Congress at the University of Illinois, Neil Reichline, editor of the *U.C.L.A. Daily Bruin*, kept his staff up night after night to discuss Harris' ideas on education, and through the pages of the *Bruin* brought about a great surge of interest in reform. "I was confronted by him and he blew my mind," Reichline recalls. "Dave's views on educational reform, on the Vietnam war, on the draft, are not based on political expediency. They follow naturally from his life-style, his mentality. His concern for his 'soul,' for his values, and for himself as a valuable person are manifested in his concern for the communities that he exists in, whether they are his school, city, or nation. He confronts you with this mentality, this concern for community, and you just can't pass over it without some self-examination, some thought on your role as a human being and how you're going to relate to other human beings. You can't meet Dave Harris and not change your life in some way." Ed Robinson, the president who cut the cord between the student government and the administration at the University of Michigan, describes him this way: "Not only is Harris intelligent, he takes the next step and applies that intelligence to thinking about his surroundings, and then he takes another step and draws some conclusions, and then he takes the farthest step and acts on the basis of those conclusions. In this step-by-step progress we fall down somewhere, most of us." The students are not alone: David Harris was one of several persons invited to participate in a meeting on students and the draft, called by Kingman Brewster, President of Yale. And in the editorial offices of *The Stanford Daily*, a file card, on the wall for months after David's resignation, read: "I don't know what Dave's reasons are for resigning and maybe that's beside the point. His A.S.S.U. administration has taken its toll on him and, I think in the long run beneficially, on official Stanford. But he's been there long enough for all of us to see his real stature, his authentic qualities of greatness. How often do you see a man who, in being himself, can help you be and find yourself; in whom you're able to detect no deviousness at all; whose compassion is no less compassionate for being unsentimental; who cares like hell about the world he lives in and can somehow go on loving and believing in the people who inhabit it, even while he protests the ways we go on lousing it up? For all his sharp, unremitting criticism—in part, of course, because of it— all of us, and all of Stanford, and the whole college and university scene in America are better for having him where he's been." The card was signed B. Davie Napier, Dean of the Chapel and Professor of Religion.

On the front door of the pale-green shingle house in the Negro neighborhood of East Palo Alto hung a penciled sign reading: Go Around to the Back Door. (His study room is in the back of the house, I learned a few minutes later, and if any other tenant of the house had been playing a record loudly, my knock would have gone unheard.) He opened the front door anyway, because two neighbor children, roaming in and out, saw me from an upstairs window as I made my way through the high grass; I heard them calling to him. He is a tall and strong-bodied young man with thick, blond hair, sideburns—the beard is gone, he shaved it off one day for whatever significant or insignificant reason —pale blue eyes, rimless glasses, and a substantial moustache that makes him appear a few years older than his twenty-one. He had interrupted his part-time job at Kepler's bookstore, owned by a prominent pacifist, to meet me. On the bright yellow wall of the living room hung a large photo of Charlie Chaplin with cane and derby, and a restaurant stove took up a good part of the floor space, a relic of the time Harris and the other tenants of the house were implementing plans—failed ones—to open a small café in Palo Alto. The windows of his study looked out on a huge, fallen tree, an old blue bus with flowered curtains, serving as bedrooms for one of the students of that communal house, and more high grass. The two neighbor boys, grammar-school age and loud talkers, gazed in from the hallway until they were asked to close the door. Out in another room a Bob Dylan record began and someone shouted from the kitchen, "The water's boiling!" An old suede jacket, mended carefully in a dozen places, hung from the closet door, boots were strewn on the floor, and a mother cat and four kittens lay atop a soft pile of clothes in a corner of the open closet.

The young man in the sagging, upholstered chair under the small photograph of Gandhi was scheduled to address in four days a massive peace mobilization in San Francisco. A senior, one of five students majoring in Social Thought among thirty in the Honors Program, an independent study program for self-motivated students, he was also teaching a class at the Free University of Palo Alto called "A Life of Peace and Liberation in the U.S." Ashes fell from his cigarette into the crevices of the chair—his fingers are nicotine stained down to the middle knuckles—and as we talked books slid from the chair's wide curved arms. On the windowsill and on the shelf were Nietzsche, Kierkegaard, A. J. Muste, the Upanishad. I asked him about his use of the I Ching, the ancient Chinese Book of Changes.

"We never just open it and read it like a book," he said. "We treat it like a friend around here. We treat it like a living thing." Would he turn to it before his speech? To oblige me he turned to it then, first tossing three Chinese coins onto the rug six times. The result of this encounter with chance led him to the hexagram that in turn directed him to a page of the text:

"The weight of the great is excessive. The load is too heavy for the strength of the supports. . . . It is an exceptional time and situation; Therefore extraordinary measures are demanded. It is necessary to find a way of transition as quickly as possible, and to take action. This promises success. For although the strong element is in excess, it is in the middle, that is, at the center of gravity, so that a revolution is not to be feared. Nothing is to be achieved by forcible measures. The problem must be solved by gentle penetration to the meaning of the situation. . . . Then the changeover to other conditions will be successful. It demands real superiority; therefore the time when the great preponderates is a momentous time."

"It's like taking a sighting off the top of a wave," he explained. "It gives you a sense of the forces of life around you and finds your relationship to those forces for that moment."

His heavy build, Levis and sideburns suggest a farm laborer in the town of Fresno, California, where he grew up, the son of an attorney, and worked in the parking sheds; or they suggest a figure in an old labor photograph of the West, posing by dray horses and by timber. "He used to wear a big buckle on his belt," one of his friends was later to tell me, "and when he spoke he was always shifting it up because his Levis were over-washed and loose. They were washed so much they were faded out to grey." He probably resembles his grandfathers and probably hopes that he does. One was a wood craftsman in Fresno— "I go over to his workshop—he's dead now but his workshop is still there—and pick up scraps of what he'd been doing. I have a goblet he made on a lathe, the walls of the wood are thin as glass—all out of one piece." The other grandfather worked in the open-pit copper mines in Utah. He talks with a fast mixture of beat jargon, academic terms, and words in common usage, and there is an accent that's Southwest, the rural parts.

Up to a few years ago a university for the offspring of California aristocracy, Stanford—its arcaded yellow stone buildings on an almost unbelievable number of acres of thick grass, oaks, and date palms—now has endowment funds sufficient to grant scholarships to the sons and daughters of the less affluent, and Harris is one of these recipients. When he came to Stanford in 1963 he was, according to his own description, an all-American frosh type, a state finalist in competitive speech from Fresno High who made innocuous speeches of no content, and a three-year veteran on the football team. Mississippi hit in that year, and the freshman dormitory at Stanford became a communication center for the South. In the Fall of 1964, in his sophomore year, he went South with a carload of Stanford students. With four others he entered Quitman County, Northwest Mississippi, wilderness territory. Their lives were constantly threatened and one of that group was kidnapped and beaten. "Essentially, when I was in Mississippi it wasn't as big a thing as when I got back, because when I got back I really started thinking about what I'd done there. Mississippi blew my mind. From there I got involved in the whole anti-war activity, from there is was a natural educational progression. The South wasn't just a boil on the face of America. The hate and brutality there were indigenous to the way America lives."

At evening programs on the campus he spoke about Mississippi, he spoke against the draft, against the war in Vietnam, and he criticized the educational system at Stanford. "It's all one thing. Once someone gets involved in Peace there's no turning back from it, it's a style of life, not something considered politics removed from one. It makes dealing with others a very direct expression of one's being." In his junior year he was approached by a group of students to run for president of the student body. He agreed to run in order to force the other candidates to face the issues, but he preferred to lose. He won, in the largest balloting in Stanford's history. "The platform was a long list of changes based on the attitude that Stanford is not educating and has no understanding of what education is. Students have no right of control over their own lives. It's a system calculated on the impotence of the students in that it makes everything the student does something outside himself. What that does is teach people to be powerless. We started from the initial statement that education is something that happens in your mind, the mind learning itself, learning how to use itself. It's a very inner process and the function that teachers traditionally serve in most of the cultures of the world—where they haven't gotten to modern industrial teaching which is essentially a training mechanism—is one of spiritual guidance. Not only should a teacher know things but he should have an understanding, a wisdom about things, beyond simply knowing them. So that a teacher provides himself as a mirror to the other person's mind and gives that person a glimpse into his own mind so he can then start educating himself. That's what education is and it isn't this whole social system at Stanford, the superficialities. They rigidify the students here into cogs for the great American wheel. Most people who teach at colleges are doing it for very simple security reasons and they don't like people to rock the boat even though they make a big thing about intellectual inquiry and all that. A professor will allow you to put down the administration but will get offended if you say the faculty is irrelevant, which they are, by and large, except for maybe ten people, and they're relevant as people because they've developed a style of living that really has relevance to other lives. Then we talked about who runs the universities, that they shouldn't belong to the trustees because they should belong to the people who are really involved in the spiritual process of learning, they should belong to the students and anyone who wants to enter into it." One of the other planks of the platform was the abolition of fraternities. "It's all one thing." Nothing is separable from the rest.

After his election, Harris met for the first time with J. E. Wallace Sterling, President of Stanford. He went into the latter's office with beard, work shirt, Levis, and moccasins. "He has a smooth way of dealing with people," Harris told me. "He never made it clear to me that he might have been dismayed by me."

As president of the student body, Harris led a Stanford delegation to the National Student Association Congress and proposed to the liberal caucus—roughly about one half of the five hundred people there—a resolution calling for immediate withdrawal of U.S. troops from Vietnam. Debate in the caucus lasted until four-thirty in the morning. The resolution failed; the one that passed the caucus and eventually the Congress called for a ceasefire and negotiations, and drew this comment from Harris: "If you come out with this resolution, you will be saying that you feel strongly about the war but you don't want to say it." Another resolution proposed by Harris, calling for abolition of the draft and formation of a draft-resistance movement, was also softened by the liberal caucus and passed by the Congress. After some "soul sessions" a radical caucus was formed and walked out on the liberal caucus. For liberals Harris has no favorable word. "They recite all the American virtues—'We are loyal American citizens who believe in America, La de da de da de da. . . .' They fall on their knees to President Johnson and say, 'Please reconsider, there may be something wrong with the war.' That way of doing things—bribing people, getting to their egos, all kinds of insidious things. What they're doing is further entrenching the whole attitude that brought this war on." On the N.S.A., in particular: "The only time members ever get together is for that Congress where they pass policy declarations and nobody does anything about them. The rest of the time it's run by a kind of oligarchic bureaucracy. Most of the people who go to N.S.A. and involve themselves look upon themselves as future Congressmen and Senators."

At the end of February, 1967, Harris resigned from the presidency of the Stanford student body. "The job had become a trap for my mind," he explained to me. "I'd done my bit for education. I'd given over two hundred speeches at Stanford and was repeating myself. I'd lost real communication with students because they treated me like a famous figure, they'd just sit and watch me do it and weren't putting themselves on the line." Another reason he gave at the time of resignation was: "My contribution has basically been to say things to the community that up to this point the community was afraid to say to itself. I was just a spokesman for a basic way of seeing the university that I felt had to be articulated if there was going to be any healthy notion of education."

I asked him to name the literature that was most meaningful for him. The list was long, including "almost every religious document," among them the Buddhist scriptures, the Bible, Lao-Tzu's *The Way of Life,* Gandhi, Jung, Fromm, Marcuse, Marx, as sociologist rather than economist, Cassirer. Of the novelists—Faulkner, Joyce, Conrad and of the poets—Tagore, Lorca. "They all come closer to understanding man than anyone else, in their own unique fashion." He writes poetry himself and some of it has been used in a poetry class that another of the student-tenants, Bill Shurtleff, teaches in the garage, where he also sleeps. A small volume of the combined poetry of Jeffrey Shurtleff, an honor student in the humanities, and David Harris is being put together within a cover designed for it by the photographers of the group, students Lary Goldsmith and Otto Schatz; the name given this enterprise—The Peace and Liberation Commune Press.

Harris came to his decision about the draft alone. He belongs to no organization, only the one he and some other students at Stanford and Berkeley have founded—the Bay Area Organizing Committee for Draft Resistance. His first step against the draft was his participation in the sit-in in President Sterling's office, protesting Stanford's acceptance of draft tests. "Student deferments are immoral," he said at that time. "They weed out the people who can afford an education." In June, 1966, he sent back his student deferment, intending to apply for a conscientious-objector status, but not on a religious basis. A few months after he gave up his deferment, he made his decision about the draft, alone one summer night in his study. "I was just sitting there when all of a sudden, just out of the back of my mind, came the statement: Well, you're not going to cooperate with them. My first thought about jail really frightened me, I'd never thought about going to jail for a principle against the draft. But from then on I knew what my principle was. I sent them a letter, then, saying I believed myself to be more of a conscientious objector than the law allows because I didn't believe in the law. I said I was going to break that law. The law is immoral and there's no being moral within an immoral law."

Reclassified 1A, Harris took his pre-induction physical in his hometown, Fresno. "I knew I wasn't going to go along with them, but I wanted to see what they did, who went into the Army. I got to the last table and the doctor there said, 'Hey, Mac, this is the guy Harris, he's the guy who's going to refuse.'" Harris was informed by mail that he was fit; a month later he was informed that he was not. The board had changed its mind, classifying him 1Y—temporary physical or psychological disability—until September, 1967, at which time it will reconsider classifying him back to 1A and Harris will fail to honor the directive to appear for another physical. "What I think about Peace in my own mind, how fully I'm understanding it, helps the growth of Peace in the world. In that sense what I'm doing is a very religious thing. I can't go out and talk about Peace if I don't feel in my own mind that I'm living it as fully as I can. So it's simply a question for me of keeping my own sense of integrity, which is what allows me to do all this against the war and against American society as it is now. It's essentially my own feeling of integrity. I think that any movement is better for the fact that the people in it are following their highest understanding, and if that means going to jail . . . I feel that I couldn't talk about the draft if I wasn't out in a position facing jail. We have an obligation to speak to the people of the United States, and the act of going to prison is itself a statement and a much more powerful one to the American consciousness than taking a C.O. or going to Canada. I have a basic hang-up about being run out of any place. I was run out of too many places in Mississippi."

I asked him if he had his speech prepared for the mobilization on Saturday. He said that he never prepared speeches. "I don't speak about anything that has no relevance to my life. I usually meditate before I speak. You get your mind down to a single point, a pinpoint, and when you reach the pinpoint you go through and come out clean, everything starts opening up and filling out, a fresh vision of everything. In speaking, I try to get to that pinpoint and then I get up and speak. Two years ago meditation was far from my life. I developed it from more and more contact with Eastern thinking, Eastern music. They have a whole different rhythm to their thinking, a much slower, a more cyclical kind of rhythm, and my life just started getting into that kind of rhythm. I'm calmer now, I used to get frenzied. Everything that happens isn't earth-shaking. It's like a quantum jump, you break through into a new world. I think there's a danger, though, in the American, the Western, reaction to Eastern thinking. They try to make themselves Easterners, which to my mind is illegitimate. You can't run around being an Indian if you're an American, you're not part of that culture. You go to the Haight-Ashbury, it's all very speeded up, very hectic, which is the exact opposite of what I associate with Eastern thinking. I'm not saying you can't learn from it, but what they take is the rote form and they think they've reached Eastern thought when all they've got are the cultural mechanisms. American society understands life in terms of fetishes and can only understand the spirit as a fetish. The people of Haight-Ashbury should ask themselves how much of what they're doing is fetish ridden. Then the culture there is organized around drugs and I think drugs are not a spiritual vortex. There's a great danger in their seeing things in terms of drugs. Love exists regardless of acid. Drugs can be useful but the nature of that activity is a minimal one. Acid stands knee-high to Peace. The son of a British Prime Minister—about a month before he died of an overdose of heroin he was talking to some friends about shooting smack and he said, 'At Cambridge everything is just around the corner. But when you go into your room and tie-off and shoot-up, everything is right there in your lap.' The real problem is how can you make a culture that's right there in someone's lap."

He talked about the war in Vietnam: "Johnson is having a hard time holding the whole thing together. I think his next move is a big escalation, invade Laos and Thailand and Cambodia and North Vietnam, and to do that he's going to have to double his manpower there and that's when the big climax is going to come, because all those people who are on student deferments are going to get called. If they escalate, there's not going to be a student deferment for anybody except engineers and medical students, and all those people in school now are going to be faced with that question by next year. He's going to try doing it first without being repressive, then he's going to get this opposition from the youth and he'll try to clamp down. The chances of anybody saying the kind of things we're saying now in a year—they'll harass you and bust you. That is, if you start getting people, and it's clear we're starting to get people."

He is positive their phone is tapped. "I know from Mississippi how it sounds, anything can foul up your phone when they put a tap in. In Mississippi we could hear the sheriff moving around in his office. I don't know who they're tapping for—one of the guys who lives here was subpoenaed by H.U.A.C. last summer in Washington for organizing that Stanford blood drive for the North Vietnamese civilians and I'm doing my Peace thing. They interrogated me when I came back from Mississippi because I was saying things about an agent back there who called me a nigger lover. They're meticulous. Every time we have a rally at Stanford there's always an F.B.I. agent there with his camera, with telescopic lens, taking pictures of everybody."

On Saturday morning, April 15, the marchers gathered at the foot of Market Street, filling up all the side streets for blocks, and when I found David Harris he was with his friends from Stanford and Berkeley, handing out, each from an armload, the Draft Resistance Committee's "We Refuse to Serve" declarations. By the time the students, numbering one-half to two-thirds of the 65,000 marchers, got started, the head of the procession had already reached Kezar Stadium, four miles away. Long hair and beards, if not the rule, were common in that massive contingent, along with fringed buckskin boots and the heavy kind, sheepskin vests, massed strings of beads. The placard, AMERICA, GO BACK, YOU'RE GOING THE WRONG WAY, may have verbalized one meaning, at least, of the costumes: they were out of the West of the last century of a time before this country went that wrong way—if any reckoning can be made of the time when any country took that turn—and the new frontier these students were advocating was way out beyond the one the late President gave that name to. The rest of the world was no territory for a General by the Dr. Strangelove name of West! More Land! but a great frontier for the spirit. The fragrance of incense sticks drifted through the air that was sometimes misty, sometimes clear and warm, and the Eye of God, the diamond-shaped colored-yarn symbol the Mexican Indians carry through their fields, was carried here down the main street. I saw Harris first on one corner, then another as he moved along between the students and the spectators. He was usually findable, being taller than most, but sometimes obscured by the placards and banners.

From a high-sided truck, Country Joe and the Fish, with beards, sheepskin vests, shoulder-length hair, a fur cap on one, and green peace signs painted on their cheeks, rolled out a tremendous rock dirge that set an hypnotic, solemn pace for the mass of students and resounded against the grey facades down the side streets and up Market Street and against the nudie movie where life-size cutouts of a soldier and marine were up on the marquee along with, "This is U.S. Servicemen Appreciation Week," and where *A Good Time with a Bad Girl* was showing. Further along the way, out near the stadium, musical accompaniment was furnished by three young men beating pots and pans up on a sixth floor balcony and by a Bob Dylan record blaring full volume out of wide-open apartment windows where two elderly women sat with their elbows on the sills, and by a girl serenely sitting on a concrete wall and singing in a high, clear voice "Krishna . . . Hari."

By the time Harris reached the stadium most of the marchers were already in the bleachers and the speakers assembled on the platform out in the center of the green oval field. With him up there were Mrs. Martin Luther King, Julian Bond, the Georgia legislator, Robert Vaughn, the Man from U.N.C.L.E., Judy Collins, several clergymen, others. He was the only one in Levis and Levi jacket. He spoke very little to those on either side of him, then not at all as he began his meditation. While the others rose and spoke to the filled stadium, their voices blaring out in several directions through the clusters of red loudspeakers on the field, I saw him bend his head to his knees for a time. When I looked again he was sitting upright, his legs crossed, and one foot shaking restlessly.

Country Joe and the Fish, out of their truck and down on the track, struck up with electric organ, guitars, and voice their *I-Feel-Like-I'm-Fixin'-to-Die Rag*, familiar to students since the early Vietnam march in Berkeley in 1965 that was halted at the Oakland border by a line of helmeted police. On the track before them a crowd gathered and couples danced to that ragtime mockery of wartime acquiescence.

> Come on all of you big strong men:
> Uncle Sam needs your help again,
> He's got himself in a terrible jam:
> Way down yonder in Vietnam.
> So put down your books and pick up a gun:
> We're gonna have a whole lot'a fun.
> 'Cause it's one, two, three. "What are we fightin' for?"
> "Don't ask me I don't give a damn";
> Next Stop is Vietnam
> And it's five, six, seven, open up the pearly gates
> There ain't no time to wonder why.
> Whoopie! We're all gonna die!

Just before Harris began to speak, down across the field and into the parking lot out of sight behind the stadium wall drifted a black-clad parachutist from an unseen source, his white and black and yellow chute inscribed with the word LOVE.

Harris loomed over the microphone, his face and voice impassioned: "We have to realize we're mistaken if we call this war Johnson's war or if we call this war the Congress' war. This war is a logical extension of the way America has chosen to live in the world. This war is the logical end of the American system that we've built, and I think that as young people facing that war, as young people who are being confronted with the choice of being in that war or not, we have an obligation to speak to this country, and that statement has to be made in this way: That this war will not be made in our names, that this war will not be made with our hands, that the prisons of the United States will be full of young people who will not honor the orders of murder. . . ."

When he had finished his speech he strode out across the green field to an exit, like a man with no time to lose.

## 23. KING OF THE STATUS DROPOUTS

### Tom Wolfe

*Tom Wolfe, author of* The Kandy-Kolored Tangerine-Flake Stream-
line Baby, The Electric Kool-Aid Acid Test, *and other books, offers
here considerable insight, not only into the appearance and behavior of a major figure in American popular culture but also into the
meaning of his impact on the American scene.*

Thirty-nine years old! A recluse! Bonafide! Doesn't go out, doesn't see
the light of day, doesn't put his hide out in God's own unconditioned
Chicago air for months on end; *years.* Right this minute, one supposes, he
is somewhere there in the innards of those forty-eight rooms, under
layers and layers of white wall-to-wall, crimson wall-to-wall, Count
Basie-lounge leather, muffled, baffled, swaddled, shrouded, closed in,
blacked out, shielded by curtains, drapes, wall-to-wall, blond wood,
screens, cords, doors, buzzers, dials, Nubians—he's down in there, the
living Hugh Hefner, 150 pounds, like the tender-tympany green heart of
an artichoke.

He is revolving counterclockwise on his bed. The bed is round and
has a motor in it like a turntable. His head is . . . floating to the left. His
own TV camera is in there in the bedroom, right nearby, not a TV set,
a *camera,* putting . . . God knows what on videotape.

Look, Hef, while I've got you—*While I've got you?* This dapper little
fellow, Lee Gottlieb, of Playboy, Inc., and some other fellow with a very
wide nutty-looking Big Lunch tie on have made their way into the
innards of Hefner's mansion, to the edge of Hefner's bed, in fact, but
they haven't *got* Hugh Hefner. Nobody's *got* Hugh Hefner, Hefner is at
the center of the world. He is deep down inside his house—at the center
of his bed. The center of the world!

Gottlieb and the man in the Big Lunch tie are right there, holding
attaché cases, folders, notebooks, very much the businessmen here at
eleven o'clock, standing up in the white wall-to-wall by the bed. Boy,
that is a bed and a half. It is round, a circle, $7\frac{1}{2}$ feet across, the biggest
roundest bed in the history of the world, fitting into a bank of curving
cabinets, and Hefner is at the controls. Dials in the headboard!

His knees are in the middle of the bed, dug down into the salmon

*Source:* "King of the Status Dropouts," reprinted with the permission of Farrar,
Straus and Giroux, Inc., from *The Pump House Gang* by Tom Wolfe. Copyright ©
1966 by The World Journal Tribune Corp.; copyright © 1964, 1965, 1966 by The
New York Herald Tribune, Inc.

percales. His hands are on the dials in the headboard and his back is bent over like a wire with a silk saffron bathrobe over it. Hefner is dressed for the day in his pajamas, bathrobe and slippers. Well, now—he is the creator of the $48-million-a-year *Playboy* magazine and club empire. Considering all that, he looks—well, kind of thin and pale; etiolate. But so what? Never mind the old idea of the *Playboy* world as a lot of girls from Akron with their gouda goodies lying all over a polar bear rug in front of the hearth. The whole thing is . . . the dials!

Hefner is thin and pale, but he has energy—his hands go after the dials. God, will he stop for just one second? Look, Hef—

Hefner pulls open a black leather headrest in the headboard, it opens on a hinge, revealing a panel of dials, and his hands are on the controls. Just—

> . . . a . . .
>> . . . little . . .
>>> . . . twist . . .
>>>> . . . here . . .

—a motor starts. The whole bed, the whole 7½-foot bed, starts going around like a phonograph. An efficient little turntable down under there somewhere is going

> . . . irr . . .        . . . irr . . .        . . . irr . . .

The whole thing starts revolving with Hefner in the middle on all fours. Suddenly he snaps upright. Heeee! He grins, his mouth pulls up into his head about three inches, his cheeks fold in, his high cheekbones slide out, his eyes turn on like a pair of pencil flashlights. He says,

"It goes 33⅓, 45 and 78!"

Gottlieb and Big Lunch stand there. Hefner's head is floating over this way.

"This changes the whole room!" Hefner says, on the way around. "It makes it three different rooms! It changes your entire field of vision, so that you—This is the hi-fi area!"

Hefner's head, his wiry back, his saffron bathrobe, float past the hi-fi area. His eyes burn like two gas-range pilot lights on top of his cheekbones. Hefner turns on with the most unselfconscious, hot-nerves enthusiasm, smiling, laughing, running over the top of his own words, batting around nervously—*This is the hi-fi area.* Damned right it is; such nice smooth, thick low cabinets, one can stand there and just look and almost feel how smooth, how thick, what a gleaming galaxy of speakers, tubes, rheenters, wheepers, flottees and . . . dials must be behind the panel doors.

Hefner's thin jaws open, heading counterclockwise at two miles an hour: "This is the—living area—" he gestures toward the hearth and fireplace, nicely sculptured and garlanded and so forth—"this can be great some afternoon, you know, the fireplace—there are some *damned romantic* afternoons in here, I'll tell you!"

. . . irr . . .

. . . irr . . .

. . . irr . . .

"This is the conversation area—"

*Conversation area.* Over here, not 10 feet away from the bed, is a TV camera, not a set but a camera, a big gleaming Ampex television camera, for instantaneous transmission into a TV screen set into the wall there, or for videotapes of . . . God knows what.

Big Lunch says, "What's that for?"

"I have a whole $40,000 Ampex videotaping console," says Hefner, "so I figured I might as well have the camera, too. It would be like having a tape recorder and no microphone."

"But why is it in the bedroom?"

"Well—" Hefner smiles, his cheekbones come out, his eyes turn on— "Who knows when something *very beautiful* might happen in this bedroom!"

Gawdam, it's going to crash, the bed, it's going to crash into a Nasal Mist Helmet. The Nasal Mist Helmet is like a clear fiberglass space helmet. One puts it on over the head to combat head colds. A part of the helmet, the straps or something, is hanging over the edge of the cabinets that inclose the bed, and the headboard is about to hit that and the hi-fi muffler earphones and, damn, all this other apparatus up there. But Hefner is a quick fellow, like a hot wire, a lot of energy! His body snaps back, he is on all fours again, he catches the helmet in one hand, the earphones in the other. The bed comes to a stop with Hefner on all fours, like a scrambling going on.

Big Lunch Tie is saying to Gottlieb, "Listen, I'm sorry you have to stay out here this late on my account."

"No," says Gottlieb, "I wanted to come out here anyway. I've got some things I want to ask Hef about. Since he never comes to the office anymore—you know, you have to get in here to see him when you can."

Hefner has his arms full of apparatus, wires, fiberglass, tubes, and looks over his shoulder at Gottlieb. Gottlieb brightens.

"I was just telling him, Hef," he says, "I have to catch you in here when I can!"

"You don't go to the office at all?" says Big Lunch.

"I don't go out of the *house* at all!" Hefner says. A very enthusiastic fellow! His eyes go up to about 150 watts and he watches to see if all this is registering. "I'm a contemporary recluse! When was the last time I left this house, Lee? Three and a half months ago?"

"Um, there was Tony Bennett."

"That's right," says Hefner, "I went to Soldier Field to see Tony Bennett. I went to see Frank Sinatra, too. They're friends of mine, and that was the only way I was going to be able to see them. But generally— before that I must not have been out of here for three and a half months; I don't know, the last time was—I flew somewhere. Where was it I flew, Lee?"

"Los Angeles, Hef. About the only time Hef sees Chicago is when he's riding to the airport to go somewhere else!"

Hefner sits on the edge of the bed. Nice platinum-hazy light shines down from recessed rheostat dim-dim lovelies in the ceiling. His bathrobe collapses in nice highlife folds.

"How many times have I been out of this house in the last two years?" he says. He leans over and puts his head down practically between his knees. A wiry guy! "About nine times," he says, answering himself. Then—

*—heeewack—*

—he snaps upright, he pulls that great angular smile into his face, his cheekbones move out.

"But I don't need to leave here. Why should I? I've got more right here now inside this house than most people ever find in a lifetime!"

—his eyes turn on—old shining Ampex moon—"I've got everything I want right here. This place is run like a hotel. I mean, I'll take you down and show—No, it isn't! Hotels shut off about two o'clock in the morning, you want to get something—This place is run like a hotel ought to be run. It goes 24 hours a day. There's a full kitchen staff 24 hours a day, a chef, anytime I wake up, I can get anything I want. I've got a staff of 25 people here on a 24-hour schedule. I've got an Ampex engineer on the staff! That's right! There's so much equipment in here, I had to have a—this must be the only house in the country with an Ampex engineer on the staff! I sent him to the Ampex school in San Francisco. He's on 24-hour call."

He stares at the "hi-fi area" and glances at the TV camera. Then he stands up and stretches. Big Lunch's mouth opens, he's cranking up a question. Hefner leans forward and puts his head down, to concentrate.

"When did this all start?" says Big Lunch.

*—heewack—*

*—lights—*

—Hefner snaps upright and starts explaining, "Well, it got to the point where I was practically working around the clock over there at the office.

I was doing nothing but working over there, eating, sleeping, getting up again, and working some more, so I decided, why not, I'd move the whole operation to the house and enjoy life.

"This operation is so personalized," says Hefner, "people are always trying to reach me, for everything. This way I can cope with that. I don't take calls anymore, I just return them. I don't have any In boxes and Out boxes. I don't have to arrange my life by other people's *hours*. I don't always have to be in some boring conference. I don't have to go through business lunches and a lot of formalities. I don't even shave if I don't feel like it. I don't have to get dressed. I don't have to put on a shirt and a tie and a suit every day. I just put on a *bathrobe!*"

Hefner smiles. Then he dims down his eyes.

"You know," he says, "people get the idea I'm a Barnum or something, putting on a show. People come by here, and you can tell—they want to find a flaw in it all. They want to think I can't be happy. They want to think it's got to be a lousy, unprofitable life I'm leading. Well, I can tell you something. It's a *damned full life!*"

"Do you get any new clothes, suits and things?"

"No, it's a funny thing"—Hefner's mouth pulls back up into his lit-up smile—"I don't seem to wear out many suits this way. You know! But it is rough on bathrobes. This must be about the third one since—"

One can imagine Hefner's tailor in there with the old measuring tape running down Hefner's wiry spine with his old stubby left thumb on the nape of Hefner's neck with the curly sprouts of Hefner's hair, where it's long in back, curling over the knuckle—making another bathrobe, a bathrobe, not a suit. Lollygag Heaven!

But who in New York will get all this? The idea of the high life in New York, when one owns a $48-million-a-year business, the idea is the old idea of *being seen*. There is always something like Monday night, the social night, at the Metropolitan Opera. Some five-foot-four chauffeur from Queens opens up the Cadillac door, and out comes Mr. Wonderful's patent-leather right pump with the grosgrain bow on it and his knuckly atrophied little right ankle. Then *she* emerges, all gold-thread slipper and alabaster and Chanel, careful, don't let that little weighted canvas Chanel hem ride up and show all that bad stuff just above the back of the knee where the colloidal tissue has dried up like old mutton, and then the swaddled little bellies and the hunkering little shoulders, and everybody at the entrance looks to see whose heads will be stuck on top of these grand stalks. It's the . . . Trailer Truck King! the Jake Seat King! the publisher's skull-faced son! it's Lennie the B! it's Jason the Mason! it's Rudy! Wendy! Jackie! Kitty! Kiki!—*seen* again, on *top* still, still winning the competition.

New York keeps trying to hang onto this, the old feudal, patrimonial idea of status hierarchies, the being seen, meeting the right people and all of that. Practically nobody here realizes what is going on out there—God, they know the term, *out there*, the English say the same thing here, *out here* they say when they get to New York—what is going on out there in Chicago, in Columbus, Ohio; in Houston, Los Angeles, San Francisco. They're all out there, with Hugh Hefner at the very forefront, living the new life style: contemporary recluse.

The New York style, this whole business, of asserting superiority, observing esoteric status lines, making symbolic gestures of rank, of living with snobbery, if one will—all this has rather acutely embarrassed large masses of Americans who have become well-to-do since World War II.

Either they are middling people making a good living in bureaucracies, usually private bureaucracies, Massachusetts Mutual, Monsanto, Union Carbide, Metropolitan Life, any of tens of thousands of firms. Or else they are the new working class, men who have "working class" jobs so far as status goes but middle-class incomes, boilermakers making $15,000 or better a year, people like that.

In either case, these people have the money to make it in the old status competition. They have all the objects it used to take to make it socially, grand-looking homes, cars, big lawns, well-dressed children, rugs in every room. They can *afford* parties, evenings out, big weekends, status striving in all its forms—but they don't have the talent and the inclination for it. They're not up to the effort of competing socially in the old terms. They feel uncomfortable with the old status system, inherited from Europe. It makes one feel not snobbish, but curiously insecure, to try to assert one's status, even in petty matters like tipping in restaurants. Some crewcut Million Dollar Club life insurance salesman is in a coffee shop with the wife, the bill comes and—damn! he knew it! he doesn't have the right change to leave a tip and he'll have to go up to the cash register and pay the bill and get change and come back and leave the tip. But if they leave the table, the waiter, such a dour unforgiving-look dark little man with no teeth on top—he'll think they're going off without leaving any tip. So he starts up toward the cash register, and his wife gets up to follow, and he wheels around and starts jabbing toward her with his finger: Get back there! Get back there to the table! and so she heads back there and sits down, my poor fumbling hubby, he has left her there as a tip hostage for the Waiter King—

They are the new middle class with few of the old Babbitt status drives; a *lumpen* middle class. All these people might have had no choice. They have been stuck with the old European status system, the way their forebears always had been. But then—beautiful, bounteous, glorious war! —World War II started off a chain of good times and advances in electronic technology that is now enabling millions to live the full life as status dropouts: dropping out of conventional status competition in order to start their own league—in the privacy of the home, as it were.

The new lumpen middle class is gloriously bored with the old idea of *going out* and enriching one's life vicariously with spectacles, with concerts, plays, stage shows, speeches, lodge meetings, hustings, debates, prize fights, balls, luncheons and so on. And they have found a way to avoid *going out* and going through a lot of the old status tests involving face-to-face meetings with Mr. So-and-so on the street, admission to this or that club, sitting here or there in whatever restaurant it is, patronizing this or that shop.

The new status dropouts can pull it off precisely because twentieth-century technologies have made it possible for them to lead a full life—a *damned full life* here!—without *going out* amongst the community. Notably, the automobile, the telephone, the radio, television and all the electronic wonders of the new home.

They can turn their own households into the *stage*, only a stage this time with themselves at the center of it, isolated, insulated within discreet and rather marvelous electronic worlds. When it *does* come to going out, the lumpen middle class finds it intensely more pleasurable, more of a treat, to go to an auto show or a hi-fi show or to simply browse about in department store furniture sections or discount bazaars. These are spectacles—but spectacles in which you get in there and vicariously put all these great objects around yourself at your own homestead, and the hell with those tired old pretentious spectacles that Beckett, Arthur Miller or even Otto Preminger still put on. What the hell are they all about? As the movie industry itself knows quite well, only children, people 25 and under, *go out* to the movies anymore.

Only one man, at least, in exemplary fashion, has lived out the new style for all to see, the king of the status dropouts, exactly! Hugh Hefner.

Hefner has had the publicity and financial success to compete for status at the highest level. And yet the whole thing has been somehow *infra dig* by orthodox, European-style, Eastern status standards. First of all, Hefner is completely Midwestern. He was born in a God-fearing but socially only fair-to-middling family in Chicago. He went to the University of Illinois. His first and only marriage—he was separated in 1954, divorced in 1959—was not "social." But, mainly the source of his money has always carried a taint in traditional status terms: *Playboy*, a "skin magazine," as they say at Yale, and the Playboy Clubs, "those Bunny houses."

Worse still, he accomplished it all in Chicago, if one can imagine that. And even Chicago has been a little frosty about it. The Chicago *Daily News* recently published a list called "The 62 Best People in Chicago." This amounted to a status roster based not only on ancestry and corporate rank but on recent accomplishment. Almost anyone of any prominence in Chicago made it, but Hugh Hefner did not, despite the fact that he is perhaps the most successful entrepreneur Chicago has had since 1945 and certainly the best known.

Hefner has been the most successful new magazine publisher since World War II. He started out with $600 of his own money and $2,000 he borrowed and now has a business that grosses $48 million a year. *Playboy* magazine's circulation keeps on going up, from 742,000 in 1956 to 1,117,000 in 1960 to 1,877,000 in 1963 to almost 4,500,000 currently. Three-fourths of it is newsstand sales, which is the most profitable kind of circulation to have. Convincing people to subscribe and then mailing the magazines out to subscribers is expensive. *Playboy* sells for 75 cents a copy and does something no other slick magazine can manage; namely, it turns a profit on newsstand income all by itself. Hefner claims that all the advertising revenue is gravy, pure profit, and it is prodigious, up from $8 million in 1964 to an estimated $17 million for 1966.

Hefner opened the first Playboy Club in Chicago in 1960. Today, when Playboy people go abroad, they speak of it as World Headquarters. By 1963 Hefner had founded seven clubs and the membership was about 250,000. Today he has 17 clubs with more than 600,000 members. There are two full-scale foreign Playboy clubs, one in Jamaica and one, with gambling, on Park Lane in London. He has also taken over one of Chicago's most famous skyscrapers, the Palmolive Building—without even leaving The House to look at it—with a 63-year, $2.7 million leasehold and converted it into The Playboy Building. There, every night, the old Palmolive Beacon, previously the Lindbergh beacon, revolves on top with a searchlight jet pilots can see 500 miles away.

Hugh Hefner is not "best people," however. By the old status standards he still doesn't rank, and he seems to sense it.

Hefner has had little taste for New York-style status competition or even the rabbity reflection of New York-style that goes on in Hollywood. For one thing, Hefner's *clothes* have never fit really well. His dinner jackets have been a little horse-collary and everything. Hefner has an apartment in New York—and has been in it twice. He also has an apartment in the making, in Los Angeles, with walls that revolve, converting rooms from libraries into bars into swimming pools into sauna baths, or something of the sort—but already that is . . . more like it.

Hefner's genius has been to drop out of the orthodox status competition and to use money and technology and to convert his habitat into a stage and to get on the stage, not in the spectator seats, and to be the undisputed hero himself. Through the more and more sophisticated use of machines, Hefner, and to a lesser degree millions of . . . *homemakers* outside of New York, have turned their homes into wonderlands, almost complete status spheres all their own. Certain basic technologies, the car, the telephone, television, radio, have enabled them to keep in touch with the basic realities of the . . . *outside world*, such as making a living, keeping in touch and so forth.

In or out of Chicago, of course, people can hardly think of Hefner without a picture of all those buttery-cheeked girls with their goudas protruding, the Playmates of the Month, folding out like hometown odalisques, and, more recently, movie stars, Carol Baker, Carol Lynley, Ursula Andress, Elke Sommer, with their real Movie Star mary poppins, their natural born aureolae, their *nature*, right there in rougey color in *Playboy*. Or, in the Playboy Clubs, the Bunnies, in satin Victorian corsets with *their* mammiforms floating in iron cups, melting vanilla custard, and their gouda buttocks décolletage squeezed out behind.

To account for Hefner's astonishing success—well, the *Playboy* aura of sex, by itself, is not enough. One must add another picture that has been shown often enough in *Playboy*—a large, *secure* bed, settled in a windowless corner, with smooth mellow walls, in a heavy wooden frame, low, smooth, modern—surrounded by smooth mellow-wood cabinets, with sliding panels that slide back to reveal *dials*. No girls anywhere in the picture! Just paradise; a bed, a fortress of smooth wood, windowless walls, and dials.

What Hefner has been offering is not merely a fantasy of some kind of potentate's serving of sex but also a fantasy of a potentate's control of the environment—all of a sudden made plausible by the new lumpen middle-class style of life. *Playboy* is running a series of picture features called "*Playboy* Pads." It shows the living quarters, apartments chiefly, of *Playboy* readers that measure up, in some degree, to the ideal environment *Playboy* is promoting. All of them are lesser versions of Hefner's own forty-eight-room dream-house—they have the same smooth, thick modernity, the wall-to-wall, the smooth thick cabinets, the rheostat lights, spiral staircases, and . . . the *dials*, the hi-fi, the projectors, the TV set into the wall. The décor, this ideal *Playboy* décor, is really a throwback to that vague concept known as 1930s or *Moderne* modern. It was an interim style whose smooth, thick surfaces finished off the old aristocratic style with its antique flutings, moldings and crested devices, redolent of feudal status competition. Yet it came before Modernity itself developed into a new kind of elite status competition with such delicate, esoteric stuff as Corbu chairs, Mies coffee tables, Paul Rudolph stairways, white walls, and wan waxy green interior-decorator plants.

Hefner moved into his mansion in 1960. The mansion or The House, as people in the Playboy organization usually call it, is at 1340 North State Parkway.

Inside, in the afternoon, *he* is asleep. Hefner's geographic position, whether he's horizontal, on his feet, sitting down, is a major piece of information, inside the House and at the *Playboy* office. He just got up, he just went to bed, he is in there working on The Philosophy—but Hefner does these things at unusual hours, which is to say, whenever he feels like it. He just went to bed; at 2:30 in the afternoon. He just got up; at 11 p.m. He is asleep; and one can sit underneath the fluorescent lights, over a gray metal desk, at the *Playboy* office over on East Ohio Street and imagine *him* with his head mashed down in the downy percale with his eyes closed and one arm writhed up under his cheek. He is working on the Playboy Philosophy while one is brushing one's teeth and watching the wispy red tide from the gums.

The official explanation of Hefner's long day-into-night night-into-day sessions in The House is that he is in there working incessantly on The Philosophy. And it is true that Hefner does devote enormous energy to this apparently endless project. The Philosophy is a solemn dissertation by Hefner on the absurdity of Victorian sex codes in the modern world. To the Eastern intellectuals, at any rate, the whole thing seems like a naïve and tedious set-to with a colossus that somebody or other must have killed off about 40 years ago. Nevertheless, Hefner has taken it through 23 installments in *Playboy* and figures he is only half through. It continues to draw a heavy mail response, much of it favorable comments—apostate thrill!—by ministers. The white wall-to-wall in the living room of Hefner's bedroom suite is covered with great hummocks of research material, marked "Sodomy," "Homosexuality," "Adultery" and so forth. He clodhops through it all and works away on a streamlined typewriter, sitting there in his pajamas and bathrobe. Actually, The Philosophy seems to be a rather conventional status performance by Hefner. The Philosophy imputes deep moral purpose to his enterprises, legitimizes them, in Weberian terms, just as the libraries helped Andrew Carnegie feel better about the whole thing. But so what? Just inches away, at all times, are the dials and the wonders of The House.

There is always a guide in The House, such as Michele, the dark-haired *dame d'honneur*, and the Nubians. Hefner has a staff of Negro servants in black-and-white livery, all tall, powerful-looking, wide in the shoulders, narrow in the waist, with close-cropped hair, all standing by straight, silent, all these silent Nubian powerhouses standing around there.

The guide, whoever, goes on about the sweet, modern up-to-date *venery* of the establishment. There are rooms and dormitories high up in The House on the top two floors where about 30 Bunnies from the Chicago Playboy Club live. Alex and Sandra or Carl and Deborah—a significant look here—they are unmarried—some such couple is currently staying up there somewhere. And the parties here—well, if a boy and girl hit it off and what they want to do is go off hand-in-hand and climb the great stairs, well nobody *says* anything, or they might say something, but nobody cares. Or when couples are in swimming—and here Michele has but to beckon, and a great silent Nubian comes over, bends at the waist, out from his white cuff comes a big black thongy hand and wrist and he pulls up a trap door in the floor of the main party room, the great hall, and one looks down into the Woo Grotto, a section of the swimming pool on the level below, a secluded pool in which *concupiscent* young bubbas can swim in the warm honey chlorine.

⸱And yet none of the sweet warm honey venery of The House can quite compare with the true motif of The House—namely, the apparatus, the *dials*, the glorious controlled environment. Somehow just having silent Nubians reaching down with a belt of thongy wrist and starched cuff to open trap doors looking down into pools—that is the motif of The House.

Look, Hef, while I've got you—

Gottlieb has a few things he would like to go over with Hef. Big Lunch keeps cutting his eyes over at the TV camera Hefner has here in the corner near the big-boy round bed. Hefner is on his feet with his velvet slippers nestled in the wall-to-wall. He is lively, full of juice. His body snaps around a little.

Hefner suddenly propels himself toward the doorway, looking back for a moment and grinning. He comes back in a moment with a bottle of Pepsi-Cola in his hand. He tilts it up and down the gullet. Hefner always has a couple of Pepsi-Colas when he gets up. He drinks about twelve a day.

Hef—in a James Bond world. The contemporary recluse—the Consumer King! Hef—at the center of the world, amid the dials. And one can almost see the ultimate—appealing!—the Consumer King, his smile pulled on, his eyes lit up, his head back, sinking back into the middle of the biggest, roundest bed in the history of the world, reaching his hands back

... just a bit, to the dials, and then—

          ... irr ...    ... irr ...    ... irr ...

—that great bed starts turning, into an orbit of its own, with the Ampex videotape on right there, coming over the screen, a videotape of a *very beautiful* thing that happened right there in that room, at the center of the world, the perfect moment, renewed with every revolution of the bed, every revolution of a ... *controlled* universe, with one's own self as king, dropped, not *out*, but *in*, to the perfect rotation, around and around, in ever-decreasing concentric circles, toward ... nirvana, *ambrosia*, while, following one's own perfect orbit, out there, for all to see, is the ... *Playboy beacon!*—up on top of the yes! Playboy Building, sweeping the heavens of America with the two-billion-candlepower beam of American Hefnerism and the perfect ... irr ... irr ... irr ...

## 24. THE DEVIL'S THUMB

### Peter L. Sandberg

*A teacher of writing at Northeastern University, Peter L. Sandberg edited the city magazine in Phoenix, Arizona before moving east in 1966. His work has appeared in* The Literary Review, Saturday Review, Playboy, *and other publications. He was once active in mountaineering, and many of his stories deal with that sport, including the one reprinted here.*

Past midnight, Meyer woke again to the noise of the bat-like birds that shot past the narrow ledge, their high-pitched sounds like rushing pinwheels. He had fallen forward in the ropes that held him in a seated position so that his upper body now hung over the ledge, and when he opened his eyes he saw the desert floor 800 feet below him and the orange smudges that were the spectators' fires. Across the desert, the moon lay its imperfect light on the dark basalt mountains to the east, and the night sky was light and marked with gauzy streaks of cloud.

Meyer eased himself back until all his weight was on the ledge, his back resting on the wall of rock behind him. He saw that Devar had not moved. The older man sat five feet away, tied in to the same narrow ledge, his back straight and stiff against the wall, his eyes open, his teeth clamped tightly on the stem of his unlit pipe. Meyer could smell the whiskey, and in Devar's gaunt face, in the arched bone of his nose and white unblinking eyes, he saw again the signs of sorrow and what he thought now was some kind of madness.

"We can climb soon," he said.

The older man nodded, but did not answer.

"I wish we could start now," Meyer said. "I feel good; I've slept enough."

The birds rushed by again and a gust of wind brightened the fires far below the ledge. Meyer guessed there were a hundred people down there, asleep in their trucks and tents. They had come to see Devar climb the Devil's Thumb which, if he made it, would be one of the really great climbs of his long career. They had not come to see Meyer who was young and not yet well known; but he knew he could climb well and he wished more than anything that just once Devar would give him the lead.

*Source:* "The Devil's Thumb," Peter L. Sandberg. Reprinted by permission of the author.

He glanced to his left and saw the older man, his mournful and whiskered face bold in the half light of the moon. Funny duck that Devar. He climbed well enough, but he had brought more whiskey than water and he never talked. The tremendous enthusiasm Meyer had felt when Devar had written him and asked him to second this climb had long since faded to disappointment. Meyer knew what a hero should be, and the old man did not measure up. He had no idea how Devar had chosen him from all the promising young climbers in Colorado, but he already wished it had not happened. There was no excitement in following in the wake of this unapproachable veteran.

It was their third night on the Thumb, and in three days climbing from dawn until dusk they had made 800 feet. Above, the pinnacle rose 300 feet more. It was the highest unclimbed tower left in the southwest and of the many climbers who had tried to make the first ascent only two others had gone higher than this, and they had fallen to death from the Finger Traverse which crossed the rock 100 feet above Meyer's head. He squinted down and saw moonlight reflected from the quilted panels of a camper truck far below him, its dimensions toylike in the distance. The birds shot by the ledge and the wind moved Devar's parka, making it flap like a window shade on a breezy summer night. Before long, the sun would begin to rise and the two men would resume the climb. Meyer thought of this impatiently and made up dreams of what he would do if Devar gave up the lead. Before many minutes passed, he had fallen against the ropes asleep.

Three hours later, when it was still night, the older man shook him awake. He had set their breakfast between them on the ledge, pemmicum and jerky, a mix of brown sugar and raisins, and one of the pint-sized flasks of water. They ate in silence, Meyer eating rapidly, eager to be finished, Devar eating slowly, as if by habit. When they were done, Meyer stuffed the empty flask and the plastic bags that had held the food into a crack at the seam where the ledge met the wall. He then filled a small climbing pack with food, water, and a first aid kit; they would leave their two large packs on this ledge to pick up on their descent. When Meyer finished; the two men made ready to climb.

Meyer said, "Today we'll be on the summit."

Devar did not answer.

When their preparations were over, Devar stood ten feet to the right of Meyer, facing the rock. In the rock, midway between them at a height of five feet above the ledge, was the piton Devar had been anchored to during the night. It was a six-inch Austrian angle piton driven to its ring in a tight horizontal crack. An aluminum carabiner was snapped to the ring, but Devar was no longer tied to it. One end of a 150-foot nylon rope was passed three times around his waist and tied with a bowline knot. The rope went from his waist freely through the carabiner to Meyer. Meyer now stood on the ledge, still tied to his own anchor piton. He faced Devar and held the rope so that it passed from his left hand across his back to his right hand and from there to the remaining rope which was coiled on the ledge at his feet. He wore gloves and his attitude was that of a man holding the reins of a horse. 800 feet below him he could see the toylike autos and trucks and the shreds of smoke above the fires. He could not yet see the sun that was coming up in back of the black mountains, but the sky was lightening and the stars were fading and when the wind blew, it was warm and carried fragments of conversation from the people who were up and starting their breakfasts.

The itch to trade places with Devar burned hotly in Meyer, the sureness that he could climb as well as the older man whose name was known to every climber in the country, that given the chance he could lead the Thumb and be the first ever to stand on its summit.

"I'm ready," Devar said.

"Climb," Meyer answered.

Devar began. The first twenty feet were easy. He climbed smoothly and swiftly, and Meyer paid out the rope. Twenty feet above the ledge, the angle of rock steepened to 85 degrees and the system of cracks that Devar was following began to thin out, providing him with fewer and less adequate holds. He stopped. Circling his body from right shoulder to left hip was a short length of rope to which were clipped two dozen carabiners, and hanging from each carabiner were one or two pitons of different shape and size. Devar unclipped one piton. It looked like a tapering steel tent peg with an eye drilled through the wide end. He placed it part way into a thin vertical crack in the rock above his left shoulder and then, removing a hammer from a leather loop on his belt, he drove the piton into the crack until only the eye was showing. Then he snapped a carabiner through the eye. The carabiner was aluminum and looked like a link from a large chain except that it had a spring gate which could be pressed open and snapped shut.

Devar clipped his rope into the carabiner so that when he climbed, the rope would run freely up from the ledge through the carabiner to his waist. If he fell, Meyer would hold the rope, and the piton, if it stayed in the crack, would stop the fall.

"How is it?" Meyer shouted.

"All right," Devar said.

Devar began climbing again. The angle of rock rose to 90 degrees. In ten feet, he drove another piton. Meyer could hear the sound coming down through the rock, the rising metallic pitch that sounded like a spike being driven into green wood and meant the piton was tight in the crack. He knew that for himself there was nothing to equal leading a high and difficult pitch, finding a workable route and setting the pitons well. Belaying the leader was second best, like paddling bow in a canoe, or flying a plane from the co-pilot's seat. Meyer flexed his hands and leaned against the rock with his left shoulder.

Now the rope ran up from the ledge freely through the first carabiner and freely through the second to Devar's waist. Meyer watched, working the rope. Devar moved up slowly toward the traverse. Over the black mountains, the sun rose huge and orange and out of all proportion to the sky. On the desert, 800 feet below Meyer's right foot, he saw figures begin to move, dark gesticulating specks against the yellow earth. Whereas in the beginning he had found it necessary to pay out the rope swiftly to keep up with Devar, he now paid it out very slowly.

As Devar inched up toward the traverse, he drove in more pitons and clipped in to them. Once, he was on the same holds for twenty minutes, and when he finally moved up he moved less than a foot and it was another twenty minutes before he moved again. Meyer felt the wind warm against his face. On the desert floor, he saw the specks move, together and away from each other, into and out of cars, toward and away from the base of the rock. He knew that many of them had binoculars and were watching Devar as he moved up toward the traverse. He wondered whether he could lead the pitch as well as the older man, and whether he could lead it better. The sun rose steadily into the sky, growing smaller and hotter. Devar's sweat fell eighty feet to the ledge where Meyer stood paying out the rope which now ran freely up through nine carabiners to Devar's waist. The drops of sweat evaporated on the warm rock at his feet. One day, he thought, I will lead and the crowds will be there and someone else will follow.

In two and one half hours the older man had reached a small ledge just below the start of the traverse, had driven an anchor piton and had tied himself to it with a short length of rope. He stood on the ledge, facing out, and Meyer heard him call "Off Belay."

Standing on the bivouac ledge, Meyer untied from his anchor piton. Then, with his hammer, he struck the head of the piton back and forth and up and down until it was loose in the crack, and then he gripped the carabiner and shook it until he was able to pull the piton from the crack. He clipped the carabiner and piton to a short loop of rope that hung from his shoulder, and stepped along the ledge to Devar's original piton which he also knocked out of the crack. As he did these things, Devar took up the rope so there was no slack between the two men.

"Ready to climb," Meyer called.

"Climb," Devar answered.

The two men were joined by the long rope. It was tied around Meyer's waist and went from there freely up through the series of carabiners to the ledge, 100 feet above, where Devar held it across his back and in his left and right hands, taking in the slack as Meyer climbed. Meyer felt sun on his back and the rock warm and grainy under his hands. When he reached Devar's first piton, he stood balanced on small holds and knocked the piton loose, drawing it out of the crack and clipping it to the short rope looped over his shoulder. When he looked up, he could see the worn cleated soles of Devar's climbing shoes where they extended beyond the thin ledge, and when he looked down beyond his own shoes he could see the desert 820 feet below and the specks of people moving around, and the larger objects that were the cars and trucks. He felt supremely confident and his irritation at being second on the rope almost disappeared in the joy of climbing up the steep and difficult pitch.

As he climbed up toward Devar, he removed the pitons and carabiners that the older man had placed. He climbed much more swiftly than Devar had climbed. The rope ran straight from his waist up to the ledge where Devar held it, taking in the slack as Meyer moved up so that if Meyer came off his holds he would not fall but would hang by the rope until he regained his holds. As second, it was his job to remove all the pitons Devar had placed and to cover the route as quickly as possible. If a piton did not come out readily, he called for direct aid. Then Devar would take in all the slack until the rope was very tight between them and Meyer would lean back on the rope with his feet braced on the wall, the way a window washer leans against a safety belt, both hands free to work the piton.

Forty minutes after he began climbing, he reached the ledge where Devar stood. He had climbed the pitch quickly, but he had also evaluated the difficulty of each move and the adequacy of the pitons Devar had set. He rated the pitch at 5.9 by the Sierra Club scale, which meant it was difficult in the extreme. He understood why so many men had turned back from the pitch and he was confident that if he had led it he would have made it and that he would have done it more quickly than Devar.

"You climbed that well," Devar said.

"Thanks. I was climbing second; it's not the same. You did the work."

Devar stood next to him on the ledge, his long face bristling with whiskers, sweat sparkling in the hollows of his eyes. He did not answer Meyer's compliment, and once again the younger man felt disappointment. Devar could not be reached. He was remote, isolated, uncommunicative. Meyer tried again.

"Now the traverse," he said. He could not hide his enthusiasm; the traverse was all that stood between them and the summit. That the first two men who tried to cross it had been killed meant only that they had been unlucky.

Again, Devar did not respond. They changed the belay. Meyer stood tied in to the anchor piton and faced Devar. Devar, no longer tied in to the anchor piton but still tied to the end of the 150 foot rope, moved to the end of the ledge and looked up at the Finger Traverse. It was a much thinner ledge, sixty feet long and tapered like a pool cue. The wide end was just above Devar's head and the thin end was sixty feet to his left. There, another big ledge began at the level of the one on which he now stood. It was that opposing ledge that Devar would have to reach, and he could do so only by swinging along the traverse.

"I'm ready," Devar said.

"Climb," Meyer said.

Devar selected a piton and held it between his teeth, and he put his hammer in the breast pocket of his parka. Then he reached up and gripped the ledge and swung out so that he hung by his fingers, 900 feet above the ground. Moving swiftly, he slid his left hand as far as he could reach to the left, and then slid his right hand to meet it. He moved this way for thirty feet and then he stopped. Hanging by the fingers of his left hand, he took the piton he had clenched in his teeth and forced it by hand into a crack just below the traverse ledge. When it was wedged, he took out his hammer and drove the piton tightly into the crack and clipped a carabiner to it. Then, still hanging by the fingers of his left hand, he clipped the climbing rope into the carabiner and called for direct aid. Meyer took in the rope, keeping it very tight, and Devar, with both hands now on the traverse ledge, pulled himself up until the knot at his waist was close to the carabiner. Then he let go and hung from the piton.

Meyer watched him. The older man opened and closed his hands, working the cramps out of them. His eyes were closed and when he opened them he looked across the thirty feet left of the traverse and closed his eyes again. Meyer stood, holding the rope tightly. 900 feet below the edge of his left shoe, he could see the specks grouped now and motionless on the desert floor. He wanted Devar to succeed on the traverse simply because he would never wish for another man's failure. But short of this, he would have given anything to be in the older man's place.

They had been on the wall four days, each day hotter than the last. Now the sun beat against the rock and the heat was terrible. Devar hung from the piton, his arms limp at his sides, his eyes closed. Meyer waited, the rope tight in his hands and across his back, passing over the short rope that tied him to the wall and crossing the traverse to Devar. When the wind blew, it was warm and sometimes carried voices although Meyer could not distinguish the words. He knew Devar had been right to drive the piton. The other man who had tried the traverse had tried to go all the way to the far ledge and gotten forty-five feet across and had fallen. The force of that fall had torn his belayer from the rock. It was right to put the piton in midway on the traverse, but Meyer knew what it had taken, like doing a chinup with the fingers of one hand and hanging a full minute, maybe longer. Admiration for Devar's strength and skill mingled with his disappointment in the man.

When Devar reached up and gripped the traverse ledge, he called "Climbing." Meyer relaxed his hold on the rope and paid out slack to Devar. Devar swung along the ledge by his fingertips, his feet scraping against the wall, dislodging grit and chips of rock that drifted down 900 feet like pieces of confetti. Meyer let out the rope. His heart was pumping and he mumbled encouragement to the older man. Devar got fifteen feet beyond the piton he had driven below the center of the traverse. Then he paused, scraping the narrowing ledge with the nails of his left hand, trying to get a decent hold. His movements were rapid, those of a man who is counting his time in seconds. Finally he found a hold and hung from it by the first joints of the fingers of his left hand and brought his right hand to meet his left. He hung that way for a few seconds, 900 feet above the desert, his hands together and at arms length above his head, his feet dangling. Then he glanced at Meyer and said, "I'm going to fall."

Meyer nodded and braced himself on his ledge. When Devar fell, he fell like a sack of wheat straight down until his weight hit the piton, and then he swung across the wall like a pendulum of a clock. Meyer let the rope run a few feet to soften the impact of the fall and brought him to a gradual stop. Devar swung back and forth in long arcs, pushing himself away from the wall with his hand until he gradually slowed and came to a stop, hanging like a plumb weight twenty feet below the traverse piton.

Meyer shouted, "You're a lousy bird!" He was relieved that the older man was safe.

Devar looked up. There was no fear in his expression, but there was irritation. Above him, the wall was smooth, but running diagonally from where he hung to the ledge where Meyer stood was a series of cracks and small nubbins of rock. Devar found holds and began to climb toward Meyer. Meyer worked the rope as Devar climbed up. It took the older man twenty minutes to reach the ledge. When he did, the rope was running from Meyer, across the traverse to the piton, and back to Devar.

"I'll have to rest," Devar said.

Meyer nodded. From the small climbing pack he got out some chocolate and a water flask, and Devar ate and drank. The sky was bright and cloudless and waves of heat shimmered over the desert so that the outlines of the basalt mountains were indistinct and had the appearance of something seen in a mirage. 900 vertical feet below the ledge, the black ciphers waited motionless for Devar to try again.

When he did, he moved swiftly and passed the traverse piton and went twenty feet beyond it before he fell. This time he fell suddenly, without warning Meyer, dropping again like a sack of wheat and penduluming across the wall. The rope scorched Meyer's gloves as he let it run and slowed it down and braked it. This time it took Devar thirty minutes to regain the ledge where Meyer stood. His hands were bleeding. Meyer looked away from him; he did not want to see the old man's eyes.

Then Devar said, "I'm ready."

Hanging by his fingers, he swung across the traverse, past the piton, fifteen feet, twenty feet, until he was five feet from the opposing ledge. For a few seconds he hung there, unable to go further, and watched fiercely as his fingers uncurled and began to slip from the ledge. Then he fell again. This time he hung from the rope a long while, and when he began climbing it took him forty minutes to reach the ledge where Meyer stood. When he reached the ledge he did not say anything for a while. His hands were raw and bleeding, his face was cut and his parka was torn below the left shoulder.

"I don't think I can go again," he said finally.

Meyer felt suddenly helpless and, because he did not know what else to do, he began talking.

"It looks like it will have to be climbed," he said "As much as we can see of the wall below the traverse, there are small nicks and nubbins, not much, but enough to take the edge of a klettershoe. Suppose a man were to go hand over hand to the piton and then rest on direct aid, not a little while but for a long time, and while he was resting he could study the wall from the piton to the far ledge. It's only thirty feet; a few key holds, especially in the last five feet, would take stress off the hands and arms. It might go that way."

Meyer talked on, and while he talked he busied himself with the canteen and chocolate, preparing a snack for the older man. He was upset and didn't know why, and talking was all he could think of to do.

"I think it will go," he said. "You almost had it the last time, five feet more, but you couldn't find anything for your feet." He glanced down at Devar's feet and saw again that the man's shoes were worn. "Your boots are pretty old, the edges are rounded and the soles are probably getting soft. You could wear mine, they may be a little big, but we could wrap your feet with cloth." He steadied himself on the thin ledge and, using a small pocket knife, he cut a sleeve off his own shirt, tore it in two pieces, and put the cloth in his teeth. Then he raised one boot and carefully untied his shoelace. Devar watched him, breathing more easily now, the sweat bright in the hollows of his eyes. "You'll have to take yours off," Meyer said. "We'll trade one at a time."

Devar removed one boot, wrapped his foot with the half sleeve that Meyer gave him, and put on Meyer's shoe, tying the laces very tight.

"How does it feel?" Meyer asked.

The older man moved his foot beyond the ledge until only a quarter of an inch of the sole touched the rock; then he let it take his weight. "Good," he said.

When they completed the exchange of shoes, Devar rested thirty more minutes and then moved out on the traverse. Hand over hand, he crossed easily to the piton, pulled himself up and called for direct aid. Meyer took in all the slack and held the rope hard against his back. Devar let go of the traverse ledge and hung from the piton. He rested for fifteen minutes, and while he rested he studied the wall below the opposing ledge. Finally, Meyer heard his call that he was ready to climb.

He moved swiftly across the remaining section of the traverse until he was five feet from the opposing ledge. Meyer paid out the rope, his teeth clenched, his heart beating very hard, his eyes fastened on the man who hung by his hands, 900 feet above the desert.

Slowly, Devar moved his right foot to a hold which must have been very small, and Meyer saw that it took part of his weight. The sun beat down, and sweat glistened from Devar's face and from the corded muscles of his forearms, and spread out in stains along the side of his parka. Again slowly, he moved his left foot until it found a hold, and he let it take part of his weight. He was now spreadeagled on the wall, holding on with the tips of his fingers and a fraction of the sole of each shoe.

He lay his cheek against the rock. Meyer watched him. He knew the spectators were watching, too, wondering whether the old man would make it or not.

Five feet to the left of Devar's foot, the broad ledge lay hot in the bright sun, a ledge on which no man had ever stood. The next move was critical; Meyer knew if Devar fell again he would be finished. He held the rope lightly in both hands and felt the tips of his fingers pulse, and it was as if the rope carried his own blood to the older man.

When Devar moved again, he moved his right hand along the traverse ledge until it reached his left, and he tensed the fingers of both hands. Then, moving swiftly, he hung from his fingers and raised his left foot from its hold and let his right foot come to it. Then, easing part of his weight onto his right foot, he moved his left hand as far as he could and found a hold. For a moment he wavered, and then he brought his right hand to his left and, stretching as far as he could with his left foot, he reached the broad ledge and stepped lightly on to it, swinging by his hands across the remaining gulf.

Meyer made no gesture or sound, but smiled as he held the rope; and he felt the wind blow up the face and heard the sounds of people shouting. Above Devar's ledge, a series of wide cracks and shelves went to the summit of the Thumb; the difficult moves were over. The older man climbed up fifty feet above the traverse so Meyer would have a safe belay. He anchored himself to a comfortable ledge and took in the slack. Meyer heard his call to climb.

Before climbing, Meyer looked east across the desert to the black mountains and then straight down almost a thousand feet and saw the people moving on the sand; and it occurred to him what it might be like to reach the end of a long career, a time which he could only vaguely imagine when he too might become uncommunicative and bring whiskey and sit sleepless through the long nights, bivouaced on a high wall.

Then, in Devar's old shoes, which were very tight for him, he crossed the traverse easily and well.

### Commentary: Distance, Concern, and Point of View in "The Devil's Thumb"

Peter Sandberg manages his language very nicely. There is, I have always suspected, something about such a skill that resides in the genes. The last line of the story, for instance. If you are not born knowing that the phrase should read "easily and well," and not "well and easily," then all the writer's conferences and advanced composition courses you can get, will help you no more than earrings on a gold fish. Such genetic good fortune does not insure success as a writer, but its absence is a definitive prophecy of failure.

Sandberg has that, the *sine qua non* of authorship. And he knows how to make a story, how to put it together, concentrating on the action and the events, letting the story tell itself. But I quarrel with his narrative point of view. The essence of what happens is, of course, that Meyer grows up, in a sense, replaces Devar, becomes a better climber on this particular venture and thus metaphorically as well as literally walks (or in this case climbs) in the old man's shoes. Shoes too tight (he'd outgrown them) but shoes in which he made the climb "easily and well."

The real movement of the story is not in the events that embody this change, but in young Meyer's growing awareness of the meaning of the events and his slow perception of his own mortality, a perception which culminates with his recognition that there would come a time "when he too might become uncommunicative and bring whiskey and sit sleepless through the long nights, bivouaced on a high wall." Of the internal story we seem to get too little. We are far away from both of them and we don't get to know Meyer well enough to care too much whether he achieves a perception of life's processes, or not. In fact, I was slightly surprised to discover at the story's end that it was not Devar, but Meyer whose story this was. I should have known this earlier. Perhaps a first personal point of view would have been better. Perhaps not. I hesitate to instruct Peter in a trade he knows better than I, as I would hesitate to tell Henry Aaron how to hit a curve ball. Though in either case I have the right to point out the occasions when they miss.

R. B. P.

### Response: "The Devil's Thumb" in Retrospect—Can There Be Too Much Detail?

Although it has been some years since I wrote this story, I remember very well the circumstances under which I produced it and what I hoped to accomplish in it.

From 1958 to 1962, I had been active in mountaineering and had written a number of stories with this general background. But because of the rather complicated techniques involved, the variety of equipment, its uses, and the nuances of position, say, on a vertical wall between the belayer and the belayed, I had never tried to describe a high-angle rock climb. It seemed to me that in order to make the technical aspects of such a climb understandable to a reader who had only a vague idea of the sport or no idea at all would bog me down in such detail that the other elements of the story—the essential matters of plot, character, theme, and so forth—would suffer. Nevertheless, I wanted to try, and it was with this motivation that I wrote "The Devil's Thumb."

I think it is fair to say that in one sense I succeeded. If the uninitiated reader is patient enough to read my description of equipment and techniques (for example, "The carabiner was aluminum and looked like a link from a large chain except that it had a spring gate which could be pressed open and snapped shut" or "Devar clipped his rope into the carabiner so that when he climbed, the rope would run freely up from the ledge through the carabiner to his waist. If he fell . . ."); if the reader is patient enough with this, he can learn how a high-angle climb is carried out. But it is also fair to say· that the story suffers from this emphasis on expertise. The authorial voice is too insistent, too much in evidence, always reminding us that on the one hand we have a potentially exciting story about two potentially interesting characters; and on the other hand—and always getting between us and that story and those characters—a meticulous presentation of rock-climbing technique which more properly belongs in a manual on the sport.

Professor Parker's criticism of the story suggests one way it could be improved. Were a certain amount of the expertise jettisoned and the rest put from Meyer's point of view rather than from the author's (for example, "Meyer let his eye follow the rope, up from his own waist, through the carabiners, 100 feet up to the ledge where Devar held it across his back . . ."), the reader would get what he needed of the picture and would not be swamped in dry detail. Meyer could become more the center of the story, and the pace overall would pick up.

As for the origins of the piece, it grew in part out of experience. In 1962 I participated in a climb of Shiprock, a 2000-foot monolith that rises from the desert floor in the northwest corner of New Mexico. It is the only significant climb I have been on which, at one point, requires the climber to climb down 100 feet in order to go up, and up 100 feet in order to go down. It is a long, fatiguing climb (we began at dawn, finished after dusk), spectacularly exposed at times; and I used many of the details of its setting (but not of the climb itself) in "The Devil's Thumb." A few weeks later I was badly injured in a fall from another rock and have since given the sport up. But it is a rigorous and splendid sport, and I still write about it, think about it, and hold a certain envy of those people I know who still go up there on high walls and enjoy the nuances of technique that I tried, with only partial success, to set down here.

P. L. S.

# The Liberation of Women

The essays in this section are argumentative, and the single short story seems clearly to suggest a conviction about womanhood being urged. The analysis of "Livvie" underscores the argumentative quality of the story by showing the mode of contrast by which the story develops, a mode which, by presenting two opposing possibilities, arrives at a conclusion.

Irving Howe's response to Kate Millett ("The Middle Class Mind of Kate Millett") is also clearly argumentative as is the analysis that follows it. The Howe essay is developed by refuting Miss Millett's assertions in more or less the order in which she makes them. The commentary on Howe's response uses his indictment of Miss Millett's essay as a bad example, a kind of club to belabor the intellectuals at large.

Simone de Beauvoir's introduction to *The Second Sex* begins as any argument ought to, with a definition of terms. "But first we must ask: what is a woman?" In the process of answering that question she associates woman with Jews and Negroes and thus defines them, without yet saying so specifically, as an oppressed class. Her argument continues closely, partly through the examination of the implications of language, partly through the quotation of authority, to her conclusion that women are the second sex, the *Other* not yet an equal part of the human race.

Betty Friedan, on the other hand, argues very directly and simply from her own first-hand experience, either with the problems that the feminine mystique presents or with people she's interviewed who have encountered such problems. The value of such an approach is that it gives a sense of immediacy and expertise (I was there, I suffered) which first personal accounts always give. But she also balances her personal experience with the experience of those interviewed. She thus avoids being accused of subjective misinterpretation. Furthermore, by illustrating from the experience of several generations, Ms. Friedan manages to make clear that the problem is now newly come on the human scene.

Of Kate Millett's argument, "The Theory of Sexual Politics," Irving Howe's essay would seem ample commentary. Here, perhaps, it is sufficient merely to point out that Miss Millett, like Mme. de Beauvoir, has set out to establish a definition (in this case not of women, but of women's relationship to men), that her technique of argumentation relies to a considerable extent on the techniques of literary analysis, and that one of the adversary skills she employs very skillfully is the art of

**225**

convincing assertion. As here: "Coitus can scarcely be said to take place in a vacuum; although of itself it appears a biological and physical activity, it is set so deeply within the larger context of human affairs that it serves as a charged microcosm of the variety of attitudes and values to which culture subscribes." Of course, we say. It is so confidently, so professionally said that we are inclined to pass right along, accepting the given as if it were just that. One telling touch is the inarguable truism with which the assertion begins. Few would argue that coitus does take place in vacuum. Yet as one examines the statement one might wish, at least, to withhold total commitment, for it is an assertion of such sweeping magnitude that if we pay attention to it, we may wish to have immediate evidence to support it. But so well said is it, that we have no such wish.

In his argument, which is largely a response to Kate Millett, Lionel Tiger in "Male Dominance . . ." begins with what one might call the old disarm-the-opposition trick (one that Irving Howe also employs). To call it a trick is not to impugn the legitimacy of its use, nor to question the sincerity of the expression. It is simply to highlight the fact that it is a standard and emulable technique. "The feminists' angry rebuke to us males could not be more correct or more justified," Lionel Tiger begins. He goes on to list the areas in which the "feminists" have every reason to complain. "However," he concludes at the end of his first paragraph, "if you want to change a system you have got to understand it." The argument then develops from that basis. We agree, in other words, on the situation. What we are debating is the causes. This approach does several things. As suggested, it disarms the opposition. It also leads the discussion into Tiger's field of competence (he's an anthropologist). And insofar as the world of men is the system (as the "feminists" have contended) which must be changed, then it must be (on the feminist argument that you must be of the gender to explain the gender) explained by a man.

There is considerably more to the matter or argument than this brief introduction could cover. But most of the rules of argumentation are implicit in the selections that follow, as well as a good deal of information about the movement toward the liberation of women.

## 25. WHAT IS A WOMAN?

### Simone de Beauvoir

*Simone de Beauvoir is a French writer, intellectual, associate of
Sartre and Richard Wright, and articulator of a feminine point of
view that has profoundly influenced recent feminist writers like
Kate Millett.*

For a long time I have hesitated to write a book on woman. The subject
is irritating, especially to women; and it is not new. Enough ink has been
spilled in the quarreling over feminism, now practically over, and perhaps we should say no more about it. It is still talked about, however,
for the voluminous nonsense uttered during the last century seems to
have done little to illuminate the problem. After all, is there a problem?
And if so, what is it? Are there women, really? Most assuredly the
theory of the eternal feminine still has its adherents who will whisper
in your ear: "Even in Russia women still are *women*"; and other erudite
persons—sometimes the very same—say with a sigh: "Woman is losing
her way, woman is lost." One wonders if women still exist, if they will
always exist, whether or not it is desirable that they should, what place
they occupy in this world, what their place should be. "What has become
of women?" was asked recently in an ephemeral magazine.[1]

But first we must ask: what is a woman? "*Tota mulier in utero,*" says
one, "woman is a womb." But in speaking of certain women, connoisseurs declare that they are not women, although they are equipped with
a uterus like the rest. All agree in recognizing the fact that females exist
in the human species; today as always they make up about one half of
humanity. And yet we are told that femininity is in danger; we are ex-
horted to be women, remain women, become women. It would appear,
then, that every female human being is not necessarily a woman; to be
so considered she must share in that mysterious and threatened reality
known as femininity. Is this attribute something secreted by the ovaries?
Or is it a Platonic essence, a product of the philosophic imagination? Is a
rustling petticoat enough to bring it down to earth? Although some
women try zealously to incarnate this essence, it is hardly patentable. It
is frequently described in vague and dazzling terms that seem to have
been borrowed from the vocabulary of the seers, and indeed in the

*Source:* "What Is a Woman?" from *The Second Sex,* by Simone de Beauvoir, translated by H. M. Parshley. Copyright 1952 by Alfred A. Knopf, Inc. Reprinted by
permission of the publisher.

[1] *Franchise,* dead today.

times of St. Thomas it was considered an essence as certainly defined as the somniferous virtue of the poppy.

But conceptualism has lost ground. The biological and social sciences no longer admit the existence of unchangeably fixed entities that determine given characteristics, such as those ascribed to woman, the Jew, or the Negro. Science regards any characteristic as a reaction dependent in part upon a *situation*. If today femininity no longer exists, then it never existed. But does the word *woman*, then, have no specific content? This is stoutly affirmed by those who hold to the philosophy of the enlightenment, of rationalism, of nominalism; women, to them, are merely the human beings arbitrarily designated by the word *woman*. Many American women particularly are prepared to think that there is no longer any place for woman as such; if a backward individual still takes herself for a woman, her friends advise her to be psychoanalyzed and thus get rid of this obsession. In regard to a work, *Modern Woman: The Lost Sex*, which in other respects has its irritating features, Dorothy Parker has written: "I cannot be just to books which treat of woman as woman. . . . My idea is that all of us, men as well as women, should be regarded as human beings." But nominalism is a rather inadequate doctrine, and the antifeminists have had no trouble in showing that women simply *are not* men. Surely woman is, like man, a human being; but such a declaration is abstract. The fact is that every concrete human being is always a singular, separate individual. To decline to accept such notions as the eternal feminine, the black soul, the Jewish character, is not to deny that Jews, Negroes, women exist today—this denial does not represent a liberation for those concerned, but rather a flight from reality. Some years ago a well-known woman writer refused to permit her portrait to appear in a series of photographs especially devoted to women writers; she wished to be counted among the men. But in order to gain this privilege she made use of her husband's influence! Women who assert that they are men lay claim none the less to masculine consideration and respect. I recall also a young Trotskyite standing on a platform at a boisterous meeting and getting ready to use her fists, in spite of her evident fragility. She was denying her feminine weakness; but it was for love of a militant male whose equal she wished to be. The attitude of defiance of many American women proves that they are haunted by a sense of their femininity. In truth, to go for a walk with one's eyes open is enough to demonstrate that humanity is divided into two classes of individuals whose clothes, faces, bodies, smiles, gaits, interests, and occupations are manifestly different. Perhaps these differences are superficial, perhaps they are destined to disappear. What is certain is that right now they do most obviously exist.

If her functioning as a female is not enough to define woman, if we decline also to explain her through "the eternal feminine," and if nevertheless we admit, provisionally, that women do exist, then we must face the question: what is a woman?

To state the question is, to me, to suggest, at once, a preliminary answer. The fact that I ask it is in itself significant. A man would never get the notion of writing a book on the peculiar situation of the human male.[2] But if I wish to define myself, I must first of all say: "I am a woman"; on this truth must be based all further discussion. A man never begins by presenting himself as an individual of a certain sex; it goes without saying that he is a man. The terms *masculine* and *feminine* are used symmetrically only as a matter of form, as on legal papers. In actuality the relation of the two sexes is not quite like that of two electrical poles, for man represents both the positive and the neutral, as is indicated by the common use of *man* to designate human beings in general; whereas woman represents only the negative, defined by limiting criteria, without reciprocity. In the midst of an abstract discussion it is vexing to hear a man say: "You think thus and so because you are a woman"; but I know that my only defense is to reply: "I think thus and so because it is true," thereby removing my subjective self from the argument. It would be out of the question to reply: "And you think the contrary because you are a man," for it is understood that the fact of being a man is no peculiarity. A man is in the right in being a man; it is the woman who is in the wrong. It amounts to this: just as for the ancients there was an absolute vertical with reference to which the oblique was defined, so there is an absolute human type, the masculine. Woman has ovaries, a uterus; these peculiarities imprison her in her subjectivity, circumscribe her within the limits of her own nature. It is often said that she thinks with her glands. Man superbly ignores the fact that his anatomy also includes glands, such as the testicles, and that they secrete hormones. He thinks of his body as a direct and normal connection with the world, which he believes he apprehends objectively, whereas he regards the body of woman as a hindrance, a prison, weighed down by everything peculiar to it. "The female is a female by virtue of a certain *lack* of qualities," said Aristotle; "we should regard the female nature as afflicted with a natural defectiveness." And St. Thomas for his part pronounced woman to be an "imperfect man," an "incidental" being. This is symbol-

---

[2] The Kinsey Report [Alfred C. Kinsey and others: *Sexual Behavior in the Human Male* (W. B. Saunders Co., 1948)] is no exception, for it is limited to describing the sexual characteristics of American men, which is quite a different matter.

ized in Genesis where Eve is depicted as made from what Bossuet called "a supernumerary bone" of Adam.

Thus humanity is male and man defines woman not in herself but as relative to him; she is not regarded as an autonomous being. Michelet writes: "Woman, the relative being. . . ." And Benda is most positive in his *Rapport d'Uriel*: "The body of man makes sense in itself quite apart from that of woman, whereas the latter seems wanting in significance by itself. . . . Man can think of himself without woman. She cannot think of herself without man." And she is simply what man decrees; thus she is called "the sex," by which is meant that she appears essentially to the male as a sexual being. For him she is sex—absolute sex, no less. She is defined and differentiated with reference to man and not he with reference to her; she is the incidental, the inessential as opposed to the essential. He is the Subject, he is the Absolute—she is the Other.[3]

The category of the *Other* is as primordial as consciousness itself. In the most primitive societies, in the most ancient mythologies, one finds the expression of a duality—that of the Self and the Other. This duality was not originally attached to the division of the sexes; it was not dependent upon any empirical facts. It is revealed in such works as that of Granet on Chinese thought and those of Dumézil on the East Indies and Rome. The feminine element was at first no more involved in such pairs as Varuna-Mitra, Uranus-Zeus, Sun-Moon, and Day-Night than it was in the contrasts between Good and Evil, lucky and unlucky auspices, right and left, God and Lucifer. Otherness is a fundamental category of human thought.

Thus it is that no group ever sets itself up as the One without at once setting up the Other over against itself. If three travelers chance to occupy the same compartment, that is enough to make vaguely hostile "others" out of all the rest of the passengers on the train. In small-town

[3] E. Lévinas expresses this idea most explicitly in his essay *Temps et l'Autre*. "Is there not a case in which otherness, alterity [*altérité*], unquestionably marks the nature of a being, as its essence, an instance of otherness not consisting purely and simply in the opposition of two species of the same genus? I think that the feminine represents the contrary in its absolute sense, this contrariness being in no wise affected by any relation between it and its correlative and thus remaining absolutely other. Sex is not a certain specific difference . . . no more is the sexual difference a mere contradiction. . . . Nor does this difference lie in the duality of two complementary terms, for two complementary terms imply a pre-existing whole. . . . Otherness reaches its full flowing in the feminine, a term of the same rank as consciousness but of opposite meaning."

I suppose that Lévinas does not forget that woman, too, is aware of her own consciousness, or ego. But it is striking that he deliberately takes a man's point of view, disregarding the reciprocity of subject and object. When he writes that woman is mystery, he implies that she is mystery for man. Thus his description, which is intended to be objective, is in fact an assertion of masculine privilege.

eyes all persons not belonging to the village are "strangers" and suspect; to the native of a country all who inhabit other countries are "foreigners"; Jews are "different" for the anti-Semite, Negroes are "inferior" for American racists, aborigines are "natives" for colonists, proletarians are the "lower class" for the privileged.

Lévi-Strauss, at the end of a profound work on the various forms of primitive societies, reaches the following conclusion: "Passage from the state of Nature to the state of Culture is marked by man's ability to view biological relations as a series of contrasts; duality, alternation, opposition, and symmetry, whether under definite or vague forms, constitute not so much phenomena to be explained as fundamental and immediately given data of social reality."[4] These phenomena would be incomprehensible if in fact human society were simply a *Mitsein* or fellowship based on solidarity and friendliness. Things become clear, on the contrary, if, following Hegel, we find in consciousness itself a fundamental hostility toward every other consciousness; the subject can be posed only in being opposed—he sets himself up as the essential, as opposed to the other, the inessential, the object.

But the other consciousness, the other ego, sets up a reciprocal claim. The native traveling abroad is shocked to find himself in turn regarded as a "stranger" by the natives of neighboring countries. As a matter of fact, wars, festivals, trading, treaties, and contests among tribes, nations, and classes tend to deprive the concept *Other* of its absolute sense and to make manifest its relativity; willy-nilly, individuals and groups are forced to realize the reciprocity of their relations. How is it, then, that this reciprocity has not been recognized between the sexes, that one of the contrasting terms is set up as the sole essential, denying any relativity in regard to its correlative and defining the latter as pure otherness? Why is it that women do not dispute male sovereignty? No subject will readily volunteer to become the object, the inessential; it is not the Other who, in defining himself as the Other, establishes the One. The Other is posed as such by the One in defining himself as the One. But if the Other is not to regain the status of being the One, he must be submissive enough to accept this alien point of view. Whence comes this submission in the case of woman?

There are, to be sure, other cases in which a certain category has been able to dominate another completely for a time. Very often this privilege depends upon inequality of numbers—the majority imposes its rule upon

4 See C. Lévi-Strauss: *Les Structures élémentaires de la parenté*. My thanks are due to C. Lévi-Strauss for his kindness in furnishing me with the proofs of his work, which, among others, I have used liberally in Part II.

*The Liberation of Women*  **231**

the minority or persecutes it. But women are not a minority, like the American Negroes or the Jews; there are as many women as men on earth. Again, the two groups concerned have often been originally independent; they may have been formerly unaware of each other's existence, or perhaps they recognized each other's autonomy. But a historical event has resulted in the subjugation of the weaker by the stronger. The scattering of the Jews, the introduction of slavery into America, the conquests of imperialism are examples in point. In these cases the oppressed retained at least the memory of former days; they possessed in common a past, a tradition, sometimes a religion or a culture.

The parallel drawn by Bebel between women and the proletariat is valid in that neither ever formed a minority or a separate collective unit of mankind. And instead of a single historical event it is in both cases a historical development that explains their status as a class and accounts for the membership of *particular individuals* in that class. But proletarians have not always existed, whereas there have always been women. They are women in virtue of their anatomy and physiology. Throughout history they have always been subordinated to men,[5] and hence their dependence is not the result of a historical event or a social change—it was not something that *occurred*. The reason why otherness in this case seems to be an absolute is in part that it lacks the contingent or incidental nature of historical facts. A condition brought about at a certain time can be abolished at some other time, as the Negroes of Haiti and others have proved; but it might seem that a natural condition is beyond the possibility of change. In truth, however, the nature of things is no more immutably given, once for all, than is historical reality. If woman seems to be the inessential which never becomes the essential, it is because she herself fails to bring about this change. Proletarians say "We"; Negroes also. Regarding themselves as subjects, they transform the bourgeois, the whites, into "others." But women do not say "We," except at some congress of feminists or similar formal demonstration; men say "women," and women use the same word in referring to themselves. They do not authentically assume a subjective attitude. The proletarians have accomplished the revolution in Russia, the Negroes in Haiti, the Indo-Chinese are battling for it in Indo-China; but the women's effort has never been anything more than a symbolic agitation. They have gained only what men have been willing to grant; they have taken nothing, they have only received.[6]

[5] With rare exceptions, perhaps, like certain matriarchal rulers, queens, and the like.—Tr.

[6] See Part II, ch. viii.

The reason for this is that women lack concrete means for organizing themselves into a unit which can stand face to face with the correlative unit. They have no past, no history, no religion of their own; and they have no such solidarity of work and interest as that of the proletariat. They are not even promiscuously herded together in the way that creates community feeling among the American Negroes, the ghetto Jews, the workers of Saint-Denis, or the factory hands of Renault. They live dispersed among the males, attached through residence, housework, economic condition, and social standing to certain men—fathers or husbands —more firmly than they are to other women. If they belong to the bourgeoisie, they feel solidarity with men of that class, not with proletarian women; if they are white, their allegiance is to white men, not to Negro women. The proletariat can propose to massacre the ruling class, and a sufficiently fanatical Jew or Negro might dream of getting sole possession of the atomic bomb and making humanity wholly Jewish or black; but woman cannot even dream of exterminating the males. The bond that unites her to her oppressors is not comparable to any other. The division of the sexes is a biological fact, not an event in human history. Male and female stand opposed within a primordial *Mitsein*, and woman has not broken it. The couple is a fundamental unity with its two halves riveted together, and the cleavage of society along the line of sex is impossible. Here is to be found the basic trait of woman: she is the Other in a totality of which the two components are necessary to one another.

One could suppose that this reciprocity might have facilitated the liberation of woman. When Hercules sat at the feet of Omphale and helped with her spinning, his desire for her held him captive; but why did she fail to gain a lasting power? To revenge herself on Jason, Medea killed their children; and this grim legend would seem to suggest that she might have obtained a formidable influence over him through his love for his offspring. In *Lysistrata* Aristophanes gaily depicts a band of women who joined forces to gain social ends through the sexual needs of their men; but this is only a play. In the legend of the Sabine women, the latter soon abandoned their plan of remaining sterile to punish their ravishers. In truth woman has not been socially emancipated through man's need—sexual desire and the desire for offspring—which makes the male dependent for satisfaction upon the female.

Master and slave, also, are united by a reciprocal need, in this case economic, which does not liberate the slave. In the relation of master to slave the master does not make a point of the need that he has for the other; he has in his grasp the power of satisfying this need through his own action; whereas the slave, in his dependent condition, his hope and fear, is quite conscious of the need he has for his master. Even if the need is at bottom equally urgent for both, it always works in favor of the oppressor and against the oppressed. That is why the liberation of the working class, for example, has been slow.

Now, woman has always been man's dependent, if not his slave; the two sexes have never shared the world in equality. And even today woman is heavily handicapped, though her situation is beginning to change. Almost nowhere is her legal status the same as man's,[7] and frequently it is much to her disadvantage. Even when her rights are legally recognized in the abstract, long-standing custom prevents their full expression in the mores. In the economic sphere men and women can almost be said to make up two castes; other things being equal, the former hold the better jobs, get higher wages, and have more opportunity for success than their new competitors. In industry and politics men have a great many more positions and they monopolize the most important posts. In addition to all this, they enjoy a traditional prestige that the education of children tends in every way to support, for the present enshrines the past—and in the past all history has been made by men. At the present time, when women are beginning to take part in the affairs of the world, it is still a world that belongs to men—they have no doubt of it at all and women have scarcely any. To decline to be the Other, to refuse to be a party to the deal—this would be for women to renounce all the advantages conferred upon them by their alliance with the superior caste. Man-the-sovereign will provide woman-the-liege with material protection and will undertake the moral justification of her existence; thus she can evade at once both economic risk and the metaphysical risk of a liberty in which ends and aims must be contrived without assistance. Indeed, along with the ethical urge of each individual to affirm his subjective existence, there is also the temptation to forgo liberty and become a thing. This is an inauspicious road, for he who takes it—passive, lost, ruined—becomes henceforth the creature of another's will, frustrated in his transcendence and deprived of every value. But it is an easy road; on it one avoids the strain involved in undertaking an authentic existence. When man makes of woman the *Other*, he may, then, expect her to manifest deepseated tendencies toward complicity. Thus, woman may fail to lay claim to the status of subject because she lacks definite resources, because she feels the necessary bond that ties her to man regardless of reciprocity, and because she is often very well pleased with her role as the *Other*.

[7] At the moment an "equal rights" amendment to the Constitution of the United States is before Congress.—Tr.

But it will be asked at once: how did all this begin? It is easy to see that the duality of the sexes, like any duality, gives rise to conflict. And doubtless the winner will assume the status of absolute. But why should man have won from the start? It seems possible that women could have won the victory; or that the outcome of the conflict might never have been decided. How is it that this world has always belonged to the men and that things have begun to change only recently? Is this change a good thing? Will it bring about an equal sharing of the world between men and women?

These questions are not new, and they have often been answered. But the very fact that woman *is the Other* tends to cast suspicion upon all the justifications that men have ever been able to provide for it. These have all too evidently been dictated by men's interest. A little-known feminist of the seventeenth century, Poulain de la Barre, put it this way: "All that has been written about women by men should be suspect, for the men are at once judge and party to the lawsuit." Everywhere, at all times, the males have displayed their satisfaction in feeling that they are the lords of creation. "Blessed be God . . . that He did not make me a woman," say the Jews in their morning prayers, while their wives pray on a note of resignation: "Blessed be the Lord, who created me according to His will." The first among the blessings for which Plato thanked the gods was that he had been created free, not enslaved; the second, a man, not a woman. But the males could not enjoy this privilege fully unless they believed it to be founded on the absolute and the eternal; they sought to make the fact of their supremacy into a right. "Being men, those who have made and compiled the laws have favored their own sex, and jurists have elevated these laws into principles," to quote Poulain de la Barre once more.

Legislators, priests, philosophers, writers, and scientists have striven to show that the subordinate position of woman is willed in heaven and advantageous on earth. The religions invented by men reflect this wish for domination. In the legends of Eve and Pandora men have taken up arms against women. They have made use of philosophy and theology, as the quotations from Aristotle and St. Thomas have shown. Since ancient times satirists and moralists have delighted in showing up the weaknesses of women. We are familiar with the savage indictments hurled against women throughout French literature. Montherlant, for example, follows the tradition of Jean de Meung, though with less gusto. This hostility may at times be well founded, often it is gratuitous; but in truth it more or less successfully conceals a desire for self-justification. As Montaigne says, "It is easier to accuse one sex than to excuse the other." Sometimes what is going on is clear enough. For instance, the

Roman law limiting the rights of women cited "the imbecility, the instability of the sex" just when the weakening of family ties seemed to threaten the interests of male heirs. And in the effort to keep the married women under guardianship, appeal was made in the sixteenth century to the authority of St. Augustine, who declared that "woman is a creature neither decisive nor constant," at a time when the single woman was thought capable of managing her property. Montaigne understood clearly how arbitrary and unjust was woman's appointed lot: "Women are not in the wrong when they decline to accept the rules laid down for them, since the men make these rules without consulting them. No wonder intrigue and strife abound." But he did not go so far as to champion their cause.

It was only later, in the eighteenth century, that genuinely democratic men began to view the matter objectively. Diderot, among others, strove to show that woman is, like man, a human being. Later John Stuart Mill came fervently to her defense. But these philosophers displayed unusual impartiality. In the nineteenth century the feminist quarrel became again a quarrel of partisans. One of the consequences of the industrial revolution was the entrance of women into productive labor, and it was just here that the claims of the feminists emerged from the realm of theory and acquired an economic basis, while their opponents became the more aggressive. Although landed property lost power to some extent, the bourgeoisie clung to the old morality that found the guarantee of private property in the solidity of the family. Woman was ordered back into the home the more harshly as her emancipation became a real menace. Even within the working class the men endeavored to restrain woman's liberation, because they began to see the women as dangerous competitors—the more so because they were accustomed to work for lower wages.[8]

In proving woman's inferiority, the antifeminists then began to draw not only upon religion, philosophy, and theology, as before, but also upon science—biology, experimental psychology, etc. At most they were willing to grant "equality in difference" to the *other* sex. That profitable formula is most significant; it is precisely like the "equal but separate" formula of the Jim Crow laws aimed at the North American Negroes. As is well known, this so-called equalitarian segregation has resulted only in the most extreme discrimination. The similarity just noted is in no way due to chance, for whether it is a race, a caste, a class, or a sex that is reduced to a position of inferiority, the methods of justification are the same. "The eternal feminine" corresponds to "the black soul" and to "the Jewish character." True, the Jewish problem is on the

[8] See Part II, pp. 106–8.

whole very different from the other two—to the anti-Semite the Jew is not so much an inferior as he is an enemy for whom there is to be granted no place on earth, for whom annihilation is the fate desired. But there are deep similarities between the situation of woman and that of the Negro. Both are being emancipated today from a like paternalism, and the former master class wishes to "keep them in their place"—that is, the place chosen for them. In both cases the former masters lavish more or less sincere eulogies, either on the virtues of "the good Negro" with his dormant, childish, merry soul—the submissive Negro—or on the merits of the woman who is "truly feminine"—that is, frivolous, infantile, irresponsible—the submissive woman. In both cases the dominant class bases its argument on a state of affairs that it has itself created. As George Bernard Shaw puts it, in substance, "The American white relegates the black to the rank of shoeshine boy; and he concludes from this that the black is good for nothing but shining shoes." This vicious circle is met with in all analogous circumstances; when an individual (or a group of individuals) is kept in a situation of inferiority, the fact is that he *is* inferior. But the significance of the verb *to be* must be rightly understood here; it is in bad faith to give it a static value when it really has the dynamic Hegelian sense of "to have become." Yes, women on the whole *are* today inferior to men; that is, their situation affords them fewer possibilities. The question is: should that state of affairs continue?

Many men hope that it will continue; not all have given up the battle. The conservative bourgeoisie still see in the emancipation of women a menace to their morality and their interests. Some men dread feminine competition. Recently a male student wrote in the *Hebdo-Latin*: "Every woman student who goes into medicine or law robs us of a job." He never questioned his rights in this world. And economic interests are not the only ones concerned. One of the benefits that oppression confers upon the oppressors is that the most humble among them is made to *feel* superior; thus, a "poor white" in the South can console himself with the thought that he is not a "dirty nigger"—and the more prosperous whites cleverly exploit this pride.

Similarly, the most mediocre of males feels himself a demigod as compared with women. It was much easier for M. de Montherlant to think himself a hero when he faced women (and women chosen for his purpose) than when he was obliged to act the man among men—something many women have done better than he, for that matter. And in September 1948, in one of his articles in the *Figaro littéraire*, Claude Mauriac—whose great originality is admired by all—could[9] write regard-

[9] or at least he thought he could.

ing woman: *"We* listen on a tone [*sic!*] of polite indifference . . . to the most brilliant among them, well knowing that her wit reflects more or less luminously ideas that come from *us."* Evidently the speaker referred to is not reflecting the ideas of Mauriac himself, for no one knows of his having any. It may be that she reflects ideas originating with men, but then, even among men there are those who have been known to appropriate ideas not their own; and one can well ask whether Claude Mauriac might not find more interesting a conversation reflecting Descartes, Marx, or Gide rather than himself. What is really remarkable is that by using the questionable *we* he identifies himself with St. Paul, Hegel, Lenin, and Nietzsche, and from the lofty eminence of their grandeur looks down disdainfully upon the bevy of women who make bold to converse with him on a footing of equality. In truth, I know of more than one woman who would refuse to suffer with patience Mauriac's "tone of polite indifference."

I have lingered on this example because the masculine attitude is here displayed with disarming ingenuousness. But men profit in many more subtle ways from the otherness, the alterity of woman. Here is miraculous balm for those afflicted with an inferiority complex, and indeed no one is more arrogant toward women, more aggressive or scornful, than the man who is anxious about his virility. Those who are not fear-ridden in the presence of their fellow men are much more disposed to recognize a fellow creature in woman; but even to these the myth of Woman, the Other, is precious for many reasons.[10] They cannot be blamed for not cheerfully relinquishing all the benefits they derive from the myth, for they realize what they would lose in relinquishing woman as they fancy her to be, while they fail to realize what they have to gain from the woman of tomorrow. Refusal to pose oneself as the Subject, unique and absolute, requires great self-denial. Furthermore, the vast majority of men make no such claim explicitly. They do not *postulate* woman as inferior, for today they are too thoroughly imbued with the ideal of democracy not to recognize all human beings as equals.

In the bosom of the family, woman seems in the eyes of childhood and youth to be clothed in the same social dignity as the adult males. Later on, the young man, desiring and loving, experiences the resistance, the

[10] A significant article on this theme by Michael Carrouges appeared in No. 292 of the *Cahiers du Sud.* He writes indignantly: "Would that there were no woman-myth at all but only a cohort of cooks, matrons, prostitutes, and bluestockings serving functions of pleasure or usefulness!" That is to say, in his view woman has no existence in and for herself; he thinks only of her *function* in the male world. Her reason for existence lies in man. But then, in fact, her poetic "function" as a myth might be more valued than any other. The real problem is precisely to find out why woman should be defined with relation to man.

independence of the woman desired and loved; in marriage, he respects woman as wife and mother, and in the concrete events of conjugal life she stands there before him as a free being. He can therefore feel that social subordination as between the sexes no longer exists and that on the whole, in spite of differences, woman is an equal. As, however, he observes some points of inferiority—the most important being unfitness for the professions—he attributes these to natural causes. When he is in a co-operative and benevolent relation with woman, his theme is the principle of abstract equality, and he does not base his attitude upon such inequality as may exist. But when he is in conflict with her, the situation is reversed: his theme will be the existing inequality, and he will even take it as justification for denying abstract equality.[11]

So it is that many men will affirm as if in good faith that women *are* the equals of man and that they have nothing to clamor for, while *at the same time* they will say that women can never be the equals of man and that their demands are in vain. It is, in point of fact, a difficult matter for man to realize the extreme importance of social discriminations which seem outwardly insignificant but which produce in woman moral and intellectual effects so profound that they appear to spring from her original nature.[12] The most sympathetic of men never fully comprehend woman's concrete situation. And there is no reason to put much trust in the men when they rush to the defense of privileges whose full extent they can hardly measure. We shall not, then, permit ourselves to be intimidated by the number and violence of the attacks launched against women, nor to be entrapped by the self-seeking eulogies bestowed on the "true woman," nor to profit by the enthusiasm for woman's destiny manifested by men who would not for the world have any part of it.

We should consider the arguments of the feminists with no less suspicion, however, for very often their controversial aim deprives them of all real value. If the "woman question" seems trivial, it is because masculine arrogance has made of it a "quarrel"; and when quarreling one no longer reasons well. People have tirelessly sought to prove that woman is superior, inferior, or equal to man. Some say that, having been created after Adam, she is evidently a secondary being; others say on the contrary that Adam was only a rough draft and that God succeeded in producing the human being in perfection when He created Eve. Woman's

---

[11] For example, a man will say that he considers his wife in no wise degraded because she has no gainful occupation. The profession of housewife is just as lofty, and so on. But when the first quarrel comes, he will exclaim: "Why, you couldn't make your living without me!"

[12] The specific purpose of Book II of this study is to describe this process.

brain is smaller; yes, but it is relatively larger. Christ was made a man; yes, but perhaps for his greater humility. Each argument at once suggests its opposite, and both are often fallacious. If we are to gain understanding, we must get out of these ruts; we must discard the vague notions of superiority, inferiority, equality which have hitherto corrupted every discussion of the subject and start afresh.

Very well, but just how shall we pose the question? And, to begin with, who are we to propound it at all? Man is at once judge and party to the case; but so is woman. What we need is an angel—neither man nor woman—but where shall we find one? Still, the angel would be poorly qualified to speak, for an angel is ignorant of all the basic facts involved in the problem. With a hermaphrodite we should be no better off, for here the situation is most peculiar; the hermaphrodite is not really the combination of a whole man and a whole woman, but consists of parts of each and thus is neither. It looks to me as if there are, after all, certain women who are best qualified to elucidate the situation of woman. Let us not be misled by the sophism that because Epimenides was a Cretan he was necessarily a liar; it is not a mysterious essence that compels men and women to act in good or in bad faith, it is their situation that inclines them more or less toward the search for truth. Many of today's women, fortunate in the restoration of all the privileges pertaining to the estate of the human being, can afford the luxury of impartiality—we even recognize its necessity. We are no longer like our partisan elders; by and large we have won the game. In recent debates on the status of women the United Nations has persistently maintained that the equality of the sexes is now becoming a reality, and already some of us have never had to sense in our femininity an inconvenience or an obstacle . Many problems appear to us to be more pressing than those which concern us in particular, and this detachment even allows us to hope that our attitude will be objective. Still, we know the feminine world more intimately than do the men because we have our roots in it, we grasp more immediately than do men what it means to a human being to be feminine; and we are more concerned with such knowledge. I have said that there are more pressing problems, but this does not prevent us from seeing some importance in asking how the fact of being women will affect our lives. What opportunities precisely have been given us and what withheld? What fate awaits our younger sisters, and what directions should they take? It is significant that books by women on women are in general animated in our day less by a wish to demand our rights than by an effort toward clarity and understanding. As we emerge from an era of excessive controversy, this book is offered as one attempt among others to confirm that statement.

But it is doubtless impossible to approach any human problem with a mind free from bias. The way in which questions are put, the points of view assumed, presuppose a relativity of interest; all characteristics imply values, and every objective description, so called, implies an ethical background. Rather than attempt to conceal principles more or less definitely implied, it is better to state them openly at the beginning. This will make it unnecessary to specify on every page in just what sense one uses such words as *superior, inferior, better, worse, progress, reaction,* and the like. If we survey some of the works on woman, we note that one of the points of view most frequently adopted is that of the public good, the general interest; and one always means by this the benefit of society as one wishes it to be maintained or established. For our part, we hold that the only public good is that which assures the private good of the citizens; we shall pass judgment on institutions according to their effectiveness in giving concrete opportunities to individuals. But we do not confuse the idea of private interest with that of happiness, although that is another common point of view. Are not women of the harem more happy than women voters? Is not the housekeeper happier than the working-woman? It is not too clear just what the word *happy* really means and still less what true values it may mask. There is no possibility of measuring the happiness of others, and it is always easy to describe as happy the situation in which one wishes to place them.

In particular those who are condemned to stagnation are often pronounced happy on the pretext that happiness consists in being at rest. This notion we reject, for our perspective is that of existentialist ethics. Every subject plays his part as such specifically through exploits or projects that serve as a mode of transcendence; he achieves liberty only through a continual reaching out toward other liberties. There is no justification for present existence other than its expansion into an indefinitely open future. Every time transcendence falls back into immanence, stagnation, there is a degradation of existence into the *"en-soi"* —the brutish life of subjection to given conditions—and of liberty into constraint and contingence. This downfall represents a moral fault if the subject consents to it; if it is inflicted upon him, it spells frustration and oppression. In both cases it is an absolute evil. Every individual concerned to justify his existence feels that his existence involves an undefined need to transcend himself, to engage in freely chosen projects.

Now, what peculiarly signalizes the situation of woman is that she— a free and autonomous being like all human creatures--nevertheless finds herself living in a world where men compel her to assume the status of the Other. They propose to stabilize her as object and to doom her to immanence since her transcendence is to be overshadowed and forever transcended by another ego (*conscience*) which is essential and sovereign. The drama of woman lies in this conflict between the fundamental aspirations of every subject (ego)—who always regards the self as the essential —and the compulsions of a situation in which she is the inessential. How can a human being in woman's situation attain fulfillment? What roads are open to her? Which are blocked? How can independence be recovered in a state of dependency? What circumstances limit woman's liberty and how can they be overcome? These are the fundamental questions on which I would fain throw some light. This means that I am interested in the fortunes of the individual as defined not in terms of happiness but in terms of liberty.

Quite evidently this problem would be without significance if we were to believe that woman's destiny is inevitably determined by physiological, psychological, or economic forces. Hence I shall discuss first of all the light in which woman is viewed by biology, psychoanalysis, and historical materialism. Next I shall try to show exactly how the concept of the "truly feminine" has been fashioned—why woman has been defined as the Other—and what have been the consequences from man's point of view. Then from woman's point of view I shall describe the world in which women must live; and thus we shall be able to envisage the difficulties in their way as, endeavoring to make their escape from the sphere hitherto assigned them, they aspire to full membership in the human race.

ed. note: The discussions promised by Ms. de Beauvoir may be found in her book, *The Second Sex.*

# 26. THE CRISIS IN WOMAN'S IDENTITY

## Betty Friedan

*Betty Friedan, since the publication, in 1963, of* The Feminine Mystique, *from which this selection is excerpted, has been one of the most important figures in the Women's Liberation Movement. Formerly the president of NOW (National Organization for Women), Ms. Friedan appears regularly on the lecture circuit on behalf of Women's Lib.*

I discovered a strange thing, interviewing women of my own generation over the past ten years. When we were growing up, many of us could not see ourselves beyond the age of twenty-one. We had no image of our own future, of ourselves as women.

I remember the stillness of a spring afternoon on the Smith campus in 1942, when I came to a frightening dead end in my own vision of the future. A few days earlier, I had received a notice that I had won a graduate fellowship. During the congratulations, underneath my excitement, I felt a strange uneasiness; there was a question that I did not want to think about.

"Is this really what I want to be?" The question shut me off, cold and alone, from the girls talking and studying on the sunny hillside behind the college house. I thought I was going to be a psychologist. But if I wasn't sure, what did I want to be? I felt the future closing in—and I could not see myself in it at all. I had no image of myself, stretching beyond college. I had come at seventeen from a Midwestern town, an unsure girl: the wide horizons of the world and the life of the mind had been opened to me. I had begun to know who I was and what I wanted to do. I could not go back now. I could not go home again, to the life of my mother and the women of our town, bound to home, bridge, shopping, children, husband, charity, clothes. But now that the time had come to make my own future, to take the deciding step, I suddenly did not know what I wanted to be.

I took the fellowship, but the next spring, under the alien California sun of another campus, the question came again, and I could not put it out of my mind. I had won another fellowship that would have com-

*Source:* "The Crisis in Woman's Identity" reprinted from *The Feminine Mystique* by Betty Friedan. By permission of W. W. Norton & Co., Inc. Copyright © 1963 by Betty Friedan.

mitted me to research for my doctorate, to a career as professional psychologist. "Is this really what I want to be?" The decision now truly terrified me. I lived in a terror of indecision for days, unable to think of anything else.

The question was not important, I told myself. No question was important to me that year but love. We walked in the Berkeley hills and a boy said: "Nothing can come of this, between us. I'll never win a fellowship like yours." Did I think I would be choosing, irrevocably, the cold loneliness of that afternoon if I went on? I gave up the fellowship in relief. But for years afterward, I could not read a word of the science that once I had thought of as my future life's work; the reminder of its loss was too painful.

I never could explain, hardly knew myself, why I gave up this career. I lived in the present, working on newspapers with no particular plan. I married, had children, lived according to the feminine mystique as a suburban housewife. But still the question haunted me. I could sense no purpose in my life. I could find no peace, until I finally faced it and worked out my own answer.

I discovered, talking to Smith seniors in 1959, that the question is no less terrifying to girls today. Only they answer it now in a way that my generation found, after half a lifetime, not to be an answer at all. These girls, mostly seniors, were sitting in the living room of the college house, having coffee. It was not too different from such an evening when I was a senior, except that many more of the girls wore rings on their left hands. I asked the ones around me what they planned to be. The engaged ones spoke of weddings, apartments, getting a job as a secretary while husband finished school. The others, after a hostile silence, gave vague answers about this job or that, graduate study, but no one had any real plans. A blonde with a ponytail asked me the next day if I had believed the things they had said. "None of it was true," she told me. "We don't like to be asked what we want to do. None of us know. None of us even like to think about it. The ones who are going to be married right away are the lucky ones. They don't have to think about it."

But I noticed that night that many of the engaged girls, sitting silently around the fire while I asked the others about jobs, had also seemed angry about something. "They don't want to think about not going on," my ponytailed informant said. "They know they're not going to use their education. They'll be wives and mothers. You can say you're going to keep on reading and be interested in the community. But that's not the same. You won't really go on. It's a disappointment to know you're going to stop now, and not go on and use it."

In counterpoint, I heard the words of a woman, fifteen years after she left college, a doctor's wife, mother of three, who said over coffee in her New England kitchen:

"The tragedy was, nobody ever looked us in the eye and said you have to decide what you want to do with your life, besides being your husband's wife and children's mother. I never thought it through until I was thirty-six, and my husband was so busy with his practice that he couldn't entertain me every night. The three boys were in school all day. I kept on trying to have babies despite an Rh discrepancy. After two miscarriages, they said I must stop. I thought that my own growth and evolution were over. I always knew as a child that I was going to grow up and go to college, and then get married, and that's as far as a girl has to think. After that, your husband determines and fills your life. It wasn't until I got so lonely as the doctor's wife and kept screaming at the kids because they didn't fill my life that I realized I had to make my own life. I still had to decide what I wanted to be. I hadn't finished evolving at all. But it took me ten years to think it through."

The feminine mystique permits, even encourages, women to ignore the question of their identity. The mystique says they can answer the question "Who am I?" by saying "Tom's wife . . . Mary's mother." But I don't think the mystique would have such power over American women if they did not fear to face this terrifying blank which makes them unable to see themselves after twenty-one. The truth is—and how long it has been true, I'm not sure, but it was true in my generation and it is true of girls growing up today—an American woman no longer has a private image to tell her who she is, or can be, or wants to be.

The public image, in the magazines and television commercials, is designed to sell washing machines, cake mixes, deodorants, detergents, rejuvenating face creams, hair tints. But the power of that image, on which companies spend millions of dollars for television time and ad space, comes from this: American women no longer know who they are. They are sorely in need of a new image to help them find their identity. As the motivational researchers keep telling the advertisers, American women are so unsure of who they should be that they look to this glossy public image to decide every detail of their lives. They look for the image they will no longer take from their mothers.

In my generation, many of us knew that we did not want to be like our mothers, even when we loved them. We could not help but see their disappointment. Did we understand, or only resent, the sadness, the emptiness, that made them hold too fast to us, try to live our lives, run our fathers' lives, spend their days shopping or yearning for things that never seemed to satisfy them, no matter how much money they cost?

Strangely, many mothers who loved their daughters—and mine was one —did not want their daughters to grow up like them either. They knew we needed something more.

But even if they urged, insisted, fought to help us educate ourselves, even if they talked with yearning of careers that were not open to them, they could not give us an image of what we could be. They could only tell us that their lives were too empty, tied to home; that children, cooking, clothes, bridge, and charities were not enough. A mother might tell her daughter, spell it out, "Don't be just a housewife like me." But that daughter, sensing that her mother was too frustrated to savor the love of her husband and children, might feel: "I will succeed where my mother failed, I will fulfill myself as a woman," and never read the lesson of her mother's life.

Recently, interviewing high-school girls who had started out full of promise and talent, but suddenly stopped their education, I began to see new dimensions to the problem of feminine conformity. These girls, it seemed at first, were merely following the typical curve of feminine adjustment. Earlier interested in geology or poetry, they now were interested only in being popular; to get boys to like them, they had concluded, it was better to be like all the other girls. On closer examination, I found that these girls were so terrified of becoming like their mothers that they could not see themselves at all. They were afraid to grow up. They had to copy in identical detail the composite image of the popular girl—denying what was best in themselves out of fear of femininity as they saw it in their mothers. One of these girls, seventeen years old, told me:

"I want so badly to feel like the other girls. I never get over this feeling of being a neophyte, not initiated. When I get up and have to cross a room, it's like I'm a beginner, or have some terrible affliction, and I'll never learn. I go to the local hangout after school and sit there for hours talking about clothes and hairdos and the twist, and I'm not that interested, so it's an effort. But I found out I could make them like me—just do what they do, dress like them, talk like them, not do things that are different. I guess I even started to make myself not different inside.

"I used to write poetry. The guidance office says I have this creative ability and I should be at the top of the class and have a great future. But things like that aren't what you need to be popular. The important thing for a girl is to be popular.

"Now I go out with boy after boy, and it's such an effort because I'm not myself with them. It makes you feel even more alone. And besides, I'm afraid of where it's going to lead. Pretty soon, all my differences will be smoothed out, and I'll be the kind of girl that could be a housewife.

"I don't want to think of growing up. If I had children, I'd want them to stay the same age. If I had to watch them grow up, I'd see myself growing older, and I wouldn't want to. My mother says she can't sleep at night, she's sick with worry over what I might do. When I was little, she wouldn't let me cross the street alone, long after the other kids did.

"I can't see myself as being married and having children. It's as if I wouldn't have any personality myself. My mother's like a rock that's been smoothed by the waves, like a void. She's put so much into her family that there's nothing left, and she resents us because she doesn't get enough in return. But sometimes it seems like there's nothing there. My mother doesn't serve any purpose except cleaning the house. She isn't happy, and she doesn't make my father happy. If she didn't care about us children at all, it would have the same effect as caring too much. It makes you want to do the opposite. I don't think it's really love. When I was little and I ran in all excited to tell her I'd learned how to stand on my head, she was never listening.

"Lately, I look into the mirror, and I'm so afraid I'm going to look like my mother. It frightens me, to catch myself being like her in gestures or speech or anything. I'm not like her in so many ways, but if I'm like her in this one way, perhaps I'll turn out like my mother after all. And that terrifies me."

And so the seventeen-year-old was so afraid of being a woman like her mother that she turned her back on all the things in herself and all the opportunities that would have made her a different woman, to copy from the outside the "popular" girls. And finally, in panic at losing herself, she turned her back on her own popularity and defied the conventional good behavior that would have won her a college scholarship. For lack of an image that would help her grow up as a woman true to herself, she retreated into the beatnik vacuum.

Another girl, a college junior from South Carolina told me:

"I don't want to be interested in a career I'll have to give up.

"My mother wanted to be a newspaper reporter from the time she was twelve, and I've seen her frustration for twenty years. I don't want to be interested in world affairs. I don't want to be interested in anything beside my home and being a wonderful wife and mother. Maybe education is a liability. Even the brightest boys at home want just a sweet, pretty girl. Only sometimes I wonder how it would feel to be able to stretch and stretch and stretch, and learn all you want, and not have to hold yourself back."

*The Liberation of Women*   **247**

Her mother, almost all our mothers, were housewives, though many had started or yearned for or regretted giving up careers. Whatever they told us, we, having eyes and ears and mind and heart, knew that their lives were somehow empty. We did not want to be like them, and yet what other model did we have?

The only other kind of women I knew, growing up, were the old-maid high-school teachers; the librarian; the one woman doctor in our town, who cut her hair like a man; and a few of my college professors. None of these women lived in the warm center of life as I had known it at home. Many had not married or had children. I dreaded being like them, even the ones who taught me truly to respect my own mind and use it, to feel that I had a part in the world. I never knew a woman, when I was growing up, who used her mind, played her own part in the world, and also loved, and had children.

I think that this has been the unknown heart of woman's problem in America for a long time, this lack of a private image. Public images that defy reason and have very little to do with women themselves have had the power to shape too much of their lives. These images would not have such power, if women were not suffering a crisis of identity.

The strange, terrifying jumping-off point that American women reach—at eighteen, twenty-one, twenty-five, forty-one—has been noticed for many years by sociologists, psychologists, analysts, educators. But I think it has not been understood for what it is. It has been called a "discontinuity" in cultural conditioning; it has been called woman's "role crisis." It has been blamed on the education which made American girls grow up feeling free and equal to boys—playing baseball, riding bicycles, conquering geometry and college boards, going away to college, going out in the world to get a job, living alone in an apartment in New York or Chicago or San Francisco, testing and discovering their own powers in the world. All this gave girls the feeling they could be and do whatever they wanted to, with the same freedom as boys, the critics said. It did not prepare them for their role as women. The crisis comes when they are forced to adjust to this role. Today's high rate of emotional distress and breakdown among women in their twenties and thirties is usually attributed to this "role crisis." If girls were educated for their role as women, they would not suffer this crisis, the adjusters say.

But I think they have seen only half the truth.

What if the terror a girl faces at twenty-one, when she must decide who she will be, is simply the terror of growing up—growing up, as women were not permitted to grow before? What if the terror a girl faces at twenty-one is the terror of freedom to decide her own life, with no one to order which path she will take, the freedom and the necessity to take paths women before were not able to take? What if those who choose the path of "feminine adjustment"—evading this terror by marrying at eighteen, losing themselves in having babies and the details of housekeeping—are simply refusing to grow up, to face the question of their own identity?

Mine was the first college generation to run head-on into the new mystique of feminine fulfillment. Before then, while most women did indeed end up as housewives and mothers, the point of education was to discover the life of the mind, to pursue truth and to take a place in the world. There was a sense, already dulling when I went to college, that we would be New Women. Our world would be much larger than home. Forty per cent of my college class at Smith had career plans. But I remember how, even then, some of the seniors, suffering the pangs of that bleak fear of the future, envied the few who escaped it by getting married right away.

The ones we envied then are suffering that terror now at forty. "Never have decided what kind of woman I am. Too much personal life in college. Wish I'd studied more science, history, government, gone deeper into philosophy," one wrote on an alumnae questionnaire, fifteen years later. "Still trying to find the rock to build on. Wish I had finished college. I got married instead." "Wish I'd developed a deeper and more creative life of my own and that I hadn't become engaged and married at nineteen. Having expected the ideal in marriage, including a hundred-per-cent devoted husband, it was a shock to find this isn't the way it is," wrote a mother of six.

Many of the younger generation of wives who marry early have never suffered this lonely terror. They thought they did not have to choose, to look into the future and plan what they wanted to do with their lives. They had only to wait to be chosen, marking time passively until the husband, the babies, the new house decided what the rest of their lives would be. They slid easily into their sexual role as women before they knew who they were themselves. It is these women who suffer most the problem that has no name.

It is my thesis that the core of the problem for women today is not sexual but a problem of identity—a stunting or evasion of growth that is perpetuated by the feminine mystique. It is my thesis that as the Victorian culture did not permit women to accept or gratify their basic sexual needs, our culture does not permit women to accept or gratify their basic need to grow and fulfill their potentialities as human beings, a need which is not solely defined by their sexual role.

Biologists have recently discovered a "youth serum" which, if fed to young caterpillars in the larva state, will keep them from ever maturing into moths; they will live out their lives as caterpillars. The expectations of feminine fulfillment that are fed to women by magazines, television, movies, and books that popularize psychological half-truths, and by parents, teachers and counselors who accept the feminine mystique, operate as a kind of youth serum, keeping most women in the state of sexual larvae, preventing them from achieving the maturity of which they are capable. And there is increasing evidence that woman's failure to grow to complete identity has hampered rather than enriched her sexual fulfillment, virtually doomed her to be castrative to her husband and sons, and caused neuroses, or problems as yet unnamed as neuroses, equal to those caused by sexual repression.

There have been identity crises for man at all the crucial turning points in human history, though those who lived through them did not give them that name. It is only in recent years that the theorists of psychology, sociology and theology have isolated this problem, and given it a name. But it is considered a man's problem. It is defined, for man, as the crisis of growing up, of choosing his identity, "the decision as to what one is and is going to be," in the words of the brilliant psychoanalyst Erik H. Erikson:

"I have called the major crisis of adolescence the identity crisis; it occurs in that period of the life cycle when each youth must forge for himself some central perspective and direction, some working unity, out of the effective remnants of his childhood and the hopes of his anticipated adulthood; he must detect some meaningful resemblance between what he has come to see in himself and what his sharpened awareness tells him others judge and expect him to be. . . . In some people, in some classes, at some periods in history, the crisis will be minimal; in other people, classes and periods, the crisis will be clearly marked off as a critical period, a kind of 'second birth,' apt to be aggravated either by widespread neuroticisms or by pervasive ideological unrest."

In this sense, the identity crisis of one man's life may reflect, or set off, a rebirth, or new stage, in the growing up of mankind. "In some periods of his history, and in some phases of his life cycle, man needs a new ideological orientation as surely and sorely as he must have air and food," said Erikson, focusing new light on the crisis of the young Martin Luther, who left a Catholic monastery at the end of the Middle Ages to forge a new identity for himself and Western man.

The search for identity is not new, however, in American thought—though in every generation, each man who writes about it discovers it anew. In America, from the beginning, it has somehow been understood that men must thrust into the future; the pace has always been too rapid for man's identity to stand still. In every generation, many men have suffered misery, unhappiness, and uncertainty because they could not take the image of the man they wanted to be from their fathers. The search for identity of the young man who can't go home again has always been a major theme of American writers. And it has always been considered right in America, good, for men to suffer these agonies of growth, to search for and find their own identities. The farm boy went to the city, the garment-maker's son became a doctor, Abraham Lincoln taught himself to read—these were more than rags-to-riches stories. They were an integral part of the American dream. The problem for many was money, race, color, class, which barred them from choice—not what they would be if they were free to choose.

Even today a young man learns soon enough that he must decide who he wants to be. If he does not decide in junior high, in high school, in college, he must somehow come to terms with it by twenty-five or thirty, or he is lost. But this search for identity is seen as a greater problem now because more and more boys cannot find images in our culture—from their fathers or other men—to help them in their search. The old frontiers have been conquered, and the boundaries of the new are not so clearly marked. More and more young men in America today suffer an identity crisis for want of any image of man worth pursuing, for want of a purpose that truly realizes their human abilities.

But why have theorists not recognized this same identity crisis in women? In terms of the old conventions and the new feminine mystique women are not expected to grow up to find out who they are, to choose their human identity. Anatomy is woman's destiny, say the theorists of femininity; the identity of woman is determined by her biology.

But is it? More and more women are asking themselves this question. As if they were waking from a coma, they ask, "Where am I . . . what am I doing here?" For the first time in their history, women are becoming aware of an identity crisis in their own lives, a crisis which began many generations ago, has grown worse with each succeeding generation, and will not end until they, or their daughters, turn an unknown corner and make of themselves and their lives the new image that so many women now so desperately need.

In a sense that goes beyond any one woman's life, I think this is the crisis of women growing up—a turning point from an immaturity that has been called femininity to full human identity. I think women had to suffer this crisis of identity, which began a hundred years ago, and have to suffer it still today, simply to become fully human.

# 27. THE THEORY OF SEXUAL POLITICS

## Kate Millett

*Born in St. Paul, Minnesota, Kate Millett has studied at the University of Minnesota, Oxford University, and received a Ph. D. in English from Columbia University. Her doctoral dissertation formed the basis for her first book Sexual Politics. The following material constitutes Part II of that book.*

The three instances of sexual description we have examined so far were remarkable for the large part which notions of ascendancy and power played within them. Coitus can scarcely be said to take place in a vacuum; although of itself it appears a biological and physical activity, it is set so deeply within the larger context of human affairs that it serves as a charged microcosm of the variety of attitudes and values to which culture subscribes. Among other things, it may serve as a model of sexual politics on an individual or personal plane.

But of course the transition from such scenes of intimacy to a wider context of political reference is a great step indeed. In introducing the term "sexual politics," one must first answer the inevitable question "Can the relationship between the sexes be viewed in a political light at all?" The answer depends on how one defines politics.[1] This essay does not define the political as that relatively narrow and exclusive world of meetings, chairmen, and parties. The term "politics" shall refer to power-structured relationships, arrangements whereby one group of persons is controlled by another. By way of parenthesis one might add that although an ideal politics might simply be conceived of as the arrangement of human life on agreeable and rational principles from whence the entire notion of power *over* others should be banished, one must confess that this is not what constitutes the political as we know it, and it is to this that we must address ourselves.

[1] The American Heritage Dictionary's fourth definition is fairly approximate: "methods or tactics involved in managing a state or government." *American Heritage Dictionary* (New York: American Heritage and Houghton Mifflin, 1969). One might expand this to a set of stratagems designed to maintain a system. If one understands patriarchy to be an institution perpetuated by such techniques of control, one has a working definition of how politics is conceived in this essay.

The following sketch, which might be described as "notes toward a theory of patriarchy," will attempt to prove that sex is a status category with political implications. Something of a pioneering effort, it must perforce be both tentative and imperfect. Because the intention is to provide an overall description, statements must be generalized, exceptions neglected, and subheadings overlapping and, to some degree, arbitrary as well.

The word "politics" is enlisted here when speaking of the sexes primarily because such a word is eminently useful in outlining the real nature of their relative status, historically and at the present. It is opportune, perhaps today even mandatory, that we develop a more relevant psychology and philosophy of power relationships beyond the simple conceptual framework provided by our traditional formal politics. Indeed, it may be imperative that we give some attention to defining a theory of politics which treats of power relationships on grounds less conventional than those to which we are accustomed.[2] I have therefore found it pertinent to define them on grounds of personal contact and interaction between members of well-defined and coherent groups: races, castes, classes, and sexes. For it is precisely because certain groups have no representation in a number of recognized political structures that their position tends to be so stable, their oppression so continuous.

In America, recent events have forced us to acknowledge at last that the relationship between the races is indeed a political one which involves the general control of one collectivity, defined by birth, over another collectivity also defined by birth. Groups who rule by birthright are fast disappearing, yet there remains one ancient and universal scheme for the domination of one birth group by another—the scheme that prevails in the area of sex. The study of racism has convinced us that a truly political state of affairs operates between the races to perpetuate a series of oppressive circumstances. The subordinated group has inadequate redress through existing political institutions, and is deterred thereby from organizing into conventional political struggle and opposition.

Quite in the same manner, a disinterested examination of our system of sexual relationship must point out that the situation between the sexes now, and throughout history, is a case of that phenomenon Max Weber

---

[2] I am indebted here to Ronald V. Samson's *The Psychology of Power* (New York: Random House, 1968) for his intelligent investigation of the connection between formal power structures and the family and for his analysis of how power corrupts basic human relationships.

defined as *herrschaft*, a relationship of dominance and subordinance.[3] What goes largely unexamined, often even unacknowledged (yet is institutionalized nonetheless) in our social order, is the birthright priority whereby males rule females. Through this system a most ingenious form of "interior colonization" has been achieved. It is one which tends moreover to be sturdier than any form of segregation, and more rigorous than class stratification, more uniform, certainly more enduring. However muted its present appearance may be, sexual dominion obtains nevertheless as perhaps the most pervasive ideology of our culture and provides its most fundamental concept of power.

This is so because our society, like all other historical civilizations, is a patriarchy.[4] The fact is evident at once if one recalls that the military, industry, technology, universities, science, political office, and finance—in short, every avenue of power within the society, including the coercive force of the police, is entirely in male hands. As the essence of politics is power, such realization cannot fail to carry impact. What lingers of supernatural authority, the Deity, "His" ministry, together with the ethics and values, the philosophy and art of our culture—its very civilization—as T. S. Eliot once observed, is of male manufacture.

If one takes patriarchal government to be the institution whereby that half of the populace which is female is controlled by that half which is male, the principles of patriarchy appear to be two fold: male shall dominate female, elder male shall dominate younger. However, just as with any human institution, there is frequently a distance between the real and the ideal; contradictions and exceptions do exist within the system. While patriarchy as an institution is a social constant so deeply entrenched as to run through all other political, social, or economic forms, whether of caste or class, feudality or bureaucracy, just as it pervades all major religions, it also exhibits great variety in history and

---

[3] "Domination in the quite general sense of power, i.e. the possibility of imposing one's will upon the behavior of other persons, can emerge in the most diverse forms." In this central passage of *Wirtschaft und Gesellschaft* Weber is particularly interested in two such forms: control through social authority ("patriarchal, magisterial, or princely") and control through economic force. In patriarchy as in other forms of domination "that control over economic goods, i.e. economic power, is a frequent, often purposively willed, consequence of domination as well as one of its most important instruments." Quoted from Max Rheinstein's and Edward Shil's translation of portions of *Wirtschaft und Gesellschaft* entitled *Max Weber on Law in Economy and Society* (New York: Simon and Schuster, 1967), pp. 323–24.

[4] No matriarchal societies are known to exist at present. Matrilineality, which may be, as some anthropologists have held, a residue or a transitional stage of matriarchy, does not constitute an exception to patriarchal rule, it simply channels the power held by males through female descent—e.g., the Avunculate.

locale. In democracies,[5] for example, females have often held no office or do so (as now) in such minuscule numbers as to be below even token representation. Aristocracy, on the other hand, with its emphasis upon the magic and dynastic properties of blood, may at times permit women to hold power. The principle of rule by elder males is violated even more frequently. Bearing in mind the variation and degree in patriarchy —as say between Saudi Arabia and Sweden, Indonesia and Red China— we also recognize our own form in the U.S. and Europe to be much altered and attenuated by the reforms described in the next chapter.

## 1. Ideological

Hannah Arendt[6] has observed that government is upheld by power supported either through consent or imposed through violence. Conditioning to an ideology amounts to the former. Sexual politics obtains consent through the "socialization" of both sexes to basic patriarchal politics with regard to temperament, role, and status. As to status, a pervasive assent to the prejudice of male superiority guarantees superior status in the male, inferior in the female. The first item, temperament, involves the formation of human personality along stereotyped lines of sex category ("masculine" and "feminine"), based on the needs and values of the dominant group and dictated by what its members cherish in themselves and find convenient in subordinates: aggression, intelligence, force, and efficacy in the male, passivity, ignorance, docility, "virtue," and ineffectuality in the female. This is complemented by a second factor, sex role, which decrees a consonant and highly elaborate code of conduct, gesture and attitude for each sex. In terms of activity, sex role assigns domestic service and attendance upon infants to the female, the rest of human achievement, interest, and ambition to the male. The limited role allotted the female tends to arrest her at the level of biological experience. Therefore, nearly all that can be described as distinctly human rather than animal activity (in their own way animals also give birth and care for their young) is largely reserved for the male. Of course, status again follows from such an assignment. Were one to

[5] Radical democracy would, of course, preclude patriarchy. One might find evidence of a general satisfaction with a less than perfect democracy in the fact that women have so rarely held power within modern "democracies."

[6] Hannah Arendt, "Speculations on Violence," *The New York Review of Books*, Vol. XII No. 4, February 27, 1969, p. 24.

analyze the three categories one might designate status as the political component, role as the sociological, and temperament as the psychological—yet their interdependence is unquestionable and they form a chain. Those awarded higher status tend to adopt roles of mastery, largely because they are first encouraged to develop temperaments of dominance. That this is true of caste and class as well is self-evident.

## 2. Biological

Patriarchal religion, popular attitude, and to some degree, science as well[7] assumes these psycho-social distinctions to rest upon biological differences between the sexes, so that where culture is acknowledged as shaping behavior, it is said to do no more than cooperate with nature. Yet the temperamental distinctions created in patriarchy ("masculine" and "feminine" personality traits) do not appear to originate in human nature, those of role and status still less.

The heavier musculature of the male, a secondary sexual characteristic and common among mammals, is biological in origin but is also culturally encouraged through breeding, diet and exercise. Yet it is hardly an adequate category on which to base political relations *within civilization*.[8] Male supremacy, like other political creeds, does not finally reside in

---

[7] The social, rather than the physical sciences are referred to here. Traditionally, medical science had often subscribed to such beliefs. This is no longer the case today, when the best medical research points to the conclusion that sexual stereotypes have no bases in biology.

[8] "The historians of Roman laws, having very justly remarked that neither birth nor affection was the foundation of the Roman family, have concluded that this function must be found in the power of the father or husband. They make a sort of primordial institution of this power; but they do not explain how this power was established, unless it was by the superiority of strength of the husband over the wife, and of the father over the children. Now, we deceive ourselves sadly when we thus place force as the origin of law. We shall see farther on that the authority of the father or husband, far from having been the first cause, was itself an effect; it was derived from religion, and was established by religion. Superior strength, therefore, was not the principle that established the family." Numa Denis Fustel de Coulanges, *The Ancient City* (1894). English translation by Willard Small (1873), Doubleday Anchor Reprint, pp. 41–42. Unfortunately Fustel de Coulanges neglects to mention how religion came to uphold patriarchal authority, since patriarchal religion is also an effect, rather than an original cause.

physical strength but in the acceptance of a value system which is not biological. Superior physical strength is not a factor in political relations —vide those of race and class. Civilization has always been able to substitute other methods (technic, weaponry, knowledge) for those of physical strength, and contemporary civilization has no further need of it. At present, as in the past, physical exertion is very generally a class factor, those at the bottom performing the most strenuous tasks, whether they be strong or not.

It is often assumed that patriarchy is endemic in human social life, explicable or even inevitable on the grounds of human physiology. Such a theory grants patriarchy logical as well as historical origin. Yet if as some anthropologists believe, patriarchy is not of primeval origin, but was preceded by some other social form we shall call pre-patriarchal, then the argument of physical strength as a theory of patriarchal *origins* would hardly constitute a sufficient explanation—unless the male's superior physical strength was released in accompaniment with some change in orientation through new values or new knowledge. Conjecture about origins is always frustrated by lack of certain evidence. Speculation about prehistory, which of necessity is what this must be, remains nothing but speculation. Were one to indulge in it, one might argue the likelihood of a hypothetical period preceding patriarchy.[9] What would be crucial to such a premise would be a state of mind in which the primary principle would be regarded as fertility or vitalist processes. In a primitive condition, before it developed civilization or any but the crudest technic, humanity would perhaps find the most impressive evidence of creative force in the visible birth of children, something of a miraculous event and linked analogically with the growth of the earth's vegetation.

It is possible that the circumstance which might drastically redirect such attitudes would be the discovery of paternity. There is some evidence that fertility cults in ancient society at some point took a turn toward patriarchy, displacing and downgrading female function in procreation and attributing the power of life to the phallus alone. Patriarchal religion could consolidate this position by the creation of a male God or gods, demoting, discrediting, or eliminating goddesses and constructing a theology whose basic postulates are male supremacist, and one of

---

[9] One might also include the caveat that such a social order need not imply the the domination of one sex which the term "matriarchy" would, by its semantic analogue to patriarchy, infer. Given the simpler scale of life and the fact that female-centered fertility religion might be offset by male physical strength, pre-patriarchy might have been fairly equalitarian.

whose central functions is to uphold and validate the patriarchal structure.[10]

So much for the evanescent delights afforded by the game of origins. The question of the historical origins of patriarchy—whether patriarchy originated primordially in the male's superior strength, or upon a later mobilization of such strength under certain circumstances—appears at the moment to be unanswerable. It is also probably irrelevant to contemporary patriarchy, where we are left with the realities of sexual politics, still grounded, we are often assured, on nature. Unfortunately, as the psycho-social distinctions made between the two sex groups which are said to justify their present political relationship are not the clear, specific, measurable and neutral ones of the physical sciences, but are instead of an entirely different nature—vague, amorphous, often even quasi-religious in phrasing—it must be admitted that many of the generally understood distinctions between the sexes in the more significant areas of role and temperament, not to mention status, have in fact essentially cultural, rather than biological, bases. Attempts to prove that temperamental dominance is inherent in the male (which for its advocates, would be tantamount to validating, logically as well as historically, the patriarchal situation regarding role and status) have been notably unsuccessful. Sources in the field are in hopeless disagreement about the nature of sexual differences, but the most reasonable among them have despaired of the ambition of any definite equation between temperament and biological nature. It appears that we are not soon to be enlightened as to the existence of any significant inherent differences between male and female beyond the bio-genital ones we already know. Endocrinology and genetics afford no definite evidence of determining mental-emotional differences.[11]

Not only is there insufficient evidence for the thesis that the present social distinctions of patriarchy (status, role, temperament) are physical

[10] Something like this appears to have taken place as the culture of Neolithic agricultural villages gave way to the culture of civilization and to patriarchy with the rise of cities. See Louis Mumford, *The City in History* (New York: Harcourt, Brace, 1961), Chapter One. A discovery such as paternity, a major acquisition of "scientific" knowledge might, hypothetically, have led to an expansion of population, surplus labor and strongclass stratification. There is good reason to suppose that the transformation of hunting into war also played a part.

[11] No convincing evidence has so far been advanced in this area. Experimentation regarding the connection between hormones and animal behavior not only yields highly ambivalent results but brings with it the hazards of reasoning by analogy to human behavior. For a summary of the arguments see David C. Glass (editor), *Biology and Behavior* (New York: Rockefeller University and the Russell Sage Foundation, 1968).

in origin, but we are hardly in a position to assess the existing differentiations, since distinctions which we know to be culturally induced at present so outweigh them. Whatever the "real" differences between the sexes may be, we are not likely to know them until the sexes are treated differently, that is alike. And this is very far from being the case at present. Important new research not only suggests that the possibilities of innate temperamental differences seem more remote than ever, but even raises questions as to the validity and permanence of psycho-sexual identity. In doing so it gives fairly concrete positive evidence of the overwhelmingly *cultural* character of gender, i.e. personality structure in terms of sexual category.

What Stoller and other experts define as "core gender identity" is now thought to be established in the young by the age of eighteen months. This is how Stroller differentiates between sex and gender:

"Dictionaries stress that the major connotation of *sex* is a biological one, as for example, in the phrases *sexual relations* or *the male sex*. In agreement with this, the word *sex*, in this work will refer to the male or female sex and the component biological parts that determine whether one is a male or a female; the word *sexual* will have connotations of anatomy and physiology. This obviously leaves tremendous areas of behavior, feelings, thoughts and fantasies that are related to the sexes and yet do not have primarily biological connotations. It is for some of these psychological phenomena that the term gender will be used: one can speak of the male sex or female sex, but one can also talk about masculinity and feminity and not necessarily be implying anything about anatomy or physiology. Thus, while *sex* and *gender* seem to common sense inextricably bound together, one purpose of this study will be to confirm the fact that the two realms (sex and gender) are not inevitably bound in anything like a one-to-one relationship, but each may go into quite independent ways."[12]

In cases of genital malformation and consequent erroneous gender assignment at birth, studied at the California Gender Identity Center, the discovery was made that it is easier to change the sex of an adolescent male, whose biological identity turns out to be contrary to his gender assignment and conditioning—through surgery—than to undo the educational consequences of years, which have succeeded in making the subject temperamentally feminine in gesture, sense of self, personality and interests. Studies done in California under Stoller's direc-

[12] Robert J. Stoller, *Sex and Gender* (New York, Science House, 1968), from the preface, pp. viii-ix.

tion offer proof that gender identity (I am a girl, I am a boy) is the primary identity any human being holds—the first as well as the most permanent and far-reaching. Stoller later makes emphatic the distinction that sex is biological, gender psychological, and therefore cultural: "*Gender* is a term that has psychological or cultural rather than biological connotations. If the proper terms for sex are 'male' and 'female,' the corresponding terms for gender are 'masculine' and 'feminine'; these latter may be quite independent of (biological) sex."[13] Indeed, so arbitrary is gender, that it may even be contrary to physiology: ". . . although the external genitalia (penis, testes, scrotum) contribute to the sense of maleness, no one of them is essential for it, not even all of them together. In the absence of complete evidence, I agree in general with Money, and the Hampsons who show in their large series of intersexed patients that gender role is determined by postnatal forces, regardless of the anatomy and physiology of the external genitalia."[14]

It is now believed[15] that the human fetus is originally physically female until the operation of androgen at a certain stage of gestation causes those with *y* chromosomes to develop into males. Psychosexually (e.g., in terms of masculine and feminine, and in contradistinction to male and female) there is no differentiation between the sexes at birth. Psychosexual personality is therefore postnatal and learned.

". . . the condition existing at birth and for several months thereafter is one of psychosexual undifferentiation. Just as in the embryo, morphologic sexual differentiation passes from a plastic stage to one of fixed immutability, so also does psychosexual differentiation become fixed and immutable—so much so, that mankind has traditionally assumed that so strong and fixed a feeling as personal sexual identity must stem from something innate, instinctive, and not subject to postnatal experience and learning. The error of this traditional assumption is that the power and permanence of something learned has been underestimated. The experiments of animal ethologists on imprinting have now corrected this misconception.[16]

[13] *Ibid.*, p. 9.

[14] *Ibid.*, p. 48.

[15] See Mary Jane Sherfey, "The Evolution and Nature of Female Sexuality in Relation to Psychoanalytic Theory," *Journal of the American Psychoanalytic Association*, vol. 14, January 1966, no. 1 (New York, International Universities Press, Inc.), and John Money, "Psychosexual Differentiation," in *Sex Research, New Developments* (New York, Holt, 1965).

[16] Money, op. cit., p. 12.

John Money who is quoted above, believes that "the acquisition of a native language is a human counterpart to imprinting," and gender first established "with the establishment of a native language."[17] This would place the time of establishment at about eighteen months. Jerome Kagin's[18] studies in how children of pre-speech age are handled and touched, tickled and spoken to in terms of their sexual identity ("Is it a boy or a girl?" "Hello, little fellow," "Isn't she pretty," etc.) put the most considerable emphasis on purely tactile learning which would have much to do with the child's sense of self, even before speech is attained.

Because of our social circumstances, male and female are really two cultures and their life experiences are utterly different—and this is crucial. Implicit in all the gender identity development which takes place through childhood is the sum total of the parents', the peers', and the culture's notions of what is appropriate to each gender by way of temperament, character, interests, status, worth, gesture, and expression. Every moment of the child's life is a clue to how he or she must think and behave to attain or satisfy the demands which gender places upon one. In adolescence, the merciless task of conformity grows to crisis proportions, generally cooling and settling in maturity.

Since patriarchy's biological foundations appear to be so very insecure, one has some cause to admire the strength of a "socialization" which can continue a universal condition "on faith alone," as it were, or through an acquired value system exclusively. What does seem decisive in assuring the maintenance of the temperamental differences between the sexes is the conditioning of early childhood. Conditioning runs in a circle of self-perpetuation and self-fulfilling prophecy. To take a simple example: expectations the culture cherishes about his gender identity encourage the young male to develop aggressive impulses, and the female to thwart her own or turn them inward. The result is that the male tends to have aggression reinforced in his behavior, often with significant anti-social possibilities. Thereupon the culture consents to believe the possession of the male indicator, the testes, penis, and scrotum, in itself characterizes the aggressive impulse, and even vulgarly celebrates it in such encomiums as "that guy has balls." The same process of reinforcement is evident in producing the chief "feminine" virtue of passivity.

In contemporary terminology, the basic division of temperamental trait is marshaled along the line of "aggression is male" and "passivity is

[17] *Ibid.*, p. 13.

[18] Jerome Kagin, "The Acquisition and Significance of Sex-Typing," in *Review of Child Development Research*, ed. M. Hoffman (New York, Russell Sage Foundation, 1964).

female." All other temperamental traits are somehow—often with the most dexterous ingenuity—aligned to correspond. If aggressiveness is the trait of the master class, docility must be the corresponding trait of a subject group. The usual hope of such line of reasoning is that "nature," by some impossible outside chance, might still be depended upon to rationalize the patriarchal system. An important consideration to be remembered here is that in patriarchy, the function of norm is unthinkingly delegated to the male—were it not, one might as plausibly speak of "feminine" behavior as active, and "masculine" behavior as hyperactive or hyperaggressive.

Here it might be added, by way of a coda, that data from physical sciences has recently been enlisted again to support sociological arguments, such as those of Lionel Tiger[19] who seeks a genetic justification of patriarchy by proposing a "bonding instinct" in males which assures their political and social control of human society. One sees the implication of such a theory by applying its premise to any ruling group. Tiger's thesis appears to be a misrepresentation of the work of Lorenz and other students of animal behavior. Since his evidence of inherent trait is patriarchal history and organization, his pretensions to physical evidence are both specious and circular. One can only advance genetic evidence when one has genetic (rather than historical) evidence to advance. As many authorities dismiss the possibility of instincts (complex inherent behavioral patterns) in humans altogether, admitting only reflexes and drives (far simpler neural responses),[20] the prospects of a "bonding instinct" appear particularly forlorn.

Should one regard sex in humans as a drive, it is still necessary to point out that the enormous area of our lives, both in early "socialization" and in adult experience, labeled "sexual behavior," is almost entirely the product of learning. So much is this the case that even the act of coitus itself is the product of a long series of learned responses— responses to the patterns and attitudes, even as to the object of sexual choice, which are set up for us by our social environment.

The arbitrary character of patriarchal ascriptions of temperament and role has little effect upon their power over us. Nor do the mutually exclusive, contradictory, and polar qualities of the categories "masculine" and "feminine" imposed upon human personality give rise to sufficiently serious questions among us. Under their aegis each personality becomes

---

[19] Lionel Tiger, *Men in Groups* (New York, Random House, 1968).

[20] Through instinct subhuman species might undertake the activity of building a complex nest or hive; through reflex or drive a human being might simply blink, feel hunger, etc.

little more, and often less than half, of its human potential. Politically, the fact that each group exhibits a circumscribed but complementary personality and range of activity is of secondary importance to the fact that each represents a status or power division. In the matter of conformity patriarchy is a governing ideology without peer; it is probable that no other system has ever exercised such a complete control over its subjects.

## 3. Sociological

Patriarchy's chief institution is the family. It is both a mirror of and a connection with the larger society; a patriarchal unit within a patriarchal whole. Mediating between the individual and the social structure, the family effects control and conformity where political and other authorities are insufficient.[21] As the fundamental instrument and the foundation unit of patriarchal society the family and its roles are prototypical. Serving as an agent of the larger society, the family not only encourages its own members to adjust and conform, but acts as a unit in the government of the patriarchal state which rules its citizens through its family heads. Even in patriarchal societies where they are granted legal citizenship, women tend to be ruled through the family alone and have little or no formal relation to the state.[22]

As co-operation between the family and the larger society is essential, else both would fall apart, the fate of three patriarchal institutions, the family, society, and the state are interrelated. In most forms of patriarchy this has generally led to the granting of religious support in statements such as the Catholic precept that "the father is head of the family," or Judaism's delegation of quasi-priestly authority to the male parent. Secular governments today also confirm this, as in census practices of designating the male as head of household, taxation, passports, etc. Female heads of household tend to be regarded as undesirable: the

[21] In some of my remarks on the family I am indebted to Goode's short and concise analysis. See William J. Goode, *The Family* (Englewood Cliffs, New Jersey, Prentice-Hall, 1964).

[22] Family, society, and state are three separate but connected entities: women have a decreasing importance as one goes from the first to the third category. But as each of the three categories exists within or is influenced by the overall institution of patriarchy, I am concerned here less with differentiation than with pointing out a general similarity.

phenomenon is a trait of poverty or misfortune. The Confucian prescription that the relationship between ruler and subject is parallel to that of farmer and children points to the essentially feudal character of the patriarchal family (and conversely, the familial character of feudalism) even in modern democracies.[23]

Traditionally, patriarchy granted the father nearly total ownership over wife or wives and children, including the powers of physical abuse and often even those of murder and sale. Classically, as head of the family the father is both begetter and owner in a system in which kinship is property.[24] Yet in strict patriarchy, kinship is acknowledged only through associates with the male line. Agnation excludes the descendants of the female line from property right and often even from recognition.[25] The first formulation of the patriarchal family was made by Sir Henry Maine, a nineteenth-century historian of ancient jurisprudence. Maine argues that the patriarchal basis of kinship is put in terms of dominion rather than blood; wives, though outsiders, are assimilated into the line, while sister's sons are excluded. Basing his definition of the family upon the *patria potestes* of Rome, Maine defined it as follows: "The eldest male parent is absolutely supreme in his household. His dominion extends to life and death and is as unqualified over his children and their houses as over his slaves."[26] In the archaic patriarchal family "the group consists of animate and inanimate property, of wife, children, slaves, land and goods, all held together by subjection to the despotic authority of the eldest male."[27]

McLennon's rebuttal[28] to Maine argued that the Roman *patria potestes* was an extreme form of patriarchy and by no means, as Maine had imagined, universal. Evidence of matrilineal societies (preliterate societies in Africa and elsewhere) refute Maine's assumption of the universality of agnation. Certainly Maine's central argument, as to the

---

[23] J. K. Folsom makes a convincing argument as to the anomalous character of patriarchal family systems within democratic society. See Joseph K. Folsom *The Family and Democratic Society* (New York: John Wiley, 1934, 1943).

[24] Marital as well as consanguine relation to the head of the family made one his property.

[25] Strict patriarchal descent is traced and recognized only through male heirs rather than through sister's, sons, etc. In a few generations descendants of female branches lose touch. Only those who "bear the name," who descend from male branches, may be recognized for kinship or inheritance.

[26] Sir Henry Maine, *Ancient Law* (London, Murray, 1861), p. 122.

[27] Sir Henry Maine, *The Early History of Institutions* (London), pp. 310–11.

[28] John McLennon, *The Patriarchal Theory* (London, Macmillan, 1885).

primeval or state of nature character of patriarchy is but a rather naïf[29] rationalization of an institution Maine tended to exalt. The assumption of patriarchy's primeval character is contradicted by much evidence which points to the conclusion that full patriarchal authority, particularly of the *patria potestes* is a late development and the total erosion of female status was likely to be gradual as has been its recovery.

In contemporary patriarchies the male's *de jure* priority has recently been modified through the granting of divorce,[30] protection, citizenship, and property to women. Their chattel status continues in their loss of name, their obligation to adopt the husband's domicile, and the general legal assumption that marriage involves an exchange of the female's domestic service and (sexual) consortium in return for financial support.[31]

The chief contribution of the family in patriarchy is the socialization of the young (largely through the example and admonition of their parents) into patriarchal ideology's prescribed attitudes toward the categories of role, temperament, and status. Although slight differences of definition depend here upon the parents' grasp of cultural values, the general effect of uniformity is achieved, to be further reinforced through peers, schools, media, and other learning sources, formal and informal. While we may niggle over the balance of authority between the personalities of various households, one must remember that the entire culture supports masculine authority in all areas of life and—outside of the home—permits the female none at all.

To insure that its crucial functions of reproduction and socialization of the young take place only within its confines, the patriarchal family insists upon legitimacy. Bronislaw Malinowski describes this as "the principle of legitimacy" formulating it as an insistence that "no child should be brought into the world without a man—and one man at that—

---

[29] Maine took the patriarchal family as the cell from which society evolved as gens, phratry, tribe, and nation grew, rather in the simplistic manner of Israel's twelve tribes descending from Jacob. Since Maine also dated the origin of patriarchy from the discovery of paternity, hardly a primeval condition, this too operates against the eternal character of patriarchal society.

[30] Many patriarchies granted divorce to males only. It has been accessible to women on any scale only during this century. Goode states that divorce rates were as high in Japan during the 1880s as they are in the U.S. today. Goode, *op. cit.*, p. 3.

[31] Divorce is granted to a male for his wife's failure in domestic service and consortium: it is not granted him for his wife's failure to render him financial support. Divorce is granted to a woman if her husband fails to support her, but not for his failure at domestic service or consortium. But see Karczewski versus Baltimore and Ohio Railroad, 274 F. Supp. 169.175 N.D. Illinois, 1967, where a precedent was set and the common law that decrees a wife might not sue for loss of consortium overturned.

assuming the role of sociological father."[32] By this apparently consistent and universal prohibition (whose penalties vary by class and in accord with the expected operations of the double standard) patriarchy decrees that the status of both child and mother is primarily or ultimately dependent upon the male. And since it is not only his social status, but even his economic power upon which his dependents generally rely, the position of the masculine figure within the family—as without—is materially, as well as ideologically, extremely strong.

Although there is no biological reason why the two central functions of the family (socialization and reproduction) need be inseparable from or even take place within it, revolutionary or utopian efforts to remove these functions from the family have been so frustrated, so beset by difficulties, that most experiments so far have involved a gradual return to tradition. This is strong evidence of how basic a form patriarchy is within all societies, and of how pervasive its effects upon family members. It is perhaps also an admonition that change undertaken without a thorough understanding of the socio-political institution to be changed is hardly productive. And yet radical social change cannot take place without having an effect upon patriarchy. And not simply because it is the political form which subordinates such a large percentage of the population (women and youth) but because it serves as a citadel of property and traditional interests. Marriages are financial alliances, and each household operates as an economic entity much like a corporation. As one student of the family states it, "the family is the keystone of the stratification system, the social mechanism by which it is maintained."[33]

## 4. Class

It is in the area of class that the castelike status of the female within patriarchy is most liable to confusion, for sexual status often operates in a superficially confusing way within the variable of class. In a society where status is dependent upon the economic, social and educational circumstances of class, it is possible for certain females to appear to stand higher than some males. Yet not when one looks more closely at

[32] Bronislaw Malinowski, *Sex, Culture and Myth* (New York, Harcourt, 1962), p. 63. An earlier statement is even more sweeping: "In all human societies moral tradition and the law decree that the group consisting of a woman and her offspring is not a sociologically complete unit." *Sex and Repression in Savage Society* (London, Humanities, 1927), p. 213.

[33] Goode, *op. cit.*, p. 80.

the subject. This is perhaps easier to see by means of analogy: a black doctor or lawyer has higher social status than a poor white sharecropper. But race, itself a caste system which subsumes class, persuades the latter citizen that he belongs to a higher order of life, just as it oppresses the black professional in spirit, whatever his material success may be. In much the same manner, a truck driver or butcher has always his "manhood" to fall back upon. Should this final vanity be offended, he may contemplate more violent methods. The literature of the past thirty years provides a staggering number of incidents in which the caste of virility triumphs over the social status of wealthy or even educated women. In literary contexts one has to deal with wish-fulfillment. Incidents from life (bullying, obscene, or hostile remarks) are probably another sort of psychological gesture of ascendancy. Both convey more hope than reality, for class divisions are generally quite impervious to the hostility of individuals. And yet while the existence of class division is not seriously threatened by such expressions of enmity, the existence of sexual hierarchy has been re-affirmed and mobilized to "punish" the female quite effectively.

The function of class or ethnic mores in patriarchy is largely a matter of how overtly displayed or how loudly enunciated the general ethic of masculine supremacy allows itself to become. Here one is confronted by what appears to be a paradox: while in the lower social strata, the male is more likely to claim authority on the strength of his sex rank alone, he is actually obliged more often to share power with the women of his class who are economically productive; whereas in the middle and upper classes, there is less tendency to assert a blunt patriarchal dominance, as men who enjoy such status have more power in any case.[34]

It is generally accepted that Western patriarchy has been much softened by the concepts of courtly and romantic love. While this is certainly true, such influence has also been vastly overestimated. In comparison with the candor of "machismo" or oriental behavior, one realizes how much of a concession traditional chivalrous behavior represents—a sporting kind of reparation to allow the subordinate female certain means of saving face. While a palliative to the injustice of woman's social position, chivalry is also a technique for disguising it. One must acknowledge that the chivalrous stance is a game the master group plays in elevating its subject to pedestal level. Historians of courtly love stress the fact that the raptures of the poets had no effect upon the legal or economic standing of women, and very little upon their social status.[35]

---

[34] Goode, op. cit., p. 74.

[35] This is the gist of Valency's summary of the situation before the troubadours, acknowledging that courtly love is an utter anomaly: "What regard to the social

As the sociologist Hugo Beigel has observed, both the courtly and the romantic versions of love are "grants" which the male concedes out of his total powers.[36] Both have had the effect of obscuring the patriarchal character of Western culture and in their general tendency to attribute impossible virtues to women, have ended by confining them in a narrow and often remarkably conscribing sphere of behavior. It was a Victorian habit, for example, to insist the female assume the function of serving as the male's conscience and living the life of goodness he found tedious but felt someone ought to do anyway.

The concept of romantic love affords a means of emotional manipulation which the male is free to exploit, since love is the only circumstance in which the female is (ideologically) pardoned for sexual activity. And convictions of romantic love are convenient to both parties since this is often the only condition in which the female can overcome the far more powerful conditioning she has received toward sexual inhibition. Romantic love also obscures the realities of female status and the burden of economic dependency. As to "chivalry," such gallant gesture as still resides in the middle classes has degenerated to a tired ritualism, which scarcely serves to mask the status situation of the present.

Within patriarchy one must often deal with contradictions which are simply a matter of class style. David Riesman has noted that as the working class has been assimilated into the middle class, so have its sexual mores and attitudes. The fairly blatant male chauvinism which was once a province of the lower class of immigrant male has been absorbed and taken on a certain glamour through a number of contemporary figures, who have made it, and a certain number of other working-class male attitudes, part of a new, and at the moment, fashionable life style. So influential is this working-class ideal of brute virility (or more accurately, a literary and therefore middle-class version of it) become in our time that it may replace more discreet and "gentlemanly" attitudes of the past.[37]

---

background, all that can be stated with confidence is that we know nothing of the objective relationships of men and women in the Middle Ages which might conceivably motivate the strain of love-poetry which the troubadours developed." Maurice Valency, *In Praise of Love* (Macmillan, New York, 1958), p. 5.

[36] Hugo Beigel "Romantic Love," *The American Sociological Review*, Vol. 16, 1951, p. 331.

[37] Mailer and Miller occur to one in this connection, and Lawrence as well. One might trace Rojack's very existence as a fictional figure to the virility symbol of Jack London's Ernest Everhard and Tennessee Williams' Stanley Kowalski. That Rojack is also literate is nothing more than an elegant finish upon the furniture of his "manhood" solidly based in the hard oaken grain of his mastery over any and every "broad" he can better, bludgeon, or bugger.

One of the chief effects of class within patriarchy is to set one woman against another, in the past creating a lively antagonism between whore and matron, and in the present between career woman and housewife. One envies the other her "security" and prestige, while the envied yearns beyond the confines of respectability for what she takes to be the other's freedom, adventure, and contact with the great world. Through the multiple advantages of the double standard, the male participates in both worlds, empowered by his superior social and economic resources to play the estranged women against each other as rivals. One might also recognize subsidiary status categories among women: not only is virtue class, but beauty and age as well.

Perhaps, in the final analysis, it is possible to argue that women tend to transcend the usual class stratifications in patriarchy, for whatever the class of her birth and education, the female has fewer permanent class associations than does the male. Economic dependency renders her affiliations with any class a tangential, vicarious, and temporary matter. Aristotle observed that the only slave to whom a commoner might lay claim was his woman, and the service of an unpaid domestic still provides working-class males with a "cushion" against the buffets of the class system which incidentally provides them with some of the psychic luxuries of the leisure class. Thrown upon their own resources, few women rise above working class in personal prestige and economic power, and women as a group do not enjoy many of the interests and benefits any class may offer its male members. Women have therefore less of an investment in the class system. But it is important to understand that as with any group whose existence is parasitic to its rulers, women are a dependency class who live on surplus. And their marginal life frequently renders them conservative, for like all persons in their situation (slaves are a classic example here) they identify their own survival with the prosperity of those who feed them. The hope of seeking liberating radical solutions of their own seems too remote for the majority to dare contemplate and remains so until consciousness on the subject is raised.

As race is emerging as one of the final variables in sexual politics, it is pertinent, especially in a discussion of modern literature, to devote a few words to it as well. Traditionally, the white male has been accustomed to concede the female of his own race, in her capacity as "his woman" a higher status than that ascribed to the black male.[38] Yet as

---

[38] It would appear that the "pure flower of white womanhood" has at least at times been something of a disappointment to her lord as a fellow-racist. The historic connection of the Abolitionist and the Woman's Movement is some evidence

white racist ideology is exposed and begins to erode, racism's older protective attitudes toward (white) women also begin to give way. And the priorities of maintaining male supremacy might outweigh even those of white supremacy; sexism may be more endemic in our own society than racism. For example, one notes in authors whom we would now term overtly racist, such as D. H. Lawrence—whose contempt for what he so often designates as inferior breeds is unabashed—instances where the lower-caste male is brought on to master or humiliate the white man's own insubordinate mate. Needless to say, the female of the non-white races does not figure in such tales save as an exemplum of "true" womanhood's servility, worthy of imitation by other less carefully instructed females. Contemporary white sociology often operates under a similar patriarchal bias when its rhetoric inclines toward the assertion that the "matriarchal" (e.g. matrifocal) aspect of black society and the "castration" of the black male are the most deplorable symptoms of black oppression in white racist society, with the implication that racial inequity is capable of solution by a restoration of masculine authority. Whatever the facts of the matter may be, it can also be suggested that analysis of this kind presupposes patriarchal values without questioning them, and tends to obscure both the true character of and the responsibility for racist injustice toward black humanity of both sexes.

## 5. Economic and Educational

One of the most efficient branches of patriarchal government lies in the agency of its economic hold over its female subjects. In traditional patriarchy, women, as non-persons without legal standing, were permitted no actual economic existence as they could neither own nor earn in their own right. Since women have always worked in patriarchal societies, often at the most routine or strenuous tasks, what is at issue

---

of this, as well as the incident of white female and black male marriages as compared with those of white male and black female. Figures on miscegenation are very difficult to obtain: Goode (*op. cit.*, p. 37) estimates the proportion of white women marrying black men to be between 3 to 10 times the proportion of white men marrying black women. Robert K. Merton "Intermarriage and the Social Structure" *Psychiatry*, Vol. 4, August 1941, p. 374, states that "most intercaste sex relations—not marriages—are between white men and Negro women." It is hardly necessary to emphasize that the more extensive sexual contacts between white males and black females have not only been extramarital, but (on the part of the white male) crassly exploitative. Under slavery it was simply a case of rape.

here is not labor but economic reward. In modern reformed patriarchal societies, women have certain economic rights, yet the "woman's work" in which some two thirds of the female population in most developed countries are engaged is work that is not paid for.[39] In a money economy where autonomy and prestige depend upon currency, this is a fact of great importance. In general, the position of women in patriarchy is a continuous function of their economic dependence. Just as their social position is vicarious and achieved (often on a temporary or marginal basis) through males, their relation to the economy is also typically vicarious or tangential.

Of that third of women who are employed, their average wages represent half of the average income enjoyed by men. These are the U. S. Department of Labor statistics for average year-round income: white male, $6704, non-white male $4277, white female, $3991, and non-white female $2816.[40] The disparity is made somewhat more remarkable because the educational level of women is generally higher than that of men in comparable income brackets.[41] Further, the kinds of employment open to women in modern patriarchies are, with few exceptions, menial, ill paid and without status.[42]

In modern capitalist countries women also function as a reverse labor force, enlisted in times of war and expansion and discharged in times of peace and recession. In this role American women have replaced immigrant labor and now compete with the racial minorities. In socialist

[39] Sweden is an exception in considering housework a material service rendered and calculable in divorce suits etc. Thirty-three to forty per cent of the female population have market employment in Western countries: this leaves up to two thirds out of the market labor force. In Sweden and the Soviet Union that figure is lower.

[40] U. S. Department of Labor Statistics for 1966 (latest available figures). The proportion of women earning more than $10,000 a year in 1966 was 7/10 of 1%. See Mary Dublin Keyserling "Realities of Women's Current Position in the Labor Force" in *Sex Discrimination in Employment Practices,* a report from the conference (pamphlet) University extension, U.C.L.A. and the Women's Bureau, September 19, 1968.

[41] See *The 1965 Handbook on Women Workers,* United States Department of Labor, Women's Bureau: "In every major occupational group the median wage or salary income of women was less than that of men. This is true at all levels of educational attainment." A comparison of the income received by women and men with equal amounts of schooling revealed that women who had completed four years of college received incomes which were only 47% of those paid to men with the same educational training; high school graduates earned only 38%, and grade school graduates only 33%.

[42] For the distribution of women in lower income and lower status positions see *Background Facts on Working Women* (pamphlet) U.S. Department of Labor, Women's Bureau.

countries the female labor force is generally in the lower ranks as well, despite a high incidence of women in certain professions such as medicine. The status and rewards of such professions have declined as women enter them, and they are permitted to enter such areas under a rationale the society or the state (and socialist countries are also patriarchal) rather than woman is served by such activity.

Since woman's independence in economic life is viewed with distrust, prescriptive agencies of all kinds (religion, psychology, advertising, etc.) continuously admonish or even inveigh against the employment of middle-class women, particularly mothers. The toil of working-class women is more readily accepted as "need," if not always by the working-class itself, at least by the middle-class. And to be sure, it serves the purpose of making available cheap labor in factory and lower-grade service and clerical positions. Its wages and tasks are so unremunerative that, unlike more prestigious employment for women, it fails to threaten patriarchy financially or psychologically. Women who are employed have two jobs since the burden of domestic service and child care is unrelieved either by day care or other social agencies, or by the co-operation of husbands. The invention of labor-saving devices has had no appreciable effect on the duration, even if it has affected the quality of their drudgery.[43] Discrimination in matters of hiring, maternity, wages and hours is very great.[44] In the U. S. a recent law forbidding discrimination in employment, the first and only federal legislative guarantee of rights granted to American women since the vote, is not enforced, has not been enforced since its passage, and was not enacted to be enforced.[45]

In terms of industry and production, the situation of women is in many ways comparable both to colonial and to pre-industrial peoples. Although they achieved their first economic autonomy in the industrial revolution and now constitute a large and underpaid factory population, women do not participate directly in technology or in production. What they customarily produce (domestic and personal service) has no market value

[43] "For a married woman without children the irreducible minimum of work probably takes between fifteen to twenty hours a week, for a woman with small children the minimum is probably 70–80 hours a week." Margaret Benston, "The Political Economy of Women's Liberation," Monthly Review, Vol. XXI, September 1969.

[44] See the publications of the Women's Bureau and particularly Sex Discrimination in Employment Practices (op. cit.) and Carolyn Bird, Born Female (New York: McKay, 1968).

[45] Title VII of the 1964 Civil Rights Act. The inclusion of "sex" in the law upholding the civil right of freedom from discrimination in employment was half a joke and half an attempt on the part of Southern congressmen to force Northern industrial states to abandon passage of the bill.

and is, as it were, pre-capital. Nor, where they do participate in production of commodities through employment, do they own or control or even comprehend the process in which they participate. An example might make this clearer: the refrigerator is a machine all women use, some assemble it in factories, and a very few with scientific education understand its principles of operation. Yet the heavy industries which roll its steel and produce the dies for its parts are in male hands. The same is true of the typewriter, the auto, etc. Now, while knowledge is fragmented even among the male population, collectively they could reconstruct any technological device. But in the absence of males, women's distance from technology today is sufficiently great that it is doubtful that they could replace or repair such machines on any significant scale. Woman's distance from higher technology is even greater: large-scale building construction; the development of computers; the moon shot, occur as further examples. If knowledge is power, power is also knowledge, and a large factor in their subordinate position is the fairly systematic ignorance patriarchy imposes upon women.

Since education and economy are so closely related in the advanced nations, it is significant that the general level and style of higher education for women, particularly in their many remaining segregated institutions, is closer to that of Renaissance humanism than to the skills of mid-twentieth-century scientific and technological society. Traditionally patriarchy permitted occasional minimal literacy to women while higher education was closed to them. While modern patriarchies have, fairly recently, opened all educational levels to women,[46] the kind and quality of education is not the same for each sex. This difference is of course apparent in early socialization, but it persists and enters into higher education as well. Universities, once places of scholarship and the training of a few professionals, now also produce the personnel of a technocracy. This is not the case with regard to women. Their own colleges typically produce neither scholars nor professionals nor technocrats. Nor are they funded by government and corporations as are male colleges

[46] We often forget how recent an event is higher education for women. In the U.S. it is barely one hundred years old; in many Western countries barely fifty. Oxford did not grant degrees to women on the same terms as to men until 1920. In Japan and a number of other countries universities have been open to women only in the period after World War II. There are still areas where higher education for women scarcely exists. Women do not have the same access to education as do men. The Princeton Report stated that "although at the high school level more girls than boys receive grades of "A," roughly 50% more boys than girls go to college." *The Princeton Report to the Alumni on Co-Education* (pamphlet), Princeton, N.J. 1968, p. 10. Most other authorities give the national ratio of college students as two males to one female. In a great many countries it is far lower.

and those co-educational colleges and universities whose primary function is the education of males.

As patriarchy enforces a temperamental imbalance of personality traits between the sexes, its educational institutions, segregated or co-educational, accept a cultural programing toward the generally operative division between "masculine" and "feminine" subject matter, assigning the humanities and certain social sciences (at least in their lower or marginal branches) to the female—and science and technology, the professions, business and engineering to the male. Of course the balance of employment, prestige and reward at present lie with the latter. Control of these fields is very greatly a matter of political power. One might also point out how the exclusive dominance of males in the more prestigious fields directly serves the interests of patriarchal power in industry, government, and the military. And since patriarchy encourages an imbalance in human temperament along sex lines, both divisions of learning (science and the humanities) reflect this imbalance. The humanities, because not exclusively male, suffer in prestige: the sciences, technology, and business, because they are nearly exclusively male reflect the deformation of the "masculine" personality, e.g., a certain predatory or aggressive character.

In keeping with the inferior sphere of culture to which women in patriarchy have always been restricted, the present encouragement of their "artistic" interests through study of the humanities is hardly more than an extension of the "accomplishments" they once cultivated in preparation for the marriage market. Achievement in the arts and humanities is reserved, now, as it has been historically, for males. Token representation, be it Susan Sontag's or Lady Murasaki's, does not vitiate this rule.

## 6. Force

We are not accustomed to associate patriarchy with force. So perfect is its system of socialization, so complete the general assent to its values, so long and so universally has it prevailed in human society, that it scarcely seems to require violent implementation. Customarily, we view its brutalities in the past as exotic or "primitive" custom. Those of the present are regarded as the product of individual deviance, confined to pathological or exceptional behavior, and without general import. And yet, just as under other total ideologies (racism and colonialism are somewhat analogous in this respect) control in patriarchal society would be imperfect, even inoperable, unless it had the rule of force to rely upon, both in emergencies and as an ever-present instrument of intimidation.

Historically, most patriarchies have institutionalized force through their legal systems. For example, strict patriarchies such as that of Islam, have implemented the prohibition against illegitimacy or sexual autonomy with a death sentence. In Afghanistan and Saudi Arabia the adulteress is still stoned to death with a mullah presiding at the execution. Execution by stoning was once common practice through the Near East. It is still condoned in Sicily. Needless to say there was and is no penalty imposed upon the male corespondent. Save in recent times or exceptional cases, adultery was not generally recognized in males except as an offense one male might commit against another's property interest. In Tokugawa Japan, for example, an elaborate set of legal distinctions were made according to class. A samurai was entitled, and in the face of public knowledge, even obliged, to execute an adulterous wife, whereas a chōnin (common citizen) or peasant might respond as he pleased. In cases of cross-class adultery, the lower-class male convicted of sexual intimacy with his employer's wife would, because he had violated taboos of class and property, be beheaded together with her. Upper-strata males had, of course, the same license to seduce lower-class women as we are familiar with in Western societies.

Indirectly, one form of "death penalty" still obtains even in America today. Patriarchal legal systems in depriving women of control over their own bodies drive them to illegal abortions; it is estimated that between two and five thousand women die each year from this cause.[47]

Excepting a social license to physical abuse among certain class and ethnic groups, force is diffuse and generalized in most contemporary patriarchies. Significantly, force itself is restricted to the male who alone is psychologically and technically equipped to perpetrate physical violence.[48] Where differences in physical strength have become immaterial through the use of arms, the female is rendered innocuous by her socialization. Before assault she is almost universally defenseless both by her physical and emotional training. Needless to say, this has the most far-reaching effects on the social and psychological behavior of both sexes.

[47] Since abortion is extralegal, figures are difficult to obtain. This figure is based on the estimates of abortionists and referral services. Suicides in pregnancy are not officially reported either.

[48] Vivid exceptions come to mind in the wars of liberation conducted by Vietnam, China, etc. But through most of history, women have been unarmed and forbidden to exhibit any defense of their own.

Patriarchal force also relies on a form of violence particularly sexual in character and realized most completely in the act of rape. The figures of rapes reported represent only a fraction of those which occur,[49] as the "shame" of the event is sufficient to deter women from the notion of civil prosecution under the public circumstances of a trial. Traditionally rape has been viewed as an offense one male commits upon another—a matter of abusing "his woman." Vendetta, such as occurs in the American South, is carried out for masculine satisfaction, the exhilarations of race hatred, and the interests of property and vanity (honor). In rape, the emotions of aggression, hatred, contempt, and the desire to break or violate personality, take a form consummately appropriate to sexual politics. In the passages analyzed at the outset of this study, such emotions were present at a barely sublimated level and were a key factor in explaining the attitude behind the author's use of language and tone.[50]

Patriarchal societies typically link feelings of cruelty with sexuality, the latter often equated both with evil and with power. This is apparent both in the sexual fantasy reported by psychoanalysis and that reported by pornography. The rule here associates sadism with the male ("the masculine role") and victimization with the female ("the feminine role").[51] Emotional response to violence against women in patriarchy is often curiously ambivalent; references to wife-beating, for example, invariably produce laughter and some embarrassment. Exemplary atrocity, such as the mass murders committed by Richard Speck, greeted at one level with a certain scandalized, possibly hypocritical indignation, is capable of eliciting a mass response of titillation at another level. At such times one even hears from men occasional expressions of envy or amusement. In view of the sadistic character of such public fantasy as caters to male audiences in pornography or semi-pornographic media, one might expect that a certain element of identification is by no means absent from the general response. Probably a similar collective *frisson* sweeps through racist society when its more "logical" members have perpetrated a lynching. Unconsciously, both crimes may serve the larger group as a ritual act, cathartic in effect.

---

[49] They are still high. The number of rapes reported in the city of New York in 1967 was 2432. Figure supplied by Police Department.

[50] It is interesting that male victims of rape at the hands of other males often feel twice imposed upon, as they have not only been subjected to forcible and painful intercourse, but further abused in being reduced to the status of a female. Much of this is evident in Genet and in the contempt homosexual society reserves for its "passive" or "female" partners.

[51] Masculine masochism is regarded as exceptional and often explained as latently homosexual, or a matter of the subject playing "the female role"—e.g., victim.

Hostility is expressed in a number of ways. One is laughter. Misogynist literature, the primary vehicle of masculine hostility, is both an hortatory and comic genre. Of all artistic forms in patriarchy it is the most frankly propagandistic. Its aim is to reinforce both sexual factions in their status. Ancient, Medieval, and Renaissance literature in the West has each had a large element of misogyny.[52] Nor is the East without a strong tradition here, notably in the Confucian strain which held sway in Japan as well as China. The Western tradition was indeed moderated somewhat by the introduction of courtly love. But the old diatribes and attacks were coterminous with the new idealization of woman. In the case of Petrarch, Boccaccio, and some others, one can find both attitudes fully expressed, presumably as evidence of different moods, a courtly pose adopted for the ephemeral needs of the vernacular, a grave animosity for sober and eternal Latin.[53] As courtly love was transformed to romantic love, literary misogyny grew somewhat out of fashion. In some places in the eighteenth century it declined into ridicule and exhortative satire. In the nineteenth century its more acrimonious forms almost disappeared in English. Its resurrection in twentieth-century attitudes and literature is the result of a resentment over patriarchal reform, aided by the growing permissiveness in expression which has taken place at an increasing rate in the last fifty years.

Since the abatement of censorship, masculine hostility (psychological or physical) in specifically *sexual* contexts has become far more apparent. Yet as masculine hostility has been fairly continuous, one deals here probably less with a matter of increase than with a new frankness in expressing hostility in specifically sexual contexts. It is a matter of release and freedom to express what was once forbidden expression outside of pornography or other "underground" productions, such as those of De Sade. As one recalls both the euphemism and the idealism of descriptions of coitus in the Romantic poets (Keats's *Eve of St. Agnes*), or the Victorian novelists (Hardy, for example) and contrasts it with Miller or William Burroughs, one has an idea of how contemporary literature has absorbed not only the truthful explicitness of pornography,

---

[52] The literature of misogyny is so vast that no summary of sensible proportions could do it justice. The best reference on the subject is Katherine M. Rogers, *The Troublesome Helpmate, A History of Misogyny in Literature* (Seattle, University of Washington Press, 1966).

[53] As well as the exquisite sonnets of love, Petrarch composed satires on women as the "De Remediis utriusque Fortunae" and *Epistolae Seniles*. Boccaccio too could balance the chivalry of romances (Filostrato, Ameto, and Fiammetta) with the vituperance of Corbaccio, a splenetic attack on women more than medieval in violence.

but its anti-social character as well. Since this tendency to hurt or insult has been given free expression, it has become far easier to assess sexual antagonism in the male.

The history of patriarchy presents a variety of cruelties and barbarities: the suttee execution in India, the crippling deformity of footbinding in China, the lifelong ignominy of the veil in Islam, or the widespread persecution of sequestration, the gynacium, and purdah. Phenomenon such as clitoroidectomy, clitoral incision, the sale and enslavement of women under one guise or another, involuntary and child marriages, concubinage and prostitution, still take place—the first in Africa, the latter in the Near and Far East, the last generally. The rationale which accompanies that imposition of male authority euphemistically referred to as "the battle of the sexes" bears a certain resemblance to the formulas of nations at war, where any heinousness is justified on the grounds that the enemy is either an inferior species or really not human at all. The patriarchal mentality has concocted a whole series of rationales about women which accomplish this purpose tolerably well. And these traditional beliefs still invade our consciousness and affect our thinking to an extent few of us would be willing to admit.


## 7. Anthropological: Myth and Religion

Evidence from anthropology, religious and literary myth all attests to the politically expedient character of patriarchal convictions about women. One anthropologist refers to a consistent patriarchal strain of assumption that "women's biological differences set her apart . . . she is essentially inferior," and since "human institutions grow from deep and primal anxieties and are shaped by irrational psychological mechanisms . . . socially organized attitudes toward women arise from basic tensions expressed by the male."[54] Under patriarchy the female did not herself develop the symbols by which she is described. As both the primitive and the civilized worlds are male worlds, the ideas which shaped culture in regard to the female were also of male design. The image of women as we know it is an image created by men and fashioned to suit their needs. These needs spring from a fear of the "otherness" of woman. Yet this notion itself presupposes that patriarchy has already been estab-

[54] H. R. Hays, *The Dangerous Sex, the Myth of Feminine Evil* (New York: Putnam, 1964). Much of my summary in this section is indebted to Hays's useful assessment of cultural notions about the female.

lished and the male has already set himself as the human norm, the subject and referent to which the female is "other" or alien. Whatever its origin, the function of the male's sexual antipathy is to provide a means of control over a subordinate group and a rationale which justifies the inferior station of those in a lower order, "explaining" the oppression of their lives.

The feeling that woman's sexual functions are impure is both worldwide and persistent. One sees evidence of it everywhere in literature, in myth, in primitive and civilized life. It is striking how the notion persists today. The event of menstruation, for example, is a largely clandestine affair, and the psycho-social effect of the stigma attached must have great effect on the female ego. There is a large anthropological literature on menstrual taboo; the practice of isolating offenders in huts at the edge of the village occurs throughout the primitive world. Contemporary slang denominates menstruation as "the curse." There is considerable evidence that such discomfort as women suffer during their period is often likely to be psychosomatic, rather than physiological, cultural rather than biological, in origin. That this may also be true to some extent of labor and delivery is attested to by the recent experiment with "painless childbirth." Patriarchal circumstances and beliefs seem to have the effect of poisoning the female's own sense of physical self until it often truly becomes the burden it is said to be.

Primitive peoples explain the phenomenon of the female's genitals in terms of a wound, sometimes reasoning that she was visited by a bird or snake and mutilated into her present condition. Once she was wounded, now she bleeds. Contemporary slang for the vagina is "gash." The Freudian description of the female genitals is in terms of a "castrated" condition. The uneasiness and disgust female genitals arouse in patriarchal societies is attested to through religious, cultural, and literary proscription. In preliterate groups fear is also a factor, as in the belief in a castrating *vagina dentata*. The penis, badge of the male's superior status in both preliterate and civilized patriarchies, is given the most crucial significance, the subject both of endless boasting and endless anxiety.

Nearly all patriarchies enforce taboos against women touching ritual objects (those of war or religion) or food. In ancient and preliterate societies women are generally not permitted to eat with men. Women eat apart today in a great number of cultures, chiefly those of the Near and Far East. Some of the inspiration of such custom appears to lie in fears of contamination, probably sexual in origin. In their function of domestic servants, females are forced to prepare food, yet at the same time may be liable to spread their contagion through it. A similar situation obtains with blacks in the United States. They are considered filthy and infectious, yet as domestics they are forced to prepare food for their queasy superiors. In both cases the dilemma is generally solved in a deplorably illogical fashion by segregating the act of eating itself, while cooking is carried on out of sight by the very group who would infect the table. With an admirable consistency, some Hindu males do not permit their wives to touch their food at all. In nearly every patriarchal group it is expected that the dominant male will eat first or eat better, and even where the sexes feed together, the male shall be served by the female.[55]

All patriarchies have hedged virginity and defloration in elaborate rites and interdictions. Among preliterates virginity presents an interesting problem in ambivalence. On the one hand, it is, as in every patriarchy, a mysterious good because a sign of property received intact. On the other hand, it represents an unknown evil associated with the mana of blood and terrifyingly "other." So auspicious is the event of defloration that in many tribes the owner-groom is willing to relinquish breaking the seal of his new possession to a stronger or older personality who can neutralize the attendant dangers.[56] Fears of defloration appear to originate in a fear of the alien sexuality of the female. Although any physical suffering endured in defloration must be on the part of the female (and most societies cause her—bodily and mentally— to suffer anguish), the social interest, institutionalized in patriarchal ritual and custom, is exclusively on the side of the male's property interest, prestige, or (among preliterates) hazard.

Patriarchal myth typically posits a golden age before the arrival of women, while its social practices permit males to be relieved of female company. Sexual segregation is so prevalent in patriarchy that one encounters evidence of it everywhere. Nearly every powerful circle in contemporary patriarchy is a men's group. But men form groups of their own on every level. Women's groups are typically auxiliary in character, imitative of male efforts and methods on a generally trivial or ephemeral plane. They rarely operate without recourse to male authority, church or religious groups appealing to the superior authority of a cleric, political groups to male legislators, etc.

---

[55] The luxury conditions of the "better" restaurant affords a quaint exception. There not only the cuisine but even the table service is conducted by males, at an expense commensurate with such an occasion.

[56] See Sigmund Freud, *Totem and Taboo*, and Ernest Crawley, *The Mystic Rose* (London, Methuen, 1902, 1927).

In sexually segregated situations the distinctive quality of culturally enforced temperament becomes very vivid. This is particularly true of those exclusively masculine organizations which anthropology generally refers to as men's house institutions. The men's house is a fortress of patriarchal association and emotion. Men's houses in preliterate society strengthen masculine communal experience through dances, gossip, hospitality, recreation, and religious ceremony. They are also the arsenals of male weaponry.

David Riesman has pointed out that sports and some other activities provide males with a supportive solidarity which society does not trouble to provide for females.[57] While hunting, politics, religion, and commerce may play a role, sport and warfare are consistently the chief cement of men's house comradery. Scholars of men's house culture from Hutton Webster and Heinrich Schurtz to Lionel Tiger tend to be sexual patriots whose aim is to justify the apartheid the institution represents.[58] Schurtz believes an innate gregariousness and a drive toward fraternal pleasure among peers urges the male away from the inferior and constricting company of women. Notwithstanding his conviction that a mystical "bonding instinct" exists in males, Tiger exhorts the public, by organized effort, to preserve the men's house tradition from its decline. The institution's less genial function of power center within a state of sexual antagonism is an aspect of the phenomenon which often goes unnoticed.

The men's houses of Melanesia fulfill a variety of purposes and are both armory and the site of masculine ritual initiation ceremony. Their atmosphere is not very remote from that of military institutions in the modern world: they reek of physical exertion, violence, the aura of the kill, and the throb of homosexual sentiment. They are the scenes of scarification, headhunting celebrations, and boasting sessions. Here young men are to be "hardened" into manhood. In the men's houses boys have such low status they are often called the "wives" of their initiators, the term "wife" implying both inferiority and the status of sexual object. Untried youths become the erotic interest of their elders and betters, a relationship also encountered in the Samurai order, in oriental priesthood, and in the Greek gymnasium. Preliterate wisdom decrees that while inculcating the young with the masculine ethos, it is necessary first to intimidate them with the tutelary status of the female. An anthropolo-

---

[57] David Riesman, "Two Generations," in *The Woman in America*, edited by Robert Lifton (Boston, Beacon, 1967). See also James Coleman, *The Adolescent Society*.

[58] Heinrich Schurtz, *Altersklassen und Männerbunde* (Berlin, 1902) and Lionel Tiger, *op. cit.*

gist's comment on Melanesian men's houses is applicable equally to Genet's underworld, or Mailer's U. S. Army: "It would seem that the sexual brutalizing of the young boy and the effort to turn him into a woman both enhances the older warrior's desire of power, gratifies his sense of hostility toward the maturing male competitor, and eventually, when he takes him into the male group, strengthens the male solidarity in its symbolic attempt to do without women."[59] The derogation of feminine status in lesser males is a consistent patriarchal trait. Like any hazing procedure, initiation once endured produces devotees who will ever after be ardent initiators, happily inflicting their own former sufferings on the newcomer.

The psychoanalytic term for the generalized adolescent tone of men's house culture is "phallic state." Citadels of virility, they reinforce the most saliently power-oriented characteristics of patriarchy. The Hungarian psychoanalytic anthropologist Géza Róheim stressed the patriarchal character of men's house organization in the preliterate tribes he studied, defining their communal and religious practices in terms of a "group of men united in the cult of an object that is a materialized penis and excluding the women from their society."[60] The tone and ethos of men's house culture is sadistic, power-oriented, and latently homosexual, frequently narcissistic in its energy and motives.[61] The men's house inference that the penis is a weapon, endlessly equated with other weapons, is also clear. The practice of castrating prisoners is itself a comment on the cultural confusion of anatomy and status with weaponry. Much of the glamorization of masculine comradery in warfare originates in what one might designate as "the men's house sensibility." Its sadistic and brutalizing aspects are disguised in military glory and a particularly cloying species of masculine sentimentality. A great deal of our culture partakes of this tradition, and one might locate its first statement in Western literature in the heroic intimacy of Patroclus and Achilles. Its development can be traced through the epic and the saga to the *chanson de geste*. The tradition still flourishes in war novel and movie, not to mention the comic book.

Considerable sexual activity does take place in the men's house, all

---

[59] Hays, *The Dangerous Sex.* p. 56.

[60] Géza Róheim, "Psychoanalysis of Primitive Cultural Types," *International Journal of Psychoanalysis* Vol. XIII, London, 1932.

[61] All these traits apply in some degree to the bohemian circle which Miller's novels project, the Army which never leaves Mailer's consciousness, and the homosexual subculture on which Genet's observations are based. Since these three subjects of our study are closely associated with the separatist men's house culture, it is useful to give it special attention.

of it, needless to say, homosexual. But the taboo against homosexual behavior (at least among equals) is almost universally of far stronger force than the impulse and tends to effect a rechanneling of the libido into violence. This association of sexuality and violence is a particularly militaristic habit of mind.[62] The negative and militaristic coloring of such men's house homosexuality as does exist, is of course by no means the whole character of homosexual sensibility. Indeed, the warrior caste of mind with its ultravirility, is more *incipiently* homosexual, in its exclusively male orientation, than it is *overtly* homosexual. (The Nazi experience is an extreme case in point here.) And the heterosexual role-playing indulged in, and still more persuasively, the contempt in which the younger, softer, or more "feminine" members are held, is proof that the actual ethos is misogynist, or perversely rather than positively heterosexual. The true inspiration of men's house association therefore comes from the patriarchal situation rather than from any circumstances inherent in the homo-amorous relationship.

If a positive attitude toward heterosexual love is not quite, in Seignebos' famous dictum, the invention of the twelfth century, it can still claim to be a novelty. Most patriarchies go to great length to exclude love as a basis of mate selection. Modern patriarchies tend to do so through class, ethnic, and religious factors. Western classical thought was prone to see in heterosexual love either a fatal stroke of ill luck bound to end in tragedy, or a contemptible and brutish consorting with inferiors. Medieval opinion was firm in its conviction that love was sinful if sexual, and sex sinful if loving.

Primitive society practices its misogyny in terms of taboo and mana which evolve into explanatory myth. In historical cultures, this is transformed into ethical, then literary, and in the modern period, scientific rationalizations for the sexual politic. Myth is, of course, a felicitous advance in the level of propaganda, since it so often bases its arguments on ethics or theories of origins. The two leading myths of Western culture are the classical tale of Pandora's box and the Biblical story of the Fall. In both cases earlier mana concepts of feminine evil have passed through a final literary phase to become highly influential ethical justifications of things as they are.

Pandora appears to be a discredited version of a Mediterranean fertility goddess, for in Hesiod's *Theogony* she wears a wreath of flowers and a sculptured diadem in which are carved all the creatures of land

[62] Genet demonstrates this in *The Screens*; Mailer reveals it everywhere.

and sea.[63] Hesiod ascribes to her the introduction of sexuality which puts an end to the golden age when "the races of men had been living on earth free from all evils, free from laborious work, and free from all wearing sickness."[64] Pandora was the origin of "the damnable race of women—a plague which men must live with."[65] The introduction of what are seen to be the evils of the male human condition came through the introduction of the female and what is said to be her unique product, sexuality. In *Works and Days* Hesiod elaborates on Pandora and what she represents—a perilous temptation with "the mind of a bitch and a thievish nature," full of "the cruelty of desire and longings that wear out the body," "lies and cunning words and a deceitful soul," a snare sent by Zeus to be "the ruin of men."[66]

Patriarchy has God on its side. One of its most effective agents of control is the powerfully expeditious character of its doctrines as to the nature and origin of the female and the attribution to her alone of the dangers and evils it imputes to sexuality. The Greek example is interesting here: when it wishes to exalt sexuality it celebrates fertility through the phallus; when it wishes to denigrate sexuality, it cites Pandora. Patriarchal religion and ethics tend to lump the female and sex together as if the whole burden of the onus and stigma it attaches to sex were the fault of the female alone. Thereby sex, which is known to be unclean, sinful, and debilitating, pertains to the female, and the male identity is preserved as a human, rather than a sexual one.

The Pandora myth is one of two important Western archetypes which condemn the female through her sexuality and explain her position as her well-deserved punishment for the primal sin under whose unfortunate consequences the race yet labors. Ethics have entered the scene, replacing the simplicities of ritual, taboo, and mana. The more sophisticated vehicle of myth also provides official explanations of sexual history. In Hesiod's tale, Zeus, a rancorous and arbitrary father figure, in sending Epimetheus evil in the form of female genitalia, is actually chastising him for adult heterosexual knowledge and activity. In opening

[63] Wherever one stands in the long anthropologists' quarrel over patriarchal versus matriarchal theories of social origins, one can trace a demotion of fertility goddesses and their replacement by patriarchal deities at a certain period throughout ancient culture.

[64] Hesiod, *Works and Days*, translated by Richmond Lattimore (University of Michigan, 1959), p. 29.

[65] Hesiod, *Theogony*, translated by Norman O. Brown (Indianapolis, Liberal Arts Press, 1953), p. 70.

[66] Hesiod, *Works and Days*, phrases from lines 53–100. Some of the phrases are from Lattimore's translation, some from A. W. Mair's translation (Oxford, 1908).

the vessel she brings (the vulva or hymen, Pandora's "box") the male satisfies his curiosity but sustains the discovery only by punishing himself at the hands of the father god with death and the assorted calamities of postlapsarian life. The patriarchal trait of male rivalry across age or status line, particularly those of powerful father and rival son, is present as well as the ubiquitous maligning of the female.

The myth of the Fall is a highly finished version of the same themes. As the central myth of the Judeo-Christian imagination and therefore of our immediate cultural heritage, it is well that we appraise and acknowledge the enormous power it still holds over us even in a rationalist era which has long ago given up literal belief in it while maintaining its emotional assent intact.[67] This mythic version of the female as the cause of human suffering, knowledge, and sin is still the foundation of sexual attitudes, for it represents the most crucial argument of the patriarchal tradition in the West.

The Israelites lived in a continual state of war with the fertility cults of their neighbors; these latter afforded sufficient attraction to be the source of constant defection, and the figure of Eve, like that of Pandora, has vestigial traces of a fertility goddess overthrown. There is some, probably unconscious, evidence of this in the Biblical account which announces, even before the narration of the fall has begun—"Adam called his wife's name Eve; because she was the mother of all living things." Due to the fact that the tale represents a compilation of different oral traditions, it provides two contradictory schemes for Eve's creation, one in which both sexes are created at the same time, and one in which Eve is fashioned later than Adam, an afterthought born from his rib, peremptory instance of the male's expropriation of the life force through a god who created the world without benefit of female assistance.

The tale of Adam and Eve is, among many other things, a narrative of how humanity invented sexual intercourse. Many such narratives exist in preliterate myth and folk tale. Most of them strike us now as delightfully funny stories of primal innocents who require a good deal of helpful instruction to figure it out. There are other major themes in the story:

[67] It is impossible to assess how deeply embedded in our consciousness is the Eden legend and how utterly its patterns are planted in our habits of thought. One comes across its tone and design in the most unlikely places, such as Antonioni's film *Blow-Up*, to name but one of many striking examples. The action of the film takes place in an idyllic garden, loaded with primal overtones largely sexual, where, prompted by a tempter with a phallic gun, the female again betrays the male to death. The photographer who witnesses the scene reacts as if he were being introduced both to the haggard knowledge of the primal scene and original sin at the same time.

the loss of primeval simplicity, the arrival of death, and the first conscious experience of knowledge. All of them revolve about sex. Adam is forbidden to eat of the fruit of life or of the knowledge of good and evil, the warning states explicitly what should happen if he tastes of the latter: "in that day that thou eatest thereof thou shalt surely die." He eats but fails to die (at least in the story), from which one might infer that the serpent told the truth.

But at the moment when the pair eat of the forbidden tree they awake to their nakedness and feel shame. Sexuality is clearly involved, though the fable insists it is only tangential to a higher prohibition against disobeying orders in the matter of another and less controversial appetite —one for food. Róheim points out that the Hebrew verb for "eat" can also mean coitus. Everywhere in the Bible "knowing" is synonymous with sexuality, and clearly a product of contact with the phallus, here in the fable objectified as a snake. To blame the evils and sorrows of life—loss of Eden and the rest—on sexuality, would all too logically implicate the male, and such implication is hardly the purpose of the story, designed as it is expressly in order to blame all this world's discomfort on the female. Therefore it is the female who is tempted first and "beguiled" by the penis, transformed into something else, a snake. Thus Adam has "beaten the rap" of sexual guilt, which appears to be why the sexual motive is so repressed in the Biblical account. Yet the very transparency of the serpent's universal phallic value shows how uneasy the mythic mind can be about its shifts. Accordingly, in her inferiority and vulnerability the woman takes and eats, simple carnal thing that she is, affected by flattery even in a reptile. Only after this does the male fall, and with him, humanity—for the fable has made him the racial type, whereas Eve is a mere sexual type and, according to tradition, either expendable or replaceable. And as the myth records the original sexual adventure, Adam was seduced by woman, who was seduced by a penis. "The woman whom thou gavest to be with me, she gave me of the fruit and I did eat" is the first man's defense. Seduced by the phallic snake, Eve is convicted for Adam's participation in sex.

Adam's curse is to toil in the "sweat of his brow," namely the labor the male associates with civilization. Eden was a fantasy world without either effort or activity, which the entrance of the female, and with her sexuality, has destroyed. Eve's sentence is far more political in nature and a brilliant "explanation" of her inferior status. "In sorrow thou shalt bring forth children. And thy desire shall be thy husband. And he shall rule over thee." Again, as in the Pandora myth, a proprietary father figure is punishing his subjects for adult heterosexuality. It is easy to agree with Róheim's comment on the negative attitude the myth adopts toward sexuality: "Sexual maturity is regarded as a misfortune, something that has robbed mankind of happiness . . . the explanation of how death came into the world."[68]

What requires further emphasis is the responsibility of the female, a marginal creature, in bringing on this plague, and the justice of her suborned condition as dependent on her primary role in this original sin. The connection of woman, sex, and sin constitutes the fundamental pattern of western patriarchal thought thereafter.

## 8. Psychological

The aspects of patriarchy already described have each an effect upon the psychology of both sexes. Their principal result is the interiorization of patriarchal ideology. Status, temperament, and role are all value systems with endless psychological ramifications for each sex. Patriarchal marriage and the family with its ranks and division of labor play a large part in enforcing them. The male's superior economic position, the female's inferior one have also grave implications. The large quantity of guilt attached to sexuality in patriarchy is overwhelmingly placed upon the female, who is, culturally speaking, held to be the culpable or the more culpable party in nearly any sexual liaison, whatever the extenuating circumstances. A tendency toward the reification of the female makes her more often a sexual object than a person. This is particularly so when she is denied human rights through chattel status. Even where this has been partly amended the cumulative effect of religion and custom is still very powerful and has enormous psychological consequences. Woman is still denied sexual freedom and the biological control over her body through the cult of virginity, the double standard, the prescription against abortion, and in many places because contraception is physically or psychically unavailable to her.

The continual surveillance in which she is held tends to perpetuate the infantilization of women even in situations such as those of higher education. The female is continually obliged to seek survival or advancement through the approval of males as those who hold power. She may do this either through appeasement or through the exchange of her sexuality for support and status. As the history of patriarchal culture and the representations of herself within all levels of its cultural media,

[68] Géza Róheim, "Eden," *Psychoanalytic Review*, Vol. XXVII, New York, 1940. See also Theodor Reik, *The Creation of Woman*, and the account given in Hays, *op. cit.*

past and present, have a devastating effect upon her self image, she is customarily deprived of any but the most trivial sources of dignity or self-respect. In many patriarchies, language, as well as cultural tradition, reserve the human condition for the male. With the Indo-European languages this is a nearly inescapable habit of mind, for despite all the customary pretense that "man" and "humanity" are terms which apply equally to both sexes, the fact is hardly obscured that in practice, general application favors the male far more often than the female as referent, or even sole referent, for such designations.[69]

When in any group of persons, the ego is subjected to such invidious versions of itself through social beliefs, ideology, and tradition, the effect is bound to be pernicious. This coupled with the persistent though frequently subtle denigration women encounter daily through personal contacts, the impressions gathered from the images and media about them, and the discrimination in matters of behavior, employment, and education which they endure, should make it no very special cause for surprise that women develop group characteristics common to those who suffer minority status and a marginal existence. A witty experiment by Philip Goldberg proves what everyone knows, that having internalized the disesteem in which they are held, women despise both themselves and each other.[70] This simple test consisted of asking women undergraduates to respond to the scholarship in an essay signed alternately by one John McKay and one Joan McKay. In making their assessments the students generally agreed that John was a remarkable thinker, Joan an unimpressive mind. Yet the articles were identical: the reaction was dependent on the sex of the supposed author.

As women in patriarchy are for the most part marginal citizens when they are citizens at all, their situation is like that of other minorities, here defined not as dependent upon numerical size of the group, but on its status. "A minority group is any group of people who because of their physical or cultural characteristics, are singled out from others in the society in which they live for differential and unequal treatment."[71] Only

---

[69] Languages outside the Indo-European group are instructive. Japanese, for example, has one word for man (otōko), another for woman (ōnna) and a third for human being (ningen). It would be as unthinkable to use the first to cover the third as it would be to use the second.

[70] Philip Goldberg, "Are Women Prejudiced Against Women?" *Transaction*, April 1968.

[71] Louis Wirth, "Problems of Minority Groups," in *The Science of Man in the World Crisis*, ed. by Ralph Linton (New York, Appleton, 1945), p. 347. Wirth also stipulates that the group see itself as discriminated against. It is interesting that many women do not recognize themselves as discriminated against; no better proof could be found of the totality of their conditioning.

a handful of sociologists have ever addressed themselves in any meaningful way to the minority status of women.[72] And psychology has yet to produce relevant studies on the subject of ego damage to the female which might bear comparison to the excellent work done on the effects of racism on the minds of blacks and colonials. The remarkably small amount of modern research devoted to the psychological and social effects of masculine supremacy on the female and on the culture in general attests to the widespread ignorance or unconcern of a conservative social science which takes patriarchy to be both the status quo and the state of nature.

What little literature the social sciences afford us in this context confirms the presence in women of the expected traits of minority status: group self-hatred and self-rejection, a contempt both for herself and for her fellows—the result of that continual, however subtle, reiteration for her inferiority which she eventually accepts as a fact.[73] Another index of minority status is the fierceness with which all minority group members are judged. The double standard is applied not only in cases of sexual conduct but other contexts as well. In the relatively rare instances of female crime too: in many American states a woman convicted of crime is awarded a longer sentence.[74] Generally an accused woman acquires a notoriety out of proportion to her acts and due to sensational publicity she may be tried largely for her "sex life." But so effective is her conditioning toward passivity in patriarchy, woman is rarely extrovert enough in her maladjustment to enter upon criminality. Just as every minority member must either apologize for the excesses of a fellow or condemn him with a strident enthusiasm, women are characteristically harsh, ruthless and frightened in the censure of aberration among their numbers.

[72] The productive handful in question include the following:
Helen Mayer Hacker, "Women as a Minority Group," *Social Forces*, Vol. XXX, October 1951.
Gunnar Myrdal, *An American Dilemma*, Appendix 5 is a parallel of black minority status with women's minority status.
Everett C. Hughes, "Social Change and Status Protest: An Essay on the Marginal Man," *Phylon*, Vol. X, First Quarter, 1949.
Joseph K. Folsom, *The Family and Democratic Society*, 1943.
Godwin Watson, "Psychological Aspects of Sex Roles," *Social Psychology, Issues and Insights* (Philadelphia, Lippincott, 1966).

[73] My remarks on the minority status of women are summarized from all the articles listed, and I am particularly indebted to an accomplished critique of them in an unpublished draft by Professor Marlene Dixon, formerly of the University of Chicago's Department of Sociology and the Committee on Human Development, presently of McGill University.

[74] See The Commonwealth v. Daniels, 37 L.W. 2064, Pennsylvania Supreme Court, 7/1/68 (reversing 36 L.W. 2004).

The gnawing suspicion which plagues any minority member, that the myths propagated about his inferiority might after all be true often reaches remarkable proportions in the personal insecurities of women. Some find their subordinate position so hard to bear that they repress and deny its existence. But a large number will recognize and admit their circumstances when they are properly phrased. Of two studies which asked women if they would have preferred to be born male, one found that one fourth of the sample admitted as much, and in another sample, one half.[75] When one inquires of children, who have not yet developed as serviceable techniques of evasion, what their choice might be, if they had one, the answers of female children in a large majority of cases clearly favor birth into the elite group, whereas boys overwhelmingly reject the option of being girls.[76] The phenomenon of parents' prenatal preference for male issue is too common to require much elaboration. In the light of the imminent possibility of parents actually choosing the sex of their child, such a tendency is becoming the cause of some concern in scientific circles.[77]

Comparisons such as Myrdal, Hacker, and Dixon draw between the ascribed attributes of blacks and women reveal that common opinion associates the same traits with both: inferior intelligence, an instinctual or sensual gratification, an emotional nature both primitive and childlike, an imagined prowess in or affinity for sexuality, a contentment with their own lot which is in accord with a proof of its appropriateness, a wily habit of deceit, and concealment of feeling. Both groups are forced to the same accommodational tactics: an ingratiating or supplicatory manner invented to please, a tendency to study those points at which the dominant group are subject to influence or corruption, and an assumed air of helplessness involving fraudulent appeals for direction through a show of ignorance.[78] It is ironic how misogynist literature has for centuries concentrated on just these traits, directing its fiercest enmity at feminine guile and corruption, and particularly that element of it which is sexual, or, as such sources would have it, "wanton."

As with other marginal groups a certain handful of women are accorded higher status that they may perform a species of cultural policing

---

[75] See Helen Hacker, op. cit., and Carolyn Bird, op. cit.

[76] "One study of fourth graders showed ten times as many girls wishing they could have been boys, as boys who would have chosen to be girls," Watson, op. cit., p. 477.

[77] Amitai Etzioni, "Sex Control, Science, and Society," Science, September 1968, pp. 1107–12.

[78] Myrdal, op. cit., Hacker, op. cit., Dixon, op. cit.

over the rest. Hughes speaks of marginality as a case of status dilemma experienced by women, blacks, or second-generation Americans who have "come up" in the world but are often refused the rewards of their efforts on the grounds of their origins.[79] This is particularly the case with "new" or educated women. Such exceptions are generally obliged to make ritual, and often comic, statements of deference to justify their elevation. These characteristically take the form of pledges of "femininity," namely a delight on docility and a large appetite for masculine dominance. Politically, the most useful persons for such a role are entertainers and public sex objects. It is a common trait of minority status that a small percentage of the fortunate are permitted to entertain their rulers. (That they may entertain their fellow subjects in the process is less to the point.) Women entertain, please, gratify, satisfy and flatter men with their sexuality. In most minority groups athletes or intellectuals are allowed to emerge as "stars," identification with whom should content their less fortunate fellows. In the case of women both such eventualities are discouraged on the reasonable grounds that the most popular explanations of the female's inferior status ascribe it to her physical weakness or intellectual inferiority. Logically, exhibitions of physical courage or agility are indecorous, just as any display of serious intelligence tends to be out of place.

Perhaps patriarchy's greatest psychological weapon is simply its universality and longevity. A referent scarcely exists with which it might be contrasted or by which it might be confuted. While the same might be said of class, patriarchy has a still more tenacious or powerful hold through its successful habit of passing itself off as nature. Religion is also universal in human society and slavery was once nearly so; advocates of each were fond of arguing in terms of fatality, or irrevocable human "instinct"—even "biological origins." When a system of power is thoroughly in command, it has scarcely need to speak itself aloud; when its workings are exposed and questioned, it becomes not only subject to discussion, but even to change. . . .

[79] Hughes, *op. cit.*

# 28. THE MIDDLE-CLASS MIND OF KATE MILLETT

**Irving Howe**

*Author and critic, professor at Brandeis, Stanford, Princeton, and currently at Hunter College, Irving Howe has long been a voice of sanity and style on issues of both literary and social significance. In addition to being a teacher, Howe is the editor of* Dissent.

Good causes attract poor advocates. The demands of the women's movements, at least those demands that can be brought to socioeconomic focus, are transparently just. So much so that to some people, including the more fanatical Women's Liberationists, they also seem a little dull. Equal pay for equal work, child-care centers for working mothers—these could become realities within a decade or two, and without bombs, guerrilla warfare, or even the razing of Western Civilization. But precisely because they don't lend themselves to ideological dramatics, such proposals gain little attention.

Our dominant economic classes and institutions seem to find this a satisfactory state of affairs. Just as they regard the rhetoric of black power as less troublesome than paying to build houses in black slums, so they are likely to find declamations against "sexism" less troublesome than having to raise the wages of women workers. And not only less troublesome, but also a good deal more entertaining. For at a time when boredom has become a crucial social fact, many people, especially in the professional classes, feel a need for new kinds of entertainment drawing upon ideologies of ultimate salvation and the rhetoric of desperate acts. Among segments of the intellectuals and the young there keeps growing a quasi-religious hunger for total system, total solution, total apocalypse; and soon enough ideologues appear with doctrines to match.

Kate Millett, author of *Sexual Politics*, is the latest such ideologue, and one would need a heart of stone not to be amused by the success she has won. Imagine the sheer comedy of it: a book declaring itself to be a "revolutionary" manifesto, presenting Jean Genet as a moral exemption, and with the barest lilt of the eyebrow envisaging the abolition of the family, gains for its author a not-so-small fortune, selection by the Book-of-the-Month Club, and the cover of *Time*.

*Source:* "The Middle Class Mind of Kate Millett," Irving Howe. Copyright © 1970 by Minneapolis Star and Tribune Co., Inc., Reprinted from the December 1970 issue of *Harper's Magazine* by permission of the author.

Miss Millett is a writer entirely of our moment, a figment of the *Zeitgeist*, bearing the rough and careless marks of what is called higher education and exhibiting a talent for the delivery of gross simplicities in tones of leaden complexity. Brilliant in an unserious way, she has learned at Columbia University how to "work up" a pastiche of scholarship that will impress those unable or disinclined to read with care. She has a mind of great energy but small feeling for nuance. She ranges wildly over history, politics, psychology, and anthropology, but with little respect for these disciplines in their own right. She is the ideal highbrow popularizer for the politics and culture of the New Left, at least some of whose followers like to back up mindless slogans with recondite volumes.

In all the favorable reviews of *Sexual Politics* that I have seen, not one has so much as troubled to compare the book with Simone de Beauvoir's *The Second Sex*. Now it is true that de Beauvoir's book was published in this country all of seventeen years ago, for us roughly the equivalent of a millennium. Still, anyone comparing the two books would immediately recognize the extent to which Miss Millett has drawn upon de Beauvoir's famous work. The central ideas and sentiments of *Sexual Politics* are simply appropriated, in vulgarized form, from *The Second Sex,* and reviewers with some intellectual conscience might consequently have shown restraint in praising Miss Millett's originality of thought. Those inclined to rigor might also have remarked that she has yet to master the ethic of intellectual obligation: she cites de Beauvoir twice, in relatively minor contexts, thereby avoiding the *gaffe* of pretending the earlier book doesn't exist, but at no point does she make an adequate acknowledgment of her debt.


2


At the heart of *Sexual Politics*, in the key chapter, "Theory of Sexual Politics," lies a nightmare vision of endless female subordination to and suffering at the hands of men. "Sexual dominion [is] perhaps the most pervasive ideology of our culture and provides the most fundamental concept of power." The relations between the sexes are basically political, that is, relations of power. Everything else that happens to and between men and women—from sex to love to mutual responsibility in family life —is secondary. In these relationships the status of woman is that of a "chattel," a status accorded legal sanction through marriage: "an exchange of the female's domestic service and (sexual) consortium in return for financial support." The woman is exploited for her labor and/ or used as a sexual object; and the exploiters are men.

Since sexual dominion is the very fundament, as also the *raison d'être*, of the patriarchal family and can't, indeed, be eradicated short of destroying the patriarchal family, we soon arrive at a terrifying impasse: an all-but-timeless and all-but-indestructible system of oppression, one in which "the entire culture supports masculine authority in all areas of life and—outside of the home—permits the female none at all." Why all-but-timeless and all-but-indestructible? Because the patriarchal family seems virtually coextensive with history itself; as Miss Millett must acknowledge, it has been "a basic form . . . within all societies."

This system of power, in which the woman "is customarily deprived of any but the most trivial sources of dignity or self-respect," rests primarily, in Miss Millett's judgment, on the social indoctrination of "sexual temperament," a learning process whereby little boys and girls are persuaded not merely of their differences but also of male superiority. Sometimes this process of indoctrination occurs through outright insistence upon male dominance, sometimes through brainwashing rationales for confining women to home and children, and sometimes through "the chivalrous stance . . . a game the master group plays in elevating its subject to pedestal level."

Now what needs first and foremost to be noted about this theory is that, in any precise sense of the term, it isn't a theory at all. It is a cry of woe, partly justified; and it offers a description of sexual relationships said to hold pretty much for all of human history. But a cry of woe isn't a theory, and neither is a description. For a group of statements to be given the status of a theory, good theory or bad, it must account for a complex of phenomena in respect to genesis, persistence, necessary characteristics, and relations to other phenomena. With the possible exception of the third item in this list, Miss Millett satisfies none of these requirements. To say "man is a beast" is not a theory about the nature of humanity, it is at best a statement of description; but to say "man is a beast because he is fallen in nature, or because he fails to obey the injunctions of Christianity, or because he has been brutalized by capitalist society"—that is to *begin* developing a theory. Miss Millett, however, makes no effort to account for the origins of male "sexual dominion," and more important, the reasons for its remarkable persistence and prevalence. Given her approach, she really cannot do so. She has no theory.

Miss Millett is determined to resist the view that biological and physical differences between the sexes may have determined or may still crucially determine a sequence of secondary and social differences, for she fears, rather naïvely, that any concession to biology must mean to accept as forever fixed the traditional patterns of male domination. The result is that she must fall back upon an unarticulated but strongly felt vision of conspiracy. And also upon a mode of reasoning utterly circular. Why does the patriarchal family persist through all recorded history? Because the social learning process trains us to accept it as a necessary given. But why does this learning process itself persist through history? Because it is needed for sustaining the patriarchal family. And what does Miss Millett spinning in circles illuminate here? Very little. Worse still, she presents a vision, misnamed a theory, which if taken seriously offers little hope of change or relief, for she cannot specify any historical factors, other than the "altered consciousness" of a "revolutionary" intellectual elite, which might enable us to end the dominion of patriarchy.

Let us approach the problem from a slightly different angle. Miss Millett argues that there "is no biological reason why the two central functions of the family (socialization and reproduction) need be inseparable from or even take place within it"; further, that we shouldn't take seriously the view that male physical endowment has been or remains a crucial factor in male social ascendancy. One must consequently ask: how then has so "basic a form [as] patriarchy" managed to arise and survive in just about every civilized society? If this "basic" form isn't even needed for socialization and reproduction, what is the secret of its hold? In what way can it even be considered "basic"? The questions, which follow inexorably from her assertions, seem never to trouble Miss Millett, since she writes with the thrust of the polemicist rather than the curiosity of the historian; and the punishment she thereby suffers is to create a picture, all but unknowingly, of endless female subordination from which, analytically, there seems hardly an escape. The root premise of her work, which naturally she does not care to express openly, is that women have been kept down because men have chosen to keep them down—which seems a more terrible tribute to the masculine will than any of its celebrants have ever dreamt of proposing. As a key to "the most pervasive ideology of our culture and . . . the most fundamental concept of power," this view of the life of the sexes is, let us say, a little inadequate.

Now, there have been other theories positing the centrality of social oppression in history. Marxism, for one, sees history thus far as a sequence of class struggles, though with the nature and relationships of the contending classes in constant change. Whatever one may think of this theory, the Marxist approach has one overwhelming advantage over Miss Millett's: it provides a principle of causation and change within society. Far from looking upon man's physical setting and conditions as somehow an "enemy" of the hope for social change, as Miss Millett does, the Marxist view places social change within a natural context, or more precisely, it sees mankind as making its history through the materials and within the limits provided by nature. As men gain mastery over nature and thereby free themselves from the burdens of brute labor, the internal relationships of society are transformed and men begin *to be able* to determine their own destinies in a distinctly "human" way. (At least, this avoids the simplistic either-or of biology/culture to which Miss Millett is addicted.) And while Marx believes all history to have been a history of class struggle, he is utterly scornful of those—precursors in economic terms of Miss Millett's sexual monism—who see history as a vista of undifferentiated oppression. He insists upon the crucial difference, say, between the master-slave relationship and the bourgeois-proletarian relationship: that is, he insists that historical change occurs and that historical change matters.

By contrast Miss Millett makes no concession to this central fact of history. Fixated upon the patriarchal family as if it were an all but supra-historical constant, and forced to acknowledge its omnipresence, she sketches out a grisly picture of the life of women. She makes no serious effort to differentiate among various kinds of patriarchal family (after all, there may have been and of course were enormous differences in its endless manifestations) or to differentiate among the life-styles by which women have tried to fulfill themselves at different points in history. Her method here is exactly that of "vulgar Marxism," that caricature of Marxist thought which insists that the only reality is the economic and all else, being "superstructural," must be insignificant. Thus, with a reckless thrust of the phrase, Miss Millett can dismiss chivalry as "a game the master group plays. . . ." But such "games" crucially affected the lives of millions of men and women during the Middle Ages when the cult of Mariolatry became so powerful in the church that a symbolic struggle between Mother and Son, female and male principles, was enacted among the faithful. Can one really explain such complex events as "a game the master group plays"? Isn't such historical reductionism a sign of an impoverishment of sensibility? A crude simplification such as we have come to expect in the work of Stalinist historians? It is striking that for all her far-ranging ambition of reference and passion of female defense, Miss Millett does not even list in her index, and only mentions two or three times in trivial contexts, the single most important woman in all Western history: the Virgin Mary.

A host of other questions press for consideration. The woman who worked sixteen hours a day in the Midland mines during the Industrial Revolution—was she really a "sexual object" up for "barter" to the "master group" (the wretched men who also worked sixteen hours a day in the same mines) quite in the same way as the bourgeois ladies of, say, Matisse's Paris? Does the "passivity" Miss Millett says patriarchal society induces in women characterize the American pioneer wife staking out a homestead in Oklahoma? Was the Jewish immigrant mother working in a sweatshop, often shoulder to shoulder with her equally exploited husband, "customarily deprived of any but the most trivial sources of dignity or self-respect"? Are the ladies of the Upper East Side of Manhattan simply "chattels" in the way the wives of California grape pickers are, and if so, are they "chattels" held by the same kinds of masters? Has the fact of being female been more important in the social history of most women than whether they were rich or poor, black or white, Christian or Jewish? Has the condition of women since the rise of the patriarchal family been so unvarying, so essentially the same repeated and endless story of oppression, that it can really be summoned through Miss Millett's one simple model? Have not human beings, men and women, found *some* paths to fulfillment and fraternity, *some* side alleys to decency of relationship and respect for sexual difference, even under the patriarchal curse? In short, does Miss Millett have any sense at all of the range and variety and complexity—and yes, even once in a while the humane achievements—of our history?

For what I am trying to suggest through the questions I have just asked—the list should be extended for pages—is not only that Miss Millett flattens out all history into a tapestry of "sexual dominion," not only paints a picture of the past and present depriving women of any initiative, will, or capacity, but that she systematically ignores those crucial factors of class position which have the most far-reaching impact on the life of women. Most of the time, when she speaks of women she really has in mind middle-class American women during the last thirty years. About the experience of working-class women she knows next to nothing, as in this comic-pathetic remark: "The invention of labor-saving devices has had no appreciable effect on the duration, even if it has affected the quality, of their drudgery." Only a Columbia Ph.D. who has never had to learn the difference between scrubbing the family laundry on a washboard and putting it into an electric washing machine can write such nonsense. As with most New Left ideologues, male or female, Miss Millett suffers from middle-class parochialism.

And more: she suffers from a social outlook which, despite its "revolutionary" claims, is finally bourgeois in character. She writes that "nearly all that can be described as distinctly human rather than animal activity (in their own way animals also give birth and care for their young) is largely reserved for the male." And again: "Even the modern nuclear family, with its unchanged and traditional division of roles, necessitates male supremacy by preserving specifically human endeavor for the male alone, while confining the female to menial labor and compulsory child care."

These sentences indicate that Miss Millett is at heart an old-fashioned bourgeois feminist who supposes the height of satisfaction is to work in an office or factory and not be burdened with those brutes called men and those slops called children. For one must ask: why is the male's enforced labor at some mindless task in a factory "distinctly human," while the woman bringing up her child is reduced to an "animal" level? Isn't the husband a "chattel" too? Hasn't Miss Millett ever been told by her New Left friends about the alienation of labor in an exploitative society? And is the poor bastard writing soap jingles in an ad agency performing a "human" task morally or psychologically superior to what his wife does at home, where she can at least reach toward an uncontaminated relationship with her own child? Why can't Miss Millett here remember the sentence, one of the best in her book, that appears in another context: "In conservative economies with an ethos of aggressive competition [and in other economies too!—I.H.], the 'home' seemed to offer the last vestiges of humane feeling, the only haven of communal emotion"? That animals also raise their young (in the same way? toward the same ends of socialization and ethical continuity?)—does this remarkable piece of information really deny the "distinctly human" character of women's experience in raising their children? In such remarks Miss Millett betrays a profound distortion of values, a deep if unconscious acquiescence not only to the corruptions of the bourgeois society against which she rails but to all those "masculine values" she supposes herself to be against.

What is lacking in Miss Millett's "theory of sexual politics," as throughout her book, is a felt sense of, a deep immersion in, the actualities of human experience which must always be the foundation of any useful theory. What is present in her "theory" is an imperious condescension toward all those complications of past and current experience that won't fit into her scheme, as toward all human beings who don't satisfy her categories. In a remark worthy of that other leftist snob, Herbert Marcuse, she tells us that "many women do not recognize themselves as discriminated against; no better proof could be found of the totality of their conditioning." And those women who *do* recognize themselves as discriminated against—would not Miss Millett leap to declare that "no better proof could be found of the acuteness with which they recognize the reality"? Against the imperviousness of circularity, reason is helpless.

Now, it is true that the lot of women has frequently been that of a subordinate group—though not that alone. The relationship between men and women, like other relationships in our society, does often have a strand of ugly commercialism—though not that alone and often not that predominantly. (How many of Miss Millett's readers or admirers, one wonders, would be ready to apply her categories—"chattel," "barter," "sexual object" etc.—to themselves?) Women have been exploited throughout history, but most of the time in ways quite similar to those in which men have been, and more often than not, as members of oppressed or disadvantaged classes rather than as women alone. Yet it is also true that many women have suffered a kind of super-exploitation, though this can't be understood in the gross terms of "sexual politics" but must be studied as an element in the tortuous development of mankind from the penalties of scarcity to the possibilities of plenty. And at the risk of being charged with "playing the game of the master group," let me add that even in their conditions of disadvantage women have also been able to gain for themselves significant privileges and powers. Males may have been "masters" and females "chattels," but this is perhaps the only such relationship in human history where the "masters" sent themselves and their sons to die in wars while trying to spare their "chattels" that fate.

That the relations between men and women have had and still have an element of "power" similar to that characterizing the relations between social classes is almost certainly true. But not the whole truth and very often not the most important truth. Indeed, the more closely one applies Miss Millett's "theory" to concrete instances both in history and immediate experience, the less adequate does it seem even as description. For the word "power" is very tricky in this context, and Miss Millett isn't the one to look carefully into its complexities. In any relationship of caring, people gain power over one another: the power to please, the power to hurt. Sexuality is a mode of power, and often, as history indicates (for Miss Millett, one gathers, no female face ever did launch a thousand ships . . . ), sexual power has been of a magnitude to overcome the effects of economic power. Sexuality gives up power at varying times of our lives, and often with radical inequities for which there seems to be no solution or even solace. That men have held power over women, in both the desirable and deporable senses, is a truth that was noticed before the appearance of Miss Millett's book. That women have held power over men, usually in the more desirable but often enough in quite deplorable ways, is a thought with which Miss Millett will have no commerce. And it is even possible—indeed, if one clings to some sort of tragic view of life, it is likely—that the powers we hold over one another are both of the desirable and the deplorable kinds, the two fatally and forever mixed.

Yet it would be a sad mistake, and for the women's movements a strategic folly, to suppose that the relations between men and women, so entwined with the deepest and most mysterious elements of our psychic life, can ever be understood by the sexual monism, the historical reductionism of Miss Millett.


3

From "theory" to "history"—and with similar results. Miss Millett begins with a sketch of the "sexual revolution" in nineteenth-century England that reveals immediately the poverty of her historical imagination. With the ideologist's willfulness, she keeps grafting upon the past categories of analysis and standards of judgment drawn from the immediate present, so that, as you might expect, the past is forever found wanting. The very period she begins by praising she ends by berating, since the women's movement of the nineteenth century concentrated on such practical matters as suffrage, while Miss Millett, snug with hindsight, would have preferred that they devote themselves to exposing "patriarchal ideology." But if she is serious about her idea of what a "sexual revolution" is—"an end of traditional sexual inhibitions and taboos, particularly those that threaten patriarchal monogamous marriage: homosexuality, 'illegitimacy,' adolescent, pre- and extra-marital sexuality"—then it is hard to see how she can speak of a "sexual revolution" in nineteenth-century England and America at all.

She proceeds to examine some intellectual and literary texts of this period concerning women, and John Stuart Mill, because of his unambiguous advocacy of equal rights for the sexes, stands out as an heroic figure. I think he deserves all the praise Miss Millett gives him. But since she isn't one to rest with an advantage, she must scurry about in search of a villain, naturally a male villain. And she finds him in the sad person of John Ruskin, the critic of art and society who, between his major works, wrote an essay urging that women, as guardians of sensibility and moral purity, cultivate these values at home. Poor Ruskin—how could anyone suppose him a representative figure of Victorian patriarchalism, this man notoriously askew in his own sexual life and about as distant from standard masculine assertion as Miss Millett from standard feminine submission? Here too an historian with a sense of scruple would have added that Ruskin's paean to femininity wasn't merely Victorian bilge; as a bitter opponent of industrial society, he felt that the home was the last resort for suffering human beings—hardly, of course, an adequate view but not a view simply to be ridiculed.

As historian Miss Millett enters high gear in the next section of her book, where she discusses the "sexual counterrevolution" of the last four decades, her evidence for which is first the reactionary family policies of Nazi Germany and Stalinist Russia, second the theories of Freud and his followers, and third the fiction of D. H. Lawrence, Henry Miller, and Norman Mailer.

Now, as is typical with Miss Millett, her intelligence has not played her false in supposing that there has been a counterrevolution of some sort during the past several decades: she is, after all, talking about the age of totalitarianism. But once beyond this useful generalization, she betrays the methodological sloppiness characteristic of her entire book. A few instances:

The "sexual revolution" she had previously celebrated was located mainly in England and America. The "counterrevolution" she locates mainly in Germany and Russia. Is a causal or reactive or any other kind of relation being proposed between the nineteenth-century "sexual revolution" of England and America and the twentieth-century "sexual counterrevolution" of Germany and Russia? No answer from Miss Millett. While Hitler and Stalin were pontificating about motherhood, what was meanwhile happening to the relations between men and women in the original locale of Miss Millett's "sexual revolution"?

My own sense of what was happening in England and America is that the gradual process of sexual reform through the first three decades of this century came to be felt by cultivated and humane persons—they can hardly have all been "sexists"—as a social-cultural trend bringing with it serious and unforeseen difficulties. Women seemed often to feel that their liberation, whether partial or complete, had cast them adrift, without adequate personal or public security. Men felt disturbed by the growing uncertainty as to their social roles and sexual obligations. There was much talk, some of it cant but some very serious, about "inadequacy" and "crisis of identity," reflecting a system of anxieties created by changes in sexual relations. Even persons of advanced opinions came to feel, through the bitter prodding of experience, that certain kinds of liberation (for example, the childless marriages favored by some intellectuals in the Twenties) had a strong element of sterility. As a result, there was an inclination among such people to reinforce the family structure, not by returning to the old-style Victorian patriarchy (it's a joke to imagine anyone thought that a genuine option) but by trying to establish distinctive sexual roles within a fraternal marriage. Sometimes it worked, sometimes it didn't.

Now Miss Millett can, if she wishes, dismiss all this as "sexual counterrevolution"—but only at the price of a fanatical disdain for the experience of others.

The "sexual counterrevolution" that did occur in Germany and Russia is placed by Miss Millett in an expository and, as it turns out, logical parallel to the rise of Freudianism and the writings of Lawrence, Miller, and Mailer. Intellectually, this is feckless: morally, shameful. Miss Millett never troubles to notice that the "reactionary" Freud was anathema to Hitler and Stalin, both of whom understood perfectly well that he threatened their despotism not because of one or another opinion but because of his fearlessness and skeptical openness of mind. Perhaps Miss Millett can explain the fact that Freud, whom she declares to be the theoretician of "counterrevolution," was banned in the very countries she designates as its central locale; if so, she is saving the explanation for another book.

Equally squalid is Miss Millett's linkage of Lawrence, Miller, and Mailer ("The Literary Reflection") with the "Sexual Counterrevolution" of Nazi Germany and Stalinist Russia, and then with the alleged Freudian "Reaction in Ideology"—subtitles that promise connections which the text cannot establish. Of *precisely what* were Lawrence, Miller, and Mailer. the "Literary Reflection"? The "sexual counterrevolution" in Germany and Russia? But Lawrence wrote his main books before that counterrevolution occurred. Henry Miller, a crackerbarrel American anarchist, was developing his sexual sentiments in the Twenties, again before the counterrevolution. How can writing reflect something that hasn't yet happened? Mailer, who until recently supposed he was breaking past "the last frontier" of sexual repressiveness, has been strongly influenced by the Wilhelm Reich whom Miss Millett relies on so heavily for documenting what happened in the totalitarian countries. In short, we have here an intellectual goulash that could be taken seriously only in a moment when serious standards have collapsed.

But let us turn to the "sexual counterrevolution" itself. Miss Millett quotes the standard reactionary hymns of Nazi and Stalinist propagandists. Very good; except that she contents herself with remaining strictly on the level of their ideological claims. Had Miss Millett read carefully the scholarly authorities she cites, she would have learned what even such radical critics as Herbert Marcuse have acknowledged: that in every totalitarian society there is and must be a deep clash between state and family, simply because the state demands complete loyalty from each person and comes to regard the family as a major competitor for that loyalty. For both political and nonpolitical people, the family becomes the last refuge for humane values. Thereby the defense of the "conservative" institution of the family becomes under totalitarianism a profoundly subversive act.

Now the comedy of all this is that Miss Millett prints, at one point, a footnote quoting from a book by Joseph Folsom:

"The Nazis have always wanted to strengthen the family *as an instrument of the state. State interest is always paramount.* Germany does not hesitate to turn a husband against a wife or children against parents when political disloyalty is involved. (Emphasis added.)"

Miss Millett prints this footnote but clearly does not understand it; otherwise she would recognize how completely it undermines her claim that in the totalitarian countries the "sexual counterrevolution" consisted in the reinforcement of the family.

Miss Millett seems especially ill-informed about what happened in Russia. She attacks Lenin for not finding "the sexual revolution . . . important enough to speak on," and then, with that sloppiness steadily characterizing the relation between her assertions in the text and her evidence in the footnotes, she quotes Lenin in a footnote as saying, "Perhaps one day I shall speak or write on these questions—but not now. Now all our time must be dedicated to other matters." That is, during the revolution and civil war, a time of hunger and death, Lenin felt he had more urgent obligations than to speculate on the end of the family. Similarly, Miss Millett notices that in *The Revolution Betrayed* Trotsky attacked the reactionary turn of Stalinist policy toward women, "but this," she adds, "is the hindsight of 1936." Nonsense! Trotsky was attacking the reversal of progressive state policies concerning divorce, abortion, nurseries, salaries, etc., enacted by the Bolshevik regime during the early Twenties. Does Miss Millett suppose that somehow these reforms had been adopted behind Trotsky's back?

4

It is upon Sigmund Freud that Miss Millett directs her heaviest fire. Freud has "generally been accepted as a prototype of the liberal urge toward sexual freedom," but this, we are now informed, was a delusion, since the effect of his work was to "rationalize the invidious relationship between the sexes." Yet, throughout the chapter attacking Freud as throughout the book as a whole, Miss Millett keeps employing Freudian concepts as if they were the merest axioms and specifically notes her approval of the "theories of the unconscious and infant sexuality." (Apparently, as old Freud noticed once or twice, there are times when too great an awareness of what one is doing can be burdensome.) We must then ask: how could the Freudian theories of which Miss Millett approves have left their mark on modern thought and experience without also profoundly affecting for the better—as in fact they did—"the invidious relationship between the sexes"? Could the current concern about sexual roles even have begun without the contributions of Freud?

Miss Millett opens her attack by discussing Freud's treatment of his early patients, most of whom were women. He "did not accept his patients' symptoms as evidence of a justified dissatisfaction with the limiting circumstances imposed on them by society, but as symptomatic of an independent and universal feminine tendency." Now this won't do, if only because it sets up much too crude and naïve a disjunction between what is biological and what is cultural. It won't do, because Freud tried always to work with the observed dynamics of his patients' experience rather than with fixed categories borrowed from other disciplines (whether leaning toward the biological or cultural) which he richly felt psychoanalysis could not handle. It won't do, because Freud did see in his patients' symptoms "evidence of a justified dissatisfaction," though not in the sense Miss Millett would like (the only "evidence" that ever strikes her as vital is that which gratifies her own rhetoric).

Many of Freud's early patients were women suffering from symptoms of "hysteria," often grossly somatic in nature; their troubles were related to the repressiveness of the upper-middle-class families in which they had grown up, especially to an excessive subordination to domineering fathers. What Freud tried to do was to enable them to accept their sexuality and thereby be freed from the symptoms. To the extent that he succeeded, Freud struck an oblique but powerful blow at the tyrannical aspects of the Victorian family. If anything can be described as militating against "the limiting conditions imposed by society," it is precisely this therapy—even though Freud's investigations also led him to believe that there were indeed problems deriving from a "universal feminine tendency" which were not likely to be resolved through social measures.

All this, in a notably vulgar sentence, Miss Millett summarizes as follows: "Female patients consulted him in the hope of becoming more productive in their work: in return for their fees Freud did what he could to cause them to abandon their vocations as unnecessary aberrations." And as evidence for this charge Miss Millett offers a footnote quoting from Freud:

"At no point in one's analytic work does one suffer more from the oppressive feeling that one is 'talking to the winds' than when one is trying to persuade a female patient to abandon her wish for a penis on the ground of its being unobtainable."

Now if Freud is right in supposing penis envy to be a pervasive fact of female experience, then what he is doing here—and in a voice wryly, "philosophically" sympathetic—is not engaging in vocation guidance but reflecting upon the sheer recalcitrance of human desire, the difficulties we all have in reconciling ourselves to the limitations of our being.

The theory of penis envy comes in for a special barrage from Miss Millett, and while I have no stake in this or any other Freudian notion, the issue here is one of simple intellectual responsibility. Freud writes:

"As we learn from psychoanalytic work, women regard themselves as wronged from infancy, as undeservedly cut short and set back; and the embitterment of so many daughters against their mothers derives, in the last analysis, from the reproach against her of having brought them into the world as women instead of men."

The crucial phrase is the opening one, "As we learn from psychoanalytic work . . ." For a central problem in considering Freudianism, or any other theory claiming to probe psychic life at levels deeper than those of rational consciousness, is the problem of validation. The validation of Freudian concepts cannot yet have, and perhaps can never have, the rigor to which scientific propositions are subjected (as Freud knew well, and therefore kept hoping that physiological bases might be found for his psychological constructs). For the time being, validation must depend on the accumulated and critically sorted observations of analysts for whom a notion like penis envy* is not, I should think, a fixed certainty

---

* Miss Millett offers an array of questions, and assaults about penis envy, not empirical in nature but rather concerned with internal consistency, and they are worth looking at, together with possible Freudian replies. What matters here, I would stress again, is not the "rightness" of the Freudian view, about which I cannot form a qualified judgment, but her method of intellectual discourse:
How does the little girl, discovering her lack of a penis, "make the logical jump from the sight of bathing or urination [to] knowledge that the boy masturbates with the novel article"? She makes the jump more experientially than logically, these events occurring during the years between three and five, when there is a great deal of experimentation in infantile sexuality.
"Might she not just as easily, reasoning from the naïveté of childish narcissism, imagine the penis is an excrescence and take her own body as norm?" No; since

but a usable lead by means of which to form hypotheses about the material they gather during analytic sessions.

Freud's "entire psychology of women," writes Miss Millett, "is built upon an original tragic experience—born female." This is true enough in a way and there is also a simplified truth in the claim that Freud sees women as defining their existence through their relations to men (though to say that isn't necessarily to *convict* him of a falsehood or bias). Finally, however, this is not so devastating a charge as Miss Millett supposes. For it is Freud's judgment that the psychology of men rests also on an original tragic experience—born male. Miss Millett manages to neglect the fact that in the Freudian system the theory of penis envy finds a polar equivalent and necessary balance in the theory of castration anxiety. The male is seen as being quite as heavily burdened by nature and circumstances as the female, and perhaps less well equipped to cope. In Freud's view, nature lets no one off easily. If women feel it "unjust" to be told they are conditioned by residues of their childhood envy for that "novel article"—Miss Millett's high-ironic parlance for "penis"—then men may feel it quite as "unjust" that they must live out their lives in constant anxiety as to sexual performance. Freud does, however, envisage a possibility for at least a partial relief or transcendence of these troubles, and perhaps a shade more so for women than for men. Women are said by him to be able to emerge from the hold of penis envy, in part through a strong and positive identification with their mothers. Nor, by the way, are they the only ones in the Freudian outlook who experience envy; men are seen as at times quite envious of that very passivity which Miss Millett regards as so libelous an attribution to her sex.

---

the "novel article" clearly has the power of directed stream which she discovers herself to lack, and since this power becomes associated for her with other, greater ones.

"Surely the first thing all children must notice is that mother has breasts, while father has none." Does this not impress the child as evidence of female advantage? Yes, but the female child has no breasts and the possibility of their later growth, not very clear at this stage in her development, can hardly mean much to her; while the male child does have that "novel article," and he has it now.

"It is interesting that Freud should imagine the young female's fears center about castration rather than rape—a phenomenon which girls are in fact, and with reason, in dread of, since it happens to them and castration does not." Several answers seemingly in contradiction but actually involving different layers of consciousness: (a) at this stage of infantile sexuality as Freud conceives it, female children aren't likely to have yet formed a strong idea as to rape: (b) in psychic life that which may not happen can be feared at least as much as that which does; (c) as Miss Millett has surely learned from her studies, reports of being raped by their fathers were so frequently proffered by Freud's early women patients that at first he took these literally and only later came to regard them as projective fantasies.

Why should all this outrage Miss Millett so much? She really has, I would venture, only a slight intrinsic concern with Freudianism. A major reason for her passionate assault is that, by making a simplistic leap from one order of experience (psychological) to another (social policy), she sees the theory of penis envy as the basis for an alleged Freudian belief that "the intellectual superiority of the male, constitutionally linked with the penis, is close to an ascertainable fact. . . ." And again she provides a footnote from Freud supposedly buttressing this claim:

"We often feel that when we have reached the penis wish and the masculine protest we have penetrated all the psychological strain and reached 'bedrock' and that our task is completed. And this is probably correct, for in the psychic field the biological factor is really rock bottom. The repudiation of femininity must surely be biological fact, part of the great riddle of sex."

Whatever the truth or falsity of what Freud says here, he is clearly not saying what Miss Millett claims he is saying. She simply will not read with care.

Yet, once her ideologicical assaults and manipulations are put aside, there does remain the fact that Freud's view of women, his analysis of their sexual natures and roles, doesn't happen to lend itself to the more extreme visions of the Women's Liberationists. Freud tended to believe, as Philip Riell says that "women are erotic hoarders in the male economy of culture. In the strife beween sensuality and culture, women represent the senses." To someone like Miss Millett this immediately seems an invidious distinction, for she is completely identified with the values of the bourgeois activist male, the one who performs (what she supposes to be) "distinctly human" work. But in Freud's canny and ambiguous view, those who "represent the senses" are at times far more "distinctly human." For even while regarding women as the agents of racial survival and men as the culture-creators, Freud also fears, like many other nineteenth-century European thinkers, the death of spontaneous life at the hands of an increasingly tyrannical culture, the nightmare of a rationalistic self-destruction as "the world of the senses becomes gradually mastered by spirituality." No one is obliged to accept these views, but anyone wishing to attack Freud in a serious way ought to be able, at the least, to report the complexities, the inner sequence of change and doubt, and the frequently problematic tone which characterize his work.

What shall we say, however, if we are committed to equality between the sexes and yet continue to believe that Freud remains one of the great minds of our age? It is the kind of question that divides those who want everything neatly aligned, slogan stacked against slogan, from those prepared to accept conflict and unresolved contradiction.

We can say of course that Freud was a product of his age, and that while he did more than anyone else to overcome its prejudices, inevitably he still shared some of them. If there is a streak of patriarchalism in his writing, as I suppose there is, we must recognize that fifty or sixty years ago people could not possibly see things as they are seen in 1970: that is known as historical perspective. In fairness, we must then add something Miss Millett fails to mention, that Freud greatly admired intellectual women and that the psychoanalytic movement was one of the first intellectual groups in this century to give a large number of gifted women the opportunity to fulfill themselves professionally. Still, to say this isn't enough.

We can add that Freud's views on women, especially those expressed in his more "philosophical" moments, must be separated from some clinically more cogent portions of his work. Freud would not be the first great thinker whose method can be used critically against portions of his writings. Still, to say that isn't enough.

We can then try to struggle with the fact that Freud advances conclusions as to the nature and consequence of sexual differences which rub against our progressive inclinations, but which can't, simply for that reason, be dismissed. For we must always recognize that analytically he may be right. Yet why should even this possibility create anxiety or anger? If the concepts of penis envy and castration anxiety prove, in some sense, to be valid for psychoanalysis, this surely doesn't at all affect the claims of women for socioeconomic justice—though it may affect some of the more nightmarishly utopian fantasies of writers like Miss Millett.*

Freud believed that the process of maturation for women presented

---

* The most egregious of these fantasies is Miss Millett's cavalier play with the notion of the abolition of the family. That the family, at once the most conservative of human institutions and endlessly open to social and psychological changes, has been coextensive with human culture itself and may therefore be supposed to have certain powers of endurance and to yield certain profound satisfactions to human beings other than merely satisfying the dominating impulses of the "master group," hardly causes Miss Millett to skip a phrase. Nor does the thought that in at least some of its aspects the family has protected the interests of women as against those of men.

In any case, one might suppose that Miss Millett would cast a glance at one of the very few contemporary social institutions—the Israeli *kibbutz*—where a serious effort has been made, if not to abolish the family, then at least significantly to modify its nature. Had she troubled to do so, and read the reports of, say, Stanley Diamond, an anthropologist of radical inclination, she would have had to recognize that at least in terms of psychological consequences, that is, the kind of children it brings forth, the evidence from the *kibbutz* isn't likely to persuade one that abolishing the family will greatly enrich the human race.

certain special difficulties, and perhaps these would persist in the best of societies—though to say that such difficulties seem to be rooted in biology isn't at all to say that they can't be eased by social policy and education. To persuade a woman to like herself and to accept herself sexually, which was one of Freud's aims, isn't necessarily to persuade her to stay in the kitchen—though it may well be to tell her, Miss Millett's arrogant ultimatism notwithstanding, that if she does prefer to stay at home, this doesn't stamp her as inferior or brainwashed or a "chattel" of the "master group."

Freud seemed also to believe that the biological differences, or if you prefer disadvantages, of women inclined them toward the sphere of private values and experience. Even if we suppose this to be true, why should it at all lessen our zeal—I mean the zeal of both women and men —for seeing to it that those women who enter upon careers be given every kind and equality of opportunity? I suspect, however, that what troubles Miss Millett is not merely the injustice of sexual discrimination but the very idea of sexual difference. For all that she is so passionate an advocate of the cause of women, she shows very little warmth of feeling toward actual women and very little awareness of their experience. Freud speaks in his essay on "Femininity" of the woman's "active pursuit of a passive function," and Miss Millett finds the phrase "somewhat paradoxical," thereby revealing a rather comic ignorance of essential experiences of her sex, such as the impulse toward the having of children. Indeed, the emotions of women toward children don't exactly form an overwhelming preoccupation in *Sexual Politics*: there are times when one feels the book was written by a female impersonator.

5

For what seems to trouble Miss Millett isn't merely the injustice women have suffered or the discriminations to which they continue to be subject. What troubles her perhaps most of all—so one is inclined to say after immersing oneself in her book—is the sheer existence of women. Miss Millett dislikes the psycho-biological distinctiveness of women, and she will go no further than to recognize—what choice is there, alas?— the inescapable differences of anatomy. She hates the perverse refusal of most women to recognize the magnitude of their humiliation, the shameful dependence they show in regard to (not very independent) men, the maddening pleasures they even take in cooking dinners for "the master group" and wiping the noses of their snotty brats. Raging against the notion that such roles and attitudes are biologically determined, since the very thought of the biological seems to her a way of forever reducing women to subordinate status, she nevertheless attributes to "culture" so staggering a range of customs, outrages, and evils that this "culture" comes to seem a force more immovable and ominous than biology itself.

Miss Millett lashes out against the Freudians not merely because some of them indulge in male chauvinism, but because they persist in seeing, within the common fate of humanity, a distinctive nature and role for women. Insofar as Miss Millett assaults the notion that current styles of perceiving "masculine" and "feminine" must be taken as eternal verities, I don't see that she can be faulted. Who would care to deny the attractiveness of historical variability, or the hope that men and women will be able to define themselves with greater freedom than they have in the past? But Miss Millett will not let it go at that, for she is driven by some ideological demon—the world as commune? the end of the nuclear family? the triumph of unisex?—which undermines what is sound in the cause of women's protest. In a remarkable sentence she writes:

"Removed from their contexts of social behavior, where they function to maintain an order not only of differentiation but of dominance and subordinance, the words 'masculine' and 'feminine' mean nothing at all and might well be replaced with what is biologically or naturally verifiable—male and female."

No longer is Miss Millett insisting on the probable truth that the claim for the biological determination of sexual roles has often been an excuse for reactionary laziness. She is now saying that the very idea of distinctive sexual psychologies, responses, and life patterns—in short, masculine and feminine as modes of behavior deriving from but more extensive in consequence than the elemental differences between male and female— means "nothing at all." And here she betrays a rashness such as one rarely finds in scholars who are genuinely committed to their subject.

For what is obvious to anyone who even glances at the literature on this matter—and that is all I claim to have done—is the agreement among scholars (who may agree on nothing else) that they don't yet know enough to make the kind of absolutist declaration I've just quoted from Miss Millett. There appear to be three *kinds* of difference between the sexes: the quite obvious physical and physiological ones; the more shadowy and ambiguous ones in role, attitude, and potential that are sometimes called "secondary"; and those that are culturally derived or imposed. Just as few scholars would now deny the last two in favor of the hegemony of the first, so few would deny the first two in favor of the hegemony of the third. The most problematic is of course the second, that is, those differences pertaining to behavior yet seeming to derive mainly from the physical and physiological.

Now there are moments when one is tempted to dismiss the whole matter by repeating Oscar Wilde's reply to a question about the differences between the sexes: "Madam, I can't conceive." For Wilde's remark points to a fundamental fact of our existence which ideologists forget at their peril and most other people, whatever their grave failings, do seem to remember. Together with the accumulated prejudice and mental junk of the centuries, there really is something we might call the experience, even the wisdom of the race, and it is not to be disposed of simply by fiat or will (as many revolutionists find out too late). It tells us, through the historical pattern of a sexual division of labor universal in form but sharply varying in content, that for good or ill our natures shape our conduct.

We can perhaps say with some assurance that the "secondary" sexual differences have to do with:

1. The distinctive female experience of maternity (one supposes that the act of carrying another human creature in one's body for nine months would have the profoundest behavioral consequences, what the anthropologist Malinowski calls an "intimate and integral connection with the child . . . associated with physiological effects and strong emotions").

2. The hormonic components of our bodies as these vary not only between the sexes but at different ages within the sexes and lead to a range of behavioral results, some of them manipulable, that have not yet been fully grasped.

3. The varying possibilities for work created by varying amounts of musculature and physical controls.

4. The psychological consequences of different sexual postures and possibilities (Diana Trilling writes: "This fundamental distinction between the active and passive sexual roles is an irrefutable fact in nature —the most active sexual seduction or participation on the part of a woman cannot relieve the male partner of his primary responsibility in their sexual union. To put the matter at its crudest, the male can rape the female, the female cannot rape the male").

Can we go any further? Miss Millett cites with approval a study by Dr. Eleanor Maccoby on women's intelligence which calls into serious question the notion that women are inherently less capable of doing abstract intellectual work by "pointing out [I quote Miss Millett] that the independence and ego strength necessary for first-rate achievement in certain analytical fields is completely absent from the cultural experience of nearly every girl child." Again, if we turn back to the source we see Miss Millett handling citations with her customary care. Were one to take literally what she says in the above-quoted sentence, there would be no way of explaining the increasing number of women who do have to their credit "first-rate achievement in certain analytical fields." And while it is true that Dr. Maccoby does make out a strong case for the view that much of the deficiency of female performance in certain intellectual fields is due to cultural inhibition, she is also careful to add:

"I think it is quite possible that there are genetic factors that differentiate the two sexes and bear upon their intellectual performance other than what we have thought of as innate 'intelligence.' For example, there is good reason to believe that boys are innately more aggressive than girls—and I mean aggressive in the broader sense, not just as it implies fighting, but as it implies dominance and initiative as well—and if this quality is one which underlies the later growth of analytic thinking, then boys have an advantage which girls who are endowed with more passive qualities will find difficult to overcome."

In the same way, with the same admirable tentativeness, Dr. Maccoby remarks: "We don't know what the biological underpinnings of maternal behavior are, but if you try to divide child training among males and females, we might find out that females need to do it and males don't."

Now the real question is, why should any of this trouble Miss Millett? That there are sexual differences extending beyond anatomy and into behavior—why should this be supposed to endanger the case for equality, *unless Miss Millett tacitly or explicitly accepts the male chauvinist view that the mere evidence of difference is proof of superiority?* Why cannot intelligent and humane people look upon sexual difference as a source of pleasure, one of the givens with which nature compensates us for the miseries of existence? Why must differences be seen as necessarily invidious? And even if these differences suggest the possibility that fewer women will reach "first-rate achievement" than men, why should that keep anyone from being responsive and responsible to those women who will do valuable work outside the home? Any more, say, than we should feel dismay at the possibility that an adjustment in sexual roles might decrease the number of men reaching "first-rate achievement"?

The dominating obsession of Miss Millett's book—which is to insist that all but rudimentary sexual differences are cultural rather than biological in origin—is a token of her lack of intellectual sophistication. If you insist, as she in effect does, that the biological be regarded as somehow untouched by cultural alloy, then it becomes virtually impossible to offer any biological evidence, if only because man is a creature that always exists in a culture, so that whatever we can learn about him must always be through the prism of cultural perspective. Culture is, at least in part, that which we make of our biology. If certain patterns of existence, such as the family, are invariable throughout the development of human culture, then it seems reasonable to suppose, even if it may be difficult to prove, that they satisfy requirements of our biology as these have manifested themselves through culture.

But as Miss Millett uses "biology" and "culture," they become absolutist polarities ranged in an endless battle against one another. She begins by noting quite properly that in the past the case for biological determinism has been overstated, especially in popular writings, and ends by doing pretty much the same thing for cultural determinism, though with not much more persuasive evidence. In her somewhat desperate reliance on the transforming powers of "culture," she reminds one of the thrust Morris Raphael Cohen once made against John Dewey's use of the term "experience": it was hard, said Cohen, to know what in Dewey's system was *not* experience.*

---

* Were there space enough and time, I would want to write at length about Miss Millett's way of approaching literary texts—an approach that proves women critics can be as heavy-handed and tendentious as male critics.

Thomas Hardy, in presenting Sue Bridehead, the charming and neurotic heroine of *Jude the Obscure*, shows himself "troubled and confused *vis-à-vis* the sexual revolution"—though Sue is one of the first and greatest portraits of the emancipated woman and nothing is said by Miss Millett about Hardy's still greater portrait of Tess, a magnificent figure transcending all of Miss Millett's categories. George Eliot is "stuck with the Ruskinian service ethic." Virginia Woolf "glorified two housewives." D. H. Lawrence, whose mystique of blood consciousness is read as if it were a social policy, is a virtual devil. His Lady Chatterley is never "given the personal autonomy of an occupation" (unlike all the other contemporary English ladies in both life and literature?). Mrs. Morel, the mother in *Sons and Lovers*, is "utterly deprived of any avenue of achievement" (as if that were somehow Lawrence's fault rather than an accurate reflection of what a miner's wife would have been like at the end of the nineteenth century—and apparently the raising of her family under conditions of hardship and with a drunken collapsed husband doesn't strike Miss Millett as an "achievement"). Paul Morel, "when his mother has ceased to be of service . . . quietly murders her"—an utterly grotesque distortion of what happens in the book. And as if there had never been a domineering woman in the world, Miss Millett complains of "a curious shift in sympathy between the presentation of Mrs. Morel from the early sections of the novel when she is a woman . . . 'done out of her rights' [Lawrence] as a human being . . . to the possessive matron guarding her beloved son from maturity. . . ." But this sentence itself gives a sufficient reason for the shift in narrative tone toward Mrs. Morel, as well as indicating, through the quote from Lawrence, that he did have kinds of sympathy for women which Miss Millett either won't allow or depreciates as tokens of male hostility.

It comes as a sign of Miss Millett's literary grasp that, outraged over Mrs. Morel's pleasure at ironing her son's shirts (as if Lawrence were here inventing a feeling

6

"It was the usual things of life that filled her with silent rage; which was natural inasmuch as, to her vision, almost everything that was usual was iniquitous."

This sentence was written a good many years ago by Henry James about Olive Chancellor, the feminist heroine-martyr of *The Bostonians*. Brilliant, it is also hard-spirited and a little unpleasant, for we sense a certain withdrawal of sympathy on James's part. Yet for those of us committed to the hope of changing the world, it is a sentence alive with challenge. Often enough "the usual" is iniquitous, and often enough not to feel "silent rage" toward the complacence with which the idea of "the usual" is employed to rationalize injustice is to abandon a portion of one's humanity. Yet in the history of modern intellectual life nothing has been more disastrous than this hatred of "the usual"; this disdain for what is called "one-dimensional"; this scorn for the inherited pleasures, ruses, and modes of survival by which most of us live; this nagging insistence that life be forever heroic and dramatic, even if ordinary humanity must be herded by authoritarian party bosses and ideologues to make it so. And in large measure this is the spirit that informs *Sexual Politics*.

Miss Millett's nightmare-fantasy of sexual lordship in which the man buys a woman as "sexual object" or household drudge and in which the woman submits to his ruling-class will: this parody of the Marxist vision of class dictatorship, with the woman as propertyless proletarian who can sell only her labor power or her sexual power—how much truth does it contain and what does it tell us about the realities of the life we lead? In the glistening towers of the Upper East Side of New York, in the country clubs of the O'Hara provinces, in Hollywood, in whatever places the rich enjoy their idleness, there are, I suppose, women who have sold themselves as "sexual objects" and must slink and kitten before their

---

utterly without precedent in human experience!), praise should then follow for, of all books, *Portnoy's Complaint* as "a healthy antidote to this kind of thing."

The one writer whom Miss Millett approves of as a spokesman for sexual health is Jean Genet, the portraitist of prison crime and homosexuality. His "explication of the homosexual code becomes a satire of the heterosexual one"—this on the dubious though popular premise that the extreme instance is the best illumination of the usual experience. Writes Miss Millett: "The degree to which eroticism and shame are inseparable in Genet is a nice illustration of how deeply guilt pervades our apprehension of the sexual, an unpleasant fact of sexual politics and hardly less true of heterosexual society than it is of Genet's." But *is it* hardly less true? Is the common range of human sexuality really "illustrated" by the world of Jean Genet?

That such a farrago of blunders, distortions, vulgarities, and plain nonsense could be passed by the English Department of Columbia University for the doctoral degree is an interesting fact.

masters. Among the millions of middle-class families living in suburban homes there are surely some—who can say how many? how does Miss Millett know? what has she *actually* observed of their lives?—that conform to this grotesque version of the human relationship. And among working-class families there are no doubt blunter and cruder variants of male bossdom and female submission.

But how can anyone with eyes to see and ears to listen suppose that this is the dominant and unmodulated reality of our time? Isn't Miss Millett guilty of the prime sin of the ideologue, which is always to forget that the scheme is at best an abstraction from reality and not reality itself, and that always the reality must be seen as more shaded, complicated, and ambiguous than any scheme can be? Caught up in a masochistic tremor of overdetermination, Miss Millett sees only butterflies broken by brutes, drudges exploited by gang bosses.

Again, one must say, yes of course, there are such instances, just as blacks are still sometimes lynched and often brutalized: but to fail to see the improvement in large areas of black life in America isn't merely political obtuseness of the kind to which the New Left is pledged unto death, it is the snobbism of those who will have nothing to do with the small struggles and little victories of human beings unless these are patterned to their ideologies and slogans. This is the very opposite—in spirit, in feeling, in political consequence—of genuine radicalism. It is, instead, a symptom of the contempt that today rages among our intellectual and professional classes: contempt for ordinary life, contempt for the unwashed and unenlightened, contempt for the unschooled, contempt for blue-collar workers, contempt for those who find some gratification in family life, contempt for "the usual."

You would never know from Miss Millett's book that working-class life can be marked by that easy warmth and fraternal steadiness in the relations between sexes that Richard Hoggart has sketched in *The Uses of Literacy*. You would never know from Miss Millett's book that there are a great many middle-class Americans who have struggled to find and perhaps in part found, terms of personal respect through which to share their lives. You would never know from Miss Millett's book that there are families where men and women work together in a reasonable approximation of humanness, fraternity, and even equality—at least as reasonable as one can expect in an unjust society, in a bad time, and with all the difficulties that sheer existence imposes on us.

I look about me and think of the people I know, the friends with whom I live. The women have it hard, since they try to be at one and the same time intellectuals or professionals (and they do suffer disadvantages here), mothers (and they do have to confront generational conflicts and confusions of value), attractive wives (and why not? since so many succeed), and heaven alone knows what else. But in part at least the women have it hard because, and for the same reasons that, the men have it hard. Do they have it harder than the men? Probably so. Yet these women, who seem to me among the most interesting people in the world, are struggling and fulfilled human beings creating the terms of their freedom even as they recognize the bounds of limitation that circumstance, gender, history, and fortune impose on them. "Chattels"? "Sexual objects"? Submissive to the "master group"? These are the phrases of a little girl who knows nothing about life.

Perhaps, however, I am referring to a very special group, too "enlightened" to betray the stigmata of sexual politics as Miss Millett describes them. I think back, then, to the one other world I have known well, the world of immigrant Jewish workers. I recall my mother and father sharing their years in trouble and affection, meeting together the bitterness of sudden poverty during the Depression, both of them working for wretched wages in the stinking garment center, helping one another, in the shop, on the subways, at home, through dreadful years. And I believe, indeed know, that they weren't unique, there were thousands of other such families in the neighborhoods in which we lived. Was my mother a drudge in subordination to the "master group"? No more a drudge than my father who used to come home with hands and feet blistered from his job as presser. Was she a "sexual object"? I would never have thought to ask, but now, in the shadow of decades, I should like to think that at least sometimes she was.

## Commentary: The Connection Between Saying and Doing

I think Irving Howe is on to something. His analysis of *Sexual Politics* finds the book wanting in a number of ways, and one of them is quite interesting. What Howe has done is to read the book as if it were a serious proposal. A theory that really is intended to ameliorate the condition of women. A theory, in short, to be applied. This technique makes Kate Millett appear to have a rather limited perception of the human condition. Here is an example:

"About the experience of working-class women she knows next to nothing, as in this comic-pathetic remark: 'The invention of labor-saving devices has had no appreciable effect on the duration, even if it has affected the quality, of their drudgery.' Only a Columbia Ph.D. who has never had to learn the difference between scrubbing the family laundry on a washboard and putting it into an electric washing machine can write such nonsense. As with most New Left ideologues, male or female, Miss Millett suffers from middle-class parochialism."

Right! The complaint is legitimate. But beyond the question of whether *Sexual Politics* is nonsense or not is a larger issue. Irving Howe's contribution here is to remind us that theory, however internally consistent, and however devoutly its consummation may be wished, must finally be compared with the experience, not only of the theorist, but of those whom the theory includes. It is the failure to remember this fact which has produced some truly baroque prattle from the upper parapets of academe.

Howe's insight explains to me a lot of things I had not understood. Monthly I have read the complaints of the new romantic educationists and thought "Yes! Right! There's a lot wrong with the public schools, they're destroying our children." But then I compare the actual school experience of my own two sons and I am puzzled. It's not doing too badly. There are things I don't like, there are teachers who are stupid or mean, or arrogant, or all three together. But there are many who are none of these and my kids are learning many things they would like to know, and seem quite happy.

I read of the vicious and predatory self-interest of the American businessman whose joy it is to trade peace for profit and ecological balance for economic gain. And I am appropriately appalled. But then I remember that I was once a businessman, that my father was a businessman and, as the saying goes, some of my best friends are businessmen; and none of us is a moral monster.

I read of the mindless chauvinism of the veteran's groups and despise it, but am again uneasy, because I'm a veteran and so are most of my friends and we are not particularly chauvinistic. It must be all those other veterans.

I read of the new consciousness of the American young, drug oriented, pastoral, McLuhanesquely tribal, and say there it is, the hope, or whatever, of the future. And then I look at all the people coming in and out of my classroom, and at the children in my town, and the children in my house, and they seem not much different than I was, not much smarter than I was at their age, and not a whole lot smarter than I am now. Must be the kids in the next state over, that they show on TV.

In short, the theories tend always to flit just shortly ahead of my experience, and I always thought it was me. For God's sake, could it be the theories? It could be. It often is. The problems all these theories express are real and pressing. But in many of the theorists there is a Chicken Littlesque quality that does a disservice to the problem.

As Howe has pointed out this is true of Kate Millett, but she is, I think, symptomatic. Many of the people who narrate the season of our discontent have pursued graduate degrees in the humanities and because of this they have a specialized outlook. By the time one has acquired a Ph.D. he has expended so much time, has executed such a quantity of busy work, and has endured such a barrage of academic hazing that he is inclined to take it and himself rather seriously, and assume that others will as well.

But he has never taken the subject matter seriously, in the way that he takes, say, tenure seriously, or promotion. This is probably because his studies and his research, his reading, and his writing have never been aimed at an audience larger than his teachers and his dissertation director, and perhaps a small circle of colleagues. His work is not designed to effect change, it is designed to earn merit. The subject becomes the matter that he assembles for publication in order that he may not perish. It is the sand in which he traces his involute initials. It is the stuff of his profession, and he shapes it to his design, never suspecting that maybe it should be vice versa.

What happens, of course, is that the Armageddon rhetoric which such an attitude produces convinces only the people who already believe you. For it substitutes the abstract for the concrete so often that it finally fails to distinguish between them. For the doctoral candidate and the publishing scholar the fact of the publication, the existence of the well-wrought abstraction is itself the point: not if it matters; simply if it is.

It is, in other words, not simply that such writers are parochial. But that they have tended to abstract themselves from the world of action and reaction. They have tended to forget that writing is a communicative, not a ritual act, and that ideas and actions have effects and consequences. Outside my office door is a sign that sums it all up perhaps. It says "Smash Unemployment." That used to make me nervous because I didn't know what I was supposed to do. Now, thanks to Irving Howe's insight, I realize that the writer of that slogan didn't really expect me to DO anything.

R. B. P.

## 29. MALE DOMINANCE? YES, ALAS. A SEXIST PLOT? NO.

### Lionel Tiger

*An anthropologist at Rutgers University, Lionel Tiger is perhaps best known for his study,* Men in Groups. *The negative reaction to that book by members of the new feminism elicited from Tiger this response, which appeared originally in the* New York Times Magazine.

The feminists' angry rebuke to us males could not be more correct and more justified. Women everywhere earn less money than men, possess less power over their communities than men, have more difficulty becoming eminent than men, and do so far less often; as a group they have lower status than men and less public prestige. Surely no one, myself included, would want to argue that such a situation is good or even tolerable: this must be the moral given or baseline from which all discussion of the feminist movement proceeds. However, if you want to change a system you have got to understand it.

The feminist critique is rooted in the assumption that there are no important differences between the sexes (except reproductive) which are not culturally determined and that, in fact, any differences which do exist result mainly from a universal conspiracy among males to keep females different—and inferior.

"Groups who rule by birthright are fast disappearing," says Kate Millett in her "Sexual Politics," "yet there remains one ancient and universal scheme for the domination of one birth group by another—the scheme that prevails in the area of sex." She claims that new research "suggests that the possibilities of innate temperamental differences seem more remote than ever. . . . In doing so it gives fairly concrete positive evidence of the overwhelmingly *cultural* character of gender, i.e., personality structure in terms of sexual category."

Not only do men keep women subordinate, goes the argument, they also make an elaborate pretense of placing them on a pretty pedestal—by means of literature and social science designed to make women feel they are most feminine, most productive and most natural when they raise men's children, cook men's food, share men's beds, and believe in the ideology that what's good for men and boys is best for women and girls.

As well as being of general intellectual interest, the feminists' attack on males is also one of the strongest indictments of science and the scientific method that it is possible to make. On generous scientific grounds, it seems clear to me that the evidence which feminists such as Kate Millett and Ti-Grace Atkinson use to support their case is, on balance, irresponsible in its selection and so narrowly and unfairly interpreted that it will finally do damage to the prospects of women's actual liberation.

Briefly, there is considerable evidence that differences between males and females do not result simply from male conspiracy, that they are directly related to our evolution as an animal, that they occur in such a wide variety of situations and cultures that the feminist explanation is inadequate in itself to help us understand them, and that there are biological bases for sexual differences which have nothing to do with oppressing females but rather with ensuring the safety of communities and the healthy growth of children. Furthermore, these differences reach back not only to the early states of our history as a civilization, but further back to our formative time as a species; accordingly, sexual differences in physique, hormone secretions, energy and endurance, and possibly even in ways of relating to other people, may be linked to our genetic heritage in direct and influential ways. To say that these differences have existed for a long time and have some biological basis is not —as some people too hastily conclude—to say that human beings are condemned to live in ancient arrangements with no hope of real change. But without understanding what they are and how they came about in the first place, the women and men who want to change our sexual patterns will fail.

First, we have to look at the unpleasant facts. In all communities, the central political decisions are overwhelmingly taken by males and the "public forum" is dominated by males. In a few progressive countries women may be actively involved in legislatures—for example, in Finland and Norway—but by and large the pattern is that even where females have had the vote for many years and where there is open encouragement of female political activity, the number of women participating in managing governments is tiny. The rule is, the higher up the hierarchy you look, the less likely it is you'll find a woman official. The same pattern applies in labor unions, businesses, recreational groups and religious hierarchies. All over the world armies and other fighting groups are all-male. In a few places where women are trained to fight, it remains unusual for them to join men in the front lines (except where defense of home territory is involved, as is sometimes the case for the Vietnamese, for example, and for Israelis living in some border kibbutzim). The task of forming a raiding and fighting party and leaving the home bases to attack elsewhere is universally and unexceptionally male. So is controlling other persons by force, as in police work and similar enterprises.

Other things being equal, women's work is of lower status than men's, and when women begin to move in on an occupation, it loses standing in comparison with others. Though in this country individual women have considerable power to dispose of family income and wealth, typically their investment decisions are guided by males; the products they buy and the manner in which they are stimulated to do so are managed by men. Even proponents of the kibbutz system in Israel—still the most radical, long-term effort at constructing the ideal society which we can observe—concede that insofar as relations between men and women are concerned, the result of over two generations of extremely shrewd and wholehearted effort is far from acceptable to sexual egalitarians. And in this country, those who have set up communes to avoid the effects of private property, patriarchy, restrictive sexual and familial life, and technocracy have discovered that simply because there is more heavy physical labor on the commune, the distinction between men's work and women's work is far sharper than in the larger society from which they hope to escape.

The political misfortune in this is clear. However, the scientific question remains: why is this the case? I've already noted the feminist answer: patriarchy exists because it has existed for so long and so universally. Despite enormous variation in standard of living, religious belief, economics, ecologies, political history, ideology and kinship systems of different societies, the same pattern broadly prevails *because* males have always dominated females in an effective and widespread scheme. But coming from feminists, this is a curious explanation, because it implies that all men everywhere are sufficiently clever and persistent to subdue permanently all women everywhere. If this is so, the conclusion follows mercilessly that men *should* govern. And if women so universally accept this state of affairs, then perhaps they are actually incapable of political action. That is nonsense, and unflattering to women, and unduly optimistic about male political acumen.

In all this general discussion, one of the most useful laws of science has been overlooked, the so-called Law of Parsimony (or Occam's

Razor*). This dictates that you cannot explain a behavioral phenomenon by a higher, more complex process if a lower or simpler one will do. To take a simple case: The other day in the paperback section of Brentano's in Greenwich Village, a beautiful woman was looking at books. She wore no bra and her blouse was aggressively unbuttoned; all the supposedly cerebral men around couldn't take their horn-rimmed eyes off her. Now it is possible that the reason we stared was that we had been brainwashed by sexist books like Mailer's and Henry Miller's and our male chauvinist egos were aroused by the challenge of conquest. But the law of parsimony demands we consider that since sexual attraction is a basic signaling system which all animals have, this woman was signaling something which the men around her were dutifully responding to. Obviously, there were some higher processes involved, too, but the simple erotic one was probably primary in this case.

If male dominance extends over the whole species—and has existed for so long—we seem constrained by the law of parsimony to look first into the biological information and theory at our disposal for an explanation. This includes comparative information about the other primates who exhibit many of the behavior patterns which feminists claim are unique impositions on human females by human males. It also requires us to see what effect our evolution in the past has on our behavior in the present, which feminists—along with many of the social scientists they criticize—by and large are unwilling to do.

Their reasoning derives from the Pavlovian biology of the nineteen-twenties and thirties, which taught that habit and conditioning could account for almost all men's behavior—and inherited characteristics for very little. Like the Lysenkoists in Russia and the positivists in this country, the feminists believe that changing the environments of the human animal will soon change the animal itself. For this, there is no evidence. Moreover, the argument ignores the theory that remains one of the strongest in science today—Darwin's explanation of the evolution of the species through natural selection and inheritance.

Modern biology in part represents an extremely important synthesis of sociology and genetics: we are able to understand the complicated social behavior of animals and can also work out how this behavior can be transmitted in the genetic codes. By now, many people are familiar with the work of the animal ethologists such as Konrad Lorenz, George Schal-

---

* Named after William of Occam, 14th-century English philosopher, because he frequently invoked the law of parsimony to explain phenomena. It is called his "razor" because the law, in effect, shaved away more complex, metaphysical explanations of nature provided by scholastic theologies.

ler and Jane Goodall. Through their experiments and field studies, and those of their colleagues, we have come to appreciate that higher animals other than man also live in relatively elaborate social systems, with traditions, much learning, and considerable variation among different groups of the same species. And yet there remains a central pattern of behavior which is common to a species and appears to be passed down genetically from generation to generation. Three decades ago, how this was transmitted would have been difficult to say. But now we know that the intricate DNA genetic code makes it possible for the individual to inherit not only simple physical characteristics, such as size, shape and chemical makeup, but also a whole set of propensities for particular social behavior which goes with a given physiology. And we can deduce from systematic observations of behavior that these propensities can be inhibited or released in the encounter with other members of the species, and modified over generations by the process of natural selection. This is most important, because it is a decisive advance from the notion of "instinct," which was defined as a relatively automatic matter of feeling hunger, blinking, and kicking softly at the doctor who hits one's knee with a small hammer.

Now we see that the question of what can be inherited is much more complex than we once thought, that all animals are "programed" not only to grow, come to sexual maturity, reproduce, become old and die, but also to interact with each other in rather predictable ways. Of course, there is considerable variation in how animals behave, just as there is in how they look, how quickly they run or swim, how much food they eat, and how large they grow. Just as with humans, there is considerable diversity but also a great amount of consistency and predictability.

We now want to know what the human biological inheritance is, or put another way, what is "in the wiring" of the average male and female, and how it got there. Almost certainly the most dismal difference between males and females is that men create large fighting groups, then with care, enthusiasm, and miserable effectiveness proceed to maim and kill each other. Feminists associate this grim pattern with *machismo*—the need for men to assert themselves in rough-and-tumble ways and to commit mayhem in the name of masculinity. Why men show *macho* and not women, the feminists do not wholly clarify, but the fact that women don't and men do is strikingly plain enough. Yet, among the possible reasons, there is a simple and clear biological factor the feminists overlook—the effect of the sex hormones on behavior.

In a report to a UNESCO conference on aggression I attended in Paris last May, David Hamburg of the department of psychiatry at Stanford described the role of testosterone in stimulating aggressive behavior. In experiments on primates, when both males and females are given extra testosterone, they show much more aggressive hyper-male activity. Humans have similar reactions under artificial manipulation of hormone levels. Among boys and girls before puberty, boys show more testosterone than girls. But at adolescence, the changes are startling: Testosterone in boys increases at least tenfold, and possibly as much as 30 times. On the other hand, girls' testosterone levels only double, from a lower base to begin with. These levels remain stable throughout the life cycle.

In one sense this seems unimportant, because the absolute amounts of these hormone substances are so tiny. And yet hormones are like poisons —a tiny amount can have a gross effect. Hence we see adolescent males— not only among humans but in some other primate species, too—flooded at puberty with a natural chemical which apparently stimulates marked aggressive behavior. When females are given extra amounts, their behavior—independent of socialization, advertising, the male conspiracy —becomes more male-like, more aggressive, more assertive. I choose the example of aggression to discuss "the wiring" and its effect on what we do because no one is likely to claim any longer that the male capacity for violent corporate aggression is a sign of superiority or courage in the world we live in.

Other differences, too, are not unusual in the world of little boys and girls. Parents and teachers are familiar with the marked difference in the rate of maturity between girls and boys: the girls generally outpace the boys for at least the first 14 years of life in school performance, physical control, ability to withstand disease and accident, emotional control, and capacity to engage in detailed work. The pattern persists into sexual maturity; the earlier social competence of women is widely recognized when women marry men some years older than they. Among humans the contrast in rates of maturation are nowhere as marked as in some of the primates—for example, those whose females may mature at $3\frac{1}{2}$ years of age and males at 7. As John Tanner of London University has shown in his book, "Human Growth," girls at adolescence are about 18 months ahead of boys, just as they have been physically more mature than boys at all ages from birth. These differences are tangible, measurable and cross-cultural; they must reflect in some degree the genetic heritage which underlies such predictable regularities—though it must be emphasized that we are speaking of propensities that overlap and not absolute differences.

Now what could be the advantage to the human species of this extensive difference of male-female production of testosterone—given its implication for behavior? In a real if extremely simplified sense, evolution is conditioning over time. In other words, just as dogs can be rewarded for salivating at the sound of a bell, so members of a species do things which become rewarded genetically by the greater ability of the performers of the effective actions to survive and to reproduce. So what our information about sex hormones may mean is that there was an advantage to the evolving human species in selecting males with high testosterone levels and females with much lower levels. Our new information about human evolution from archeological research gives us a reason for this difference: hunting.

From all the available evidence, hunting was the critical human adaptation as long ago as 2 million, or 14, or even 20 million years ago. We have been farming for 13,000 years at most, and until about 5,000 years ago the majority of us were hunter-gatherers. We have been industrialized for barely 200 years. For 99 per cent of our history our survival depended on what bio-anthropologist William Laughlin of the University of Connecticut calls "the master pattern of the human species."

During this vast time span, the hunting-based behavioral adaptations which distinguish us from the other primates were selected in the same way we evolved our huge higher brains, our striding walk, our upright posture, and the apparatus for speech. And one of the most important of our evolutions underlies precisely the feminists' complaint: males hunted and females did not, and my suggestion is that, in addition to other indices such as size, running and throwing ability, and endurance, the differences between male and female hormone patterns reflect this reality.

It's worth reviewing this briefly. Among the other primates, an individual who is old enough gathers virtually all the food he or she will eat. Almost no primates eat meat, and there is no division of labor as far as getting food is concerned. Among humans, however, a division of work on the basis of sex is universal. A strong explanation for this is that our hunting past stimulated a behavioral specialization—males hunted, females gathered—which is clearly still very much part of us, though often in only symbolic and contorted forms. The ancient pattern seems to persist: men and women unite to reproduce young, but they separate to produce food and artifacts. Highly volatile adolescent males are subjected to rigorous and frequently painful initiations and training in the active manly arts; females—more equable, less accident-prone, less gripped by symbolic fantasies of heroic triumph—rarely undergo initiations as violent and abusive as those males suffer. That is, it appears that females are much less truculent, much less in need of control, much less committed to extensive self-assertion. The possibility must be faced that this general characteristic of the species reflects the physiological one—that female bodies are less driven by those internal secretions which mark the rambunctious and often dangerous males.

If millions of years of evolution have a lot to do with the temperament of the individual male, it may also help explain the deep emotional ties that bind men together in groups. In a book that I published last year, "Men in Groups," I suggested that there is a biological program that results in a "bonding" between males which is as important for politics as the program of male-female bonding is for reproduction. The results of this male bonding propensity could be seen easily and everywhere: in sports, rock groups (who ever said males weren't emotional?), the American Legion, the men's houses of Indians, the secret societies of both Yale seniors and Australian aborigines and—most unhappily of all—the bizarre and fantasy-ridden male enterprises called armies.

So not only were there traditional and casual barriers to female participation in the powerful groups of human communities but more elusive and fundamental ones as well. It might take far more radical steps than we feared to approach the sexual equality we say we want.

I have said that males hunted and females gathered. This is not to imply that what females did was less valuable for survival. In his detailed studies of the Kalahari Bushmen, my colleague Richard Lee of Rutgers has shown that in this group, at least, the food women gather is 80 per cent of the diet. What the Kalahari males bring back from the hunt is useful, but not essential. How representative the Bushmen are of all hunters, and particularly of our ancestors, is another question, but Lee's general suggestion presumably applies in many hunting-gathering communities. Nonetheless, all societies make some distinction between men's work and women's work. As Cynthia Epstein of Queens College has pointed out in her excellent study, "Woman's Place" (the most sensitive and probing modern analysis of the sociology of female employment), these distinctions are not necessarily sensible or logical. Still and all, we are an animal as committed to sexual segregation for certain purposes—particularly those having to do with hunting, danger, war, and passionate corporate drama—as we are to sexual conjunction for others—in particular for conceiving and rearing children, and sharing food.

Once again, we get perspective of this matter from studying other primates. While among the other primates there is no sexual division of labor for food-getting, there is still considerable difference between what males and females do. In fact, from primatological work only now becoming available, an unexpected and fascinating body of information is emerging about encounters among primate females, their hierarchies, how they structure relationships over generations and how they learn their social roles. From the work of researchers at the Japanese Monkey Center, from Vernon Reynolds and his wife, Frankie, of Bristol University, from Jane Lancaster of Rutgers, Suzanne Ripley of the Smithsonian Institution and Phyllis Jay Dolhinow of the University of California, we are beginning to learn that there are indeed elaborate patterns of female bonding and that these are based to a large extent on kinship relationships rather than the political ones that frequently bind males. Furthermore, these kinship-like structures appear to be essential for comfortable and viable community life, and they provide security for the young in a web of affiliations which persist over their lifetimes. Hence, the core social bonds at the intimate level are mediated through the females, while at the public or political level, the central relationships remain very much a male monopoly. It is extremely unlikely for a female to assume political leadership of a group when a suitable adult male is available, even though the females may be far more experienced than a young leader-male, and though females seem perfectly capable of leading groups in interim periods when no suitable male is present.

One possible, if elusive, clue to the different social roles of male and female is suggested by research into the frequency of their smiles by Daniel G. Freedman of the Committee for the Study of Human Development at the University of Chicago. The underlying proposition is that smiling is an affiliative gesture of deference, a permissive, accommodating expression rather than a commanding or threatening one. Certainly among other primates, the smile is associated with fear, and humans too talk of the "nervous smile." Freedman and his associates found that among human infants two days old, females smiled spontaneously at a significantly higher rate than males. This was *eyes-closed smiling*—in the absence of a social relationship—and suggests the affinity for this particular motor pattern which girls have.

In another study—using the ingenious method of looking at photos of students in high school and college yearbooks since 1900—the same sexual difference was maintained. While everyone smiled less during periods of economic depression (they also had fewer babies), still the significant sexual difference persisted. And in his field studies of primates, Irven De Vore of Harvard University has found that females smile more often than males as a result of fear.

Intriguingly enough, some of the techniques of political organization which feminists are exploring suggest significant differences from conventional male procedures. For one thing, the principle of competitive, individual leadership is rejected in favor of an attempt at cooperative, group action. In their "consciousness-raising" sessions, the exchange and discussion of personal intimacies serves as a basis for eventual political activity; these groups gather in a circle, formalities are minimal and sisterhood is emphasized. In a sense, the feminist approach to politics is genuinely radical; if it works, it could well be an important contribution not only to the lives of women but to the political conduct of men and the body politic in general.

So far I have argued that the feminist critique takes for granted what important scientific evidence does not permit us to take for granted: that only explicit cultural control—in fact, conspiracy—lies behind the very great differences in certain male and female social behaviors. Feminists such at Kate Millett suggest that once upon a time there was a matriarchy that became corrupted by patriarchal force, which to this day oppresses women. However, the archeological facts available suggest that there is an unbroken line from the male-dominated primate systems I have described here through the hunting stage of our evolution—from which we have not changed genetically—to the most sophisticated and complicated, male-dominated technocratic societies.

Because they ignore biological factors (like many other reformers), the feminists run the risk of basing their legitimate demand for legal and economic equality on a vulnerable foundation. Their denial of significant physiological differences can also deter real occupational and educational success by women—a possibility that is suggested by a variety of studies of the menstrual cycle. The relationship of the cycle to social performance is by no means simple, nor is the evidence conclusive. But studies such as those done over a period of some 15 years by Katherine Dalton of University College, University of London, must be considered: One of her estimates is that roughly 40 per cent of women suffer from a variety of distressing symptoms during the final week or so of the menstrual cycle (other researchers see a higher figure). Dalton's investigation of admission to mental hospitals revealed that 46 per cent of the female admissions occurred during the seven or eight days preceding and during menstruation; at this time, too, 53 per cent of attempted suicides by females occurred.

In another of her studies, 45 per cent of industrial employes who reported sick did so during this period; 49 per cent of crimes committed by women prisoners happened at this time and so did 45 per cent of the punishments meted out to schoolgirls. Dalton also discovered that schoolgirls who were prefects and monitors doled out significantly greater numbers of punishments to others during the menstrual period, and she raises the question of whether or not this is also true of women magistrates, teachers and other figures in authority.

She presents evidence that students writing examinations during the premenstruum earn roughly 14 to 15 per cent poorer grades than they do at other times of the month. If what happens in England also happens here (there could well be cultural and psychological differences between the reactions of the two female populations), then an American girl writing her Graduate Record Examinations over a two-day period or a week-long set of finals during the premenstruum begins with a disadvantage which almost certainly condemns her to no higher than a second-class grade. A whole career in the educational system can be unfairly jeopardized because of this phenomenon. In another sphere, a study by the British Road Research Laboratory suggests that about 60 per cent of all traffic accidents of females occur during about 25 per cent of the days of the month—apparently before and during menstruation. Since women are generally safer drivers than men, certainly in the younger age groups, this may not be a considerable hazard to the public. But for individual women driving cars or writing examinations, these findings may be relevant—and important.

So the paradox is that when they deny there are meaningful differences between males and females because of such a predictable phenomenon as menstruation, feminists may help make it more difficult for women to compete openly and equally for scholarships, jobs, entry to graduate schools, and the variety of other prerequisites of wealth and status. This emphatically does not mean women shouldn't have responsible or competitive jobs; it may mean that in a community committed to genuine equal opportunity examinations and schedules of work—for example, the flying time of women pilots—could be adjusted to the realities of female experience and not, as now, wholly to the male-oriented work week and pattern. (Interestingly, Valentina Tereshkova-Nikolayeva, the first woman astronaut, affirms that women can be as capable astronauts as men, but that allowance should be made for the effect of the cycle on psychology.)

The human species is faced with two overwhelming problems—war and overpopulation. The first results from the social bonding of males, and is not our concern here. The second results from the sexual bonding of males and females. Men and women make love and have children not simply because the patriarchal conspiracy offers women no other major form of satisfaction, but because an old pattern rooted in the genetic codes and reflected in our life cycles—particularly in the flurries of adolescence—draw men and women to each other and to the infants their conjunction yields.

There is no conspiracy in becoming adolescent and sprouting breasts and becoming interested in boys in a new way. Madison Avenue did not invent the fact that female bodies and the movement and sound of women are stimulating to men. Anyone who has pushed a baby carriage down the street will know how many passers-by peek at a young infant and how quickly the presence of a baby will help strangers talk. Throughout the primates, females with newborn infants enjoy high status and babies are enormously attractive to all members of the community. Can it be that human females, who have more of a stake in maternity than males, are responding to the crisis of population and devaluation of this role in the stringent, probing, feminist way? In other words, is the rhetoric about sexual politics really political, or is it, ironically, another expression of sexual difference? More poignantly still, may it perhaps reflect also the currently drastic excess of females over males of marriageable age—because of the disruptions of the Second World War and the baby boom which followed—and hence the probability that a huge number of mature women remain "sexually unemployed" insofar as they will probably be unable to arrange reproductive lives in the limited ways our sexual rigidities allow?

Child-rearing remains the most labor-intensive task left to members of mechanized societies, and it can't be speeded up. Day-care centers for children can obviously be a sensible feature of a civilized society. But it is another thing for Kate Millett to recommend that child care be entrusted to "trained persons of both sexes"—an idea which is not promising in view of the experiences of orphanages and foster homes. As John Bowlby has argued in his book on child-rearing and deprivation, "Attachment," children need inputs of behavior as much as they require food, and there is considerable evidence that those who do not have a mother or mother-figure on which to focus their affections and security in early childhood suffer irreparable difficulty later on.

Now, it is not clear that fathers cannot do as well. Millions of children are currently being raised by fathers without wives, and it is true that adult males obviously have, as Margaret Mead has suggested, a strong interest in infants. On the other hand, the long and intimate relationship a pregnant woman has with her gestating child must prime her to respond to the child differently from even the most doting father. Even if this has not been demonstrated conclusively, it remains a possibility, just as it is possible that breast-feeding mothers—still the majority at the present time—have, in comparison to fathers, some different if not more substantial commitment to their children because of the hormonal and other physiological processes involved. And if nothing else, the fact that the whole human species has overwhelmingly elected to have children raised at least in the first years by women suggests conformity to nature rather than to male conspiracy.

There is good psychological and primatological evidence that it is necessary for young children to separate themselves increasingly from their parents as they mature. But unless the day-care program of the women's liberationists takes carefully into account what mothers know too well—the routinely incessant and innocent demands of young children for both care and encounter—then too many women who have spent too many days with this understanding will reject the more appealing aspects of the movement. A rejection of the intimacies of family life such as they are, and an implication that females interested sexually in males as husbands and progenitors are somehow inferior and don't know their own minds, can also serve only to frighten off potential supporters.

The theorists who proclaim the withering away of the state of sexual differences may well be proved as wrong as those Marxists who assumed that the state would wither away once it had changed the social arrangements of the people. The problem the feminists face is not just to change a culture and an economy, but to change a primate who is very old genetically and who seems stubbornly committed to relatively little variation in basic sexual structures. This is not to say that some change cannot and will not be achieved, if for no other reason than that the population crush may affect this animal as it has some others—by drastically altering his behavior patterns (though we may as yet be far from the densities which will seriously inhibit breeding).

In an article on the relationship between women's rights and socialism (New Left Review, November-December, 1966), the English sociologist Juliet Mitchell called the feminist struggle "The Longest Revolution." If there is to be a revolution, it will be of infinitely greater duration than Mitchell anticipated. Our biological heritage is the product of millions of years of successful adaptation and it recurs in each generation with only tiny alterations. It is simply prudent that those concerned with changing sex roles understand the possible biological importance of what they want to do, and take careful measure of what these phenomena mean. If they do not, the primary victims of their misanalysis, unfortunately, will be—as usual—women and their daughters.

# 30. LIVVIE

## Eudora Welty

*Eudora Welty was born in the South and still lives there, in Jackson, Mississippi. A member of the National Institute of Arts and Letters, she is an honorary consultant on American letters to the Library of Congress. Here in "Livvie" she presents another approach to the meaning of womanhood.*

Solomon carried Livvie twenty-one miles away from her home when he married her. He carried her away up the Old Natchez Trace into the deep country to live in his house. She was sixteen—an only girl, then. Once people said he thought nobody would ever come along there. He told her himself that it had been a long time, and a day she did not know about, since that road was a traveled road with *people* coming and going. He was good to her, but he kept her in the house. She had not thought that she could not get back. Where she came from, people said an old man did not want anybody in the world to ever find his wife, for fear they would steal her back from him. Solomon asked her before he took her, "Would she be happy?"—very dignified, for he was a colored man that owned his land and had it written down in the courthouse; and she said, "Yes, sir," since he was an old man and she was young and just listened and answered. He asked her, if she was choosing winter, would she pine for spring, and she said, "No indeed." Whatever she said, always, was because he was an old man . . . while nine years went by. All the time, he got old, and he got so old he gave out. At least he slept the whole day in bed, and she was young still.

It was a nice house, inside and outside both. In the first place, it had three rooms. The front room was papered in holly paper, with green palmettos from the swamp spaced at careful intervals over the walls. There was fresh newspaper cut with fancy borders on the mantleshelf, on which were propped photographs of old or very young men printed in faint yellow—Solomon's people. Solomon had a houseful of furniture. There was a double settee, a tall scrolled rocker and an organ in the front room, all around a three-legged table with a pink marble top, on which was set a lamp with three gold feet, besides a jelly glass with pretty hen

*Source:* "Livvie," Eudora Welty. Copyright, 1942, 1970, by Eudora Welty. Reprinted from her volume, *The Wide Net and Other Stories,* by permission of Harcourt Brace Jovanovich, Inc.

feathers in it. Behind the front room, the other room had the bright iron bed with the polished knobs like a throne, in which Solomon slept all day. There were snow-white curtains of wiry lace at the window, and a lace bedspread belonged on the bed. But what old Solomon slept sound under was a big feather stitched piece-quilt in the pattern "Trip Around the World," which had twenty-one different colors, four hundred and forty pieces, and a thousand yards of thread, and that was what Solomon's mother made in her life and old age. There was a table holding the Bible, and a trunk with a key. On the wall were two calendars, and a diploma from somewhere in Solomon's family, and under that Livvie's one possession was nailed, a picture of the little white baby of the family she worked for, back in Natchez before she was married. Going through that room and on to the kitchen, there was a big wood stove and a big round table always with a wet top and with the knives and forks in one jelly glass and the spoons in another, and a cut-glass vinegar bottle between, and going out from those, many shallow dishes of pickled peaches, fig preserves, water-melon pickles and blackberry jam always sitting there. The churn sat in the sun, the doors of the safe were always both shut, and there were four baited mouse-traps in the kitchen, one in every corner.

The outside of Solomon's house looked nice. It was not painted, but across the porch was an even balance. On each side there was one easy chair with high springs, looking out, and a fern basket hanging over it from the ceiling, and a dishpan of zinnia seedlings growing at its foot on the floor. By the door was a plow-wheel, just a pretty iron circle, nailed up on one wall and a square mirror on the other, a turquoise-blue comb stuck up in the frame, with the wash stand beneath it. On the door was a wooden knob with a pearl in the end and Solomon's black hat hung on that, if he was in the house.

Out front was a clean dirt yard with every vestige of grass patiently uprooted and the ground scarred in deep whorls from the strike of Livvie's broom. Rose bushes with tiny blood-red roses blooming every month grew in threes on either side of the steps. On one side was a peach tree, on the other a pomegranate. Then coming around up the path from the deep cut of the Natchez Trace below was a line of bare crape-myrtle trees with every branch of them ending in a colored bottle, green or blue. There was no word that fell from Solomon's lips to say what they were for, but Livvie knew that there could be a spell put in trees, and she was familiar from the time she was born with the way bottle trees kept evil spirits from coming into the house—by luring them inside the colored bottles, where they cannot get out again. Solomon had made the bottle trees with his own hands over the nine years, in labor amounting to about a tree a year and without a sign that he had any uneasiness in his heart, for he took as much pride in his precautions against spirits coming in the house as he took in the house, and sometimes in the sun the bottle trees looked prettier than the house did.

It was a nice house. It was in a place where the days would go by and surprise anyone that they were over. The lamplight and the firelight would shine out the door after dark, over the still and breathing country, lighting the roses and the bottle trees, and all was quiet there.

But there was nobody, nobody at all, not even a white person. And if there had been anybody, Solomon would not have let Livvie look at them, just as he would not let her look at a field hand, or a field hand look at her. There was no house near, except for the cabins of the tenants that were forbidden to her, and there was no house as far as she had been, stealing away down the still, deep Trace. She felt as if she waded a river when she went, for the dead leaves on the ground reached as high as her knees, and when she was all scratched and bleeding she said it was not like a road that went anywhere. One day, climbing up the high bank, she had found a graveyard without a church; with ribbon-grass growing about the foot of an angel (she had climbed up because she thought she saw angel wings), and in the sun, trees shining like burning flames through the great caterpillar nets which enclosed them. Scarey thistles stood looking like the prophets in the Bible in Solomon's house. Indian paint brushes grew over her head, and the mourning dove made the only sound in the world. Oh for a stirring of the leaves, and a breaking.of the nets! But not by a ghost, prayed Livvie, jumping down the bank. After Solomon took to his bed, she never went out, except one more time.

Livvie knew she made a nice girl to wait on anybody. She fixed things to eat on a tray like a surprise. She could keep from singing when she ironed, and to sit by a bed and fan away the flies, she could be so still she could not hear herself breathe. She could clean up the house and never drop a thing, and wash the dishes without a sound, and she would step outside to churn, for churning sounded too sad to her, like sobbing, and if it made her home-sick and not Solomon, she did not think of that.

But Solomon scarcely opened his eyes to see her, and scarcely tasted his food. He was not sick or paralyzed or in any pain that he mentioned, but he was surely wearing out in the body, and no matter what nice hot thing Livvie would bring him to taste, he would only look at it now, as if he were past seeing how he could add anything more to himself. Before she could beg him, he would go fast asleep. She could not surprise him any more, if he would not taste, and she was afraid that he was never in the world going to taste another thing she brought him—and so how could he last?

But one morning it was breakfast time and she cooked his eggs and grits, carried them in on a tray, and called his name. He was sound asleep. He lay in a dignified way with his watch beside him, on his back in the middle of the bed. One hand drew the quilt up high, though it was the first day of spring. Through the white lace curtains a little puffy wind was blowing as if it came from round cheeks. All night the frogs had sung out in the swamp, like a commotion in the room, and he had not stirred, though she lay wide awake and saying "Shh, frogs!" for fear he would mind them.

He looked as if he wanted to sleep a little longer, and so she put back the tray and waited a little. When she tiptoed and stayed so quiet, she surrounded herself with a little reverie, and sometimes it seemed to her when she was so stealthy that the quiet she kept was for a sleeping baby, and that she had a baby and was its mother. When she stood at Solomon's bed and looked down at him, she would be thinking, "He sleeps so well," and she would hate to wake him up. And in some other way, too, she was afraid to wake him up because even in his sleep he seemed to be such a strict man.

Of course, nailed to the wall over the bed—only she would forget who it was—there was a picture of him when he was young. Then he had a fan of hair over his forehead like a king's crown. Now his hair lay down on his head, the spring had gone out of it. Solomon had a lightish face, with eyebrows scattered but rugged, the way privet grows, strong eyes, with second sight, a strict mouth, and a little gold smile. This was the way he looked in his clothes, but in bed in the daytime he looked like a different and smaller man, even when he was wide awake, and holding the Bible. He looked like somebody kin to himself. And then sometimes when he lay in sleep and she stood fanning the flies away, and the light came in, his face was like new, so smooth and clear that it was like a glass of jelly held to the window, and she could almost look through his forehead and see what he thought.

She fanned him and at length he opened his eyes and spoke her name, but he would not taste the nice eggs she had kept warm under a pan.

Back in the kitchen she ate heartily, his breakfast and hers, and looked out the open door at what went on. The whole day, and the whole night before, she had felt the stir of spring close to her. It was as present in the house as a young man would be. The moon was in the last quarter and outside they were turning the sod and planting peas and beans. Up and down the red fields, over which smoke from the brush-burning hung showing like a little skirt of sky, a white horse and a white mule pulled the plow. At intervals hoarse shouts came through the air and roused her as if she dozed neglectfully in the shade, and they were telling her, "Jump up!" She could see how over each ribbon of field were moving men and girls, on foot and mounted on mules, with hats set on their heads and bright with tall hoes and forks as if they carried streamers on them and were going to some place on a journey—and how as if at a signal now and then they would all start at once shouting, hollering, cajoling, calling and answering back, running, being leaped on and breaking away, flinging to earth with a shout and lying motionless in the trance of twelve o'clock. The old women came out of the cabins and brought them food they had ready for them, and then all worked together, spread evenly out. The little children came too, like a bouncing stream overflowing the fields, and set upon the men, the women, the dogs, the rushing birds, and the wave-like rows of earth, their little voices almost too high to be heard. In the middle distance like some white-and-gold towers were the haystacks, with black cows coming around to eat their edges. High above everything, the wheel of fields, house, and cabins, and the deep road surrounding like a moat to keep them in, was the turning sky, blue with long, far-flung white mare's-tail clouds, serene and still as high flames. And sound asleep while all this went around him that was his, Solomon was like a little still spot in the middle.

Even in the house the earth was sweet to breathe. Solomon had never let Livvie go any farther than the chicken house and the well. But what if she would walk now into the heart of the fields and take a hoe and work until she fell stretched out and drenched with her efforts, like other girls, and laid her cheek against the laid-open earth, and shamed the old man with her humbleness and delight? To shame him! A cruel wish could come in uninvited and so fast while she looked out the back door. She washed the dishes and scrubbed the table. She could hear the cries of the little lambs. Her mother, that she had not seen since her wedding day, had said one time, "I rather a man be anything, than a woman be mean."

So all morning she kept tasting the chicken broth on the stove, and when it was right she poured off a nice cupful. She carried it in to Solomon, and there he lay having a dream. Now what did he dream about? For she saw him sigh gently as if not to disturb some whole thing he held round in his mind, like a fresh egg. So even an old man dreamed about something pretty. Did he dream of her, while his eyes were shut and sunken, and his small hand with the wedding ring curled close in sleep around the quilt? He might be dreaming of what time it was, for even through his sleep he kept track of it like a clock, and knew how much of it went by, and waked up knowing where the hands were even before he consulted the silver watch that he never let go. He would sleep with the watch in his palm, and even holding it to his cheek like a child that loves a plaything. Or he might dream of journeys and travels on a steamboat to Natchez. Yet she thought he dreamed of her; but even while she scrutinized him, the rods of the foot of the bed seemed to rise up like a rail fence between them, and she could see that people never could be sure of anything as long as one of them was asleep and the other awake. To look at him dreaming of her when he might be going to die frightened her a little, as if he might carry her with him that way, and she wanted to run out of the room. She took hold of the bed and held on, and Solomon opened his eyes and called her name, but he did not want anything. He would not taste the good broth.

Just a little after that, as she was taking up the ashes in the front room for the last time in the year, she heard a sound. It was somebody coming. She pulled the curtains together and looked through the slit.

Coming up the path under the bottle trees was a white lady. At first she looked young, but then she looked old. Marvelous to see, a little car stood steaming like a kettle in the field-track—it had come without a road.

Livvie stood listening to the long, repeated knockings at the door, and after a while she opened it just a little. The lady came in through the crack, though she was more than middle-sized and wore a big hat.

"My name is Miss Baby Marie," she said.

Livvie gazed respectfully at the lady and at the little suitcase she was holding close to her by the handle until the proper moment. The lady's eyes were running over the room, from palmetto to palmetto, but she was saying, "I live at home . . . out from Natchez . . . and get out and show these pretty cosmetic things to the white people and the colored people both . . . all around . . . years and years . . . Both shades of powder and rouge. . . . It's the kind of work a girl can do and not go clear 'way from home . . ." And the harder she looked, the more she talked. Suddenly she turned up her nose and said, "It is not Christian or sanitary to put feathers in a vase," and then she took a gold key out of the front of her dress and began unlocking the locks on her suitcase. Her face drew the light, the way it was covered with intense white and red, with a little patty-cake of white between the wrinkles by her upper lip. Little red tassels of hair bobbed under the rusty wires of her picture-hat, as with an air of triumph and secrecy she now drew open her little suitcase and brought out bottle after bottle and jar after jar, which she put down on the table, the mantelpiece, the settee, and the organ.

"Did you ever see so many cosmetics in your life?" cried Miss Baby Marie.

"No'm," Livvie tried to say, but the cat had her tongue.

"Have you ever applied cosmetics?" asked Miss Baby Marie next.

"No'm," Livvie tried to say.

"Then look!" she said, and pulling out the last thing of all, "Try this!" she said. And in her hand was unclenched a golden lipstick which popped open like magic. A fragrance came out of it like incense, and Livvie cried out suddenly. "Chinaberry flowers!"

Her hand took the lipstick, and in an instant she was carried away in the air through the spring, and looking down with a half-drowsy smile from a purple cloud she saw from above a chinaberry tree, dark and smooth and neatly leaved, neat as a guinea hen in the dooryard, and there was her home that she had left. On one side of the tree was her mama holding up her heavy apron, and she could see it was loaded with ripe figs, and on the other side was her papa holding a fish-pole over the pond, and she could see it transparently, the little clear fishes swimming up to the brim.

"Oh, no, not chinaberry flowers—secret ingredients," said Miss Baby Marie. "My cosmetics have secret ingredients—not chinaberry flowers."

"It's purple," Livvie breathed, and Miss Baby Marie said, "Use it freely. Rub it on."

Livvie tiptoed out to the wash stand on the front porch and before the mirror put the paint on her mouth. In the wavery surface her face danced before her like a flame. Miss Baby Marie followed her out, took a look at what she had done, and said, "That's it."

Livvie tried to say "Thank you" without moving her parted lips where the paint lay so new.

By now Miss Baby Marie stood behind Livvie and looked in the mirror over her shoulder, twisting up the tassels of her hair. "The lipstick I can let you have for only two dollars," she said, close to her neck.

"Lady, but I don't have no money, never did have," said Livvie.

"Oh, but you don't pay the first time. I make another trip, that's the way I do. I come back again—later."

"Oh," said Livvie, pretending she understood everything so as to please the lady.

"But if you don't take it now, this may be the last time I'll call at your house," said Miss Baby Marie sharply. "It's far away from any-where, I'll tell you that. You don't live close to anywhere."

"Yes'm. My husband, he keep the *money*," said Livvie, trembling. "He is strict as he can be. He don't know *you* walk in here—Miss Baby Marie!"

"Where is he?"

"Right now, he in yonder sound asleep, an old man. I wouldn't ever ask him for anything."

Miss Baby Marie took back the lipstick and packed it up. She gathered up the jars for both black and white and got them all inside the suitcase, with the same little fuss of triumph with which she had brought them out. She started away.

"Goodbye," she said, making herself look grand from the back but at the last minute she turned around in the door. Her old hat wobbled as she whispered, "Let me see your husband."

Livvie obediently went on tiptoe and opened the door to the other room. Miss Baby Marie came behind her and rose on her toes and looked in.

"My, what a little tiny old, old man!" she whispered, clasping her hands and shaking her head over them. "What a beautiful quilt! What a tiny old, old man!"

"He can sleep like that all day," whispered Livvie proudly.

They looked at him awhile so fast asleep, and then all at once they looked at each other. Somehow that was as if they had a secret for he had never stirred. Livvie then politely, but all at once, closed the door.

"Well! I'd certainly like to leave you with a lipstick!" said Miss Baby Marie, vivaciously. She smiled in the door.

"Lady, but I told you I don't have no money, and never did have."

"And never will?" In the air and all around, like a bright halo around the white lady's nodding head, it was a true spring day.

"Would you take eggs, lady?" asked Livvie softly.

"No, I have plenty of eggs—plenty," said Miss Baby Marie.

"I still don't have no money," said Livvie, and Miss Baby Marie took her suitcase and went on somewhere else.

Livvie stood watching her go, and all the time she felt her heart beating in her left side. She touched the place with her hand. It seemed as if her heart beat and her whole face flamed from the pulsing color of her lips. She went to sit by Solomon and when he opened his eyes he could not see a change in her. "He's fixin' to die," she said inside. That was the secret. That was when she went out of the house for a little breath of air.

She went down the path and down the Natchez Trace a way, and she did not know how far she had gone, but it was not far, when she saw a sight. It was a man looking like a vision—she standing on one side of the Old Natchez Trace and he standing on the other.

As soon as this man caught sight of her, he began to look himself over. Starting at the bottom with his pointed shoes, he began to look up, lifting his peg-top pants the higher to see fully his bright socks. His coat long and wide and leaf-green he opened like doors to see his high-up tawny pants and his pants he smoothed downward from the points of his collar, and he wore a luminous baby-pink satin shirt. At the end, he reached gently above his wide platter-shaped round hat, the color of a plum, and one finger touched at the feather, emerald green, blowing in the spring winds.

No matter how she looked, she could never look so fine as he did, and she was not sorry for that, she was pleased.

He took three jumps, one down and two up, and was by her side.

"My name is Cash," he said.

He had a guinea pig in his pocket. They began to walk along. She stared on and on at him, as if he were doing some daring spectacular thing, instead of just walking beside her. It was not simply the city way he was dressed that made her look at him and see hope in its insolence looking back. It was not only the way he moved along kicking the flowers as if he could break through everything in the way and destroy anything in the world, that made her eyes grow bright. It might be, if he had not appeared the way he did appear that day she would never have looked so closely at him, but the time people come makes a difference.

They walked through the still leaves of the Natchez Trace, the light and the shade falling through trees about them, the white irises shining like candles on the banks and the new ferns shining like green stars up in the oak branches. They came out at Solomon's house, bottle trees and all. Livvie stopped and hung her head.

Cash began whistling a little tune. She did not know what it was, but she had heard it before from a distance, and she had a revelation. Cash was a field hand. He was a transformed field hand. Cash belonged to Solomon. But he had stepped out of his overalls into this. There in front of Solomon's house he laughed. He had a round head, a round face, all of him was young, and he flung his head up, rolled it against the mare's-tail sky in his round hat, and he could laugh just to see Solomon's house sitting there. Livvie looked at it, and there was Solomon's black hat hanging on the peg on the front door, the blackest thing in the world.

"I been to Natchez," Cash said, wagging his head around against the sky. "*I* taken a trip, *I* ready for Easter!"

How was it possible to look so fine before the harvest? Cash must have stolen the money, stolen it from Solomon. He stood in the path and lifted his spread hand high and brought it down again and again in his laughter. He kicked up his heels. A little chill went through her. It was as if Cash was bringing that strong hand down to beat a drum or to rain blows upon a man, such an abandon and menace were in his laugh.

Frowning, she went closer to him and his swinging arm drew her in at once and the fight was crushed from her body, as a little match-flame might be smothered out by what it lighted. She gathered the folds of his coat behind him and fastened her red lips to his mouth, and she was dazzled by herself then, the way he had been dazzled at himself to begin with.

In that instant she felt something that could not be told—that Solomon's death was at hand, that he was the same to her as if he were dead now. She cried out, and uttering little cries turned and ran for the house.

At once Cash was coming, following after, he was running behind her. He came close, and half-way up the path he laughed and passed her. He even picked up a stone and sailed it into the bottle trees. She put her hands over her head, and sounds clattered through the bottle trees like cries of outrage. Cash stamped and plunged zigzag up the front steps and in at the door.

When she got there, he had stuck his hands in his pockets and was turning slowly about in the front room. The little guinea pig peeped out. Around Cash, the pinned-up palmettos looked as if a lazy green monkey had walked up and down and around the walls leaving green prints of his hands and feet.

She got through the room and his hands were still in his pockets, and she fell upon the closed door to the other room and pushed it open. She ran to Solomon's bed, calling "Solomon! Solomon!" The little shape of the old man never moved at all, wrapped under the quilt as if it were winter still.

"Solomon!" She pulled the quilt away, but there was another one under that, and she fell on her knees beside him. He made no sound except a sigh, and then she could hear in the silence the light springy steps of Cash walking and walking in the front room, and the ticking of Solomon's silver watch, which came from the bed. Old Solomon was far away in his sleep, his face looked small, relentless, and devout, as if he were walking somewhere where she could imagine the snow falling.

Then there was a noise like a hoof pawing the floor, and the door gave a creak, and Cash appeared beside her. When she looked up Cash's face was so black it was bright, and so bright and bare of pity that it looked sweet to her. She stood up and held up her head. Cash was so powerful that his presence gave her strength even when she did not need any.

Under their eyes Solomon slept. People's faces tell of things and places not known to the one who looks at them while they sleep, and while Solomon slept under the eyes of Livvie and Cash his face told them like a mythical story that all his life he had built, little scrap by little scrap, respect. A beetle could not have been more laborious or more ingenious in the task of its destiny. When Solomon was young, as he was in his picture overhead, it was the infinite thing with him, and he could see no end to the respect he would contrive and keep in a house. He had built a lonely house, the way he would make a cage, but it grew to be the same with him as a great monumental pyramid and sometimes in his absorption of getting it erected he was like the builder-slaves of Egypt who forgot or never knew the origin and meaning of the thing to which they gave all the strength of their bodies and used up all their days. Livvie and Cash could see that as a man might rest from a life-labor he lay in his bed, and they could hear how, wrapped in his quilt, he sighed to himself comfortably in sleep, while in his dreams he might have been an ant, a beetle, a bird, an Egyptian, assembling and carrying on his back and building with his hands, or he might have been an old man of India or a swaddled baby, about to smile and brush all away.

Then without warning old Solomon's eyes flew wide open under the hedgelike brows. He was wide awake.

And instantly Cash raised his quick arm. A radiant sweat stood on his temples. But he did not bring his arm down—it stayed in the air, as if something might have taken hold.

It was not Livvie—she did not move. As if something said "Wait," she stood waiting. Even while her eyes burned under motionless lids, her lips parted in a stiff grimace, and with her arms stiff at her sides she stood above the prone old man and the panting young one, erect and apart.

Movement when it came came in Solomon's face. It was an old and strict face, a frail face, but behind it, like a covered light, came an animation that could play hide and seek, that would dart and escape, had always escaped. The mystery flickered in him, and invited from his eyes. It was that very mystery that Cash with his quick arm would have to strike, and that Livvie could not weep for. But Cash only stood holding his arm in the air, when the gentlest flick of his great strength, almost a puff of his breath, would have been enough, if he had known how to give it, to send the old man over the obstruction that kept him away from death.

If it could not be that the tiny illumination in the fragile and ancient face caused a crisis, a mystery in the room that would not permit a blow to fall, at least it was certain that Cash, throbbing in his Easter clothes, felt a pang of shame that the vigor of a man would come to such an end that he could not be struck without warning. He took down his hand

and stepped back behind Livvie, like a round-eyed schoolboy on whose unsuspecting head the dunce cap has been set.

"Young ones can't wait," said Solomon.

Livvie shuddered violently, and then in a gush of tears she stooped for a glass of water and handed it to him, but he did not see her.

"So here come the young man Livvie wait for. Was no prevention. No prevention. Now I lay eyes on young man and it come to be somebody I know all the time, and been knowing since he were born in a cotton patch, and watched grow up year to year. Cash McCord, growed to size, growed up to come in my house in the end—ragged and barefoot."

Solomon gave a cough of distaste. Then he shut his eyes vigorously, and his lips began to move like a chanter's.

"When Livvie married, her husband were already somebody. He had paid great cost for his land. He spread sycamore leaves over the ground from wagon to door, day he brought her home, so her foot would not have to touch ground. He carried her through his door. Then he growed old and could not lift her, and she were still young."

Livvie's sobs followed his words like a soft melody repeating each thing as he stated it. His lips moved for a little without sound, or she cried too fervently, and unheard he might have been telling his whole life, and then he said, "God forgive Solomon for sins great and small. God forgive Solomon for carrying away too young girl for wife and keeping her away from her people and from all the young people would clamor for her back."

Then he lifted up his right hand toward Livvie where she stood by the bed and offered her his silver watch. He dangled it before her eyes, and she hushed crying; her tears stopped. For a moment the watch could be heard ticking as it always did, precisely in his proud hand. She lifted it away. Then he took hold of the quilt; then he was dead.

Livvie left Solomon dead and went out of the room. Stealthily, nearly without noise, Cash went beside her. He was like a shadow, but his shiny shoes moved over the floor in spangles, and the green downy feather shone like a light in his hat. As they reached the front room he seized her deftly as a long black cat and dragged her hanging by the waist round and round him, while he turned in a circle, his face bent down to hers. The first moment, she kept one arm and its hand stiff and still, the one that held Solomon's watch. Then the fingers softly let go, all of her was limp, and the watch fell somewhere on the floor. It ticked away in the still room, and all at once there began outside the full song of a bird.

They moved around and around the room and into the brightness of the open door, then he stopped and shook her once. She rested in silence in his trembling arms, unprotesting as a bird on a nest. Outside the redbirds were flying and criss-crossing, the sun was in all the bottles on the prisoned trees, and the young peach was shining in the middle of them with the bursting light of spring.

## Commentary: About Comparison and Contrast

I read "Livvie" last night, and twice again this morning. It is a handsome story, rich in ambiguity and implication, finely styled; and when I next teach a class in the short story, or Introduction to Literature, or Freshman English, I am going to include it. For one thing, the themes of the story intrigue me. For another, I am delighted by the characters, their relationships, their symbolic values. And, just now, I can think of no more than half a dozen other pieces of short fiction that make as careful use of setting.

But to explore any of these matters in detail would use up more space than I am allowed here, and would lead me to emphasize the story's content rather than its craft (which we have agreed should be our focus). "Livvie" fairly brims with proofs of Miss Welty's gift as writer; but I am as much taken with her use of comparison and contrast as with any of them. The story depends in large part on this rhetorical technique; and whether Miss Welty is using it in her development of setting or character, whether explicitly or implicitly, she invariably uses it well.

Among many other things in "Livvie" we are invited to compare and contrast: Solomon's blackest of black hats (which hides the pearl on the wooden peg) with Cash's lush, plum-colored hat (which is shaped like a platter); Solomon's safe (the doors of which are always shut) with Baby Marie's suitcase (which she opens triumphantly); the crape-myrtle trees (imprisoned and bare) with the peach tree (shining with leaves); the yard (out of which the grass has been pulled) with the fields (into which seeds have been sown); the mousetraps (which hold death) with Cash's pocket (which holds life); Solomon's bottles (which are empty) with Marie's bottles (which are full); the atmosphere in Solomon's house (heavy with silence) with the atmosphere of the fields (bright with noise); the name "Livvie" (its suggestion of life) with the name "Solomon" (its suggestion of death); Baby Marie's pride in her life (which brings her into contact with people) with Solomon's pride in his life (where no one will come); Livvie's photograph (of a child) with Solomon's photograph (of himself); Livvie's appetite (which allows her to eat two breakfasts) with Solomon's appetite (which allows him to eat none). . . .

And there is much more. When Miss Welty writes "He was good to her, but he kept her in the house" she is using comparison and contrast. We are invited to compare the fact of the man's "goodness" in the first clause with his action in the second. Or when, in the voice of Baby Marie, she writes "What a beautiful quilt! What a tiny old, old man!" Or when, of Livvie's view of her relationship with Solomon, she writes ". . . she could see that people never could be sure of anything as long as one of them was asleep and the other awake."

In a substantial way this story depends on a single rhetorical mode.

P. L. S.

# SECTION VI

## The Environment

# THE TONE OF A WRITER'S VOICE

It is no more than a truism to observe that when we listen to a man speak, we understand his message not only by what he says but how he says it. "Peace now" can be an indifferent, gentle, cautioning, intense, or even threatening phrase depending on how it is delivered. Similarly, the tone of a writer's voice is an essential aspect of his performance; it informs us as to the attitude he is taking toward his material and, in a way, toward us. Because it encompasses many elements of the craft of writing, tone is difficult to define; but it is not difficult to demonstrate. All of the materials in this section deal with the environment; each has its own identifiable tone. Take, for example, the following two excerpts (admittedly out of context):

"And these bureaucracies of unionized civil servants are strangling the cities. In New York City, for example, the police force has been doubled in the past fifteen years, although the population figures have remained almost constant. Fewer, not more policemen are on the line. There are supposedly six policemen for every one-to-two-block election district in Manhattan. Tell that to a New Yorker and he'll laugh at you. He hasn't seen one of those policemen on the beat for years—unless it's to protect Khrushchev or Castro or the President of the United States. And then the question is, 'Where did they all come from?' "

"Even in America, some wise men have always known how to live with the earth instead of against it. If we had more husbandmen like Thomas Jefferson and John Bartram, the American farm might have remained as stable as those of northern Europe, where the soil has been farmed for two thousand years without becoming less fertile. If our lumbermen had been foresters as sane as Gifford Pinchot, we would not have mined the forests of New England, the Great Lakes region, and the Northwest and left so many of them scrub country unproductive for generations. If our dry-land settlers and their congressmen had made use of the foresight of John Wesley Powell, there would have been no dust bowls in the shortgrass plains. If more attention had been paid to a book called *Man and Nature*, published over one hundred years ago, we would not now have to learn, little and late, the principles of ecology."

We might define the prevailing tone in the first excerpt as "cool and dryly accusatory"; and that of the second as "even and quietly urbane."

**349**

But these rather awkward labels do not tell us very much about how the respective passage got that way. Exactly what in each paragraph leads us to label it as we have? The answer as we have said is complex. It derives from the writer's use of diction, his syntax, rhetorical devices and, in part, from his attitude toward the reader.

The writer of the first excerpt is earnest. We discover that he is from his use of such words as "strangling" and "supposedly," and such phrases as "bureaucracies of unionized civil servants." The coolness of the passage results from the distance the writer maintains between himself and us ("Tell that to a New Yorker and he'll laugh at you").

The second excerpt achieves its urbanity from a sophisticated style, its complex sentences, its studied repetition of the introductory "If," its references to such larger and reputable authority as Jefferson and Powell, its use of such words as "husbandmen" and "fertile," such phrases as "to live with the earth instead of against it" and "dust bowls in the shortgrass plains." There is an unmistakable sense throughout that the writer is not really including himself among those who failed to pay attention to the lesson of history and that he is writing primarily to an audience who will understand his references and share his concern for the environment.

## 31. CONSERVATION EQUALS SURVIVAL

### Wallace Stegner

*Head of the writing program at Stanford, Wallace Stegner is a novelist and short story writer. Many of his works are set in the American West or Northwest, are distinguished among other things by their careful descriptions of the natural world, and reflect the author's lifetime concern with the environment and conservation.*

In the spring of 1969 thousands of Californians, warned by soothsayers that earthquakes impended, shut themselves up in their houses or fled to what they thought safe places, where they waited for disaster through a day and a night like nineteenth-century Millerites gathered for the Second Coming. The earth did not tremble and gape—the San Andreas fault is fairly unresponsive to soothsaying—but the gullible demonstrated one important human truth: we can be more frightened by fictions and phantasms than by the things that should really scare us to death. These frightened people huddled in houses that were sunk in air murky with poisonous smog; they should have sniffed panic with every breath they drew. Those who fled rushed past endless overcrowded subdivisions down freeways that roared with cars bumper to bumper, four lanes each way, at seventy or eighty miles an hour; they should have heard apocalypse rumbling before and beside and behind. Above the murk and the traffic the firmament split with sonic booms. The passing roadside showed them the devastated redwood groves of Eureka and Arcata. They drove past Santa Barbara, where crude oil bubbled from below the offshore drilling platforms and moved in great black rafts of tar toward the beaches; or through the Santa Clara Valley, where bulldozers pushed down prune orchards to clear the way for cheesebox housing; or up into Yosemite, where the gibbering of pre-apocalypse dementia greeted them from the thousand transistors on every campground; or down into the desert, where rallies of Hondas and Yamahas roared past in a mass frenzy called outdoor recreation.

People had every reason to turn pale, hide, flee, in the spring of 1969. But they hid or fled from the shadow of a fear, not from the true substance of their danger. From the thing that should have terrified them

*Source:* "Conservation Equals Survival," Wallace Stegner. Copyright © 1969 by American Heritage Publishing Co., Inc. Reprinted by permission from *American Heritage,* December, 1969.

there is no hiding. How do we flee from ourselves, from our incontinent fertility, our wastes and poisons, the industrial society in which we are guilty, suffering participants?

Six years ago Stewart Udall, then Secretary of the Interior, published a book summarizing the history of land use and abuse in the United States and suggesting a "land ethic" by which we might be guided. He called his book *The Quiet Crisis*; most readers probably read "quiet" as also meaning "slow," "delayed." Many probably assumed that he was talking primarily about open space and scenic beauty. To the average city dweller of the early 1960's—and more and more we all tend to be city dwellers—such concerns probably seemed minor by comparison with the cold war, the bomb, racial strife, inflation, the disintegrating cities, and much else. To people living in the ghetto these matters may have seemed, and may still seem, frivolous.

They were not frivolous—that was Mr. Udall's point. Neither were they limited to open space and scenic beauty. Neither have they remained quiet. While we watched the horizon for mushroom clouds, a funnel-shaped one came up behind us with terrifying swiftness. It is perfectly clear now that we can destroy ourselves quite as completely, if not quite so spectacularly, through continuing abuse of our environment as we can through some mad or vengeful or preventive finger on the atomic trigger. Conservation still properly concerns itself with national parks and wildernesses, but it has not for some years been confined to them. As Mr. Udall says in another context, true conservation begins wherever people are and with whatever trouble they are in.

People are everywhere, and in trouble wherever they are. It is not only amenity, not only quality of living, not only a supply of raw materials or open space for our grandchildren, that we must fight for. Paul B. Sears and William Vogt and others told us what was at stake thirty-odd years ago in the Dust Bowl years: survival. It is even more at stake now—survival of this civilization, perhaps even survival of the living world. And it is later than we think.

Even in America, some wise men have always known how to live with the earth instead of against it. If we had had more husbandmen like Thomas Jefferson and John Bartram, the American farm might have remained as stable as those of northern Europe, where the soil has been farmed for two thousand years without becoming less fertile. If our lumbermen had been foresters as sane as Gifford Pinchot, we would not have mined the forests of New England, the Great Lakes region, and the Northwest and left so many of them scrub country unproductive for generations. If our dry-land settlers and their congressmen had made use of the foresight of John Wesley Powell, there would have been no dust bowls in the shortgrass plains. If more attention had been paid to a book called *Man and Nature*, published over one hundred years ago, we would not now have to learn, little and late, the principles of ecology.

It seems to us a relatively new science, but George Perkins Marsh comprehended its basic laws as early as 1864. As a Vermont farm boy he had observed how woods, streams, lakes, ponds, swamps, plants, animals, fish, insects earthworms and weather form a flexible and dynamic system in which every part—even the earthworm—has a function. As Lincoln's ambassador to Italy, he had seen in Mediterranean countries the manmade deserts that taught him how civilizations are brought to an end. He was one of the first to point out that man is an agent of erosion and, in his book, to warn against "the dangers of imprudence and the necessity of caution in all operations which, on a large scale, interfere with the spontaneous arrangements of the organic and inorganic world."

We could have found our land ethic long ago in Marsh, or Bartram, or Powell. We could have found it in Aldo Leopold's *Sand County Almanac* (1949), one of the great love letters to the natural world.

If we read their books at all, we read them as metaphor, or as something applicable to other parts of the world or to a time centuries away. Our faith in science told us that when minerals and fossil fuels ran out, science would find substitutes; when earth's fertility declined, science would feed us on fish meal and plankton that the taste buds could not distinguish from prime ribs. We forgot Paul Sears's warning that nature is not an "inert stockroom" but "an active system, a pattern and a process." We forgot that every human act against the earth has consequences, sometimes big consequences.

One Santa Barbara with its fouled beaches and its slimed and dying sea birds and seals is enough to make a conservationist of a confirmed exploiter and force us to ask ourselves how much an oil field is worth. The poisoning of the Rhine reminds us that American rivers—including the Mississippi—have been similarly poisoned, that Lake Erie is so clogged with sewage and industrial sludge that fish cannot live in its oxygenless waters, that whole catches of the painstakingly cultivated coho salmon of Lake Michigan have been declared inedible because of the amount of DDT in their bodies, that our eagles and peregrine falcons and perhaps our pelicans as well are dying out from eating DDT-contaminated prey. The plight of the angry Dutch at the Rhine's mouth is not so different from the plight of any of us. It is dangerous to live downwind or downstream from an industrial community, and in this global world every place is ultimately downstream or downwind. Penguins at the South Pole have DDT in their livers; the Greenland icecap has a dark modern layer, courtesy of the smog blanket of Los Angeles, Tokyo, and London.

Smog has been one of our best teachers. A recent poll indicates that more than half the people of the United States think air pollution one of our most pressing problems. Most of us, on reflection, would rate water pollution as being just as serious. Hardly a river in New England runs Class A—drinkable—water. Many run Class E—sewage. And all of them have poisons washed into them from sprayed and dusted fields or forests or swamps.

We show signs of putting certain villains down: DDT, dieldrin, and the other chlorinated hydrocarbons. These so-called "hard" pesticides are man-made compounds that do not exist in nature; they were never born and they are all but eternal. Instead of dispersing and becoming harmless, they concentrate in living forms, moving from food to feeder, prey to predator, accumulating as they go.

Suppose we do ban the worst of these poisons, as we seem likely to do. What then do we do with the vast quantities already in existence? What do I do with the junk in my garden shed? Bury it in the ground? Dump it in the ocean? Incinerate it so that it can be blown around the world? Sweep it under the rug? Whatever I do with it, it is in danger of joining those amounts that already contaminate the natural world and are sneaking up on me through the food chain. It is a problem that promises to be as difficult of solution as the disposal of radioactive wastes, which have a half-life infinitely longer than that of any container in which they can be locked. Those lead canisters we sink in the sea will be cracking open one day to leak their contents into the water from which, the scientists assure us, much of our food will ultimately come.

Sooner or later our wastes and poisons become part of the garbage problem. In this high-consumption country every one of us generates 5.3 pounds of refuse a day exclusive of sewage, which is a separate problem. It is no longer possible, because of air pollution, to burn even those parts of it that are combustible. We spend more on garbage collection and disposal than on any public service except schools and roads, and still we fall behind.

Not one of our environmental problems—ecological disruption, depletion, pollution, the shrinking of healthy open space—gets anything but worse, despite all our ingenuity. For as we mine from nature more than we have a right to take, we make it possible to go on multiplying in exponential ways the real root of our difficulties: ourselves. There are too many of us now. Like bacteria, we multiply to the edge of our agar dish. When we arrive there, as many nations already have, we will either starve or strangle in our own wastes.

Unless.

Unless, being men and not bacteria, and living not in an agar dish but on a renewable earth, we apply to ourselves and our habitat the intelligence that has endangered both. That means drastically and voluntarily reducing our numbers, decontaminating our earth, and thereafter husbanding, building, and nourishing, instead of squandering and poisoning.

Some say the world will end in fire, Robert Frost wrote, some say in ice. His alternatives do not exhaust the possibilities. For destruction, overpopulation is very adequate; pollution and depletion are also great, and will suffice. If Professor Lamont Cole of Cornell is right, our large-scale burning of fossil fuels endangers the atmosphere in other ways than pollution. The percentage of oxygen in the air we breathe goes imperceptibly down as pollutants and carbon dioxide go up. We will feel it first at night, when photosynthesis stops, and in winter, when it is slowed. But ultimately we will feel it. Two conclusions emerge: fossil energy is the worst discovery man ever made, and his disruption of the carbon-oxygen cycle is the greatest of his triumphs over nature. Through thinner and thinner air we labor toward our last end, conquerors finally of even the earth chemistry that created us.

These are hard doctrines, and an America lulled by four and a half centuries of careless plenty accepts them unwillingly if at all. I myself find them difficult to accept, sitting in my woodsy shack on a bright Vermont morning, with a junco working in the balsam fir outside and a spider knitting up a captured fly in the corner of the window—weather and plants and creatures and I all going about our comfortable business. American optimism asserts itself against the doomsday demographers. I comfort myself that one demographer, Donald Bogue of the University of Chicago, predicts not a geometric progression of our numbers but a levelling off of the American population at about two hundred twenty million in the next decade, and relative stability thereafter. Japan has succeeded in controlling its population, though Tokyo in 1969 is a horror, a paradigm of the merely bearable world that we will all go through on our way to doomsday if we do not make peace with the earth and learn what conservationists have long known: that living with the earth is healthier, saner, and more rewarding than living against it.

The conservation movement that began as a small group of nature lovers working for the preservation of natural beauty has expanded in numbers and influence and broadened its areas of concern. The Sierra Club, born in the early part of this century of John Muir's fight to save

Hetch Hetchy Valley from a storage dam, has grown from ten thousand members to eighty thousand since World War II. The Wilderness Society, formed by Aldo Leopold and other ecologists to help save for science small remnants of the untouched American biota, has similarly grown. So has the Audubon Society, created to save from extinction the egrets of the Everglades. United with other groups—Izaak Walton League, National Parks Association, Federation of Western Outdoor Clubs—they have had their surge of militancy as our environmental problems thickened and the outdoors came under greater threat. They have had their victories—they blocked the proposed Echo Park Dam in Dinosaur National Monument and the Marble and Bridge Canyon dams in the Grand Canyon; they appear to have won in Red River Gorge in Kentucky; they have played watchdog on the government agencies charged with the care of the national parks and forests; they are locked in battle with Consolidated Edison over the Hudson and with Walt Disney Productions over the Mineral King. They helped make Stewart Udall's eight years as Secretary of the Interior productive of sixty-four new additions to the national park system, including four new national parks, six national seashores and two national lakeshores, seven national monuments, and dozens of historical parks and sites and recreation areas. If they have sometimes sounded alarmist, their alarm has not been unjustified.

Conservationists, being the first to comprehend ecology, are the people best equipped to spread their knowledge of how inextricably related our environmental problems are. They comprise the indispensable counterforce to industrial exploitation. They have a political base; they can swing elections; their zeal often takes precedence over party and must be wooed by both sides. If there is a hope for the American habitat and for the quality of American life, it is the hope that they represent through their capacity to educate and to get environmental sanity incorporated into law.

Froelich Rainey, Loren Eiseley, and some of their associates at the University Museum, University of Pennsylvania, are currently working on an exhibit that will demonstrate both man's disastrous effect on his environment and the single hope they see of recovering from his abuses. Their exhibit will be in three parts: the first showing the world in its natural balance, nature in full charge, man no more than one more primate; the second showing man in charge, progressing through higher and higher technologies with greater and greater damage to the earth and all its interdependent forms of life; the third, a hypothetical stage barely suggested by our present small efforts at correction and adjustment, showing man learning how to rejoin and develop in harmony with the nature he has previously slashed, burned, gutted, mined, poisoned, and overused.

What that projected exhibit is trying to come at in its third section is precisely what Leopold, Udall, and all the forces of ecology and conservation have been working toward: the development of a land ethic, a respect for the earth and its healthy relationships, a wise stewardship instead of wasteful greed, a rationing of our resources and ourselves for the purpose of promoting a sane, healthy, and renewable living place.

It is very late. But if we are not at the brink of a Spenglerian decline, with the conquest of the moon the last mad achievement of a mad society, we could be on the brink of the greatest period of human history. And it could begin with the little individuals, the kind of people many would call cranks, who insist on organically grown vegetables and unsprayed fruits, who do not pick the wild flowers, who fight against needless dams and roads. For that is the sort of small personal action that a land ethic suggests. Widespread enough, it can keep men from moving mountains.

## 32. TECHNOLOGY AND THE NATURAL ENVIRONMENT

### Barry Commoner

*Barry Commoner is a biologist who has earned his reputation as one of the originators and prime movers of the ecology boom. In dealing with an emotionally charged subject, his appeals are reasoned and factual. His most recent book,* The Closing Circle, *is a best seller.*

The architect is the designer of places for human habitation. But the habitat of man is not merely buildings, roads, and cities. It is, rather, the earth's total skin of air, water, and soil, for it is that planetary system—the biosphere—which establishes the basic conditions that support the life of man. Like all living things, human beings can survive on the earth only so long as this environment is fit to support them. What the architect designs for the use of man must therefore fit into the design of the environment.

Until recently the environment has been largely taken for granted that it will continue, as it always has, to support our life and our livelihood, providing the air that we breathe, the water that we drink, the food that we eat, and much of our industrial raw material. In the last few years, with a sudden shock, it has become apparent that modern technology is changing the environment—for the worse. The air that we now breathe in our cities can lead to respiratory disease, and lung cancer; surface waters are losing their natural capability for accommodating human wastes; environmentally induced changes in food crops are causing disease in animals, and in some instances people; human activities may threaten—depending on the outcome of two contradictory effects—either to flood the cities of the world under water from the earth's molten ice-caps, or to induce a new ice age.

I should like to review briefly what has been learned from the mounting roster of environmental problems. The lesson, I believe, is simple and grim: The environment is being stressed to the point of collapse. I believe that we are approaching, in our time on this planet, a crisis which may destroy its suitability as a place for human habitation. But I believe that we have also learned that the environmental crisis *can* be

*Source:* "Technology and the Natural Environment," Barry Commoner. Reprinted from the article, "Technology and the Natural Environment," from the June 1969 issue of *The Architectural Forum.* Copyright 1969 by Whitney Publications, Inc.

resolved if we accept a fundamental fact—that man is not designed to conquer nature, but to live in it.

The proliferation of human beings on the surface of this planet is proof of the remarkable suitability of the terrestrial environment as a place for human life. But, the fitness of the environment is not an immutable feature of the earth, having been developed by gradual changes in the nature of the planet's skin. Living things have themselves been crucial agents of these transformations, converting the earth's early rocks into soil, releasing oxygen from its water, transforming carbon dioxide into accumulated fossil fuels, modulating temperature, and tempering the rush of waters on the land. And, in the course of these transformations, the living things that populated the surface of the earth have, with the beautiful precision that is a mark of life, themselves become closely adapted to the environment they have helped to create. As a result, the environment in which we live is itself part of a vast web of life, and like everything associated with life, is internally complex, and stable, not in a static sense, but by virtue of the intricate play of internal interactions.

On a small scale, the dependence of environmental stability on the nice balance of multiple biological processes is self-evident. A hillside denuded of vegetation by fire, and thus lacking protection against the erosion of heavy rains previously afforded by the canopy of leaves and the mat of roots, can quickly shed its soil and lose its capability to support plants and harbor animals. And, on this scale, the threat of thoughtless human interventions is equally self-evident; we have long since learned that brutal lumbering or greedy exploitation of the soil can permanently alter the life-supporting properties of a forest or a once-fertile plain.

But, now, the size and persistence of environmental effects has grown with the power of modern science and the expansion of new technology. In the past, the environmental effects which accompanied technological progress were restricted to a small place and a relatively short time. The new hazards are neither local nor brief. Modern air pollution covers vast areas of the continents. Radioactive fallout from nuclear explosions is world wide. Synthetic chemicals have spread from the United States to Antarctica; some of them may remain in the soil for years. Radioactive pollutants now on the earth's surface will be found there for generations, and in the case of carbon-14, for thousands of years.

At the same time, the permissible margin for error has become very much reduced. In the development of steam engines a certain number of boiler explosions were tolerated as the art was improved. If a single comparable disaster were to occur in a nuclear power plant or in a reactor-driven ship near a large city, thousands of people might die, and a whole region rendered uninhabitable. Modern science and technology are simply too powerful to permit a trial-and-error approach.

This means that we cannot escape the responsibility of evaluating the competence of modern science and technology as a guide to human intervention in the environment. My own considered opinion is that modern science is a dangerously faulty foundation for technological interventions into nature. This becomes evident if we apply the so-called "engineering test" to it—that is, how well does it work in practice? Science represents our understanding of the natural world in which man must live.

Since, man consciously acts on the environment through technology, the compatibility of such action with human survival will, in turn, depend on the degree to which our technological practice accurately reflects the nature of the environment. We may ask, then, how successful is the understanding of nature which science now gives us as an effective guide to technological action in the natural world?

It is my contention that environmental pollution reflects the failure of modern science to achieve an adequate understanding of the natural world, which is, after all, the arena in which every technological event takes place.

The roster of the recent technological mistakes in the environment which have been perpetrated by the most scientifically advanced society in the history of man—the United States of America—is appalling:

We used to be told that radiation from the fallout produced in nuclear tests was harmless. Only now, long after the damage has been done, we know differently. The bombs were exploded long before we had even a partial scientific understanding that they would increase the incidence of harmful mutations, thyroid cancer, leukemia, and congenital birth defects.

We built the maze of highways that strangles almost every large city, and filled them with hordes of automobiles and trucks long before it was learned—from analysis of the chemistry of the air over Los Angeles—that sunlight induces a complex chain of chemical events in the vehicles' exhaust fumes, leading eventually to the noxious accumulation of smog.

For more than 40 years massive amounts of lead have been disseminated into the environment from automobile fuel additives; only now has concern developed about the resultant accumulation of lead in human beings at levels that may be approaching the toxic.

The insecticide story is well known: They were synthesized and massively disseminated before it was learned that they kill not only insects, but birds, and fish as well, and accumulate—with effects that are still largely unknown—in the human body.

Billions of pounds of synthetic detergents were annually drained into U.S. surface waters before it was learned—more than ten years too late—that such detergents are not degraded by bacterial action, and therefore accumulate in water supplies. Nor were we aware, until a few years ago, that the phosphates added to improve the cleansing properties of synthetic detergents would cause overgrowths of algae, which on their death pollute surface waters.

In the last 25 years the amount of inorganic nitrogen fertilizer used on U.S. farms annually has increased about fourteen-fold. Only in the last few years has it become apparent that this vast elevation in the natural levels of soil nutrient has so stressed the biology of the soil as to introduce harmful amounts of nitrate into foods and surface waters.

The rapid combustion of fossil fuels for power, and more recently, the invasion of the stratosphere by aircraft, are rapidly changing the earth's heat balance in still poorly understood ways. The outcome may be vast floods—or a new ice age.

And, for the future, if we make the monumental blunder, the major military powers have prepared to conduct large-scale nuclear, chemical and biological warfare—which can only result, for belligerents and neutrals, in a vast biological catastrophe.

Each of these is a technological mistake, in which an unforeseen consequence has seriously marred the value of the undertaking. In order to illustrate the origin of such failures, I should like to discuss, briefly, the homely example of sewage disposal.

In natural lakes or rivers, animal organic wastes are degraded by the action of bacteria of decay which convert them into inorganic substances: carbon dioxide, nitrates, and phosphates. In turn these substances nourish plants, which provide food for the animals. In sunlight, plants also add to the oxygen content of the water and so support animals and the bacteria of decay. All this makes up a tightly woven cycle of mutually dependent events, which in nature maintains the clarity and purity of the water, and sustains its population of animals, plants, and microorganisms.

If all goes well, this biological cycle can assimilate added organic waste materials, and, maintaining its balance, keeps the water pure. But such a complex cyclical system, with its important feedback loops, cannot indefinitely remain balanced in the face of a steadily increasing organic load. Sufficiently stressed it becomes vulnerable at certain critical points. For example, the bacteria that act on organic wastes must have oxygen, which is consumed as the waste is destroyed. If the waste load becomes too high, the oxygen content of the water falls to zero, the bacteria die, the biological cycle breaks down, the purification process collapses, and the water becomes foul.

A sewage treatment plant domesticates the microbial activities that degrade wastes in natural streams and lakes. Sewage treatment involves a primary step in which indigestible solids are removed, and secondary treatment in a tank or pond rich in microbial decay organisms. During secondary treatment the organic materials, artificially supplied with oxygen, are converted to microbial oxidation into unorganic substances. If the system works well, the resulting water is a clear, dilate solution of the inorganic products, of which nitrate and phosphate are most important. These inorganic products of sewage treatment, now free of oxygen demand, presumably can be released to rivers and lakes without causing any immediate drain on the oxygen in them.

But it has recently become apparent that this form of waste disposal technology is, to put it simply, a failure. For, in many places—for example, Lake Erie—the products of the treatment systems themselves, nitrate and phosphate, ultimately increase the organic load on the water, deplete the oxygen, and so negate the entire purpose of the system. Nitrate and phosphate are always present in natural waters—but in amounts far less than those generated by the huge waste load imposed on them by man. And at such abnormally high levels, nitrate and phosphate become a new hazard to the biological balance. These concentrated nutrients may induce a huge growth of algae—an algal "bloom." Such an abnormally dense population tends to die off with equal suddenness, again overloading the water with organic debris, and disrupting the natural cycle. To make matters worse, we are adding to the nitrate burden of surface waters by the massive use of nitrogenous chemical fertilizers, and to their phosphate burden through the use of phosphate-rich detergents.

What all this means for the U.S. as a whole is evident from the report of the Spilhaus Committee report to the President's Office of Science and Technology. According to that report:

"The oxygen-demanding fraction of domestic and industrial waste is growing much more rapidly than the efficiency of waste treatment, so that, by 1980, it is estimated the oxygen demand of treated effluents will be great enough to consume the entire oxygen content of a volume of water equal to the dry-weather flow of all the United States' 22 river basins."

Ignorance of the biology of the environment is leading to the absolute deterioration of the quality of the nation's water systems. For example, despite a steady improvement in New York City's sewage treatment facilities, since 1948, in most of the coastal waters which receive the effluent of New York City treatment plants, the numbers of human intestinal bacteria have *increased* sharply. Water at many of the city beaches contains bacterial counts which are well above the allowable public health limits. Behind this astonishing fact may be a new and hitherto unanticipated phenomenon—that intestinal bacteria, rather than dying off, as expected, when they are discharged from treatment plants into surrounding waters, actually multiply in them, because of the high concentration of bacterial nutrients, such as phosphate.

The warning is clear. We have begun to stress the self-purifying power of the Nation's surface waters to the point of biological collapse. A major cause of this impending catastrophe is our ignorance of the technological requirements of the environment and our persistent tendency to design technological instruments which do violence to these requirements.

The failure of technology is also evident in the air pollution problem. How else can we judge the matter of the recent proposal to construct a sunken expressway, capped with schools and houses, across lower Manhattan, without previous consideration of the resultant effects of carbon monoxide generated by the traffic on the school children and residents? Only *after* the plan was announced, did it become apparent that the resultant carbon monoxide levels would be sufficient to cause headaches, mental dullness, and even collapse. Or consider the potential impact of microscopic flakes of asbestos spread from building materials and the lining of air conditioning ducts into the city air. Careful studies by Dr. I. J. Selikoff of the Mount Sinai School of Medicine of New York City residents show ". . . these particles are now very common among city dwellers at this time." And it has been established that the presence of asbestos particles in the human lung is the prelude, if sufficiently concentrated, to a particular form of lung cancer.

We tolerate the operational failure of the automobile and other technological hazards to the environment only because of a peculiar social and economic arrangement—that the high costs of such failures (for example, the lives lost to lung cancer or the medical cost of smog-induced emphysema) are not charged to any given enterprise, but are widely distributed in society. As a result, these costs become so intermingled with the costs due to other agents (for example, air pollution from power plants) as to become effectively hidden and unidentifiable. This suggests that the "success" of modern technology is largely determined by its ability to meet the economic requirements of the manufacturer. Measured against the economic interests of those who bear its costs in environmental deterioration—society as a whole—technology is by no means as successful.

In the same way, nuclear bombs epitomize the exquisitely refined control that has been achieved over nuclear reactions. There is no evidence that any U.S. nuclear bomb has failed to go off or to produce the expected blast. What has been unanticipated, and the source for loud complaint, is the effect of nuclear explosions on the biology of the environment. And again, the scientists and engineers who have given us the new synthetic detergents and insecticides are clearly competent to produce the desired materials; the trouble comes when we begin to use them, as they must be, in the environment.

No one can deny, of course, that, in certain respects, modern technology is brilliantly successful. Certainly, the modern mass-produced automobile is a technological triumph—up to a point. The dividing line between success and failure is the factory door. So long as the automobile is being constructed, it is a technological success. The numerous parts are designed, shaped, fitted together—and the whole assemblage works. However, once the automobile is allowed out of the factory into the environment, it is a shocking failure. It then reveals itself as an agent which has rendered urban air carcinogenic, burdened human bodies with nearly toxic levels of carbon monoxide and lead, embedded pathogenic particles of asbestos in human lungs, and has contributed significantly to the nitrate pollution of surface waters.

I believe that we must reverse the order of relationships which now connect economic need, technology, and the biology of the natural world. In the present scheme of things, narrow economic or political needs dictate the choice of a given technological capability—construction of nuclear weapons or an expressway, synthesis of insect-killing chemicals or the manufacture of asbestos building materials. This capability is translated into a specific engineering operation and when the operation is intruded upon the natural world, a myriad of biological problems arise —and it is left to the biologists, physicians, and others concerned with the survival of living things, to cope with these hazards as best they can.

I believe that if we are to assimilate modern science into technology which is compatible with the environment that must support us, we shall need to reverse the present relationships among biology, engineering technology, and economics. We need to begin with an evaluation of human needs and desires, determine the potential of a given environment to meet them, and *then* determine what engineering operations, technological processes, and economic resources are needed to accomplish these desires, in harmony with demands of the whole natural system.

We need to reassess our attitudes toward the natural world on which our technology intrudes. Among primitive people, man is seen as a dependent part of nature, as a frail reed in a harsh world, governed by immutable processes which must be obeyed if he is to survive. The knowledge of nature which can be achieved among primitive peoples is remarkable. The African bushman lives in one of the most stringent habitats on earth; food is scarce, water even more so, and extremes of weather come rapidly. The bushman survives because he has an intimate understanding of his environment.

We who call ourselves advanced claim to have escaped from this kind of dependence on the environment. Where the bushman must squeeze water from a searched-out tuber, we get ours by the turn of the tap. Instead of trackless wastes, we have the grid of city streets; instead of seeking the sun's heat when we need it, or shunning it when it is too strong, we warm ourselves and cool ourselves with man-made machines. All this tends to foster the idea that we have made our own environment and no longer depend on the one provided by nature. In the eager search for the benefits of modern science and technology, we have become enticed into a nearly fatal illusion: that we have at last escaped from our dependence on the balance of nature.

The truth is tragically different. We have become, not less dependent on the balance of nature, but more dependent on it. If we fail to understand this inescapable fact of modern life, we shall forfeit our survival.

We are still in a period of grace. In that time, let us hope, we can all learn what the architect has long known—that the proper use of technology is not to conquer the world, but, instead, to live in it.

## Commentary: The Nuts and Bolts of Exposition

I suspect that if we were to read everything printed in English since the *Recuyell of the Historyes of Troye*, we would find that the great bulk of it had to do not with the preservation of literature, but with the dissemination of information: that is, with language reduced to its first causes of communication and persuasion, and not with what Sidney called "the sky of poetry."

Barry Commoner's article, clearly, was not written to delight us with its style or intricacy of design, its inventions and paradoxes, but to inform us of a problem and persuade us to do something about it. He has structured his article in such a basic and workmanlike way that, with one or two exceptions, it might well be a model for almost any piece of writing with a similar purpose.

    I.   Introduce the General Problem
        A. Provide framing material (paragraph no. 1)
        B. Develop in general terms (no. 2)
        C. Explain seriousness (no. 3)

II. Substantiate General Problem with Examples
   A. Lead-in paragraph (no. 4)
   B. Erosion example (no. 5)
   C. Air pollution example (no. 6)
   D. Nuclear power plant example (no. 7)

III. Introduce the Specific Problem
   A. Lead-in paragraph (no. 8)
   B. Develop in general terms (no. 9)

IV. Substantiate Specific Problem with Examples
   A. Lead-in paragraphs (nos. 10 and 11)
   B. Fallout example (no. 12)
   C. Highway and auto examples (nos. 13 and 14)
   D. Insecticide and detergent examples (nos. 15 and 16)
   E. Fertilizer example (no. 17)
   F. Aircraft example (no. 18)
   G. Military example (no. 19)

V. Develop One Example in Detail
   A. Lead-in paragraph (no. 20)
   B. Sewage disposal example (nos. 21 to 26)
   C. Conclusions (no. 27)

*Note: Paragraphs nos. 28, 29, 30, and 31 seem redundant. They add nothing of substance to the discussion and tend to detract from the energy developed by the sewage disposal example.*

VI. Conclude
   A. Suggest reordering of priorities (nos. 32 to 34)
   B. Deliver warning (nos. 35 and 36)
   C. Conclude framing material (no. 37)

A somewhat shorter essay might utilize only items III, IV, and VI of the outline; or III, IV, V, and VI. From the standpoint of how to lead in to material and how to paragraph logically, item IV of the outline is worth noting. Also worth noting is the fact that the movement of the article is always from the general to the particular.

P. L. S.

## 33. THE AGE OF EFFLUENCE

### Editors of Time

*Time is a weekly news magazine founded by Briton Hadden and Henry Luce. In recent years it has included as one of its regular features an essay on a subject of contemporary and wide appeal.*


What ever happened to America the Beautiful? While quite a bit of it is still visible, the recurring question reflects rising and spreading frustration over the nation's increasingly dirty air, filthy streets and malodorous rivers—the relentless degradations of a once virgin continent. This manmade pollution is bad enough in itself, but it reflects something even worse: a dangerous illusion that technological man can build bigger and bigger industrial societies with little regard for the iron laws of nature.

The problem is much bigger than the U.S. The whole industrialized world is getting polluted, and emerging nations are unlikely to slow their own development in the interest of clearer air and cleaner water. The fantastic effluence of affluence is overwhelming natural decay—the vital process that balances life in the natural world. All living things produce toxic wastes, including their own corpses. But whereas nature efficiently decays—and thus reuses—the wastes of other creatures, man alone produces huge quantities of synthetic materials that almost totally resist natural decay. And more and more such waste is poisonous to man's fellow creatures, to say nothing of himself.

Man has tended to ignore the fact that he is utterly dependent on the biosphere: a vast web of interacting processes and organisms that form the rhythmic cycles and food chains in which one part of the living environment feeds on another. The biosphere is no immutable feature of the earth. Roughly 400 million years ago, terrestrial life consisted of some primitive organisms that consumed oxygen as fast as green plants manufactured it. Only by some primeval accident were the greedy organisms buried in sedimentary rock (as the source of crude oil, for example), thus permitting the atmosphere to become enriched to a life-sustaining mix of 20% oxygen, plus nitrogen, argon, carbon dioxide and water vapor. With miraculous precision, the mix was then maintained by plants, animals and bacteria, which used and returned the

*Source:* "The Age of Effluence," the Editors of *Time*. Reprinted by permission from *Time*, the Weekly Newsmagazine, © Time, Inc., 1968.

gases at equal rates. About 70% of the earth's oxygen is thus produced by ocean phytoplankton: passively floating plants. All this modulated temperatures, curbed floods and nurtured man a mere 1,000,000 or so years ago.

To primitive man, nature was so harsh and powerful that he deeply respected and even worshiped it. He did the environment very little damage. But technological man, master of the atom and soon the moon, is so aware of his strength that he is unaware of his weakness—the fact that his pressure on nature may provoke revenge. Although sensational cries of impending doom have overstated the case, modern man has reached the stage where he must recognize that real dangers exist. Indeed, many scholars of the biosphere are now seriously concerned that human pollution may trigger some ecological disaster.

For one thing, the impact of human pollutants on nature can be vastly amplified by food chains, the serial process by which weak creatures are typically eaten by stronger ones in ascending order. The most closely studied example is the effect of pesticides, which have sharply improved farm crops but also caused spectacular kills of fish and wildlife. In the Canadian province of New Brunswick, for example, the application of only one-half pound of DDT per acre of forest to control the spruce budworm has twice wiped out almost an entire year's production of young salmon in the Miramichi River. In this process, rain washes the DDT off the ground and into the plankton of lakes and streams. Fish eat the DDT-tainted plankton; the pesticide becomes concentrated in their bodies, and the original dose ultimately reaches multifold strength in fish-eating birds, which then often die or stop reproducing. DDT is almost certainly to blame for the alarming decrease in New England's once flourishing peregrine falcons, northern red-shouldered hawks and black-crowned night herons.

In the polluting sense, man is the dirtiest animal, and he must learn that he can no longer afford to vent smoke casually into the sky and sewage into rivers as he did in an earlier day, when vast reserves of pure air and water easily diluted a waste-disposal process that clearly has limits. The winds that ventilate earth are only six miles high; toxic garbage can kill the tiny organisms that normally clean rivers. Today, industrial America is straining the limits.

One massively important factor is that the U.S. consumer actually consumes nothing; he merely uses things, and though he burns, buries, grinds or flushes his wastes, the material survives in some form, and technology adds to its longevity. The tin can used to rust away; now comes the immortal aluminum can, which may outlast the Pyramids. Each year, the U.S. produces 48 billion cans, plus 28 billion long-lived bottles and jars. Paced by hardy plastic containers, the average American's annual output of 1,600 lbs. of solid waste is rising by more than 4% a year. Disposal already costs $3 billion a year.

All this effluence is infinitely multiplied in big cities—and 70% of Americans live on only 10% of the country's total land area. Every day, New York City dumps 200 million gallons of raw sewage into the Hudson River. Each square mile of Manhattan produces 375,000 lbs. of waste a day; the capital cost of incinerating that 1-sq.-mi.-output is $1.87 million, and 30% of the residue drifts in the air as fly ash until it settles on the citizens.

The sheer bulk of big cities slows the cleansing winds; at the same time, rising city heat helps to create thermal inversions (warm air above cold) that can trap smog for days—a crisis that in 1963 killed 400 New Yorkers. Cars complete the deadly picture. While U.S. chimneys belch 100,000 tons of sulfur dioxide every day, 90 million motor vehicles add 230,000 tons of carbon monoxide (52% of smog) and other lethal gases, which then form ozone and peroxyacetyl nitrate that kill or stunt many plants, ranging from orchids to oranges. Tetraethyl lead in auto exhausts affects human nerves, increasing irritability and decreasing normal brain function. Like any metal poison, lead is fatal if enough is ingested. In the auto's 70-year history, the average American's lead content has risen an estimated 125-fold, to near maximum tolerance levels. Arctic glaciers now contain windwafted lead.

By the year 2000, an estimated 90% of Americans will live in urban areas and drive perhaps twice as many cars as they do now. The hope is that Detroit will have long since designed exhaust-free electric or steam motors. Another hope is nuclear power to generate electricity in place of smoggy "fossil fuels" (oil, coal), but even with 50% nuclear power, U.S. energy needs will so increase by 2000 that fossil-fuel use may quadruple. Moreover, nuclear plants emit pollution: not only radioactive wastes, which must be buried, but also extremely hot water that has to go somewhere and can become a serious threat to marine life.

Industry already devours water on a vast scale—600,000 gal. to make one tone of synthetic rubber, for example—and the resultant hot water releases the dissolved oxygen in rivers and lakes. This kills the oxygen-dependent bacteria that degrade sewage. Meanwhile, the country's ever-mounting sewage is causing other oxygen-robbing processes. By 1980, these burdens may well dangerously deplete the oxygen in all 22 U.S. river basins. The first massive warning is what happened to Lake Erie, where overwhelming sewage from Detroit and other cities cut the oxygen content of most of the lake's center to zero, turning a once magnificently productive inland sea into a sink where life is catastrophically diminished. With state and federal aid, the cities that turned Erie's tributaries into open sewers are now taking steps to police the pollution, and if all goes well, Erie may be restored to reasonable life in five or ten years.

But the problem goes on. Though one-third of U.S. sewage systems are below health standards, improving them may also kill lakes. The problem is that treated sewage contains nitrate and phosphate, fertilizing substances, widely used in agriculture that make things worse in overfertilized lakes. Though nitrate is normally harmless in the body, intestinal bacteria can turn it into nitrite, a compound that hinders hemoglobin from transporting oxygen to the tissues, causing labored breathing and even suffocation.

It seems undeniable that some disaster may be lurking in all this, but laymen hardly know which scientist to believe. As a result of fossil-fuel burning, for example, carbon dioxide in the atmosphere has risen about 14% since 1860. According to Ecologist Lamont C. Cole, man is thus reducing the rate of oxygen regeneration, and Cole envisions a crisis in which the amount of oxygen on earth might disastrously decline. Other scientists fret that rising carbon dioxide will prevent heat from escaping into space. They foresee a hotter earth that could melt the polar icecaps, raise oceans as much as 400 ft., and drown many cities. Still other scientists forecast a colder earth (the recent trend) because man is blocking sunlight with ever more dust, smog and jet contrails. The cold promises more rain and hail, even a possible cut in world food. Whatever the theories may be, it is an established fact that three poisons now flood the landscapes: smog, pesticides, nuclear fallout.

Finding effective antidotes will take a lot more alertness to ecological consequences. What cities sorely need is a systems approach to pollution: a computer analysis of everything that a total environment—greater Los Angeles, for example—is taking in and giving out via air, land, water. Only then can cities make cost-benefit choices and balance the system. Equally vital are economic incentives, such as taxing specific pollutants so that factories stop using them. Since local governments may be loath to levy effluence charges, fearing loss of industry, the obvious need is regional cooperation, such as interstate river-basin authorities to enforce scientific water use. Germany's Ruhr River is ably governed this way. A shining U.S. example is the eight-state Ohio River Valley Water Sanitation Commission, which persuaded 3,000 cities and industries to spend $1 billion diverting 99% of their effluent to sewage plants.

Similar "air shed" action is starting between some smog-bound states and is considered preferable to federally imposed air standards, which might not fit local climate conditions. Still, far greater federal action—especially money—is urgently needed to help cities build all kinds of waste-treating facilities. In fact, the Secretary of the Interior really ought to be the Secretary of the Environment. To unify federal leadership, he might well be given charge of the maze of rival federal agencies that now absurdly nibble only at their own slice of the pollution mess.

One of the prime goals in attacking pollution ought to be a vast shrinkage of the human impact on other creatures. The war on insects, for example, might actually go a lot better without chemical pesticides that kill the pests' natural enemies, such as birds. One of the best strategies is to nurture the enemies so they can attack the pests; more insect-resistant crops can also be developed. Florida eliminated the screw-worm fly not by spraying but by sterilizing hordes of the male flies, then liberating them to produce infertile eggs. A still newer method is the use of sex attractants to lure male insects into traps and thus to their death.

Above all, man should strive to parallel natural decay by recycling—reusing as much waste as possible. Resalvaging already keeps 80% of all mined copper in circulation. But U.S. city incinerators now destroy about 3,000,000 metric tons of other valuable metals a year; magnetic extractors could save the metal and reduce incineration by 10%. The packaging industry could do a profound service by switching to materials that rot—fast. The perfect container for mankind is the edible ice-cream cone. How about a beer container that is something like a pretzel? Or the soft-drink bottle that, when placed in the refrigerator, turns into a kind of tasty artificial ice? Soft drinks could also come in frozen form, as popsicles with edible sticks.

To cut air pollution, a Japanese process can be used to convert fly ash into cinder blocks. Since the market is too small for commercial success, public subsidies would make sense; recovering waste at the source is almost always cheaper than cleanup later. There are some real prospects of profit in reconstituting other waste. Take sulfur, for example, which is in short supply around the world. While 26 million tons are mined a year, smokestacks belch 28 million tons of wasted sulfur dioxide, which could easily be trapped in the stack and converted to sulfuric acid or even fertilizer. Standard Oil of California is already profitably recovering the refinery sulfur waste that pollutes streams.

To reduce smog over cities, one of the most visible and worst forms of pollution, smog-causing power plants might be eliminated from densely populated areas. Why not generate electricity at the fuel source —distant oil or coal fields—and then wire it to cities? On the other hand, industrialization must not be taken to distant places that can be better used for other purposes. Industrializing Appalachia, for example, would smogify a naturally hazy region that settlers aptly named the Smokies. The right business for Appalachia is recreation; federal money could spur a really sizable tourist industry.

Sometimes pollution can even help recreation. In flat northeastern Illinois, for instance, the handsomest recreation area will soon be Du Page County's fast-rising 118-ft. hill and 65-acre lake—artfully built on garbage fill. One form of pollution could even enhance—rather than spoil—water sports. Much of the nation's coastline is too cold for swimming; if marine life can be protected, why not use nuclear plant heat to warm the water? Or even create underwater national parks for scuba campers?

Ideally, every city should be a closed loop, like a space capsule in which astronauts reconstitute even their own waste. This concept is at the base of the federally aided "Experimental City" being planned by Geophysicist Athelstan Spilhaus, president of Philadelphia's Franklin Institute, who dreams of solving the pollution problem by dispersing millions of Americans into brand-new cities limited to perhaps 250,000 people on 2,500 acres of now vacant land. The pilot-city, to be built by a quasi-public corporation, will try everything from reusable buildings to underground factories and horizontal elevators to eliminate air-burning cars and buses. The goal is a completely recycled, noise-free, pure-air city surrounded by as many as 40,000 acres of insulating open countryside. "We need urban dispersal," says Spilhaus, "not urban renewal."

In the search for solutions, there is no point in attempting to take nature back to its pristine purity. The approach must look forward. There is no question that just as technology has polluted the country, it can also depollute it. The real question is whether enough citizens want action. The biggest need is for ordinary people to learn something about ecology, a humbling as well as fascinating way of viewing reality that ought to get more attention in schools and colleges. The trouble with modern man is that he tends to yawn at the news that pesticides are threatening remote penguins or pelicans; perhaps he could do with some of the humility toward animals that St. Francis tried to graft onto Christianity. The false assumption that nature exists only to serve man is at the root of an ecological crisis that ranges from the lowly litterbug to the lunacy of nuclear proliferation. At this hour, man's only choice is to live in harmony with nature, not conquer it.

## Commentary: Topic Sentences and Their Support

What is one of the best of the traditional ways to open an essay? With a question of course. This is a particularly useful approach to an essay that explores a problem, as this *Time* essay does. Opening with a question at least partially determines the organization of what follows. If step one is a question, step two should be an answer (as in this analysis), and the rest of paragraph one provides the answer to its lead sentence. The opening sentence of the first paragraph thus serves double duty: it sets the subject and design of the whole essay and serves as the specific topic sentence of the first paragraph. What are the advantages of opening with a question? One is that your audience may read on in order to find out the answer. This depends on the question. If the opening question were, "How come Bayonne is so messy?" not everyone would read on. Another advantage, and perhaps a more important one, has already been suggested. It proposes an organizing pattern for you: ask a question —give the answer. If it is a big question (such as, "What ever happened to America the beautiful?") there may be a number of answers and you have a whole essay all organized. But what if the question is at least partially rhetorical, as *Time*'s was? What if the answer is in some ways as rhetorical as the question (for example, "It got polluted")? How does one develop an essay out of that? One develops the rhetorical answer. That is, one shows the ways in which America got polluted. One defines concretely the problem that the answer stated generally. This is what *Time* has done.

The organization of each paragraph reflects that pattern: a general assertion supported by concrete evidence, or developed by detailed example. Consider paragraph three. The essential assertion there is that, though he tends to ignore the fact, man is dependent on the biosphere. The rest of the paragraph is devoted to showing how this came about, how conditions necessary for current life are the product of forces which began 400 million years ago. Or consider another example: paragraph eight. The first sentence asserts that effluence is multiplied in large cities and proceeds to support that assertion with statistics that make the assertion seem inarguable: "70% of Americans live on 10% of the country's total land area"; "New York dumps 200 million tons of waste into the Hudson River," and so on. In fact, so orderly are the editors of *Time* in their organization that a list of the opening sentences of the paragraphs would serve as a rather good outline of the essay. Try it and see. You might also observe that the paragraph you have just read here is organized on the same principle: beginning with an assertion about

*Time's* paragraph organization and then giving several excerpts from the essay to prove the assertion.

But there is more. If you were to list the topic sentences of each paragraph you would see that there is a larger overall organization. That, after the introductory paragraph, the essay divides in two parts. Part two begins with paragraph fourteen, the lead sentence of which is "Finding effective antidotes will take a lot more alertness to ecological consequences." While part one (the first thirteen paragraphs) has described the problem, part two (the last eight) suggests solutions. What could be more logical? An essay on a problem begins by describing the problem in detail and follows with proposals to solve it. The same organizing pattern would take place in a doctor's diagnosis, a mechanic's appraisal, a architect's plan, an inventor's initial notes. The organizing pattern is nothing more than inductive reasoning, also known as the scientific method.

Hypothetically the writer of the *Time* essay went through the most elementary thinking process in our culture. He noticed that America was not so beautiful anymore and wondered why. He analyzed the problem. He proposed a solution. Given the subject matter and the intent of the essay one is hard put to imagine another way of writing the essay.

This is not to say that anyone could write the essay. *Time* magazine is the product of highly skilled professional hands. The management of language is sophisticated (for example, the image of a degraded virgin land in paragraph one) and the easy marshaling of evidence demonstrates considerable research. The pun in the title is an inventive one. In short, most beginning writers, and a good many others, cannot aspire to write as well as *Time's* group journalists. But anyone able to reason inductively can organize an essay as well. And should.

R. B. P.

## 34. CITIES CAN WORK

### Edward N. Costikyan

*Edward N. Costikyan, a New York attorney and former leader of the Democratic Committee of New York County, is author of* Behind Closed Doors: Politics in the Public Interest.

Why are the mayors all quitting?
Why are the cities all broke?
Why are the people all angry?
Why are we dying of smoke?
Why are the streets unprotected?
Why are the schools in distress?
Why is the trash uncollected?
How did we make such a mess?
                    *Anon*

This bit of verse sums up with commendable clarity and directness the problems of the cities as we enter a new decade. The answers are less clear, and the solutions still more obscure. But a misunderstanding of the causes of the trouble has led most urbanologists to a wholly ineffective and unlikely cure. For the nearly universal prescription would have the federal government provide massive financial assistance and take over as many city governmental functions as can possibly be palmed off upwards.

I doubt that the federal government will provide money in sufficient amounts to reconstruct our cities within the near future. Although some of a city's money problems, such as the costs of welfare, properly are financed in whole, instead of only in part, by the federal government, massive increases in federal aid would *not* solve a city's problems, but rather would be quickly ingested by the money-consuming monster that city government can become. Therefore, the causes of the crisis within our cities demand a different type of federal help for two reasons: The predominant cause of city crises is the collapse and destruction of the political machine. The second cause is the shortage of a supply of cheap labor essential to the growth and life of any city.

*Source:* "Cities Can Work," Edward N. Costikyan. From April 4, 1970 *Saturday Review.* Copyright 1970, Saturday Review, Inc.

The political machine was the institutional backbone of city government during the period in which our cities were built. It played a multitude of governmental roles. And it gave the average citizen the direct access to government services, which he cannot find today.

The base of the machine was the captain of the election district or precinct. He was in charge of a one- to two-block area for the party. And he was in charge year round. If a resident had a problem—a leaking ceiling, no water or heat, a son in trouble with the law, a shortage of cash or food—he turned to his neighbor the captain. The captain, if he himself could not deal with the problem, took the constituent to "the leader" at the local clubhouse. There the problem was explained, and the leader undertook to solve it. If it was a leaky roof, the leader called someone he knew in the appropriate city department—often someone the leader had placed there—explained the problem, and got action.

This power of lateral invasion into the bureaucracy made efficient administration of a large city possible. It kept the bureaucracy hopping. But it also encouraged corruption. The average citizen, however, was willing to tolerate a degree of corruption as the price of his having ready access to government services. But the more affluent members of society (the backbone of every reform movement), seeing in this lateral access to government services (and not needing those services) potential and actual corruption, set out to destroy that access and the system that produced it.

By and large, these efforts have succeeded in their intent. But we will never know whether their success represents, on balance, progress or retrogression, for all the histories of the political machines and their workings have been written from a reform orientation. It should be observed, however, in the absence of fairer contemporaneous data, that the political machines built the cities, paved their streets, dug their sewers, and piped their water supply systems. Furthermore, under the administration of the machines, mass transit systems, school systems, and massive developments of new housing were constructed.

It would be laughable to suggest that any of our present city administrations could accomplish one-tenth of what the political machines accomplished during the period from the Civil War to World War I.

The machine was also the source of manpower to staff the city government. Of course, the city jobs available to the machine were part of its lifeblood. But the reservoir of people with some training in city government was also a resource for the city—a resource whose absence today has contributed to the "mess" referred to in the verse. People untrained in government try to learn what it is all about while on the job, wandering in and out of office at a pace that staggers the minds of the citizenry. By and large, these untrained people find themselves unable to effectively control or direct the bureaucracy, and frequently they quit in frustration.

The reform answer to the machine as the personnel pool for government was the creation of a competing source of manpower: civil service. As long as civil service and the machine remained in competition for the staffing of the government, the administrative result was good. But with the collapse of the machine, civil service has monopolized the field, and the administrative results have been disastrous, for the bureaucracies have a double layer of protection that deprives any elected official of the power to get the bureaucrats to do their jobs. One layer is the impossibility of firing a civil servant. The other is the civil service unions, which have such power over the city—in the absence of alternative sources of manpower—that in the final analysis the bureaucracies are in a position to dictate to elected officials and their appointees. The bureaucrats can specify what they will and will not do (such as inspect boilers during a cold wave), what they will wear, and where they will work. The elected official (or his appointee) is at their mercy.

And these bureaucracies of unionized civil servants are strangling the cities. In New York City, for example, the police force has been doubled in the past fifteen years, although the population figures have remained almost constant. Fewer, not more policemen are on the line. There are supposedly six policemen for every one- to two-block election district in Manhattan. Tell that to a New Yorker and he'll laugh at you. He hasn't seen one of those policemen on the beat for years—unless it's to protect Khrushchev or Castro or the President of the United States. And then the question is, "Where did they all come from?"

There are fewer than 3,000 policemen assigned to duty on New York City streets (in cars or on foot) at any one time. (Put aside whether those assigned are where they are supposed to be.) One night last year, according to former Mayor Robert Wagner, there was not a single policeman on duty on the streets of Brooklyn. And the cost of all this "protection" has been estimated to be about $39 per citizen in New York City, as compared with about $13 per capita in a city of 100,000 people. When Mayor John Lindsay tried to change an archaic state statute that stipulated police be assigned to only three equal shifts, the police union first fought him in the state legislature, and lost. Ultimately, however, the union won by simply refusing to go along, and the fourth shift, which increases the number of police on duty during high crime periods, is now "voluntary" and is paid overtime.

The same phenomena of high costs, large numbers of employees with few on the line, rigidity, and immunity from discipline by elected officials or their appointees are found in every city department.

The cost of all this leaps and leaps. In New York City, the cost of providing essential services goes up every year by about 15 per cent, while revenues rise by less than 5 per cent. The result is the annual budget gap with which city dwellers are familiar, and which causes the cry for more federal money. New York City's budget, at $3-billion in 1965, is more than double that five years later. This $3-billion increase has not been absorbed by the cost of new services, but by the cost of existing programs. More federal aid will not solve the problem created by the capacity of the present bureaucracies to absorb more and more money for the same, or perhaps less, service.

The destruction of the political machine has left the unionized civil service bureaucracies with the same control over the life of the city that the machine once enjoyed and abused sufficiently to lead to the growth of civil service.

Finally, the destruction of the machine has left some governmental functions without anyone to perform them. The city's election machinery, for example, was once operated by the political parties. The parties, rather than the city, not only trained the election inspectors but paid them (the city paid a pittance, and still does, but the parties no longer can transform this pittance into reasonable compensation). The parties saw that the polls were open when they should be, and that the voting machines worked. True, the parties sometimes abused their power. There were conflicts of interest in primary elections where one faction or another selected the inspectors. (In the first primary in which I was elected a district leader, my opponent selected the thirty-two Democratic inspectors who, with thirty-two Republican ones, operated our sixteen polling places. I won, nonetheless.)

But the parties no longer are capable of performing this governmental function. And although some critics attribute breakdowns in the electoral machinery to the venality of the political machine, in fact, it is the result of incompetence.

The political consequences of the destruction of the machine are far more obvious than the governmental ones. The wave of upset victories in recent city primaries and elections all over the country is the obvious product of the death of the political party machines and party loyalty and party discipline.

The solution to all this is *not* the re-creation of the political machines, an impossible task given the level of competence of their present leaders and personnel. Rather it is to stimulate alternative methods of performing the necessary governmental and political functions that the machines once performed.

The second major cause of the crisis of the cities has been the loss of a supply of cheap labor. This loss has not only escalated municipal government costs, but has posed the most serious threat to the capacity of the cities to survive.

Eliel Saarinen in his book *The City: Its Growth, Its Decay, Its Future* pointed out that the basic function of a city is to provide places for people to live and work. Indeed, without places to live, there can be no city.

The loss of a supply of cheap labor has eliminated the capacity of the city (here I mean not the city government, but the totality of its institutions) to provide the places for people to live. In New York City, residential construction has come to a halt—literally, not figuratively, for construction capital and labor can far more profitably be devoted to commercial construction, where rents of $16 per year per square foot can be earned.

Unless some solution is found to this problem, the city is doomed to a slow death as its existing supply of residential housing decays and becomes uninhabitable, and the city's people are pushed out.

The second major problem created by the loss of a supply of cheap labor has already been noted—the 15 per cent increase in the costs of city government each year. Once city employment was attractive to ambitious young men as well as to security-seeking citizens. There was a surplus of cheap labor. Jobs were impermanent in a non-unionized volatile economy, and many offered little in the way of a future. Lower paying government jobs were attractive. They provided security and a step up the ladder. That is no longer true. To get people to work for it, the city must now compete with and attempt to match the private sector. As a result, the costs of city government have skyrocketed, and will continue to skyrocket sufficiently to absorb all that giant transfusion of federal aid to the cities that everyone calls for, and that is supposed to be on the way.

Again, the solution is not to re-create a supply of cheap labor by having a nice little recession (a solution the Nixon administration more and more appears to be pursuing). Rather the creation of alternative work forces, not drawn from the existing high cost labor supply, seems essential.

So much for the causes of the crisis. What are the cures?

On the governmental level, the first task is to create a device to perform the function once provided by the machine of giving the citizen direct lateral access to his government. The most popular proposal to accomplish this has been called decentralization. I prefer to call it reallocation of government functions. The proposal is that each government function will be assigned to the lowest and smallest governmental entity qualified to perform it. Under this approach, basic government services, such as police patrolling, street cleaning, and parking and housing enforcement, will be overseen by a local administrator in charge of a district of about 100,000 people. Other services, such as those dealing with air and water pollution, would be administered on a regional basis. In between, city or county governments would perform those functions they are best capable of.

The details of such a reorganization of city government are far too complex to deal with here. But essential to the proposal is the notion that the local administrator be elected by and be responsible to the voters whose streets he is supposed to keep clean and safe, that the existing civil service bureaucracies be eliminated, that their functions and personnel be reassigned to the appropriate level of government—local, city, county, or regional—and that the elected administrator of each level of government be given substantially greater power over those he supervises than city officials now have over unionized civil servants, who also possess a fair amount of political power.

Finally, the proposal envisages the creation of local district councils consisting of approximately eighty committeemen. These committeemen would each represent an election district (or precinct)—one to two city blocks (about 1,500) people). The committeemen would be part-time city employees elected by their neighbors. They would act much as the old captain did; if there were a problem about a leaky roof or a dirty street, the committeeman would be the person to see. He would have direct access to the local administrator, as his predecessor the captain had to the leader. Similar proposals have been made elsewhere. In Los Angeles, a similar recent proposal gives the committeeman the unwieldy but descriptive title of "neighborhoodman."

Since the committeeman would be an elected official, he would be far more sensitive to constituents' problems than any remote unionized civil servant downtown. And if the committeeman was *not* more sensitive, he could hardly survive the next election.

It is hoped that this reallocation of government functions will achieve a number of salutary effects:

1. Humanizing the presently impersonal government furnished by most cities to their citizenry;
2. Eliminating the bureaucratic rigidity and waste of manpower that have characterized increasingly centralized city government;
3. Placing responsibility for city government on identifiable individuals subject to popular control and, when appropriate, to removal from office by those they are supposed to be serving;

4. Reducing the cost of government by eliminating the layers of administrators, which result, for example, in less than 10 per cent of the New York City Police Department's personnel (and analogous percentages in other departments) performing line duty.

Without such a reorganization of city government, I do not believe massive federal aid—if it ever comes—will solve the problems of the cities. And, although the cities need the money, I'd rather not wait for it. Instead, I would suggest that two other steps be taken by the federal government to help cities solve the basic problem of staying alive.

First: On the city governmental level, there is a tremendous need for short-term, vigorous, young manpower to deal with the emergencies that every city constantly faces and the special emergencies it faces from time to time. The city's existing manpower cannot meet or effectively deal with these emergencies.

Consider: If teachers make demands that a city cannot or should not accept, and they go on strike, what happens? The city capitulates, and up go the costs of government. If there is a cold wave and a rash of complaints about lack of heat, and building inspectors cannot keep up with the volume or refuse to try, what happens? People stay cold. If sanitationmen go on strike and there is a health crisis, what happens? Unless the mayor can find a way to blame it on the governor, the city capitulates.

And what of the many areas in every city similar to those in New York City, such as Bedford-Stuyvesant in Brooklyn, Harlem in Manhattan, and Hunts Point in the Bronx, where local government has broken down and the city's total existing manpower, even if it were working at full strength, could not deal with a particular area's problems unless it worked sixteen hours a day and disregarded the remainder of the city?

The answer to all these situations is a special emergency force, consisting of young men and women who would devote two to three years of their lives to serving their city just as they are now asked to serve their country. They could quickly be given sufficient knowledge of city government to spot housing violations and to file complaints. They could move into a problem area, take it over house by house, and clean it up. They could provide extra police protection in high crime areas; collect garbage, if that were necessary; patrol the streets, if that were necessary; arrest narcotics pushers (which would be necessary); and bring help and guidance to the oppressed city dwellers who live in degradation. They could collect the rents, and make the repairs the absent landlords refused to make. Some could first complete their educations and then bring medical and legal services to the people and places that need it. No picnic, it would be hard and sometimes dangerous work. What mayor would not rejoice at such an emergency force?

The possibilities are limitless. It is clear that a force such as this is necessary if the cities are ever going to undo the damage that time, bureaucracy, and lack of money and manpower have already done.

Federal sponsorship of such a program, including financial help and especially exemption from the draft, would do more to revitalize our cities than any big gobs of money we are likely to see from Washington.

The most rewarding dividend, however, would be a generation of graduates of the emergency force. Undoubtedly, some would stay in government. And all would have a working knowledge of the problems of government that would act as a bulwark against the electoral appeal of the demagogues we can confidently expect to proliferate as television increasingly becomes politics' principal medium of communication. Furthermore, it might supply some of the meaning to life that so many of our young people seem to be seeking.

Second: the housing problem. If city governments were to operate to perfection but their present failure to build and maintain residential housing were to continue, the cities would soon die, for private enterprise, using the money and manpower available at present, simply cannot meet the cities' housing needs.

When a similar condition existed during the 1930s in the electric industry in the South, the federal government found a solution. Through the Tennessee Valley Authority and the Rural Electrification Administration, the federal government did what private industry could not do. And, while TVA was a yardstick, it was more than that; it was a stimulus to industrial growth and expansion throughout the entire South.

The cities need a federal yardstick program to build housing at rational costs. If industry and labor cannot do the job—and they simply cannot, given today's costs—let the federal government do what it did in the South in the 1930s: unabashedly go into the business of doing what the private sector cannot do.

This move would raise many problems. Vested interests in some labor unions would protest, as would construction firms and bankers. But basically all construction labor, building companies, and real estate bankers are at present devoting their efforts to commercial projects. They cannot build or finance housing at commercial construction costs, and they have not set up for themselves two scales of costs that would permit the production of expensive commercial buildings and less expensive housing. Accordingly, the cost of building housing is the same as the cost of building commercial structures, but the returns on commercial construction are many times higher. Small wonder that housing construction has stopped and private financing for housing has dried up, while new office buildings spring up one after another.

We need a federal yardstick operation with self-renewing federal money, and, if necessary, the creation of a new housing construction work force to build the millions of dwellings the cities will need in the coming years. The creation of such a housing work force might well go a long way toward solving the impasse between the black man and the existing construction unions. There is no stimulus like competition, or even the threat of it, to produce action where action is needed.

This kind of federal assistance would be far more effective than the pie-in-the-sky massive assistance most urbanologists call for. For as cities get larger and larger, their actions more and more seem to resemble those of the dinosaur—or what we imagine the dinosaur to have been in its declining years: large, clumsy, slow-moving, unable to deal with small enemies, too big to be viable, afflicted with hardening of the arteries. The extinction of the dinosaur ultimately resulted from its inability to function and to regenerate itself.

Cities are already in that condition. They are not performing their basic purpose of providing places for people to live, and because of this failure they are dying. Hungry dinosaurs would probably have been kept alive a little longer if there had been a beneficent federal government to provide food. But extinction would have remained the dinosaur's fate.

Our cities will survive and be governable only if those we elect have effective power over those who are supposed to do the work, only if those we elect are responsible and accountable to the people who elect them, and only if the federal government gives the kind of help that will make manpower available to do the work that survival requires.

## 35. TOO MANY PEOPLE

### Paul R. Ehrlich

*Dr. Paul R. Ehrlich is a professor of biology at Stanford University
where he specializes in population problems. The author of numerous writings on the subject, he is best known for his book* The
Population Bomb, *a chapter of which we have reprinted here.*

Americans are beginning to realize that the undeveloped countries of the
world face an inevitable population-food crisis. Each year food production in undeveloped countries falls a bit further behind burgeoning
population growth, and people go to bed a little bit hungrier. While
there are temporary or local reversals of this trend, it now seems inevitable that it will continue to its logical conclusion: mass starvation. The
rich are going to get richer, but the more numerous poor are going to get
poorer. Of these poor, a minimum of three and one-half million will
starve to death this year, mostly children. But this is a mere handful
compared to the numbers that will be starving in a decade or so. And it
is now too late to take action to save many of those people.

In a book about population there is a temptation to stun the reader
with an avalanche of statistics. I'll spare you most, but not all, of that.
After all, no matter how you slice it, population is a numbers game. Perhaps the best way to impress you with numbers is to tell you about the
"doubling time"—the time necessary for the population to double in size.

It has been estimated that the human population of 6000 B.C. was
about five million people, taking perhaps one million years to get there
from two and a half million. The population did not reach 500 million
until almost 8,000 years later—about 1650 A.D. This means it doubled
roughly once every thousand years or so. It reached a billion people
around 1850, doubling in some 200 years. It took only 80 years or so for
the next doubling, as the population reached two billion around 1930.
We have not completed the next doubling to four billion yet, but we now
have well over three billion people. The doubling time at present seems
to be about 37 years.[1] Quite a reduction in doubling times: 1,000,000
years, 1,000 years, 200 years, 80 years, 37 years. Perhaps the meaning
of a doubling time of around 37 years is best brought home by a theo-

*Source:* "Too Many People" from *The Population Bomb* (revised edition), by Dr.
Paul R. Ehrlich. Copyright © 1968, 1971 by Paul R. Ehrlich. Reprinted by permission of Ballantine Books, Inc.

retical exercise. Let's examine what might happen on the absurd assumption that the population continued to double every 37 years into the indefinite future.

If growth continued at that rate for about 900 years, there would be some 60,000,000,000,000,000 people on the face of the Earth. Sixty million billion people. This is about 100 persons for each square yard of the Earth's surface, land and sea. A British physicist, J. H. Fremlin,[2] guessed that such a multitude might be housed in a continuous 2,000-story building covering our entire planet. The upper 1,000 stories would contain only the apparatus for running this gigantic warren. Ducts, pipes, wires, elevator shafts, etc., would occupy about half of the space in the bottom 1,000 stories. This would leave three or four yards of floor space for each person. I will leave to your imagination the physical details of existence in this ant heap, except to point out that all would not be black. Probably each person would be limited in his travel. Perhaps he could take elevators through all 1,000 residential stories but could travel only within a circle of a few hundred yards' radius on any floor. This would permit, however, each person to choose his friends from among some ten million people! And, as Fremlin points out, entertainment on the worldwide TV should be excellent, for at any time "one could expect some ten million Shakespeares and rather more Beatles to be alive."

Could growth of the human population of the Earth continue beyond that point? Not according to Fremlin. We would have reached a "heat limit." People themselves, as well as their activities, convert other forms of energy into heat which must be dissipated. In order to permit this excess heat to radiate directly from the top of the "world building" directly into space, the atmosphere would have been pumped into flasks under the sea well before the limiting population size was reached. The precise limit would depend on the technology of the day. At a population size of one billion billion people, the temperature of the "world roof" would be kept around the melting point of iron to radiate away the human heat generated.

But, you say, surely Science (with a capital "S") will find a way for us to occupy the other planets of our solar system and eventually of other stars before we get all that crowded. Skip for a moment the virtual certainty that those planets are uninhabitable. Forget also the insurmountable logistic problems of moving billions of people off the Earth. Fremlin has made some interesting calculations on how much time we could buy by occupying the planets of the solar system. For instance, at any given time it would take only about 50 years to populate Venus, Mercury, Mars, the moon, and the moons of Jupiter and Saturn to the same population density as earth.[3]

What if the fantastic problems of reaching and colonizing the other planets of the solar system, such as Jupiter and Uranus, can be solved? It would take only about 200 years to fill them "Earth-full." So we could perhaps gain 250 years of time for population growth in the solar system after we had reached an absolute limit on Earth. What then? We can't ship our surplus to the stars. Professor Garrett Hardin[4] of the University of California at Santa Barbara has dealt effectively with this fantasy. Using extremely optimistic assumptions, he has calculated that Americans, by cutting their standards of living down to 18% of its present level, could in *one year* set aside enough capital to finance the exportation to the stars of *one day's* increase in the population of the world.

Interstellar transport for surplus people presents an amusing prospect. Since the ships would take generations to reach most stars, the only people who could be transported would be those willing to exercise strict birth control. Population explosions on space ships would be disastrous. Thus we would have to export our responsible people, leaving the irresponsible at home on Earth to breed.

Enough of fantasy. Hopefully, you are convinced that the population will have to stop growing sooner or later and that the extremely remote possibility of expanding into outer space offers no escape from the laws of population growth. If you still want to hope for the stars, just remember that, at the current growth rate, in a few thousand years everything in the visible universe would be converted into people, and the ball of people would be expanding with the speed of light.[5] Unfortunately, even 900 years is much too far in the future for those of us concerned with the population explosion. As you shall see, the next *nine* years will probably tell the story.

Of course, population growth is not occurring uniformly over the face of the Earth. Indeed, countries are divided rather neatly into two groups: those with rapid growth rates, and those with relatively slow growth rates. The first group, making up about two-thirds of the world population, coincides closely with what are known as the "undeveloped countries" (UDCs). The UDCs are not industrialized, tend to have inefficient agriculture, very small gross national products, high illiteracy rates and related problems. That's what UDCs are technically, but a short definition of undeveloped is "starving." Most Latin American, African, and Asian countries fall into this category. The second group consists, in essence, of the "developed countries" (DCs). DCs are modern, industrial nations, such as the United States, Canada, most European countries, Israel, Russia, Japan, and Australia. Most people in these countries are adequately nourished.

Doubling times in the UDCs range around 20 to 35 years. Examples of these times (from the 1968 figures just released by the Population Reference Bureau) are Kenya, 24 years; Nigeria, 28; Turkey, 24; Indonesia, 31; Philippines, 20; Brazil, 22; Costa Rica, 20; and El Salvador, 19. Think of what it means for the population of a country to double in 25 years. In order just to keep living standards at the present inadequate level, the food available for the people must be doubled. Every structure and road must be duplicated. The amount of power must be doubled. The capacity of the transport system must be doubled. The number of trained doctors, nurses, teachers, and administrators must be doubled. This would be a fantastically difficult job in the United States—a rich country with a fine agricultural system, immense industries, and rich natural resources. Think of what it means to a country with none of these.

Remember also that in virtually all UDCs, people have gotten the word about the better life it is possible to have. They have seen colored pictures in magazines of the miracles of Western technology. They have seen automobiles and airplanes. They have seen American and European movies. Many have seen refrigerators, tractors, and even TV sets. Almost all have heard transistor radios. They *know* that a better life is possible. They have what we like to call "rising expectations." If twice as many people are to be happy, the miracle of doubling what they now have will not be enough. It will only maintain today's standard of living. There will have to be a tripling or better. Needless to say, they are not going to be happy.

Doubling times for the populations of the DCs tend to be in the 50-to-200-year range. Examples of 1968 doubling times are the United States, 63 years; Austria, 175; Denmark, 88; Norway, 88; United Kingdom, 140; Poland, 88; Russia 63; Italy, 117; Spain, 88; and Japan, 63. These are industrialized countries that have undergone the so-called demographic transition—a transition from high to low growth rate. As industrialization progressed, children became less important to parents as extra hands to work on the farm and as support in old age. At the same time they became a financial drag—expensive to raise and educate. Presumably these are the reasons for a slowing of population growth after industrialization. They boil down to a simple fact—people just want to have fewer children.

This is not to say, however, that population is not a problem for the DCs. First of all, most of them are overpopulated. They are overpopulated by the simple criterion that they are not able to produce enough food to feed their populations. It is true that they have the money to buy food, but when food is no longer available for sale they will find the money rather indigestible. Then, too, they share with the UDCs a serious problem of population distribution. Their urban centers are getting more and more crowded relative to the countryside. This problem is not as severe as it is in the UDCs (if current trends should continue, which they cannot, Calcutta could have 66 million inhabitants in the year 2000). As you are well aware, however, urban concentrations are creating serious problems even in America. In the United States, one of the more rapidly growing DCs, we hear constantly of the headaches caused by growing population: not just garbage in our environment, but over-crowded highways, burgeoning slums, deteriorating school systems, rising crime rates, riots, and other related problems.

From the point of view of a demographer, the whole problem is quite simple. A population will continue to grow as long as the birth rate exceeds the death rate—if immigration and emigration are not occurring. It is, of course, the balance between birth rate and death rate that is critical. The birth rate is the number of births per thousand people per year in the population. The death rate is the number of deaths per thousand people per year.[6] Subtracting the death rate from the birth rate; and ignoring migration, gives the rate of increase. If the birth rate is 30 per thousand per year, and the death rate is 10 per thousand per year, then the rate of increase is 20 per thousand per year (30−10=20). Expressed as a percent (rate per hundred people), the rate of 20 per thousand becomes 2%. If the rate of increase is 2%, then the doubling time will be 35 years. Note that if you simply added 20 people per thousand per year to the population, it would take 50 years to add a second thousand people (20×50=1,000). But the doubling time is actually much less because populations grow at compound interest rates. Just as interest dollars themselves earn interest, so people added to populations produce more people. It's growing at compound interest that makes populations double so much more rapidly than seems possible. Look at the relationship between the annual percent increase (interest rate) and the doubling time of the population (time for your money to double):

| Annual percent increase | Doubling time |
|:---:|:---:|
| 1.0 | 70 |
| 2.0 | 35 |
| 3.0 | 24 |
| 4.0 | 17 |

Those are all the calculations—I promise. If you are interested in more details on how demographic figuring is done, you may enjoy reading Thompson and Lewis's excellent book, *Population Problems.*[7]

There are some professional optimists around who like to greet every sign of dropping birth rates with wild pronouncements about the end of the population explosion. They are a little like a person who, after a low temperature of five below zero on December 21, interprets a low of only three below zero on December 22 as a cheery sign of approaching spring. First of all, birth rates, along with all demographic statistics, show short-term fluctuations caused by many factors. For instance, the birth rate depends rather heavily on the number of women at reproductive age. In the United States the current low birth rates soon will be replaced by higher rates as more post World War II "baby boom" children move into their reproductive years. In Japan, 1966, the Year of the Fire Horse, was a year of very low birth rates. There is widespread belief that girls born in the Year of the Fire Horse make poor wives, and Japanese couples try to avoid giving birth in that year because they are afraid of having daughters.

But, I repeat, it is the relationship between birth rate and death rate that is most critical. Indonesia, Laos, and Haiti all had birth rates around 46 per thousand in 1966. Costa Rica's birth rate was 41 per thousand. Good for Costa Rica? Unfortunately, not very. Costa Rica's death rate was less than nine per thousand, while the other countries all had death rates above 20 per thousand. The population of Costa Rica in 1966 was doubling every 17 years, while the doubling times of Indonesia, Laos, and Haiti were all above 30 years. Ah, but, you say, it was good for Costa Rica—fewer people per thousand were dying each year. Fine for a few years perhaps, but what then? Some 50% of the people in Costa Rica are under 15 years old. As they get older, they will need more and more food in a world with less and less. In 1983 they will have twice as many mouths to feed as they had in 1966, if the 1966 trend continues. Where will the food come from? Today the death rate in Costa Rica is low in part because they have a large number of physicians in proportion to their population. How do you suppose those physicians will keep the death rate down when there's not enough food to keep people alive?

One of the most ominous facts of the current situation is that roughly 40% of the population of the undeveloped world is made up of people *under 15 years old.* As that mass of young people moves into its reproductive years during the next decade, we're going to see the greatest baby boom of all time. Those youngsters are the reason for all the ominous predictions for the year 2000. They are the gunpowder for the population explosion.

How did we get into this bind? It all happened a long time ago, and the story involves the process of natural selection, the development of culture, and man's swollen head. The essence of success in evolution is reproduction. Indeed, natural selection is simply defined as differential reproduction of genetic types. That is, if people with blue eyes have more children on the average than those with brown eyes, natural selection is occurring. More genes for blue eyes will be passed on to the next generation than will genes for brown eyes. Should this continue, the population will have progressively larger and larger proportions of blue-eyed people. This differential reproduction of genetic types is the driving force of evolution; it has been driving evolution for billions of years. Whatever types produced more offspring became the common types. Virtually all populations contain very many different genetic types (for reasons that need not concern us), and some are always outreproducing others. As I said, reproduction is the key to winning the evolutionary game. Any structure, physiological process, or pattern of behavior that leads to greater reproductive success will tend to be perpetuated. The entire process by which man developed involves thousands of millenia of our ancestors being more successful breeders than their relatives. Facet number one of our bind—the urge to reproduce has been fixed in us by billions of years of evolution.

Of course through all those years of evolution, our ancestors were fighting a continual battle to keep the birth rate ahead of the death rate. That they were successful is attested to by our very existence, for, if the death rate had overtaken the birth rate for any substantial period of time, the evolutionary line leading to man would have gone extinct. Among our apelike ancestors, a few million years ago, it was still very difficult for a mother to rear her children successfully. Most of the offspring died before they reached reproductive age. The death rate was near the birth rate. Then another factor entered the picture—cultural evolution was added to biological evolution.

Culture can be loosely defined as the body of non-genetic information which people pass from generation to generation. It is the accumulated knowledge that, in the old days, was passed on entirely by word of mouth, painting, and demonstration. Several thousand years ago the written word was added to the means of cultural transmission. Today culture is passed on in these ways, and also through television, computer tapes, motion pictures, records, blueprints, and other media. Culture is all the information man possesses except for that which is stored in the chemical language of his genes.

The large size of the human brain evolved in response to the development of cultural information. A big brain is an advantage when dealing with such information. Big-brained individuals were able to deal more successfully with the culture of their group. They were thus more successful reproductively than their smaller-brained relatives. They passed on their genes for big brains to their numerous offspring. They also added to the accumulating store of cultural information, increasing slightly the premium placed in brain size in the next generation. A self-reinforcing selective trend developed—a trend toward increased brain size.[8]

But there was, quite literally, a rub. Babies had bigger and bigger heads. There were limits to how large a woman's pelvis could conveniently become. To make a long story short, the strategy of evolution was not to make a woman bell-shaped and relatively immobile, but to accept the problem of having babies who were helpless for a long period while their brains grew after birth.[9] How could the mother defend and care for her infant during this unusually long period of helplessness? She couldn't, unless Papa hung around. The girls are still working on that problem, but an essential step was to get rid of the short, well-defined breeding season characteristic of most mammals. The year-round sexuality of the human female, the evolution of the family group, all are at the roots of our present problem. They are essential ingredients in the vast social phenomenon that we call sex. Sex is not simply an act leading to the production of offspring. It is a varied and complex cultural phenomenon penetrating into all aspects of our lives—one involving our self-esteem, our choice of friends, cars, and leaders. It is tightly interwoven with our mythologies and history. Sex in man is necessary for the production of young, but it also evolved to ensure their successful rearing. Facet number two of our bind—our urge to reproduce is hopelessly entwined with most of our other urges.

Of course, in the early days the whole system did not prevent a very high mortality among the young, as well as among the older members of the group. Hunting and food-gathering is a risky business. Cavemen had to throw very impressive cave bears out of their caves before the men could move in. Witch doctors and shamans had a less than perfect record of treating wounds and curing disease. Life was short, if not sweet. Man's total population size doubtless increased slowly but steadily as human populations expanded out of the African cradle of our species.

Then about 8,000 years ago a major change occurred—the agricultural revolution. People began to give up hunting food and settled down to grow it. Suddenly some of the risk was removed from life. The chances of dying of starvation diminished greatly in some human groups. Other threats associated with the nomadic life were also reduced, perhaps balanced by new threats of disease and large-scale warfare associated with the development of cities. But the overall result was a more secure existence than before, and the human population grew more rapidly. Around 1800, when the standard of living in what are today the DCs was dramatically increasing due to industrialization, population growth really began to accelerate. The development of medical science was the straw that broke the camel's back. While lowering death rates in the DCs was due in part to other factors, there is no question that "instant death control," exported by the DCs, has been responsible for the drastic lowering of death rates in the UDCs. Medical science, with its efficient public health programs, has been able to depress the death rate with astonishing rapidity and at the same time drastically increase the birth rate; healthier people have more babies.

The power of exported death control can best be seen by an examination of the classic case of Ceylon's assault on malaria after World War II. Between 1933 and 1942 the death rate due directly to malaria was *reported* as almost two per thousand. This rate, however, represented only a portion of the malaria deaths, as many were reported as being due to "pyrexia."[10] Indeed, in 1934–1935 a malaria epidemic may have been directly responsible for fully half of the deaths on the island. In addition, malaria, which infected a large portion of the population, made people susceptible to many other diseases. It thus contributed to the death rate indirectly as well as directly.

The introduction of DDT in 1946 brought rapid control over the mosquitoes which carry malaria. As a result, the death rate on the island was halved in less than a decade. The death rate in Ceylon in 1945 was 22. It dropped 34% between 1946 and 1947 and moved down to ten in 1954. Since the sharp postwar drop it has continued to decline and now stands at eight. Although part of the drop is doubtless due to the killing of other insects which carry disease and to other public health measures, most of it can be accounted for by the control of malaria.

Victory over malaria, yellow fever, smallpox, cholera, and other infectious diseases has been responsible for similar plunges in death rate throughout most of the UDCs. In the decade 1940–1950 the death rate declined 46% in Puerto Rico, 43% in Formosa, and 23% in Jamaica. In a sample of 18 undeveloped areas the average decline in death rate between 1945 and 1950 was 24%.

It is, of course, socially very acceptable to reduce the death rate. Billions of years of evolution have given us all a powerful will to live. Intervening in the birth rate goes against our evolutionary values. During all those centuries of our evolutionary past, the individuals who had the most children passed on their genetic endowment in greater quantities than those who reproduced less. Their genes dominate our heredity today. All our biological urges are for more reproduction, and they are all too often reinforced by our culture. In brief, death control goes with the grain, birth control against it.

In summary, the world's population will continue to grow as long as the birth rate exceeds the death rate; it's as simple as that. When it stops growing or starts to shrink, it will mean that either the birth rate has gone down or the death rate has gone up or a combination of the two. Basically, then, there are only two kinds of solutions to the population problem. One is a "birth rate solution," in which we find ways to lower the birth rate. The other is a "death rate solution," in which ways to raise the death rate—war, famine, pestilence—*find us*. The problem could have been avoided by *population control*, in which mankind consciously adjusted the birth rate so that a "death rate solution" did not have to occur.

## NOTES

1. Since this was written, 1968 figures have appeared, showing that the doubling time is now 35 years.

2. J. H. Fremlin, "How Many People Can the World Support?" *New Scientist*, October 29, 1964.

3. To understand this, simply consider what would happen if we held the population constant at three billion people by exporting all the surplus people. If this were done for 37 years (the time it now takes for one doubling) we would have exported three billion people—enough to populate a twin planet of the Earth to the same density. In two doubling times (74 years) we would reach a total human population for the solar system of 12 billion people, enough to populate the Earth and three similar planets to the density found on Earth today. Since the areas of the planets and moons mentioned above are not three times that of the Earth, they can be populated to equal density in much less than two doubling times.

4. "Interstellar Migration and the Population Problem." *Heredity* 50: 68–70, 1959.

5. I. J. Cook, *New Scientist*, September 8, 1966.

6. The birth rate is more precisely the total number of births in a country during a year, divided by the total population at the midpoint of the year, multiplied by 1,000. Suppose that there were 80 births in Lower Slobbovia during 1967, and that the population of Lower Slobbovia was 2,000 on July 1, 1967. Then the birth rate would be:

$$\text{Birth rates} = \frac{(80 \text{ total births in L. Slobbovia in 1967})}{2,000 \text{ (total population, July 1, 1967)}} \times 1,000$$

$$= .04 \times 1,000 = 40$$

Similarly if there were 40 deaths in Lower Slobbovia during 1967 the death rate would be:

$$\text{Death rate} = \frac{40 \text{ (total deaths in L. Slobbovia in 1967)}}{2,000 \text{ (total population, July 1, 1967)}} \times 1,000$$

$$= .02 \times 1,000 = 20$$

Then the Lower Slobbovian birth rate would be 40 per thousand, and the death rate would be 20 per thousand. For every 1,000 Lower Slobbovians alive on July 1, 1967, 40 babies were born and 20 people died. Subtracting the death rate from the birth rate gives us the rate of natural increase of Lower Slobbovia for the year 1967. That is, $40 - 20 = 20$; during 1967 the population grew at a rate of 20 people per thousand per year. Dividing that rate by ten expresses the increase as a percent (the increase per hundred per year). The increase in 1967 in Lower Slobbovia was two percent. Remember that this rate of increase ignores any movement of people into and out of Lower Slobbovia.

7. McGraw-Hill Book Company, Inc., New York, 1965.

8. Human brain size increased from an apelike capacity of about 500 cubic centimeters (cc) in *Australopithecus* to about 1,500 cc in modern *Homo sapiens*. Among modern men small variations in brain size do not seem to be related to significant differences in the ability to use cultural information, and there is no particular reason to believe that our brain size will continue to increase. Further evolution may occur more readily in a direction of increased efficiency rather than increased size.

9. This is, of course, an oversimplified explanation. For more detail see Ehrlich and Holm, *The Process of Evolution*, McGraw-Hill Book Company, Inc., New York, 1963.

10. These data and those that follow on the decline of death rates are from Kingsley Davis's "The Amazing Decline of Mortality in Underdeveloped Areas," *The American Economic Review*, Vol. 46, pp. 305–318.

# 36. MAGNILOQUENT MYTHOLOGY

## from Asphalt

*Asphalt is a trade publication delivered quarterly by The Asphalt Institute, "an international, nonprofit association sponsored by members of the petroleum asphalt industry to serve both users and producers of asphaltic materials through programs of engineering service, research and education." Membership in the institute is limited to refiners of asphalt from crude petroleum.*

YOU have probably seen him—syndicated columnist Herb Block's character, "the Highway Lobby"—a fat fellow, invariably chomping a cigar, riding in a vehicle, hauling bags of money around and running over John Q. Public with a degree of relish. Mr. Block has talent, and to some his anti-highway cartoons are bitterly amusing.

But the plain truth is that "the Highway Lobby" is a figment of the cartoonist's imagination. There is no such thing, even though the mythical body has been described by columnists and cartoonists from the late Drew Pearson upward. The implication that there is a multi-billion-dollar syndicate of corporation and industrial interests conspiring to make the United States a paved-over province is in fact utter nonsense, even damaging nonsense, because denigration of the nation's highway builders and their works clears the way for diversion of highway funds—contributed solely by highway users—to purposes unrelated to roads and highways.

The myth of a sinister highway lobby, and other absurdities about highways, are designed solely to discredit national and state highway programs.

Fortunately, there are organizations willing and able to challenge the mythmakers, among them the Highway Users Federation for Safety and Mobility, The Road Information Program (TRIP), the American Road Builders' Association, and the American Association of State Highway Officials. The first-named organization, HUFSAM, has mounted an intensive campaign to debunk the mythology and acquaint the public with the facts, viz.:

MYTH: *"Highway groups are bent on paving over the country."*
FACT: In the past 50 years the United States population has doubled, yet the total road system mileage since 1948, for example, has increased by less than 10 percent, and today all surfaced highways, roads and streets

together occupy less than one percent of the nation's tital land area. At the present construction rate it would take 10,000 years to "pave over the country."

MYTH: *"Highway modernization should be opposed, in favor of mass transportation."*

FACT: For most of America, highways *are* mass transportation. In urban areas of 50,000 or more population, 99 percent of all person trips are by rubber-tired vehicles. Road and street improvements are needed to increase efficiency and convenience. In some of the largest metropolitan areas fixed rail transit is also needed to serve high-density corridors, but the backbone of total transportation is highways.

MYTH: *"Highways bulldoze people out of their homes and businesses with callous disregard of the consequences."*

FACT: Highway departments are required by law to relocate families and businesses in equal or better quarters and to pay home-owners up to $15,000 above fair market value for their homes, as well as to provide other social services.

MYTH: *"Highways ruin the environment."*

FACT: On the contrary, one out of every eight federal-aid highway dollars is spent to *enhance* the environment. Every year more than 1.5 million trees and seedlings are planted along highway rights of way. Many blighted urban areas have been "rescued" by the construction of modern freeways and parkways with contiguous renewal projects.

MYTH: *"Highways despoil parks, forests and scenic areas that should be left for the enjoyment of the people."*

FACT: How can you enjoy anything you cannot get to? Highways open to millions of families the natural beauty and recreational values of vast areas of this great country. Scenic areas now benefit all the people—rich and not-so-rich alike.

MYTH: *"The Highway Trust Fund is a sacrosanct pork-barrel, using the taxpayers' money to subsidize roads."*

FACT: Not a penny from the U.S. Treasury goes into the Highway Trust Fund. It is the money that highway users pay "in trust" for modern, safe roads. Like a fare box: if you ride, you pay, in proportion to your use of the roads and highways through taxes on fuel, tires and other automotive needs.

A recently-conducted public opinion survey on the question of roads indicated that a whopping 80 percent of the public has a favorable impression of the nation's highway system, and that an even greater majority feels that current highway progress is proceeding "about right" or "too slowly." Nevertheless, many transportation decision-makers could take heed of the clamorous mythmakers and their insupportable contentions, to public disadvantage.

This year, 1972, undoubtedly will be a decisive one in which the future of American highways will be debated and decided. We therefore applaud and endorse the efforts of the organizations seeking to ensure that magniloquent mythology plays no part in the deliberations affecting highways —for these are lifelines vitally essential to the nation's economy, integrity, and well-being.

## Commentary: A Letter to the Editor

PEOPLE AGAINST THE EAST-WEST HIGHWAY
| Box 191 | Rural | New Hampshire | 71170 |
|---------|-------|---------------|-------|

January 21, 1972

Editor
ASPHALT magazine
Asphalt Institute Building
College Park
Maryland 20740

Dear Sir:

I read with interest your editorial "Magniloquent Mythology" which appears in your January issue (Volume 24, No. 1). As editor of a trade publication it is your job, of course, to promote the sales of asphalt and asphaltic materials; but it seems to me you have rather outdone yourself in this most recent piece. May I be permitted to respond to some of your remarks?

First I hope we can agree it is perfect nonsense to state, as you have done, that there is no such thing as a Highway Lobby. The READER'S DIGEST, certainly a conservative and "pro-industry" journal, carried an article titled "Let's Put the Brakes on the Highway Lobby" as early as May 1969. Reputable opinion on both sides of the roadbuilding issue not only agree there is such a lobby, but also that it is one of the most powerful lobbies in the country, second only, perhaps, to that which promotes weaponry and defense. From the standpoint of argument, you are on safer ground when you state later that there is no such thing as a "sinister Highway Lobby." That obviously becomes a matter of point of view. You and I might look at the same large bear coming our way, and you might say, "He's just a friendly old bear"; and I might say, "Maybe so, but he looks hungry as hell to me."

So let us agree that there is a Highway Lobby (whether evil or benign) and go on to deal with some of the statistics you have cited in its defense. You have used as your authority an organization called HUFSAM. I will use as mine Mr. Ben Kelley who has been an executive with the Federal Highway Administration and who wrote a fine book not long ago titled THE PAVERS AND THE PAVED. HUFSAM and Mr. Kelley while not addressing themselves to precisely the same questions do provide contrasting views.

HUFSAM: "At the present construction rate it would take 10,000 years to 'pave over the country'."

KELLEY: Each year Americans "pave more than 20,000 miles of new highways that consume at least 200,000 acres of land . . ." The Interstate System alone has in it enough concrete "to build six sidewalks to the moon."

HUFSAM: "For most of America, highways <u>are</u> mass transportation. In urban areas of 50,000 or more population, 99 percent of all person trips are by rubber-tired vehicles."

KELLEY: Because of the earmarked Federal Highway Trust Fund which can only be spent for new road construction "the United States today can claim the most impressive system of superhighways the world has ever known—along with a collection of run-down railroads, limping urban transit services, and archaic local streets and roads that have been starved of public funding support . . ."

HUFSAM: "Highway departments are required by law to relocate families and businesses in equal or better quarters . . ."

KELLEY: Highway departments each year "displace more than 56,000 people."

HUFSAM: ". . . one out of every eight federal-aid highway dollars is spent to <u>enhance</u> the environment."

KELLEY: Each mile of Interstate consumes "about forty-three acres of land." The Interstate System alone will consume "as much land as the country now devotes to all its county and municipal parks."

HUFSAM: "A recently conducted public opinion survey on the question of roads indicated that a whopping 80 percent of the public has a favorable impression of the nation's highway system . . ."

KELLEY: "According to the Harris poll, the public is demonstrating a 'widespread desire . . . to make greater use of mass transportation facilities'."

Now my letter is rapidly becoming as long-winded as your article, and

I will quit here while I am ahead. We have recently had the good fortune to help stop a proposed half-billion dollar highway across the three northern New England states which if constructed would have destroyed thousands of acres of some of the most beautiful rural country in the United States, and would have served no useful purpose except saving a man in upper New York State about 50 minutes of driving time on his hell-bent-for-election way to the coast of Maine. A pox on him; and on you sir. The next time that old bear comes lumbering up from Washington, wearing all of his bureaucratic hats, we will light after him with slingshots and pitchforks and double-barrel shotguns; and we will not be satisfied until he has turned tail.

In the meantime, all best wishes.


                    And Very Truly yours,

                    *[signature]*

                    Peter L. Sandberg/Chairman

                    PEOPLE AGAINST THE EAST-WEST HIGHWAY

cc: all concerned citizens

enc: one sprig of wintergreen (which, as you may know, grows better
     when not under asphalt)

PLS/me

## 37. CAN WE BUST THE HIGHWAY TRUST?

### Denis Hayes

*Stanford University graduate Denis Hayes is already a well-known environmentalist. He was a director of Earth Day 1970, has served as a national coordinator of Environmental Action, and continues to sit on the programming council of National Educational Television. Having hitchhiked around the world, he has seen various ecological problems firsthand. One of primary concern is that of modern mass transportation versus the automobile.*

Two-thirds of the land encompassed by the city of Los Angeles is covered by freeways and roads and streets and parking lots and gasoline stations and automobile salesrooms and private garages and other appurtenances of automobiling. Fumes from automobile exhaust pipes have turned the skies above the city a weird shade of yellowish green, obscuring the nearby purple-mountained majesty. On many days of every year the accumulated smog is so unbearable that school children are not allowed to play outdoors. Last year someone placed a hand-lettered sign at the city limits reading: BREATHING IS UNHEALTHY FOR CHILDREN AND OTHER GROWING THINGS. Emphysema, a lung disease caused by gases and particulates in the air, has killed 12 per cent more people every year for the past twenty years. The death toll from crashing automobiles is staggering. The city grows relentlessly noisier, dirtier, and uglier.

Why is this affront to public decency tolerated?

According to advertisements written and distributed at considerable expense by automobile makers, gasoline salesmen, and road builders, it is because the private automobile is an unsurpassed convenience for all of us—because it takes us wherever we need or want to go more quickly than we could get there by any other means of transportation, and in the most pleasing fashion imaginable.

But people who drive or ride private automobiles through Los Angeles rarely if ever enjoy the experience. Any trip into, within, or out of the city is hard work at best and at worst a grating ordeal. All involved suffer a similar fate. They inch their exasperated way up waiting lines at freeway entrances, stand almost motionless bumper to bumper for as

*Source:* "Can We Bust the Highway Trust?" Denis Hayes. From June 5, 1971 *Saturday Review.* Copyright 1971 Saturday Review, Inc.

long as two hours at a time, find all available parking spaces filled upon reaching the central city, and ultimately arrive back home disgusted and exhausted by the compulsive aggressiveness that has come to characterize automobiling. Instead of enjoying an exhilarating exercise in personal freedom, the motorist endures a sweaty war of nerves.

The inhabitants of Watts and the Chicano barrios of East Los Angeles have never had any illusions about the private automobile's fundamental hostility to the simple humanity that once was found in cities. The asphalt-paved culture surrounding these people brings them no pleasure. Few of them have automobiles of their own, and they live at the end of the line. Only there is no line. No streetcar, no subway. Only occasional buses travel the roads, and those who cannot afford wheels must either hitch a ride from someone who has wheels or walk. These people see more than the fact that transportation in Los Angeles is inefficient, unhealthy, and ugly. They see that it discriminates against the young, the old, and the crippled as well as against the poor.

If the private automobile's degrading effect on Los Angeles were unique, the phenomenon would merit an exhaustive analysis as a dangerous inversion of social values. But it is not unique. No major city in the country has escaped automobile poisoning. Atlanta, Baltimore, Boston, Charleston, Chicago, Cleveland, Detroit, Indianapolis, Memphis, Milwaukee, Minneapolis, Nashville, Newark, New Orleans, New York, Philadelphia, Phoenix, Seattle, and Washington, D.C. (to name only a prominent score), all display the same symptoms of debilitation; all have been weakened by the same dehumanizing fever.

Plainly, something must be done to arrest the spread of this technological malady. Plainly, too, that something must somehow restrict the growth of highways, for automobilitis is carried by highways. Every American motorist contributes to acceleration of the epidemic through the gasoline, tire-sales, and other auto-use taxes he pays into the federal government's Highway Trust Fund.

Since 1956, money in the Highway Trust Fund( it totals about $5-billion a year) has been sequestered for the exclusive purpose of building roads, principal emphasis going to an interstate highway network linking all the nation's cities that have populations greater than 50,000. Planned at first to stretch more than 41,000 miles and to be completed by 1972, the system is now targeted at 42,500 miles and is certain to be extended in length until the year 1977.

In the beginning, interstate highways were intended only to *connect* the cities. Later, the purpose was restated to include *passage through* the cities. Of course, the cost of the highway increases progressively as the core of the city is approached and traversed. Yet, any piece of interstate highway, no matter how extravagant, costs the city or state that builds it only 10 cents on the dollar. The other 90 cents is paid by the Highway Trust Fund. Although buses, subways, and railroad trains carry many times more people than private automobiles do, cities and states preferring those facilities must pay from 33 cents to 50 cents on the dollar. With urban tax sources shrinking steadily because of the amount of productive land eaten up by roads and parking spaces, local government officials find it hard to raise 33-cent dollars or 50-cent dollars when 10-cent dollars are so much more readily available.

The simplest cure for automobilitis in the cities, then, is to bust the Highway Trust Fund and to release its monies on a fair, competitive footing for whatever means of conveyance proves most adaptable to human sensitivities.

Can the Highway Trust be busted? I believe that it can be. Furthermore, I am convinced that it will be when enough people understand how the Highway Trust is wrecking America, not only esthetically but economically and spiritually.

This understanding cannot be expected overnight, nor even in a year or two. Mainstream America has exulted in its love affair with the private automobile for too long. The automobile is a truer symbol of the essence of America than is the bald eagle, Uncle Sam, or apple pie. The automobile is glamorous. It is sexy. It is the dream of every high school kid. Model kits, magazines, even popular music enshrine it. Adults put it at the top of the scale of values they use to judge the neighbors and themselves. The highest expression of national grandeur is the pretentious coat of arms on the new Cadillac.

The automobile is a powerful economic force. Directly and indirectly, it provides jobs for one in every five employed persons.

The automobile takes most Americans to work, and returns them home. It picks up supplies at the supermarket, transports the kids to and from school, and facilitates the rites of passage when Johnny turns sixteen.

With chrome teeth glistening beneath its glassy eyes, the automobile is perceived as the most indispensable commodity in contemporary American life. One questionnaire frankly identified the automobile as the cause of most air pollution, the cause of nerve-racking traffic congestion, the cause of 50,000 deaths every year, the cause of displacement of tens of thousands of home owners, and the cause of destruction of irreplaceable open spaces; then the individuals to whom the questionnaire was addressed were asked: "Is it worth it?" Eighty-five per cent of the 5,000 persons sampled said yes.

It must be admitted that the automobile does provide a unique and desirable freedom on lengthy, leisurely trips. Ninety per cent of all Americans who took vacations last year went by automobile. Forty million Americans visited national parks last year, and more than 95 per cent of them arrived in automobiles. Even for short-haul amusement, automobiles are still almost unalloyed blessings to millions of residents of the countryside, isolated towns, and small cities. The Saturday drive to market, the Sunday afternoon tour of the rural neighborhood—though infinitely rarer than in the early days of automobiling—continue as happy rituals for thousands of families.

In short, abolition of the automobile is impractical for the present and the foreseeable future. Limitation of use of the automobile in big cities, however, is inevitable. Environmental Protection Agency Administrator William D. Ruckelshaus said as much in his recent public warning that EPA has no intention of lifting the stringent ceilings on air pollution that have been set for 1975. Chicago, Denver, Los Angeles, New York, Philadelphia, and Washington won't be able to lower the carbon monoxide content of air in their streets to the designated levels without adopting extraordinary measures. Ruckelshaus predicted "some rather drastic changes in . . . commuting habits." Outright prohibition of automobiles during peak traffic hours was one of the alternatives he foresaw. Others were mandatory car pools and greater reliance on mass-transit facilities.

Where is the money for the mass-transit facilities to come from when the cities are heading for bankruptcy? President Richard Nixon's plan for sharing federal revenue with the states proposes to give at least $525-million a year for mass-transit facilities and to free as much of $2-billion a year additional as the states and cities wish to put into mass transit. Neither the cities nor the states would have to pay out anything to get those dollars, which would come from the Highway Trust Fund, the Airport and Airway Trust Fund, and general tax revenues. "Despite our technological capacity, we do not enjoy a fully balanced transportation system in modern America, particularly in our larger cities," the President explained to Congress in a special transportation message last March. "A balanced transportation system is essentially one that provides adequate transportation not just for *some* of the people in a community but for *all* the people in a community. . . . We have relied too much in our cities on cars and on highways; we have given too little attention to other modes of travel. Approximately 94 per cent of all travel in urbanized areas is by automobile; yet, about 25 per cent of our people —especially the old, the very young, the poor, and the handicapped— don't drive a car." After that token acknowledgment that the future of the country does not rest on more highways, Mr. Nixon advised Congress to leave the Highway Trust in charge of interstate roads "at this time."

Being several years short of my thirtieth birthday, I would take special pleasure in reporting that the young activists who engineered the Earth Day events of April 22, 1970, were the first to appreciate the central role of the Highway Trust in urban blight and air pollution. However, such a report would fall short of accuracy. A fortyish, white, middle-income housewife who lives in a predominantly black neighborhood in northeast Washington, D. C., is the earliest public antagonist of the Highway Trust known to me. She is Mrs. Angela Rooney, wife of an art professor at Catholic University, cultural center of the community of Brookland.

Seven years or so ago, Mrs. Rooney became aware that if plans then on the drawing board should materialize, as they seemed about to do, a six-lane interstate highway launched in Maine and headed for Florida would pour 200,000 automobiles and trucks a day through a string of seven towns, including Brookland. Scores of homes would be flattened to open the route.

Mrs. Rooney was not a rich woman, nor even well-to-do. But she loved her home and her town. She sat down at her kitchen table, lifted the telephone off its cradle, fingered the dial, and began spreading the news to neighbors and friends. Before she finished her marathon, a new organization existed. The Emergency Committee on the Transportation Crisis, it was called, and it had a motto: "Not one more inch of freeway."

Now Washington, D.C., is the only city of its size in the country that is not crossed north-south and east-west by interstate freeways. Highway Trust lobbyists look upon this exceptional situation as a national disgrace. Mrs. Rooney strikes them as a misguided relic of the Stone Age who is trying to knock automobiles off the road with a rolled-up newspaper. But Mrs. Rooney is not intimidated by their taunts.

At one point in her crusade, sixty-nine houses were emptied of tenants and boarded up in preparation for the coming freeway. Mrs. Rooney wrote letters and typed leaflets faster than ever. Not to be outdone by his wife, Professor Rooney headed a band of people who reoccupied the abandoned homes. When the professor went to jail for that, Mrs. Rooney returned to the telephone and extended the span of her calls to long distance. At the end of that burst of activity, she was executive secretary of another organization: the National Coalition on the Transportation Crisis, with the same motto as the Emergency Committee on the Transportation Crisis: "Not one more inch of freeway."

Today Mrs. Rooney is under her physician's orders to slow down her war against the Highway Trust for the sake of her health. By this time, thousands on the District of Columbia think of her as a secular saint.

Several court suits have been brought to prevent freeways from penetrating Washington either in the direction of Brookland or at other points of the compass.

I don't share Mrs. Rooney's objective of stopping all freeway construction everywhere. That is a decision I believe each community has a right to make for itself. I think it is enough to break up the Highway Trust and to make its monies available for bus lines, subways, railroads, aircushion vehicles, and other means of transport as well as for highways. If this is done—if 10-cent dollars are spread across the board—I am sure that many states and smaller cities and towns will continue to ask for freeways. Fair enough, if that is what the people really want. It is equally fair for citizens of the big cities to have what they want and need.

The people patently are not making such choices today. Some decisions are being made by Congress purely at the behest of the highway lobby. In Washington, for example, enough residents favored subways over freeways to persuade the Mayor and municipal council of the District of Columbia to ask Congress for subway construction funds. Congress authorized an expenditure of $34.2-million.

Sensing that the subways would make the freeways unnecessary, the road lobby hurried to its friends in Congress with a plea that the Washington subways be stopped. Congressman William Natcher of Kentucky, chairman of the District of Columbia subcommittee of the House Appropriations Committee, tightly bottled the subway appropriation (of money already approved by the Congress) in his committee and announced that he would keep it there until freeway opponents agreed to end their opposition to construction of a proposed "Three Sisters" bridge over the Potomac River. That bridge, named for a trio of small islands on its route, is the key to a complex of freeway interchanges that would destroy the graceful pattern of one of the finest assemblages of national monuments on earth.

The antiquated and autocratic Congressional committee machinery had been used before, in a somewhat similar fashion, to protect the Highway Trust from the popular will. The National Committee on Natural Resources, a long established conservation lobby, tried in 1965 to have Highway Trust spending stretched to cover costs of roadside beautification, including abolition of billboards. After that effort failed, another try was made in 1966. That, too, failed, but a third attempt was made in 1968, and it produced a Congressional authorization for the purpose sought. In spite of the personal interest and influence of President Lyndon Johnson's wife, Lady Bird, a Congressional conference committee quietly killed the appropriation.

Shortly after Earth Day 1970 a new voice was heard in the highway arena: that of Earth Day's primary organizer, Environmental Action. One hundred and fifty of its representatives attended the National Conference on Environmental Action inspired by the late Walter Reuther at Black Lake, Michigan, in July 1970, and there began developing tactics to drive the automobile from the inner city. Sponsored jointly by the Alliance for Labor Action and the Methodist Church, the meeting had been planned for June but was delayed by Reuther's unexpected death. The conferees agreed to support as an ultimate goal the total removal of the automobile from the central-city environment. The closing of a single street in each big city for a few hours every day was indicated as an opening tactic, and New York City's Environmental Protection Commissioner, Jerome Kretchmer, encouraged the conferees by reporting Mayor John Lindsay's intention to close the exclusive shopping section of Fifth Avenue to traffic every Saturday in the month of July.

The activists left Black Lake resolved to attack automobilitis with every resource at their disposal. But the newborn organization was living from hand to mouth. Other than enthusiasm, the only resource it had was ingenuity in popularizing little-appreciated ecological facts in such a way as to arouse public reaction. Turning first to politics, we compiled a list of what we called a "Dirty Dozen" Congressmen whose voting records on environmental issues were insupportably bad.

Among the "Dirty Dozen" we named a veteran of thirteen terms in the House of Representatives, Maryland Democrat George Fallon, chairman of the House Public Works Committee. The chairmanship provided him with a strategic post from which to act as chief watchman over the Highway Trust Fund. He had in fact invented the Highway Trust, and he behaved toward his brain child in the manner of an excessively jealous parent. As such parents often do, he misjudged the force of opinions differing from his own. He especially undercalculated the opposition of residents of Baltimore to an interstate freeway that Highway Trust backers were trying to bash through one of the most stable middle-income black neighborhoods in the city.

We put all the fiery words that Environmental Action could muster behind Fallon's Democratic party primary election challenger, Paul Sarbanes, a former member of the Maryland State House of Delegates. Meanwhile, the Friends of the Earth, an outspoken group of environmental lobbyists, encouraged emergence of an affiliate called the League of Conservation Voters, and the league contributed $8,000 to help pay Sarbanes's expense. Poetic justice then intervened in the form of the worst visitation of smog the Eastern Seaboard had suffered in many years. Sarbanes reminded voters that smog is chiefly due to the automobile and that automobiles are hogging the countryside because of the

10-cent highway-building dollars strewn about by Fallon's Highway Trust.

When Fallon lost his bid for renomination last September, we saw for the first time a fair chance to bust the Highway Trust. In the month immediately before the Maryland primary, the Congressional Joint Economic Committee's subcommittee on economy in government, chaired by Senator William Proxmire of Wisconsin, had issued a report urging that the Highway Trust Fund be phased out of existence. Although the committee had no power to do more than recommend, the tiny staff of Environmental Action felt encouraged by even that much gain, and it turned its skills to the sharpening of teeth in Senator Edmund S. Muskie's 1970 Clean Air Law. The stunning effect of that honing can be read in the subsequent prediction by EPA's Ruckelshaus that the law's post-1975 pollution limit will force diminution of private automobile traffic in the nation's six biggest cities.

The vote of no confidence from his Maryland constituents did not prevent Congressman Fallon from wielding the authority of the House Public Works Committee chairmanship to keep the Highway Trust going. He used his lame-duck period to extend the life of the Highway Trust Fund from 1972 to 1977.

Fallon at last disappeared from the House with the reorganization of Congress in January 1971. His successor as Public Works Committee chairman was John Blatnik of Minnesota, who told news reporters he intends to review the whole question of the Highway Trust Fund's place in America's current urban crisis. The actions he ultimately must take may be simplified for him by happenings in the Senate, which already is considering four omens: (1) the 1971 Economic Report, which reiterates last year's urging of a phase-out of the Highway Trust Fund and pleads that plans for the phase-out be drafted now; (2) introduction by Massachusetts Senator Edward Kennedy of a bill to replace the Highway Trust Fund with a transportation trust fund designed to subsidize all types of urban transit facilities on an equal footing; (3) another bill submitted by Illinois Senator Charles Percy, authorizing the governors of the fifty states to spend their shares of Highway Trust monies as the governors think best; and (4) the appointment of Indiana Democratic liberal Birch Bayh as chairman of the Senate Public Works subcommittee on roads, coupled with the appointment to that subcommittee of Democratic Presidential front-runner Muskie.

As the Presidential campaign warms up, Senate hearings on broad transportation issues seem well within reach of sustained initiative. Sensing the challenge in these circumstances, two young environmental activists last February took on the job of organizing a Highway Action

Coalition. They were Barbara Reid, Midwestern regional director of Earth Day 1970, and Bob Waldrop of the Sierra Club. He had been sniping at the Highway Trust since the National Committee on Natural Resources made its first futile move back in 1965; she had been a worker in the late Bobby Kennedy's Presidential nomination campaign, an educational staffer at the Conservation Foundation, head of Environmental Action's 1970 clean air alliance with Senator Muskie, and a major activist in the Coalition Against the SST.

As co-directors of the Highway Action Coalition, Barbara and Bob first enlisted the support of the Sierra Club and Environmental Action. Then they drafted Environmental Action's Linda Katz, a University of Michigan graduate trained in labor union grass-roots lobbying techniques, to coordinate the HAC activities. Next they obtained the participation in HAC of Friends of the Earth, the League of Conservation Voters, the Wilderness Society, and Zero Population Growth. This gave HAC an initial membership of about 300,000. An introductory letter went out to these people in March. It got straight to the point:

"More than 60 per cent of the total land area of most large American cities is devoted to the movement and storage of the automobile. Not only do cars in cities fail to transport people effciently (as we all know from experience in rush-hour traffic jams) but, in addition, cars are the major source of urban air pollution. What's more, land that is taken out of private ownership to be used for streets or freeways is removed from the all-important tax base, thus contributing to the financial crisis of urban areas. Another major problem in cities is housing. At a time when we desperately need new units, we are tearing down existing dwellings to build new roads. No less important are the psychological effects of cars in cities. Our consciousness is assaulted daily by the thousands of automobiles competing for space to drive and park in downtown areas.

"Cities are not the only areas where the values of the automobile and new road construction are in question. The ecologically destructive form of land use known as 'suburban sprawl' is directly attributable to a random frenzy of road building. And, looking beyond the suburbs, the single greatest threat to the survival of our nation's forests and other wild areas is roads and automobile traffic."

The letter assured its readers that HAC does "not propose that people be prevented from using their cars or that states be prevented from building new roads." Rather, the proposal "is that people and states be given the option to utilize good public transportation if they so choose." The pernicious role of the Highway Trust Fund was succinctly described:

"The sacrosanct Highway Trust Fund . . . is a self-perpetuating mechanism. Money flows automatically into the fund, mainly from the 4-cent per gallon gasoline tax. The more the American public drives, the more gas is used. This causes the trust fund to grow, bringing about the construction of new highways. New highways encourage more people to use automobiles more often. Every time a road gets crowded, the need for another road is proclaimed. And so by circular and self-perpetuating mechanisms, we are buried under concrete. Meanwhile, . . . the more people get into the habit of driving, the less likely they are to make use of mass transit. This causes bus and train patronage to fall off. The transit companies are forced to raise fares, causing many riders to switch to automobiles. All of these effects are snowballing . . . to the chagrin of those who cannot or do not drive cars."

The HAC letter promised distribution of "a complete citizen action handbook" during the summer of 1971. But recipients of the letter did not wait for the handbook. Between 100 and 125 citizen groups already actively involved in debates over local transportation crises wrote to declare their allegiance to HAC.

There was a loud encouraging ring to one message from San Francisco. It came from citizens who had raised such a rumpus that the Mayor and city council stopped the Embarcadero Freeway dead in mid-course in 1968, accepting as a penalty the loss of $280 million in Highway Trust monies.

Cheering news also came from the Committee for the Preservation of Overton Park. Overton Park is a 342-acre sweep of wilderness in the midst of Memphis, Tennessee. The Committee for Preservation of Overton Park has existed, on and off, since 1957, when a proposal first was made to push a six-lane interstate highway across the park in order to shorten the automobiling distance between the center of Memphis and the city's eastern suburbs. The real local reason for the road was obscured by claims that this was a defense highway—not an unusual tactic for the Highway Trust.

The space required for the road lay between the zoo and the remainder of the park, which includes a nine-hole golf course, an outdoor theater, an art academy, bridle paths, nature trails, picnic grounds, and 170 acres of forest.

Because of the tenacity of the Committee for the Preservation of Overton Park, construction of the road through the park has been repeatedly delayed. In 1968, the U.S. Secretary of Transportation agreed with Memphis city officials that the project should be started. This action sent the Committee for Preservation of Overton Park to Federal

District Court. When the court upheld the right of the DOT Secretary to proceed, an appeal was taken to the Sixth Circuit Court of Appeals, which sustained the District Court decision. Another appeal was taken to the Supreme Court of the United States, and that body ruled in October 1970 that the DOT Secretary had failed to fulfill the intent of Congress. It was clear, the Justices held, that parklands (not just those in Memphis but everywhere in the country) are not to be taken for highway purposes unless no other feasible alternate routes are available and even then only after all possible steps have been taken to minimize damage to the environment. The DOT Secretary had not demonstrated the absence of alternatives in the case of Overton Park.

Response to the HAC letter uncovered another blow for freedom from the Highway Trust. After twenty-eight years of controversy, a proposal to plunge a freeway across the Great Smoky Mountains National Park had finally been killed.

A myriad of motives merged as the HAC recruitment list grew. In Eastham, Massachusetts, there was "Operation Roadblock." It was put in motion by the Eastham Board of Selectmen, the local Historical Society, the Jaycees, the Garden Club, the Conservation Commission, the Rod and Gun Club, and the Natural Resources Trust of Eastham to stop a four-lane limited access highway that would cut Eastham in half, threaten the water supply, alter its drainage pattern, and loose a tempest of traffic noise. The Valley Transportation Coalition in Phoenix, Arizona, is determined to save the valley in which Phoenix lies from "being paved over as solidly as Los Angeles." A moratorium on all new highway construction in Milwaukee and rural southeastern Wisconsin is being sought by environmentalists there. The League to Save Lake Tahoe is opposed to any new highways in the Tahoe basin of California. In Denver, citizen resentment against smog that veiled the mountains from view for 100 days last year has led to an application for federal subsidy of an air-cushioned-vehicle mass-transit system to serve Denver's 8,500-square-mile transportation district. The Mid-North Association of Chicago has vowed to fight all new roads through the city's Lincoln Park area. Father John Hinkley is leading a coalition of low-income groups against freeways that would destroy their neighborhoods in Boston. The Community Park Coalition of the University of Pennsylvania is opposing university efforts to pave a small public park and convert it to a parking lot. Jonathan von Ranson, editor of the West Hartford News, is campaigning against an interstate road that would drive through a reservoir and cleave a four-mile square of wilderness in Connecticut. Marc D. Hiller of Environmental Action-Zero Population Growth in Pittsburgh reports a campaign to halt a highway headed through the center of Duff Park in Murrysville, Pennsylvania. The Oregon Environmental Council is trying to stop construction of a sixteen-story parking garage in downtown Portland.

This motley company of crusaders has a common adversary: the highway lobby, an amorphous and sometimes uneasy alliance of interests—many of whom have little formal contact with one another. It is difficult to define where the highway lobby begins and ends because the automobile is so completely woven through the fabric of American life. Clearly, the highway lobby contains the highway builders—the contractors, the construction unions, the manufacturers of asphalt and concrete and steel and construction equipment. They belong to overlapping organizations, such as the American Road Builders Association and the Associated General Contractors of America. The highway lobby also includes those state organizations and officials whose very future depends upon the construction and maintenance of an ever-expanding system of roads and highways. These are most effectively represented by the American Association of State Highway Officials, a fifty-year-old organization with an enormous capacity to generate political pressure back home in the district of any recalcitrant Congressman.

Other members of the highway lobby include automobile manufacturers, makers of automobile accessories, the petroleum industry, the American Automobile Association, and even traditional adversaries such as the American Trucking Association and the International Brotherhood of Teamsters. The lobby has less obvious members, too. Land speculators sometimes make more money off highways than do contractors. Chains of roadside restaurants and motels are inevitably linked to the future of the highway. Then there are the people who repair the roads, who clean the roads, who erect billboards along the roads. Although not technically a part of the lobby, the National Highway Users Conference cannot be overlooked. Founded in 1932 by Alfred P. Sloan, the conference includes virtually every business in America that uses cars or trucks.

Although not ready to tackle the highway lobby head on and count on winning, HAC nonetheless is a force to reckon with. To the extent that a goal can be agreed on and energies can be at least loosely coordinated, the new coalition can have an important effect. Whether individual hopes call for monorails, air-cushion vehicles, gravity-vacuum-tube subways, electromagnetic propulsion systems, turbojet trains, or dial-a-bus-from-home systems, the common need is to achieve a shift in public attitudes toward transport financing.

As I noted earlier, the Highway Trust Fund has been extended to 1977. There is no realistic way to alter that fact. In my opinion, energies now should be focused on converting that fund into a general transportation trust fund for the duration of its existence and allow this $5-billion a year to be spent on any and all forms of transport at the 9-to-1 matching terms reserved to date for highways.

It is critically important that we not move irresponsibly. Nor must we allow our thinking to become rigid, our thoughts doctrinaire. The shape, and much of the very nature, of the modern city was determined by reliance on the automobile. Any new transportation system receiving massive federal assistance is likely to exert a similar far-reaching influence.

We can, however, state quite boldly just what interest we wish to serve. Not the interest of Detroit, or of the petroleum or tire industries, or of the builders of highways. Not the urban planners' and academic rhetoricians' compulsive need for vindication of theories. Not the political fortunes of any particular band of elected representatives. Our goal must be no less than the ultimate best interest of the whole people.

What can *you* do? Join an existing group and help to fire it up. Or, if no group exists, start one. Spread the message around. Never refuse an invitation to speak on the subject. Testify at public hearings. Petition your local government bodies. If you are just getting interested in the field, read *Earth Tool Kit, Super Highway-Super Hoax,* and *Road to Ruin.* Get your facts in order first. Don't pull your punches after that. Weaken the Highway Trust from within if you can, perhaps by joining the American Automobile Association and exerting your privileges as a member to introduce new ideas. Find out where your Congressman stands on this issue (i.e., how he votes). Question him about it when he appears in public on his visits home.

Don't be afraid of occasional street theater. Remember the story about the San Francisco hippie who put a dime in a parking meter and lay down for an hour's sleep in the little plot of land he had just rented from the city. Imagine the result in Manhattan if 1,000 anti-freeway partisans arrived one morning at 7:30 with folding chairs and "rented" all the available parking space on several major streets for two hours.

The address of the Highway Action Coalition is Suite 731, 1346 Connecticut Avenue N.W., Washington, D.C. 20036. Your name will be added to its mailing list on request, and you will be kept informed about transportation activities in the Congress. If you belong to a local group that is trying to obtain reconsideration of a freeway project, HAC will welcome whatever news of it you can offer.

## 38. WATER

### Edward Abbey

*Edward Abbey has lived most of his life in the Southwest. He has taught philosophy at the University of New Mexico, has written several books, including* The Brave Cowboy *and* Fire on the Mountain, *and has worked as a park ranger in Arches National Monument Park near Moab, Utah. This last experience provided material for Abbey's book* Desert Solitaire *from which this selection has been taken.*

"THIS WOULD be good country," a tourist says to me, "if only you had some water."

He's from Cleveland, Ohio.

"If we had water here," I reply, "this country would not be what it is. It would be like Ohio, wet and humid and hydrological, all covered with cabbage farms and golf courses. Instead of this lovely barren desert we would have only another blooming garden state, like New Jersey. You see what I mean?"

"If you had more water more people could live here."

"Yes sir. And where then would people go when they wanted to see something besides people?"

"I see what you mean. Still, I wouldn't want to live here. So dry and desolate. Nice for pictures but my God I'm glad I don't have to live here."

"I'm glad too, sir. We're in perfect agreement. You wouldn't want to live here, I wouldn't want to live in Cleveland. We're both satisfied with the arrangement as it is. Why change it?"

"Agreed."

We shake hands and the tourist from Ohio goes away pleased, as I am pleased, each of us thinking he has taught the other something new.

The air is so dry here I can hardly shave in the mornings. The water and soap dry on my face as I reach for the razor: aridity. It is the driest season of a dry country. In the afternoons of July and August we may get thundershowers but an hour after the storms pass the surface of the desert is again bone dry.

It seldom rains. The geography books credit this part of Utah with an annual precipitation of five to nine inches but that is merely a sta-

*Source:* "Water" from *Desert Solitaire* by Edward Abbey. Copyright © 1968 by Edward Abbey. Used with permission of McGraw-Hill Book Company.

tistical average. Low enough, to be sure. And in fact the rainfall and snowfall vary widely from year to year and from place to place even within the Arches region. When a cloud bursts open above the Devil's Garden the sun is blazing down on my ramada. And wherever it rains in this land of unclothed rock the runoff is rapid down cliff and dome through the canyons to the Colorado.

Sometimes it rains and still fails to moisten the desert—the falling water evaporates halfway down between cloud and earth. Then you see curtains of blue rain dangling out of reach in the sky while the living things wither below for want of water. Torture by tantalizing, hope without fulfillment. And the clouds disperse and dissipate into nothingness.

Streambeds are usually dry. The dry wash, dry gulch, *arroyo seco*. Only after a storm do they carry water and then but briefly—a few minutes, a couple of hours. The spring-fed perennial stream is a rarity. In this area we have only two of them, Salt Creek and Onion Creek, the first too salty to drink and the second laced with arsenic and sulfur.

Permanent springs or waterholes are likewise few and far between though not so rare as the streams. They are secret places deep in the canyons, known only to the deer and the coyotes and the dragonflies and a few others. Water rises slowly from these springs and flows in little rills over bare rock, over and under sand, into miniature fens of wire grass, rushes, willow and tamarisk. The water does not flow very far before disappearing into the air and under the ground. The flow may reappear farther down the canyon, surfacing briefly for a second time, a third time, diminishing in force until it vanishes completely and for good.

Another type of spring may be found on canyon walls where water seeps out between horizontal formations through cracks thinner than paper to support small hanging gardens of orchids, monkeyflower, maidenhair fern, and ivy. In most of these places the water is so sparingly measured that it never reaches the canyon floor at all but is taken up entirely by the thirsty plant life and transformed into living tissue.

Long enough in the desert a man like other animals can learn to smell water. Can learn, at least, the smell of things associated with water— the unique and heartening odor of the cottonwood tree, for example, which in the canyonlands is the tree of life. In this wilderness of naked rock burnt to auburn or buff or red by ancient fires there is no vision more pleasing to the eyes and more gratifying to the heart than the translucent acid green (bright gold in autumn) of this venerable tree. It signifies water, and not only water but also shade, in a country where shelter from the sun is sometimes almost as precious as water.

*Signifies* water, which may or may not be on the surface, visible and available. If you have what is called a survival problem and try to dig for this water during the heat of the day the effort may cost you more in sweat than you will find to drink. A bad deal. Better to wait for nightfall when the cottonwoods and other plants along the streambed will release some of the water which they have absorbed during the day, perhaps enough to allow a potable trickle to rise to the surface of the sand. If the water still does not appear you may then wish to attempt to dig for it. Or you might do better by marching farther up the canyon. Sooner or later you should find a spring or at least a little seep on the canyon wall. On the other hand you could possibly find no water at all, anywhere. The desert is a land of surprises, some of them terrible surprises. Terrible as derived from terror.

When out for a walk carry water; not less than a gallon a day per person.

More surprises. In places you will find clear-flowing streams, such as Salt Creek near Turnbow Cabin, where the water looks beautifully drinkable but tastes like brine.

You might think, beginning to die of thirst, that any water however salty would be better than none at all. Not true. Small doses will not keep you going or alive and a deep drink will force your body to expend water in getting rid of the excess salt. This results in a net loss of bodily moisture and a hastening of the process of dehydration. Dehydration first enervates, then prostrates, then kills.

Nor is blood, your own or a companion's, any adequate substitute for water; blood is too salty. The same is true of urine.

If it's your truck or car which has failed you, you'd be advised to tap the radiator, unless it's full of Prestone. If this resource is not available and water cannot be found in the rocks or under the sand and you find yourself too tired and discouraged to go on, crawl into the shade and wait for help to find you. If no one is looking for you write your will in the sand and let the wind carry your last words and signature east to the borders of Colorado and south to the pillars of Monument Valley— someday, never fear, your bare elegant bones will be discovered and wondered and marveled at.

A great thirst is a great joy when quenched in time. On my first walk down into Havasupai Canyon, which is a branch of the Grand Canyon, never mind exactly where, I took with me only a quart of water, thinking that would be enough for a mere fourteen-mile downhill hike on a warm day in August. At Topocoba on the rim of the canyon the temperature was a tolerable ninety-six degrees but it rose about one degree for each mile on and downward. Like a fool I rationed my water, drank frugally, and could have died of the heatstroke. When late in the afternoon I finally stumbled—sun-dazed, blear-eyed, parched as an old bacon rind—upon that blue stream which flows like a miraculous mirage down the floor of the canyon I was too exhausted to pause and drink soberly from the bank. Dreamily, deliriously, I waded into the waist-deep water and fell on my face. Like a sponge I soaked up moisture through every pore, letting the current bear me along beneath a canopy of overhanging willow trees. I had no fear of drowning in the water—I intended to drink it all.

In the Needles country high above the inaccessible Colorado River there is a small spring hidden at the heart of a maze of fearfully arid grabens and crevasses. A very small spring: the water oozes from the grasp of moss to fall one drop at a time, one drop per second, over a lip of stone. One afternoon in June I squatted there for an hour—two hours?—filling my canteen. No other water within miles, the local gnat population fought me for every drop. To keep them out of the canteen I had to place a handkerchief over the opening as I filled it. Then they attacked my eyes, drawn irresistibly by the liquid shine of the human eyeball. Embittered little bastards. Never have I tasted better water.

Other springs, more surprises. Northeast of Moab in a region of gargoyles and hobgoblins, a landscape left over from the late Jurassic, is a peculiar little waterhold named Onion Spring. A few wild onions grow in the vicinity but more striking, in season, is the golden princess plume, an indicator of selenium, a mild poison often found in association with uranium, a poison not so mild. Approaching the spring you notice a sulfurous stink in the air though the water itself, neither warm nor cold, looks clear and drinkable.

Unlike most desert waterholes you will find around Onion Spring few traces of animal life. Nobody comes to drink. The reason is the very good one that the water of Onion Spring contains not only sulfur, and perhaps selenium, but also arsenic. When I was there I looked at the water and smelled it and ran my hands through it and after a while, since the sampling of desert water is in my line, I tasted it, carefully, and spat it out. Afterwards I rinsed my mouth with water from my canteen.

This poison spring is quite clear. The water is sterile, lifeless. There are no bugs, which in itself is a warning sign, in case the smell were not sufficient. When in doubt about drinking from an unknown spring look for life. If the water is scummed with algae, crawling with worms, grubs, larvae, spiders and liver flukes, be reassured, drink hearty, you'll get nothing worse than dysentery. But if it appears innocent and pure, beware. Onion Spring wears such a deceitful guise. Out of a tangle of poison-tolerant weeds the water drips into a basin of mud and sand, flows from there over sandstone and carries its potent solutions into the otherwise harmless waters of the creek.

There are a number of springs similar to this one in the American desert. Badwater pool in Death Valley, for example. And a few others in the canyonlands, usually in or below the Moenkopi and Shinarump formations—mudstone and shales. The prospector Vernon Pick found a poison spring at the source of the well-named Dirty Devil River, when he was searching for uranium over in the San Rafael Swell a few years ago. At the time he needed water; he *had* to have water; and in order to get a decent drink he made something like a colander out of his canteen, punching it full of nail holes, filling it with charcoal from his campfire and straining the water through the charcoal. How much this purified the water he had no means of measuring but he drank it anyway and although it made him sick he survived, and is still alive today to tell about it.

There are rumors that when dying of the thirst you can save your soul *and* body by extracting water from the barrel cactus. This is a dubious proposition and I don't know anyone who has made the experiment. It might be possible in the Sonoran desert where the barrel cactus grows tall as a man and fat as a keg of beer. In Utah, however, its nearest relative stands no more than a foot high and bristles with needles curved like fishhooks. To get even close to this devilish vegetable you need leather gloves and a machete. Slice off the top and you find inside not water but only the green pulpy core of the living plant. Carving the core into manageable chunks you might be able to wring a few drops of bitter liquid into your cup. The labor and the exasperation will make you sweat, will cost you dearly.

When you reach this point you are doomed. Far better to have stayed at home with the TV and a case of beer. If the happy thought arrives too late, crawl into the shade and contemplate the lonely sky. See those big black scrawny wings far above, waiting? Comfort yourself with the reflection that within a few hours, if all goes as planned, your human flesh will be working its way through the gizzard of a buzzard, your essence transfigured into the fierce greedy eyes and unimaginable consciousness of a turkey vulture. Whereupon you, too, will soar on motionless wings high over the ruck and rack of human suffering. For most of us a promotion in grade, for some the realization of an ideal.

In July and August on the high desert the thunderstorms come. Mornings begin clear and dazzling bright, the sky as blue as the Virgin's cloak, unflawed by a trace of cloud in all that emptiness bounded on the north by the Book Cliffs, on the east by Grand Mesa and the La Sal Mountains, on the south by the Blue Mountains and on the west by the dragon-tooth reef of the San Rafael. By noon, however, clouds begin to form over the mountains, coming it seems out of nowhere, out of nothing, a special creation.

The clouds multiply and merge, cumuli-nimbi piling up like whipped cream, like mashed potatoes, like sea foam, building upon one another into a second mountain range greater in magnitude than the terrestrial range below.

The massive forms jostle and grate, ions collide, and the sound of thunder is heard over the sun-drenched land. More clouds emerge from empty sky, anvil-headed giants with glints of lightning in their depths. An armada assembles and advances, floating on a plane of air that makes it appear, from below, as a fleet of ships must look to the fish in the sea.

At my observation point on a sandstone monolith the sun is blazing down as intensely as ever, the air crackling with dry heat. But the storm clouds continue to spread, gradually taking over more and more of the sky, and as they approach the battle breaks out.

Lightning streaks like gunfire through the clouds, volleys of thunder shake the air. A smell of ozone. While the clouds exchange their bolts with one another no rain falls, but now they begin bombarding the buttes and pinnacles below. Forks of lightning—illuminated nerves—join heaven and earth.

The wind is rising. For anyone with sense enough to get out of the rain now is the time to seek shelter. A lash of lightning flickers over Wilson Mesa, scorching the brush, splitting a pine tree. Northeast over the Yellowcat area rain is already sweeping down, falling not vertically but in a graceful curve, like a beaded curtain drawn lightly across the desert. Between the rain and the mountains, among the tumbled masses of vapor, floats a segment of a rainbow—sunlight divided. But where I stand the storm is only beginning.

Above me the clouds roll in, unfurling and smoking billows in malignant violet, dense as wool. Most of the sky is lidded over but the sun remains clear halfway down the west, shining in under the storm. Overhead the clouds thicken, then crack and split with a roar like that of cannonballs tumbling down a marble staircase; their bellies open—too late to run now—and the rain comes down.

*Comes down:* not softly not gently, with no quality of mercy but like heavy water in buckets, raindrops like pellets splattering on the rock, knocking the berries off the junipers, plastering my shirt to my back, drumming on my hat like hailstones and running in a waterfall off the brim.

The pinnacles, arches, balanced rocks, fins and elephant-backs of sandstone, glazed with water but still in sunlight, gleam like old gray silver

**418**  *Order and Diversity*

and everything appears transfixed in the strange wild unholy light of the moment. The light that never was.

For five minutes the deluge continues under the barrage of thunder and lightning, then trails off quickly, diminishing to a shower, to a sprinkling, to nothing at all. The clouds move off and rumble for a while in the distance. A fresh golden light breaks through and now in the east, over the turrets and domes, stands the rainbow sign, a double rainbow with one foot in the canyon of the Colorado and the other far north in Salt Wash. Beyond the rainbow and framed within it I can see jags of lightning still playing in the stormy sky over Castle Valley.

The afternoon sun falls lower; above the mountains and the ragged black clouds hangs the new moon, pale fragment of what is to come; in another hour, at sundown, Venus too will be there, planet of love, to glow bright as chromium down on the western sky. The desert storm is over and through the pure sweet pellucid air the cliff swallows and the nighthawks plunge and swerve, making cries of hunger and warning and—who knows?—maybe of exultation.

Stranger than the storms, though not so grand and symphonic, are the flash floods that follow them, bursting with little warning out of the hills and canyons, sometimes an hour or more after the rain has stopped.

I have stood in the middle of a broad sandy wash with not a trickle of moisture to be seen anywhere, sunlight pouring down on me and on the flies and ants and lizards, the sky above perfectly clear, listening to a queer vibration in the air and in the ground under my feet—like a freight train coming down the grade, very fast—and looked up to see a wall of water tumble around a bend and surge toward me.

A wall of water. A poor image. For the flash flood of the desert poorly resembles water. It looks rather like a loose pudding or a thick dense soup, thick as gravy, dense with mud and sand, lathered with scuds of bloody froth, loaded on its crest with a tangle of weeds and shrubs and small trees ripped from their roots.

Surprised by delight, I stood there in the heat, the bright sun, the quiet afternoon, and watched the monster roll and roar toward me. It advanced in crescent shape with a sort of forelip about a foot high streaming in front, making hissing sucking noises like a giant amoeba, nosing to the right and nosing to the left as if on the spoor of something good to eat. Red as tomato soup or blood it came down on me about as fast as a man could run. I moved aside and watched it go by.

A flick of lightning to the north
where dun clouds grumble—
while here in the middle of the wash

black beetles tumble
and horned toads fumble
over sand as dry as bone
and hard-baked mud and glaring stone.

Nothing here suggests disaster
for the ants' shrewd play;
their busy commerce for tomorrow
shows no care for today;
but a mile away
and rolling closer in a scum of mud
comes the hissing lapping blind mouth of the flood.

Through the tamarisk whine the flies
in pure fat units of conceit
as if the sun and the afternoon
and blood and the smells and the heat
and something to eat
would be available forever, never die
beyond the fixed imagination of a fly.

The flood comes, crawls thickly by, roaring
with self-applause, a loud
spongy smothering liquid avalanche:
great ant-civilizations drown,
worlds go down,
trees go under, the mud bank breaks
and deep down underneath the bedrock shakes.

A few hours later the bulk of the flood was past and gone. The flow
dwindled to a trickle over bars of quicksand. New swarms of insect life
would soon come to recover the provinces of those swept away. Nothing
had changed but the personnel, a normal turnover, and the contours of
the watercourse, that not much.

Now we've mentioned quicksand. What is quicksand anyway? First
of all, quicksand is *not* as many think a queer kind of sand which has
the hideous power to draw men and animals down and down into a
bottomless pit. There can be no quicksand without water. The scene of
the sand-drowned camel boy in the movie *Lawrence of Arabia* is pure
fakery. The truth about quicksand is that it is simply a combination of
sand and water in which the upward force of the water is sufficient to
neutralize the frictional strength of the particles of sand. The greater the
force and saturation, the less weight the sand can bear.

Ordinarily it is possible for a man to walk across quicksand, if he keeps moving. But if he stops, funny things begin to happen. The surface of the quicksand, which may look as firm as the wet sand on an ocean beach, begins to liquefy beneath his feet. He finds himself sinking slowly into a jelly-like substance, soft and quivering, which clasps itself around his ankles with the suction power of any viscous fluid. Pulling out one foot, the other foot necessarily goes down deeper, and if a man waits too long, or cannot reach something solid beyond the quicksand, he may soon find himself trapped. The depth to which he finally sinks depends upon the depth and the fluidity of the quicksand, upon the nature of his efforts to extricate himself, and upon the ratio of body weight to volume of quicksand. Unless a man is extremely talented, he cannot work himself in more than waist-deep. The quicksand will not *pull* him down. But it will not let him go either. Therefore the conclusion is that while quicksand cannot drown its captive, it could possibly starve him to death. Whatever finally happens, the immediate effects are always interesting.

My friend Newcomb, for instance. He has only one good leg, used to wear a brace on the other, can't hike very well in rough country, tends to lag behind. We were exploring a deep dungeon-like defile off Glen Canyon one time (before the dam). The defile turned and twisted like a snake under overhanging and interlocking walls so high, so close, that for most of the way I could not see the sky. The floor of this cleft was irregular, wet, sandy, in places rather soupy, and I was soon far ahead and out of sight of Newcomb.

Finally I came to a place in the canyon so narrow and dark and wet and ghastly that I had no heart to go farther. Retracing my steps I heard, now and then, a faint and mournful wail, not human, which seemed to come from abysmal depths far back in the bowels of the plateau, from the underworld, from subterranean passageways better left forever unseen and unknown. I hurried on, the cries faded away. I was glad to be getting out of there. Then they came again, louder and as it seemed from all sides, out of the rock itself, surrounding me. A terrifying caterwauling it was, multiplied and amplified by echoes piled on echoes, overlapping and reinforcing one another. I looked back to see what was hunting me but there was only the naked canyon in the dim, bluish light that filtered down from far above. I thought of the Minotaur. Then I thought of Newcomb and began to run.

It wasn't bad. He was in only a little above the knees and sinking very slowly. As soon as he saw me he stopped hollering and relit his pipe. Help, he said, simply and quietly.

What was all the bellowing about? I wanted to know. I'm sorry, he said, but it's a horrible way to die. Get out of that mud, I said, and let's get out of here. It ain't just mud, he said. I don't care what it is, get out of there; you look like an idiot. I'm sinking, he said.

And he was. The stuff was now halfway up his thighs.

Don't you ever read any books? I said. Don't you have sense enough to know that when you get in quicksand you have to lie down flat? Why? he asked. So you'll live longer, I explained. Face down or face up? he asked next.

That stumped me. I couldn't remember the answer to that one. You wait here, I said, while I go back to Albuquerque and get the book.

He looked down for a moment. Still sinking, he said; please help?

I stepped as close to him as I could without getting bogged down myself but our extended hands did not quite meet. Lean forward, I said. I am, he said. All the way, I said; fall forward.

He did that and then I could reach him. He gripped my wrist and I gripped his and with a slow steady pull I got him out of there. The quicksand gurgled a little and made funny, gasping noises, reluctant to let him go, but when he was free the holes filled up at once, the liquid sand oozing into place, and everything looked as it had before, smooth and sleek and innocent as the surface of a pudding. It was in fact the same pool of quicksand that I had walked over myself only about an hour earlier.

Quicksand is more of a menace to cattle and horses, with their greater weight and smaller feet, than it is to men, and the four-legged beasts generally avoid it when they can. Sometimes, however, they are forced to cross quicksand to reach water, or are driven across, and then the cattleman may have an unpleasant chore on his hands. Motor vehicles, of course, cannot negotiate quicksand; even a four-wheel-drive jeep will bog down as hopelessly as anything else.

Although I hesitate to deprive quicksand of its sinister glamour I must confess that I have not yet heard of a case where a machine, an animal or a man has actually sunk *completely* out of sight in the stuff. But it may have happened; it may be happening to somebody at this very moment. I sometimes regret that I was unable to perform a satisfactory experiment with my friend Newcomb when the chance presented itself; such opportunities come but rarely. But I needed him; he was among other things a good camp cook.

After the storms pass and the flash floods have dumped their loads of silt into the Colorado, leaving the streambeds as arid as they were before, it is still possible to find rainwater in the desert. All over the slickrock country there are natural cisterns or potholes, tubs, tanks and basins sculptured in the soft sandstone by the erosive force of weathering, wind and sand. Many of them serve as little catchment basins during rain and a few may contain water for days or even weeks after a storm, the length of time depending on the shape and depth of the hole and the consequent rate of evaporation.

Often far from any spring, these temporary pools attract doves, ravens and other birds, and deer and coyotes; you, too, if you know where to look or find one by luck, can slake your thirst and fill your water gourd. Such pools may be found in what seem like the most improbable places: out on the desolate White Rim below Grandview Point, for example, or on top of the elephant-back dome above the Double Arch. At Toroweap in Grand Canyon I found a deep tank of clear sweet water almost over my head, countersunk in the summit of a sandstone bluff which overhung my campsite by a hundred feet. A week after rain there was still enough water there to fill my needs; hard to reach, it was well worth the effort. The Bedouin know what I mean.

The rain-filled potholes, set in naked rock, are usually devoid of visible plant life but not of animal life. In addition to the inevitable microscopic creatures there may be certain amphibians like the spadefoot toad. This little animal lives through dry spells in a state of estivation under the dried-up sediment in the bottom of a hole. When the rain comes, if it comes, he emerges from the mud singing madly in his fashion, mates with the handiest female and fills the pool with a swarm of tadpoles, most of them doomed to a most ephemeral existence. But a few survive, mature, become real toads, and when the pool dries up they dig into the sediment as their parents did before, making burrows which they seal with mucus in order to preserve that moisture necessary to life. There they wait, day after day, week after week, in patient spadefoot torpor, perhaps listening—we can imagine—for the sound of raindrops pattering at last on the earthen crust above their heads. If it comes in time the glorious cycle is repeated; if not, this particular colony of *Bufonidae* is reduced eventually to dust, a burden on the wind.

Rain and puddles bring out other amphibia, even in the desert. It's a strange, stirring, but not uncommon thing to come on a pool at night, after an evening of thunder and lightning and a bit of rainfall, and see the frogs clinging to the edge of their impermanent pond, bodies immersed in water but heads out, all croaking away in tricky counterpoint. They are windbags: with each croak the pouch under the frog's chin swells like a bubble, then collapses.

Why do they sing? What do they have to sing about? Somewhat apart from one another, separated by roughly equal distances, facing outward from the water, they clank and croak all through the night with tireless perseverance. To human ears their music has a bleak, dismal, tragic quality, dirgelike rather than jubilant. It may nevertheless be the case that these small beings are singing not only to claim their stake in the pond, not only to attract a mate, but also out of spontaneous love and joy, a contrapuntal choral celebration of the coolness and wetness after weeks of desert fire, for love of their own existence, however brief it may be, and for joy in the common life.

Has joy any survival value in the operations of evolution? I suspect that it does; I suspect that the morose and fearful are doomed to quick extinction. Where there is no joy there can be no courage; and without courage all other virtues are useless. Therefore the frogs, the toads, keep on singing even though we know, if they don't, that the sound of their uproar must surely be luring all the snakes and ringtail cats and kit foxes and coyotes and great horned owls toward the scene of their happiness.

What then? A few of the little amphibians will continue their metamorphosis by way of the nerves and tissues of one of the higher animals, in which process the joy of one becomes the contentment of the second. Nothing is lost, except an individual consciousness here and there, a trivial perhaps even illusory phenomenon. The rest survive, mate, multiply, burrow, estivate, dream, and rise again. The rains will come, the potholes shall be filled. Again. And again. And again.

More secure are those who live in and around the desert's few perennial waterholes, those magical hidden springs that are scattered so austerely through the barren vastness of the canyon country. Of these only a rare few are too hot or too briny or too poisonous to support life— the great majority of them swarm with living things. Here you will see the rushes and willows and cottonwoods, and four-winged dragonflies in green, blue, scarlet and gold, and schools of minnows in the water, moving from sunlight to shadow and back again. At night the mammals come—deer, bobcat, cougar, coyote, fox, jackrabbit, bighorn sheep, wild horse and feral burro—each in his turn and in unvarying order under the declaration of a truce. They come to drink, not to kill or be killed.

Finally, in this discussion of water in the desert, I should make note of a distinctive human contribution, one which has become a part of the Southwestern landscape no less typical than the giant cactus, the juniper growing out of solid rock or the red walls of a Navajo canyon. I refer to the tiny oasis formed by the drilled well, its windmill and storage tank. The windmill with its skeleton tower and creaking vanes is an object of beauty as significant in its way as the cottonwood tree, and the open tank at its foot, big enough to swim in, is a thing of joy to man and beast, no less worthy of praise than the desert spring.

Water, water, water. . . . There is no shortage of water in the desert but exactly the right amount, a perfect ratio of water to rock, of water to sand, insuring that wide, free, open, generous spacing among plants and animals, homes and towns and cities, which makes the arid West so different from any other part of the nation. There is no lack of water here, unless you try to establish a city where no city should be.

The Developers, of course—the politicians, businessmen, bankers, administrators, engineers—they see it somewhat otherwise and complain most bitterly and interminably of a desperate water shortage, especially in the Southwest. They propose schemes of inspiring proportions for diverting water by the damful from the Columbia River, or even from the Yukon River, and channeling it overland down into Utah, Colorado, Arizona and New Mexico.

What for? "In anticipation of future needs, in order to provide for the continued industrial and population growth of the Southwest." And in such an answer we see that it's only the old numbers game again, the monomania of small and very simple minds in the grip of an obsession. They cannot see that growth for the sake of growth is a cancerous madness, that Phoenix and Albuquerque will not be better cities to live in when their populations are doubled again and again. They would never understand that an economic system which can only expand or expire must be false to all that is human.

So much by way of futile digression: the pattern is fixed and protest alone will not halt the iron glacier moving upon us.

No matter, it's of slight importance. Time and the winds will sooner or later bury the Seven Cities of Cibola and the ruins of the others, all of them, under dunes of glowing sand, over which blue-eyed Navajo bedouin will herd their sheep and horses, following the river in winter, the mountains in summer, and sometimes striking off across the desert toward the red canyons of Utah where great waterfalls plunge over silt-filled, ancient, mysterious dams.

Only the boldest among them, seeking visions, will camp for long in the strange country of the standing rock, far out where the spadefoot toads bellow madly in the moonlight on the edge of doomed rainpools, where the arsenic-selenium spring waits for the thirst-crazed wanderer, where the thunderstorms blast the pinnacles and cliffs, where the rust-brown floods roll down the barren washes, and where the community of the quiet deer walk at evening up glens of sandstone through tamarisk and sage toward the hidden springs of sweet, cool, still, clear, unfailing water.

## Commentary: Creative Control—Edward Abbey (and Others) on the Environment

Picture this, if you will. It is a Sunday afternoon in winter, March 12 to be precise. My wife and I are sitting in the front room of our place which rests on the eastern shore of a lake in New Hampshire. The walls of the room are dark walnut, the ceiling high and white, the rafters exposed. There are several avocado-green bookcases that hold books and other things: a potbellied mandolin that neither of us can play; an aquarium with Angel fish; a picture of a pretty child for whom, not too long ago, I tried to build a cradle. There is a Franklin stove, vintage 1875, in which a small fire burns. A lady spaniel, quite deaf now, sleeps on a hassock just under the sill of the picture window that looks out on the lake. The lake is frozen to a depth of two feet and is snow-covered. On the close bank there is an old, hollowed out maple tree which houses a family of red squirrels. I am interested in those red squirrels and would like to tell you something about them.

Red squirrels have a fondness for meat. If you put a beetle and an acorn in front of them, they would eat the beetle first and then the acorn. A gray squirrel might eat the acorn first. I know this because I happen to have a book at my side called *American Wildlife and Plants: A Guide to Wildlife Food Habits* by Martin, Zim, and Nelson. That is a pretty specialized kind of book, and it doesn't tell me much more about the red squirrel than what I have just told you. But I'll bet Edward Abbey could, because he is just about as close and careful and knowledgeable an observer of nature as I have ever read. What is it, really, that makes Abbey's nature writing so good? (I am assuming you liked him too; I hope you did, even if you are not an environmental nut like some of the rest of us.)

One thing that makes Abbey good is that he knows just about all there is to know about the desert. He has not only read a lot, he has also been there and seen and heard and touched things for himself. He knows exactly what he is talking about and because he does, he is extremely instructive. If we were to list everything he teaches us in this one chapter from *Desert Solitaire* our list would be long and would include such diverse things as the true nature of quicksand, and the life cycle of the spadefoot toad. In the hands of some writers, these materials would wind up as dry as the desert itself; but Abbey is always, it seems to me, very much aware of his reader, and this also accounts in part for his success. He does not allow himself to get bogged down in meaningless detail. He keeps things moving along, keeps changing the pace in such a way that, although we are receiving a great deal of information, we are not crushed under the weight of boredom unleashed by so many similar books. (Think of the dullest, driest, most pedantic writer you have ever read and imagine what he would do with the spadefoot toad.)

Abbey plays an active role in his materials. His hat fills up with water, gnats assault his eyes, people talk to him, he talks to them. He is real. He has opinions about things. When he wants to let us know what quicksand is like, he sticks his friend Newcomb in there and lets us see it all and hear it all firsthand. When he feels like writing a poem, he writes a poem. It may not be a very good poem, but old Abbey liked it and put it in, and we like him for doing that. And somehow, although he cares very much about the environment, and knows how much of it we have already destroyed and how perilously close we are to destroying what is left; *somehow* he manages not to preach, or lose his temper, or die of a coronary, but keeps his equanimity, his sense of humor, his wry fatalism: ". . . the pattern is fixed and protest alone will not halt the iron glacier moving upon us. No matter, it's of slight importance." Admirable. Absolutely admirable.

Now if you will remember, my wife and I are sitting in the front room of our place which rests on the eastern shore of a lake in New Hampshire. Until a few minutes ago we were spending a quiet afternoon. My wife was reading the *Times* which she bought at a newstand in Rochester. I was working on an essay due at the publisher's in three days. Then, one after another, sixteen ski-machines went by, snarling, spitting, shrieking, howling, screaming like F-100's at full throttle: one, two, three, four, five, six, seven, eight, nine, ten, eleven, twelve, thirteen, fourteen, fifteen, SIXTEEN! The red squirrels have leapt terrified into the hollow tree. The Angel fish are quaking behind the filter in the aquarium. The strings of the mandolin are vibrating. Only the spaniel is impervious; she will not raise her head until the exhaust fumes begin to filter in under the door; then she will sit up and sneeze.

"Try to control yourself," my wife tells me.

"*Bleep-bleep!*"

"It's Sunday. They're just having fun. They'll be gone tomorrow."

"*Bleep-bleep!*"

"I know, dear. You've said it all before."

"But now there's a dunderhead in a *Volkswagen*, racing after them . . ."

"That's new."

"I'm going to get some grenades."

"If you feel *that* strongly about it, why don't you write an article?"

"I've already started."

"How does it begin?"

"*People who buy ski-machines should be horsewhipped. People who sell them should be shot.*"

"I think you better read some more Abbey."

"*Bleep-bleep!*"

But my wife is right. This bellowing is not going to get those fish out from behind the aquarium filter, or those squirrels out of the hollow maple tree. And tomorrow *is* Monday. And where would I go to get a grenade anyway? Ed? Do you really think the morose and fearful are doomed to quick extinction?

P. L. S.

## 39. THE CLEVELAND WRECKING YARD

### Richard Brautigan

*Poet and author Richard Brautigan lives in San Francisco where he is fast becoming one of the brightest lights in contemporary writing. Of his work, critic John Ciardi says, "Brautigan manages effects the English novel has never produced before." Anyone inclined to doubt that is urged to read* In Watermelon Sugar, *a lovely and inventive work; and* Trout Fishing in America, *a chapter of which appears below.*

Until recently my knowledge about the Cleveland Wrecking Yard had come from a couple of friends who'd bought things there. One of them bought a huge window: the frame, glass and everything for just a few dollars. It was a fine-looking window.

Then he chopped a hole in the side of his house up on Potrero Hill and put the window in. Now he has a panoramic view of the San Francisco County Hospital.

He can practically look right down into the wards and see old magazines eroded like the Grand Canyon from endless readings. He can practically hear the patients thinking about breakfast: I hate milk, and thinking about dinner: I hate peas, and then he can watch the hospital slowly drown at night, hopelessly entangled in huge bunches of brick seaweed.

He bought that window at the Cleveland Wrecking Yard.

My other friend bought an iron roof at the Cleveland Wrecking Yard and took the roof down to Big Sur in an old station wagon and then he carried the iron roof on his back up the side of a mountain. He carried up half the roof on his back. It was no picnic. Then he bought a mule, George, from Pleasanton. George carried up the other half of the roof.

The mule didn't like what was happening at all. He lost a lot of weight because of the ticks, and the smell of the wildcats up on the plateau made him too nervous to graze there. My friend said jokingly that George had lost around two hundred pounds. The good wine country around Pleasanton in the Livermore Valley probably had looked a lot better to George than the wild side of the Santa Lucia Mountains.

*Source:* "The Cleveland Wrecking Yard" from *Trout Fishing in America* by Richard Brautigan. Copyright © 1967 by Richard Brautigan. A Seymour Lawrence Book/ Delacorte Press. Reprinted by permission of the publisher.

My friend's place was a shack right beside a huge fireplace where there had once been a great mansion during the 1920s, built by a famous movie actor. The mansion was built before there was even a road down at Big Sur. The mansion had been brought over the mountains on the backs of mules, strung out like ants, bringing visions of the good life to the poison oak, the ticks, and the salmon.

The mansion was on a promontory, high over the Pacific. Money could see farther in the 1920s, and one could look out and see whales and the Hawaiian Islands and the Kuomintang in China.

The mansion burned down years ago.

The actor died.

His mules were made into soap.

His mistresses became bird nests of wrinkles.

Now only the fireplace remains as a sort of Carthaginian homage to Hollywood.

I was down there a few weeks ago to see my friend's roof. I wouldn't have passed up the chance for a million dollars, as they say. The roof looked like a colander to me. If that roof and the rain were running against each other at Bay Meadows, I'd bet on the rain and plan to spend my winnings at the World's Fair in Seattle.

My own experience with the Cleveland Wrecking Yard began two days ago when I heard about a used trout stream they had on sale out at the Yard. So I caught the Number 15 bus on Columbus Avenue and went out there for the first time.

There were two Negro boys sitting behind me on the bus. They were talking about Chubby Checker and the Twist. They thought that Chubby Checker was only fifteen years old because he didn't have a mustache. Then they talked about some other guy who did the twist forty-four hours in a row until he saw George Washington crossing the Delaware.

"Man, that's what I call twisting," one of the kids said.

"I don't think I could twist no forty-four hours in a row," the other kid said. "That's a lot of twisting."

I got off the bus right next to an abandoned Time Gasoline filling station and an abandoned fifty-cent self-service car wash. There was a long field on one side of the filling station. The field had once been covered with a housing project during the war, put there for the shipyard workers.

On the other side of the Time filling station was the Cleveland Wrecking Yard. I walked down there to have a look at the used trout stream. The Cleveland Wrecking Yard has a very long front window filled with signs and merchandise.

There was a sign in the window advertising a laundry marking machine for $65.00. The original cost of the machine was $175.00. Quite a saving.

There was another sign advertising new and used two and three ton hoists. I wondered how many hoists it would take to move a trout stream.

There was another sign that said:

THE FAMILY GIFT CENTER,
GIFT SUGGESTIONS FOR THE ENTIRE FAMILY

The window was filled with hundreds of items for the entire family. Daddy, do you know what I want for Christmas? What, son? A bathroom. Mommy, do you know what I want for Christmas? What, Patricia? Some roofing material.

There were jungle hammocks in the window for distant relatives and dollar-ten-cent gallons of earth-brown enamel paint for other loved ones.

There was also a big sign that said:

USED TROUT STREAM FOR SALE.
MUST BE SEEN TO BE APPRECIATED.

I went inside and looked at some ship's lanterns that were for sale next to the door. Then a salesman came up to me and said in a pleasant voice, "Can I help you?"

"Yes," I said. "I'm curious about the trout stream you have for sale. Can you tell me something about it? How are you selling it?"

"We're selling it by the foot length. You can buy as little as you want or you can buy all we've got. A man came in here this morning and bought 563 feet. He's going to give it to his niece for a birthday present," the salesman said.

"We're selling the waterfalls separately of course, and the trees and birds, flowers, grass and ferns we're also selling extra. The insects we're giving away free with a minimum purchase of ten feet of stream."

"How much are you selling the stream for?" I asked.

"Six dollars and fifty-cents a foot," he said. "That's for the first hundred feet. After that it's five dollars a foot."

"How much are the birds?" I asked.

"Thirty-five cents apiece," he said. "But of course they're used. We can't guarantee anything."

"How wide is the stream?" I asked. "You said you were selling it by the length, didn't you?"

"Yes," he said. "We're selling it by the length. Its width runs between five and eleven feet. You don't have to pay anything extra for width. It's not a big stream, but it's very pleasant."

"What kinds of animals do you have?" I asked.

"We only have three deer left," he said.

"Oh . . . What about flowers?"

"By the dozen," he said.

"Is the stream clear?" I asked.

"Sir," the salesman said, "I wouldn't want you to think that we would ever sell a murky trout stream here. We always make sure they're running crystal clear before we even think about moving them."

"Where did the stream come from?" I asked.

"Colorado," he said. "We moved it with loving care. We've never damaged a trout stream yet. We treat them all as if they were china."

"You're probably asked this all the time, but how's fishing in the stream?" I asked.

"Very good," he said. "Mostly German browns, but there are a few rainbows."

"What do the trout cost?" I asked

"They come with the stream," he said. "Of course it's all luck. You never know how many you're going to get or how big they are. But the fishing's very good, you might say it's excellent. Both bait and dry fly," he said smiling.

"Where's the stream at?" I asked. "I'd like to take a look at it."

"It's around in back," he said. "You go straight through that door and then turn right until you're outside. It's stacked in lengths. You can't miss it. The waterfalls are upstairs in the used plumbing department."

"What about the animals?"

"Well, what's left of the animals are straight back from the stream. You'll see a bunch of our trucks parked on a road by the railroad tracks. Turn right on the road and follow it down past the piles of lumber. The animal shed's right at the end of the lot."

"Thanks," I said. "I think I'll look at the waterfalls first. You don't have to come with me. Just tell me how to get there and I'll find my own way."

"All right," he said. "Go up those stairs. You'll see a bunch of doors and windows, turn left and you'll find the used plumbing department. Here's my card if you need any help."

"Okay," I said. "You've been a great help already. Thanks a lot. I'll take a look around."

"Good luck," he said.

I went upstairs and there were thousands of doors there. I'd never seen so many doors before in my life. You could have built an entire city out of those doors. Doorstown. And there were enough windows up there to build a little suburb entirely out of windows. Windowville.

I turned left and went back and saw the faint glow of pearl-colored light. The light got stronger and stronger as I went farther back, and then I was in the used plumbing department, surrounded by hundreds of toilets.

The toilets were stacked on shelves. They were stacked five toilets high. There was a skylight above the toilets that made them glow like the Great Taboo Pearl of the South Sea movies.

Stacked over against the wall were the waterfalls. There were about a dozen of them, ranging from a drop of a few feet to a drop of ten or fifteen feet.

There was one waterfall that was over sixty feet long. There were tags on the pieces of the big falls describing the correct order for putting the falls back together again.

The waterfalls all had price tags on them. They were more expensive than the stream. The waterfalls were selling for $19.00 a foot.

I went into another room where there were piles of sweet-smelling lumber, glowing a soft yellow from a different color skylight above the lumber. In the shadows at the edge of the room under the sloping roof of the building were many sinks and urinals covered with dust, and there was also another waterfall about seventeen feet long, lying there in two lengths and already beginning to gather dust.

I had seen all I wanted of the waterfalls, and now I was very curious about the trout stream, so I followed the salesman's directions and ended up outside the building.

O I had never in my life seen anything like that trout stream. It was stacked in piles of various lengths: ten, fifteen, twenty feet, etc. There was one pile of hundred-foot lengths. There was also a box of scraps. The scraps were in odd sizes ranging from six inches to a couple of feet.

There was a loudspeaker on the side of the building and soft music was coming out. It was a cloudy day and seagulls were circling high overhead.

Behind the stream were big bundles of trees and bushes. They were covered with sheets of patched canvas. You could see the tops and roots sticking out the ends of the bundles.

I went up close and looked at the lengths of stream. I could see some trout in them. I saw one good fish. I saw some crawdads crawling around the rocks at the bottom.

It looked like a fine stream. I put my hand in the water. It was cold and felt good.

I decided to go around to the side and look at the animals. I saw where the trucks were parked beside the railroad tracks. I followed the road down past the piles of lumber, back to the shed where the animals were.

The salesman had been right. They were practically out of animals. About the only thing they had left in any abundance were mice. There were hundreds of mice.

Beside the shed was a huge wire birdcage, maybe fifty feet high, filled with many kinds of birds. The top of the cage had a piece of canvas over it, so the birds wouldn't get wet when it rained. There were woodpeckers and wild canaries and sparrows.

On my way back to where the trout stream was piled, I found the insects. They were inside a prefabricated steel building that was selling for eighty-cents a square foot. There was a sign over the door. It said

## INSECTS

SECTION **VII**

*Popular Culture*

# ENDINGS

Perhaps the best exit line in English is that uttered by Hamlet at his death, "The rest is silence." Everyone that writes has surely at one time or another wished he'd written it, or at least could use it. For everyone who writes must wrestle with the exit line just as vigorously as the playwright. Each poem, story, or essay must end—and the rest is, at least temporarily, silence. What lingers on is the effect of (for instance) the essay, and most writers are unusually diligent in making a good first impression (see the introduction to Section IV, "The Search For Values"), and a memorable departure. "The Simple Art of Murder," in this section, ends in a particularly powerful way and its ending is analyzed in some detail. The point that the analysis makes is one worth reiterating here: that a writer is not likely to end well unless he thinks well ahead of time about how he wants to end.

There are several standard endings, the most obvious being the one that summarizes and the one that concludes. There is a distinction. The summary merely restates succinctly what has been said as does Burt Korall's ending in "Music of Protest." The conclusion is more than a summary, however. It resolves a problem or offers a judgement based on the material that has gone before. A conclusion is the interpretation of evidence that the essay has provided. Of this, the ending of Marshall McLuhan's essay "Media Hot and Cold" is a reasonable example. The final sentence begins with "so" used here to mean "therefore" or "consequently" and we see that McLuhan is giving us a new piece of information based on that which has gone before.

The ending to Robert Brustein's essay on theater ("Three Playwrights and a Protest") is a somewhat more specific device: the rhetorical question. It leaves you in other words thinking about something. It serves a summary function, it suggests a conclusion (the phrasing of the question would make it difficult to answer Brustein's questions affirmatively), but Brustein does not have a solution to the problem he has posited in his essay, beyond a rejection of the proposals that others have made (that is, Hanley, Jones, and Albee). Brustein obviously feels that a third alternative must appear, and perhaps his ending is but a kind of beginning to another dialogue which his essay has inspired. Or so at least he might hope.

Robert Parker's essay on the mass media uses a different ploy. It invokes authority. While the Frost quote that concludes the essay is applicable (Parker is arguing for a realistic rather than idealistic approach to the evaluation of television), it is also persuasive. It puts Parker on the side of Frost and hence the angels, it acts subtly as a kind of endorsement of the essay by one of the great figures of our literature. It is a variation on the technique of ending which Franklin Roosevelt once referred to as "giving them the God business."

Beginning writers very often write elaborate endings that are simply rather ill-fashioned rehashes of what they've already said better. Experienced writers often suggest a very simple expedient. Don't write a final paragraph, or if you must, cross it out and let the final draft end without it. Tom Wolfe does this in a way. His essay contains so many charged moments that one has the feeling he could have stopped at any of the occasions when he asked rhetorically, "What if he is right?" The entire ending situation is a perfect miniature of Wolfe's technique and style (see the analysis on p. 494), intermixing profundity and mendacity, juxtaposing the new Freud with the silicone breasts, and once more raising, this final time for the reader to ponder the most meaningful of questions: "What If He's Right?"

The matter of endings is extensive; the selections here sampled are but a few examples from many. Getting an essay to end with a bang not a whimper is a matter of technique, of skill, sometimes simply of cleverness and verbal trickery. But if a writer is unable, after some thought, to fashion a powerful exit line, then perhaps he should simply stop. Like this.

# 40. THE SIMPLE ART OF MURDER

## Raymond Chandler

*Raymond Chandler was brought up and educated in England, though he was born in Chicago, Illinois. During World War I he served in the Canadian Armed Forces and after the war was an oil executive. At age 45, he turned to writing fiction. His seven novels about a private eye named Philip Marlowe elevated the hard-boiled detective novel to the level of serious art. It is Marlowe to whom Chandler clearly refers in the last pages of this essay.*

Fiction in any form has always intended to be realistic. Old-fashioned novels which now seem stilted and artificial to the point of burlesque did not appear that way to the people who first read them. Writers like Fielding and Smollett could seem realistic in the modern sense because they dealt largely with uninhibited characters, many of whom were about two jumps ahead of the police, but Jane Austen's chronicles of highly inhibited people against a background of rural gentility seem real enough psychologically. There is plenty of that kind of social and emotional hypocrisy around today. Add to it a liberal dose of intellectual pretentiousness and you get the tone of the book page in your daily paper and the earnest and famous atmosphere breathed by discussion groups in little clubs. These are the people who make best sellers, which are promotional jobs based on a sort of indirect snob appeal, carefully escorted by the trained seals of the critical fraternity, and lovingly tended and watered by certain much too powerful pressure groups whose business is selling books, although they would like you to think they are fostering culture. Just get a little behind in your payments and you will find out how idealistic they are.

The detective story for a variety of reasons can seldom be promoted. It is usually about murder and hence lacks the element of uplift. Murder, which is a frustration of the individual and hence a frustration of the race, may have, and in fact has, a good deal of sociological implication. But it has been going on too long for it to be news. If the mystery novel is at all realistic (which it very seldom is) it is written in a certain spirit of detachment; otherwise nobody but a psychopath would want to write

*Source:* "The Simple Art of Murder" from *The Simple Art of Murder.* Copyright 1950 by Raymond Chandler. Reprinted by permission of the publisher, Houghton Mifflin Co.

it or read it. The murder novel has also a depressing way of minding its own business, solving its own problems and answering its own questions. There is nothing left to discuss, except whether it was well enough written to be good fiction, and the people who make up the half-million sales wouldn't know that anyway. The detection of quality in writing is difficult enough even for those who make a career of the job, without paying too much attention to the matter of advance sales.

The detective story (perhaps I had better call it that, since the English formula still dominates the trade) has to find its public by a slow process of distillation. That it does do this, and holds on thereafter with such tenacity, is a fact; the reasons for it are a study for more patient minds than mine. Nor is it any part of my thesis to maintain that it is a vital and significant form of art. There are no vital and significant forms of art; there is only art, and precious little of that. The growth of populations has in no way increased the amount; it has merely increased the adeptness with which substitutes can be produced and packaged.

Yet the detective story, even in its most conventional form, is difficult to write well. Good specimens of the art are much rarer than good serious novels. Second-rate items outlast most of the high-velocity fiction, and a great many that should never have been born simply refuse to die at all. They are as durable as the statues in public parks and just about as dull.

This fact is annoying to people of what is called discernment. They do not like it that penetrating and important works of fiction of a few years back stand on their special shelf in the library marked "Bestsellers of Yesteryear" or something, and nobody goes near them but an occasional shortsighted customer who bends down, peers briefly and hurries away; while at the same time old ladies jostle each other at the mystery shelf to grab off some item of the same vintage with such a title as *The Triple Petunia Murder Case* or *Inspector Pinchbottle to the Rescue*. They do not like it at all that "really important books" (and some of them are too, in a way) get the frosty mitt at the reprint counter while *Death Wears Yellow Garters* is put out in editions of fifty or one hundred thousand copies on the newsstands of the country, and is obviously not there just to say goodbye.

To tell you the truth, I do not like it very much myself. In my less stilted moments I too write detective stories, and all this immortality makes just a little too much competition. Even Einstein couldn't get very far if three hundred treatises of the higher physics were published every year, and several thousand others in some form or other were hanging around in excellent condition, and being read too.

Hemingway says somewhere that the good writer competes only with the dead. The good detective story writer (there must after all be a few) competes not only with all the unburied dead but with all the hosts of the living as well. And on almost equal terms; for it is one of the qualities of this kind of writing that the thing that makes people read it never goes out of style. The hero's tie may be a little out of the mode and the good gray inspector may arrive in a dogcart instead of a streamlined sedan with siren screaming, but what he does when he gets there is the same old futzing around with timetables and bits of charred paper and who trampled the jolly old flowering arbutus under the library window.

I have, however, a less sordid interest in the matter. It seems to me that production of detective stories on so large a scale, and by writers whose immediate reward is small and whose meed of critical praise is almost nil, would not be possible at all if the job took any talent. In that sense the raised eyebrow of the critic and the shoddy merchandising of the publisher are perfectly logical. The average detective story is probably no worse than the average novel, but you never see the average novel. It doesn't get published. The average—or only slightly above average—detective story does. Not only is it published but it is sold in small quantities to rental libraries and it is read. There are even a few optimists who buy it at the full retail price of two dollars, because it looks so fresh and new and there is a picture of a corpse on the cover.

And the strange thing is that this average, more than middling dull, pooped-out piece of utterly unreal and mechanical fiction is really not very different from what are called the masterpieces of the art. It drags on a little more slowly, the dialogue is a shade grayer, the cardboard out of which the characters are cut is a shade thinner, and the cheating is a little more obvious. But it is the same kind of book. Whereas the good novel is not at all the same kind of book as the bad novel. It is about entirely different things. But the good detective story and the bad detective story are about exactly the same things, and they are about them in very much the same way. There are reasons for this too, and reasons for the reasons; there always are.

I suppose the principal dilemma of the traditional or classic or straight deductive or logic and deduction novel of detection is that for any approach to perfection it demands a combination of qualities not found in the same mind. The coolheaded constructionist does not also come across with lively characters, sharp dialogue, a sense of pace, and an acute use of observed detail. The grim logician has as much atmosphere as a drawing board. The scientific sleuth has a nice new shiny laboratory, but I'm sorry I can't remember the face. The fellow who can write you a vivid and colorful prose simply will not be bothered with the coolie labor of breaking down unbreakable alibis.

The master of rare knowledge is living psychologically in the age of the hoop skirt. If you know all you should know about ceramics and Egyptian needlework, you don't know anything at all about the police. If you know that platinum won't melt under about 3000° F. by itself, but will melt at the glance of a pair of deep blue eyes if you put it near a bar of lead, then you don't know how men make love in the twentieth century. And if you know enough about the elegant *flânerie* of the prewar French Riviera to lay your story in that locale, you don't know that a couple of capsules of barbital small enough to be swallowed will not only not kill a man—they will not even put him to sleep if he fights against them.

Every detective story writer makes mistakes, of course, and none will ever know as much as he should. Conan Doyle made mistakes which completely invalidated some of his stories, but he was a pioneer, and Sherlock Holmes after all is mostly an attitude and few dozen lines of unforgettable dialogue. It is the ladies and gentlemen of what Mr. Howard Haycraft (in his book *Murder for Pleasure*) calls the Golden Age of detective fiction that really get me down. This age is not remote. For Mr. Haycraft's purpose it starts after the First World War and lasts up to about 1930. For all practical purposes it is still here. Two thirds or three quarters of all the detective stories published still adhere to the formula the giants of this era created, perfected, polished, and sold to the world as problems in logic and deduction.

These are stern words, but be not alarmed. They are only words. Let us glance at one of the glories of the literature, an acknowledged masterpiece of the art of fooling the reader without cheating him. It is called *The Red House Mystery*, was written by A. A. Milne, and has been named by Alexander Woollcott (rather a fast man with a superlative) "one of the three best mystery stories of all time." Words of that size are not spoken lightly. The book was published in 1922 but is timeless, and might as easily have been published in July, 1939, or, with a few slight changes, last week. It ran thirteen editions and seems to have been in print, in the original format, for about sixteen years. That happens to few books of any kind. It is an agreeable book, light, amusing in the *Punch* style, written with a deceptive smoothness that is not so easy as it looks.

It concerns Mark Ablett's impersonation of his brother Robert, as a hoax on his friends. Mark is the owner of the Red House, a typical laburnum-and-lodge-gate English country house. He has a secretary who encourages him and abets him in this impersonation, and who is going to murder him if he pulls it off. Nobody around the Red House has ever seen Robert, fifteen years absent in Australia and known by repute as a no-good. A letter is talked about (but never shown) announcing Robert's arrival, and Mark hints it will not be a pleasant occasion. One afternoon, then, the supposed Robert arrives, identifies himself to a couple of servants, is shown into the study. Mark goes in after him (according to testimony at the inquest). Robert is then found dead on the floor with a bullet hole in his face, and of course Mark has vanished into thin air. Arrive the police, who suspect Mark must be the murderer, remove the debris, and proceed with the investigation—and in due course, with the inquest.

Milne is aware of one very difficult hurdle and tries as well as he can to get over it. Since the secretary is going to murder Mark, once Mark has established himself as Robert, the impersonation has to continue and fool the police. Since, also, everybody around the Red House knows Mark intimately, disguise is necessary. This is achieved by shaving off Mark's beard, roughening his hands ("not the hands of a manicured gentleman"—testimony), and the use of a gruff voice and rough manner.

But this is not enough. The cops are going to have the body and the clothes on it and whatever is in the pockets. Therefore none of this must suggest Mark. Milne therefore works like a switch engine to put over the motivation that Mark is such a thoroughly conceited performer that he dresses the part down to the socks and underwear (from all of which the secretary has removed the maker's labels), like a ham blacking himself all over to play Othello. If the reader will buy this (and the sales record shows he must have), Milne figures he is solid. Yet, however light in texture the story may be, it is offered as a problem of logic and deduction.

If it is not that, it is nothing at all. There is nothing else for it to be. If the situation is false, you cannot even accept it as a light novel, for there is no story for the light novel to be about. If the problem does not contain the elements of truth and plausibility, it is no problem; if the logic is an illusion, there is nothing to deduce. If the impersonation is impossible once the reader is told the conditions it must fulfill, then the whole thing is a fraud. Not a deliberate fraud, because Milne would not have written the story if he had known what he was up against. He is up against a number of deadly things, none of which he even considers. Nor, apparently, does the casual reader, who wants to like the story—hence takes it at its face value. But the reader is not called upon to know the facts of life when the author does not. The author is the expert in the case.

Here is what this author ignores:

1. The coroner holds formal jury inquest on a body for which no legal

competent identification is offered. A coroner, usually in a big city, will sometimes hold inquest on a body that *cannot* be identified, if the record of such an inquest has or may have a value (fire, disaster, evidence of murder). No such reason exists here, and there is no one to identify the body. Witnesses said the man said he was Robert Ablett. This is mere presumption, and has weight only if nothing conflicts with it. Identification is a condition precedent to an inquest. It is a matter of law. Even in death a man has a right to his own identity. The coroner will, wherever humanly possible, enforce that right. To neglect it would be a violation of his office.

2. Since Mark Ablett, missing and suspected of the murder, cannot defend himself, all evidence of his movements before and after the murder is vital (as also whether he has money to run away on); yet all such evidence is given by the man closest to the murder and is without corroboration. It is automatically suspect until proved true.

3. The police find by direct investigation that Robert Ablett was not well thought of in his native village. Somebody there must have known him. No such person was brought to the inquest. (The story couldn't stand it.)

4. The police know there is an element of threat in Robert's supposed visit, and that it is connected with the murder must be obvious to them. Yet they make no attempt to check Robert in Australia, or find out what character he had there, or what associates, or even if he actually came to England, and with whom. (If they had, they would have found out he had been dead three years.)

5. The police surgeon examines a body with a recently shaved beard (exposing unweathered skin) and artificially roughened hands, but it is the body of a wealthy, soft-living man, long resident in a cool climate. Robert was a rough individual and had lived fifteen years in Australia. That is the surgeon's information. It is impossible he would have noticed nothing to conflict with it.

6. The clothes are nameless, empty, and have had the labels removed. Yet the man wearing them asserted an identity. The presumption that he was not what he said he was is overpowering. Nothing whatever is done about this peculiar circumstance. It is never even mentioned as being peculiar.

7. A man is missing, a well-known local man, and a body in the morgue closely resembles him. It is impossible that the police should not at once eliminate the chance that the missing man *is* the dead man. Nothing would be easier than to prove it. Not even to think of it is incredible. It makes idiots of the police, so that a brash amateur may startle the world with a fake solution.

The detective in the case is an insouciant amateur named Anthony Gillingham, a nice lad with a cheery eye, a nice little flat in town, and that airy manner. He is not making any money on the assignment, but is always available when the local gendarmerie loses its notebook. The English police endure him with their customary stoicism, but I shudder to think what the boys down at the Homicide Bureau in my city would do to him.

There are even less plausible examples of the art than this. In *Trent's Last Case* (often called "the perfect detective story") you have to accept the premise that a giant of international finance, whose lightest frown makes Wall Street quiver like a chihuahua, will plot his own death so as to hang his secretary, and that the secretary when pinched will maintain an aristocratic silence—the old Etonian in him, maybe. I have known relatively few international financiers, but I rather think the author of this novel has (if possible) known fewer.

There is another one, by Freeman Wills Crofts (the soundest builder of them all when he doesn't get too fancy), wherein a murderer, by the aid of make-up, split-second timing and some very sweet evasive action, impersonates the man he has just killed and thereby gets him alive and distant from the place of the crime. There is one by Dorothy Sayers in which a man is murdered alone at night in his house by a mechanically released weight which works because he always turns the radio on at just such a moment, always stands in just such a position in front of it, and always bends over just so far. A couple of inches either way and the customers would get a rain check. This is what is vulgarly known as having God sit in your lap; a murderer who needs that much help from Providence must be in the wrong business.

And there is a scheme of Agatha Christie's featuring M. Hercule Poirot, that ingenious Belgian who talks in a literal translation of school-boy French. By duly messing around with his "little gray cells" M. Poirot decides that since nobody on a certain through sleeper could have done the murder alone, everybody did it together, breaking the process down into a series of simple operations like assembling an egg beater. This is the type that is guaranteed to knock the keenest mind for a loop. Only a halfwit could guess it.

There are much better plots by these same writers and by others of their school. There may be one somewhere that would really stand up under close scrutiny. It would be fun to read it, even if I did have to go back to page 47 and refresh my memory about exactly what time the second gardener potted the prize-winning tea-rose begonia. There is nothing new about these stories and nothing old. The ones I mentioned are all English because the authorities, such as they are, seem to feel that the English writers had an edge in this dreary routine and that the Americans, even the creator of Philo Vance, only make the Junior Varsity.

This, the classic detective story, has learned nothing and forgotten nothing. It is the story you will find almost any week in the big shiny magazines, handsomely illustrated, and paying due deference to virginal love and the right kind of luxury goods. Perhaps the tempo has become a trifle faster and the dialogue a little more glib. There are more frozen daiquiris and stingers and fewer glasses of crusty old port, more clothes by *Vogue* and décors by *House Beautiful*, more chic, but not more truth. We spend more time in Miami hotels and Cape Cod summer colonies and go not so often down by the old gray sundial in the Elizabethan garden.

But fundamentally it is the same careful grouping of suspects, the same utterly incomprehensible trick of how somebody stabbed Mrs. Pottington Postlethwaite III with the solid platinum poniard just as she flatted on the top note of the "Bell Song" from *Lakmé* in the presence of fifteen ill-assorted guests; the same ingénue in fur-trimmed pajamas screaming in the night to make the company pop in and out of doors and ball up the timetable; the same moody silence next day as they sit around sipping Singapore slings and sneering at each other, while the flatfeet crawl to and fro under the Persian rugs, with their derby hats on.

Personally I like the English style better. It is not quite so brittle and the people as a rule just wear clothes and drink drinks. There is more sense of background, as if Cheesecake Manor really existed all around and not just in the part the camera sees; there are more long walks over the downs and the characters don't all try to behave as if they had just been tested by MGM. The English may not always be the best writers in the world, but they are incomparably the best dull writers.

There is a very simple statement to be made about all these stories: they do not really come off intellectually as problems, and they do not come off artistically as fiction. They are too contrived, and too little aware of what goes on in the world. They try to be honest, but honesty is an art. The poor writer is dishonest without knowing it, and the fairly good one can be dishonest because he doesn't know what to be honest about. He thinks a complicated murder scheme which baffled the lazy reader, who won't be bothered itemizing the details, will also baffle the police, whose business is with details.

The boys with their feet on the desks know that the easiest murder case in the world to break is the one somebody tried to get very cute with; the one that really bothers them is the murder somebody thought of only two minutes before he pulled it off. But if the writers of this fiction wrote about the kind of murders that happen, they would also have to write about the authentic flavor of life as it is lived. And since they cannot do that, they pretend that what they do is what should be done. Which is begging the question—and the best of them know it.

In her introduction to the first *Omnibus of Crime*, Dorothy Sayers wrote: "It [the detective story] does not, and by hypothesis never can, attain the lofiest level of literary achievement." And she suggested somewhere else that this is because it is a "literature of escape" and not "a literature of expression." I do not know what the loftiest level of literary achievement is: neither did Aeschylus or Shakespeare; neither does Miss Sayers. Other things being equal, which they never are, a more powerful theme will provoke a more powerful performance. Yet some very dull books have been written about God, and some very fine ones about how to make a living and stay fairly honest. It is always a matter of who writes the stuff, and what he has in him to write it with.

As for "literature of expression" and "literature of escape"—this is critics' jargon, a use of abstract words as if they had absolute meanings. Everything written with vitality expresses that vitality: there are no dull subjects, only dull minds. All men who read escape from something else into what lies behind the printed page; the quality of the dream may be argued, but its release has become a functional necessity. All men must escape at times from the deadly rhythm of their private thoughts. It is part of the process of life among thinking beings. It is one of the things that distinguish them from the three-toed sloth; he apparently—one can never be quite sure—is perfectly content hanging upside down on a branch, not even reading Walter Lippmann. I hold no particular brief for the detective story as the ideal escape. I merely say that *all* reading for pleasure is escape, whether it be Greek, mathematics, astronomy, Benedetto Croce, or The Diary of the Forgotten Man. To say otherwise is to be an intellectual snob, and a juvenile at the art of living.

I do not think such considerations moved Miss Dorothy Sayers to her essay in critical futility.

I think what was really gnawing at Miss Sayers' mind was the slow realization that her kind of detective story was an arid formula which could not even satisfy its own implications. It was second-grade literature because it was not about the things that could make first-grade literature. If it started out to be about real people (and she could write about them—her minor characters show that), they must very soon do unreal things in order to form the artificial pattern required by the plot.

When they did unreal things, they ceased to be real themselves. They became puppets and cardboard lovers and papier-mâché villains and detectives of exquisite and impossible gentility.

The only kind of writer who could be happy with these properties was the one who did not know what reality was. Dorothy Sayers' own stories show that she was annoyed by this triteness; the weakest element in them is the part that makes them detective stories, the strongest the part which could be removed without touching the "problem of logic and deduction." Yet she could not or would not give her characters their heads and let them make their own mystery. It took a much simpler and more direct mind than hers to do that.

In *The Long Week End*, which is a drastically competent account of English life and manners in the decades following the First World War, Robert Graves and Alan Hodge gave some attention to the detective story. They were just as traditionally English as the ornaments of the Golden Age, and they wrote of the time in which these writers were almost as well known as any writers in the world. Their books in one form or another sold into the millions, and in a dozen languages. These were the people who fixed the form and established the rules and founded the famous Detection Club, which is a Parnassus of English writers of mystery. Its roster includes practically every important writer of detective fiction since Conan Doyle.

But Graves and Hodge decided that during this whole period only one first-class writer had written detective stories at all. An American, Dashiell Hammett. Traditional or not, Graves and Hodge were not fuddy-duddy connoisseurs of the second-rate; they could see what went on in the world and that the detective story of their time didn't; and they were aware that writers who have the vision and the ability to produce real fiction do not produce unreal fiction.

How original a writer Hammett really was it isn't easy to decide now, even if it mattered. He was one of a group—the only one who achieved critical recognition—who wrote or tried to write realistic mystery fiction. All literary movements are like this; some one individual is picked out to represent the whole movement; he is usually the culmination of the movement. Hammett was the ace performer, but there is nothing in his work that is not implicit in the early novels and short stories of Hemingway.

Yet, for all I know, Hemingway may have learned something from Hammett as well as from writers like Dreiser, Ring Lardner, Carl Sandburg, Sherwood Anderson, and himself. A rather revolutionary debunking of both the language and the material of fiction had been going on for some time. It probably started in poetry; almost everything does. You can take it clear back to Walt Whitman, if you like. But Hammett applied it to the detective story, and this, because of its heavy crust of English gentility and American pseudo-gentility, was pretty hard to get moving.

I doubt that Hammett had any deliberate artistic aims whatever; he was trying to make a living by writing something he had firsthand information about. He made some of it up; all writers do; but it had a basis in fact; it was made up out of real things. The only reality the English detection writers knew was the conversational accent of Surbiton and Bognor Regis. If they wrote about dukes and Venetian vases, they knew no more about them out of their own experience than the well-heeled Hollywood character knows about the French Modernists that hang in his Bel-Air Château or the semi-antique Chippendale-cum-cobbler's bench that he uses for a coffee table. Hammett took murder out of the Venetian vase and dropped it into the alley; it doesn't have to stay there forever, but it looked like a good idea to get as far as possible from Emily Post's idea of how a well-bred debutante gnaws a chicken wing.

Hammett wrote at first (and almost to the end) for people with a sharp, aggressive attitude to life. They were not afraid of the seamy side of things; they lived there. Violence did not dismay them; it was right down their street. Hammett gave murder back to the kind of people that commit it for reasons, not just to provide a corpse; and with the means at hand, not hand-wrought dueling pistols, curare and tropical fish. He put these people down on paper as they were, and he made them talk and think in the language they customarily used for these purposes.

He had style, but his audience didn't know it, because it was in a language not supposed to be capable of such refinements. They thought they were getting a good meaty melodrama written in the kind of lingo they imagined they spoke themselves. It was, in a sense, but it was much more. All language begins with speech, and the speech of common men at that, but when it develops to the point of becoming a literary medium it only looks like speech. Hammett's style at its worst was as formalized as a page of *Marius the Epicurean*; at its best it could say almost anything. I believe this style, which does not belong to Hammett or to anybody, but is the American language (and not even exclusively that any more), can say things he did not know how to say, or feel the need of saying. In his hands it had no overtones, left no echo, evoked no image beyond a distant hill.

Hammett is said to have lacked heart; yet the story he himself thought the most of is the record of a man's devotion to a friend. He was spare, frugal, hard-boiled, but he did over and over again what only the best writers can ever do at all. He wrote scenes that seemed never to have been written before.

With all this he did not wreck the formal detective story. Nobody can; production demands a form that can be produced. Realism takes too much talent, too much knowledge, too much awareness. Hammett may have loosened it up a little here, and sharpened it a little there. Certainly all but the stupidest and most meretricious writers are more conscious of their artificiality than they used to be. And he demonstrated that the detective story can be important writing. *The Maltese Falcon* may or may not be a work of genius, but an art which is capable of it is not "by hypothesis" incapable of anything. Once a detective story can be as good as this, only the pedants will deny that it *could* be even better.

Hammett did something else; he made the detective story fun to write, not an exhausting concatenation of insignificant clues. Without him there might not have been a regional mystery as clever as Percival Wilde's *Inquest*, or an ironic study as able as Raymond Postgate's *Verdict of Twelve*, or a savage piece of intellectual double-talk like Kenneth Flaring's *The Dagger of the Mind*, or a tragi-comic idealization of the murderer as in Donald Henderson's *Mr. Bowling Buys a Newspaper*, or even a gay Hollywoodian gambol like Richard Sale's *Lazarus No. 7*.

The realistic style is easy to abuse: from haste, from lack of awareness, from inability to bridge the chasm that lies between what a writer would like to be able to say and what he actually knows how to say. It is easy to fake; brutality is not strength, flipness is not wit, edge-of-the-chair writing can be as boring as flat writing; dalliance with promiscuous blondes can be very dull stuff when described by goaty young men with no other purpose in mind than to describe dalliance with promiscuous blondes. There has been so much of this sort of thing that if a character in a detective story says "Yeah," the author is automatically a Hammett imitator.

And there are still a number of people around who say that Hammett did not write detective stories at all—merely hard-boiled chronicles of mean streets with a perfunctory mystery element dropped in like the olive in a martini. These are the flustered old ladies—of both sexes (or no sex) and almost all ages—who like their murders scented with magnolia blossoms and do not care to be reminded that murder is an act of infinite cruelty, even if the perpetrators sometimes look like playboys or college professors or nice motherly women with softly graying hair.

There are also a few badly scared champions of the formal or classic mystery who think that no story is a detective story which does not pose a formal and exact problem and arrange the clues around it with neat labels on them. Such would point out, for example, that in reading *The Maltese Falcon* no one concerns himself with who killed Spade's partner, Archer (which is the only formal problem of the story), because the reader is kept thinking about something else. Yet in *The Glass Key* the reader is constantly reminded that the question is who killed Taylor Henry, and exactly the same effect is obtained—an effect of movement, intrigue, cross-purposes, and the gradual elucidation of character, which is all the detective story has any right to be about anyway. The rest is spillikins in the parlor.

But all this (and Hammett too) is for me not quite enough. The realist in murder writes of a world in which gangsters can rule nations and almost rule cities, in which hotels and apartment houses and celebrated restaurants are owned by men who made their money out of brothels, in which a screen star can be the finger man for a mob, and the nice man down the hall is a boss of the numbers racket; a world where a judge with a cellar full of bootleg liquor can send a man to jail for having a pint in his pocket, where the mayor of your town may have condoned murder as an instrument of money-making, where no man can walk down a dark street in safety because law and order are things we talk about but refrain from practicing; a world where you may witness a holdup in broad daylight and see who did it, but you will fade quickly back into the crowd rather than tell anyone, because the holdup men may have friends with long guns, or the police may not like your testimony, and in any case the shyster for the defense will be allowed to abuse and vilify you in open court, before a jury of selected morons, without any but the most perfunctory interference from a political judge.

It is not a fragrant world, but it is the world you live in, and certain writers with tough minds and a cool spirit of detachment can make very interesting and even amusing patterns out of it. It is not funny that a man should be killed, but it is sometimes funny that he should be killed for so little, and that his death should be the coin of what we call civilization. All this still is not quite enough.

In everything that can be called art there is a quality of redemption. It may be pure tragedy, if it is high tragedy, and it may be pity and irony, and it may be the raucous laughter of the strong man. But down these mean streets a man must go who is not himself mean, who is neither tarnished nor afraid. The detective in this kind of story must be such a man. He is the hero; he is everything. He must be a complete man and a common man and yet an unusual man. He must be, to use a rather weathered phrase, a man of honor—by instinct, by inevitability, without thought of it, and certainly without saying it. He must be the best man in his world and a good enough man for any world. I do not care much about his private life; he is neither a eunuch nor a satyr; I think he might seduce a duchess and I am quite sure he would not spoil a virgin; if he is a man of honor in one thing, he is that in all things.

He is a relatively poor man, or he would not be a detective at all. He is a common man or he could not go among common people. He has a sense of character, or he would not know his job. He will take no man's money dishonestly and no man's insolence without a due and dispassionate revenge. He is a lonely man and his pride is that you will treat him as a proud man or be very sorry you ever saw him. He talks as the man of his age talks—that is, with rude wit, a lively sense of the grotesque, a disgust for sham, and a contempt for pettiness.

The story is this man's adventure in search of a hidden truth, and it would be no adventure if it did not happen to a man fit for adventure. He has a range of awareness that startles you, but it belongs to him by right, because it belongs to the world he lives in. If there were enough like him, the world would be a very safe place to live in, without becoming too dull to be worth living in.

**Commentary: Plan Ahead**

As a prose stylist Raymond Chandler may not be peerless, but his peers are hardly legion. While style would seem a simple matter, it is not. It is the articulation of a man, and how one controls (though it doesn't necessarily compel) how one writes. One reason that Chandler writes this way is that Chandler thinks this way, but the writing is not automatic. It is the conscious creation of a man who is concerned not only with expressing himself but with expressing an idea, and has exercised his considerable talent to a considerable degree to do so. Consider the third paragraph from the end of the essay.

"In everything that can be called art there is a quality of redemption. It may be pure tragedy, if it is high tragedy, and it may be pity and irony, and it may be the raucous laughter of the strong man. But down these mean streets a man must go who is not himself mean, who is neither tarnished nor afraid. The detective in this kind of story must be such a man. He is the hero; he is everything. He must be a complete man and a common man and yet an unusual man. He must be, to use a rather weathered phrase, a man of honor—by instinct, by inevitability, without thought of it, and certainly without saying it. He must be the best man in his world and a good enough man for any world. I do not care much about his private life; he is neither a eunuch nor a satyr; I think he might seduce a duchess and I am quite sure he would not spoil a virgin; if he is a man of honor in one thing, he is that in all things."

Parts of the third sentence have been lifted out of context to serve as the title for at least two books (for example, Piri Thomas's novel of New York Barrio life, *Down These Mean Streets*) and the entire paragraph is often and justly celebrated as a triumph of style. One of the charms of the sentence is that all of the multiple meanings of the phrase "mean streets" are available and appropriate to what the paragraph is saying. The phrase is just right. But it was no happy accident. Chandler prepared for it a long time back by planting the phrase early in the essay. Some two pages earlier he says of the kind of characters Dashiell Hammett wrote of, "Violence did not dismay them; it was right down their street." And one page prior he tells us that some think Hammett wrote only "hardboiled chronicles of mean streets," and two paragraphs earlier he comments that "the realist in murder writes of a world in which . . . no man can walk down a dark street in safety. . . ." In other words Chandler knew precisely where he was going back at least as far as his paragraph 45. Perhaps the phrase "right down their street" gave rise to the phrase "mean streets," and its repetition. Or perhaps Chandler had thought of the phrase "mean streets" as he walked down one ten years ago and had saved it for the right time. Whatever, it is clear that he carefully engineered its progress to the culminating statement. To recognize this is to recognize that an essay is not, any more than a novel or a poem, a series of happy coincidences. It is the careful work of a man who understands not only what he's writing now but what he's going to say later. That is skill—not art, nor even personality.

Someone who had read this essay without reading Chandler's would be prone to suspect Chandler of mechanistic and repetitious writing. But only if one had read the analysis, not the work. For Chandler's skill is such that in each instance of the use of the "street" figure it is so appropriate and natural to the context that few readers are conscious of its previous use when they encounter it the last time, but simultaneously they are not puzzled, they do not ask: What mean streets? The reference, "down these mean streets" is after all remote (back to the previous page). But the image of a civilization scarred with shabby and hostile streets has become part of our consciousness as we read, and when we come to the reference it is perfectly natural.

So compelling is Chandler's style, in fact, that we may be convinced not because he's reasonable but because he's evocative. You might analyze the paragraph quoted above in terms of its logic: how much is assertion, how much is evidence. What Chandler has done in this essay, is quite simply to create a speaker whose wit, grace, irreverence, and charm we so admire that we are much inclined to accept his opinions as though they were fact, and share them with the vigor of a small boy when he agrees with his worshipped older brother. But this is the subject for another essay, this one having said what it set out to. And that is quite enough.

R. B. P.

# 41. THREE PLAYWRIGHTS AND A PROTEST

## Robert Brustein

*The Dean of the School of Drama at Yale, and the holder of a Ph. D. from Columbia, Robert Brustein is one of the most respected drama critics now writing. His books include* The Theater of Revolt: Studies in the Modern Drama, *and* Seasons of Discontent *from which this selection is taken.*

Three new plays by the younger generation of American dramatists compel a protest from me.

*Slow Dance on the Killing Ground.* William Hanley's melodrama has one arresting moment, which occurs right after the rise of the curtain. The scene is a neighborhood candy store on a dark, deserted street; the proprietor, a middle-aged German, is taking inventory. Suddenly, a Negro enters, obviously eluding pursuers, dressed in a black cape, string tie, sneakers, and dark glasses. As played by the gifted Clarence Williams III, he is a sinister figure, hunched like a monkey, and ambulating with the balletic grace of a junkie Charlie Chaplin. The most conspicuous element in his costume is an umbrella, the point of which has been sharpened for a kill, and it is not long before he is menacing the storekeeper with this improvised weapon, muttering wild irrelevancies in a hip, auto-didactic verbal style. Accounts of the psychopathic killer known as the Umbrella Man have prepared us for the brutal attack which must follow—but the expected blow never falls. Instead, the Negro sits down, removes his glasses, changes his ominous tone, and—employing a highly eloquent vocabulary (he has, he tells us, an IQ of 187)—initiates a three-hour talkathon, quoting from Gide and Kafka, and analyzing the roots of his own behavior: he suffers from insufficient mother love!

Mr. Hanley's game might be called Truth without Consequences; his rules are to evoke an evil reality, culled from some recent headline, and then to soften this reality with psychological bromides, self-conscious motive-mongering, and sentimental evasions. This technique he applies not only to Negro crime but to a large number of our current theatrical obsessions: Jewish victimization, German guilt, Appearance versus Reality, the Need for Commitment to Something Higher than the Self, and (with the entrance later of a young girl in search of an abortion) the Importance of Loving the Life Inside Your Body. Mr. Hanley's play, in short, is like a catalogue of contemporary Broadway themes and conventions, but in order to include them all, the playwright is forced to sacrifice consistency of character, unity of form, and logical continuity. What begins as a melodrama eventually becomes a disquisitory debate, a sex comedy, and a soap opera: each of the three acts seems totally independent of the other two; and the characters must function in a host of different roles, the Umbrella Man, for example, acting as confessor, confidant, orator, psychological counselor, social worker, and judge, in sequence. At the end, he returns to his original role as menace, when he reveals that he has murdered his mother. But by this time, all credibility has been swallowed up in the drama's sententious molasses, where every speech is italicized, and every line is a curtain line. This is Mr. Hanley's first Broadway effort, and the significant thing about it is how a dramatist so new to the street could have so quickly become privy to all its commercial secrets.

*The Slave* and *The Toilet*. While Hanley's play reveals a jaded talent, these two karate blows by LeRoi Jones display no talent at all—they are inspired primarily by race hatred. Larry Rivers' set for *The Toilet* consists of seven urinals; the scene is the boys' john of a predominantly Negro high school. There students congregate, during pauses in the educational process, to exchange insults and obscenities, and to gang up on unprotected students, usually "whiteys." The major victim of *The Toilet* is a Puerto Rican homosexual who, having sent a love letter to one of the Negroes, is brutally beaten, and then tossed, bleeding and unconscious, into one of the urinals. The Negro he loves—and who helped to mug him—returns surreptitiously at the end to cradle the victim's head in his lap and to sob over his prostrate form. This maudlin conclusion reveals a soft chink in the author's spiky armor, but still the play is not a drama but a psychodrama, designed for the acting out of sado-masochistic racial fantasies.

*The Slave* projects these fantasies into a Genet-like war between White and Black, which the Negroes are on the verge of winning. The play concerns the visit of the Negro military leader, once a poet and intellectual, to the home of his former (white) wife and her present husband, a white university professor. Before long, the Negro has, predictably, maligned the professor's liberalism and his manhood ("Professor No-Dick"), rabbit-punched him to the ground, and emptied his revolver into his body, while leaving the woman lying dead under the debris of her exploded home. The play, to say the least, is out of control, and its language is full of semi-literate blather ("I have killed for all times any creative impulse I will ever have by the depravity of my murderous philosophies"). The decay of Western culture—to which the playwright frequently alludes in *The Slave*—is nowhere better exemplified than in the unwarranted favor this culture has lavished on LeRoi Jones, because he has shown little theatrical purpose beyond the expression of a raging chauvinism, and few theatrical gifts beyond a capacity to record the graffiti scrawled on men's room walls.

*Tiny Alice.* Edward Albee has called his new play a "mystery story," a description which applies as well to its content as to its genre. The work is certainly very mystifying, full of dark hints and riddling allusions, but since it is also clumsy and contrived, and specious in the extreme, the mystery that interested me most was whether the author was kidding his audience or kidding himself. *Tiny Alice* may well turn out to be a huge joke on the American culture industry; then again, it may turn out to be a typical product of that industry. The hardest thing to determine about "camp" literature, movies, and painting is the extent of the author's sincerity. A hoax is being perpetrated, no doubt of that, but is this intentional or not? Is the contriver inside or outside his own fraudulent creation? Does Andy Warhol really believe in the artistic validity of his Brillo boxes? *Tiny Alice* is a much more ambitious work than the usual variety of camp, but it shares the same ambiguity of motive. For while some of Albee's obscurity is pure playfulness, designed to con the spectator into looking for nonexistent meanings, some is obviously there for the sake of a sham profundity in which the author apparently believes.

My complaint is that Albee has not created profundity, he has only borrowed the appearance of it. In *Tiny Alice*, he is once again dealing with impersonation—this time as a metaphor for religious faith—and once again is doing most of the impersonating himself. The central idea of the play—which treats religious ritual as a form of stagecraft and playacting—comes from Jean Genet's *The Balcony*; its initial device—which involves a wealthy woman handing over a fortune in return for the sacrifice of a man's life—comes from Duerrenmatt's *The Visit*; its symbolism —revolving around mysterious castles, the union of sacred and profane, and the agony of modern Christ figures—is largely taken from Strindberg's *A Dream Play*; and its basic tone—a metaphysical rumble arising out of libations, litanies, and ceremonies created by a shadowy hieratic trio—is directly stolen from T. S. Eliot's *The Cocktail Party*. The play, in short, is vitually a theatrical echo chamber, with reverberations of Graham Greene, Enid Bagnold, and Tennessee Williams being heard as well; but Albee's manipulation of these sources owes more to literature than to life, while his metaphysical enigmas contribute less to thematic perception than to atmospheric fakery.

To approach *Tiny Alice* as a coherent work of art, therefore, would be a mistake, since, in my opinion, most of it is meaningless—a frozen portent without an animating event. There are thematic arrows, to be sure, planted throughout the play: allusions to the imperfectibility of human knowledge, appearance and reality, the unreachableness of God, but all these ultimately point down dead-end streets, or are bent and twisted by leaden paradoxes. Let me, in consequence, try to discharge my duties to the play simply by outlining the plot.

In return for a bequest of two billion dollars—presented to a waspish Cardinal by a bitchy Lawyer who used to be his schoolfellow—a lay brother in the Roman church named Julian is sent to the home of Alice, the millionairess who donated the money. Alice later turns out to be a priestess in the service of a god (or goddess) named Alice, for whom she is acting as surrogate. She is also identified with the Virgin Mother (the Lawyer has suggestions of Satan), even though she seems to have slept with everybody, including her butler (named Butler), who functions as a kind of hierophant. Alice, Lawyer, and Butler all live in a gigantic castle, which represents the universe. Inside one room is a perfect miniature model of this castle, called "The Wonders of the World," and inside the "Wonders," presumably, is another miniature—and so forth, on the principle of Chinese boxes. The possibility arises that the actual castle is merely a model within an even larger room, which is itself only a miniature, *ad infinitum*. The "Wonders," however, is not only a symbol of the expanding universe, but also an altar, to which the mysterious threesome pray, and inside which the god Alice may reside (thus, "tiny" Alice).

Slowly, it is revealed that this priestly trio is preparing Julian for a ritual sacrifice. He will eventually be forced to re-enact the death of Christ, a role for which he qualifies not by virtue of any moral beauty, visionary power, or special sanctity, but rather because of certain pathological attributes. He longs to debase himself, is subject to hallucinations, and enjoys masochistic fantasies of being bloodied by gladiators and eaten by lions. His martyrdom, however, comes in quite a different way. First, he is seduced by Alice; then she marries him; then deserts him; and finally the Lawyer shoots him. Now the Passion begins, accompanied by a hailstorm of religious symbols. Julian, dying, is held, like Jesus in the Pietà, by a blue-cloaked Alice, who begs him to accept the godhead of Alice. Julian refuses at first, and is left in isolation. Then, in what may be one of the longest death scenes on record (it is surely among the dullest), he cries "Alice, oh Alice, why hast thou forsaken me?" and stumbles—arms outstretched in crucifixion—against the "Wonders of the World." Accepting Alice at the last, he expires, to the accompaniment of heartbeats and breathing amplified over a loudspeaker.

The only thing that might redeem a concept like this from its own pretentiousness is some kind of theatrical adroitness; but I regret to say that Albee's customary ingenuity has deserted him here. The language, first of all, is surprisingly windy, slack, sodden, and repetitive; the jokes are childishly prurient ("The organ is in need of use," says the sexually undernourished Julian upon visiting the chapel); and the usual electricity of an Albee quarrel has degenerated—when it is employed in the opening scene between the Cardinal and the Lawyer—into mere nagging. Furthermore, Albee has not been able to exploit his own devices sufficiently. The miniature castle is a good conceit; but it functions more for obfuscation than for theatrical effect, being used to good advantage only once (when the chapel catches fire). And finally, the play vacillates between excessive fruitiness and excessive staginess, whether Julian is being enfolded within the wrapper of the naked Alice (and disappearing somewhere near her genital region), or being gunned down by the Lawyer in a manner reminiscent of Victorian melodrama.

As for the production, it staggers under the ponderousness of the play. John Gielgud is probably one of the few actors in the world capable of disguising the ludicrousness of his role; but he is forced to maintain a pitch of exaltation, bordering on hysteria, throughout the entire evening, and even he cannot prevent his speeches from sounding monotonous. Irene Worth, the most charming of actresses, is warm and compassionate as Alice, and John Heffernan has a wry, laconic quality as the butler, but the production, as a whole, does not work, for the director, Alan Schneider, has been unable to find a convincing histrionic equivalent for the portentous style of the writing. Only William Ritman's setting, a massive affair with huge wooden doors and expansive playing area, is really very satisfying, for it supplies that sense of solidity and substantiality that the play so sorely lacks.

These three plays are fairly representative of the kind of theatre being produced by our younger dramatists, and therein lies my protest: Whatever their superficial differences, they are all possessed by a subterranean nihilism. Hanley, Jones, and Albee seem to be preoccupied with important contemporary concerns—the position of minority groups, the Negro revolution, Existential *Angst*, the loss of faith—but some essential commitment is seriously lacking, and the central questions are invariably skirted. What results is less an artistic quest than a fashionable posture or personal exhibition, with the playwright producing not masterpieces but conversation pieces. This, to be sure, is the characteristic art of our time. Now that the cultural revolution has become an arm of big business, the mass media, and the fashion magazines, values have all but disappeared from artistic creation, and a crowd of hipsters and their agents are cynically exploiting the fears and pretensions of a semi-educated public. But while the nihilism of Pop Art, for example, is relatively open, the theatre continues to simulate values and feign commitments: it will not be long before these masks fall too. The collapse of the original Lincoln Center Repertory Company signifies the end of the theatre of the thirties, and the extinction of its dreams—but I dread the nightmare that is coming to take its place. Must we choose between a discredited Establishment and a careerist avant-garde? Are the only alternatives to be between the collapsed idealism of the old and the secret cynicism of the new?

## 42. MEDIA HOT AND COLD

### Marshall McLuhan

*Marshall McLuhan, who holds a Ph. D. from Cambridge University, has expanded well beyond the traditional limits of academic publication with a series of books on communication that has brought him to national prominence. Among them are* The Gutenberg Galaxy, The Mechanical Bride, The Medium Is the Message, *and* Understanding Media: The Extension of Man *from which the following selection was taken.*

"The rise of the waltz," explained Curt Sachs in the *World History of the Dance*, "was a result of that longing for truth, simplicity, closeness to nature, and primitivism, which the last two-thirds of the eighteenth century fulfilled." In the century of jazz we are likely to overlook the emergence of the waltz as a hot and explosive human expression that broke through the formal feudal barriers of courtly and choral dance styles.

There is a basic principle that distinguishes a hot medium like radio from a cool one like the telephone, or a hot medium like the movie from a cool one like TV. A hot medium is one that extends one single sense in "high definition." High definition is the state of being well filled with data. A photograph is, visually, "high definition." A cartoon is "low definition," simply because very little visual information is provided. Telephone is a cool medium, or one of low definition, because the ear is given a meager amount of information. And speech is a cool medium of low definition, because so little is given and so much has to be filled in by the listener. On the other hand, hot media do not leave so much to be filled in or completed by the audience. Hot media are, therefore, low in participation, and cool media are high in participation or completion by the audience. Naturally, therefore, a hot medium like radio has very different effects on the user from a cool medium like the telephone.

A cool medium like hieroglyphic or ideogrammic written characters has very different effects from the hot and explosive medium of the phonetic alphabet. The alphabet, when pushed to a high degree of abstract visual intensity, became typography. The printed word with its specialist intensity burst the bonds of medieval corporate guilds and monasteries, creating extreme individualist patterns of enterprise and monopoly. But the typical reversal occurred when extremes of monopoly brought back the corporation, with its impersonal empire over many lives. The hotting-up of the medium of writing to repeatable print intensity led to nationalism and the religious wars of the sixteenth century. The heavy and unwieldy media, such as stone, are time binders. Used for writing, they are very cool indeed, and serve to unify the ages; whereas paper is a hot medium that serves to unify spaces horizontally, both in political and entertainment empires.

Any hot medium allows of less participation than a cool one, as a lecture makes for less participation than a seminar, and a book for less than dialogue. With print many earlier forms were excluded from life and art, and many were given strange new intensity. But our own time is crowded with examples of the principle that the hot form excludes, and the cool one includes. When ballerinas began to dance on their toes a century ago, it was felt that the art of the ballet had acquired a new "spirituality." With this new intensity, male figures were excluded from ballet. The role of women had also become fragmented with the advent of industrial specialism and the explosion of home functions into laundries, bakeries, and hospitals on the periphery of the community. Intensity or high definition engenders specialism and fragmentation in living as in entertainment, which explains why any intense experience must be "forgotten," "censored," and reduced to a very cool state before it can be "learned" or assimilated. The Freudian "censor" is less of a moral function than an indispensable condition of learning. Were we to accept fully and directly every shock to our various structures of awareness, we would soon be nervous wrecks, doing double-takes and pressing panic buttons every minute. The "censor" protects our central system of values, as it does our physical nervous system by simply cooling off the onset of experience a great deal. For many people, this cooling system brings on a lifelong state of psychic *rigor mortis*, or of somnambulism, particularly observable in periods of new technology.

An example of the disruptive impact of a hot technology succeeding a cool one is given by Robert Theobald in *The Rich and the Poor*. When Australian natives were given steel axes by the missionaries, their culture, based on the stone axe, collapsed. The stone axe had not only been scarce but had always been a basic status symbol of male importance. The missionaries provided quantities of sharp steel axes and gave them to women and children. The men had even to borrow these from the women, causing a collapse of male dignity. A tribal and feudal hierarchy of traditional kind collapses quickly when it meets any hot medium of the mechanical, uniform, and repetitive kind. The medium of money or wheel or writing, or any other form of specialist speedup of exchange and information, will serve to fragment a tribal structure. Similarly, a very much greater speed-up, such as occurs with electricity, may serve to restore a tribal pattern of intense involvement such as took place with the introduction of radio in Europe, and is now tending to happen as a result of TV in America. Specialist technologies detribalize. The non-specialist electric technology retribalizes. The process of upset resulting from a new distribution of skills is accompanied by much culture lag in which people feel compelled to look at new situations as if they were old ones, and come up with ideas of "population explosion" in an age of implosion. Newton, in an age of clocks, managed to present the physical universe in the image of a clock. But poets like Blake were far ahead of Newton in their response to the challenge of the clock. Blake spoke of the need to be delivered "from single vision and Newton's sleep," knowing very well that Newton's response to the challenge of the new mechanism was itself merely a mechanical repetition of the challenge. Blake saw Newton and Locke and others as hypnotized Narcissus types quite unable to meet the challenge of mechanism. W. B. Yeats gave the full Blakean version of Newton and Locke in a famous epigram:

Locke sank into a swoon;
The garden died;
God took the spinning jenny
Out of his side.

Yeats presents Locke, the philosopher of mechanical and lineal associationism, as hypnotized by his own image. The "garden," or unified consciousness, ended. Eighteenth-century man got an extension of himself in the form of the spinning machine that Yeats endows with its full sexual significance. Woman, herself, is thus seen as a technological extension of man's being.

Blake's counterstrategy for his age was to meet mechanism with organic myth. Today, deep in the electric age, organic myth is itself a simple and automatic response capable of mathematical formulation and expression, without any of the imaginative perception of Blake about it. Had he encountered the electric age, Blake would not have met its challenge with a mere repetition of electric form. For myth *is* the instant vision of a complex process that ordinarily extends over a long period. Myth is contraction or implosion of any process, and the instant speed of electricity confers the mythic dimension on ordinary industrial and social action today. We *live* mythically but continue to think fragmentarily and on single planes.

Scholars today are acutely aware of a discrepancy between their ways of treating subjects and the subject itself. Scriptural scholars of both the Old and New Testaments frequently say that while their treatment must be linear, the subject is not. The subject treats of the relations between God and man, and between God and the world, and of the relations between man and his neighbor—all these subsist together, and act and react upon one another at the same time. The Hebrew and Eastern mode of thought tackles problem and resolution, at the outset of a discussion, in a way typical of oral societies in general. The entire message is then traced and retraced, again and again, on the rounds of a concentric spiral with seeming redundancy. One can stop anywhere after the first few sentences and have the full message, if one is prepared to "dig" it. This kind of plan seems to have inspired Frank Lloyd Wright in designing the Guggenheim Art Gallery on a spiral, concentric basis. It is a redundant form inevitable to the electric age, in which the concentric pattern is imposed by the instant quality, and overlay in depth, of electric speed. But the concentric with its endless intersection of planes is necessary for insight. In fact, it is the technique of insight, and as such is necessary for media study, since no medium has its meaning or existence alone, but only in constant interplay with other media.

The new electric structuring and configuring of life more and more encounters the old lineal and fragmentary procedures and tools of analysis from the mechanical age. More and more we turn from the content of messages to study total effect. Kenneth Boulding put this matter in *The Image* by saying, "The meaning of a message is the change which it produces in the image." Concern with *effect* rather than *meaning* is a basic change of our electric time, for effect involves the total situation, and not a single level of information movement. Strangely, there is recognition of this matter of effect rather than information in the British idea of libel: "The greater the truth, the greater the libel."

The effect of electric technology had at first been anxiety. Now it appears to create boredom. We have been through the three stages of alarm, resistance, and exhaustion that occur in every disease or stress of life, whether individual or collective. At least, our exhausted slump after the first encounter with the electric has inclined us to expect new problems. However, backward countries that have experienced little permeation with our own mechanical and specialist culture are much better able to confront and to understand electric technology. Not only have backward and nonindustrial cultures no specialist habits to overcome in their encounter with electromagnetism, but they have still much of their traditional oral culture that has the total, unified "field" character of our new electromagnetism. Our old industrialized areas, having eroded their oral traditions automatically, are in the position of having to rediscover them in order to cope with the electric age.

In terms of the theme of media hot and cold, backward countries are cool, and we are hot. The "city slicker" is hot, and the rustic is cool. But in terms of the reversal of procedures and values in the electric age, the past mechanical time was hot, and we of the TV age are cool. The waltz was a hot, fast mechanical dance suited to the industrial time in its moods of pomp and circumstance. In contrast, the Twist is a cool, involved and chatty form of improvised gesture. The jazz of the period of the hot new media of movie and radio was hot jazz. Yet jazz of itself tends to be a casual dialogue form of dance quite lacking in the repetitive and mechanical forms of the waltz. Cool jazz came in quite naturally after the first impact of radio and movie had been absorbed.

In the special Russian issue of *Life* magazine for September 13, 1963, it is mentioned in Russian restaurants and night clubs, "though the Charleston is tolerated, the Twist is taboo." All this is to say that a country in the process of industrialization is inclined to regard hot jazz as consistent with its developing programs. The cool and involved form of the Twist, on the other hand, would strike such a culture at once as retrograde and incompatible with its new mechanical stress. The Charleston, with its aspect of a mechanical doll agitated by strings, appears in Russia as an avant-garde form. We, on the other hand, find the *avant-garde* in the cool and the primitive, with its promise of depth involvement and integral expression.

The "hard" sell and the "hot" line become mere comedy in the TV age, and the death of all the salesmen at one stroke of the TV axe has turned the hot American culture into a cool one that is quite unacquainted with itself. America, in fact, would seem to be living through the reverse process that Margaret Mead described in *Time* magazine (September 4, 1954): "There are too many complaints about society having to move too fast to keep up with the machine. There is great advantage in moving fast if you move completely, if social, educational, and recreational changes keep pace. You must change the whole pattern at once and the whole group together—and the people themselves must decide to move."

Margaret Mead is thinking here of change as uniform speed-up of motion or a uniform hotting-up of temperatures in backward societies. We are certainly coming within conceivable range of a world automatically controlled to the point where we could say, "Six hours less radio in Indonesia next week or there will be a great falling off in literary attention." Or, "We can program twenty more hours of TV in South Africa next week to cool down the tribal temperature raised by radio last week." Whole cultures could now be programmed to keep their emotional climate stable in the same way that we have begun to know something about maintaining equilibrium in the commercial economies of the world.

In the merely personal and private sphere we are often reminded of how changes of tone and attitude are demanded of different times and seasons in order to keep situations in hand. British clubmen, for the sake of companionship and amiability, have long excluded the hot topics of religion and politics from mention inside the highly participational club. In the same vein, W. H. Auden wrote, ". . . this season the man of goodwill will wear his heart up his sleeve, not on it. . . . the honest manly style is today suited only to Iago" (Introduction to John Betjeman's *Slick But Not Streamlined*). In the Renaissance, as print technology hotted up the social *milieu* to a very high point, the gentleman and the courtier (Hamlet—Mercutio stye) adopted, in contrast, the casual and cool nonchalance of the playful and superior being. The Iago allusion of Auden reminds us that Iago was the *alter ego* and assistant of the intensely earnest and very non-nonchalant General Othello. In imitation of the earnest and forthright general, Iago hotted up his own image and wore his heart on his sleeve, until General Othello read him loud and clear as "honest Iago," a man after his own grimly earnest heart.

Throughout *The City in History*, Lewis Mumford favors the cool or casually structured towns over the hot and intensely filled-in cities. The great period of Athens, he feels, was one during which most of the democratic habits of village life and participation still obtained. Then burst forth the full variety of human expression and exploration such as was later impossible in highly developed urban centers. For the highly developed situation is, by definition, low in opportunities of participation, and rigorous in its demands of specialist fragmentation from those who would control it. For example, what is known as "job enlargement" today in business and in management consists in allowing the employee more freedom to discover and define his function. Likewise, in reading a detective story the reader participates as co-author simply because so much has been left out of the narrative. The open-mesh silk stocking is far more sensuous than the smooth nylon, just because the eye must act as hand in filling in and completing the image, exactly as in the mosaic of the TV image.

Douglas Cater in *The Fourth Branch of Government* tells how the men of the Washington press bureaus delighted to complete or fill in the blank of Calvin Coolidge's personality. Because he was so like a mere cartoon, they felt the urge to complete his image for him and his public. It is instructive that the press applied the word "cool" to Cal. In the very sense of a cool medium, Calvin Coolidge was so lacking in any articulation of data in his public image that there was only one word for him. He was real cool. In the hot 1920s, the hot press medium found Cal very cool and rejoiced in his lack of image, since it compelled the participation of the press in filling in an image of him for the public. By contrast, F.D.R. was a hot press agent, himself a rival of the newspaper medium and one who delighted in scoring off the press on the rival hot medium of radio. Quite in contrast, Jack Paar ran a cool show for the cool TV medium, and became a rival for the patrons of the night spots and their allies in the gossip columns. Jack Paar's war with the gossip columnists was a weird example of clash between a hot and cold medium such as had occurred with the "scandal of the rigged TV quiz shows." The rivalry between the hot press and radio media, on one hand, and TV on the other, for the hot ad buck, served to confuse and to over-heat the issues in the affair that pointlessly involved Charles van Doren.

An Associated Press story from Santa Monica, California, August 9, 1962, reported how

"Nearly 100 traffic violators watched a police traffic accident film today to atone for their violations. Two had to be treated for nausea and shock. . . .

"Viewers were offered a $5.00 reduction in fines if they agreed to see the movie, *Signal* 30, made by Ohio State police.

"It showed twisted wreckage and mangled bodies and recorded the screams of accident victims."

Whether the hot film medium using hot content would cool off the hot drivers is a moot point. But it does concern any understanding of media. The effect of hot media treatment cannot include much empathy or participation at any time. In this connection an insurance ad that featured Dad in an iron lung surrounded by a joyful family group did more to strike terror into the reader than all the warning wisdom in the world. It is a question that arises in connection with capital punishment. Is a severe penalty the best deterrent to serious crime? With regard to the bomb and the cold war, is the threat of massive retaliation the most effective means to peace? Is it not evident in every human situation that is pushed to a point of saturation that some precipitation occurs? When all the available resources and energies have been played up in an organ-ism or in any structure there is some kind of reversal of pattern. The spectacle of brutality used as deterrent can brutalize. Brutality used in sports may humanize under some conditions, at least. But with regard to the bomb and retaliation as deterrent, it is obvious that numbness is the result of any prolonged terror, a fact that was discovered when the fallout shelter program was broached. The price of eternal vigilance is indifference.

Nevertheless, it makes all the difference whether a hot medium is used in a hot or a cool culture. The hot radio medium used in cool or non-literate cultures has a violent effect, quite unlike its effect, say in England or America, where radio is felt as entertainment. A cool or low literacy culture cannot accept hot media like movies or radio as entertainment. They are, at least, as radically upsetting for them as the cool TV medium has proved to be for our high literacy world.

And as for the cool war and the hot bomb scare, the cultural strategy that is desperately needed is humor and play. It is play that cools off the hot situations of actual life by miming them. Competitive sports between Russia and the West will hardly serve that purpose of relaxation. Such sports are inflammatory, it is plain. And what we consider entertainment or fun in our media inevitably appears as violent political agitation to a cool culture.

One way to spot the basic difference between hot and cold media uses is to compare and contrast a broadcast of a symphony performance with a broadcast of a symphony rehearsal. Two of the finest shows ever released by the CBC were of Glenn Gould's procedure in recording piano recitals, and Igor Stravinsky's rehearsing the Toronto symphony in some of his new work. A cool medium like TV, when really used, demands this involvement in process. The neat tight package is suited to hot media, like radio and gramophone. Francis Bacon never tired of contrasting hot and cool prose. Writing in "methods" or complete packages, he contrasted with writing in aphorisms, or single observations such as "Revenge is a kind of wild justice." The passive consumer wants packages, but those, he suggested, who are concerned in pursuing knowledge and in seeking causes will resort to aphorisms, just because they are incomplete and require participation in depth.

The principle that distinguishes hot and cold media is perfectly embodied in the folk wisdom: "Men seldom make passes at girls who wear glasses." Glasses intensify the outward-going vision, and fill in the feminine image exceedingly, Marion the Librarian notwithstanding. Dark glasses, on the other hand, create the inscrutable and inaccessible image that invites a great deal of participation and completion.

Again, in a visual and highly literate culture, when we meet a person for the first time his visual appearance dims out the sound of the name, so that in self-defense we add: "How do you spell your name?" Whereas, in an ear culture, the *sound* of a man's name is the overwhelming fact, as Joyce knew when he said in *Finnegans Wake*, "Who gave you that numb?" For the name of a man is a numbing blow from which he never recovers.

Another vantage point from which to test the difference between hot and cold media is the practical joke. The hot literary medium excludes the practical and participant aspect of the joke so completely that Constance Rourke, in her *American Humor*, considers it as no joke at all. To literary people, the practical joke with its total physical involvement is as distasteful as the pun that derails us from the smooth and uniform progress that is typographic order. Indeed, to the literary person who is quite unaware of the intensely abstract nature of the typographic medium, it is the grosser and participant forms of art that seem "hot," and the abstract and intensely literary form that seems "cool." "You may perceive, Madam," said Dr. Johnson, with a pugilistic smile, "that I am well-bred to a degree of needless scrupulosity." And Dr. Johnson was right in supposing that "well-bred" had come to mean a white-shirted stress on attire that rivaled the rigor of the printed page. "Comfort" consists in abandoning a visual arrangement in favor of one that permits casual participation of the senses, a state that is excluded when any one sense, but especially the visual sense, is hotted up to the point of dominant command of a situation.

On the other hand, in experiments in which all outer sensation is withdrawn, the subject begins a furious fill-in or completion of senses that is sheer hallucination. So the hotting-up of one sense tends to effect hypnosis, and the cooling of all senses tends to result in hallucination.

## 43. WHAT IF HE'S RIGHT?

### Tom Wolfe

*There are few more striking prose styles than the one employed by Tom Wolfe. A former scholar (Ph. D., Yale, 1957), and newspaper reporter (Springfield* Union, Washington Post, New York Herald Tribune), *Tom Wolfe has published several collections of essays including* The Pump House Gang, *from which the following was taken.*

I first met Marshall McLuhan in the spring of 1965, in New York. The first thing I noticed about him was that he wore some kind of a trick snap-on necktie with hidden plastic cheaters on it. He was a tall man, 53 years old, handsome, with a long, strong face, but terribly pallid. He had gray hair, which he combed straight back. It was a little thin on top, but he could comb it into nice sloops over the ears. Distinguished-looking, you might say. On the other hand, there were the plastic cheaters. A little of the plastic was showing between his collar and the knot of the tie. I couldn't keep my eye off it. It's the kind of tie you buy off a revolving rack in the Rexall for about 89¢. You just slip the plastic cheaters—they're a couple of little stays sticking out of the knot like wings—you slip them under your collar and there the tie is, hanging down and ready to go, Pree-Tide.

We were having lunch, five of us, out back in the garden of the French restaurant called Lutèce, at 249 East 50th Street. Lutèce is a small place but one of the four or five most fashionable restaurants in New York, I suppose. Certainly it is one of the most expensive. It is so expensive, only your host's menu has the prices listed. Yours just has a list of the dishes. That way you won't feel guilty about it. They put decanters of distilled water on the tables at Lutèce and they have a real wine steward. It is one of those places in the East Fifties in Manhattan where the Main Biggies and the Fashionable Matrons convene for the main event of the weekday, the Status Lunch. Executives, culturati, rich women who are written up in *Women's Wear Daily*, illuminati of all sorts meet there in a marvelous chorale of King Sano and Eastern Honk voices. The women walk in looking an ice-therapy 45, force-starved, peruked and lacquered at the hairdresser's, wearing peacock-colored Pucci dresses signed "Emilio" up near the throat, taking in "the crowd," sucking their cheeks in for the entrance, and calling Lutèce's owner by his first name, which is André, in a contralto that has been smoke-cured by fifteen to twenty years of inhaling King Sanos, the cigarette of New York Society women. The men come in wearing lozenge-shaped cuff links with real links and precious metal showing on the inside as well as the outside of the cuffs, not those Swank-brand gizmos that stick through and click, and they start honking over André and each other, speaking in a voice known as the Eastern boarding-school honk, a nasal drawl mastered by Nelson Rockefeller, Huntington Hartford, and Robert Dowling, among other eminent Americans. It was grand here, as I say. All honks and smoke-cured droning.

Our table was not the most illustrious, but it was in there trying: a movie actress; the daughter of one of the richest women in America; one of New York's top editors; and, of course, McLuhan. McLuhan, however, was not a celebrity at that time. I doubt that anybody else in the restaurant had ever heard of him.

And vice versa. McLuhan could not have been more oblivious of the special New York grandeur he had landed in. I don't think he noticed the people at all. He was interested in the little garden, or rather its thermodynamics, the way it was set out here in the heat of the noonday sun.

"The warmth steps up the tactile sense and diminishes the visual," he told us presently—as nearly as I can remember his words—I was following the plastic cheater. "It is more involving. It obliterates the distance between people. It is literally more 'intimate.' That's why these so-called garden restaurants' work."

Just before he made this sort of statement—and he was always analyzing his environment out loud—he would hook his chin down over his collarbone. It was like an unconscious signal—*now!* I would watch the tie knot swivel over the little telltale strip of plastic. It was a perfect Rexall milky white, this plastic.

At the time I didn't realize that McLuhan had been brought here, to New York, to Lutèce also, to be introduced to *haute New York*. He was about to make his debut, after a fashion. He was about to change from Herbert Marshall McLuhan, 53-year-old Canadian English professor, to *McLuhan*. He certainly didn't act like it, however. It had all been planned, but not by him. To him there was no *haute New York*. It was all past tense in this town. Toward the end of the meal his chin came down, the knot swiveled over the plastic—voices droned and honked richly all around us—and he turned his eyeballs up toward the great office buildings that towered above our little thermodynamic enclave.

"Of course, a city like New York is obsolete," he said. "People will no longer concentrate in great urban centers for the purpose of work. New York will become a Disneyland, a pleasure dome . . ."

Somehow, plastic cheaters and all, he had the charisma of a haruspex, the irresistible certitude of the monomaniac. I could see New York turning into a huge Astrodome with raggy little puberteens in white Courrèges boots giggling and shrieking and tumbling through the atmosphere like the snow in one of those Christmas paperweights you turn upside down—

What if he's right What . . . if . . . he . . . is . . . right W-h-a-t i-f h-e i-s r-i-g-h-t

|   |    | R |   |
|---|----|---|---|
| W |    | I |   |
| H | IF | G | ? |
| A | HE | H |   |
| T | IS | T |   |

Quite a few American businessmen, it turned out, were already wondering the same thing. There were many studs of the business world, breakfast-food-package designers, television-network creative-department vice presidents, advertising "media reps," lighting-fixture fortune heirs, patent lawyers, industrial spies, we-need-vision board chairmen—all sorts of business studs, as I say, wondering if McLuhan was . . . right. At the time McLuhan was a teacher working out of a little office off on the edge of the University of Toronto that looked like the receiving bin of a second-hand bookstore, grading papers, *grading papers,* for days on end, getting up in the morning, slapping the old Pree-Tide tie on, teaching English, grading more papers—

*But what if*—large corporations were already trying to put McLuhan in a box. Valuable! Ours! Suppose he *is* what he sounds like, the most important thinker since Newton, Darwin, Freud, Einstein, and Pavlov, studs of the intelligentsia game—suppose he *is* the oracle of the modern times—*what if he is right?*—he'll be in there, in our box.

IBM, General Electric, Bell Telephone, and others had been flying McLuhan from Toronto to New York, Pittsburgh, all over the place, to give private talks to their hierarchs about . . . this unseen world of electronic environment that *only he sees fully.* One corporation offered him $5,000 to present a closed-circuit—*ours*—television lecture on the ways the products in its industry would be used in the future. Another contributed a heavy subsidy to McLuhan's Centre for Culture and Technology at the University of Toronto, which, despite the massive name, was at that time largely McLuhan's genius and some letterhead stationery. One day in New York, McLuhan was staying at Howard Gossage's suite at the Lombardy Hotel. Gossage is a San Francisco advertising man. McLuhan was staying there and representatives of two national weekly magazines called up. Both offered him permanent offices in their buildings, plus fees, to do occasional consulting work. Just to have him in the box, I guess—

"What should I do, Howard?" says McLuhan.

"Take 'em both!" says Gossage. "You need offices on both sides of town. Suppose you get caught in traffic?"

McLuhan looks puzzled, but Gossage is already off into his laugh. This Gossage has a certain wild cosmic laugh. His eyes light up like Stars of Bethlehem. The laugh comes in waves, from far back in the throat, like echoes from Lane 27 of a bowling alley, rolling, booming far beyond the immediate situation, on to . . .

. . . in any case, McLuhan never failed to provoke this laugh. Perhaps because there were really two contradictory, incongruous McLuhans at this point. Even his appearance could change markedly from situation to situation. One moment he would look like merely the English teacher with the Pree-Tide tie on, naïve, given to bad puns derived from his studies of *Finnegans Wake* and worse jokes from God knows where, a somewhat disheveled man, kindly, disorganized—the very picture of the absent-minded professor. The next moment he would look like what he has, in fact, become: the super-savant, the Freud of our times, the omniscient *philosophe*, the unshakable dialectician. That was whenever the subject was The Theory, which it usually was. On those occasions the monologue began, and McLuhan was, simply, the master. He preferred Socratic dialogues, with six to ten people in attendance. A Socratic dialogue, like a Pentecostal sermon, is a monologue punctuated by worshipful interruptions. "Marshall is actually very polite," said one of his friends, meaning to be kind. "He always waits for your lips to stop moving."

Among his business clients, McLuhan was always that, monomaniac and master. The business studs would sit in their conference rooms under fluorescent lights, with the right air-conditioned air streaming out from behind the management-style draperies. Upward-busting hierarch executives, the real studs, the kind who have already changed over from lie-down crewcuts to brushback Eric Johnston-style Big Boy haircuts and from Oxford button-downs to Tripler broadcloth straight points and have hung it all on the line, an $80,000 mortgage in New Canaan and a couple of kids at Deerfield and Hotchkiss—hung it all on the line on knowing exactly what this corporation is all about—they sit there with the day's first bloody mary squirting through their capillaries—and this man with a plastic cheater showing at the edge of the collar, who just got through *grading papers*, for godsake, tells them in an *of-course* voice, and with *I'm-being-patient* eyes, that, in effect, politely, they all know just about exactly . . . nothing . . . about the real business they're in—

"—Gentlemen, the General Electric Company makes a considerable portion of its profits from electric light bulbs, but it has not yet discovered that it is not in the light bulb business but in the business of moving information. Quite as much as A.T.&T. Yes. *Of-course I-am-willing-to-be-patient.* He pulls his chin down into his neck and looks up out of his long Scotch-lairdly face. Yes. The electric light is pure information. It is a medium without a message, as it were. Yes. Light is a self-contained communications system in which the medium is the message. *Just think that over for a moment—I-am-willing-to-be—*When IBM discovered that it was not in the business of making office equipment or business machines—

————but that it was in the business
of processing
information,
then it began
to navigate
with
clear
vision.
Yes."

Swell! But where did *this* guy come from? What is this—cryptic, Delphic saying: *The electric light is pure information.*

Delphic! *The medium is the message. We are moving out of the age of the visual into the age of the aural and tactile. . . .*

It was beautiful. McLuhan excelled at telling important and apparently knowledgeable people they didn't have the foggiest comprehension of their own bailiwick. He never did it with any overtone of now-I'm-going-to-shock-you, however. He seemed far, far beyond that game, out on a threshold where all the cosmic circuits were programmed. I can see him now, sitting in the conference room on the upper deck of an incredible ferryboat that Walter Landor, one of the country's top package designers, has redone at a cost of about $400,000 as an office and design center. This great package design flagship nestles there in the water at Pier 5 in San Francisco. The sun floods in from the Bay onto the basket-woven wall-to-wall and shines off the dials of Landor's motion-picture projection console. Down below on the main deck is a whole simulated supermarket for bringing people in and testing package impact—and McLuhan says, almost by the way:

"Of course, packages will be obsolete in a few years. People will want tactile experiences, they'll want to feel the product they're getting—"

But!—

McLuhan's chin goes down, his mouth turns down, his eyes roll up in his *of-course* expression: "Goods will be sold in *bins*. People will go right to bins and pick things up and *feel* them rather than just accepting a package."

Landor, the package designer, doesn't lose his cool; he just looks— *what if he is right?*

*. . . The human family now exists under conditions of a global village. We live in a single constricted space resonant with tribal drums . . .* That even, even, even voice goes on—

—McLuhan is sitting in the Laurent Restaurant in New York with Gibson McCabe, president of *Newsweek,* and several other high-ranking communications people, and McCabe tells of the millions *Newsweek* has put into reader surveys, market research, advertising, the editorial staff, everything, and how it paid off with a huge rise in circulation over the past five years. McLuhan listens, then down comes the chin: "Well . . . of course, your circulation would have risen about the same anyway, the new sensory balance of the people being what it is . . ."

*Print gave tribal man an eye for an ear.*

McLuhan is at the conference table in the upper room in Gossage's advertising firm in San Francisco, up in what used to be a firehouse. A couple of newspaper people are up there talking about how they are sure their readers want this and that to read—McLuhan pulls his chin down into his neck:

"Well . . . of course, people don't actually *read* newspapers. They get into them every morning like a hot bath."

Perfect! Delphic! Cryptic! Aphoristic! Epigrammatic! With this even, even, even voice, this utter scholarly aplomb—with *pronouncements*—

The phone rings in Gossage's suite and it's for McLuhan. It is a man from one of America's largest packing corporations. They want to fly McLuhan to their home office to deliver a series of three talks, one a day, to their top management group. How much would he charge?

McLuhan puts his hand over the receiver and explains the situation to Gossage.

"How much should I charge?"

"What do you usually get for a lecture?" says Gossage.

"Five hundred dollars."

"Tell him a hundred thousand."

McLuhan looks appalled.

"Oh, all right," says Gossage. "Tell him fifty thousand."

McLuhan hesitates, then turns back to the telephone: "Fifty thousand."

Now the man on the phone is appalled. That is somewhat outside the fee structure we generally project, Professor McLuhan. They all call him Professor or Doctor. We don't expect you to prepare any new material especially for us, you understand, and it will only be three talks—

"Oh—well then," says McLuhan, "twenty-five thousand."

Great sigh of relief. Well! That is more within our potential structure projection, Professor McLuhan, and we look forward to seeing you!

McLuhan hangs up and stares at Gossage, nonplussed. But Gossage is already off into the cosmic laugh, bounding, galloping, soaring, eyes ablaze—*imas alla!—imas alla!* just over the next skyline!—El Dorado, Marshall! Don't you understand!—

Looking back, I can see that Gossage, but not McLuhan, knew what was going to happen to McLuhan over the next six months. Namely, that this 53-year-old Canadian English teacher, gray as a park pigeon, would suddenly become an international celebrity and the most famous man his country ever produced.

McLuhan rose up from out of a world more obscure, more invisible, more unknown to the great majority of mankind than a Bantu village or the Southeast Bronx. Namely, the EngLit academic life. Tongaland and the Puerto Rican slums may at least reek, in the imagination, of bloodlust and loins oozing after sundown. EngLit academia, so far as the outside world is concerned, neither reeks nor blooms; an occasional whiff of rotting tweeds, perhaps: otherwise, a redolence of nothing. It is a world of liberal-arts scholars, graduate schools, *carrels,* and monstrous baby-sitting drills known as freshman English. It is a far more detached life than any garret life of the artists. Garret life? Artists today spend their time calling up Bloomingdale's to see if the yellow velvet Milo Laducci chairs they ordered are in yet.

English-literature scholars start out in little cubicles known as carrels, in the stacks of the university libraries, with nothing but a couple of metal Klampiton shelves of books to sustain them, sitting there making scholarly analogies—detecting signs of Rabelais in Sterne, signs of Ovid in Pound, signs of Dickens in Dostoevsky, signs of nineteenth-century flower symbolism in Melville, signs of Schlegelianism in Coleridge, signs of the Oral-narrative use of the conjunctive in Hemingway, signs, analogies, insights—always *insights*—golden *desideratum!*—hunched over in silence with only the far-off sound of Maggie, a Girl of the Stacks, a townie who puts books back on the shelves—now she is all right, a little lower-class-puffy in the nose, you understand, but . . . —only the sound of her to inject some stray, *sport* thought into this intensely isolated regimen. In effect, the graduate-school scholar settles down at an early age, when the sap is still rising, to a life of little cubicles, little money, little journals in which his insights, if he is extremely diligent, may someday be recorded. A Volkswagen, a too-small apartment, Department Store Danish furniture with dowel legs—before he is 30 his wife will have begun to despise him as a particularly sad sort of failure, once the cultural charisma of *literature* has lost its charm. How much better to have failed at oil prospecting or the diaper-service game than at . . . practically nothing!

McLuhan graduated from the University of Manitoba in 1933, then went to England and took another B.A. at Cambridge (in 1936; and, eventually, a doctorate, in 1942). At Cambridge in the thirties the literati were keen on PopCult. Movies, advertising, radio, display art were something to be analyzed as a "Language," a kind of technological Creole that was understood instinctively (*ProleSlob!*) among the masses. It was up to the literati to discern its grammar and syntax (*O Gauche-Kick!*). Wyndham Lewis had written extensively on popular culture. F. R. Leavis had written *Culture and Environment.* Joyce's *Finnegans Wake,* Eliot's *The Waste Land* and Pound's *Cantos* seemed, in the fellows rooms of Cambridge, to be veritable nigger nightclubs of PopCult. Lewis, particularly, influenced McLuhan.

In 1936 McLuhan took his first teaching job, at the University of Wisconsin. He immediately found himself in one of the most exquisitely squalid hells known to middle-class man: freshman English at a Midwestern university. The teacher's evidently serious interest in the likes of Donne, Shakespeare, or Milton marks him at once, of course, as a pedantic and therefore all the more hopeless fool. One thing the poor nit can do in this situation is assign *The Old Man and the Sea, Of Mice and Men,* or some other storybook in words of one syllable and hope that will hold the little bastards for ten or twelve weeks.

McLuhan, however, had pride and ambition. He resorted to the GaucheKick PopCult of Cambridge. He showed the little bastards advertisements, the same advertisements their gummy little brains soaked up every day outside the classroom. What do these ads *really* convey? he would ask.

It works. It is a nice stratagem. Others have used it effectively, too, notably Orwell in essays like "The Art of Donald McGill." One presents a Gotham Gold Stripe nylon-stockings ad showing a pair of slick and shimmering female legs on a pedestal. Or a Lysol vaginal-wash ad showing a gorgeous woman in an evening dress sinking into a pool whose ripples are inscribed Doubt, Inhibitions, Ignorance, Misgivings. Or a Bayer aspirin ad showing a drum majorette wearing a military helmet and jackboots and carrying a mace-like baton captioned: "In 13.9 seconds a drum majorette can twirl a baton twenty-five times . . . but in only TWO SECONDS Bayer Aspirin is ready to go to work!" What is the true language of these ads? What do they *really* convey? Why, the wedding of sex and technology (The Mechanical Bride), the break-down of the sexual object, Woman, into component machine parts: the Bakelite legs on a pedestal, the antiseptic, B.O.-free plastic vagina; the "goose-stepping combination of military mechanism and jackbooted eroticism."

Yes! *It is written—but I say unto you . . .* From Wisconsin McLuhan went to the University of St. Louis, Assumption University (Windsor, Ontario), and St. Michael's College of the University of Ontario. Along the way he became something of a charismatic figure in the phlegmy grim dim world of EngLit academia. He attracted circles of students and spoke to student groups, *extra curricula*, both in lectures and in Socratic gatherings. He showed slides of ads, comic strips, and newspapers, ex-ploring the hidden language of "the folklore of industrial man," as he called it.

After Wisconsin, every institution McLuhan taught in was Roman Catholic. In the mid-1930's he had become a convert to Catholicism. His parents were Scotch-Irish Protestants from western Canada. McLuhan was apparently influenced by Catholic intellectuals in England, notably Chesterton and Hopkins. Twenty years later he was to discover a piece of PopCult that was to him a strangely Catholic and catholic force in the world: TV.

In 1951 McLuhan published his "industrial folklore" material in a book, *The Mechanical Bride*. The book went virtually unnoticed, then out of print, and he was left with stacks of copies himself. In 1966, be-fore the book was republished as a $2.95 paperback, copies brought $40 and $50 apiece.

Compared to his two major books, *The Gutenberg Galaxy* (1962) and *Understanding Media* (1964), *The Mechanical Bride* is embarrassingly moralistic. It is written with the conventional nineteenth-century, anti-industrial bias of *the literary man,* a term McLuhan would later associate with the worst sort of intellectual obtuseness and rear-guardism. *The Mechanical Bride* is explicitly presented as a book designed to help Western man protect himself from the hidden persuasions of Madison Avenue, the press, and Showbiz. "Why not use the new commercial education as a means to enlightening its intended prey? Why not assist the public to observe consciously the drama which is intended to operate upon it unconsciously?"

*The Mechanical Bride,* however, as a book about folklore and the "collective public mind," led McLuhan more and more toward the work of anthropologists and historians. Certainly one of the great influences on his thinking was his friend and colleague at the University of Toronto, Edmund Carpenter, an anthropologist with whom he edited a book called *Explorations in Communication.*

Two books were published by university presses in 1950 and 1951 that changed McLuhan's life, I suppose you could say. They were *Empire and Communications* and *The Bias of Communication,* by Harold Innis. Innis was at the University of Toronto at the time. Innis gave McLuhan the basic insight of his career, which he was to compress into the aphorism: *The medium is the message.* You seldom hear anything about Innis in the many critiques of McLuhan. This is not McLuhan's fault, however. He gave Innis full credit in the *Gutenberg Galaxy* (p. 50): "Innis also explained why print causes nationalism and not tribalism; and why print causes price systems and markets such as cannot exist without print. In short, Harold Innis was the first person to hit upon the process of change as implicit in the forms of media technology. The present book is a footnote of explanation to his work."

McLuhan was also influenced by Henri Bergson. He adapted some of Bergson's theories about the central nervous system. They impressed Aldous Huxley as well. Bergson had the idea that the brain is a "reducing valve." The senses, he said, send an overwhelming flood of information to the brain which the brain then filters down to an orderly trickle it can manage for the purpose of survival in a highly competitive world. Modern man, he believed, has become so rational, so utilitarian, so devoted to the classification of information for practical purposes, that the trickle becomes very thin and distilled, indeed, though efficient. Meantime, said Bergson, modern man has screened out the richest and most wondrous part of his experience without even knowing it. Implicit in this theory is the idea that sometime in the past primitive man experienced the entire rich and sparkling flood of the senses fully. It ties in with one of the most ancient metaphysical beliefs: the belief that out there somewhere, beyond the veil that blinds our egocentric modern minds, is our forgotten birthright, a world of wholeness, unity, and beauty. As a Roman Catholic, incidentally, McLuhan found the idea very congenial: "The Christian concept of the mystical body—all men as members of the body of Christ— this becomes technologically a fact under electronic conditions." *The All-in-One.*

McLuhan's great stroke was to bring Innis's and Bergson's ideas forward, beyond print, beyond the confines of the scholarly past, and into the present, like an anthropologist. In short, he turned their ideas on to PopCult, to television, motion pictures, radio, and telephone, the computer, photography, xerography: *the media.*

McLuhan had plenty of Pop-Cult to look at in the 1950's. He had a house full of children. In 1939 he had married Corinne Lewis, an American actress. They had two sons and four daughters. They took over the place. Inside—TV, record players, radios, telephones, and children—while McLuhan wrote of tribal man and the Gutenberg revolution; of space and time and the collision of civilizations; of the seamless web and the electronic unification of mankind; on a ping-pong table in the back yard.

McLuhan is fond of quoting Daniel Boorstin's dictum, "The celebrity is a person who is known for his wellknownness." That pretty much describes McLuhan himself. McLuhan is one of those intellectual celebrities, like Toynbee or Einstein, who is intensely well known as a name, and as a *savant,* while his theory remains a grand blur. Part of the difficulty is that McLuhan is presented to the world as "the communications theorist." His first book, *The Mechanical Bride,* was a book about communication. Since then McLuhan has barely dealt with communication at all, at least if you define communication as "interchange of thought or opinions." He is almost wholly concerned with the effect of the means of communication (the medium) on the central nervous system. His theory falls squarely in a field known as cognitive psychology, even though his interests cut across many fields. Modern cognitive psychology is highly scientific devoted to complex physiological experiments. McLuhan isn't. In fact, he is a theoretical cognitive psychologist.

This is made quite clear in *The Gutenberg Galaxy. Understanding Media* is really a chapbook for *The Gutenberg Galaxy's* theory.

The theory, as I say, concerns the central nervous system. McLuhan makes a set of assumptions, à la Bergson, about how the central nervous system processes information. He believes that humans have a "sensory balance"—a balance between the five senses: sight, hearing, touch, smell, and taste. This balance, he says, changes according to the environment. For example, if the visual sense is dimmed, the auditory sense intensifies (as in the blind); if the auditory sense is increased, the sense of touch diminishes (as when a dentist puts earphones on a patient, turns up the sound, and thereby reduces his sensitivity to pain). Great technological changes, he goes on to say, can alter these "sensory ratios" for an entire people. McLuhan is concerned chiefly with two of these great technological changes: (1) the introduction of print in the fifteenth century (reputedly by Johann Gutenberg) and the spread of literacy in the next four hundred years: (2) the introduction of television in the twentieth.

Print, says McLuhan, stepped up the visual sense of Western man at the expense of his other senses. It led, he says, to "the separation of the senses, of functions, of operations, of states emotional and political, as well as of tasks." This, he says, had overwhelming historical consequences: nationalism and nationalist wars (cultural fragmentation); the modern army, industrialism and bureaucracy (fragmentation of tasks); the market and price structure (economic fragmentation), individualism and the habit of privacy (fragmentation of the individual from the community)—and schizophrenia and peptic ulcers (caused by the fragmentation of both intellect and action from emotion); pornography (fragmentation of sex from love); the cult of childhood (fragmentation by age); and a general impoverishment of man's intuitive and artistic life (because of the fragmentation of the senses). And those are but a few of the results he mentions.

Enter TV. Television and the electric media generally, says McLuhan, are reversing the process; they are returning man's sensory ratios to the pre-print, pre-literate, "tribal" balance. The auditory and tactile senses come back into play, and man begins to use all his senses at once again in a unified, "seamless web" of experience. (Television, in McLuhan's psychology, is not primarily a visual medium but "audio-tactile.") The world is becoming a "global village," to use one of his happy phrases.

The immediate effects of TV on the central nervous system, says McLuhan, may be seen among today's young, the first TV generation. The so-called "generation gap," as he diagnoses it, is not a state of mind but a neurological fact. It is a disparity between a visual, print-oriented generation and its audio-tactile, neo-tribal offspring. School dropouts, he says, are but the more obvious casualties among a great mass of "psychic dropouts." These are children educated by the electric media to have unified, all-involving sensory experiences. They sit baffled and bored in classrooms run by teachers who fragment knowledge into "subjects," disciplines, specialities, and insist on the classification of data (rather than "pattern recognition," which is the principle of computers). This means, he says, that the educational system must be totally changed. In the long run, he says, the new neural balance will cause total change in everything anyway: "Total Change, ending psychic, social, economic, and political parochialism. The old civic, state, and national groupings have become unworkable. Nothing can be further from the spirit of the new technology than 'a place for everything and everything in its place.' You can't *go* home again." Many of the implications of the theory are very cheery, indeed: no more bitter nationalism—instead, the global village; no more shutout, ghetto-pent minority groups (racial fragmentation)—instead, all "irrevocably involved with, and responsible for," one another; no more tedious *jobs* (mechanistic fragmentation)—instead, all-involving *roles*; no more impoverished intuition (fragmented senses)—instead, expanded, all-embracing sensory awareness; and so on. Man made whole again!

## MAN MADE WHOLE AGAIN

I gazed upon the printed page.
It tore me limb from limb.
I found my ears in Mason jars.
My feet in brougham motorcars,
My khaki claws in woggy wars—
But in this cockeyed eyeball age
I could not find my soul again.
Vile me.
*And then—*
   I touched a TV dial
*And—pop!—*
   it made me whole again.

To a clinical neurologist or psychologist, McLuhan's neurology is so much air. McLuhan's subject matter, as I say, is not communication but the central nervous system. The central nervous system is today perhaps the greatest dark continent of the physical sciences. Precious little is known about even the crudest neural functions. It was not until the 1950's that experimenters discovered, piecemeal, through experiments in several countries, the actual processes by which even so primitive an impulse as hunger is transmitted through the brain (Neal Miller in America, W. R. Hess in Switzerland, Konorski in Poland, Anand in India, *et alii*). It has taken half a century, since the development of the technique of stereotaxic needle implants, to reach even such tiny thresholds as this. It was not until 1962 that physiologists, using microelectrodes, discovered how the eye transmits shapes to the brain. To move from this level to the postulate that TV is altering the neural functions of entire peoples or even one person—this could only strike a clinician as romanticism.

McLuhan, however, was ready for the criticism. He insisted he was not presenting a self-contained theory but making "probes." He sees himself as trying to open up the dark continent for systematic exploration by others. He says he is not drawing conclusions but using what facts are available as "means of getting into new territories." He even says that if he could persuade enough investigators to study the effect of the new technologies systematically, he would gladly return whence he came, viz., to "literary studies." At the same time, he has sought to give his theory some scientific underpinning by setting up psychological studies of sample groups in Canada and Greece, studying their "sensory balance" before and after the coming of TV to their locales. The Canadian study has been completed, and I understand that the results, unpublished as of this writing (January, 1968), were inconclusive.

What, then, has been the nature of McLuhan's extraordinary splash? It certainly has not been scientific, despite the fact that he now characterizes himself as a scientist, speaks of the "clinical spirit," and compares his methods to those of modern psychiatry, metallurgy, and structural analysis.

A clue, I think, may be found in the parallels between McLuhan's history and Freud's. In any historical perspective the two men are contemporaries (Freud died in 1939). Both have come forth with dazzling insights in a period (1850 to the present) of tremendous intellectual confusion and even convulsion following what Nietzsche called "the death of God"; and Max Weber, "the demystification of the world." Both men explain *all* in terms of—*Santa Barranzá! something common as pig tracks! under our very noses all the time! so obvious we never stepped back to see it for what it was!* Freud: sex. McLuhan: TV. Both men electrified—outraged!—the intellectuals of their time by explaining the most vital, complex, cosmic phases of human experience in terms of such low-life stuff: e.g., the anus; the damnable TV set. The biggest howl Freud ever caused was with a two-page paper that maintained that anal sensations in infancy were capable of imprinting a man's mature personality in a quite specific way. Freud was the subject of as much derision in his day as McLuhan in his; and, like McLuhan, benefited from it. Freud said to Jung: "Many enemies, much honor"; McLuhan might well say the same. After all, where there's smoke, there's . . . *what if he is right?* McLuhan said to his disciple and amanuensis, Gerald Stearn: "No one believes these factors have any effect whatever on our human reactions. It's like the old days when people played around with radium. They painted watch dials and licked the brushes. They didn't believe radium could affect people."

Freud, of course, was a doctor of medicine and a trained clinician and a more certifiably scientific thinker than McLuhan. But Freud, like Mc-Luhan, strove after the cosmic insight. The more rigorous psychologists today, as well as most research physicians, regard Freud as a romanticist, almost a metaphysician. They cast the old boy as a sort of Viennese Bishop Berkeley. There is a suspicion that Freud poked *around—aha! very significant!*—amid the plump velvet and florid warps and woofs of a few upperbourgeois Viennese households, including his own—*Dad, that bugger, seduced my sis*—and then rerouted his insights through the front door of the clinic as findings explaining the behavior of all mankind. One cannot help but wonder something of the sort about McLuhan. Here sits the master out back at the ping-pong table. And there, inside the house, sit the kids, gazing at their homework—amid a raging, encapsulating sensory typhoon of TV sets, transistor radios, phonographs, and telephones—and yet they make it through school all the same—*Very significant!* Amazing, even. A neo-tribal unity of the senses. "The family circle has widened. The worldpool of information fathered by electric media—movies, Telstar, flight—far surpasses any possible influence Mom and Dad can now bring to bear."

### PING-PONG

I walked into the living room.
They rocked me with a stereo boom.
No haven here downstairs at all.
Nymphets frug on my wall-to-wall
And boogaloo in my private den
And won't let poor work-a-daddy in.
How glorious!
*Übermenschen!* golden gulls!
With transistor radios plugged in their skulls.
Radiant! with an Elysian hue
From the tubercular blue of the television.
Such a pure Zulu euphoria
Suffuses their hi-fi sensoria!
How glorious.
I shall stand it long as I can,
This neo-tribal festival.
Their multi-media cut-up,
The audio-pervasion of their voices,
Leaves me with two choices:
Shall I simply make them shut up—

Or . . . extrapolate herefrom the destiny
Of Western Man?

Freud and McLuhan both became celebrities at the same period of life, their early fifties, and under similar circumstances. Both began with rather obscure cliques of academic followers. Freud had a little group of adherents who held discussions every Wednesday night in his waiting room and were known as the "Psychological Wednesday Society." McLuhan had his adherents in several Canadian universities, and they, plus Americans interested in his work, often met in his home. If one were to choose a precise date for Freud's emergence as a public figure, it would probably be April 26, 1908, when a *Zusammenkunft fur Freud'sche Psychologie* (Meeting for Freudian Psychology) was held in the Hotel Bristol in Salzburg, with Jung, Adler, Stekel, and others in attendance. In McLuhan's case it would be January 30, 1964, when faculty members of the University of British Columbia staged what was known to his followers as a "McLuhan Festival" in the university armory. They suspended sheets of plastic from the ceiling, forming a maze. Operators aimed light projections at the plastic sheets and at the people walking through them. A movie projector showed a long, meaningless movie of the interior of the empty armory. Goofy noises poured out of the loudspeakers, a bell rang, somebody banged blocks of wood together up on a podium. Somebody else spewed perfume around. Dancers flipped around through the crowds, and behind a stretch fabric wall—a frame with a stretch fabric across it—there was a girl, pressed against the stretch fabric wall, like a whole wall made of stretch pants, and *undulating* and humping around back there. Everybody was supposed to come up and *feel it*—the girl up against the stretch fabric—to understand the "tactile communication" McLuhan was talking about.

Neither event, the Meeting for Freudian Psychology or the McLuhan Festival, received any very great publicity, but both were important if esoteric announcements that *this* is the new name to be reckoned with. As Freud says . . . As McLuhan says . . . McLuhan's friend, Carpenter, had already put it into words: "McLuhan is one of the epic innovators of the electronic age. His *Gutenberg Galaxy* is the most important book in the social sciences of this generation, overshadowing in scope and depth any other contribution."

Both Freud and McLuhan attracted another obscure but important source of support: young artists and young literary intellectuals who saw them as visionaries, as men "who divined the famed riddle" (Sophocles. *Oedipus Rex*), to quote from a medallion that Freud's Wednesday Society friends gave him on his fiftieth birthday in 1906. Both McLuhan and Freud present scientific theories, but in an ancient priestly-aristocratic idiom that literary and artistic souls find alluring. Both buttress their work with traditional literary erudition. Freud, of course, presents his most famous insight in the form of a literary conceit, i.e., "the Oedipus complex." To sense Freud's strong literary bias, one has only to read ten pages of Freud and then ten pages of Pavlov. The difference in mental atmospheres, the literary vs. the clinical, stands out at once. Freud had the typical literary respect for artistic genius. He depicted the artist as one who has the power to express openly and faithfully the world of fantasy—the link between the conscious and the unconscious—that ordinary mortals grasp only fitfully in daydreams. Freud became the patron saint of the Surrealists, who saw themselves as doing just that (Dali visited Freud shortly before Freud's death, sketched him, and told him that surrealistically his cranium was reminiscent of a snail).

McLuhan, of course, was trained as a literary scholar. He begins *The Gutenberg Galaxy* with three chapters carrying out a somewhat abstruse analysis of *King Lear*. A la Freud's Oedipus, he begins his discussion of "sensory ratios" with a Greek legend (the myth of Cadmus: the Phoenician who sowed dragon's teeth—and up sprang armed men; and introduced the alphabet to Greece—and up sprang specialism and fragmentation of the senses). It is all quite literary, this neurology. Joyce, Matthew Arnold, Dr. Johnson, Blake, Ruskin, Rimbaud, Pope, Cicero, Dean Swift, Montaigne, Pascal, Tocqueville, Cervantes, Nashe, Marlowe, Shakespeare, Ben Jonson, St. Augustine—they twitter and gleam like celebrities arriving by limousine.

Artists, meanwhile, have precisely the same role in McLuhan's galaxy as in Freud's. They are geniuses who detect the invisible truths intuitively and express them symbolically. They are divine *naturals*, gifted but largely unconscious of the meaning of their own powers. McLuhan sees artists as mankind's "early warning system." They possess greater unity and openness of the senses and therefore respond earlier to the alteration of the "sensory ratios" brought about by changes in technology. McLuhan today is the patron saint of most "mixed-media" artists and of many young "underground" moviemakers (for such dicta as "The day of the story line, the plot, is over"). He was very much the patron saint of the huge "Art and Technology" mixed-media show staged by Robert Rauschenberg and others at the 27th Street Armory in New York in 1967. The artists, incidentally, are apparently willing to overlook McLuhan's theory of how they register their "early warning." It is a rather retrograde performance, as McLuhan sees it. The "avant garde" of each period, he says, is actually always one technology behind. Painters did not discover The Landscape until the early nineteenth century, when the intrusion of machine-age industrialism caused them to see the technology of agriculture—i.e., The Land—as an art form for the first time. They did not discover machine forms (cubism) until the electric age had begun. They did not discover mass-produced forms (pop Art: Roy Lichtenstein's comic strips, Andy Warhol's Campbell Soup cans) until the age of the conveyor belt had given way to the age of electronic circuitry. McLuhan says that this is the early warning, nevertheless—and the idea has made artists happy.

Older literary intellectuals, however, have reacted to McLuhan with the sort of *ressentiment*, to use Nietzsche's word, that indicates he has hit a very bad nerve. The old guard's first salvo came as far back as July, 1964, with a long piece by Dwight Macdonald. It contained most of the objections that have become so familiar since then: the flat conclusion that McLuhan writes nonsense (a typical reaction to Freud), that his style is repetitive and "boring," that he is anti-book and for the new barbarism (TV, electronic brains), or, obversely, that he is amoral, has no values. Once again the example of Freud comes to mind. After Freud's Clark University lectures were published, the Dean of the University of Toronto said: "An ordinary reader would gather that Freud advocates free love, removal of all restraints, and a relapse into savagery." In fact, of course, Freud savaged and very nearly exterminated traditional philosophy, the queen of the sciences throughout the nineteenth century. What was left of the lofty metaphysics of God, Freedom and Immortality, if they were products of the anus and the glans penis?

McLuhan, in turn, has been the savager of the literary intellectuals. He has made the most infuriating announcement of all: You are irrelevant.

He has hit a superannuated target. The literary-intellectual mode that still survives in the United States and England today was fashioned more than 150 years ago in Regency England with the founding of magazines such as the *Edinburgh Review*, the *Quarterly*, *Blackwood's*, the *London Magazine*, the *Examiner* and the *Westminster Review*. They became platforms for educated gentlemen-amateurs to pass judgment in a learned way on two subjects: books and politics. This seemed a natural combination at the time, because so many literati were excited by the French Revolution and its aftermath (e.g., Byron, Wordsworth, Shelley, Hazlitt, Francis Jeffrey). The *Edinburgh Review* had covers of blue and buff, the Whig colors. Remarkably, the literary-intellectual mode has remained locked for more than a century and a half in precisely that format: of books and moral protest, by gentlemen-amateurs, in the British polite-essay form.

McLuhan has come forth as a man with impeccable literary credentials of his own to tell them that the game is all over. He has accused them of "primitivism" and ignorance of the nature of the very medium they profess to value: the book; they "have never thought for one minute about the book as a medium or a structure and how it related itself to other media as a structure, politically, verbally, and so on. . . . They have never studied any medium." He has challenged them to come to grips, as he has, with the objective, empirical techniques of exploration developed in the physical and social sciences in the past fifty years; if the literary intellectual continues to retreat from all this into the realm of values, says McLuhan, "he's had it."

This has been the sorest point for the literary fraternities, as he calls them. During the past five years their response to the overwhelming sweep of scientific empiricism has been *the literary retrenchment*—an ever more determined retrenchment into the moralist stance of the Regency literati ("intellectual" protest against the tyrants and evils of the times). Literary intellectuals even sound the cry in so many words today, asserting that the task of the intellectual in a brutal age is the preservation of sacred values (e.g., Naom Chomsky's manifesto, "The Responsibility of the Intellectuals," in *The New York Review of Books*). Macdonald, for example, has devoted the past two decades of his career to the *retrenchment*. He has been busily digging in against all forms of twentieth-century empiricism, from sociology to linguistics. He even sallied forth against so conservative and benign an intrusion of empiricism into the literary world as the third edition of Webster's Dictionary— on the quaint grounds that it had abdicated its moral responsibility to referee Good vs. Evil in grammar and diction. All the while, from inside the trench, he has been running up the flag of "values."

McLuhan's Nietzschean (*Beyond Good and Evil*) "aphorisms and entr'actes" on this subject have been particularly galling: "For many years I have observed that the moralist typically substitutes anger for perception. He hopes that many people will mistake his irritation for insight. . . . The mere moralistic expression of approval or disapproval, preference or detestation, is currently being used in our world as a substitute for observation and a substitute for study. People hope that if they scream loudly enough about 'values' then others will mistake them for serious, sensitive souls who have higher and nobler perceptions than ordinary people. Otherwise, why would they be screaming? . . . Moral bitterness is a basic technique for endowing the idiot with dignity."

Even more galling to the literati, I suspect, is that there is no medium they can turn to, books or otherwise, esoteric or popular, without hearing the McLuhan dicta thundering at them, amid the most amazing fanfare. *Ecce Celebrity.*

McLuhan's ascension to the status of international celebrity has been faster than Freud's, due in no small part to the hyped-up tempo of *the media* today—and the fact that the phenomenon of Freud himself had already conditioned the press to exploit the esoteric guru as a star. Freud's ascension was more gradual but quite steady. His emergence, at the Meeting for Freudian Psychology, was in 1908. By 1910 his writings prompted barrages of heated reviews in both American and European intellectual journals, sometimes running to more than a hundred pages apiece. In 1915 his two essays, "Thoughts for the Times on War and Death," were a popular hit and were widely reprinted. By 1924 he was very definitely *Freud*; both the Chicago *Tribune* and the Hearst newspapers offered him huge sums, private ocean liners, etc., to come to the United States and make a psychoanalysis of the sensational thrill-killers, Leopold and Loeb (he declined).

Both Freud and McLuhan experienced their great publicity booms after trips to the United States, however. Freud's followed a series of lectures at Clark University in Worcester, Massachusetts, in 1909 on the twentieth anniversary of its founding. When his boat landed in New York on August 27, he was mentioned, and merely mentioned, in only one newspaper, and as "Professor Freund of Vienna," at that. By the time he sailed for Europe on September 21, he had his first honorary doctorate (from Clark) and was well on the way to becoming a proper sensation and outrage.

McLuhan's pivotal trip to the U.S. came in May, 1965. As I say, American corporations had already begun to import him for private lectures. The publication of *Understanding Media* in 1964 had prompted that. There was first of all the sheer intriguing possibility—*what if he is right?* There was also the strange wrong-side-of-the-tracks sense of inferiority such firms seem to feel toward the academic and intellectual worlds. Any scholar with good credentials who will take a serious, vaguely optimistic, or even neutral interest in the matters of the business world, e.g., technology, will be warmly received. McLuhan's May, 1965, trip to New York, however, was at the behest of two rather extraordinary men from San Francisco, Howard Gossage and Dr. Gerald Feigen.

Gossage is a tall, pale advertising man with one of the great heads of gray hair in the U.S.A., flowing back like John Barrymore's. Feigen is a psychiatrist who became a surgeon; he is dark and has big eyes and a gong-kicker mustache like Jerry Colonna. He is also a ventriloquist and carries around a morbid-looking dummy named Becky. Gossage and Feigen started a firm called Generalists, Inc., acting as consultants to people who can't get what they need from specialists because what they need is the big picture. Their first client was a man who was stuck with an expensive ski lift in Squaw Valley that was idle half the year. They advised him to start a posh and rather formal restaurant-nightclub up the slope that could be reached only by ski lift. So he did. It was named High Camp and immediately became all the rage. One thing that drew Gossage and Feigen to McLuhan was his belief that the age of specialists (fragmentation of intellect) was over.

Gossage and Feigen invested about $6,000 into taking McLuhan around to talk to influential people outside the academic world, chiefly in the communications and advertising industries, on both coasts. Gossage says they had no specific goal (no fragmentation; open field). They just wanted to play it "fat, dumb and happy" and see what would happen.

So in May 1965 they had a series of meetings and lunches set up for McLuhan, at Laurent, Lutèce, and other great expense-account feasteries of the East Fifties in Manhattan, with men of the caliber of Gibson McCabe. The first meetings and a cocktail party in Gossage's suite at the Lombardy were set for a Monday. McLuhan never showed up. Gossage finally got him on the telephone in Toronto that evening. Marshall, what the hell are you doing—

"I'm grading papers."

"Grading papers?"

"And waiting for the excursion rate."

"The excursion rate! What excursion rate?"

—the midweek excursion rate on the airlines. He could save about $12 round-trip if he didn't come to New York until Tuesday morning.

"But Marshall, you're not even *pay*ing for it!"

—but that was the English prof with the Pree-Tide tie. He had a wife and six children and thirty years behind him of shaving by on an English teacher's pay. So there he was in the bin, grading papers, scratching away—

"Listen," says Gossage, "there are so many people willing to invest money in your work now, you'll never have to grade papers again."

"You mean it's going to be fun from now on?" says McLuhan.

"Everything's coming up roses," says Gossage.

By January, 1966, the McLuhan boom was on, and with a force, as I say, that McLuhan himself never dreamed of. I remember seeing McLuhan in August, 1965, in Gossage's firehouse offices in San Francisco. Gossage and Feigen were putting on their own "McLuhan Festival," as they called it. They invited small groups of influential West Coast people in for Socratic dialogues with McLuhan every morning and every afternoon for a week. One afternoon McLuhan was sitting at the round table in Gossage's own big, handsome office with half a dozen people, Gossage,

Feigen, Mike Robbins of Young & Rubicam, Herbert Gold the novelist, Edward Keating, then editor and publisher of *Ramparts* magazine, and myself. Someone asked McLuhan what he thought of a large-scale communications conference that happened to be going on in San Francisco at that moment, at the Hilton Hotel, with a thousand scholars in attendance, headed by the renowned semanticist, S. I. Hayakawa.

"Well . . ." said McLuhan, pulling his chin in and turning his eyes up, "they're working from very obsolete premises, of course. Almost by definition."

By definition?

"Certainly. By the time you can get a thousand people to agree on enough principles to hold such a meeting, conditions will already have changed. The principles will be useless."

The Hayakawa conference . . . evaporated.

I thought of this remark four months later. McLuhan had a long-standing invitation to speak before the regular monthly luncheon meeting of a New York advertising group. This group always met in a banquet room off the mezzanine of the Plaza Hotel. Attendance was seldom more than a hundred. Suddenly McLuhan's appearance took on the proportions of a theater opening by a blazing new star. The luncheon had to be transferred to the Plaza's grand ballroom—and was attended by . . . a thousand.

McLuhan, as I look back on it, was magnificent that day. Rather than gratify the sudden popular clamor, he stood up at the podium and became his most cryptic, Delphic, esoteric, Oriental self. He was like a serious-faced Lewis Carroll. Nobody knew what the hell he was saying. I was seated at a table with a number of people from Time-Life, Inc. Several of them were utterly outraged by the performance. They sighed, rolled their eyeballs, then actually turned their chairs around and began conversing among themselves as he spoke. It could not have been more reminiscent of the Freud phenomenon fifty years before. *Many enemies, much honor!*

I have heard friends of McLuhan say that his publicity boom has become so intense, he is in danger of overexposure and trivialization. Perhaps; certainly some of his recent gestures, such as an article in *Look* on "The Future of Sex" (co-authored by a *Look* editor), have sounded trivial enough. But I think that all in all he has handled the whole thing like a champion. Like Freud, he never stops to debate a point ("I want observations, not agreement"). Mainly, he has just continued to pour it on, in every medium he can get hold of, books, magazines, TV, radio, lectures, seminars, symposia. He has even broken through the meaning barrier. As late as the winter of 1965–66 people from the Canadian Broadcasting Company told me they would like to put McLuhan on Canadian TV, but they felt he would be unintelligible to their audience. Today that objection would be a laugh, even at the CBC. It would be like saying, We can't show Richard Burton—he doesn't finish his sentences.

McLuhan's monomania for his theory—and his consecrated pursuit of it amid the whole spume of his celebrity—has lent him a weird peace. It is the peace of the eye of the hurricane or of what Professor Silenus, the architect, describes in Evelyn Waugh's *Decline and Fall.* Professor Silenus describes life as being like one of those whirling discs at the old amusement parks. They are like a gigantic phonograph record, 50 feet across. You get on the disc and it starts spinning, and the faster it goes, the more centrifugal force builds up to throw you off it. The speed on the outer edge of the disc is so great you have to hold on for dear life just to stay on. The closer you can get to the center of the disc, the slower the speed is and the easier it is to stand up. In fact, theoretically, at the very center there is a point that is completely motionless. In life, most people won't get on the disc at all. They shouldn't get on. They don't have the nerve or the *élan.* They just sit in the stands and watch. Some people like to get on the outer edge and hang on and ride like hell— that would be people like McLuhan's madman impresarios, Gossage and Feigen. Others are standing up and falling down, staggering, lurching toward the center. And a few, a very few, reach the middle, that perfect motionless point, and stand up in the dead center of the roaring whirly-gig as if nothing could be clearer and less confused—that would be McLuhan.

Yes. I once took McLuhan to a Topless Lunch in San Francisco. This was at a place on North Beach called the Off Broadway, where the waitresses served lunch bare-breasted. Gossage, Feigen, and Herb Caen, the famous San Francisco columnist, joined us. All of us had heard about the Topless Lunch, but none of us had ever seen it. I found out that a curious thing happens when men walk for the first time into a room full of nude girls. Namely, they are speechless. I saw it happen many times that afternoon. The whole vocabulary of masculine humor about female nudity is actually based on the premise that they are partly clothed, that much is being revealed, but by no means all. When men walk into a restaurant and find a dozen girls walking around in nothing but flesh-colored cache-sexes and high heels, they just don't know what to say— not even a sophisticated boulevardier like Caen. Everyone was struck dumb; everyone, that is to say, except McLuhan.

Inside of thirty seconds McLuhan had simply absorbed the whole scene into . . . the theory. He tucked his chin down.

"Well!" he said. "Very interesting!"

"What's interesting, Marshall?"

"They're wearing *us*." He said it with a slight shrug, as if nothing could be more obvious.

"I don't get it, Marshall."

"We are their clothes," he said. "We become their environment. We become extensions of their skin. They're wearing *us*."

We sat down. The place was packed with businessmen. It was kept in a black-light gloom, apparently to spare embarrassment, just like in the old burlesque houses. Except that huge heavy expense-account lunches were being served by bare-breasted waitresses. Their breasts dangled and jiggled and sweated over your plate as they stretched in the meat crush to hand out the soups, the salads, the bread, and cocktails. You could barely see the plate in front of you, only glistening breasts in a nightgown gloom. It was a pure nutball farce, that was all one could seem to get out of it. Unless you were McLuhan.

"When you dim the visual sense," he said, "you step up the sense of taste. That's why these so-called 'dim-lit restaurants' work. That's why they are literally 'intimate.' You are brought together sensually and sensorially, forced out of the isolation of the visual man."

Later on we fell to discussing the relative charms of our sweating seraglio houris, and Caen happened to single out one girl as "good-looking"—

"Do you know what you said?" said McLuhan. "Good-*looking*. That's a visual orientation. You're separating yourself from the girls. You are sitting back and *looking*. Actually, the light is dim in here. This is meant as a *tactile* experience, but visual man doesn't react that way."

Everyone looks to McLuhan to see if he is joking, but it is impossible to tell in the tactile night. All that is clear is that . . . yes, McLuhan has already absorbed the whole roaring whirligig into the motionless center.

Just after the meal, the Off Broadway presented its Style Show. This consisted of several girls with enormous tits—"breasts" just doesn't say it—blown up by silicone injections and sticking clear out of the various gowns and lingerie they were "modeling." All the while a mistress of ceremonies was at a microphone giving a parody version of that feathery female commentary you hear at fashion shows. "And here is Denise," she would say, "in her lace chemise"—and a young thing comes forward with a pair of prodigious dugs swollen out in front of her, heavily rouged about the nipples, and a wispy little stretch of lace dripped over her shoulder and tied with a bow at her neck. "This latest creation," says the M.C., "is made of *heavy-duty* Belgian lace . . . for that so, so *neces-sary extra* support . . ."

After the show, McLuhan calls to the M.C., the woman at the micro-phone—she was clothed, by the way—he calls her over to our table and says to her, "I have something you can use in your *spiel*."

"What's that?" she says. Her face starts to take on that bullet-proof smile that waitresses and barmaids put on to cope with middle-aged wiseguys.

"Well, it's this," said McLuhan—and I have to mention that Topless performers had recently been brought into court in San Francisco in a test case and had won the trial—"It's this," says McLuhan. "You can say, you can tell them"—and here his voice slows down as if to emphasize the utmost significance—"*The topless waitress is the opening wedge of the trial balloon!*"

Then he looks at her with an unfathomable smile.

Her smile, however, freezes. The light goes out in her eyes. She sud-denly looks like an aging pole-axed ewe. She stares at McLuhan without a word or an expression—

But of course!

—*what if he is right?*


## Commentary: On Believing the Narrator; the Technique of Credibility

The first picture I ever saw of Tom Wolfe was on the back of a paper-back collection of his essays, OH wow! He looked as if he'd paused on the way to a Truman Capote Masquerade to pose, standing with a walk-ing stick, one slim ankle crossed over the other with the tip of the toe in a frozen pirouette. Elegant!

The thing I noticed was the boots. The kind that look like high but-toned shoes kind of, shaped very tight over the ankle. They were prob-ably Fryes but I'd seen some just like them in a Flagg Brothers window.

The rest of him was without flaw, white wasp-waisted Oscar de la Renta suit with six-inch lapels, Harry Cotler shirt, a Countess Mara Big Lunch Tie, and a white Cavanaugh hat with the Bill Blass headband. Dandy! But it was the boots, I couldn't stop speculating on them. In the picture there was no indication of how he got them on, or having accomplished that how he got them off. I imagined them being molded to his feet in a Flagg Brothers fitting room, in the back, the way they mold ski boots, and him spending the rest of his life walking about elegantly in them; in the shower, in bed, struggling to get his Jaime Romain flares over them, getting ready for a lunch with some Main Biggies and Now People at the most exclusive restaurant in the mid-fifties.

```
How                                    on?  How? How? How?
   does                                    them
      he                                      get
      get                                      he
      them                                   did
      off?    How
```

I've never solved the problem and it haunts me. But I have finally settled it, in a way, by assuming a man who writes as well and as cleverly as Tom Wolfe, can get his boots on and off, somehow. And Tom Wolfe surely does write well. Part of his skill is the care with which he elevates his narrative voice above the crowd. Here, in his essay on McLuhan, and again in his essay on Hugh Hefner (p. 198), he carefully belittles his subject.

The technique is a simple one. At the very beginning of his essay on McLuhan, Wolfe plants the image of the Pree-Tide tie. It is a superb stroke, for it captures in a concrete image the incongruity that Wolfe sees in McLuhan, the unworldly scholar bursting onto the high finance, *haute New York* scene. But it also helps cut McLuhan down to size, make him seem a little ridiculous. The reader, following the progress of the Pree-Tide image through the essay, will recognize that it serves again and again this function. Clever.

However, if McLuhan is shabbily genteel, Wolfe is not. Even without the neat-o picture on the back of the paperback among the promo blurbs, we would know that Wolfe was not shabbily genteel, and would not wear a tie with plastic cheaters. His horrified fascination with the tie is enough evidence. But there's much more. Wolfe's description of the other people in Lutèce reveals a sure knowledge of how the beautiful people dress. To recognize a Pucci dress is to reveal that you are knowledgeable. To know that King Sano is "the cigarette of New York Society women," to explain to us about "the Eastern boarding-school honk" is to let us know that Wolfe has moved in those circles and recognizes it from experience with the likes of Nelson Rockefeller and Huntington Hartford. A telling point: Wolfe comments on the society matrons "calling Lutèce's owner by his first name" and then adds, "which is André," revealing that, of course, he too knows Andre. I wonder if Andre's boots are removable? Or if he wears boots? Surely not to work.

As the essay develops Wolfe slowly makes everyone else in the essay— McLuhan, the "many studs of the business world," Howard Gossage (of the "wild, cosmic laugh")—everyone, I say, in the essay seem faintly ridiculous. He sees through the pretensions of "upward-bursting, hierarch executives, the real studs, the kind who have already changed over from lie down crew cuts to brushback Eric Johnston-style Big Boy haircuts and from Oxford button-downs to Tripler broadcloth straight points and have hung it all on the line, an $80,000 mortgage in New Canaan and a couple of kids at Deerfield and Hotchkiss. . . ." Tom Wolfe sees through them, he's not taken in, just as he understands and, indeed, patronizes McLuhan. Tom Wolfe is in the know. He understands what McLuhan's effect is, and why the executives flock to him. He is above his subject matter, and since he is, he is finally the voice of authority in the essay. His complete credibility is not the result of logical reasoning or the presentation of evidence, but results from the fact that everyone in the essay but its speaker seems at least a bit ridiculous, and this by a guy who has to sleep in his form-fitted shoes. Amazing.

This is not to suggest that we do not get a good deal of insight into both McLuhan and the response to him. Nor is this meant to imply that Wolfe is somehow to be condemned for his technique. We get a good deal of insight into the paradox of the two McLuhans, "the English teacher with the Pree-tide tie on" and "the omniscient *philosophe*." We also get considerable information about McLuhan's theory, and the response of the business world to it. And we get this in the most amusing possible way; but the impact of Wolfe's essay finally depends on the care with which he makes himself credible by making everyone else incredible. And our convictions about McLuhan ought to include a recognition of how Wolfe helped form them.

R. B. P.

## 44. THE MUSIC OF PROTEST

### Burt Korall

*A frequent contributor to the* Saturday Review, *and a critic of popular music, Burt Korall represents a trend in criticism which is ascending. He examines popular culture as a way of coming to a larger understanding of the American experience. Here he examines the youth revolution of the 1960s and 1970s through the implications of its music.*

Youth damns the past, defines the diseased present, and demands change. Their outrage and defiance takes various forms—from direct confrontation and protest, satire, love in the face of hate, to drugs and dropping out. What remains constant is a flood of commentary—youth taking the world's pulse and their own, using music to purge themselves, while increasingly irritating and provoking the forces of reaction. In essence, they function as an alarm clock for the country and march to the tune of their aspirations, hoping to attain sanity, reason, physical and mental mobility, love and, most important, realistic appraisal on a mass level.

Having overrun popular music and realized its power as a tool, they are cementing a link with an increasingly large audience through the country and the world. It is a matter of record that music representative of the tidal wave of youth sells more heavily than any other kind—and not only to youngsters. Cultural lag doesn't seem a problem in this era of multiple communication, even in more provincial areas.

The music of youth, like their clothes and hair styles, simultaneously singularizes and isolates them, while lending tribal strength. Nothing new; swing music of the 1930s and be-bop ten years later spawned analogous figures which, for simplicity's sake, we will call hipsters. They, too, had their own folkways, manner of dressing, language, and lived on the periphery of the establishment.

One major difference, however, separates today's rag-tagger from the hipster of old. Living away from the illness of the establishment is primary to today's young—at least until they can motivate some radical changes. The old-time hipster, on the other hand, put down the world as unbearably square but still was part of it. Politics and the expression of the need for radical metamorphosis were not his bag. Comfortable in his own orbit, where everything was familiar and relaxed, the hipster dismissed the square as funny and unfeeling. They couldn't dig him; they

*Source:* "The Music of Protest," Burt Korall. From November 16, 1968 *Saturday Review.* Copyright 1968 Saturday Review, Inc.

didn't know how. Proudly, but with a hint of finger-popping hostility, he ambled down Main Street in big town and small, flaunting his difference and his cool.

The rag-tag generation finds no humor in the mistakes and cop-outs of the conforming armies. Sleeping, easily fooled, bigoted people are a travesty, they say, and are responsible for the relative chaos in which we live. Anything but cool, youth senses what is wrong and how things should be. They find muscle in their growing numbers and the possibilities implicit in grouping for attack on the status quo, and in the attack itself. As for a sharply definitive sense of identity—that's another matter. The search continues. For the moment, the method, culminating in revelation, has not been found. The young of earlier generations fostered the idea that they knew who they were. "Today's youth have no such delusion," critic Albert Goldman declares. "But lacking any clear-cut sense of identity has only made them more keenly aware of everyone else's."

Cross-ventilation of ideas and techniques combined with the inner and outer ferment in the country have produced a radical change in popular music—now a fascinating, if sometimes troubled mixture of elements, which truly reflects our present position. What Goldman has deemed the "Rock Age"—the period in which we live—indeed has been a time of assimilation. Musically it has "assimilated everything in sight, commencing with the whole of American music: urban and country blues, gospel, hillbilly, Western, 'good-time' (the ricky-tick of the Twenties), and Tin Pan Alley. It has reached across the oceans for the sounds and rhythms of Africa, the Middle East, and India. It has reached back in time for the baroque trumpet, the madrigal, and the Gregorian Chant; and forward into the future for electronic music and the noise collages of *musique concrète*. By virtue of its cultural alliances, the Beat has also become the pulse of pop culture."

It remains to be determined whether music-song is a powerful, provocative instrument, which aids the cause of change. Does our contemporary musical amalgam, itself implicit protest against the limited popular music of the past, make its point?

There is widespread disparity of opinion concerning the cogency of musical protest. Critic John Cohen states that "topical songs are like newspapers; pertinent to the latest developments, bearing the latest ideas, and ending up in the garbage can." It is his contention that "for young people in the cities, the topical songs have become abstract emotional substitutes for what is going on in the world; and although this can be a good factor when it stimulates people to action, more often it is a delusion." By making such connections, he explains, "topical songs blind young people into believing they are accomplishing something in their own protest, when, in fact, they are doing nothing but going to concerts, record stores, and parties at home."

Admittedly, protest music diminishes in impact once the crisis in question is past. It does, however, serve as a source of strength, unification, and expression when the battle is raging. Music's depth of importance within the civil rights movement earlier in this decade is a matter of history. It converted many to the cause in a manner that signs, demonstrations, and other means did not. Even more important, the songs solidified the chain of commitment among the followers. Northern writers, including the ever present Peter Seegar, Phil Ochs, Tom Paxton, and Len Chandler, among others, personalized the struggle, giving their own reactions to various situations. They spoke of injustices and what had to be done. The Southern freedom singers and writers, working within the Afro-American tradition, using gospel and rhythm and blues forms and songs, with lyrics to fit each occasion, also cut deeply and made their point, leaving an enduring mark. One has only to refer back to the tremendous effect of "We Shall Overcome."

At the base of today's musical protest, casting a giant shadow that sometimes goes unnoticed by current practitioners, are generations of black blues singers and players—disenfranchised, alienated, and imprisoned, who had their say, if sometimes obliquely, and broke through, using the only medium at their disposal, music. Equally influential in casting the current shapes and forms for contemporary comment were individuals of conscience and compassion who sang of injustice and helped people find answers to pressing questions in their songs.

The prototypical figure in the latter category is the late Woody Guthrie, a truth-teller about whom Tom Paxton had said: "The most important thing Woody gave us was courage to stand up and say the things we believe." A ramblin' man who wandered through his beloved land, he was devoted to causes—some deemed radical; however, with time on our side, it is plain to see that all Guthrie wanted to do was make us aware of the country's good points and bad, while bringing us closer to it. His thoughts, generally couched in simple, human terms, are accessible to all. Through more than 1,000 songs, he strung the history of the America he knew—from the deprivations of the Depression through the first post-World War II years, until his illness began to take hold of him and prove prohibitive on his talent.

Those who register complaint and desperation today are not far removed in spirit from Guthrie and other bards of yesterday, like black artists Big Bill Broonzy and Leadbelly, who spoke out of their experience and tried to bring mass focus to inequality and the number of sicknesses in the land. Today, however, the voices of dissent are louder, for cause; we cannot wait any longer for the rapport to develop whereby we can live with one another. It is either pass down an inheritance of absurd reality or change direction.

Amidst the hurt, disappointment, and hopelessness, there seems reason for limited optimism. The 1960s have been crucial years in the journey to a new reality. An extended period of silence, repression, and resultant welling up of feeling came to an end. A revolution broke out in music—and the other arts as well—paralleling the turmoil throughout the national and international structure. Folk artists in America again began speaking openly, following years of black lists and red channels. With the coming of Ornette Coleman and the emergence and development of John Coltrane, jazz again became a maverick. On the heels of an era concerned with consolidation and progressive rediscovery of roots, after the death of Charlie Parker in 1955, the ground breakers reached out, touching new bases. They provoked the young to look to their feelings. The music, though unfinished in many of its aspects and chaotic to the uninitiated, motivated a complete re-examination of existing guidelines, and challenges us to think about our lives and what the future will offer.

Some sage, for lack of a more ornate description, deemed it "The New Thing." An oversimplification, but appropriate for a sudden turning in the road. Bringing into play a variety of techniques from diverse musical and extra-musical sources, the practitioners mutate and revamp the jazz we know playing havoc on its identity. Exactly what will emerge remains to be heard; it's certain that jazz, by nature an evolving form, can never be the same. The revolution continues. To accept it wholly, completely discarding yesterdays, seems out of the question. To open one's self to its positive aspects and prospects is a necessity. A highly contemporary manifestation, it certainly has been instrumental in shaking jazz loose from a progressive case of nostalgia, a malaise which could envelop and incapacitate the music and its players.

It comes clear that it is no longer possible to separate music and life as it really is. Politics, sexuality, racial pride, deep and true feelings have entered popular music to stay. Our youth is central to this metamorphosis.

Bob Dylan has been *the* standard-bearer of the 1960s. A stylistic son of Woody Guthrie at the beginning of his career, he stepped forward in 1961 and initiated a stream of comment that continues to this day. Particularly at the outset he noted in no uncertain terms the hypocrisy of this country and the need for vigorous change. Using the narrative form, in the tradition of Guthrie, his first records echoed with the meaninglessness of life, the impossibility of racial inequality, the imminence of death, as man moved further and further from himself. It was time to take hold, NOW.

Deemed a poet by some, a prophet by others, a self-propelled mediocrity by still others, Dylan caught the tenor of the times in his songs. Innocence was a thing of the past. No longer was it possible to live with soda shoppe morality and answers which had nothing to do with pressing questions. He realized that isolation from true reality was as unbearable as the reality itself. Yet this did not prohibit him from immersing himself in surrealistic pessimism. After clearly indicating the world in his "Blowin' in the Wind," he turned to an inverted mode of writing, couching his point of view within a rush of words and images, oblique and abstract, often approaching hallucinations: dreams more frightening than reality. This is the subterranean Dylan, living in song in a demimonde of "haunted, frightened trees"; dwarfs; clowns who seem blind; intransigent policemen. On occasion he surfaced to sing of love relationships (often unfulfilling) and to express youth's alienation from the older, reactionary generation who simply won't understand what it's all about, as on "It's Alright, Ma, I'm Only Bleeding." Dylan, the observer, would make things right if he could, but the governing forces block renewal of effort.

With the release early this year of *John Wesley Harding* (Columbia CS 9604), his first album after a silence of a year and a half, he gives evidence of having thrown aside the recent past in favor of rebirth and a new maturity. The electrified accompaniment that served his purposes prior to his near-fatal accident has been unplugged. His songs are concise rather than sprawling. The imagery, if still opaque, is not as dreamlike, nor just for him alone. His morality, accessible at every turn and almost religious in aspect, guides him in sharply defining good as opposed to that which is intrinsically evil. The nature of his songs and delivery are devoid of obvious artifice and the false "cool" and stances of the public person. Placing a heavy emphasis on country simplicity in vocally and instrumentally projecting his feelings, the songwriter-singer again acoustic-guitarist is back in the world. A new Dylan? Hardly. He's just a bit more direct, relaxed, open. His means and manner may change but he retains a unity of image. He is the questioning and needling voice of the 1960s.

Dylan's colleagues in the pop realm, like him, are the products of many influences and pressures. With few exceptions, their comment and mode of vocal and instrumental performances bear the marks of the black man—his inflections, mannerisms, and accents. But taken as a whole, popular music, 1968, reflects urban and provincial attitudes, sounds, and rhythms native to black and white, a spillover of techniques from traditional and contemporary classical music and foreign cultures. It is a democracy in sound—as free and flexible as the world we yearn for. It logically follows that the lyrics for this universal popular music would be as emancipated, outspoken, and diverse as the music itself.

This is very much the case. We have moved into wide-ranging application of words since swinging around the corner into the 1960s, with contexts running from the decisively concrete to abstraction. This is a considerable distance from the nonsense syllables and one-dimensional lyrics which characterized much of the song produce of the Fifties. The songsmiths aspire to be equal to the times.

Whatever the degree of accessibility of the wordage, the creator's need to link up with his audience is strongly sensed. Often, however, he will make the listeners work to achieve communion, benevolently allowing multiple interpretations of his message or lack of one, intimating that in life everyone doesn't see everything the same way. At their ultimate in surrealism and ambiguity, Dylan, the Beatles, and the acid rock groups i.e., Jefferson Airplane—might initially cloud the mind with a crazy quilt of images. But they do draw you to them within the maelstrom and engage your capacities in a search that frequently is as exciting and fulfilling as the revelation that sometimes lies at the end of the trip. Observers have paralleled the experience with the drug turn on—an analogue not without basis in fact. The drug phenomenon is very much with us and figures in the music of youth. The maze and confusion out of which we try to make sense also structures the music and is part of its structure. Therefore, the music is singularly relevant, because it contains in its own form what's happening in and around us. If anything is true of contemporary popular music, it is the intent of its makers to set life to music.

Surprisingly, the prime movers are white—surprising only in that their black brethren have far more reason to build bandwagons. But there is reason for this. White people are freer and have less to lose. The black man generally remains repressed and is less inclined to show his true face—musically, anyway. Make no mistake, however, his protest is there for all who will take time to reach and find his soul. One has only to pay special heed to the sound and words of the blues. And sometimes the mask slips, as on this old-time entry:

> Well, I drink to keep from worrying and I laugh to keep from crying, (twice)

I keep a smile on my face so the public won't know my mind.
Some people think I am happy but they sho' don't know my mind,
(twice)
They see this smile on my face, but my heart is bleeding all the time.[1]

Admittedly, the turn of events in this decade has motivated the black man to speak more directly in his music, and to abandon to some extent the protective code and inside terminology of the past. Race pride and anger is felt in some of his songs, as well as the need to throw off strictured yesterdays. Lou Rawls, a modern black singer, with roots in gospel and the blues, gives urgent voice to these feelings in "They Don't Give Medals (to Yesterday's Heroes)"—a song by two white writers, Burt Bachrach and Hal David, which serves black aspiration well.

They don't give medals to yesterday's heroes,
Yesterday's over and I got to live for today,
I'm goin' places and nothing can stand in my way.[2]

Songs of burning inquiry, confrontation, and accusation are now written and performed by black people . . . and heard more and more often. Billy Taylor's "I Wish I Knew How It Would Feel to Be Free" has extraordinary currency and is increasingly performed and recorded. The musing, black folk artist-songwriter Richie Havens screams out the query, "Why must we wait until morning to wake up and BE?" in his scalding song, "No Opportunity Necessary, No Experience Needed." Otis Redding bemoans the lack of change in his hit, "Dock of Bay." James Brown, Soul Brother Number 1, raises his voice in the cause of black pride on his "Say It Loud—I'm Black and I'm Proud." Julius Lester, the literate and deeply expressive black songsmith and artist, takes a militant stance, espousing a strong front against the oppressor and the death of stereotypes: "Gonna get me a gun and shoot Aunt Jemima dead." Nina Simone often casts a skewering glance at bedridden society. Her record of Martha Holmes's "Turning Point," an eye-opening comment on the existing distance between the races, is a recommended experience. Perhaps the most touching song, rendering with rare clarity the situation in the black ghetto, is the relatively unheralded "Cracker-

[1] "Bleeding Heart Blues," by Amos Castor. Used by permission of Northern Music Co., a division of MCA Entertainment, Inc. All rights reserved.

[2] "They Don't Give Medals" (to Yesterday's Heroes), by Burt Bachrach and Hal David. © Copyright 1966 Blue Seas Music, Inc. /Jac Music Co., Inc. Permission granted by Publisher.

box Livin'," by Howlett Smith, as interpreted by singer Ernie Andrews in his Dot album *Soul Proprietor*.

> Crackerbox livin'—ain't no kind of livin',
> What is this hole you charge for?
> What is this hole we're much too large for?
> Lord of the land, won't you understand,
> We'll trade you places just for the day,
> Maybe your kids can chase the rats away,
> Maybe your kids don't need some place to play.[3]

Inhibition on a really major scale, however, has not been broken. Black song, drenched in blues, with the throb and sob of the church at its core, remains a reflection of ephemeral Saturday night freedom—an act of love and despair, a flash of energy in a long darkness. Centering on black people's major source of strength—the love relationship, physically solidified—it soothes hurt and repairs dwindling dignity. "Baby, baby, baby," cries prototypical Aretha Franklin, echoing black men and women through their painful past in America. "Don't send me no doctor fillin' me up with all those pills/Got me a man named Dr. Feelgood/That man takes care of all my pains and ills."[4]

The young, rebellious white, unlike his black counterpart, is unfettered. For him, however, this freedom is but part of an overall delusion. He feels trapped by the traditions and legacies of the past.

Confusion reigns. Truth and honesty are at a premium. A valid way of life is sought. To this end, the young explorer rolls across a wide spectrum of subject matter and musical means and mannerisms. He experiments with ideology and sounds, often shaping answers in the process. But they always are open to change; flexibility is part of the concept. Though his protest and comment is less centralized than his soul brother's, his objective is essentially the same. Hope is implicit in the negation of past and present mistakes—the hope for an apocalypse, which will make the blind see, the intractable feel, the world's fearful face change.

Fear is the underlying feeling motivating the young. It's everywhere, openly shared. "What's becoming of the children?" people ask in a

---

[3] "Crackerbox Livin'," by Howlett Smith, Hilkert Music.

[4] "Dr. Feelgood," by Aretha Franklin and Ted White Publishers: Fourteenth Hour Music, 1721 Field Street, Detroit, Michigan.

Simon and Garfunkel song. "What has become of the world?" would be a more pertinent question. Moreover, if things go on the way they have, will it be here at all? Turmoil and violence, at every turn. A heavily theatrical and ritualistic rock group called The Doors, featuring lead singer Jim Morrison, is archtypical in its bold statement of the existing situation. Mounting a saturation bombardment attack in words, lights, and amplified sound, leveling listeners into submissiveness, the unit projects the fear embedded in the young, and all of us for that matter, Listen to "When the Music's Over."

> . . . For the music is your special friend,
> Dance on fire as it intends,
> Music is your only friend,
> Until the end,
> Until the end,
> Until
> THE END![5]

Threading one's way through the mountains of recent recordings, the temper of the times and the matters of concern are multiply revealed. The Vietnam war is a primary subject. A yearning for peace is predominant. "Honor is without profit in its own country," declare The Split Level in the song, "Speculator," included in the group's recent Dot album. Kenny Rankin, a Mercury artist, singing Fred Neil's song, "The Dolphin," underscores the crucial fact: "Peace gonna come only when hate is gone." It seems indicated that songs will continue to pour from the cauldron until the situation in Southeast Asia is eased. Joan Baez inevitably will lead the voices of nonviolence and peace—just as inevitably as songs taking the opposite stance, like Barry Sadler's "The Ballad of the Green Berets," will be created.

The gap in understanding between young and not so young consistently is mirrored in music. Razor-sharp satirists, who laugh to keep from crying, like Frank Zappa's Mothers of Invention, define the situation with a sneering smile, lending it dimensions it would not otherwise have. In a song called "Mom & Dad," Zappa goes for the heart, querying parents: "Ever take a minute just to show a real emotion? . . . Ever tell your kids you're glad that they think?" Country Joe and The Fish, a San Francisco group deeply involved in today's swirl, also waves the ammonia bottle under the collective nose of America. Though its mate-

---

[5] "When The Music's Over," words and music by The Doors. © Copyright 1967 by Nipper Music Company, Inc.

rial has a comedic exterior and unit treatment deepens the satiric quality, these fellows aren't fooling around.

Loneliness also is a frequent song subject. "All the lonely people/ Where do they all come from," the Beatles wonder. Confusion and the bureaucracy of life also crops up often, as in Arlo Guthrie's "Alice's Restaurant." The positive power of love to turn people away from their destructive proclivities is still another notable theme. ". . . plant them now, never a better time," Buffy Sainte-Marie says in her song, "The Seeds of Brotherhood." Record after record reveals the inner plight and acute sensitivity of today's youth and the world in which they live. The warnings are there to be understood.

In recent months, however, pop music of protest has taken on a much more affirmative tone. Songs define what might be as opposed to expressing a condition. The recent assassinations of Martin Luther King and Robert Kennedy certainly contributed to this reversal. Seemingly artists and the industry as a whole have realized that there is no other alternative and concluded, exclusive of one another, to use music affirmatively, hopefully for a positive result.

Within a short space of time over a dozen items have been released—all statements of hope and faith in the underlying strength and possibility of the country. Included in this number are Laura Nyro's "Save the Country," James Brown's "America is My Home," a rash of inspirational songs—notably treatment of "The Impossible Dream" from *Man of La Mancha*—and the Kim Weston album, *This is America.*

Whatever the plight of America, its music indicates that the people are reaching out to find it and themselves. Some want revolution; others desire yesterday. Certainly things cannot stay the same. Take a look around. Listen to today's music. It's all there.

# 45. A THING IS WHAT IT IS AND NOT SOMETHING ELSE: TELEVISION IN AMERICA

## Robert B. Parker

*Robert B. Parker is an Assistant Professor of English at Northeastern University. Before pursuing an academic career, Parker was a partner in a Boston-based advertising firm. A free-lance writer and editor, he is the author of* The Personal Response to Literature, *"The Prince and the King: Shakespeare's Machiavellian Cycle," "The Function and Maintenance of the Gravity Feed Oil Burner Nozzle," "The Maltese Banana," and other works. His field of expertise is the Twentieth-Century Violent Hero.*

Whether or not the medium is the message it surely controls the message (you don't make a novel out of clay, a sculpture out of print). All of us seem willing to agree with that assertion except when it comes to the mass media. Then we look at "Bonanza" and say, "*Hamlet* it ain't." That's like looking at Picasso's *Guernica* and saying *"War and Peace* it ain't." Ain't, nor was meant to be. The mass media are not in conspiracy to make sows' ears out of silk purses. Television is trying to sell the sponsor's product. You are not required to like that fact, but no sensible appraisal of television is likely to be made if you don't, at least, accept the fact. A thing is what it is, and not something else.

Television, radio, newspapers, and magazines are media through which sellers communicate with buyers. That they are other things as well in no way changes the fact that they are this. Thus the question facing a man who writes for such a medium, or who produces or directs, who writes continuity, or lays out photos is not, How can I create art? but, as it is with a man who works in any medium, How can I create art within the limits of my medium, that is without violating its function and thus destroying it? It is a remarkably useful thing to know, for instance, that most newspapers are made up on sheets on which the advertising space has been laid out first, and the news is squeezed around it. The question is not universally that of presenting all the news that's fit to print. It is, upon occasion, a matter of printing all the news that will fit. It is very helpful to remember that if you have a 39-week contract for a television series you cannot very well contrive the death of the hero in episode eleven no matter how artistically necessary that might be. Nor can you write a play that runs one hour and seventeen minutes because, of course, television time isn't sold that way. You've got to fit your ultimate statement about the nature of the human experience into the prepackaged slots: a half hour, an hour, an hour and a half: with time enough to pause for commercial messages at the appropriate interval.

If you write a play in which a character is killed when a tire blows out, then you'll never get sponsored by Firestone. Should you write a series dealing with economic exploitation in Latin America you probably won't sell it to United Fruit. If your detective is slugged with a coke bottle you can forget the beverage and bottle industry. Until the Marlboro man rode into the sunset few people died of lung cancer in the hospital dramas. The list can be multiplied infinitely, and thus a writer preparing a script which he hopes to sell must very carefully avoid including something that will offend a sponsor. Since he often doesn't know in advance who the sponsor might be, his options become quite narrow. If your spy lights a bomb with the end of his cigar, you can kiss Dorothy Muriel goodbye as a sponsor. If the villain practices insurance fraud and gets away with it, you'll be in no hands of Allstate. If one can't get sponsored, one doesn't appear and one's work of art becomes as real as the sound a tree makes when it falls in an empty forest. One cigarette company insisted that cigarettes be treated nicely on shows it sponsored. The camera could never show them being stubbed out, flipped away, stepped on, or otherwise brutalized. There are even more Wagnerian examples but we needn't belabor the point.

Not only does the sponsor concern himself that his product be treated well, but he also often concerns himself that his product appear in a pleasing context, and not one that may associate his product with something unpleasant, with something, God preserve us, controversial. If one sponsors a program in which leftist views are presented, might one be associated with leftists and thereby lose the Davenport, Iowa market? If one sponsors a program with right-wing overtones, does one lose Berkeley? If the program is about an anti-Semite does one lose the Bronx? Even "Sermonette" probably gets hate mail from the atheists.

Consider then the problem you face if you've decided to write a television play, part of a series (discounting the difficulty of getting anyone to read it; most television scripts are, as it were, staff written). A consideration of contemporary issues may offend a segment of the buying public and thus make it more difficult to get a sponsor. If someone is to die, it must be in a way that uses no product (drownings are good, the water lobby is not active; falling off cliffs has the same charm). You must make it fit into exactly thirty, sixty, or ninety minutes (including commercial time) with the action arranged so that one may pause for a message without unduly disrupting the flow; in other words, in an hour show one needs three minor climaxes before the final one.

In short, television programming falls into the realm that Samuel Johnson once described in reference to a woman preaching. It is like a dog walking on its hind legs: the remarkable thing being not that it is done well, but that it is done at all.

The effect of all this is, of course, rather serious. What comes on the screen is thus very frequently a pasteurized, deodorized, air-conditioned, germ-free version of life that appears to have come into being untouched by human hands. Scored with a laugh track and dancing gaily down the exact middle of a yellow brick road, the world that television pictures is one in which father always does know best, and the kids after some humorous failures to do so, finally listen to him.

That such a picture of the world, endlessly reiterated, can have serious adverse effect on viewers whose world (the real one) does not match up to the electronic one has been often and convincingly argued. It need not be further insisted on here. It is almost certainly so. What may be suggested here is that one should, at least, know one's enemy. Television is not a disease; it's one symptom in a syndrome. Mass productive capability requires a mass market to support it. Mass market requires continual needs-creation. This was not always true. Perhaps, at first there was a man who made a good mousetrap. He put out a sign that said "Good Mousetraps For Sale" and the world shortly beat a path to his door. Now there are 136 men who build equally good (and, indeed, indistinguishable) mousetraps, and since there is no special reason why you should buy mine instead of someone else's I've got to invent one. This is the function of advertising, to create a market, to invent a reason why you should buy one mousetrap rather than another when, in fact, there is no reason.

Since there's no real reason to buy my mousetrap, one of the things I need to do is associate it with things that give you a positive feeling: success, nature, squeaky-clean sex, money, familial love, courage, America, popularity. I do this both by the nature of my advertising, and by the nature of the context in which my advertisement appears. I create for my mousetrap a positive image. When you see it on the shelf you feel good about it and buy it. Anything that gives you a negative feeling is to be fled as the hound of hell.

Now to all of this there is shapely and convincing logic. My own experience suggests that sales executives who worry about such things (they are, after all, paid to), overrate the effect of their own advertising program (the agencies who prepare the advertising programs are not likely to argue with them), but my experience may have misled me, and the theory is, at least, a sound one, as far as it goes. Unfortunately, of course, it needs to go further. And does not. Those who oppose it, oppose it on the grounds of a counter theory that is equally simplistic: television is a vast wasteland. It aims at the lowest common denominator. It should not pander to American tastes; it should shape them. Stuff like that. It's like condemning cancer. It moves us no closer to a cure, but it gives us the good feeling of having done so.

The problem is not simply in craven account executives and greedy sponsors. It lies in the very heart of our success at contriving the mass-production-mass-marketing-mass-consuming economy. I am not prepared to offer an alternative system at the moment. But until I am, I shall refrain from bemoaning the fact that a western draws a bigger Nielsen than *Hamlet* and content myself with seeing what we can do to make it a better western.

"The fact," Robert Frost once said, "is the sweetest dream of all."

## Commentary: A Problem of Analogy

A writer does not always have to be like Caesar's wife. If he is good at what he does he can take liberties as, I think, Robert Parker takes them here. I am not sure, for example, I think there is any proper analogy that can be drawn between "Bonanza" and *Hamlet*, and *Guernica* and *War and Peace*. That is like comparing oranges and apples. *Hamlet* is a play; "Bonanza" is also a play. The difference between them is in quality, not in kind. *Guernica* is a painting; *War and Peace* a novel. The difference between them is in kind, not quality.

Nor am I sure I understand just what Parker means when he says "the medium . . . surely controls the message . . .", at least not if he means television cannot or will not produce and deliver a distinguished "Hamlet" as, at least once in recent memory, it has done (with sponsor).

What I do understand in this article is an altogether refreshing and overall persuasive appeal to face the facts of life as they pertain to television programming in general, facts of life too often ignored by ivory tower critics who either rail against or sniff at each season's offerings. Parker puts the well-earned needle to this rather silly balloon. Television, as he points out, depends for its life on advertising. And for as long as this is true, everything else that pertains on the small screen is no more or less than can be expected. While we may yearn for more *Hamlets*, let us indeed write better westerns.

In sum, the strength of this article depends not on flawless analogy, but recognition of truth. Worth reading, I think.          P. L. S.

## Response: Impropriety for Emphasis?

I was thirty and twice a father when I quit advertising to study full time for my Ph. D. The decrease in my income was awesome and my doctoral studies were often interrupted while I engaged both the sheriff and the wolf at my front door. That is over now, and like military service, seems amusing in retrospect. What I remember vividly about it all was the frequency with which, gleeful, and a little smug, both my fellow Ph. D. candidates and my professors would assume I had suffered profound moral revulsion and, tired of prostituting myself (like Holden Caulfield's brother), had turned my back on Mammon and set out in the service of God.

I seemed the material counterpart of their most profound suspicions. I was like a reformed whore in a convent, and they probed me for salacious revelation: accounts stolen, unprincipled backstabbing, and the struggle of copywriters, red in tooth and claw, to succeed to the throne of the copy chief.

Unfortunately, I was so busy trying to pay the mortgage and underwrite my kid's allergy shots that I hadn't enough time left to invent something to feed their fantasies. So I would always shrug and say, "I didn't like it," when asked why I left. But I remember those people very well and I remember their incomprehension when I said that the university community didn't seem a lot different. I still see that look when I say such things to colleagues, and I was thinking about it when I wrote my essay on television. It accounts for the liberties that Peter Sandberg has caught me taking.

It is true that the difference between *Guernica* and *War and Peace* is a difference in kind, but I was willing to make the improper analogy to suggest as strongly as I could to those incomprehending faces the degree to which television is not theater, or the novel, or Lincoln Center, or "Ode on a Grecian Urn." It is cash and carry, profit and loss, and maybe it's not so bad for what it is. The real test is not whether television produces distinguished *Hamlet*s (I agree, it does, occasionally), but whether we can upgrade "The Dating Game." Maybe we cannot, but we shall not until we recognize that television is what it is and not something else.

R. B. P.